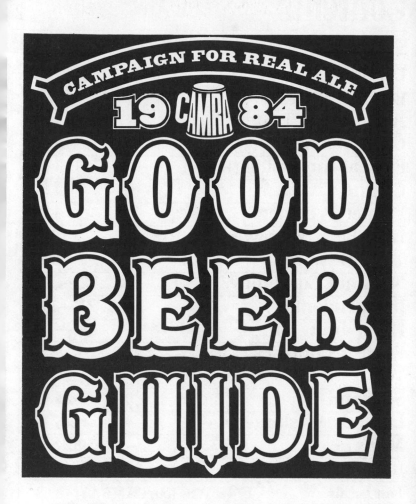

CAMPAIGN FOR REAL ALE

19 CAMRA 84

GOOD BEER GUIDE

The Good Beer Guide
1984

Edited by
Neil Hanson

CAMRA

Campaign for Real Ale,
34 Alma Road, St Albans,
AL1 3BW

Contents

Editor Neil Hanson. **Production Editor** Cathy Totman. **Breweries Section** edited by Brian Glover. **Additional research and editorial** by: Danny Blyth, John Buckby, Paul Carter, Jenny Greenhalgh, Neil Harris, Peter Lerner, Tony Millns, Pat O'Neill, Ted Sharp and Tim Webb. **Design** by Barron Hatchett, Manchester. **Cover photograph** by Bryan Bane, Manchester: Mirror by Trevor Hatchett and Garsons Glamour Glass **Published** by CAMRA, Campaign for Real Ale Limited, 34 Alma Road, St Albans, Herts, AL1 3BW. **Printed** in Great Britain at the University Press, Cambridge. ISBN 0 950 3340 9 X ISSN 0265 0681

The Good Beer Guide 1984

WELCOME TO the 1984 *Good Beer Guide* – the eleventh, the biggest and, we hope, the best yet. The *GBG* lists over 5,000 pubs throughout Britain and Ireland that serve consistently good draught beer. It's *not* a comprehensive list of all 30,000 British pubs selling real beer – they're covered by the local guides listed inside the back cover.

Though the quality of the beer is paramount, the *GBG* is much more than just a list of places to drink in. It tells you where to eat, where to stay overnight, which pubs have rooms for children, which have open fires, and gives you lots of other information to increase your drinking pleasure when travelling, holidaying or just looking for a different pub for a night out.

Every pub in the country selling real ale is regularly visited by CAMRA members, and the *GBG* offers you a wide choice of pubs to visit in towns and villages all over the country. Wherever you are, you're never far from a *GBG* pub – and they range from country inns to plush hotels, back street locals to high street bistros.

Hundreds of pubs are removed from the *GBG* every year. A few stop selling real ale and a few fall below an acceptable standard. In others, a new landlord may have taken over who needs time to establish a record of keeping his beer well, or it may simply be that there are several pubs in the area serving excellent beer and each must take its turn. The fact that a pub is not included in the *GBG* is not necessarily an indication that its beer does not reach CAMRA's high standards. If you visit a pub that you think should be in the *GBG*, however, please let us know on the recommendation form provided on page 320. These suggestions will be passed to the local CAMRA branch to consider for the next year's *Good Beer Guide*.

As well as giving you the choice of over 5000 pubs to visit, this *GBG* also points to several reasons why a strong Campaign for Real Ale is still needed.

Parts of the country are still beer deserts, but just as important are issues like pub closures, brewery takeovers and mergers, false advertising, restrictive licensing hours, the disappearance or dilution of regional varieties of beers and the unchanging dominance of the brewing industry by the major national companies. These issues pose a continuing threat to a unique institution – the British pub – which can only be successfully challenged by a vital and effective consumer organisation – CAMRA.

There are further details about CAMRA and an application form on pages 318–319. Don't leave it to others – membership costs only £7 – a small price to pay to support the work of 'Europe's most successful consumer movement', which has fought many successful battles, but still has the war to win.

Drooping Brews

Is British beer getting blander?

CAMRA's 1983 AGM certainly thought so. Two motions, both overwhelmingly passed, called for opposition of the trend to blandness, and for an improvement in the quality of the beer being brewed and served. Evidence of the trend has come from all over Britain – and some famous names are appearing in the dock.

In Liverpool, Higson's beer seems to have shared the general decline of the area. Following brewhouse changes, it's no longer so bitter and distinctive.

In Manchester it's suggested that the original gravity of Boddingtons pale, yet flavourful bitter has recently been reduced. One punster has said that "they're prostituting their good name by selling their Boddy"!

Over in Nottingham, there's been much debate on the once astringent hoppiness of Shipstone's bitter.

Surpassing Mediocrity

The regional brews of the Bass group – Brew X, Brew XI, and the ubiquitous Stones – have come in for forthright criticism as "characterless, insipid, and utterly unappealing". CAMRA's Chairman, in his annual report, said that Bass's draught beer line-up was of "surpassing mediocrity."

Even the famous Draught Bass, billed as "one of the great ales of England", has been having problems. After the demise of the Burton Union Room, and the change to brewing Draught Bass in conical fermenters, the taste stability of the beer has gone – ironically, because the whole reputation of Bass was founded on a beer whose taste matured on the voyage to India, and whose flavour was stable even through extremes of temperature. The new Draught Bass seems more trouble-free – it's less likely to work vigorously – but it doesn't keep its magnificent flavour so well.

CAMRA will not stand by uncomplaining while once-distinctive beers are reduced to the unmemorable level of something like Greenall Whitley's so-called "Local Bitter". There's no point in campaigning to preserve real ale that isn't worth drinking.

The brewers argue that the recession is the main cause of this trend to blandness. Beer consumption and production has fallen to the level of 1972, and in an attempt to keep their share of the market, some brewers have deliberately aimed for middle-of-the-road beers which the great mass of drinkers won't find objectionable. The chances are, of course, that they won't find them particularly appealing either – but the brewery marketing experts reckon that by brewing ales of a highly distinctive character and flavour, the appeal is limited to a relatively small sector of the market, and there is a risk of putting off people who find too much flavour difficult to take.

Watering the Beer

There is another side to the argument, however. Less duty is paid the lower the original gravity of the beer, so by reducing the strength of its beer, a brewery can increase its profits without raising its prices. It's rather like a publican watering the beer except that the publican's action is illegal whereas the brewery's is simply 'good business'.

Another reason advanced has a degree of historical irony. It's argued that CAMRA has been too successful in converting people from drinking keg beer – because these converts, used to the bland and sweet taste of most keg beers, tend to go for the middle-of-the-road beers or the slightly sweetish ones, not the highly-distinctive "bitter bitters" like Bateman's XB. So, it is alleged, the real ale market is simply responding to the genuine taste preferences of the keg converts.

It's also claimed that one of the reasons for blandness is poor quality – beer not being kept properly because of inexpert cellarmanship. The very success of CAMRA has led, say the cynics, to real ale being introduced into lots of pubs where the landlord has no experience of keeping it. The downward spiral then starts – the beer isn't very good, so few people drink it, so the turnover is low, so the beer isn't very good...The flavour of real ale is certainly very dependent on good cellarmanship, and neglect results in mediocre ale.

The rising popularity of that nadir of bland tastelessness and indistinguishability, British-brewed ersatz "lager" provides another reason for blandness. Just as British high streets have been deluged with fast-food outlets selling McDogsbreath's blandburgers in polystyrene containers, so our pubs have been inundated with thinner, paler, colder, blander, less distinctive so-called "lagers". Though these draught "lagers" usually have exotic continental names, they're actually brewed in exotic locations like Tadcaster, Warrington, Reading, Luton, and Northampton. Their taste is nothing like as full and distinctive as the higher-gravity continental equivalents, and they appeal to immature palates not used to strong and rich flavours. Lager drinkers always ask for "lager", not a brand by name – they're more or less all the same, and all bland.

Fast Drink

Real ale drinkers' palates are getting blander along with the rest of the population's, say the marketing pundits. The question remains whether the trend towards blander food and drink reflects a genuine change in the nation's tastes or other factors such as the importance of the youth market to food and drink manufacturers. The young are the big spenders in pubs, and their palates are inevitably unsophisticated. They are likely to prefer fast food and fast drink, particularly when their preferences are so assiduously shaped and strengthened by the industry's vast promotions expenditure.

Sales of some beers which have got blander have certainly increased, but the trend to blandness is less than half the story. The blander beers are far outnumbered by new beers with highly distinctive flavours. These beers come – encouragingly – from a very wide range of breweries. Many individualistic ales are produced by the new small breweries, especially the flourishing home-brew-pubs.

New small breweries have achieved considerable success in tastings – for instance, the awards won by Golden Hill Brewery's Exmoor Ale and West Riding's Tyke Bitter at CAMRA's Great British Beer Festivals. Obviously they would not stay in business without substantial market support from drinkers who like their widely-varied beers.

Quality Product

The great majority of small to medium-sized independent brewers are also unwavering in their commitment to a quality product. They know that if the taste of their beer changed markedly for the worse, their regulars would vote with their feet. Some brewers have definitely improved the taste and distinctiveness of their beers – Tolly's Original and Paine's 41, for instance, are markedly better than they were.

Even a couple of the major brewery groups have introduced more distinctive real ales. Allied have brought back the hoppy Benskins to partner Ind Coope's rather unremarkable bitter, and the new Taylor-Walker "Mainline" beers have been well received. The new beers from regional companies in the Grand Metropolitan group, though high-priced, are fine brews.

CAMRA will continue to fight for good quality, distinctive flavourful beers. If the British beer-drinker still recognises and wants quality and value for money, the good ales will drive out the bad. If not, we may well find that we're drowning in a tide of bland and boring imitation Euro-fizz in 20 years time – and we'll only have ourselves to blame.

Good ale flourishes in even the most unexpected parts of the British Isles. A few years ago I sat nervously in the back of a Volvo estate car with Dublin number plates that was being driven at break-neck speed through the streets of Belfast. We were en route for the first and so far only Good Beer Guide press reception in Northern Ireland.

The reception was in the Linen Hall, a rare outlet for cask beer in the region. Across the road from the bar, a member of the RUC, in jet-black uniform, eyed the Dublin-registered car with suspicion, his finger hovering on the trigger of his gun. We hurried inside to the welcome cheer of the bar. A pint of cask beer, I thought, would calm the nerves that other beers cannot reach.

Irish Pride

A glass of Hilden Ale was pushed into my hand in the spacious back room set aside for the reception. It was my first encounter with the beer from Lisburn in County Antrim. I marvelled at the clear, tawny colour, the proud head and the clean, refreshing taste, a splendid, skilful blend of malt and hops.

I was introduced to Hilden's brewer, Brendan Dobbin, a name that conjured up images of patient dedication, loyalty and devotion. "I hope you won't feel insulted," I said, "but your beer tastes remarkably like Fuller's London Pride." A slow smile spread across his face. "That is exactly what I was trying to achieve," he said.

A beer brewed in Co Antrim to taste remarkably similar to Fuller's prize ale from Chiswick shows how difficult it is to draw a beer map of Britain. I have long tired of simplistic descriptions that suggest that all Scottish beers are dark and malty, West Midlands ales sweet and lightly hopped, and London bitters exceptionally sharp and uncompromising. The more you travel the country in search of good beer the more you are convinced that no two ales are alike unless, like

Brendan Dobbin, you set out to recreate a beer that you think is the last word in perfection.

The great pleasure and wonder of British draught beer is its ability to offer brews that, even within small and compact areas, astonish the drinker by their sheer difference. In East Anglia, there is no possible confusion between Adnams' tangy bitter, Tolly Cobbold's light, refreshing bitter and smooth, malty Original and Green King's nutty IPA and rich, heady Abbot.

Smooth Landlord

The Lake District offers both Jennings bitter, sharp, yellowy and hoppy, and Hartley's darker and maltier brew. Yorkshire is scarcely a small and compact area but a vast region of three counties with such marvelously differing brews as Theakston's sharp bitter, Sam Smith's sweetish Old Brewery, Ward's, Stone's, Webster's and Darley's fine, distinctive ales, and, of course, Tetley's renowned and shockingly dry bitter. If I had to choose my favourite from Yorkshire's collection then I would plump for the lesser-known but splendid beers from Timothy Taylor of Keighley, especially that smooth, creamy Landlord.

Dark Mild

I am conscious that, so far, I have mentioned only bitters. Bitter is thought of as the "typical" British beer, yet the strength of our main beer style lies not in some identikit taste from Truro to Thurso but in its myriad, subtle varieties. If there is a beer style that does have some unity of palate throughout the islands then it must be dark mild, a style threatened with extinction and hanging on to the mash tun by its fingertips.

From Maclay's 60 shilling in the north to Courage's Heavy in Plymouth, from Adnams' in the East through Ansell's in the Midlands, from Brain's Dark in Wales to Higson's in the north-west, there is a definable British tradition of jet-black, rich ales with a warm, deep flavour made possible by the use of roasted barley. Dark milds are not necessarily sweet – Adnams' mild, for example, is a well-hopped, refreshing drink – but the relative thinness of these ales comes as something of a shock to a palate expecting, from the colour in the glass, the punch of Guinness stout.

Declining Milds

The best and the worst dark milds I have drunk both came from London: Fuller's Hock and Young's Best Malt Ale. Both have gone the way of all casks, a sad reflection of declining interest in mild beers. Youngs of Wandsworth brew some magnificent bitters but their mild was a watery product that tasted rather like a liquid version of a Mars Bar. But Fuller's Hock was a delicious, satisfying, bitter-sweet beverage, a quite exceptional beverage. It lingers on now in a carbonated container version, which Fullers – tut, tut – sometimes serve by dummy handpumps. Like Young's mild, sales of Hock had fallen so low that it was no longer a viable proposition for the brewery in cask form.

Slutching Brews

A true light mild is merely a distant relation of dark mild, except when brewers adopt, for me, the dubious practice of adding caramel to the one to produce the other. It is difficult to say where a light mild ends and a low-gravity bitter starts – why, for example, Burt's 1030 degrees gravity LB from the Isle of Wight, or Whitbread's West Country Pale Ale, Ruddle's Bitter, Devenish's Bitter or Buckley's Standard, all around 1031 or 1032 degrees – should be classified as bitters while ales of equivalent or higher gravity weigh in as milds. Possibly it is because light bitters are more astringently hoppy; they certainly make good session or "slutching" brews. I am sad that Hall and Woodhouse in Dorset have

phased out their 1031 Badger, a quality ale that did not deserve its dismissive nickname of "boy's bitter".

But where the genuine light milds are concerned there is no doubt that the best I have supped is McMullen's AK from Hertford. It is a fruity, tasty ale, the ideal lunchtime sup or the starter for an evening.

Mention of light bitters does throw up at least one strong regional style. Hall and Woodhouse were not alone in brewing "boy's bitter". Eldridge Pope, Palmer, Devenish and Wadworth produce beers in the West Country that, while low in gravity, have a tasty, hoppy character. But try as hard as I can, I find it hard to lay down firm patterns for the rest of Britain.

Heavies

Scottish 70 and 80 shilling "heavies", it is true, have a tendency to be darkish and malty. The best of the breed must be Belhaven's 80 shilling, a beer so superb that is a wonder that a company beset by boardroom upheavals and Miss World boob-eramas could manage to produce it. Belhaven belongs to a definable trend that includes Younger, McEwan, Drybrough and the new Arroll's Ale, but in Alloa Maclay's heavies have a distinctly more hoppy edge and the new Tennent 80 shilling has a light and delightfully subtle palate that suggests that Bass, the parent company, is attempting to create a typical Burton-style ale in the Scottish heartland.

Drinker's Mecca

The Manchester region, often described as the beer drinker's Mecca – perhaps as a result of the imbiber's tendency to genuflect towards the nearest brewery at sunset – defies any attempt to impose a regional style. It is hard to find or imagine beers more diverse in taste and character than the likes of Hyde, "Joseph's" (Holt), John Willy Lees, Boddingtons, Oldham,

Wilson, Greenall or Robinson. The last-named, from Stockport, brews for my money one of the stand-out beers in Britain, the beautifully sharp best bitter. Yet one man's fine beer is another's poison: a former CAMRA HQ colleague refused to touch it on pain of death on the grounds that it was "too sweet".

Prince of Ales

Sweetness is claimed to be characteristic of West Midlands beers. It is true of the ubiquitous Brew XI but I find Ansell's bitter to be pleasantly hopped, Davenport's to be an excellent dry, quenching brew and Banks's and Hanson's smooth and nutty. Close at hand in the East Midlands Marston produce arguably the prince of ales in Pedigree, the last genuine "union" beer, a system in which the beer ferments in vast oak casks, frothing up pipes into trays where it circulates over a constantly regenerating yeast strain. I can only marvel at the superb, delicate palate of Pedigree and bewail the demise of the union-room Bass and Worthington Bitter.

Wells Farrago

Down from the Midlands, taking in Everard's excellent ales in Leicester and Ruddle's fiercely independent brews in Rutland, and into the Home Counties. McMullen, already mentioned for their light-mild, also brew a good, chewy strong bitter while in Bedford Charles Wells produce a tawny bitter that divides drinkers more than any other beer I know. While I delight in the hoppy, well-balanced palate of the beer, otherwise good friends refuse even to enter a Wells' pub.

And so into London, now short on genuine local ales though the capital is bombarded with beer from every nook and cranny of the country. Fullers and Youngs kept the cask flag flying bravely through the lean years of the keg ascendancy but Whitbread have decamped to their Luton fizzery and Courage's heavily vamped "Cockney" best bitter is now trunked up the motorway from Bristol. Fortunately, Watneys now brew and serve cask beer with some fervour and a clutch of mini-breweries and home-brew pubs add to jolly toping. Sadly, the beer of my East End youth, Charrington IPA, is now a bowdlerised, Brummified tipple.

My remit is a short article, not a tome. It is impossible to do justice to the variety of British beer here. I can only mention in passing the joys of the Thames valley, with Brakspear, Morrells, Morland and Hook Norton, the tongue-tingling pleasures of Shepherd Neame in the heart of the Kentish hop fields, and, a long leek's throw west, the there's-lovely beers of Wales, in particular Felinfoel's delicious bitter.

Bottled Jewel

There are strong bitters, such as the mind-blowing Fuller's ESB, rich, heavy old ales in the class of the legendary Old Peculier, and barley wines so rich and strong that, in the case of the bottled Thomas Hardy's Ale, they have to be "laid down" like fine wine for several years.

In case this quick canter through the brewing land is thought to be Guinnless, special mention must be reserved for that bitter-sweet bottled jewel from Dublin and Park Royal, produced with loving care and allowed to reach full maturity and true taste in its small container. Bottled Guinness is one of the brewing marvels of the world.

Naturally-conditioned beer is alive and well. In spite of the best efforts of the accountants and marketing department of the giant brewing conglomerates and the incursions of over-promoted, over-carbonated and over-priced mock lagers, cask beer has revived and survived. It is ready to cheer you in all its multi-faceted glory throughout the British isles, even in beleaguered Belfast.

Roger Protz

A Matter of Taste

Take a mouthful of beer. Roll it round your mouth. Swallow it (it's too expensive to spit out). How would you describe its taste? The chances are that if you venture more than a couple of words you'll feel an uncomfortable sense of embarrassment crawling over you.

The language of taste tends to be associated with snobbery, pretentiousness, and writing worthy of "Pseuds' Corner". Everyone knows Thurber's cartoon in "Men, Women and

Dogs", with the overbearing host announcing grandly to his guests as he pours the wine: "It's a naive domestic burgundy without any breeding, but I think you'll be amused by its presumption." The risks and pitfalls are there for those who try to discuss the taste of beer as well.

It is important to be able to describe the taste of beer, however. First of all, it's important because that's why most people drink beer – for the taste. It's also the reason why people *don't* drink beer – witness the lager-drinker who said he didn't like beer "because you can taste it afterwards".

It's important also for a consumer group like CAMRA to be able to talk intelligently about the taste of beer. If the customer wants to persuade breweries to produce beers he likes, he has to be able to say what they should taste like. Reductions and improvements in quality, manifest themselves in subtle differences of taste – and these have to be spotted and described.

It's also important for the brewers. Marketing studies based on customer preference, and day-to-day quality control tastings, are impossible without experienced tasters and the language of taste.

Though beer's main appeal is to the taste, it awakens the appetite by appealing to various senses. It appeals to sight: think of a fine amber-coloured draught bitter, or the dark body and creamy head of a stout. It appeals to smell, usually by a hoppy aroma. And the sense of satisfaction and well-being promoted by the stomach-filling volume and alcoholic content of a couple of pints shouldn't be neglected.

None of this will matter in the slightest if, when you actually take a mouthful of the stuff, it tastes like washing-up liquid, disinfectant, cough mixture, or cold tea. Such extremes of taste are easily described. It's the delicate nuances that are difficult

to capture in words, and the lack of a precise and well-used vocabulary of taste in English is a major obstacle.

What is needed is a set of words that provides a notation for taste sensations, quite independent of the subjective judgement whether an individual actually *likes* that flavour or not.

This raises the question of whether – in such a highly subjective area as taste – there can be such a thing as a common agreed language. No two people can be entirely certain that they taste and mean the same thing – they may use different words for the same taste, and the same word for different tastes.

In recent years, considerable progress has been made in establishing a language of taste. In America, research has focussed on analysis of the chemical compounds which influence the flavour of beer. In England, work has centred on the linguistic classification of flavours.

Morton Meilgaard, Director of Research and Development at the Stroh Brewing Company in Detroit, has established links between the various acids, sugars, alcohols, esters and other substances which make up beer, and the range of flavour perceived in beer.

Even if beer can be broken down into all the chemical components which contribute flavour, Meilgaard doubts whether the laboratory machine will ever replace taste panels of human beings. This is because a machine could analyse the parts, but it could never taste the whole thing – and then pronounce whether or not it liked the overall taste! The human tongue can. A marvellously sensitive instrument of taste, it has 9000 taste buds, each with 10–15 taste cells.

There may be no well-used and co-ordinated vocabulary of taste in English, but there are hundreds of words that describe tastes, some of them unusual and surprising, like "cardboardy" and "cabbagey", some well-known like "rubbery" or "rancid", and some specialised like "aldehydic" and "ribes" (curranty, hence "Ribena"). One problem of the language of taste is that it tends, like Freudian psychology, towards the pathological. It's easier to taste and describe the distinctive nasty off-flavours than the pleasant

ones. Hence there are many more words for disease than there are for normality.

At the Brewing Research Foundation at Lyttel Hall, near Nutfield in Surrey, J F. Clapperton and C. E. Dalgliesh have developed a key-word system for classifying beer tastes. This involved a painstaking search of the Oxford English Dictionary for all words describing aroma and flavour. Clusters of synonyms were then analysed, and a central key-word chosen which incorporates the sense of several synonyms. The Brewing Research Foundation claim that the 44 key-words describe all the aromas and flavours perceptible in any beer. The flavour of any one beer can normally be characterised by around 25 key-words, describing its aroma, taste and after-taste, which build up its "flavour profile".

Extensive taste-panel tests have proved that the key-word system can help record consumer judgements and preferences with a much greater degree of consistency, because it provides a common language based on agreed definition of tastes. This work takes flavour analysis a long way beyond the classification of the four "primary tastes" – sweet, salt, bitter and sour. And it takes it into an area where the customer can tell the brewer what beer he likes – and precisely *how* he likes it to taste.

The language of flavour gives the beer-drinker a way of expressing his choice, by telling the brewer what he wants to drink – not the other way round!

Cellarmanship

In days of old when men were bold, most pubs brewed their own beer. In the nineteenth century the organisation, equipment and technology of brewing underwent a considerable change, with effects which are still being felt today.

With the new style of pubs came a new profession, that of cellarman. Looking after a cellar full of casks, connected by a tangle of piping to beer engines in as many as four or five bars was a full time, skilled job. It is a pity that a growing number of landlords in 1984 seem to have lost interest in this part of their craft.

The dramatic increase in the number of real ale pubs in recent years has been accompanied in many cases by a decline in the quality of the ale available. Some landlords think that a pint of antique, vinegary beer, will satisfy the customer as long as it comes from a fancy handled beer engine. Unfortunately some customers seem to agree – too few of us are willing to reject the pint that is not worth drinking.

What is required to get the perfect pint onto the bar? Certainly no magic; just some practical common sense, a respect for hygiene and a modest amount of labour. Absolutely the first essential is to choose the proper size of cask to suit the volume of trade. Brewers supply traditional ale in casks of many sizes, normally in multiples of nine gallons, from the smallest nine gallon firkin, through the eighteen gallon kilderkin to the thirty six gallon barrel (the only cask that should be so called).

A few considerate brewers still supply tiny four and a half gallon pins, but these are becoming uneconomic to handle, since, unlike almost any other product, the purchaser of beer pays no financial penalty for buying in small quantities. One barrel will cost exactly the same as four firkins even though these will have cost the brewer virtually four times the labour to clean and fill and several times the capital to buy. Brewers keep up this expensive practice to encourage their licensees to choose a cask size which, once started, will be emptied within one or two days. Unfortunately a minority of lazy landlords consider that using large casks will be less work – less cask changing, more cellar space, but with worse beer as a result.

Having got the size of the casks right, the landlord has to treat them with care and respect. If at all possible (space and cash-flow permitting), the beer should be allowed to mature undisturbed in the cellar for a week or so before being vented. Venting releases the excess gas produced in the beer during the all-important secondary fermentation. As soon as this dissolved gas has escaped, a process that normally takes twenty four hours or so, the beer is ready for use.

From now on the two problems are to prevent further gas being lost (the beer going flat) and to prevent contamination (the beer going sour). The traditional method of achieving the first objective is the hard spile, a wooden peg that is inserted into the shive hole whenever the cask is not in use. Once again, laziness leads to abuse as casks are frequently left open from venting until they are empty. The last customers get some pretty flat, characterless beer.

Contamination of beer in the cask can come from two sources, airborne organisms and infections introduced by the publican returning poor beer to the cask. Provided the cellar is kept scrupulously clean (it is a perishable food store after all), airborne infection is rarely a problem if the right cask sizes are being used. Returning beer to casks, however, is a widespread practice resulting in a great deal of beer that is mediocre or worse.

There is a lot of confusion about this practice, which is widely and erroneously believed to be illegal. All that is illegal is to put beer of a different type back into a cask – bitter into mild, for example, although this habit is common enough. Returning beer to the cask cannot be condemned out of hand, it can be acceptable when collecting good beer from a venting but very lively cask, and when drawing off good beer from engines and pipes (lines), at the end of a session.

In both cases the beer must be collected in a sterilised bucket and then filtered back immediately into a cask that is at least half full. The essential is that filtering back should only ever be used with perfectly good beer. In all too many cases, what goes back is a mixture of slops, ends of already soured casks or even dregs from unfinished glasses. Lest this should be thought to be only a problem in pubs selling real beer, it should be noted that allegedly tamper-proof kegs are routinely opened by unsavoury landlords to return used beer.

The last stop in the ale's journey to your glass is the dispensing system – the beer engine and its connecting pipes. The Victorians had solid lead pipes of many hundredweights to haul around the cellar, pumps with leather pistons and even

cleaners using caustic mixtures – a health officer's nightmare.

Today the lines are smooth bore transparent plastic, cleaners are non-toxic detergents and the pumps are mostly stainless steel, glass or plastic.

Nevertheless yeast still deposits in the pipework and pumps, and weekly cleaning is the minimum acceptable regime. Apart from a permanent coarseness of taste and lack of clarity, the tell-tale signs of dirty lines and pumps are small fluffy lumps of yeast in the glass and often a poor head with a 'scummy' appearance containing small white flecks.

Indifferent cellarmanship can ruin a superb product. If you get a poor pint, complain. If the landlord won't change it, change your pub. If we don't insist on the best possible quality of beer, served and kept in the best possible condition, we are not only condemning ourselves to some joyless drinking, we are also providing the breweries with the perfect excuse for a fresh keg assault on our pubs.

Cellarmanship – a full booklet of practical advice on all aspects of the subject relating to real ale is available from CAMRA's head office, 34 Alma Road, St Albans, for 75p including postage.

Announce to your fellow-regulars in the Rat & Armpit in Glueworks Street that you've changed your name from Shufflebottom to von Straubenzee, and that you expect henceforth to be treated as an European aristocrat. The immediate response will be of hoots of laughter and derision, and cries of 'Right lads, off with his majesty's keks and pass the Cherry Blossom.'

Yet set up a lager brewery behind the Blagdon gasworks, and your advertising agency will be only too happy to persuade these same regulars to swallow the claim that this Blagdon brew is actually Junkerbrau, Yodelpils or Belgebier.

Raise criticism of the advertising industry and the outcry is predictable. Agencies are quick with the glib claim that advertisements exist only to inform consumers about the choice of products available to them. This is cant. Advertising exists to create demand through manipulation, building a product image with which the target audience can be persuaded to identify.

In the case of breweries the target audience is young people who are important targets because they have a good deal of spending power, are more malleable and, most important, are far less price conscious than their elders.

The big brewers have invested massively in lager brewing capacity and an equally massive investment in advertising is needed to keep the plant running. No expense is spared to convince pub customers that the watery, carbonated liquid they are paying through the nose for, is the 'in' drink to have.

The power of the advertisers and their clients is insidious and far reaching, for those who pay the piper call the tune.

There is, of course, the Advertising Standards Authority, which exists, as they tell us in their own advertisements, to ensure that adverts are legal, decent, honest and truthful. The ASA is the advertisers' poodle, a sop to public opinion to ensure that no government will set up a truly independent body to control the advertising industry. It is also a poodle with no teeth, with no power to sanction or punish firms who overstep even its miserably lax standards.

The ASA is further devalued by its slowness to act. Most advertising campaigns are short-lived affairs, with new slogans or concepts being introduced in a matter of weeks or months. The ASA regularly shuts the stable door after the horse has gone. It is not enough for the advertiser to promise not to do it again, the damage has already been done.

Any member of the public can write to the ASA and complain about a poster or newspaper or magazine advertisement. It does not cover television or radio commercials, which are dealt

Fizzical Impossibilities

with by the IBA, or hoardings not displayed on 'paid for' space. If a brewery chooses to advertise a product on hoardings owned by the brewery, or on the walls of the company's thousands of pubs, the ASA will not act. The ASA will also not handle any complaints regarding company-produced promotional material, or point-of-sale products such as drip mats, pub decorations or in-house poster campaigns.

If the content of an ad is queried, the advertisers will say the claims made are so exaggerated or amusing that no rational person could take them seriously. If that is really so, why should such hyper-rational people be spending such vast sums of money to spread their message?

Virtually all lagers are promoted as if they are continental. In fact none of the widely available brands of lager in this country are brewed abroad and none are brewed to the same recipe as their foreign forebears. These lagers are not directly advertised as foreign brewed, but the suggestion is planted through the use of continental names, words and images.

Courage's lager, Hofmeister, for example, is hardly a name suggestive of its origins – a beer factory on the M4 near Reading. Watneys advertised their new draught lager, Fosters, by claiming that it was 'Fresh up from down under'. In fact it comes from Mortlake, so unless their slogan is rhyming slang for some other method of producing lager, the claim is misleading.

The ASA's guidelines for advertising alcohol make clear that the impression should not be given that drinking improves one's prowess in any way. Yet in Harp adverts a quick-witted 'hero' talks his way out of trouble and successfully pinches another man's date; Heineken is alleged to refresh the parts; Bass' Black Label is sold on the claim that it enables the drinker to eat four of what Ian Botham can only eat three of. Complain to the ASA and they fall back on their 'so exaggerated or amusing' formula.

To link drink with sex is absolutely forbidden. It is, therefore, entirely coincidental that the results of a survey suggesting that some women thought that lager drinkers were 'better in bed' should have been released a week before Watney's began a massive promotion of an 'International Lager Festival'. So international was the event that all but one of the lagers was brewed by Watneys in this country and the other one was bottled here.

Many lagers are sold as diet or 'lite' lagers. Though they are often lower in carbohydrate, they are actually just as fattening as any other beer. Lagers are also bad value for money. They are heavily chilled to conceal their lack of flavour, and not only are they consistently 10p and more a pint over the price of bitter and mild, they are also much weaker in alcoholic strength. The brewers pay less duty on weak beers than strong ones, so the actual greater profit is even more than the apparent price differential. No wonder they are so keen to promote lager sales.

When the large brewers do condescend to promote beer it is usually canned or keg beer that they push. Keg Watney Mann's beer is marketed as 'traditional ale in cans' and Whitbread have concocted an organisation, 'the campaign for real value', whose acronym CANVA appears an obvious attempt to associate their inferior canned beer with the quality image of CAMRA.

With an advertising investment running at tens of millions a year, the large brewers are able to report that lager sales to people under 35 are now running at approaching four pints in every ten sold. They will no doubt, continue to spend an annual king's ransom on promoting the products that they want to make. Unfortunately we only seem to want to buy them when their advertisers have 'informed' us about them in their own inimitable way.

Canine CAMRA

If you get down to the Woods today, you're in for a big surprise. Ben, the pub dog at the Last Inn, Hengoed, near Oswestry, really can sort out the Woods from the trees.

Give him a row of dishes, one containing real beer and the rest whatever variety of beers, lagers and stouts you care to proffer, and after a brief sniff round, Ben will unerringly zero in on the real stuff and polish off the lot. Ben prefers Woods Special Bitter, but if that's off, he is willing to drink most other real ales and he'll usually give the guest beers brought in by landlord Jim Heaton a try. If there's no real beer on offer, however, he'll turn up his nose at the lagers and keg bitters and walk out in disgust.

Ben's greatest moment (until his appearance in the Good Beer Guide) came when the BBC descended on the Last Inn to film him for That's Life. First the entire lighting, sound, camera, production, editorial, secretarial and free lunch departments set up their equipment. Then followed an interminable series of rehearsals, run throughs and 'let's try that again, loves', until at last the team were ready for the final take.

Unfortunately Ben had worked his way through some four pints of Woods during the

1. *Counsel approaches the bar – one dish contains Woods Special Bitter, the others 'well known brands'*

2. *This one smells like Piths*

3. *You trying to poison me?*

rehearsals, and had retired to a corner to sleep it off. The BBC crew were reduced to patrolling the car park in relays with him for the next couple of hours until he'd sobered up enough to complete the final take.

Ben developed his remarkable talents young. At the age of one he had his elbows on the bar beside the regulars. Sometimes he'd have a drink with them, sometimes he wouldn't, so the Heatons decided to find out which beers he would drink. They lined him up with a sample from each pump, Ben ignored the rest, supped the Woods and a star was born.

Now aged two, Ben is still very much a social drinker, having a pint when a customer offers him one, but often going a few days without touching a drop. In tribute to his moderation, he has absolutely no trace of a beer gut.

Ben's talents aren't likely to endear him to some of our larger breweries. The fake continental image of their lagers obviously doesn't fool a dog who is part Great Dane himself, and when it comes to keg beers like John Piths, Ben clearly feels it isn't even fit for a dog to drink.

4. The dognosis is complete – this one's the Woods, the rest are trees – and we know what dogs do to trees

5. Three more pints please, Doris

6. Our hero rests from his labours – in tests 9 out of 10 dogs can tell the difference between real beer and Piths

The British pub has evolved over centuries. The Roman taverna, the Saxon ale-houses, the monastic hospices, the coaching inns, gin shops, beer houses, gin palaces, and present day pubs are all variations on a theme that is uniquely British. In no other country do the drinking places have the warmth, the character and the central place in the life of the community of the British pub.

In every pub from the highest to the lowest, the qualities that go to make a good pub have remained constant down the years – good beer, well kept and well served, a cheerful, friendly landlord, a bite to eat, warmth, comfort and good conversation, and a blazing open fire which not only contributes its heat, but also adds greatly to the character and ambience of a pub.

The first public houses were simply the kitchens of houses where the traveller could find refreshment by the warmth of a blazing fire. As ale houses and inns developed, the inglenook or alcove by the fire became a central feature giving a place to eat, drink and talk, out of the winter cold. It is no longer necessary or usually possible to sit in the fireplace, but an open fire remains the focal point of a typical pub, providing warmth and a cheerful welcome for the thirsty traveller. So it is probably not so surprising to find that, coinciding with the real beer revival in Britain's pubs in recent years – and with much the same motivation – has come a pronounced swing-back to 'real fire' heating.

Responding in many cases to

may surprise you to know that a pub with an open fire is one of the best ways to avoid it. The aromas of everything from cigarettes to hikers socks are drawn out of a room by a roaring open fire. If the fire's roar is sufficiently loud it has the added advantage of drowning out the wartime reminiscences of the resident pub bore as well.

To encourage the trend towards more real fires in pubs, the Solid Fuel Advisory Service has been conducting a successful campaign persuading publicans to open up disused chimneys and fireplaces and install modern fires. As a result there will be many hundreds of new glowing pub hearths to greet customers in those long, cold winter evenings.

customer demand and with active encouragement from the coal industry's promotional body, the Solid Fuel Advisory Service, many breweries and landlords are now installing or re-instating open fires as an aid to the appeal of their pubs old and new.

Solid fuel heating fits into every sort of surrounding from an old country inn to a brand new town pub. There are several smokeless fuels as well as coal, and a range of fires that will do everything from running the central heating to cooking mouth-watering meals.

If smoke gets in your eyes it

Whether you're in a moorland inn, a post-house with an inglenook or a modern town tavern, wherever you go, a pub with a real fire provides the warmest welcome. Look out for the colourful 'Warmest Welcome' sign on the door of your local and note the real fire symbol in this Good Beer Guide.

A real fire is also perfect to go home to, whether you just want a glowing living room fire or whole house central heating. For further information write to the Solid Fuel Advisory Service, Hobart House, Grosvenor Place, London SW1X 7AE.

Malting

Beer begins in the barley fields. The harvested barley is taken to the maltings, where the grains are steeped in water and than laid out, three of four inches deep, on a malting floor. In the warmth, the grains germinate and enzymes begin to break down their starch content into sugars. At this point, the barley grains are dried in hot air at 140 °F, which stops germination. The grain is then 'kilned' – or roasted. The higher the temperature in the kiln, the darker the roast, and the more colour and flavour the malted barley has.

Milling

The malted barley is ground coarsely between rollers in a malt mill. The resulting 'grist' must not be too fine and floury, or it will form a sticky paste when water is added. Nor must it be too lumpy, or the sugars in the grain will not dissolve fully in the mash.

Water

Water – called 'liquor' by brewers – is a vital ingredient of beer. Mineral salts in water help the enzymes convert the starch in the malted barley into fermentable sugars in the mash, and act as a yeast nutrient in fermentation. Different beer styles are best brewed with different waters – pale ales with Burton water full of magnesium salts, dark beers like stout and porter with London water, and Pilsner beers with very soft water.

Mashing

The 'grist' and 'hot liquor' are run together into the mash tun and left to stand – or 'mash' – for up to two hours at about 152 °F. In the thick porridgy mash, the enzymes complete the conversion of the starch into natural soluble sugars. The hot sweet liquid, called 'wort', is then drained off through the slotted plates in the base of the mash tun. The grain in the tun is 'sparged' – or sprinkled – with more hot liquor to ensure maximum possible extraction of the sugars.

Hops

Hops – climbing plants, related botanically to hemp and nettles – give beer its bitter flavour and hoppy aroma. Hops are picked in the early autumn and dried in oast houses. The dry hops are packed in huge sacks, called 'pockets', and transported to the brewery, where they must be kept cool and dry.

Copper

The hot sweet wort from the mash tun is boiled for about 90 minutes with the hops in the copper. Boiling extracts the essential flavour compounds from the leaves and seed-cones of the hops.

Hop back and cooler

After boiling, the hops are separated from the wort in the 'hop back', which acts as a strainer. The hop leaves settle at the perforated base of the hop back, and form a filter bed which catches the trub. Some brewers put a scattering of fresh hops on the floor of the hop back to boost aroma. The clear hopped wort coming out of the hop back is still very hot, before it can be fermented, it has to be cooled in a simple heat exchange device, called a 'paraflow cooler'.

Spent hops and grain

Brewing is a very efficient process. The spent grain is usually sold to local farmers for pig or cattle feed, the spent hops go for garden fertiliser and the excess yeast created during fermentation is sold off to make yeast extracts.

Yeast

Yeast is a one-celled fungus which grows by ingesting the sugars from the wort, metabolising them into alcohol and carbon dioxide, and splitting or budding to form new cells. During this fermentation process, the yeast multiplies many times, and the brewer collects samples to keep for the next brew. Brewing yeast adapts to its environment, and if taken from one brewery to another will mutate, sometimes undesirably.

Fermentation

The warm hopped wort is run from the paraflow into a fermenting vessel. At this stage, the Customs and Excise Officer takes a sample to find out the original gravity of the wort before fermentation. The higher the original gravity, the more potential alcohol in the finished beer – and the more duty the brewer must pay. Then the yeast is added – or 'pitched', and the gravity of the brew drops steadily. When it is down to about a quarter of the starting figure, the brewer ends fermentation by cooling the wort and skimming off the yeast head.

Racking and fining

The 'green beer' is run from the fermenting vessel into large conditioning tanks, or straight into racking machines from which casks are filled. Often a handful of dry hops are added to the cask to improve the hoppy 'nose' of the beer. For several days, a slow secondary fermentation takes place as the remaining yeast continues working on the residual sugars. This produces slightly more alcohol, natural carbon dioxide which gives the beer condition and life, and, most importantly, flavour changes which simply do not happen in filtered and pasteurised keg and bright beer. In a word, real ale is *matured*. Just before the cask is despatched from the brewery, a shot of finings is added. After the cask is vented, the finings clear the yeast, leaving a clear beer in the peak of condition and with a mature flavour – REAL ALE.

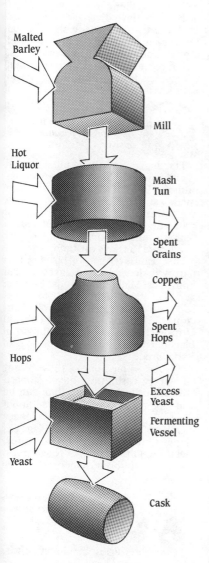

Malted Barley

Mill

Hot Liquor

Mash Tun

Spent Grains

Copper

Spent Hops

Hops

Excess Yeast

Fermenting Vessel

Yeast

Cask

Return of the local hero in Britain's brave new world of beer

"We at Conglomerate Brewing are not entirely deaf to the beer drinkers' demands."

A MAP of Britain's breweries in 1960 would have covered 358 operating companies. Ten years later our cartographer would have saved on ink and effort as there were around 200. With the number decreasing every year.

Over 150 independent breweries vanished during this period – and by 1972 the Big Six national combines dominated the market, producing four out of every five pints, most of them keg. Which is where CAMRA came in.

But a map today would once again tax the map maker's arm, for since the real ale revival gathered pace, over 100 new free trade brewers have set up along with 50 home-brew pubs. And despite some casualties in this brave new world of brewing, the numbers are increasing every month.

"We have spent considerable money researching our product range and its position in the market place."

From a trickle of pioneers in the early and mid-Seventies, this pint-size revolution has exploded into a major industry itself, with several plant manufacturers and brewing consultants competing for the new small brewery business.

And while some have been content to brew just for their own pub or a few local houses, others, like Butcombe near Bristol or Broughton in Scotland, have carved themselves a fair slice of the free trade. Above all, almost every one of them has concentrated on producing traditional beer.

In total, they may only account for a small percentage of Britain's beer production – but they bring much-needed variety to our bars, often brewing specialist ales larger brewers would never consider.

If brewing at the hop roots is looking surprisingly healthy, takeover storm clouds are gathering again over the larger mash tuns.

In the past decade few breweries have been taken over. The Big Six, believing further concentration would be blocked, have diversified into other food and leisure areas, while the real ale revival restored the fortunes of many traditional family breweries. But in recent years ambitious regional companies have begun to snap up their less forceful fellows.

"And I can confidently tell you that after much thought, we have produced the answer..."

The biggest of them all, Greenall Whitley, bought Shipstone of Nottingham in 1978, the same year northern rivals Vaux took over Darleys in South Yorkshire. Then in 1982 Boddingtons collared Manchester neighbours Oldham, and Robinsons of Stockport swallowed Hartleys of Cumbria.

Last year Davenports of Birmingham narrowly fended off a takeover bid from West Midlands 'friends' Banks's, and as the Guide went to press Ellerman Lines were selling off Camerons of Hartlepool and Tolly Cobbold of Ipswich. While Matthew Brown of Blackburn were buying Theakstons of Yorkshire.

At least so far none of these recent take-over casualties have stopped brewing. Which is more than can be said for many of the traditional breweries entrusted to the tender mercies of the Big Six. In the Eighties alone Courage have closed three, including John Smiths at Newark last year, and Whitbread a mere seven (see P27).

"Our cask bitter is now to be sold under 12 different local names."

Fewer breweries inevitably mean fewer genuine local ales, however hard some companies try to produce ten different beers from one remote plant. It is the local variations that make Britain's beers so fascinating. Which is why the appearance of new local breweries, after decades of decline, is so welcome.

Brian Glover

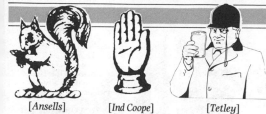

[Ansells]   [Ind Coope]   [Tetley]

ALLIED BREWERIES

It was back in the tense takeover years of the early Sixties that, in 1961, Allied Breweries was formed through the merger of existing national brewers, Ind Coope, with Ansells of the Midlands and Tetley-Walker in the North.

The new giant became Britain's second largest brewing group after Bass, and for a long time put all its energy behind keg brands like Double Diamond and Skol. However, in recent years, Allied have proved the most adventurous and progressive of the national combines.

Following the launch of Burton Ale in 1976, the company has increasingly supported traditional beers, including launching a number of new local brews. In the South, the group has masked its once-prominent name, Ind Coope, under a shower of old brewery titles like Benskins, Friary Meux, Taylor-Walker and Halls.

In the N.West a new company, Peter Walker, has been formed on Merseyside to run a chain of 75 highly-traditional pubs, with its own unique cask mild and bitter. 1983 saw Nicholson's chain of free houses in London, now owned by Allied, selling a variety of real ales.

The clock has turned full circle, right down to acquiring a home-brew pub near Ormskirk, Lancashire, the New Fermor Arms, and setting up others in Newark and Leeds, with more to follow in Yorkshire. They even launched a cask-conditioned lager, Gold Cross, served by handpump.

But the clock cannot go back completely. This author remembers one of his first jobs, after joining the staff of CAMRA, was to witness the demolition of Benskins' brewery in Watford. The names may have returned, but the new beers are chiefly brewed at Burton or Romford, and the stream of 1037 bitters has not been distinguished.

Perhaps the most welcome beers have been the more distinctive Mainline for Taylor-Walker in London – and Allied's new Scottish-brewed cask beer, Archibald Arrol's 70/-. Launched late in 1982, it marks a major breakthrough as the first real ale from the Alloa Brewery.

Now the new marketing companies need their own brewing plants. Nicholsons are planning such a venture, and Halls, with their long transport lines in the S.West, would certainly benefit. They are already due to open a brewery in Oxford. It is also time the Aylesbury Brewery began to brew again after 40 years.

For underneath the tun full of names, Allied have surprisingly few breweries – only six altogether including the Wrexham lager brewery – having closed Ansells Brewery in Birmingham in 1981.

How one irreverent artist, working on an Allied house magazine, sees the new marketing companies in the S.East.

IND COOPE ALLOA, Whins Road, Alloa, Clackmannanshire, Scotland. ✆ 23539.
Archibald Arrol's 70/- (1037) – now in 84 outlets.

IND COOPE BURTON, Station Street, Burton-upon-Trent, Staffs. ✆ 45320.
Mild (1031)
Bitter (1037)
Burton Ale (1047.5)
Ansells Mild (1035.5)
Ansells Bitter (1037)
ABC Bitter (1037)
Hall's Harvest Bitter (1037)
Like Romford, brews a wide range of beers for Ansells and the various southern marketing companies without breweries. In the East Midlands also runs the **Maple Leaf** home-brew pub in Newark brewing **Maple Leaf Bitter** (1037).

IND COOPE ROMFORD, High Street, Romford, Essex. ✆ 66088.
Brewers Bitter (1037)
Benskins Bitter (1037)
Friary Meux Bitter (1037)
Taylor-Walker Bitter (1037)
Taylor-Walker Mainline (1041)

JOSHUA TETLEY, PO Box 142, Hunslet Road, Leeds. ✆ 435282.
Mild (1032)
Falstaff Best (1032)
Bitter (1035.5)
Real ale is available in nearly 80 per cent of the 1,100 tied houses. There is also one malt-extract home-brew pub, the *Station*, Guiseley, Leeds, producing **Guiseley Gyle** (1045), with two more about to open at the *New Inn*, Harrogate and the *Rose and Crown*, York.

TETLEY-WALKER, Dallam Lane, Warrington, Cheshire. ✆ 31231.
Tetley Mild (1032)
Tetley Bitter (1035.5)
Walker Mild (1032)
Walker Bitter (1033)
Walker Best Bitter (1035.5)
Real ale in about half the 820 pubs. Also owns the *New Fermor Arms* home-brew pub, Rufford, Ormskirk, producing **Blezards Bitter** (1040).

WREXHAM Lager Brewery, Wrexham, N.Wales. Brews the new handpumped lager **Gold Cross** (1040).

The historic Burton Union room is now shut down.

BASS

Bass is probably the most famous name in British brewing. When huge companies were unheard of, it was a national brewer, sending its beers by rail throughout the land from Burton-upon-Trent. Back in 1927 it merged with that equally eminent name, Worthington.

But it was in the Sixties that it swelled into Britain's biggest brewer. First, Canadian entrepreneur Eddie Taylor swept through the country taking over 16 breweries to form Northern United Breweries. In 1961 United merged with Charringtons, later adding Tennents of Scotland. At the same time Bass merged with Mitchells and Butlers of Birmingham. Then in 1967 the toby jug and the red triangle joined to form Bass Charrington, controlling 20 per cent of the brewing industry and some 10,000 pubs.

This huge concern often boasts that it is the biggest brewer of cask-conditioned beer in the world. But in practice it has proved slow and unwieldy. An executive from a rival company once described Bass as "the dull boy of the class". Instead of being the leader, it has turned into a bulky also-ran.

Take the case of its most famous beer, Draught Bass, a brew long revered by drinkers, which was uniquely produced on the Burton Union system, involving continuous fermentation in large oak casks. This method gave the beer – including bottled Worthington White Shield – its distinctive character. But in 1982 Bass declared they could not afford the upkeep and closed their historic Number 2 brewery at Burton.

Now Draught Bass is brewed like other beers – and in the view of many drinkers tastes like other beers. It is no longer out on its own but one of a crowd. Only a short-sighted brewery could have trampled on centuries of tradition in this way. For the cost of a lager advertising campaign, they have lowered the colours of their flagship brand.

And it is a loss Bass could well have done without, for many of their other traditional beers have never been highly regarded. Brew X in the North and Brew XI in the Midlands taste like they sound, beers that never gained enough character to deserve more than a number.

Where Bass have really fallen behind is in their failure to improve their range of cask beers by introducing new local brands. Burton-brewed Worthington Bitter was tragically withdrawn in the East Midlands, while Crown has disappeared in the S.East. Only in the past year has the clumsy giant begun to move.

First came Fussell's Bitter for the S.West, followed by a real breakthrough in Scotland with the appearance of Tennent's own cask beer, Heriot Brewery 80/-.

But Bass have a long way to go if they are to rebuild their reputation, now left hanging on such brews as their excellent cask Stones from Sheffield (not to be confused with the much more widely available keg version).

BASS BURTON, High Street, Burton-upon-Trent, Staffs. ✆ 45301.
Draught Bass (1044)
Worthington White Shield (1051) – a naturally-conditioned bottled ale.

BASS RUNCORN, Cheshire and **BASS ALTON,** Hampshire – no real ale.

BASS TADCASTER, Tower Brewery, Tadcaster, N.Yorks. ✆ 832361.
Best Mild XXXX (1031)
Extra Light or **Toby Light** (1031)
Tower or **Cask Bitter** (1036)
Blackpool Best Mild (1036)
Altogether Bass own over 2,000 houses in the North of England, over half selling at least one cask beer. Some pubs in the N.West also take Jennings Bitter from Cumbria.

MITCHELLS & BUTLERS, Cape Hill Brewery, PO Box 27, Birmingham 16. ✆ 021 558 1481.
Mild (1035)
Brew XI (1040)
Three-quarters of the 1700 pubs sell real ale.

M&B HIGHGATE Brewery, Sandymount Road, Walsall, W.Midlands. ✆ 23168.
Highgate Mild (1036)
Highgate Best (1036)
Highgate Old Ale (1055)

M&B SPRINGFIELD Brewery, Wolverhampton, W.Midlands. ✆ 54551.
Springfield Bitter (1037)
Charrington IPA (1039)

STONES, Cannon Brewery, Rutland Road, Sheffield. ✆ 29331.
Stones Best Bitter (1038.3)
Cannon Special (1050)
Bass also run the Hope and Anchor brewery in Sheffield.

TENNENT Caledonian Breweries, Wellpark Brewery, Glasgow ✆ 041 552 6552 and Heriot Brewery, Roseburn Terrace, Edinburgh ✆ 031 337 1361.
Heriot Brewery 80/- (1042)

WELSH Brewers, Crawshay Street, Cardiff. ✆ 33071.
Hancocks or **Worthington Pale Ale** (1033)
Worthington Dark (1034)
Hancock's HB or **Worthington BB** (1037)
Fussell's Bitter (1038)
More than 350 of the 500 tied houses serve real ale.

National Combines

COURAGE

The story of Courage today is very much a tale of two companies. In the South, despite the closure of their historic London brewery on the south bank of the Thames and the opening of a huge keg brewery in Berkshire to replace the old Simonds brewery in Reading, Courage are still firmly wedded to cask beer.

All their traditional beer for the S. East may have to come up the motorway from Bristol...but it arrives in force in the shape of the excellent Best Bitter and Directors. Courage Western itself, with its Ale House scheme and other activities, has widely promoted real ale. And there is still another brewery in the far west at Plymouth, full of tradition, brewing the distinctive, dark Heavy in addition to Best. Though how long either the mild or the brewery will survive is a cause for constant concern.

But if the picture is relatively rosy in the South, it is dark and gloomy in the North, where John Smiths of Tadcaster, Courage's northern arm, continues to stick its head in its kegs and refuses to brew real ale for its pubs. It is the only major brewery in the country to treat its customers with contempt in this way. Every other one, following the recent introduction of real ales from North Country of Hull and Mansfield breweries, allow their drinkers at least one traditional beer.

John Smiths say they recognise that there is a demand for traditional beer, but do not believe it is sufficient to justify investment. Their attitude is hard to fathom when they live next door to their highly successful traditional relatives, Samuel Smith.

To add to the shame of the Magnet sign, John Smiths last year closed their ancient brewery in Newark. They have now killed brewing completely in this Nottinghamshire town, just like they once destroyed one of Yorkshire's more famous beers, Barnsley Bitter.

Part of the Imperial group with 5,300 pubs

COURAGE Central, The Brewery, Worton Grange, Berkshire. No real ale.

COURAGE Western, Regent Road, Bedminster, Bristol. ☎ 666944.
Bitter Ale (1030)
Best Bitter (1039)
Directors (1046)
1,200 pubs sell real ale.

COURAGE Western, Regent Brewery, Stonehouse, Plymouth, Devon. ☎ 20481.
Heavy (1032)
Best Bitter (1039)

JOHN SMITHS, Tadcaster, N. Yorks. ☎ 832091. No real ale since 1974.

* Courage also brew a powerful bottle-conditioned **Imperial Russian Stout** (1104)

SCOTTISH & NEWCASTLE

Scottish and Newcastle Breweries, the result of a merger in 1960 between Scottish Brewers and Newcastle Breweries, owe their national standing to their penetration of the free trade. For in terms of the numbers of pubs, they own less than the major regional brewery, Greenall Whitley, with few houses outside their strongholds in the N. East and Scotland.

That national position was carved out by their keg beers – Younger's Tartan and McEwan's Export – but with the swing back to traditional beer they have been slow to react, only promoting their real ales in the past few years, which have also seen the reintroduction of the distinctive dark Younger's No 3.

The free trade itself has become much more competitive, with the result that S&N have turned out a string of disappointing profit performances. This, coupled with their relative small size – they only own 1,485 pubs – means they have become the centre of continuous takeover rumours.

NEWCASTLE Breweries, Tyne Brewery, Newcastle. No real ale.

SCOTTISH Brewers, New Fountain Brewery, Edinburgh.
McEwan 70/- or **Younger's XXPS Scotch** (1036.5)
McEwan 80/- or **Younger's IPA** (1042.2)
Younger's No 3 (1043)

SCOTTISH Brewers, Holyrood Brewery, Edinburgh. ☎ 031 556 2591. No real ale. To close 1986.

ROYAL Brewery, Moss Side, Manchester. No real ale.

GUINNESS

Guinness, Park Royal Brewery, London NW10. ☎ 01 965 7700.
The world-renowned Irish stout brewers own no pubs nor produce a cask beer. Draught Guinness is all keg. Yet they provide a welcome 'friend' in every bar with their bottle-conditioned **Guinness Extra Stout** (1042)

WATNEY

If one name will always be linked with CAMRA, then it's Watneys, the villain of the piece in the early Seventies, who attracted much of the Campaign's venom through their appalling Red keg beer and red pub policies. Much to their discomfort they became universally dubbed 'Grotneys'.

But if there is more joy in heaven over one repented sinner than over all those who stayed pure, then CAMRA today should be dancing in Watney pub doorways.

In London, the renamed Watney Combe Reid has not only introduced its own traditional beers into the vast majority of its pubs, but also added one of the most famous real ales, Ruddles County; Trumans have introduced a full range of cask beers including a mild; Wilsons of Manchester have converted almost completely to handpumps; Drybroughs have watered the Scottish desert with two real ales.

The list of achievement is impressive, but Watneys can never completely escape their black Red history. Their notorious takeover trail has left them with massive monopolies in Norfolk and Northamptonshire, resulting in constant conflict over pub closures and lack of choice.

And the price the drinker has had to pay for these improvements has sometimes been too great, particularly in their Chef and Brewer managed houses. Ruddles at a pound a pint may leave the average customer wondering whether Watneys are trying to put him back into the red in another way.

And while Watney's renamed South Coast company, Phoenix, may be introducing guest beers from independent breweries like Burts and Gales besides their own Ushers, in Yorkshire Websters have been dragging their feet.

Their popular bitter may now be widely available throughout the South on handpump, but in their own pubs pressurised beer still rules most of the bars. And to add insult to injury, the company has even changed the recipe to an altogether blander brew for its own local drinkers.

Watney, Mann, Truman is a subsidiary of Grand Metropolitan, the hotel and leisure group.

DRYBROUGH, Cragmillar, Edinburgh. ☎ 031 661 6161.
Pentland (1036)
Drybrough's Eighty (1042)

NORWICH Brewery, Rouen Road, Norwich. ☎ 60222.
Bullard's Mild (1035)
Norwich Castle (1037)
Also brew for Manns of the E. Midlands and Phoenix on the S. Coast:
Manns IPA (1038.1)
Manns Bitter (1039.7)
570 of the 800 pubs in the Midlands serve real ale.
Tamplins Bitter (1038)

TRUMAN, Brick Lane, London E1. ☎ 01 377 0020.
Prize Mild (1034)
Bitter (1036)
Best Bitter (1045)
Sampson Hanbury's Extra Strong Ale (1055)
600 of the 900 houses serve cask beer.

USHERS, Parade House, Trowbridge, Wilts. ☎ 63171.
PA (1031)
Best Bitter (1038)
Founder's Ale (1045)
570 of the 680 pubs serve cask beer.

WATNEY COMBE REID, Stag Brewery, Mortlake, London SW14. ☎ 01 876 3434.
London Bitter (1037.5)
Stag Bitter (1044)
Real ale in over 80 per cent of the 1,500 pubs.

WEBSTER, Fountain Head Brewery, Ovendon Wood, Halifax, W. Yorks. ☎ 63451.
Dark Mild (1032)
Yorkshire Light (1033.8)
Yorkshire Bitter (1037.5)
A third of the 295 houses serve real ale.

WILSONS, Monsall Road, Newton Heath, Manchester 10. ☎ 061 205 2345.
Original Mild (1032.1)
Original Bitter (1036)
Gold Medal (1042)
About 600 of the 720 houses serve real ale.

"WE'VE GOT BENSKINS, TAYLOR WALKER, FRIARY MEUX, ROMFORD BREWERY, WILSONS, WEBSTERS, NORWICH BITTER, TAMPLINS, FREMLINS, FLOWERS, STRONGS, WETHEREDS, AND POMPEY ROYAL — WHAT WOULD YOU LIKE ?"

"A PINT OF WATNEYS"

WHITBREAD

Whitbread were once regarded within the industry as the most gentle of the giants. Independent breweries, threatened with takeover, could shelter from the advancing storm under the historic London company's 'umbrella' – this meant allowing good, old Colonel Whitbread a sizeable share stake in return for protection.

Some independent companies like Boddingtons, Marstons and Devenish still carry the mark today while managing to maintain their freedom. But inevitably others lost control to their major shareholder and were absorbed into the Whitbread group.

There they did not find life as safe as expected. Between 1960 and 1971, Whitbread closed 15 breweries including such famous names as Campbell, Hope and King in Edinburgh, Flowers of Stratford-upon-Avon and Cobbs in Kent, whose fine Georgian brewery was also needlessly demolished. In recent years, as the major new keg breweries at Magor in S. Wales and Samlesbury in Lancashire, have come on stream, many of the remaining traditional breweries have been boarded up or bulldozed down.

- Strong's Brewery, Romsey, Hants – shut June 81.
- Phoenix Brewery, Kent – shut Nov. 81.
- Tiverton Brewery, Devon – shut Feb. 82.
- Ely Brewery, Cardiff – shut April 82.
- Threlfalls Brewery, Liverpool – shut October 82.
- Kirkstall Brewery, Leeds – shut January 83.
- Brickwood's Brewery, Portsmouth – shut Sept. 83.

And there is no guarantee that the axe has stopped swinging. What odds that Chester's Salford Brewery will still be alive next year? Ironically, at the same time Whitbread have set up ten home-brew pubs scattered throughout the country.

Within what remains of the group, traditional beers have long taken a back seat behind the promotion of lagers and national keg brands like Trophy and the new Whitbread Best Bitter. This is particularly true in the North where the company has struggled to present a convincing range of real ales, the latest change seeing the short-lived Queen's Ale from Sheffield replaced by a cask version of Trophy.

In the South, Fremlins and Wethereds present a much more reassuring picture while Cheltenham has become virtually an all real ale brewery. The main problems there – besides the demise of traditional mild – lie in pricing and the destruction of some excellent pubs.

In surveys conducted by CAMRA, Whitbread have consistently been found to be Britain's most expensive brewery, pricing their beers to the limit, even above other national combines. As their marketing men say, Whitbread beers reach the parts other beers cannot reach – the bottom of your wallet. On the pub side there has been growing concern at the treatment meted out to some of their houses, notably ones changed beyond recognition into Beefeater steakhouses.

ESTᴰ 1742

WETHERED, High Street, Marlow, Bucks. ☎ 6969.
Wethered Bitter (1035.6)
SPA or **Special** (1041.6).
Winter Royal (1056.6)
Real ale in all 200 houses.

WHITBREAD CHESTERS, Cook Street, Salford, Manchester. ☎ 061 832 8344.
Chester's Best Mild (1033).
Chester's Best Bitter (1034)
Sold as **Dutton's Bitter** further north.

WHITBREAD CASTLE EDEN, Co. Durham. ☎ 431.
Castle Eden Ale (1041)
Durham Ale (1037)

WHITBREAD E. PENNINES, Exchange Brewery, Sheffield. ☎ 71101.
BYB (1032)
Trophy (1037)

WHITBREAD FLOWERS, Monson Avenue, Cheltenham, Glos. ☎ 0242 21401.
West Country Pale Ale (1030)
Strong Country Bitter (1037.8)
Whitbread Bitter (1037)
Flowers Original (1044)
Pompey Royal (1046.9)
Now the only traditional brewery serving the S. West from Hampshire to Wales.

WHITBREAD FREMLINS, Court Street, Faversham, Kent. ☎ 533311.
Fremlins Bitter (1037)
Tusker (1046)
More than 85 per cent of the 750 outlets serve the beer traditionally.

WHITBREAD S. EAST, The Brewery, Oakley Road, Luton, Beds. ☎ 53231. No real ale

WHITBREAD MAGOR, S. Wales and **SAMLESBURY**, Lancs. Major new plants that brew no real ale.

Whitbread also now have a growing number of malt extract home-brew pubs - *Alford Arms*, Frithsden, Herts; *Streets of London*, E. Molesey, Surrey; *Fellows, Morton & Clayton Brewhouse*, Nottingham; *Frog and Parrot*, Sheffield; *Lass O'Gowrie*, Manchester; *Fox and Newt*, Leeds; *Dog & Parrot*, Newcastle; *Railway*, Burgess Hill, Sussex; *The Gate*, Southampton and *Old Swan*, Cheltenham, Glos.

Breweries

ABBEY, Danes Hill Road, Lound, Retford, Notts. ☎ 818932.
Begun in 1981 serving free trade in Notts and S. Yorks with **Quail Bitter** (1036) and **Drystone Bitter** (1044).

ADNAMS, Sole Bay Brewery, Southwold, Suffolk. ☎ 722424/5/6.
E. Anglia's famous seaside brewery still producing beer 'with the tang of seaweed' for its 68 houses which all serve real ale. Also widely available in the S.East free trade.
Mild (1034) – dark and malty.
Bitter (1036) – well-hopped and distinctive.
Old (1042) – a dark winter brew.

AFAN, Brunell Ind. Estate, Cwmavon, Port Talbot, W. Glamorgan. ☎ 0639 895320.
Begun in 1982 serving S. Wales free trade with **XXX** (1032) and **Afan Bitter** (1040).

ALEXANDRA, 19 North St., Portslade, Brighton, Sussex. ☎ 0273 421922.
Begun 1982 serving S. Coast free trade plus 3 tied houses.
Tom Becket's Pale (1035), **Bitter** (1039), **Best** (1044) and **Special** (1049).

ALICE Brewery, Harbour Road, Inverness. ☎ 0463 220572.
Ambitious project to serve the Scottish Highlands. Began last year brewing **Alice Ale** (1038).

ANN STREET Brewery, St Helier, Jersey. ☎ 31561. No real ale.

ARCHERS, London Street, Swindon, Wilts. ☎ 46789.
Enterprising new brewery begun in 1979 serving an area from London to Bristol. Now has two tied houses besides over 60 free trade outlets.
Village Bitter (1035) – light and sweetish.
Best Bitter (1040) – smooth and well-hopped.
Golden (1048) – full-flavoured and hoppy.
Headbanger (1065) – dark, strong and malty.

ARKELL, Kingsdown Brewery, Swindon, Wilts. ☎ 823026.
This family brewery has gradually abandoned its previous top pressure policy, so that now 49 of its 63 houses sell real ale.
John Arkell Bitter or **BB** (1033.5) – light and hoppy.
BBB (1038.5) – a fuller-bodied, distinctive bitter.
Kingsdown Ale (1050) – a strong, bitter brew.

ASHFORD, Unit 125, Ellingham Way, Ashford, Kent. ☎ 0233 41477.
Begun last year on a very small scale brewing **Harvest Best Bitter** (1040) and **Spencer's Strong Draught** (1045).

ASTON MANOR, Thimble Lane, Aston, Birmingham. ☎ 021 328 4336.
Begun last year by former Ansells workers on an ambitious scale, concentrating on supplying beer in large plastic bottles for supermarkets.
Aston Manor Mild (1037) and **Bitter** (1039).

BAILEYS, Crowcroft, Leigh Sinton, Malvern, Worcs. ☎ 0886 33254.
Begun last year next door to Malvern Chase, another new brewery.
Bailey's Best Bitter (1040). NB. Bailey's Stout brewed by Gwent.

BALLARDS, Cumbers Farm, Rogate, Petersfield, Hants. ☎ 073080 301.
Despite the postal address, this country brewery is actually in W. Sussex. Begun in 1980 and now serving over 30 free houses in this border area.
Best Bitter (1042) – well-balanced and nutty.
Wassail (1060) – strong, malty brew.

BANKS'S, Park Brewery, Lovatt Street, Wolverhampton, W.Midlands. ☎ 711811.
With Hanson's makes up Wolverhampton and Dudley Breweries. Famous for its mild and the fact that all 700-plus tied houses serve cask beer. Looking to expand, hence its unsuccessful bid for Davenports of Birmingham last year.
Mild (1036) – medium dark, smooth and malty.
Bitter (1038) – full-bodied and well hopped.

BANKS & TAYLOR, The Brewery, Shefford, Beds. ☎ 0462 815080.
Begun 1982 serving 40 outlets including some Whitbread pubs and one tied house with **SPA** (1034) and **Shefford Bitter** (1038).

BATEMAN, Salem Bridge Brewery, Wainfleet, Skegness, Lincs. ☎ 880317.
One of Britain's true family breweries, maintaining close links with
the local community including sustaining many small Fenland pubs.
Nearly all 104 houses sell their 'Good Honest Ales' without pressure.
Mild (1032) – a smooth, creamy dark mild.
XB (1037) – a distinctive, well-hopped bitter.
XXXB (1048) – a powerful, malty ale.

BATES, Western Units, Pottery Road, Bovey Tracey, Devon. ☎ 0626 833706.
Begun last year brewing **Bates Bitter** (1039).

BATHAM, Delph Brewery, Brierley Hill, W. Midlands. ☎ 77229.
Hidden behind one of the Black Country's most famous pubs, the
'Bull and Bladder', this small family firm has managed to survive
brewing excellent beer for its eight pubs.
Mild (1036) – dark and tasty.
Bitter (1043) – distinctive and full-bodied.
Delph Strong Ale (1054) – a Christmas ale.

BELHAVEN Brewery, Dunbar, East Lothian, Scotland. ☎ 62734.
Scotland's best-known independent brewery, which has had a
turbulent but colourful history in recent years. Currently
controlled by Eric Morley of Miss World fame. Supplies some 200
Scottish outlets.
60/- Light (1031) – dark and malty.
70/- Heavy (1036) – beautiful, well-balanced bitter.
80/- Export (1042) – heavy, distinctive bitter.
90/- Strong Ale (1070) – occasional rich brew.

BERROW, Coast Road, Burnham-on-Sea, Somerset. ☎ 027 875 345.
Begun 1982 brewing **BBBB** (1038) for few free houses.

BIG LAMP, Summerhill St., Westgate Road, Newcastle-upon-Tyne. ☎ 0632 614227.
The only new free trade brewery in the N. East, begun in 1982 selling **Big Lamp Bitter**
(1040).

BLACKAWTON, Washbourne, Totnes, Devon. ☎ 080 423 339.
One of the earliest new small breweries dating from 1977 now
brewing for 45 free trade outlets in S. Devon.
Blackawton Bitter (1037) – hoppy and well-rounded.
Headstrong (1048) – dark and malty winter brew.

BLOSSOMWARD, Elvington Ind. Estate, York. ☎ 0759 72334.
Begun 1981 as Kingsley Brewery and taken over by new owners last year. Brew
Blossomward Bitter (1038).

BODDINGTONS, Strangeways Brewery, Manchester M60. ☎ 061 831 7881.
Manchester's most famous brewing son, which fought off an Allied
takeover attempt in the early 70's. Then in 1982 swallowed
near-neighbours Oldham Brewery. All 281 tied houses serve real ale,
but locals are concerned that the bitter has lost some of its distinctive
character.
Mild (1033) – dark and full-flavoured.
Bitter (1035) – popular straw-coloured bitter.

BODMIN, Higher Tawna Farm, Cardinham. ☎ 312.
Tiny brewery begun in 1982 serving few outlets in mid-Cornwall with **Bell Bitter** (1038).

*The figure after each beer (eg. 1037) is the Original Gravity of the brew, which
gives an indication of strength. As a very rough rule of thumb, you can say that
a 1040 beer will contain four per cent alcohol, a 1050 five per cent etc. An ordinary
strength bitter is between 1035–39.*

Breweries

BORDER Brewery, Wrexham, Clwyd. ☎ 265444.
North Wales only established independent, brewing a range of low-gravity beers, usually served under pressure, except in 33 of the 170 pubs.
Mild (1032.4) – dark and nutty.
Exhibition (1034.4) – light and flavourful.
Bitter (1035.4) – light and malty.
4X Mild (1035.5) – dark and sweet.
Old Master (1037.6) – new, all-malt bitter.

BOURNE VALLEY, North Way, Walworth, Andover, Hants. ☎ 3669.
Begun in 1978 by former CAMRA national chairman. Now owns two pubs besides serving 35 local outlets.
Weaver's Bitter (1037) – hoppy and refreshing.
Andover Ale (1040) – distinctive, hoppy brew.
Henchard's Bitter (1045) – new, stronger bitter.
Wallop (1055.9) – a dark strong winter brew.

BRAIN, Old Brewery, St. Mary Street, Cardiff, S. Glamorgan. ☎ 399022.
As much a part of Wales as Rugby Union and Max Boyce. These distinctive beers are served traditionally in all their 100-plus pubs.
Dark (1035) – a smooth and malty mild.
Bitter (1035.3) – light and well-flavoured.
SA (1042) – full-bodied, malty bitter.

BRAKSPEAR, The Brewery, Henley-on-Thames, Oxfordshire. ☎ 3636.
Deservedly popular brewery with some of the most unspoilt pubs near London. All but one of the 125 houses serve real ale.
Mild (1031) – thin but hoppy.
Bitter (1035) – sweeter than of old.
Special (1043) – rich distinctive bitter.
Old or **XXXX** (1043) – a traditional old ale.

BRIGHTLINGSEA, Dale Hall Estate, Lawford, Manningtree, Essex. ☎ 6259.
Begun in 1982 serving 35 local outlets with **Brightlingsea Best Bitter** (1037) and **Strong Brew** (1051).

BROUGHTON Brewery, Broughton, Biggar, Lanarkshire. ☎ 08994 345.
One of the most significant and successful new breweries now supplying over 200 outlets in Scotland's keg wastes. Begun 1980.
Greenmantle Ale (1038) – tasty and distinctive.

MATTHEW BROWN, PO Box 5, Lion Brewery, Blackburn, Lancs. ☎ 52471.
Large, N. West brewery with an increasing commitment to real ale, now available in 160 of their 550 tied houses. Also brew lager at their Lakeland brewery in Workington.
Lion Mild (1031) – dark and nutty.
Lion Bitter (1036) – well-balanced and malty.
John Peel (1040) – well-hopped, light-coloured bitter.

BUCKLEY, Gilbert Road, Llanelli, Dyfed. ☎ 58441.
Traditional dispense can be found in over half the 180 houses scattered throughout S. West Wales. Also has a major stake in neighbours Felinfoel.
Standard Bitter (1031) – well-balanced.
Mild (1032) – dark and fruity.
Best Bitter (1036) – full-flavoured.
Gold (1042) – new, stronger bitter.

BURT, High Street, Ventnor, Isle of Wight. ☎ 852153.
One of Britain's most remarkable breweries that has managed to survive, serving real ale in six of its 11 pubs, despite the lowest prices in the South of England! Also available in five Watney houses.
LB (1030) – a fine light bitter.
DMA (1030) – darkish, unusual mild.
VPA (1040) – hoppy, distinctive bitter.
4X (1040) – a winter old ale.

BURTON BRIDGE, Bridge St., Burton-upon-Trent, Staffs. ☎ 36596.
Begun in 1982 by former Ind Coope workers to challenge the major
brewers in their home town. Over 35 outlets including own brewery
bar.

IPA (1036) – well-hopped pale ale.
Bridge Bitter (1042) – distinctive hoppy beer.
Porter (1045) – dark and fruity.
Burton Festival (1055) – a strong ale.

BURTONWOOD, Forshaws Brewery, Burtonwood, Cheshire. ☎ 09252 4281.
Traditional regional brewery near Warrington with 280 widely
scattered pubs including some in N. Wales, 224 of them offering real
ale. A rare Light Mild lost last year.

Dark Mild (1032) – pleasant, rich flavour.
Bitter (1036.5) – a light, creamy bitter.

BUTCOMBE Brewery, Butcombe, Blagdon, Avon. ☎ 027 587 2240.
Along with Broughton, the most successful of the new breweries,
set up in 1978 by a former Courage Western managing director. One
tied house and over 100 free trade outlets around Bristol.

Butcombe Bitter (1038) – light and clean tasting.

CAMERON, Lion Brewery, Hartlepool, Cleveland. ☎ 66666.
The N. East's major brewers of real ale, available in over half their
500 houses. At the time of going to press, its future was uncertain
as parent company Ellerman Lines had put the brewery up for sale.

Lion Bitter (1036) – a tasty, hoppy brew.
Strongarm (1042) – a fine malty bitter.

CASTLETOWN, Victoria Road, Castletown, Isle of Man. ☎ 822561.
One of the two independent breweries to satisfy the Manx thirst,
producing excellent real 'Ale of Man' under the islands Pure Beer
Act (only malt, hops and sugar) for its 35 pubs. All but one sell real
ale.

Mild (1036) – dark version of the bitter. Rare in cask.
Bitter (1036) – a fine, refreshing, fruity brew.

CANTERBURY Brewery, 28 St. Radigunds, Canterbury, Kent. ☎ 60352.
First of the new breweries in Kent in 1979, it has recently moved
site. Two tied houses plus 15 free trade outlets in E. Kent.

Canterbury Ale (1038) – distinctively hoppy.
Buff's Bitter (1050) – full-bodied beer.

CESTRIAN, Pinfold Estate, Buckley, Clwyd. ☎ 0244 549441.
Begun in 1981 just inside the N. Wales border, now brewing for 40
outlets, over half of them off-licences. Also bottled beer.

Cestrian Best Bitter (1039) – a smooth bitter.

CHILTERN, Nash Lee Road, Terrick, Aylesbury, Bucks. ☎ 029 661 3647.
Begun in 1980. Now supplying widespread outlets including some
Aylesbury Brewery pubs and British Rail mainline stations in
London.

Chiltern Ale (1036) – distinctive, bitter beer.
Beechwood Bitter (1043) – full-bodied and nutty.

CHUDLEY, 1a Saltram Crescent, Maida Vale, London W9. ☎ 01 969 7832.
Former Courage brewer set up on his own after the closure of
Courage's London brewery in 1981. Now serves over 40 free trade
outlets.

Local Line Bitter (1038) – pleasant and well-balanced.
Lord's Strong Ale (1050) – distinctive and full-flavoured.
Draught Excluder (1070) – dark, smooth winter ale.

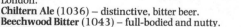

*This brewery section contains only the independent regional and local companies.
For the beers and breweries of the 'Big Six' national combines see P23–27. For
home-brew houses see P47–48.*

Breweries

CIRENCESTER Brewery, Workshops, Cirencester, Glos. ☎ 0285 61450.
Begun last year brewing **Cirencester Bitter** (1040) for a few outlets.

CLARK, Westgate Brewery, Wakefield, W. Yorks. ☎ 0924 373328.
Drinks wholesale company which began brewing again in 1982, and
now brew for 40 free houses and clubs including their own tied
house.
Clark's Traditional Bitter (1038.5) – refreshing and well-hopped.

COTLEIGH, The Old Brewery, Wiveliscombe, Somerset. ☎ 0984 24066.
Begun in Devon in 1979 before moving to present site alongside Golden Hill Brewery.
Supply 50 outlets in the S. West.
Nutcracker (1036) – hoppy, dark ale.
Tawny Bitter (1040) – smooth and hoppy.
Old Buzzard (1048) – a strong winter brew.

CROUCH VALE, Redhills Road, S. Woodham Ferrers, Chelmsford, Essex. ☎ 322744.
Begun in 1981 by CAMRA enthusiasts. Now supply 50 free trade
outlets from Kent to Cambridgeshire.
Woodham Bitter (1034.9) – a light bitter
Best Bitter (1038.9) – well-hopped and malty.
Strong Anglian Special (1048) – deceptively powerful.

CROWN Brewery, Pontyclun, Mid-Glamorgan. ☎ 0443 225453.
Formerly the South Wales Clubs Brewery, specialising in the club
trade where the bulk of the beer is pressurised. Now also supplies
some free trade pubs using traditional dispense.
Crown Pale Ale (1033) – a light bitter.
4X (1033) – a pleasant dark mild.
SBB (1036) – hoppy and bitter.

DARLEY, Thorne, Doncaster, S. Yorks. ☎ 812331.
Family brewery taken over by Vaux of Sunderland in 1978, who
also own nearby Wards of Sheffield. Slowly turning off the gas
bottles; 43 of the 62 pubs now sell unpressurised beer.
Dark (1032) – a pleasant, malty brew.
Thorne Best Bitter (1038) – splendid, full-flavoured bitter.

DAVENPORTS Brewery, Bath Row, Birmingham. ☎ 021 643 5021.
Birmingham's last independent brewery, famous for its unique 'Beer
at Home' service, hit the headlines last year when it successfully
fought off a takeover bid from Banks's of Wolverhampton. Nearly
all its 124 scattered houses now serve draught beer.
Mild (1034.5) – dark and malty.
Bitter (1038.9) – well-balanced and hoppy.

DEMPSEYS, Jamestown Ind. Estate, Inchicore, Dublin 8. ☎ 725899.
Eire's first new small brewery begun last year, brewing **Demspey's Real Ale** (1037) for
59 outlets in the Dublin area. Also now **Porter** (1034).

DEVANHA, Old Station Yard, Alford, Aberdeenshire. ☎ 0336 2393.
A welcome addition to the new brewery revival in N. East Scotland, begun in 1982.
Triple X (1043) – dark and very malty.

DEVENISH, Weymouth Brewery, Weymouth, Dorset. ☎ 74511.
And Redruth Brewery, Redruth, Cornwall. ☎ 213591.
The major 'seaside' brewers of the S. West with over 350 houses
and two breweries in Dorset and Cornwall. Gradually turning off the
top pressure; 139 out of 183 pubs served from Weymouth now offer
real ale, and the majority of the 176 pubs from Redruth.
John Devenish Bitter (1032) – a pleasant light brew.
Wessex Best Bitter (1042) – smooth and hoppy (Weymouth).
Cornish Best Bitter (1042) – full-bodied brew (Redruth).

DONNINGTON Brewery, Stow-on-the-Wold, Glos. ☎ 30603.
Probably Britain's most picturesque brewery set in an old mill alongside a lake. At its best the taste of the beer, served by handpump in their 17 Cotswold stone pubs, matches the beauty of the buildings and their surroundings.
XXX (1033) – rare dark mild.
BB (1035) – a beautiful light bitter.
SBA (1040) – a full-bodied bitter.

ELDRIDGE POPE, Dorchester Brewery, Dorchester, Dorset. ☎ 64801.
Boasts the strongest naturally-conditioned bottled beer in the country – Thomas Hardy's Ale (1126). A growing number of the 180 tied houses now seel the 'Huntsman' draught beers unpressurised.
Dorchester Bitter (1032.5) – light but well-balanced.
Dorset Original IPA (1041) – a well-hopped beer.
Royal Oak (1048) – full-bodied malty brew.

ELGOOD, North Brink Brewery, Wisbech, Cambridgeshire. ☎ 583160.
Tucked-away brewery in the flatlands near The Wash selling real ale in the majority of its 55 pubs. Like many other southern breweries, the company discontinued cask mild last year.
Bitter (1037) – refreshing well-regarded brew.

EVERARDS Tiger Brewery, Burton-upon-Trent, Staffs. ☎ 63563.
Although brewing in Burton, the company's headquarters are in Leicester, at Castle Acres, Narborough (☎ 891010). Once producing only processed beers, it now offers a full range of real ales in over half the 140 houses.
Burton Mild (1033) – a dryish dark mild.
Beacon (1036) – well-balanced light bitter.
Tiger (1041) – a tasty best bitter.
Old Original (1050) – a malty, finely hopped ale.

FAILSWORTH, Oldham Road, Newton Heath, Manchester. ☎ 061 682 2509.
Rare new brewery in Manchester, challenging the might of neighbouring Wilsons.
Failsworth Original (1036) and **Strong** (1044).

FEDERATION, N. Clubs Federation Brewery, Dunston, Newcastle. ☎ 609023.
No real ale. Bright beers only from this N. East brewery now expanding into the free pub trade throughout the country.

FELINFOEL Brewery, Llanelli, Dyfed. ☎ 3356/7.
Britain's champion brewers in the past, this famous Welsh brewery sadly serves its beers without pressure in fewer than a quarter of its 75 tied houses.
Mild (1032) – dark and malty.
Bitter (1034) – light and hoppy.
Double Dragon (1041) – a highly distinctive bitter.

FIVE TOWNS, Trent Trading Park, Botteshaw St., Hanley, Staffs. ☎ 262705.
A new brewery begun last year, named after the towns of the Potteries. **Bursley Bitter** (1040).

FRANKLINS, Gardeners Arms, Bilton Lane, Bilton. N. Yorks.
Small brewery behind a free house near Harrogate serving a few outlets since 1980.
Franklin's Bitter (1038) – bitter and fruity.

FULLER, Smith and Turner, Griffin Brewery, Chiswick, London W4. ☎ 01 9934 3691.
One of only two independent brewers in the Capital to survive the takeovers of the Sixties. Now buying up pubs to the West of London. Serves its award-winning real ales in 84 of its 127 houses.
Chiswick Bitter (1035.5) – pleasant, light bitter.
London Pride (1041.5) – tasty, fruity beer.
ESB (1055.75) – Extra Special Bitter in every sense.

GALES, Horndean, Portsmouth, Hants. ☎ 594050.
Traditional brewery with a fine range of cask beers and real ale in all 99 pubs. Produces the only naturally-conditioned beer sold in a corked bottle – **Prize Old Ale** (1095).
XXXL (1030) – light mild. **XXXD** (1030) – rare dark mild.
BBB (1037) – a hoppy bitter with malty aftertaste.
XXXXX (1045) – dark, sweet winter brew.
HSB (1051) – full-bodied distinctive bitter.

Breweries

GIBBS MEW, Anchor Brewery, Milford Street, Salisbury, Wilts. ☎ 29244.
One of Britain's more unusual breweries, running many of its 70
pubs like free houses. Also owns Robert Porter bottling and beer
wholesaling company in London.
Wiltshire Bitter (1036) – new light hoppy bitter.
Premium Bitter (1039) – malty and fuller bodied.
Bishop's Tipple (1066) – barley wine that would have most clerics
on their knees.

GLENNY, The Crofts, Witney, Oxon. ☎ 0993 2574.
New brewery set up last year in part of Clinch's Old Eagle Brewery. **Eagle Bitter** (1037).

GOACHER'S, Hayle Mill Cottages, Bockingford, Maidstone, Kent. ☎ 682112.
First new brewery to revive Maidstone's once-proud brewing history. **Goacher's Maidstone Ale** (1040).

GODSON, Black Horse Brewery, Chisenhale Road, Bow, London E3. ☎ 01 980 0604.
Britain's most travelled brewery, which began in Hackney in 1977
and has since moved site a number of times. Almost merged with
Tisbury last year.
Best Bitter (1036) – light, hoppy bitter.
Black Horse (1047.8) – unusual, malty brew.
Stock Ale (1084) – smooth, tawny old ale.

GOLDEN HILL, Wiveliscombe, Somerset. ☎ 0984 23798.
Has the unique distinction of winning the Best Bitter award at
CAMRA's Great British Beer Festival only months after starting in
1980. Serves 60 outlets in the S. West.
Exmoor Ale (1039) – a malty, well-balanced beer.

GOOSE EYE, Laycock, Keighley, W. Yorks. ☎ 605807.
Began brewing again last year after a break of 18 months.
Goose Eye Mild (1033) and **Bitter** (1038).

GREENE KING, Westgate Brewery, Bury St. Edmunds, Suffolk. ☎ 63222
and The Brewery, Biggleswade, Beds. ☎ 313935.
East Anglia's largest regional brewery, brewing both in Suffolk and
Bedfordshire. Also own Rayments of Hertfordshire. Famous for its
robust Abbot Ale, but sadly the company pressurise their excellent
beers in over 60% of their 827 pubs. Also supply Grays of
Chelmsford's 50 pubs in Essex.
XX (1030.8) – malty dark mild. **KK** (1030.8) – pleasant light mild.
IPA (1035) – a full-flavoured bitter.
Abbot Ale (1048) – full-bodied and distinctive.
Christmas Ale (1053) – seasonal dark ale.

GREENALL WHITLEY, Wilderspool Brewery, PO Box 2, Warrington, Cheshire. ☎ 51234.
Britain's largest regional brewery by far with 1,119 pubs in the N.
West besides owning Shipstone of Nottingham and Wem of
Shropshire. Although about half the pubs serve real ale, the
company has been heavily criticised by CAMRA because of its
undistinguished beers and trend towards tank beer and chilled and
filtered mild. None of its 50 houses in Cumbria serve real ale.
Local Mild (1033.7) – dark and sweet.
Local Bitter (1038) – pleasant but characterless.

GUERNSEY Brewery, South Esplanade, St Peter Port, Guernsey. ☎ 20143.
One of two breweries on this Channel island serving stronger than
usual real ales in 25 of their 30 tied houses owing to the excise duty
uniquely being levied on quantity not strength.
LBA Mild (1036.6) – dark and sweet.
Draught Bitter (1045) – full-flavoured and hoppy.

GWENT, Little Mill, Pontypool, Gwent. ☎ 049 528 681.
South Wales first new brewery opened in 1981. Serves 25 free trade outlets in Gwent
and Glamorgan. Occasionally brews Bailey's Stout.
Silverthorne's Bitter (1034), **Special** (1040), **Exhibition** (1054) and **Druid's Ale** (1072).

GWYNEDD, Gaerwen, Anglesey, Gwynedd. ☎ 0248 77410.
The only brewery on Anglesey set up by a N. Wales hotel chain in 1980. Supplies their three hotels and 25 free houses.
Menai Mild (1034), **Anglesey Bitter** (1037) and **Snowdon Strong** (1043).

HALL & WOODHOUSE, The Brewery, Blandford Forum, Dorset. ☎ 52141.
More usually known as 'Badger Beer' – they also own Panda soft drinks – the company runs 156 pubs along the South Coast, 120 of them serving real ale. Have recently been changing their range of beers.
Hector's Bitter (1034) – a new bitter replacing the Badger 'boys'.
Badger Best Bitter (1041) – well-hopped and full-bodied.
Tanglefoot (1048) – lightish-coloured strong ale.

HANSONS, High Street, Dudley, W. Midlands. ☎ 57731.
The other half of Wolverhampton and Dudley Breweries (see Banks's) which brews similar but separate beers to its Big Brother. The only major brewery – Julia Hanson – named after a woman.
Mild (1036) – medium dark and malty.
Bitter (1038) – light but well-hopped.

HARDINGTON, Mandeville Arms, Hardington Mandeville, Somerset. ☎ 093586 2418.
Pub brewery begun in 1979 that has expanded into the free trade, now supplying 15 local outlets. Brews own 'real' lager, Landsdorf.
Hardington Best Bitter (1037) – well-balanced.
Somerset Special (1045) – fuller-bodied beer.
Hardington Horrors (1055) – a new strong winter brew.

HARDYS & HANSONS, Kimberley Brewery, Nottingham. ☎ 383611.
This brewery – the result of a merger in 1930 between two neighbouring firms in Kimberley – serves real ale in the majority of its 200 houses, but increasingly uses top-pressure dispense.
Best Mild (1035.4) – a dark, sweet brew.
Best Bitter (1038.6) – distinctive, well-hopped beer.

HARTLEY, Old Brewery, Ulverston, Cumbria. ☎ 53269.
Family firm famous for its 'Beers from the Wood', which was taken over by the larger family firm of Robinsons of Stockport in 1982. Still brewing real ale for its 55 pubs and some Whitbread houses.
Mild (1031) – smooth and dark.
Bitter (1031) – smooth and light.
XB (1040) – strong, well-flavoured bitter.

HARVEY, Bridge Wharf Brewery, Cliff High St., Lewes, E. Sussex. ☎ 71222.
Traditional family brewery producing a wide range of real ales for their 28 pubs. Also brew for the other Lewes firm of Beards.
XX (1030) – pleasant dark mild.
Pale Ale (1033) – well-hopped light bitter.
BB (1040) – well-balanced with a nutty flavour.
XXXX (1043) – tasty, dark winter brew.

HAWTHORNE, Alfred Street Trading Estate, Gloucester.
Began as home-brew pub at the Norfolk House Hotel in Gloucester in 1978, before last year becoming a free trade brewery on a new site.
Glevum Mild (1035), **Gloucester Bitter** (1038) and **Severnside Stunner** (1066).

HERALD, Old Stables, Millburn Road, Coleraine, Co. Derry. ☎ 0265 57117.
Begun last year as N. Ireland's second much-needed traditional brewery. **Herald Ale** (1036).

HEREWARD, Blenheim Way, Market Deeping, Lincs. ☎ 0778 34769.
Lincolnshire's first new brewery started last year, supplying local free trade. Also selling **Hereward Bitter** (1038) across 'the border' into Cambridgeshire.

Many famous names are not included in this section nor in the brewery listings under National Combines (P23–27). Companies like Charrington, Benskins and Manns have lost their breweries and now operate as marketing companies running chains of pubs while their beers are brewed elsewhere. This includes independents like Beards of Lewes, Heavitree of Exeter and Melbourn of Stamford.

Breweries

HERMITAGE, Main Road, Hermitage, Emsworth, W. Sussex. ☎ 71533.
Brewery attached to the confusingly-named Sussex Brewery public
house since 1981, supplying the pub and local free trade.
Hermitage Bitter (1040) – smooth and well-balanced.
Best Bitter (1048) – hoppy, stronger bitter.
Lumley Old Ale (1049) – dark, malty winter brew.

HIGSONS Brewery, 127 Dale Street, Liverpool. ☎ 051 236 1255.
Scouse city's only independent brewery, which serves unpressurised
cask beer in half of its 160 houses. But following the building of a
new brewhouse, the bitter has lost its distinctive hoppiness.
Mild (1032) – well-balanced dark beer.
Bitter (1038) – palatable shadow of a great bitter.

HILDEN Brewery, Hilden House, Lisburn, Co. Antrim. ☎ 08462 3863.
N. Ireland's brave new brewery, the first to brew traditional beer in Ulster for decades
when it began in 1981.
Linenhall Special (1035) and **Hilden Ale** (1040).

HOLDEN, Hopden Brewery, George St., Woodsetton, Dudley, W. Midlands. ☎ 09073 2051
One of the small long-established family breweries of the Black
Country, producing a good range of real ales for all their 15 tied
houses.
Mild (1036) – dark and well-balanced.
Bitter (1039) – a hoppy bitter.
Special (1052) – full-bodied, sweetish bitter.
Old Ale (1080) – powerful, occasional dark brew.

HOLT, Derby Brewery, Empire St., Cheetham, Manchester M3. ☎ 061 834 3285.
Traditional family firm which recently moved into the free trade.
Brews one of Britain's true bitters of character. Real ale in all 88
tied houses, often delivered in hogsheads (54-gallon barrels) such
is its popularity and low price.
Mild (1033.4) – dark, malty and bitter.
Bitter (1039) – superior, distinctive bitter brew.

HOME Brewery, Mansfield Road, Daybrook, Nottingham. ☎ 269741.
Another company famous for providing value for money, with real
ale available in most of the 400 pubs stretching throughout the E.
Midlands up to S. Yorkshire.
Mild (1036.1) – dark and malty.
Bitter (1038.7) – popular and consistent.

HOOK NORTON Brewery, Hook Norton, Banbury, Oxon. ☎ 737210.
One of the most delightful traditional tower breweries in Britain,
with all 34 country pubs serving real ale, a few on blanket pressure.
Mild (1032) – light and fruity.
Best Bitter (1036) – distinctive and hoppy.
Old Hookey (1049) – genuine dark old ale.

HOSKINS, Beaumanor Road, Leicester. ☎ 61122.
Old family concern with one pub at Market Bosworth and an
off-licence at the brewery, which was taken over last year by wine
merchants, the Saffron Waldon Vineyard Company.
Mild (1033) – sweet and dark.
Bitter (1039) – full-flavoured.
Old (1039) – darker occasional brew.

HYDES Anvil Brewery, Moss Lane West, Moss Side, Manchester. ☎ 061 226 1317.
The smallest of the long-established Manchester breweries serving
its real 'Anvil' ales in all 50 tied houses, which are largely to be found
in the south of the city.
Mild (1032) – dark. **Best Mild** (1034) – light and hoppy.
Bitter (1036.6) – full-flavoured bitter.
Anvil Strong Ale (1080) – rich winter brew.

JENNINGS, Castle Brewery, Cockermouth, Cumbria. ☎ 823214.
A true traditional brewery in the far N. West whose excellent real
ales are not only available in all 91 tied houses, but also in a number
of Bass houses in the region.
Mild (1033) – dark and mellow.
Bitter (1035) – a distinctive bitter brew.

KING & BARNES, 18 Bishopric, Horsham, W. Sussex. ☎ 69344.
Well-regarded Sussex family brewery which serves real ale in all its
58 country houses. Runs a popular 'passport' scheme round its pubs.
Sussex Mild (1034.5) – smooth and malty dark mild.
Sussex Bitter (1034.5) – a well-hopped bitter.
Old Ale (1047.5) – a malty winter ale.
Draught Festive (1050.5) – strong, full-flavoured bitter.

LEES, Greengate Brewery, Middleton Junction, Manchester. ☎ 061 643 2487.
One of Manchester's clutch of surviving independent breweries, with
128 tied houses in the north of the city, 121 of them serving real
ale.
GB Mild (1032) – medium-dark mild.
Bitter (1038) – full-flavoured and malty.
Moonraker (1072) – guaranteed to launch you into orbit.

LEICESTER Brewery, High Street, Syston, Leics.
Set up last year to serve the club trade. No real ale.

LEITH, Arthur Street, Leith, Edinburgh. ☎ 031 554 5347.
Begun 1982 serving the Scottish Capital's free trade with **Leith Heavy** (1039).

LITCHBOROUGH, Alvis Way, Royal Oak Estate, Daventry, Northants. ☎ 3171.
The pioneer of the new brewery revolution begun by a redundant
Watney brewer Bill Urquart in 1974 in the village of Litchborough.
In 1980 the company changed hands and moved to the present site.
Northamptonshire Bitter (1036) – a malty bitter.
Tudor Ale (1044) – new, stronger, fruity brew.

LORIMER & CLARK, Caledonian Brewery, Slateford Road, Edinburgh. ☎ 031 337 1286.
A subsidiary of Vaux of Sunderland which lost its tied houses in
Scotland when they were sold to Allied Breweries. Now the unique
coal-fired brewery supplies the free trade besides selling its 70/- in
Vaux houses in N. East England as Lorimer's Best Scotch.
70/- Ale (1036) – well-balanced brew.
80/- Ale (1043) – full-bodied and flavoursome.
Caledonian (1077) – an occasional rich strong ale.

MACLAY, Thistle Brewery, Alloa, Scotland. ☎ 723387.
One of Scotland's two remaining independent breweries after the
takeover typhoon swept through the country, supplying real ale to
15 of its 25 houses and an appreciative free trade.
60/- Light (1030) – a flavoursome dark beer.
70/- Heavy (1035) – a well-hopped brew.
80/- Export (1040) – a well-balanced beer.

McMULLEN, 26 Old Cross, Hertford. ☎ 54911.
Hertfordshire family brewery currently building a second brewhouse.
After long favouring top pressure, it is increasingly serving the 'real
McCoy' in its 157 houses.
AK Mild (1033) – popular brew, more of a light bitter.
Country Bitter (1041) – fruity and distinctive.

MALVERN CHASE, Sherridge, Leigh Sinton, Worcs. ☎ 0886 33254.
Begun 1981 and taken over by new owner last year. **Chase Ale** (1040) available in 40
free houses.

Breweries

Very few breweries now treat their customers with contempt by brewing no real ale. Mansfield Brewery (below) and North Country of Hull (opposite) are both recent converts which have started satisfying ALL their drinkers. The one glaring exception is John Smiths of Tadcaster, Courage's northern arm, which still refuses to produce cask beer. Other odd-ones-out include the two Jersey breweries and the clubs brewery, Federation, in Newcastle.

MANSFIELD Brewery, Littleworth, Mansfield, Notts. ☎ 25691.
One of CAMRA's recent converts which began brewing real ale again in 1982 after a gap of ten years. But still very much on a trial basis, being only available in about 14 of the 200 pubs and some free trade.
4XXXX Bitter (1045) – well-balanced creamy beer.

MARKET Brewery, Park Street, Southwark, London SE1. ☎ 01 407 2495.
Begun as malt extract home-brewhouse for adjacent Market Porter pub. Now full mash for free trade and two tied houses.
Beach's Borough Bitter (1038) and **Southwark Special** (1049).

MARSTON, Thompson and Evershed, Shobnall Road, Burton-upon-Trent, Staffs. ☎ 3113
One of Britain's great traditional brewers with nearly 700 pubs stretching from Cumbria to Hampshire. Now the only brewery using the unique Burton Union system of brewing since Bass closed their plant down.
Capital (1030) – a light mild. **Mercian Mild** (1032) – dark and fruity.
Burton Bitter (1037) – well-balanced bitter.
Pedigree (1043) – full-bodied and smooth.
Merrie Monk (1043) – powerful, darker brew.
Owd Rodger (1080) – heavy, rich ale.

MARTLET, 44 Hammonds Drive, Eastbourne, E. Sussex. ☎ 642430.
One of the larger new breweries, begun in 1979, surprisingly taken over by Tisbury in 1982. Serves some 40 free houses.
Brighton Bitter (1036) – pleasant, hoppy bitter.
Brighton Specal (1040) – well-balanced and full-flavoured.
Regency Bitter (1048) – strong and well-hopped.
Old Devil (1055) – a dark, malty winter brew.

The Martlet Brewery

MAULDON, Addison Road, Sudbury, Suffolk. ☎ 0787 311055.
Former Watney brewer revived the name of his family brewery in 1982 to brew **Mauldon's Bitter** (1037) for 35 free trade outlets.

MENDIP, Shadows Factory, Temple Cloud, Avon. ☎ 0761 52938.
Begun in 1978 by a former Courage brewer and now run in partnership with local licensees. Serves 20 free trade outlets plus one tied house.
Bristol Bitter (1035) – light and well-hopped.
Mendip Special (1040) – richer, nutty beer.

MICKLES, Victoria Works, Walkern, Stevenage, Herts.
Begun near Luton in 1982 but moved to this new site last year.
Birch Bitter (1038) and **Oak Bitter** (1048).

MINERS ARMS Brewery, Westbury-sub-Mendip, Somerset. ☎ 074 987 719.
The first new home-brew house in 1973 (in Priddy), producing naturally-conditioned bottled beer, which in 1981 moved site and switched to brewing draught beer for the free trade under the same name.
Own Ale (1040) – a well-balanced beer.

MITCHELLS, Moor Lane, Lancaster. ☎ 63773.
One of Lancaster's two independent breweries, selling real ale in virtually all its 51 tied houses, many in the pub-packed city itself.
Mild (1034.8) – dark and smooth.
Bitter (1036) – a malty brew.
ESB (1044.8) – round and full-bodied.

MOLE'S, Merlin Way, Bowerhill, Melksham, Wilts. ☏ 0225 708842.
Begun in 1982 by a former Usher's brewer and a soft drinks firm to produce **Mole's Bitter** (1040) for the local trade.

MOORHOUSE'S Burnley Brewery, Moorhouse St., Burnley, Lancs. ☏ 22864.
A long-established producer of hop bitters which in 1979 began
brewing beer. Two years later the company was taken over by the
Hutchinson leisure group, and the beers are now marketed
nationwide.

Premier Bitter (1036) – smooth and full-flavoured.
Pendle Witches Brew (1050) – potent, malty bitter.

MORLAND, 40 Ock Street, Abingdon, Oxon. ☏ 20770.
Substantial Thames valley brewery with handpumps in more than
half the 215 tied houses. But a large proportion of these use a cask
breather.

Mild (1032) – refreshing dark ale.
Bitter (1035) – dry and bitter.
Best Bitter (1042) – full-flavoured and well-hopped.

MORRELL, Lion Brewery, St. Thomas Street, Oxford. ☏ 242013.
The famous university city's only brewery produces one of the widest
ranges of real ales in the country for its 140 pubs, though a few
houses use blanket pressure.

Light (1031.6) – refreshing. **Dark Mild** (1032.6) – hard to find.
Bitter (1036) – subtle beer. **200 Ale** (1038) – bicentenary brew.
Varsity (1041) – well-balanced, malty bitter.
Celebration (1066) – occasional brew. **College** (1073) – winter ale.

NAILSEA, Southfield Road, Nailsea, Avon. ☏ 0272 857642.
One of the throng of new breweries in the Bristol area, begun in 1980
by a former licensee. Supplies 35 free trade outlets.

Jacobs Best Bitter (1040) – a distinctive, light, hoppy beer.
LG (1031) – a low-gravity brew.

NEW FOREST, Old Lyndhurst Road, Cadnam, Hants. ☏ 0703 812766.
Set up in 1979 by a soft drinks company, the brewery concentrates
on supplying Woodman keg beers to the Southampton club trade,
but also brews two real ales for 25 outlets.

New Forest Real Ale (1036) – well-balanced beer.
Keeper's Bitter (1040) – new stronger brew.

NORTH COUNTRY, Silvester St., Hull, N. Humberside. ☏ 0482 223461.
An unusual brewery, producing only filtered beers for decades – until 1982 when it
launched Riding Bitter, which is soon expected to be in over half the 210 houses.
Formerly the Hull Brewery, it was renamed after being taken over by Northern Foods.
Riding Bitter (1038) – a new cask bitter.

OAK Brewery, Merseytown Road, Ellesmere Port, Cheshire. ☏ 051 356 0950.
Begun in 1982 in one of England's worst remaining 'desert' areas for real ale.
XL Bitter (1035), **Oak Best Bitter** (1040), **Old Oak Ale** (1046) and **Porter** (1050).

OKELL, Falcon Brewery, Douglas, Isle of Man. ☏ 3034.
The larger of the two indepedent breweries in the Island, brewing
real ale under the unique Manx Pure Beer Act for virtually all its
71 tied houses. Has an impressive Victorian brewhouse.

Mild (1035.2) – dark and smooth.
Bitter (1035.9) – a well-hopped, dryish brew.

OLDHAM, Brewery, Coldhurst Street, Oldham, Manchester. ☏ 061 6248305.
Taken over by neighbours Boddingtons in 1982. There were fears
that Oldham's own real ales would disappear. Now outlets appear
to be on the increase. Currently in 25 of the 87 pubs with many more
selling Boddies Bitter.

Mild (1031.7) – malty and dark.
Bitter (1037.2) – pale and full-flavoured.

OLD MILL Brewery, Mill Street, Snaith, Humberside. ☎ 0405 861813.
Begun by former Wilson's production director last year, brewing **Old Mill Traditional Bitter** (1037).

PAINE, James Paine Brewery, Market Square, St. Neots, Cambs. ☎ 0480 216160.
Formerly owned by Paine's maltsters and millers, the brewing side was taken over by new owners in 1982 and renamed James Paine. Real ale in 13 of the 16 pubs.

Mild (1032) – a pleasant brew.
XXX (1036) – smooth, medium bitter.
St. Neots Bitter (1041) – creamy and well-hopped.
EG (1047) – full-bodied and malty.

PALMER, West Bay Road, Bridport, Dorset. ☎ 22396.
The only thatched brewery in the country in a seaside setting. Sadly only 17 of the 70 houses serve the beers without pressure.

BB (1030.4) – light, pleasant bitter.
IPA (1039.5) – well-balanced bitter.
Tally Ho (1047) – an occasional brew.

PARADISE Brewery, Paradise Park, Hayle, Cornwall. ☎ 0736 753365.
Unusual new brewery set up in a bird park in 1981. The brewery is behind the one tied house, the Bird in Hand.

Paradise Bitter (1040) – a pleasant beer.
Artists Ale (1055) – smooth and full-bodied.
Victory Ale (1070) – strong, rich brew.

PENRHOS, Kington, Herefordshire. ☎ 0544 230720.
Begun in 1977 with help from Terry Jones of Monty Python fame, next door to a restored Tudor pub and restaurant. Uses own computer-controlled brewing system.

Penrhos Bitter (1038) – a bitter brew.
Jones First Brew (1048) – stronger, malty ale.
Porter (1050) – dark, distinctive beer.

PENSANS, Little Chysauster Farm, Gulval, Penzance, Cornwall.
Tiny new brewery set up in 1982 by the brewer from the famous Blue Anchor home-brew house in Helston, producing '**Coref Pensans**' (1045).

PHILLIPS, Greyhound Brewery, Marsh Gibbon, Bucks. ☎ 08697 365.
New brewery set up at a country pub near Bicester in 1981. But now not only supplying the Greyhound but also the local free trade.

Heritage Bitter (1036) – a fruity, well-hopped bitter.
Ailrics Old Ale (1045) – smooth, nutty brew.

PILGRIM Brewery, Hurst Place, Woldingham, Surrey. ☎ 2505.
Surrey's only new free trade brewery, begun in 1982. Now supplying 15 local outlets.
Surrey Bitter (1038) – a hoppy, light bitter.
Progress (1042) – a malty, full-bodied beer.

POOLE, 32 Sterte Avenue, Poole, Dorset. ☎ 682345.
This South coast county's only new brewery – it already has four established independent companies – which last year added a home-brew pub called the Brewhouse in Poole High Street. Supplies 20 free trade outlets.

Dolphin Best Bitter (1038) – a distinctive hoppy brew.

PRIORY, George Street, Newark Notts. ☎ 706448.
Begun in 1977 as Westcrown and taken over by a Leicestershire licensee in 1980 when the name was changed to Priory. Brews for one tied house and 20 free trade outlets.
Priory Pride or **Bitter** (1036) – lightly-hopped brew.
Ned Belcher's Bitter (1040) – a mellow beer.

RANDALL, Vauxlaurens Brewery, St. Julians Av., St. Peter Port, Guernsey. ☎ 20134.
Guernsey's smaller brewery, operating under the 'Bobby Ales' sign rather than the 'Pony Ales' mark of the Guernsey Brewery. Half of the 18 tied houses sell real ale.
Best Mild (1036) – a dark, unusual brew.
Best Bitter (1044) – light and distinctive.

RANDALL Vautier, Clare Street, St. Helier, Jersey. ☎ 73541.
No real ale. Attempted own brew now discontinued. Some houses stock Draught Bass.

RAVEN, 35 Vine Street, Brighton, E. Sussex. ☎ 699444.
Began brewing again last year under new owners after a gap of 12 months. Serves local free trade.
Raven Bitter (1038) and **Best Bitter** (1048).

RAYMENT, Furneux Pelham, Buntingford, Herts. ☎ 027 978 671.
Small village brewery subsidiary of Greene King serving real ale in 20 of its 24 pubs in Hertfordshire and Essex. Plus expanding free trade.
BBA (1036) – distinctive and refreshing.

RED KITE, Glanyrafon, Aberystwyth, Dyfed. ☎ 617590.
The only brewery in central Wales, begun in 1982 brewing **Red Kite Original** (1040) for 20 free trade outlets.

RIDLEY, Hartford End, Chelmsford, Essex. ☎ 0371 820316.
Essex's only remaining, long-established, independent brewery, selling real ale in all 65 houses from a tucked-away country brewery. Also supplies off-licences of Cooks of Halstead.
XXX (1034) – dark and distinctive mild.
PA (1034) – beautifully balanced bitter of character.
Bishops (1080) – strong Christmas barley wine.

RINGWOOD, Minty's Yard, New Street, Ringwood, Hants. ☎ 87629.
Begun by one of the fathers of the new brewery revolution, Peter Austin, who has helped many others to start brewing. Supplies two tied houses and 60 free trade outlets.
Ringwood Best Bitter (1040) – hoppy and full-bodied.
Fortyniner (1049) – a heavy, malty brew.
4X Porter (1049) – a dark, dry winter brew.
Old Thumper (1060) – well-hopped, strong bitter.

ROBINSON, Unicorn Brewery, Stockport, Manchester. ☎ 061 480 6571.
Major family brewery with over 300 houses serving real ale, which in 1982 took over Hartleys of Ulverston in Cumbria. Pubs concentrated in S. Manchester and Cheshire with some in N. Wales.
Best Mild (1032) – sometimes darkened with extra caramel.
Bitter (1035) – well-balanced brew.
Best Bitter (1042) – full-bodied and well-hopped.
Old Tom (1079) – strong, smooth winter brew.

ROYAL TUNBRIDGE WELLS, Grange Road, Rusthall, T. Wells, Kent. ☎ 35832.
Begun in 1982 brewing for 30 free trade outlets in Kent and Sussex.
RPA (1036), **Royal Bitter** (1041) and **Entire** (1055).

RUDDLE, Langham, Oakham, Rutland, Leics. ☎ 56911.
Probably the most famous real ale brewery – with a far from traditional trade. It sold all its pubs except one to concentrate on supermarkets and the free trade. Now also supplies over 200 Watney houses in London.
Bitter (1032) – excellent light bitter.
County (1050) – full-flavoured rich brew.

Breweries

St. AUSTELL Brewery, St. Austell, Cornwall. ☎ 4444.
Popular 'holiday' brewery that in the past has relied on keg, but in recent years has widened its range of real ales by adding two stronger brews. The majority of the 132 houses now sell real ale.
BB (1031) – a light bitter.
XXXX (1034) – rare dark mild.
Tinners Bitter (1038) – a well-hopped malty bitter.
Hicks Special (1050) – a rich distinctive bitter.

SELBY, Millgate, Selby, N. Yorks. ☎ 702826.
An old family brewery that began brewing again in 1972 after a gap of 18 years. Only a few scattered free trade outlets.
Best Bitter (1039) – a hoppy brew bottled as **No. 1**.

SEVENOAKS Brewery, Crown Point Inn, Seal Chart, Kent. ☎ 0732 810222.
Began as home-brew pub in 1981 but now supplying a few free houses.
Sevenoaks Best Bitter (1038) and **Crown Point BB** (1038).

SHEPHERD NEAME, 17 Court Street, Faversham, Kent. ☎ 532206.
The only survivor of the hop county's once-proud host of independent breweries, serving real ale in most of its 250 houses. Has been buying up pubs, notably in London.
Mild (1031) – sweet but thin.
Bitter (1036) – fine, well-hopped brew.
Stock (1037) – a full-bodied ale.
Best Bitter (1039) – distinctive hoppy bitter.

SHIPSTONE, Star Brewery, New Basford, Nottingham 785074.
Taken over by regional giant Greenall Whitley of Warrington in 1978 since when the recipe of the distinctive bitter has been modified. Real ale in virtually all 270 houses.
Mild (1034.6) – dark and well-hopped.
Bitter (1038.6) – popular and refreshing.

SIMPKISS, Dennis Brewery, Brierley Hill, W. Midlands. ☎ 77576.
One of the Black Country's old family firms, serving real ale in 15 of its 16 houses. Has recently been trying guest beers.
Bitter (1037) – well-hopped and malty.
Supreme (1041) – new darker bitter.
Old (1050) – fruity and full-bodied.

SMILES, Colston Yard, Colston Street, Bristol, Avon. ☎ 297350.
Avon's first new brewery dating from 1977, now supplying over 50 free trade outlets and one tied house from its city centre site.
Pale Ale (1036) – distinctive light ale.
Best Bitter (1040) – full-bodied and hoppy.
Exhibition (1051) – strong, well-rounded bitter.

SAMUEL SMITH, Old Brewery, Tadcaster, N. Yorks. ☎ 832225.
Not to be confused with its larger neighbour, John Smith, which produces no real ale. Yorkshire's oldest brewery still produces 'beer from the wood' for the majority of its 300 scattered pubs including some in London, although there is only one solitary real ale. Also supplies the 38 pubs of Melbourn's former brewery in Stamford, Lincolnshire.
Old Brewery Bitter (1038.9) – full-bodied and malty.

SOUTHSEA, Old Lion Brewery, Pitcroft Lane, Portsmouth, Hants. ☎ 699943.
Begun in 1982 in the premises of an old Portsmouth brewery.
Bosun's Dark (1032), **Captain's Bitter** (1042), **Admiral's Ale** (1050) and **1066** (1066).

STRATHALBYN, 70 Beardmore Way, Clydebank Ind. Estate, Dalmuir. ☎ 041 941 2070.
Begun in 1982 to challenge the keg stronghold of Glasgow. **Strathalbyn Ale** (1038) is now available in 45 outlets in the West of Scotland.

SUMMERSKILLS, The Manor, Ringmore, Kingsbridge, Devon. ☎ 054 881 641.
The only brewery in Britain set up in a vineyard! Began brewing **Bigbury Best Bitter** (1042) last year for a few local outlets.

SWANNELLS, Numbers Farm, Station Road, Kings Langley, Herts. ☎ 65076.
Begun in 1982 by a former partner in another Hertfordshire brewery, Victoria.
Dark Ale (1034), **Bitter** (1038), **Best** (1048), **Swan Ale** (1055) and **Old Licky** (1072).

TAP Brewery, 27–31 Duke Street, Norwich. ☎ 617967.
Began as the Star Brewery behind the well-known Star free house in Norwich. Reopened last year on the same site with a new name and under new management.
Mild (1033), **Tap 40** (1040), **Norfolk Nog** (1043) and **Royal Flush** (1053).

TAYLOR, Knowle Spring Brewery, Keighley, W. Yorks. ☎ 603139.
The fame of Timothy Taylor's quality ales – which have won a barrel full of Championship medals – stretches far beyond W. Yorkshire and their 28 pubs. One of the widest ranges of real ales including a porter.
Golden Best (1033) – light and malty.
Mild (1033) – darker version of the Best.
Best Bitter (1037) – well-hopped bitter.
Landlord (1042) – distinctive, full-bodied bitter.
Porter (1043) – occasional rich brew.
Ram Tam (1043) – fruity winter ale.

THEAKSTON, Wellgarth, Masham, Ripon. N. Yorks. ☎ 89544. And Bridge Street, Carlisle, Cumbria. ☎ 24467.
Yorkshire Dales brewery, renowned for its Old Peculier, which sprang to prominence with the real ale revival, and subsequently bought the former State brewery in Carlisle to meet free trade demand. Sold off some of its pubs but now building up estate again. Currently has 12 houses.
Light Mild (1032.5) – dry and nutty.
Dark Mild (1032.5) – darker version.
Best Bitter (1038) – light but distinctive (the only Carlisle brew).
XB (1045) – new stronger bitter.
Old Peculier (1058.5) – notorious, rich and heavy.

THOMPSONS'S, London Inn, West Street, Ashburton, Devon. ☎ 52478.
Begun in 1981 supplying just their own pub, but now they are expanding the brewery to drive into the free trade around Dartmoor.
Aysheberton Mild (1034) – hoppy, dark ale.
Bitter (1040) – full-bodied and hoppy.
IPA (1045) – dark and bitter.

THWAITES, Star Brewery, Blackburn, Lancashire. ☎ 54431.
Excellent Lancashire brewery providing real ale in 95 per cent of its 360 houses. The quality of beers was underlined by the bitter being voted Best Draught Beer in Britain at the brewers own exhibition, Brewex, last year.
Mild (1031) – nutty and dark.
Best Mild (1033) – excellent malty brew.
Bitter (1035.5) – creamy and hoppy.

TISBURY, The Old Brewery, Church St., Tisbury, Wilts. ☎ 0747 870666.
An unusually ambitious new brewery which began in 1980 by floating shares on the stock market. Taken over by an investment company last year, which also now controls Martlet of Eastbourne. One tied house and free trade.
Local Bitter (1037) – light and well-hopped.
Heavy Bitter (1045) – well-balanced brew.
Old Grumble (1060) – stong winter ale.

Breweries

TOLLY COBBOLD, Cliff Brewery, Ispwich, Suffolk. ☎ 56751.
Suffolk's major brewery which has considerably improved its range
of beers. Real ale now in 75 per cent of the 350 pubs. Like Camerons,
a subsidiary of Ellerman Lines, and up for sale as the Guide went
to press.
Mild (1032) – sweet and malty.
Bitter (1034) – subtle and pleasantly dry.
Original (1036) – well-hopped, flavoursome bitter.
Old Strong (1046) – rich, fruity winter brew.

TRAQUAIR HOUSE, Innerleithen, Peeblesshire, Borders. ☎ 830323.
Historic Scottish brewery set in an ancient manor house and still run by the Laird.
Previously known for his rich, strong bottled beer, Peter Maxwell-Stuart has now
launched a lower-gravity draught beer for the free trade.
Bear Ale (1050) – new draught ale.
Traquair House Ale (1075) – usually bottled but occasionally on draught.

TROUGH Brewery, Louisa Street, Idle, Bradford, W. Yorks. ☎ 613450.
Begun in 1981 brewing value-for-money beers for the club trade,
but have since built up a tied estate of four houses.
Black Hog Mild (1033) – dark and tasty.
Trough Bitter (1035.5) – refreshing bitter.
Wild Boar Bitter (1039) – full-bodied beer.

VAUX, Sunderland, Tyne & Wear. ☎ 76277.
Britain's second largest regional brewing group which also owns
Darley and Ward in S. Yorkshire and Lorimer in Scotland. 135 of
Vaux's own 462 pubs sell real ale, including Lorimer's Best Scotch.
Sunderland Draught Bitter (1040) – light, soft bitter.
Samson (1042.3) – flavoursome, sharp bitter.

VICTORIA, Broadmeads, Ware, Herts. ☎ 68332.
Begun in 1981 in an old maltings and now brewing for 55 outlets
from Cambridge to Kent.
Bitter (1037) – a light, hoppy beer.
Special (1043) – smooth, malty ale.
Hellfire (1063) – reaches parts other beers never consider.

VICTORIA BREWERY

WADWORTH, Northgate Brewery, Devizes, Wilts. ☎ 3361.
Delightful market town brewery whose excellent 6X is popular in
the free trade throughout the South. Solidly traditional, with all but
one of the 142 houses selling real ale.
Devizes Bitter – a light bitter.
IPA (1035) – a hoppier brew.
6X (1041) – a splendid, malty bitter.
Old Timer (1053) – heavy and fruity.

WARDS, Sheaf Brewery, Ecclesall Road, Sheffield S11. ☎ 78787.
Taken over by Vaux of Sunderland in 1972, this S. Yorkshire
brewery sells real ale in half of its 100 pubs. Last year stopped
producing its short-lived light ale, Sheaf.
Best Mild (1034) – dark and malty.
Sheffield Best Bitter (1038.7) – full-bodied and malty.

WELLS Brewery, Havelock Street, Bedford. ☎ 65100.
This regional company completely rebuilt its brewery on a new site
and is now building up its tied estate, even in London. Two-thirds
of the 273 pubs serve cask beer without pressure.
Eagle Bitter (1035) – a consistent bitter beer.
Bombardier (1042) – a full-bodied bitter.

WEM Brewery, Wem, Shrewsbury, Shropshire. ☎ 32415.
A subsidiary of Greenall Whitley of Warrington which has largely remained untouched by the regional giant, serving real ale in all its 200 houses.
Pale Ale (1034) – pleasant, light bitter.
Mild (1036) – dark and creamy.
Best Bitter (1039) – full-bodied and distinctive.

WESTMORLAND, Cross Croft, Appleby, Cumbria. ☎ 0930 52197.
Begun in 1979 as Appleby Brewery and taken over just over a year later by a Lancaster wines and spirits company. Supplies 20 free trade outlets plus one tied house.
Slater's Bitter (1037) – well-balanced, malty brew.
Cumberland Strong (1050) – a full-bodied ale.

WEST RIDING, Bradley Mills, Huddersfield, W. Yorks. ☎ 44262.
Begun by local CAMRA members in 1980 and has since carried off a string of awards from the Great British Beer Festival. Supplies one tied house and local free trade.
Light Mild (1033) – refreshing.
Dark Mild (1033) – smooth and nutty.
West Riding Bitter (1037) – a well-balanced bitter.
Tyke Best Bitter (1041) – full-bodied hoppy brew.

WINKLE'S Saxon Cross Brewery, Harpur Hill, Buxton, Derby. ☎ 0298 71720.
Begun in 1979 serving the local free trade and now concentrating on building up a chain of tied houses.
Mild (1037) – dark and malty.
Bitter (1037) – well-hopped brew.
BVA (1037) – pale 'house' beer, known under various names.

WOOD, Plough Inn, Wistanstow, Craven Arms, Shropshire. ☎ 05882 2523.
Begun in 1980 behind a pub but now supplying over 30 outlets in this border area.
Parish Bitter (1037) – refreshing, light bitter.
Wood's Special (1043) – full-flavoured, sweetish bitter.

WOODFORDE, Spread Eagle Brewery, Erpingham, Norfolk. ☎ 0263 78152.
Begun in 1981 in Norwich, bringing much-needed choice to this Watney dominated region, before moving to the present site last year. Supplies 30 free trade outlets plus own pub.
Broadsman Bitter (1036) – light but full-flavoured.
Wherry Best Bitter (1041) – pale and malty.
Norfolk Porter (1042) – distinctive, dark and hoppy.
Festival Ale (1052) – strong winter ale.

YATES & JACKSON, Brewery Lane, Lancaster. ☎ 34166.
The smaller of the two independent breweries that dominate the Lancashire county town, providing real ale in all 40 tied houses.
Mild (1030.8) – dark and dry.
Bitter (1035.8) – truly bitter.

YOUNG, Ram Brewery, Wandsworth, London SW18. ☎ 01 870 0141.
Last but not least is one of the most warmly regarded breweries in the country, which stood alone against the keg tide in the Capital in the early Seventies. All 138 houses offer real ale, with a new low-gravity brew, Young John's Ale, replacing the mild last year.
Young John's Ale (1030) – new value-for-money brew.
Bitter (1036) – light and bitter.
Special (1046) – full-flavoured and distinctive.
Winter Warmer (1055) – strong old ale.

ALL NATIONS (Mrs Lewis's), Coalport Road, Madeley, Shropshire.
☏ 0952 585747.
Pale Ale (1032)
One of four home-brew pubs left by the early Seventies before the new wave arrived. The others are the Blue Anchor, Old Swan and Three Tuns.

ANCHOR INN, High Street, Upton-on-Severn, Worcs. ☏ 068 46 2146.
Jolly Roger Bitter (1035)
Severn Bore Special (1045)
Old Anchor Ale (1060)

BEER ENGINE, Newton St. Cyres, Exeter, Devon.
☏ 039 285 282.
Rail Ale (1037)
Piston Bitter (1044)

BLUE ANCHOR, Coinagehall Street, Helston, Cornwall.
☏ 032 65 6281.
Medium (1050),
BB (1053)
Special (1060)
Summer Special (1066)
Historic thatched home brewery producing powerful ales.

BREWHOUSE, High Street, Poole, Dorset.
High Street Mild (1035)
High Street Bitter (1036)
Bosun Bitter (1048)
Owned by Poole Brewery.

BRIDGE HOUSE, 218 Tower Bridge Road, London SE1.
☏ 01 403 2276.
Bermondsey Bitter (1036)
Bridge Special (1045)
007 (1055)

BRIDGEWATER ARMS, Little Gaddesden, Berkhamsted, Herts.
☏ 2408.
Bridgewater Best (1035)
Special (1040)

CASTLE HOTEL, Downham Market, Norfolk. ☏ 0366 382157.
Downham Bitter (1036) – malt extract.

DOWN ROYAL, Ballindery Road, Lisburn, N. Ireland.
☏ 08462 82473.

ONCE virtually all beer in this country was brewed on the premises of the public house. Gradually 'common' or commercial brewers sprang up serving more than one pub, but home-brew houses remained a feature of every town and locality.

A hundred years ago there were still 12,417 home-brew pubs recorded in Britain. But then, as the common brewers began to build up their tied estates, these unique bars with their own beers disappeared.

By the early Seventies they were in serious danger of extinction. Only four remained hidden in the depths of Cornwall, Shropshire and the Black Country. But with the appearance of CAMRA and the revival of interest in real beer, so the dying art of brewing on a small scale was resurrected, nearly always to produce traditional beer.

Now there are over 50 home-brew pubs. This list only contains those that brew essentially for themselves. Others, that brew behind a pub but concentrate on supplying the free trade, have been included in the main list of independent regional brewers.

Even the national brewers have jumped on this dray wagon, with Whitbread, Allied and Watneys now all running their own home-brew pubs. Details of these are included in the National Combines section.

Down Royal Local (1037)
Export (1043)
Special (1046) – summer, (1060) – winter.

FERRET & FIRKIN in the Balloon up the Creek, 114 Lots Road, London SW10. ☏ 01 352 6645.
Stoat Bitter (1036)
Ferret Ale (1045)
Dogbolter (1060)
Balloonatic Broth (1075)
One of a chain of six crazy 'Firkin' home-brew pubs set up by David Bruce in London and Bristol.

FLEECE & FIRKIN, 12 St. Thomas Street, Bristol.
☏ 277150.
Bootlace Bitter (1038)
Best Bristol (1045)
Dogbolter (1060)
Black Sheep (1075)

FOUR KEYS, Station Road, Wadhurst, Sussex.
☏ 089 288 2252.

4X Bitter (1036)
Stallion (1045) – malt extract beers.

FOX & FIRKIN, 316 Lewisham High Street, London SE13.
☏ 01 690 8925.
Blackheath (1036)
Bruce's Bitter (1045)
Dogbolter (1060)

FOX & HOUNDS, Barley, Royston, Herts.
☏ Barkway 459.
Nathaniel's Special (1034)
Nog (1040)
Hogshead (1043)

FOX & HOUNDS, Stottesdon, Shropshire.
☏ 074 632 222.
DDD (1040)
Dasher's Disaster (1048)
Also available in a few other pubs.

FROG & FIRKIN, 41 Tavistock Crescent, London W11.
☏ 01 727 9250.
Tavistock (1036)
Bullfrog (1045)
Dogbolter (1060)

FROG & FRIGATE, 33 Canute Road, Southampton, Hants.
☏ 332231
Frog's Original (1040)
Croaker (1050)
One of two home-brew pubs owned by Ringwood

Home-brew Pubs

Brewery, the other is the Mash Tun.

GATE, Swan Bottom, The Lee, Bucks.
℡ 024 020 368.
Carr's Best Bitter (1041)

GLOBE, Main Street, Fishguard, Dyfed, Wales.
℡ 0348 872500.
Black Fox Bitter (1038) – malt extract.

GOOSE & FIRKIN, 47 Borough Road, Southwark, London SE1.
℡ 01 403 3590.
Elephant Ale (1038)
Borough Bitter (1045)
Dogbolter (1060)
The first and only Bruce house brewing with malt extract.

HALL CROSS, Hallgate, Doncaster, S. Yorks.
℡ 28213.
Stocks Best Bitter (1037)
Stocks Select (1044)
Stocks Wake (1064)

HATCHET INN, Winkfield, Windsor, Berks. ℡ 0344 882303.
Woodman's Bitter (1037) – malt extract.

KING'S ARMS, Market Place, Bishop Auckland, Co. Durham. ℡ 661296
Weard Ale (1038)

LION, Pawsons Road, Croydon, London.
℡ 01 684 2978.
Croydon Bitter (1036)
Burke's Best Bitter (1044)
Also available at the Hole in the Wall, Waterloo.

LONG BARN, Cippenham Lane, Cippenham, Berks.
℡ 0753 21396.
Stallion Bitter (1037)
Barnstormer (1048)

MASH TUN, Eastgate Street, Winchester, Hants.
℡ 61440.
Mash Tun Bitter (1038)
Austin GT (1049)

MASON ARMS, South Leigh, Witney, Oxon.
℡ 0993 2485.
Sowlye Ale (1040) – malt extract.
One of the first of the new wave of home-brew pubs, begun in 1974.

NELSON, Skipton Road, Harrogate, N. Yorks.
℡ 0423 500340.
Oliver John's Bitter (1038) – malt extract.

OLD SWAN (Ma Pardoe's), Halesowen Road, Netherton, Dudley, W. Midlands.
℡ 0384 53075.
Bitter (1034)
One of the great institutions of Black Country drinking.

PHEASANT, Gestingthorpe, Essex.
℡ 0787 61196.
Pheasant Bitter (1036) – malt extract

PHEASANT & FIRKIN, 166 Goswell Road, London EC1.
℡ 01 253 7429.
Bruce's Mild (1037)
Pheasant Bitter (1038)
Barbarian (1045)
Firkin Ale (1052)
Dogbolter (1060)

PIER HOTEL, Town Pier, Gravesend, Kent.
℡ 0474 67193
Clipper (1040)
Gravedigger (1050)
Buccaneer (1065)
Lifebuoy (1076)

PIG & WHISTLE, Privett, Alton, Hants.
℡ 073 088 323
Joshua Privett Bitter (1043)
BDS (1055)
Also brew for two other pubs in Southampton in the same company, the Compton Arms and the Pub-in-the-Park.

PITFIELD Brewery, The Beer Shop, Pitfield Street, London N1.
℡ 01 739 3701.
Pitfield Bitter (1038)
Hoxton Heavy (1048)
Dark Star (1050)
Britain's only brewery in an off-licence

PLOUGH, Bodicote, Banbury, Oxon.
℡ 0295 62327
Jim's Brew (1037)
No. 9 (1045)

QUEEN'S HEAD, St. James Street, Monmouth, Gwent, Wales.
℡ 0600 2767.
Ten Thirty Five (1035)
Piston Bitter (1045)

RIDGEWOOD INN, Uckfield, Sussex.
℡ 0825 2795.
Old Oak Bitter (1038)

ROYAL CLARENCE, Burnham-on-Sea, Somerset.
℡ 0278 783138.
KC Bitter (1038)

ROYAL INN, Horsebridge, Tavistock, Devon.
℡ 082 287 214.
Tamar Ale (1039)
Horsebridge Best (1045)
Heller (1060)

SAIR, Lane Top, Linthwaite, Huddersfield, W. Yorks.
℡ 0484 842370.
Linfit Mild (1033)
Linfit Light (1033)
Linfit Bitter (1036)
Old Eli 1050)

TAVERN, Newnham Bridge, Worcs.
℡ 058 479 331
Bartlett's Mild (1040)
Bartlett's Bitter (1042)
Set up by former Black Country family brewer Bob Bartlett, producing some of the best value-for-money beers.

JOHN THOMPSON Inn, Ingleby, Derbyshire.
℡ 033 16 3426.
Shires Bitter (1035)
JTS XXX (1045)
Award-winning pub brewery named after the landlord. JTS XXX is sold in the free trade as **Lloyd's Country Bitter**, where **Derby Bitter** (1038) is also marketed.

THREE TUNS, Bishop's Castle, Shropshire.
℡ 0588 638797
Mild (1035)
XXX (1042)
Steamer (1045)
Historic home-brew pub.

Almondsbury 14E8

10.30–2.30; 6–10.30 (11 F, S and summer)

Bowl
Church Road, Lower Almondsbury (off A38)
℡ 612757
Morning opening: 11
Courage Bitter, Best Bitter, Directors H
Old-world inn next to church
🚗♣🅿️🍴🔥🅱️Ⓖ🕙Ⓢ

Backwell 14D9

10–2.30; 6–10.30 (11 F, S)

Rising Sun
West Town Road
℡ Flax Bourton 2215
Draught Bass
Welsh Fussell's Best Bitter H
'Brewers Tudor' roadhouse with contrasting bars
🚗♣🅿️🅱️Ⓖ🍴Ⓢ

Bath 15E9

10.30–2.30; 5.30–10.30 (11 F, S)

Coeur de Lion
17 Northumberland Place
Morning opening: 11
Devenish Bitter, Wessex Best Bitter H
Tiny pub in attractive passageway Ⓢ≷

Garrick's Head
8 St. John's Place
Courage Best Bitter, Directors H
Theatrical pub 🎵🅿️Ⓢ

King William
Thomas Street (A4)
Brain SA
Cotleigh Tawny Bitter
Hall & Woodhouse Badger Best Bitter
Marston Pedigree
Smiles Exhibition H
Street-corner pub with good selection of beers 🚗🎵♣🍴Ⓢ

Larkhall Inn
The Square, Larkhall (off A4)
Courage Bitter, Best Bitter, Directors H
Distinctive pub of character; unusual brass handpumps
🚗🎵♣🍴🍴

Midland
14 James Street West
℡ 25029
Courage Bitter, Best Bitter H
Large, wood-panelled town pub 🎵♣🅱️Ⓖ🍴Ⓢ

New Westhall
Upper Bristol Road (A4)
℡ 25432
Butcombe Bitter
Marston Burton Bitter, Pedigree, Merrie Monk, Owd Rodger H
Lively atmosphere, splendid cellar 🍴🎵♣🅱️Ⓖ🅱️

Olde Farmhouse
Lansdown Road
Butcombe Bitter
Ind Coope Burton Ale
Marston Pedigree
Wadworth 6X
Whitbread Flowers Original Bitter H
Lively local of great character; 9 beers always available
🍴♣🅿️🍴Ⓢ

Pulteney Arms
37 Daniel Street ℡ 63923
Usher PA, Best Bitter H & G
Founders Ale H
Sidestreet local with gas lighting 🎵♣🅱️Ⓖ🍴Ⓢ

Railway Brewery
Wells Road (A367)
Draught Bass
Whitbread WCPA, Flowers Original Bitter H
Convivial local on southern slopes overlooking city
🎵♣🅿️🍴Ⓢ≷

Richmond Arms
7 Richmond Place, Lansdown
Courage Bitter, Best Bitter
Taunton Cider G
Out-of-the-way pub in Georgian terrace 🎵♣🅿️🍴Ⓢ

Rose & Crown
6 Brougham Place, St. Saviours Road, Larkhall
Courage Best Bitter
Felinfoel Double Dragon
Marston Capital, Pedigree H
Friendly out-of-town local
🎵♣🅱️🍴Ⓢ

Smiths
11–12 Westgate Buildings
℡ 330470
Eldridge Pope Dorchester Bitter, IPA, Royal Oak H
Spacious central pub, good atmosphere 🍴♣🅱️🅱️Ⓖ🍴🍴Ⓢ≷

Blagdon 5F1

10.30–2.30; 6–10.30 (11 F, S)

New Inn
Church Street (off A368)
℡ 62475
Morning opening: 11
Draught Bass
Wadworth Devizes Bitter, 6X, Old Timer H
Antique-festooned lounge, garden with superb lake views
🚗♣🅿️🅱️Ⓖ🍴Ⓢ

Bristol 14D9

10.30–2.30; 5.30–10.30 (11 F, S)

Annexe Inn
Nevil Road, Bishopston, 7
Courage Bitter, Best Bitter, Directors H
Converted skittle alley; interesting bottle collection
🎵♣🅿️🍴Ⓢ

Bay Horse
Lewins Mead, 1 ℡ 291319
Davenports Mild, Bitter E
Spacious, comfortable pub, handy for bus station 🎵♣Ⓖ🍴Ⓢ

Bell Inn
151 East Street, Bedminster, 3 (A38) ℡ 667135
Wadworth Devizes Bitter, 6X, Old Timer H
Basic split-level pub on main shopping street 🍴🎵♣Ⓖ🍴Ⓢ

Clifton
Regent Street, Clifton, 8
℡ 739286
Draught Bass
Welsh Fussell's Best Bitter H
Busy, two-bar local with separate restaurant bar 🎵♣Ⓖ🍴

Farm
30 Hopetoun Road, Ashley Vale, St. Werburghs, 2
℡ 43622
Evening opening: 6
Usher PA, Best Bitter, Founders Ale H
Quiet and 'rural', near St. Werburgh's city farm
🍴🎵♣🅿️Ⓖ (must book) Ⓢ

Horse & Groom
St Georges Road, 1
Morning opening: 11
Courage Best Bitter, Directors H
Small open-plan local with Toulouse Lautrec-style murals
🎵♣🅿️Ⓢ

Nova Scotia
Nova Scotia Place, Hotwells
Courage Bitter, Best Bitter, Directors H
Quayside pub with nautical flavour 🍴🎵♣🅿️🅱️Ⓖ🍴🍴

Old Duke
45 King Street, 1 ℡ 277137
Opens at 11 am and 6 pm
Courage Best Bitter, Directors H
Open-plan pub with nightly jazz, often crowded 🍴🅿️Ⓖ

All pubs in King Street serve real ale

Phoenix
Wellington Road, St. Judes, 2
Draught Bass
Halls Harvest Bitter H
Wadworth 6X, Old Timer G
Modernised local near multi-storey car park 🍴🎵♣🅿️Ⓢ

Pride of the Forest
Unity Street, Old Market, 2
℡ 298109
Wadworth IPA, 6X, Old Timer H
Small and comfortable
🎵♣Ⓖ🍴Ⓢ

Sherberts
29 Old Market Street, 2
Wadworth IPA, 6X H
Basic local on one of Bristol's oldest thoroughfares 🎵♣Ⓖ🍴

Victoria
20 Chock Lane, Westbury-on-Trym, 9 ℡ 500441

Opens at 11 am and 7 pm
Draught Bass
**Wadworth Devizes Bitter, 6X,
Old Timer** �H
Bustling local with young
clientele ♪♣⊞℘℞Ⓖ♥Ⓢ

Windmill
14 Windmill Hill, Bedminster,
3 ☎ 665510
Opens at 11 am and 6.30 pm
Davenports Bitter �H
Basic split-level suburban
local ♪♣℘℞Ⓖ♥Ⓢ⇌

Butcombe 14D9

10.30–2.30; 6.30–10.30 (11 F, S)
Mill Inn
Courage Bitter, Best Bitter Ⓖ
Cosy, unspoilt former mill in
rustic setting ♨♪♣♠Ⓢ

Camerton 5G1

10.30–2.30; 6–11
Camerton Inn
Meadgate (B3115)
Wadworth 6X
Welsh Fussell's Best Bitter �H
Pleasant roadside inn
♪♣♠♥

Chipping Sodbury
15E8

10.30–2.30; 5.30–10.30 (11 F, S)
Portcullis
Horse Street (A432)
☎ 312004
**Courage Best Bitter,
Directors** �H
Taunton Cider Ⓖ
Comfortable, traditional inn
♨℘⊟℞Ⓖ♥Ⓢ

Churchill 5F1

10.30–2.30; 6–10.30 (11 F, S)
Crown
Skinners Lane (off A38)
Courage Best Bitter
Felinfoel Double Dragon Ⓖ
Unspoilt farmhouse at foot of
Mendips ♨♣♥♠

Clandown 5G1

10.30–2.30; 6–11
Lamb
Old Fosseway (off A367)
☎ Radstock 32150
Evening opening: 7
Halls Harvest Bitter �H
Taunton Cider Ⓖ
Large, popular village pub
♪♣♠⊟℞Ⓖ♥Ⓢ

Clapton-in-Gordano
14D8

10.30–2.30; 6–10.30 (11 F, S)
Black Horse
Clevedon Lane (off M5 and
A369)
Courage Bitter, Best Bitter Ⓖ
Bulmer & Taunton Cider �H
Old country pub full of
character
♨♣⊞℘♠℞♥Ⓢ

Clevedon 14C9

10.30–2.30; 6–10.30 (11 F, S)
Bristol Hotel
Chapel Hill ☎ 872073
**Courage Bitter, Best Bitter,
Directors** �H
Extensive facade hides
unassuming bars; separate
restaurant ♪♣℘♠⊞Ⓖ♥Ⓢ

Compton Martin 5F1

11–2.30; 6–11
Ring O' Bells
(A368) ☎ West Harptree 284
Evening opening: 7
Butcombe Bitter
Marston Pedigree �H
Large local, good food and
garden ♨♪♣⊞℘♠℞Ⓖ♥Ⓢ

Congresbury 14D9

10.30–2.30; 6–10.30 (11 F, S)
Old Inn
St. Pauls Causeway (off A370)
Butcombe Bitter
Welsh Worthington Pale Ale
Whitbread Flowers
Original Bitter �H
15th-century inn with
matchbox collection ♣℘♠Ⓖ♥

Dundry 14D9

10.30–2.30; 6–10.30 (11 F, S)
Carpenters Arms
Wells Road (off A38) OS
565664 ☎ Bristol 640415
Butcombe Bitter
Courage Bitter, Directors
Devenish Wessex Best Bitter �H
Perched on hill overlooking
Bristol ♪♣℘♠♠Ⓖ♥Ⓢ♠

Hanham 14E9

10.30–2.30; 6–10.30 (11 F, S)
Blue Bowl
High Street ☎ Bristol 673280
**Courage Bitter, Best Bitter,
Directors** Ⓖ
Tastefully refurbished
15th-century alehouse
♪℘♠Ⓖ♥

Hinton 15E8

10–2.30; 6.30–10.30 (11 F, S)
Bull
(Off A46) OS 735768
☎ Abson 2332
**Wadworth Devizes Bitter, 6X,
Old Timer** �H
Friendly country pub
♨♣♠℘♠℞Ⓖ♥Ⓢ

Hinton Charterhouse 5H1

10.30–2.30; 5.30–10.30 (11 F, S)
Rose & Crown
(B3110)
☎ Limpley Stoke 2153
Opens at 11 am and 6 pm
Draught Bass
Marston Pedigree
Wadworth 6X
Welsh Worthington Pale Ale Ⓖ

Busy local with oak-panelled
bar ♪♣℘♠℞Ⓖ

Kendleshire 14E8

10.30–2.30; 5.30–10.30 (11 F, S)
Golden Heart
Down Road
☎ Winterbourne 773152
**Courage Best Bitter,
Directors** ⊞
Attractive old-world coaching
inn ♨♣℘♠Ⓖ♥

Keynsham 14E9

10.30–2.30; 5.30–11
Crown
63 Bristol Road (A4135)
☎ 2150
Courage Bitter, Best Bitter ⊞
Breweriana collection and fine
home-made fare
♪♣⊞℘♠⊟℞Ⓖ♥Ⓢ♠⇌

Littleton-on-Severn
14E7

10.30–2.30; 6–10.30 (11 F, S and summer)
White Hart
☎ Thornbury 412275
Opens at 12 noon and 7 pm
Archer Village Bitter
Eldridge Pope Royal Oak
Smiles Best Bitter ⊞
Local cider Ⓖ
16th-century pub, frequent
guest beers
♪♣℘♠℞Ⓖ♥Ⓢ♠♠

Long Ashton 14D9

10.30–2.30; 6.30–10.30 (11 F, S)
Miners Rest
42 Providence Lane (off
B3128) ☎ 3449
Courage Bitter, Best Bitter
Taunton Cider Ⓖ
Excellent cottage pub with
fine views
♨♪℘♠℞Ⓖ♥Ⓢ

Midford 5H1

10.30–2.30; 5.30–10.30 (11 F, S)
Hope & Anchor
(B3110) ☎ 832296
Opens at 11 am and 6 pm
Draught Bass
**Hall & Woodhouse Hectors's
Bitter, Tanglefoot**
**Marston Pedigree, Owd
Rodger** ⊞
Oak-beamed lounge in
300-year-old pub
♨♣⊞℘♠Ⓖ♥Ⓢ

Midsomer Norton
5G1

10.30–2.30; 6–11
White Hart
The Island
Draught Bass
**Welsh Worthington Pale Ale,
Fussell's Best Bitter** ⊞
Taunton Cider Ⓖ
Popular pub with warm local
atmosphere
♨♪♣℘℞Ⓖ♥Ⓢ

Monkton Combe 15F9

11–2.30; 6–10.30 (11 F, S)
Wheelwrights Arms
☎ Limpley Stoke 2287
Wadworth 6X
Whitbread WCPA [H] **Bitter** [G]
Pleasant village local in picturesque valley
🔥♪♣✿🚗▦[R]☾❧🍷Ⓢ

Oldbury-on-Severn 14E7

10.30–2.30; 6–10.30 (11 F, S and summer)
Anchor
☎ Thornbury 413331
Morning opening: 11.30
Butcombe Bitter
Marston Pedigree
Theakston Best Bitter [H]
Bulmer Cider [G]
Attractive Severnside pub; frequent guest beers
🔥♣✿🚗☾❧🍷Ⓢ

Old Down 14E8

10.30–2.30; 6–10.30 (11 F, S and summer)
Fox
The Inner Down (off A38)
OS 617873
Draught Bass
Davenports Bitter
Whitbread Flowers Original Bitter [H]
Old stone-built village local with excellent garden
🔥♣✿🚗Ⓢ

Paulton 5G1

10.30–2.30; 6–11
Somerset Inn
Bath Road (off B3355)
☎ Midsomer Norton 412828
Courage Bitter, Best Bitter, Directors
Taunton Cider [H]
Friendly cosy pub, good food
♪♣✿🚗☾🍷

Pensford 14E9

10.30–2.30; 6–11
Rising Sun
Church Street (off A37)
☎ Compton Dando 402
Opens at 11 am and 7 pm
Halls Harvest Bitter
Ind Coope Burton Ale
Bulmer Cider [H]
Riverside local with fine garden
🔥♪♣▦✿🚗[R]☾❧🍷Ⓢ♿

Rickford 5F1

10–2.30; 6–10.30 (11 F, S)
Plume of Feathers
(A368) ☎ 62409
Morning opening: 11
Courage Bitter, Best Bitter [H]
Taunton Cider [G]
Picturesque and unspoilt pub in streamside hamlet
🔥♪♣▦✿▦[R]🍷Ⓢ♿

Ridgehill 14D9

10–2.30; 6–10.30 (11 F, S)
Crown
(Off A3130) ☎ Lulsgate 2388
Draught Bass
Wadworth Devizes Bitter, 6X [H]
Fine food, facilities, views and value 🔥♪♣✿🚗[R]☾❧Ⓢ

Southstoke 5H1

10.30–2.30; 5.30–10.30 (11 F, S)
Pack Horse
(Off B3110)
Evening opening: 6
Courage Bitter, Best Bitter [H]
Coates Cider [G]
Popular, unspoilt 15th-century village pub; three shove-halfpenny tables
🔥⌐♣✿🍷Ⓢ

Stanton Drew 14D9

10.30–2.30; 6.30–11
Druids Arms
(Off A368)
Courage Bitter, Best Bitter, Directors [H]
Stone-built 'cottage' local by druids monument 🔥♪♣✿🚗🍷Ⓢ

Stoke Gifford 14E8

10.30–2.30; 5.30–10.30 (11 F, S)
Beaufort Arms
55 North Road (off A4174)
☎ Bristol 691187
Courage Bitter, Best Bitter, Directors [H]
Thriving, substantial village local ♪♣✿🚗☾❧🍷Ⓢ🚆

Thornbury 14E7

10–2.30; 6–10.30 (11 F, S and summer)
White Lion
High Street (B4061)
☎ 412126
Courage Bitter, Best Bitter, Directors [H]
Fine old pub with unusual Georgian frontage
⌐♣✿[R]☾❧🍷Ⓢ

Try also: Swan (Courage)

Westerleigh 15E8

10.30–2.30; 6–10.30 (11 F, S)
Olde Inn
Westerleigh Road (off B4465)
OS 698797 ☎ Chipping Sodbury 312344
Courage Best Bitter, Directors [H]
Taunton Cider [G]
Fine two-bar local near church 🔥⌐▦✿🚗[R]☾❧🍷Ⓢ♿⛺

Weston-super-Mare 14C9

10.30–2.30; 6–10.30 (11 F, S and summer)
Britannia
118 High Street ☎ 32629
Courage Best Bitter, Directors [H]
Cosmopolitan pub
♪♣✿☾❧Ⓢ♿

Heron
Locking Road (A370)
☎ 22218
Courage Best Bitter, Directors [H]
Large, well-appointed suburban roadhouse
⌐♪♣▦✿🚗[R]☾🍷⛺

Imperial
South Parade
Evening opening: 7
Courage Best Bitter, Directors [H]
Comfortable, friendly Regency-style lounge ♪♣▦♿

Long John Silver
73 Beach Road, Sand Bay
☎ 23367
Wadworth Devizes Bitter, 6X [H] **Old Timer** [G]
Split-level pub with scenic bay views ⌐♪♣▦✿🚗[R]☾🍷Ⓢ⛺

Major From Glengarry
10–14 Upper Church Road
☎ 29594
Butcombe Bitter
Golden Hill Exmoor Ale
Marston Pedigree
Wadworth 6X [H]
Good atmosphere and good food. Range of beers may vary
♪♣▦✿[R]☾❧🍷Ⓢ

Phoenix
4 Richmond Street ☎ 413176
Eldridge Pope Dorchester Bitter, Royal Oak [H]
Bistro with pub atmosphere
♪♣▦[R]☾❧Ⓢ🚆

Willsbridge 14E9

10.30–2.30; 5.30–10.30 (11 F, S)
Queens Head
Willsbridge Hill (A431)
Opens at 11 am and 7 pm
Courage Bitter, Best Bitter [H]
Friendly wood-panelled village local near Bitton steam railway ♪♣▦🚗🍷Ⓢ

Yatton 14D9

10.30–2.30; 6–10.30 (11 F, S)
Butchers Arms
High Street (off B3133)
Courage Bitter, Best Bitter
Bulmer Cider [G]
Small, traditional local ♣✿☾🍷🚆

WARMEST WELCOME
♦ A REAL FIRE PUB ♦

The 🔥 symbol denotes a pub with a real solid fuel fire

Ampthill 17E6

10.30–2.30; 6–11
Queens Head
Woburn Street (A507)
✆ 402267
Wells Eagle Bitter Ⓗ
Pleasantly renovated local
♨♪♣⌂Ⓖ❶Ⓢ♿

Aspley Guise 16E7

10.30–2.30; 6–11
Weathercock
High Street (A5130)
Greene King IPA, Abbot Ⓗ
Welcoming pub by Woburn
Sands station ♨♪♣⌂♠Ⓖ❶Ⓢ⇌

Aspley Heath 16E7

10.30–2.30; 6–11
Royal Oak
Church Road (off A5130)
✆ Milton Keynes 584007
Morning opening: 11.30
Greene King XX, IPA, Abbot Ⓗ
Congenial, low-ceilinged pub
♣⌂♠Ⓖ (Mon–Fri)

Barton-le-Clay 17F7

10.30–2.30; 6–11
Speed the Plough
Pulloxhill Turn (A6)
Tolly Cobbold Bitter,
Original Ⓗ Old Strong Ⓖ
Well kept and comfortable
♨⌂Ⓖ

Bedford 17E6

10.30–2.30; 5.30–11
Bull
259 London Road (A600)
✆ 55719
Greene King XX, IPA, Abbot Ⓔ
Friendly local with good food
♨♪♣⌂♠ⒶⒼ❶Ⓢ

Castle
Newnham Street (east of A6)
Wells Eagle Bitter,
Bombardier Ⓗ
Comfortable pub with
attractive walled garden
♪♣⌂Ⓖ (Mon–Fri) 🏠Ⓢ

Fleur de Lis
12 Mill Street (east of A6)
Evening opening: 6
Wells Eagle Bitter Ⓗ
Excellent town pub, 100 yards
east of Debenham's corner
♪♣🅷⌂Ⓡ⌂ (Mon–Sat)

Phoenix
45 St Johns Street (A600)
✆ 52862
Wells Eagle Bitter Ⓗ
Sizeable alehouse by busy
roundabout ♪♣⌂♠⌂❶Ⓢ⇌

Swan
403 Goldington Road
(A428) ✆ 59595
Aylesbury ABC Bitter
Draught Bass
Morrell Light Ale Ⓗ
Good pub on large green, east
of town ♨♪♣⌂♠ⒶⓇⒼ❶Ⓢ

Beeston 17F6

10.30–2.30; 6–11
Cross
High Road (A1 northbound)
✆ Sandy 80024
Greene King IPA Ⓗ
Small roadside local with quiet
lounge and pool-mad tap
♪♣⌂Ⓖ❶Ⓢ

Biggleswade 17F6

10.30–2.30; 6–11
Coach & Horses
Shortmead Street (off A1)
Greene King XX, IPA, Abbot Ⓗ
Lively pub north of town
centre ♪♣♠Ⓐ⌂⇌

Crown
34 High Street (off A1)
✆ 312228
Greene King IPA, Abbot Ⓗ
Hotel opposite market square
♪♣🅷♠ⒶⒹⒼ❶⇌

Broom 17F6

10.30–2.30; 6–11
Cock
High Street (off B658)
Greene King IPA Ⓖ
As pubs once were, skittles but
no bar ♨♣🅷ⒶⓇ

Campton 17F6

11–2.30; 7–11
White Hart
Mill Lane (off A507)
✆ Hitchin 812657
Wells Eagle Bitter Ⓗ
Bombardier Ⓖ
Fine pub with friendly hosts
♪♣⌂♠Ⓖ❶Ⓢ

Cardington 17F6

11–2.30; 6–11
Exeter Arms
Southill Road (off A603) ✆ 207
Greene King IPA 🅷 & Ⓖ
Popular village pub with
emphasis on games
♨♪♣🅷♠ⒶⓇⒼ❶Ⓢ

Carlton 16E5

10.30–2.30; 5.30–11
Fox
High Street (off A428)
✆ Bedford 720235
Wells Eagle Bitter Ⓗ
Friendly local with
enthusiastic landlady; worth a
detour ♪♠Ⓖ❶Ⓢ

Clapham 17E6

10.30–2.30; 5.30–11
Fox & Hounds
(A6) ✆ Bedford 52889
Wells Eagle Bitter Ⓗ
Tastefully refurbished three-
bar pub ♪♣♠Ⓖ (Mon–Fri) 🏠

Clophill 17F6

10.30–2.30; 6–11
Green Man
The Green (off A6)

✆ Silsoe 60352
Morning opening: 11
Greene King KK, IPA, Abbot Ⓗ
16th century local on village
green ♨♪♣♠Ⓖ❶Ⓢ

Stone Jug
Back Street (off A6)
✆ Silsoe 60526
Adnams Bitter
Banks & Taylor Shefford
Bitter, SPA
Courage Best Bitter,
Directors Ⓗ
Popular pub in village
backwater, regular guest
beers ♨♪♣♠ⒶⓇⒼ❶Ⓢ

Deadmans Cross 17F6

11–2.30; 6–11
Red Lion
(A600) OS 110420
✆ Haynes 381
Lunchtime opening: 12 noon
Evening opening: 7 (winter)
Wethered Bitter Ⓗ Winter
Royal Ⓖ
Whitbread Flowers Original
Bitter Ⓗ
Friendly local with large
garden, good home cooking
♨♪♣♠ⒶⓇⒼ❶Ⓢ♿Ⓐ

Deepdale 17F6

10.30–2.30; 6–11
Locomotive
(B1042) ✆ Potton 260365
Wells Eagle Bitter,
Bombardier Ⓗ
Bulmer Cider Ⓖ
Bright country pub near RSPB
♨♣♠Ⓖ❶Ⓢ

Dunton 17G6

11–2.30; 6–11
March Hare
High Street (off A1)
✆ Biggleswade 313852
Wethered Bitter
Whitbread Flowers
Original Bitter Ⓗ
Smart country pub, good
blackboard menu
♨♪♣♠Ⓖ❶Ⓢ

Eggington 16E7

10–2.30; 6–11
Horseshoes
Benskins Bitter Ⓗ
Splendid little pub with
vintage MGs ♨♪♣♠ⒶⓇ🏠Ⓢ Ⓐ

Everton 17F6

11–2.30; 7–11
Thornton Arms
1 Potton Road OS 202512
Wells Eagle Bitter,
Bombardier Ⓗ
Bright village pub
♪♣♠ⒶⓇⓈ Ⓐ

Flitwick 17E7

11–2.30; 6–11
Blackbirds
High Street (A5120)

Wethered Bitter Ⓗ
Smart one-bar pub with public section
🍴♪♣🅿🍺Ⓛ (not Sat) Ⓢ≥

Houghton Conquest 17E6

10.30–2.30; 6–11
Royal Oak
High Street
✆ Bedford 740459
Wells Eagle Bitter Ⓗ
Popular local in centre of village 🍴♪♣🅱🍺Ⓡ
Ⓛ🍺 (must book) 🍺Ⓢ🏕

Kempston Green End 17E6

10.30–2.30; 5.30–11
Shoulder of Mutton
Green End Road OS 009476
Greene King XX, IPA Ⓖ
Rural setting; popular pub for dominoes and shove halfpenny 🍴♣🅿🍺

Kempston West End 17E6

10.30–2.30; 5.30–11
Three Horseshoes
West End Road, West End (B560) OS 997482
Greene King KK, IPA Ⓖ
Pleasant country pub
🍴♣🅿Ⓢ

Keysoe 17F5

10.30–2.30; 6–11
Chequers
Brook End (B660) OS 077633
✆ Riseley 678
Adnams Bitter
Everard Old Original
Hook Norton Best Bitter
Wethered Bitter Ⓗ
Large, comfortable pub, popular for food
🍴♪♣🅱🅿🍺Ⓡ Ⓛ🍺🍺

Langford 17F6

10.30–2.30; 6–11
Red Cow
High Street (A6001)
Greene King IPA Ⓗ
Good honest basic local 🍴♪♣🍺

Leighton Buzzard 16E7

10–2.30; 6–11
Cross Keys
Market Square (off A418)
✆ 373033
Evening opening: 7
Benskins Bitter
Ind Coope Burton Ale Ⓗ
Imposing pub with good bar food and restaurant
♪♣🅱🅿🍺ⓇⓁ🍺🍺

White Lion
87 North Street (A418)
Morning opening: 11

**Wells Eagle Bitter,
Bombardier** Ⓗ
Welcoming local ♪♣🅿Ⓛ Ⓢ

Luton 17F7

10.30–2.30; 5.30–10.30 (11 F, S)
Great Northern
63 Bute Street
Ind Coope Bitter Ⓗ
Great little pub, full of character ♪🍺🍺Ⓢ≥

Mother Redcap
80 Latimer Road (off A6)
Greene King IPA, Abbot Ⓗ
Recently renovated ♪♣ⒼⓁ🅱≥

Maulden 17E6

10.30–2.30; 6–11
Commander in Chief
Clophill Road, Hall End (A507) ✆ Silsoe 60764
Wells Eagle Bitter Ⓗ
Bombardier (occasional) Ⓖ
Small pub, big welcome
♪♣🅿ⒼⓁ🍺🍺Ⓢ🅱

White Hart
Ampthill Road (A507)
✆ Silsoe 402306
Wethered Bitter Ⓗ
Old thatched pub with frequent live jazz
🍴♪♣🅿ⒼⓁ🍺🍺🅱

Melchbourne 17E5

11–2.30; 6.30–11
St Johns Arms
Knotting Road (off A6)
OS 029662 ✆ Riseley 238
Greene King IPA, Abbot Ⓗ
Excellent pub, former gamekeeper's lodge
🍴♪♣🅱🅿🍺ⒺⒼⓁ🍺 (not Wed)
🍺Ⓢ🅱🏕

Milton Ernest 17E5

10.30–2.30; 5.30–11
Queens Head
1 Rushden Road (A6)
**Wells Eagle Bitter,
Bombardier** Ⓗ
Pre-Tudor pub; try hole-in-the-ground darts
♪♣🅿🍺🍺

Moggerhanger 17F6

10.30–2.30; 6–11
Guinea
Bedford Road (A603)
**Wells Eagle Bitter,
Bombardier** Ⓗ
Spacious, comfortable roadhouse with bar billiards
♪♣🅿ⒼⓁ (Mon–Sat) 🍺

Old Warden 17F6

11–2.30; 6–11
Hare & Hounds
High Street ✆ Northhill 225
**Wells Eagle Bitter,
Bombardier** Ⓗ
Comfortable country pub in picturesque village
🍴♪♣🅿🍺ⓇⓁ🍺🍺Ⓢ

Pavenham 16E5

10.30–2.30; 5.30–11
Cock
High Street (off A6)
Morning opening: 11.30
Greene King IPA, Abbot Ⓗ
Lively village pub with a warm welcome 🍴♣🅿🍺🍺Ⓢ

Pegsdon 17F7

10.30–2.30; 6–11
Live and Let Live
(B655)
Greene King XX, IPA, Abbot Ⓔ
Well-run pub in scenic surroundings 🍴♣♪🅿🍺🍺Ⓢ🅱

Potton 17G6

10.30–2.30; 6–11
George & Dragon
Market Square (B1042)
Benskins Bitter
Ind Coope Burton Ale Ⓗ
Old town-centre pub ♪🍺🍺Ⓢ

Pulloxhill 17E7

10.30–2.30; 6–11
Cross Keys
High Street ✆ Flitwick 712442
**Wells Eagle Bitter,
Bombardier** Ⓗ
500-year-old inn with restaurant attached
🍴🅱🔥🅿🍺ⓇⓁ🍺🍺🅱🏕

Renhold 17F5

190.30–2.30; 6–11
Polhill Arms
25 Wilden Road, Salph End (off A428) OS 082527
Greene King KK, IPA Ⓗ
Splendidly sited, west of straggling village
🍴♣🅿🍺Ⓡ Ⓛ (Mon–Fri)

Ridgmont 17E7

10.30–2.30; 6–11
Rose & Crown
89 High Street (A418) ✆ 245
**Wells Eagle Bitter,
Bombardier** Ⓗ
Excellent pub catering for all tastes 🍴♪♣🅱🅿🍺ⓇⓁ🍺🍺Ⓢ🅱🏕

Sandy 17F6

10.30–2.30; 6–11
Bell
Station Road (off A1) ✆ 80267
Greene King IPA, Abbot Ⓗ
Open-plan local, handy for RSPB headquarters
🍴♪♣🅿🍺Ⓛ≥

Sharnbrook 16E5

10.30–2.30; 5.30–11
Fordham Arms
Templars Way (off A6)
✆ Bedford 781357
Evening opening: 6
Wethered Bitter Ⓗ
Large, pleasant pub with attractive garden
🍴♣🅿🍺Ⓛ🍺 (Mon–Sat) 🍺Ⓢ

Swan with Two Nicks
High Street (off A6)
☎ Bedford 781585
Wells Eagle Bitter, Bombardier ⊞
Friendly welcome at this village local
🏤🎵🍴🚗🅿�🚌🕒🌙🍷Ⓢ

Shefford · 17F6
10.30–2.30; 6–11
Bridge
50 High Street (A507)
Wells Eagle Bitter, Bombardier ⊞
Tastefully refurbished pub with cordial atmosphere
🏤🍴🎵🚗🅿🕒🌙🍷Ⓢ

Shillington 17F7
10.30–2.30; 6–11
Crown
High Road ☎ 667
Wethered Bitter, Winter Royal Whitbread Flowers Original Bitter Bulmer Cider ⊞
Welcoming pub with fine fireplace 🏤🎵🍴🚗🅿🕒🌙🍷Ⓢ⛺

Musgrave Arms
Aspley End Road
Greene King XX, IPA, Abbot Ⓖ
Superb traditional pub, little touched by progress
🏤🚗🅿🍷

Silsoe 17F7
11–2.30; 6–11
Star & Garter
☎ 60250
Wethered Bitter ⊞
Welcoming village local
🏤🎵🍴🚗🅿🚌🕒🌙🍷Ⓢ

Slip End 17F8
10.30–2.30; 6–10.30 (11 F, S)
Royal Exchange
30 Church Road
Adnams Bitter Webster Yorkshire Bitter Wells Eagle Bitter, Bombardier ⊞
One-bar pub, formerly the New Royal; disco 3 nights a week 🎵🍴🚗🅿🕒

Southill 17F6
11–2.30; 6–11
White Horse
(Off B568) OS 148418
☎ Hitchin 813364
Wethered Bitter ⊞
Country pub near Southill Park and Shuttleworth collection 🏤🍴🚗🅿🚗🚌🕒🌙🍷Ⓢ

Steppingley 17E7
10.30–2.30; 6–11
Drovers Arms
Flitwick Road
Opens at 11 am and 6.30 pm

Wells Eagle Bitter ⊞
Good local with collections of Toby jugs and darts trophies
🏤🎵🍴🚗🅿

Stevington 17E5
10.30–2.30; 5.30–11
Royal George
Silver Street (off A428)
☎ Oakley 2184
Wells Eagle Bitter, Bombardier ⊞
Converted saddlery, near 18th-century windmill
🏤🎵🚗🅿🕒🌙Ⓢ

Studham 17E8
11–2.30; 6.30–10.30 (11 F, S)
Bell Inn
Dunstable Road
☎ Whipsnade 872460
Benskins Bitter ⊞
Fine old pub near Whipsnade zoo, guest beer
🏤🎵🍴🚗🅿🚗🚌🕒🌙Ⓢ♿⛺

Tebworth 17E7
11–2.30; 6–10.30 (11 F, S)
Queens Head
The Lane
☎ Toddington 4101
Wells Eagle Bitter, Bombardier ⊞
Friendly and high spirited
🏤🎵🍴🚗🅿🚗🚌🕒🌙Ⓢ♿

Tempsford 17F6
10.30–2.30; 6–11
Anchor
(A1) ☎ Biggleswade 40233
Everard Tiger Greene King IPA Manns IPA Ruddle County Bulmer Cider ⊞
Large riverside free house, vast garden and excellent carvery
🍴🎵🍴🚗🅿🚌🕒🌙Ⓢ⛺

White Hart
61 Station Road (off A1 east)
☎ Biggleswade 40358
Wells Eagle Bitter ⊞
Friendly local near the Anchor
🏤🎵🍴🚗🅿🚗🚌🕒🌙 (must book)
🌙Ⓢ

Toddington 17E7
10.30–2.30; 6–10.30 (11 F, S)
Sow & Pigs
Church Square (A5120)
☎ 3089
Greene King XX Ⓖ (occasional), **IPA, Abbot** Ⓖ
Friendly and atmospheric, nothing quite like it
🏤🚗🅿🚗🕒🌙🍷 (must book) Ⓢ

Turvey 16E6
11–2.30; 5.30–11
Three Fyshes
(A428) ☎ 264
Adnams Bitter Draught Bass

Marston Pedigree ⊞ **Owd Rodger** Ⓖ
Wells Eagle Bitter ⊞
Blands Cider Ⓖ
Homely free house with beams and inglenooks; guest beers 🏤🎵🍴🚗🅿🚗🚌🕒🌙🍷Ⓢ

Westoning 17E7
10.30–2.30; 6–11
Chequers
Park Road (A5120) ☎ Flitwick 713125
Wethered Bitter Whitbread Flowers Original Bitter ⊞
Pleasantly renovated thatched house 🏤🎵🍴🚗🅿🚗🚌🕒🌙🍷Ⓢ

Willington 17F6
10.30–2.30; 5.30–11
Crown
17 Station Road (off A603)
Greene King IPA, Abbot ⊞
Village local close to the lock and Tudor dovecote
🎵🍴🚗🅿🍷

Woburn 16E7
10–2.30; 6–11
Black Horse
1 Bedford Street (A418) ☎ 210
Marston Burton Bitter Young Special Bitter ⊞
Popular pub with good food
🚗🅿🕒🌙Ⓢ

Woodside 17F8
11–2.30; 6–10.30 (11 F, S)
Plough
Woodside Road
Wethered Winter Royal Ⓖ
Whitbread Flowers Original Bitter ⊞
Well-run pub with fine garden for children
🏤🎵🍴🚗🚗🅿🚗🕒🍷Ⓢ

Wootton 17E6
10.30–2.30; 5.30–11
Black Horse
7 Potters Cross (off A5140)
Wells Eagle Bitter ⊞
Homely village pub off the beaten track 🏤🚗🅿🚗🅿🍷

Chequers
Hall End (off A5140)
☎ Bedford 768394
Evening opening: 6
Wells Eagle Bitter, Bombardier ⊞
Welcoming 16th-century oak-beamed pub
🏤🎵🍴🚗🅿🚗🕒🌙🍷Ⓢ

Wrestlingworth 17G6
11–2.30; 6–11
Chequers
High Street (B1042)
Greene King IPA ⊞ **Abbot** Ⓖ
Cosy village pub with large open fire and many brasses
🏤🎵🍴🚗🅿🍷Ⓢ

Aldworth 6E2

10.30–2.30; 6–10.30 (11 F, S)

Bell
(Off B4009)
Closed Mondays
Arkell BBB, Kingsdown Ale
Hall & Woodhouse
Badger Best Bitter
Morland Mild Ⓗ
Timeless rural gem
🛏🍴🖾🏃🏠🎱🛈

Binfield 7G2

10.30–2.30; 5.30–10.30 (11 F, S)

Victoria Arms
Terrace Road North (off
B3034) ✆ Bracknell 3856
Evening opening: 6
Fuller Chiswick Bitter, London
Pride, ESB Ⓗ
Renovated pub with
interesting bottle collection
🛏🍴🖾🏃🏠🄶🎱 (not Sun)🍴

Bracknell 7G2

10.30–2.30; 5.30–10.30 (11 F, S and summer)

Horse & Groom
Bagshot Road (A322)
✆ 22444
Evening opening: 6
Courage Best Bitter,
Directors Ⓗ
Former hunting lodge,
crammed with young
executives 🎵🍴🏃🏠🄶🎱🛈

Market Inn
Station Road ✆ 51734
Friary Meux Bitter
Ind Coope Burton Ale Ⓗ
Former station hotel with
contrasting bars
🎵🍴🖾🏃🏠🄻🎱🛈🚻

Royal Oak
London Road (A329)
Courage Best Bitter,
Directors Ⓗ
Small old pub, lively
atmosphere🎵🍴🏃🏠🛈

Silver Birch
Birch Hill Road (off
A322/3095) ✆ 57318
Evening opening: 6
Morland Mild, Bitter, Best
Bitter Ⓗ
Popular modern pub with
three contrasting bars
🎵🍴🏃🄶🛈🖾

Burchetts Green 7F2

10.30–2.30; 6–10.30 (11 F, S)

Red Lion
Applehouse Hill, Henley Road
(A423)
Brakspear Pale Ale, Special
Bitter, Old Ⓗ
Popular country pub used by
locals and travellers 🛏🏃🏠

Caversham 7F2

10.30–2.30; 6–10.30 (11 F, S)

Prince of Wales
76 Prospect Street (A4155)
✆ Reading 472267
Brakspear Mild, Bitter, Special
Bitter Ⓗ
Popular, welcoming pub
🎵🍴🍴🏃🏠🎱🛈

Chaddleworth 6D2

10.30–2.30; 6.30–10.30 (11 F, S)

Ibex
OS 416774 ✆ 311
Courage Best Bitter Ⓗ
Country pub of character,
imaginative food
🛏🍴🖾🏃🏠🄻🄶🛈🍴

Charvil 7F2

10.30–2.30; 6–10.30 (11 F, S)

Lands End
Park Lane OS 781748
✆ Reading 340700
Brakspear Pale Ale, Special
Bitter, Old Ⓗ
Remote but popular pub,
worth finding
🎵🍴🍴🖾🏃🄶🛈🍴

Cippenham 7G2

10.30–2.30; 5.30–10.30 (11 F, S)

Long Barn
Cippenham Lane (off M4 exit
6/A4) ✆ Slough 21390
Morning opening: 11.30;
Saturday evening opening: 7
Brakspear Pale Ale, Old
Long Barn Stallion,
Barnstormer
Morland Bitter Ⓗ
Pricey but popular home-brew
pub 🖾🏃🄶🍴🛈

Cockpole Green 7F2

10.30–2.30; 6–10.30 (11 F, S and summer)

Old Hatch Gate
(Off A321/A423) OS 798803
Brakspear Mild, Special Bitter,
Old Ⓗ
Unspoilt and basic; opens late
🛏🍴🍴🏃🛈

Cold Ash 6E2

10–2.30; 6–10.30 (11 F, S)

Castle
✆ Thatcham 63232
Morning opening: 11
Courage Best Bitter,
Directors Ⓗ
Busy village local, good public
bar🎵🍴🖾🏃🄶🛈

Donnington 6D2

10–2.30; 6–10.30 (11 F, S)

Fox & Hounds
Oxford Road (Old A34)
✆ Newbury 40540
Morning opening: 10.30
Courage Best Bitter,
Directors Ⓗ
Lively pub near local
scramblers' circuit
🛏🍴🍴🖾🏃🄻🄶🍴🛈

East Ilsley 6D2

10–2.30; 6–10.30 (11 F, S)

Crown & Horns
(Off A34) ✆ 205
Morning opening: 11
Bourne Valley Best Ilsley Bitter
Brakspear Pale Ale
Fuller ESB
Morland Bitter
North Country Riding Bitter
Usher Best Bitter
Wadworth 6X
Wethered Bitter Ⓗ
Roomy village pub
🛏🍴🖾🏃🏠🄶🛈

Fifield 7G2

10.30–2.30; 6–10.30 (11 F, S)

Rising Sun
Forest Green (B3024)
OS 909764
Morland Mild, Bitter, Best
Bitter Ⓗ
Comfortable, friendly country
pub 🍴🏃🏠🛈

White Hart
Fifield Road
Morland Mild, Bitter, Best
Bitter Ⓗ
🎵🍴🏃🏠🛈🏕

Finchampstead 7F3

10.30–2.30; 5.30–10.30 (11 F, S and summer)

Queens Oak
Church Lane (off B3016)
OS 793640
Morning opening: 11
Brakspear Pale Ale, Special
Bitter, Old Ⓗ
Popular pub with garden
barbecue Sunday lunchtimes
🎵🍴🍴🖾🏃🄶

Frilsham 6E2

11–2.30; 6–10.30 (11 F, S)

Pot Kiln
OS 553731
✆ Hermitage 201366
Arkell BBB Ⓗ
Courage Directors Ⓖ
Morland Bitter, Best Bitter Ⓗ
Remote old pub in wooded
countryside
🛏🍴🖾🏃🏠🄶🍴🛈

Great Shefford 6D2

10–2.30; 6–10.30 (11 F, S)

Swan
(A338) ✆ 271
Morning opening: 10.30
Courage Best Bitter,
Directors Ⓗ
Lively village pub with
riverside garden
🎵🍴🖾🏃🄶🍴 (not Mon)🍴🛈

Hermitage 6D2

10–2.30; 6–10.30 (11 F, S)

Fox
(B4009)
✆ 201545
Morning opening: 11
Draught Bass
Morland Bitter, Best Bitter
Wadworth Old Timer Ⓗ
Attractive pub with fine patio
🛏🎵🍴🏃🏠🍴🛈

Berkshire

Hungerford 6C3

10–2.30; 6–10.30 (11 S)

Beer
Charnham Street (A4)
☎ 82512
Morning opening: 10.30
Arkell BBB, Kingsdown Ale
Morland Bitter [H]
Comfortable 13th-century hotel with convivial bar
🏠♪⊞🍴🚗■[R]◔◗Ⓢ

Try also: Railway Tavern (Usher); **Tally Ho** (Wadworth)

Hurley 7F2

10–2.30; 6–10.30 (11 F, S)

Black Boy
Henley Road (A423)
☎ Littlewick Green 4212
Brakspear Pale Ale, Old [H]
16th-century beamed tavern, emphasis on food 🏠🍴🚗◔◗Ⓢ

Hurst 7F2

10.30–2.30; 5.30–10.30 (11 F, S and summer)

Green Man
Hinton Road (off A321)
OS 801741
Opens at 11 am & 6 pm
Brakspear Pale Ale, Special Bitter, Old [G]
Pleasant oak-beamed village pub 🏠♪♣🍴🚗

Inkpen 6C3

10–2.30; 6–10.30 (11 F, S)

Swan
Lower Green OS 359643
☎ 326
Opens at 11 am & 6.30 pm
Hall & Woodhouse Badger Best Bitter
Wethered Bitter (summer), **SPA** [G]
Welcoming country pub near Combe Gibbet 🏠♪🍴🚗◔◗Ⓢ

Jealotts Hill 7G2

10.30–2.30; 5.30–10.30 (11 F, S and summer)

New Leathern Bottle
(A3095) OS 869733
☎ Bracknell 21282
Courage Best Bitter [H]
Small pub with friendly atmosphere 🏠♣🍴🚗◔🍷

Kintbury 6D3

10–2.30; 6–10.30 (11 F, S)

Crossways
Inkpen Road OS 385653
☎ 58398
Marston Burton Bitter, Pedigree, Merrie Monk
Wadworth 6X
Bulmer Cider [E]
Smart country hostelry, formerly a school ♪🍴🚗[R]◔◗Ⓢ

Knowl Hill 7F2

10–2.30; 6–10.30 (11 F, S)

Seven Stars
Bath Road (A4)
☎ Littlewick Green 2967
Brakspear Pale Ale, Special Bitter, Old [H]
Superb traditional roadside pub 🏠♣⊞🍴🚗[R]🍷

Long Lane 6D2

10–2.30; 6–10.30 (11 F, S)

Lamb
(B4009)
Wethered Bitter, SPA, Winter Royal [H]
Attractive long, narrow one-bar pub
🏠♪♣🍴🚗◔◗Ⓢ

Maidenhead 7G2

10–2.30; 6–10.30 (11 F, S)

Cricketers
Park Street
Morland Mild, Bitter, Best Bitter [H]
Modernised pub behind the town hall ♣🍷Ⓢ⇌

North Star
North Town Road
Wethered Bitter, SPA [H]
Honest, friendly local ♣🍴

North Star
Westborough Road (off A4)
Courage Best Bitter [H]
Memories of old Nicholson's brewery in saloon bar
♪♣🍷Ⓢ

Pond House
Bath Road (A4) ☎ 27178
Wethered Bitter, SPA [H]
Modern local 1 mile west of town centre ♣🍴🚗◔🍷Ⓢ

Marsh Benham 6D3

10.30–2.30; 6–10.30 (11 F, S and summer)

Red House
(Off A4) ☎ Newbury 41637
Brakespear Mild [G] **Pale Ale, Special Bitter** [H] **Old** [G]
Hall & Woodhouse Badger Best Bitter, Tanglefoot [H]
Lively pub in old estate hamlet; superb home cooking
ſ♣🍴🚗[R]◔◗Ⓢ

Midgham 6E3

10.30–2.30; 6–10.30 (11 F, S)

Coach & Horses
☎ Woolhampton 3384
Bath Road (A4)
Wethered Bitter, SPA, Winter Royal [H]
Comfortable roadside inn, excellent food
🏠♪♣🍴🚗◔◗🍷Ⓢ

Moneyrow Green 7G2

10.30–2.30; 5.30–10.30 (11 F, S)

White Hart
Near Holyport
Morland Mild, Bitter, Best Bitter [H]
Comfortable, wood-panelled pub 🏠♪♣🍴🚗◔🍷Ⓢ

Newbury 6D3

10–2.30; 6–10.30 (11 F, S)

Bacon Arms
Oxford Street (off A34)
☎ 40408
Courage Best Bitter, Directors [H]
Hotel with comfortable bar
🏠♪🚗■◔◗Ⓢ

Railway
Greenham Road (A34)
☎ 47413
Morning opening: 11
Morland Mild, Bitter, Best Bitter [H]
Friendly, renovated pub, interesting handpumps
ſ♪♣🍴🚗■[R]◔◗🍷Ⓢ⇌

Try also: Blue Ball (Halls); **Catherine Wheel** (Courage); **Globe** (Usher); **Woodpecker, Wash Water** (free)

North Street 7E2

10–2.30; 6–10.30 (11 F, S)

Thatchers Arms
(Off M4 Exit 12) OS 637724
☎ Reading 302070
Wethered Bitter, SPA, Winter Royal [H]
Rural pub in quiet backwater
🏠♪♣🍴🚗◔◗🍷Ⓢ

Old Windsor 7G2

10.30–2.30; 6–10.30 (11 F, S)

Oxford Blue
Crimp Hill
Friary Meux Bitter
Ind Coope Burton Ale [H]
Splendid rural pub, ideal for summer family outings
♪🍴🚗◔

Paley Street 7G2

10.30–2.30; 6–10.30 (11 F, S)

Royal Oak
(B3024)
Fuller Chiswick Bitter, London Pride, ESB [H]
Once owned by Fullers of Maidenhead, now by Fullers of London ♣🍴🚗◔Ⓢ

Pangbourne 7E2

10.30–2.30; 6–10.30 (11 F, S)

Cross Keys
Church Road (A340) ☎ 3268
Courage Best Bitter, Directors [H]
16th-century two-bar pub in riverside village
🏠♪♣⊞🍴■[R]◔◗🍷Ⓢ⇌

Reading 7F2

10.30–2.30; 5.30–10.30 (11 F, S)

Cambridge Arms
109 Southampton Street (A33) ☎ 81446
Morland Mild, Bitter, Best Bitter [H]
Friendly town pub
♪♣◔🍷Ⓢ

Eldon Arms
19 Eldon Terrace (off A4)
☎ 53857
Wadworth IPA, 6X, Old Timer Ⓗ
Straightforward backstreet pub with lively atmosphere
♪♣Ⓖ✦⑧

Greyhound
4 Mount Pleasant (A33)
☎ 863023
Courage Best Bitter, Directors Ⓗ
Popular, lively pub
♪♣✦🅿️🅰️Ⓖ🍴⑧

Horn
St Mary's Butts
Courage Best Bitter, Directors Ⓗ
Comfortable old town-centre pub near old brewery ♪Ⓖ⑧

Red Lion
34 Southampton Street (A33) ☎ 53243
Wethered Bitter, SPA, Winter Royal Ⓗ
Town local, emphasis on pool ♪♣Ⓡ Ⓖ✦⑧

Retreat
8 St. John's Street (off A4)
Wethered Bitter, SPA, Winter Royal Ⓗ
Convivial backstreet drinkers' pub ♪♣🍴⑧

Wallingford Arms
Caroline Street
Morland Mild, Bitter Ⓗ
Down-to-earth town local
♪♣🅰️🍴⑧

Try also: **Sweeney Todd, Castle Street** (free)

Remenham 7F2

10–2.30; 6–10.30 (11 F, S)
Two Brewers
Wargrave Road (A321)
☎ Henley 4375
Brakspear Pale Ale, Old Ⓗ
Many-roomed, comfortable inn, good atmosphere
🅰️♪✦🅿️🅰️Ⓡ Ⓖ✦⑧

Ruscombe 7F2

10–2.30; 6–10.30 (11 F, S)
Royal Oak
Cross Road (B3024)
☎ 345190
Morning opening: 11; winter evening opening: 5.30
Wethered Bitter, SPA, Winter Royal Ⓗ
Bulmer Cider Ⓖ
Large, comfortable public bar, cosy lounge/restaurant
🅰️♪✦🅿️🅰️Ⓖ✦🍴⑧

Sandhurst 7G3

10.30–2.30; 6–10.30 (11 F, S and summer)
Wellington Arms
York Town Road (A321)
☎ Yateley 872408

Brakspear Pale Ale, Special Bitter Ⓗ **Old** Ⓖ
Friendly, family pub with weekend singalongs
♪♣✦🅿️🅰️🍴⑧

Shefford Woodlands 6D2

10–2.30; 6–10.30 (11 F, S)
Pheasant
(B4000, off A338/M4)
☎ Great Shefford 284
Morning opening: 10.30
Wadworth 6X Ⓗ
Wethered Bitter, SPA Ⓗ & Ⓖ
Bulmer Cider Ⓖ
Remote country inn with 'ring the bull'
🅰️♪✦🅿️🅰️Ⓡ Ⓖ✦🍴⑧Ⓢ

Shurlock Row 7F2

10.30–2.30; 5.30–10.30 (11 F, S and summer)
Royal Oak
Hungerford Lane (off B3934)
☎ Twyford 345133
Morland Mild, Bitter, Best Bitter Ⓗ
Tastefully modernised pub
🅰️♣✦🅰️✦ (not Tue)🍴⑧

Slough 7G2

10.30–2.30; 5.30–10.30 (11 F, S)
Montagu Arms
Bath Road (A4)
Courage Best Bitter, Directors Ⓗ
Large, comfortable pub with good garden ♣✦🅰️Ⓖ🍴⑧

Wheatsheaf
Albert Street
Fuller Chiswick Bitter, London Pride, ESB Ⓗ
Recently renovated pub with own phone box ♪✦Ⓖ🍴

Speen 6D3

10–2.30; 6–10.30 (11 F, S)
Starting Gate
Bath Road (A4)
☎ Newbury 43859
Wethered Bitter Ⓗ
Modern, busy, young people's pub♪♣✦🅰️Ⓖ (Mon–Fri)🍴

Try also: **Hare & Hounds** (free)

Stanford Dingley 6E2

10.30–2.30; 6–10.30 (11 F, S)
Old Boot Inn
☎ Bradfield 744292
Arkell BBB
Everard Tiger
Fuller London Pride
Ruddle County Ⓗ
Smart, friendly country inn noted for food
🅰️♪✦🅿️🅰️Ⓡ Ⓖ✦🍴⑧

Streatley 6E2

10–2.30; 6–10.30 (11 F, S)
Bull
(A329) ☎ Goring 872507

Morning opening: 11
Usher Best Bitter, Founders Ale Ⓗ
15th-century coaching inn with restaurant ✦🅰️Ⓖ🍴⑧

Sunninghill 7G3

10.30–2.30; 5.30–10.30 (11 F, S and summer)
Cannon
London Road (A329) ☎ Ascot 20456
Morning opening: 11
Courage Best Bitter, Directors Ⓖ
Comfortably furnished two-bar pub ♪♣🅱️✦🅰️Ⓖ🍴⑧

Carpenters Arms
78 Upper Village Road ☎ Ascot 22763
Evening opening: 6
Wethered Bitter, SPA Ⓗ
Good village local with three contrasting bars
♪♣✦Ⓖ✦ (not Sun)⑧

Thatcham 6D3

10–2.30; 6–10.30 (11 F, S)
Kings Head
Broadway (off A34)
☎ 62145
Saturday evening opening: 7
Courage Best Bitter Ⓗ
Old coaching inn 🅰️♣🅰️Ⓡ🍴⑧

Try also: **Cricketers** (Usher)

Theale 7E2

10–2.30; 6–10.30 (11 F, S)
Lamb
Church Street
(off A4/M4 exit 12)
☎ Reading 302216
Courage Best Bitter, Directors Ⓖ
Friendly village pub with potty collection 🅰️♣✦🅿️🅰️Ⓡ Ⓖ✦⑧

Tilehurst 7E2

10.30–2.30; 5.30–10.30 (11 F, S)
Bear
160 Park Lane (off A4)
☎ Reading 27328
Courage Best Bitter, Directors Ⓗ
Large, friendly pub near watertower ♪♣✦🅰️🍴⑧

REAL ALE
UNREAL PRICES

Royal Oak
69 Westwood Glen
OS 661739
Halls Harvest Bitter
Ind Coope Burton Ale Ⓗ
Steep driveway, well worth
the climb
♪♣🏠Ⓖ▮

Upper Bucklebury
6E2

10.30–2.30; 6–10.30 (11 F, S)
Three Crowns
☎ Thatcham 62153
Courage Best Bitter,
Directors Ⓗ
Substantial pub with
all-round facilities for children
🏠♪♣🎪🅿🏠Ⓖ▮Ⓢ

Waltham St. Lawrence
7F2

10.30–2.30; 5.30–10.30 (11 F, S and summer)
Bell
(Off B3024)
☎ Twyford 343216
Opens at 11 am & 6 pm
Arkell BBB, Kingsdown Ale
Brakspear Mild, Pale Ale Ⓗ
Old Ⓖ
Ancient, oak-beamed pub by
the village church
🏠♣🎪🏠Ⓡ▮Ⓢ

Warfield
7G2

10.30–2.30; 5.30–10.30 (11 F, S and summer)
Shepherds House
Moss End (A3095)
OS 868728
☎ Bracknell 23341
Brakspear Special Bitter
Gale BBB, HSB
Usher Best Bitter
Wadworth 6X Ⓗ
Pub converted to restaurant,
but retaining friendly bar
♪♣🅿🏠Ⓡ🕒▮Ⓢ

Three Legged Cross
Maidenhead Road (A3095)
☎ Bracknell 21673
Courage Best Bitter,
Directors Ⓖ
Pleasantly modernised
country pub
♪🅿🏠🕒 (not Sun) Ⓢ

Wargrave
7F2

10–2.30; 6–10.30 (11 F, S and summer)
Greyhound
High Street (A321)
☎ 2556
Courage Best Bitter,
Directors Ⓗ
A friendly welcome for all
🏠♣🎪🅿🏠Ⓡ🕒▮Ⓢ≷

White Hart
High Street (A321)
☎ 2590
Wethered Bitter, SPA, Winter
Royal Ⓗ
Warm and comfortable, busy
with food
🏠♪♣🏠🕒▮Ⓢ≷

Warren Row
7F2

10.30–2.30; 6–10.30 (11 F, S)
Old House at Home
(Off A4) OS 812808
☎ Littlewick Green 2995
Brakspear Pale Ale Ⓗ **Old** Ⓖ
Classic village local, one of a
dying breed 🏠▮♪♣🏠Ⓡ▮

West Ilsley
6D2

10–2.30; 6–10.30 (11 F, S)
Harrow
☎ East Ilsley 260
Morning opening: 10.30
Morland Mild, Bitter Ⓗ
Best Bitter
Bulmer Cider Ⓖ
Downland pub by cricket
ground; try the rabbit pie
🏠♪♣🅿🏠Ⓖ🕒▮Ⓢ

White Waltham
7G2

10–2.30; 6–10.30 (11 F, S)
Beehive
High Street (off B3024)
☎ Littlewick Green 2877
Wethered Bitter, SPA Ⓗ
Two-bar village local
♪♣🏠♪ (Fri–Sun)▮

Windsor
7G2

10.30–2.30; 5.30–10.30 (11 F, S)
Mitre
Vansittart Road
Wethered Bitter, SPA, Winter
Royal Ⓗ
Lively local on fringe of tourist
area ▮♪♣▮

Prince Christian
King's Road
Brakspear Pale Ale
Fuller London Pride
Young Bitter, Special Bitter Ⓗ
Lively town-centre free house
♪🕒

Stag & Hounds
St. Leonard's Road
Courage Best Bitter,
Directors Ⓗ
16th-century pub of character
♣🅿🏠🕒

William IV
Thames Street
Courage Best Bitter,
Directors Ⓗ
Lively, oak-beamed inn near
the river ▮Ⓡ🕒≷

Winkfield
7G2

10.30–2.30; 5.30–10.30 (11 F, S and summer)
Hernes Oak
North Street (B3022)
Wethered Bitter, SPA, Winter
Royal Ⓗ
Old-style village local, popular
with young and old 🏠♣🅿🏠▮

Slug & Lettuce
Lovel Road (off A330)
☎ 883498
Friary Meux Bitter
Gale HSB
Ind Coope Burton Ale

King and Barnes Festive Ⓗ
Popular, modernised pub with
guest beers 🏠♪🅿🏠
🕒 (not Sun)🍴 (not Sun, Mon)

Winterbourne
6D2

10.30–2.30; 6–10.30 (11 F, S)
New Inn
(Off B4494)
☎ Chieveley 200
Wethered Bitter, SPA Ⓗ
Welcoming country pub,
noted for its gardens
🏠♪♣🅿🏠Ⓡ🕒🍴 (not Tue)Ⓢ♿

Wokingham
7F3

10.30–2.30; 5.30–10.30 (11 F, S and summer)
Crooked Billet
Honey Hill OS 826668
☎ 780438
Brakspear Mild, Pale Ale,
Special Bitter, Old Ⓗ
Popular country pub with
good food ♣🅿🏠🕒Ⓢ

Queens Head
The Terrace (A329) ☎ 781221
Morland Mild, Bitter, Best
Bitter Ⓗ
Lively one-bar local ♣🅿🕒Ⓢ≷

Ship
Peach Street ☎ 780389
Fuller Chiswick Bitter, London
Pride, ESB Ⓗ
Renovated old town pub
🏠♪🅿🏠🕒Ⓢ

Woodspeen
6D2

10.30–2.30; 6–10.30 (11 F, S)
Five Bells
☎ Newbury 43478
OS 451687
Courage Best Bitter,
Directors Ⓗ
Small, friendly pub in valley
hamlet 🏠♣🎪🏠🕒▮Ⓢ

World's End
6D2

10–2.30; 5.30–10.30 (11 F, S)
Langley Hall
(Old A34) OS 484763
☎ Chieveley 332
Evening opening: 6.30
Wethered Bitter, SPA, Winter
Royal Ⓗ
West Country Cider
(summer)Ⓖ
Old estate inn with ghost
🏠▮♪♣🏠Ⓖ🕒▮Ⓢ♿

WARMEST WELCOME

♦ A REAL FIRE PUB ♦

The 🏠 symbol denotes a pub
with a real solid fuel fire

Adstock 16C7

11–2.30; 6–11

Old Thatched Inn

Main Street (off A413)
Adnams Bitter
Everard Old Original
Greene King Abbot [H]
Morrell Bitter [G]
Delightful 17th-century inn, tastefully restored
🏠♪♣✿🚗[R]🎯[S]

Akeley 16C6

11–2.30; 6–10.30 (11 F, S)

Bull & Butcher

The Square (A413)
Morning opening: 12 noon
Marston Pedigree
Litchborough
Northamptonshire Bitter
Weston Cider [H]
Cosy, extended village pub; guest beers 🏠♪♣✿🚗☾◗

Amersham 16E9

10–2.30; 6–10.30 (11 F, S)

Kings Arms

High Street (A413) ☎ 6333
Benskins Bitter [H]
Ind Coope Bitter [G]
Burton Ale [H]
Fine coaching inn
🏠✿🚗[R]☾◗[S]

Queens Head

Whielden Gate (A404) ☎ 5240
Benskins Bitter
Ind Coope Burton Ale [H]
Unspoilt pub outside town
♪♣✿🚗☾🎯[S]

Aston Abbotts 16D8

10–2.30; 6–10.30 (11 F, S)

Royal Oak

Wingrave Road ☎ 262
Aylesbury ABC Bitter
Everard Tiger [H]
16th-century inn with fine brasses ♪♣⊞✿🚗▣[R]◗[S]

Aylesbury 16D8

10–2.30; 6–10.30 (11 F, S)

Bricklayers Arms

Walton Terrace ☎ 82930
Aylesbury ABC Bitter
Ind Coope Burton Ale [H]
Popular, friendly old town pub
♣✿[R]🎯🚆

White Swan

Walton Street ☎ 23933
Aylesbury ABC Bitter
Draught Bass
Morrell Mild [H]
Lively pub, popular with the younger set ♪♣[R][S]🚆

Try also: Plough & Harrow, Walton (Courage)

Beachampton 16D6

11–2.30; 6–10.30 (11 F, S)

Bell

Main Street (B4033)
☎ Milton Keynes 563861
Greene King IPA, Abbot
Manns Bitter [H]
Popular, charming village inn
♪♣✿🚗[R]☾◗🎯[S]

Bellingdon 16D9

10–2.30; 6–10.30 (11 F, S)

Bull

Bellingdon Road
Benskins Bitter
Ind Coope Burton Ale [H]
Picturesque country inn, enterprising landlord 🏠✿🚗

Bletchley 16D7

10.30–2.30; 6–11

George

16 Buckingham Road
Benskins Bitter [H]
Lively town pub ⌐♪♣🚗🎯[S]🚆

Bolter End 7F1

10–2.30; 6–10.30 (11 F, S)

Peacock

(B482) OS 797923
☎ High Wycombe 881417
Morning opening: 11
Aylesbury ABC Bitter
Draught Bass
Everard Tiger [H]
Popular country pub with good food at reasonable prices
🏠♪♣✿🚗[R]☾◗[S]

Bourne End 7G1

10.30–2.30; 6–10.30 (11 F, S)

Heart in Hand

Cores End Road (A4094)
☎ 23887
Morning opening: 11
Wethered Bitter, SPA, Winter Royal [H]
Attractive pub with excellent food
🏠♪♣✿🚗☾◗ (not Sun)[S]🚆

Buckingham 16C7

10.30–2.30; 6–11

Swan & Castle

Castle Street ☎ 3082
Marston Burton Bitter, Pedigree
Bulmer Cider [H]
Rambling, well-appointed old hotel ♪♣🚗▣[R]☾◗

Burnham 7G1

10.30–2.30; 5.30–10.30 (11 F, S)

Crispin

High Street ☎ 2827
Charrington IPA
Draught Bass [H]
Pleasant local at top of street
♪♣✿🚗☾ (Mon–Fri)[S]

Pheasant

Lent Rise Road ☎ 5843
Courage Best Bitter, Directors [H]
Small, comfortable village pub
♪♣✿🚗☾🎯[S]

Cadmore End 7F1

10.30–2.30; 6–10.30 (11 F, S)

Old Ship

(B482) OS 785927
Brakspear Pale Ale, Special Bitter, Old [G]
Tiny, unspoilt traditional country pub 🏠♣✿[S]

Chalfont St Giles 7H1

10.30–2.30; 5.30–10.30 (11 F, S)

Feathers

Dean Way (High Street) (Off A413)
Wethered Bitter, SPA, Winter Royal [H]
Dates from the Tudor period

Chenies 17E9

10.30–2.30; 6–10.30 (11 F, S)

Red Lion

(B485, off A404) OS 022981
Morning opening: 11
Ind Coope Bitter, Burton Ale [H]
Excellent three-bar local ♣🚗☾

Chesham 16E9

10–2.30; 6–10.30 (11 F, S)

Queens Head

Church Street (B485) ☎ 73769
Brakspear Pale Ale, Specal Bitter [H] **Old** [G]
Pleasant two-bar pub in old town 🏠♣✿☾🎯🚆

Colnbrook 7H2

10.30–2.30; 5.30–10.30 (11 F, S)

Red Lion

High Street (B3378) ☎ 2685
Courage Best Bitter, Directors [H]
Spendid pub, full of antiques
♪✿🚗☾[S]

Dagnall 17E8

10.30–2.30; 6–10.30 (11 F, S)

Golden Rule

Main Road South (A4146)
Greene King Abbot
Marston Pedigree
Ruddle County
Young Bitter, Special Bitter [H]
Excellent free house, handy for Whipsnade Zoo ⊞✿🚗☾[S]

Denham 7H1

10–2.30; 5.30–10.30 (11 F, S)

Falcon

Village Road (off A40)
☎ 832125
Wethered Bitter, SPA, Winter Royal [H]
Unspoilt local in tourist village
☾[S]

Farnham Royal 7G1

10.30–2.30; 5.30–10.30 (11 F, S)

Emperor of India

Blackpool Lane (off A355)
☎ Farnham Common 3006
Wethered Bitter, SPA [H]
Busy country pub, enveloped by suburbia ♪♣✿🚗☾🎯[S]

Fawley 16D9

10.30–2.30; 5.30–10.30 (11 F, S)

Walnut Tree

(Off A4155) OS 75782
☎ Turville Heath 360/617

Opens at 11 am & 6 pm
Brakspear Pale Ale, Special Bitter Ⓗ Ⓓ Ⓖ
Popular, remote pub noted for exotic bar food
♠♪♣🎁♫🅿️🅰️Ⓡ🕓🍴🅂♿

Fenny Stratford 16D7

10.30–2.30; 5.30–11
Chequers
48 Watling Street (A5)
Aylesbury ABC Bitter Ⓗ
Honest small-town boozer
♪♣♫≉

Forty Green 7G1

10.30–2.30; 6–10.30 (11 F, S)
Royal Standard of England
(Off B474) OS 923919
✆ Beaconsfield 3382
**Marston Pedigree,
Owd Rodger
Samuel Smith Old Brewery Bitter** Ⓗ
Ancient and popular – superb cold table ♠♫🅰️Ⓡ🕓🍴🅂♿

Frieth 7F1

10.30–2.30; 5.30–10.30 (11 F, S)
Prince Albert
Moor Common OS 799907
Morning opening: 10.30
Brakspear Mild, Pale Ale, Special Bitter, Old Ⓖ
Popular, friendly pub in attractive countryside
♠♣♫🅰️Ⓖ (Mon–Fri)🅂

Gerrards Cross 7H1

10.30–2.30; 5.30–10.30 (11 F, S)
Three Pigeons
Austenwood (off A413)
✆ 87291
Courage Best Bitter, Directors Ⓗ
Two bars, providing comfort or games ♪♣♫🅰️Ⓖ🅂

Great Missenden 16D9

10.30–2.30; 6–10.30 (11 F, S)
Barley Mow
Chesham Road, Hyde End (B485) OS 913012
**Arkell BBB
Hook Norton Best Bitter
Morrell Bitter** Ⓗ
Like wine, it improves year by year ♠♣🅰️

Cross Keys
High Street
**Aylesbury ABC Bitter
Draught Bass
Everard Tiger
Bulmer Cider** Ⓗ
Fascinating pub full of memorabilia ♠♪♣🅰️Ⓖ≉

Red Lion Hotel
High Street (off A413) ✆ 2208
**Everard Beacon
Fuller ESB**

**Morland Bitter, Best Bitter
Truman Sampson Hanbury's Extra Strong** Ⓗ
Recommended for food and ale ♠🅰️Ⓓ🅲Ⓖ🕓🅂≉

Great Woolstone 16D6

11–2; 5.30–11
Cross Keys
Newport Road
✆ Milton Keynes 679404
Evening opening: 6
**Wells Eagle Bitter,
Bombardier** Ⓗ
Smart, pleasantly restored thatched village pub
♪♣🅰️Ⓖ🕓🅂♿

Grendon Underwood 16C8

10–2.30; 6–10.30 (11 F, S)
Swan
Main Street (off A41) ✆ 242
Usher PA Ⓗ **Best Bitter,
Founders Ale** Ⓖ
250-year-old thatched village local, good home cooking
♠♪♣♫🅰️Ⓖ🕓🅂

Haddenham 16C8

10–2.30; 6–10.30 (11 F, S)
Kings Head
High Street (off A418)
Aylesbury ABC Bitter Ⓖ
Excellent friendly pub with locally carved inn signs
♣♫🅰️🅂

Hambleden 16D9

10–2.30; 6–10.30 (11 F, S)
Stag & Huntsman
✆ 227
Opens at 11 am & 6 pm
**Brakspear Bitter, Special Bitter
Chiltern Beechwood Bitter
Fuller London Pride
Ruddle County
Stag & Huntsman Bitter
Wadworth 6X
Bulmer Cider** Ⓗ
Old village local with restaurant and 'house' beer
♠♪♣♫🅲Ⓡ🕓🍴🅂 (not Sun)🍴🅂

Hartwell 16D6

10–2.30; 6–10.30 (11 F, S)
Bugle Horn
(A418) ✆ Aylesbury 748209
**Benskins Bitter
Ind Coope Burton Ale** Ⓗ
Attractive 17th-century former farmhouse
♠♪🎁🅰️Ⓖ🕓🅂

Hawridge 16E8

10–2.30; 6–10.30 (11 F, S)
Full Moon
Hawridge Common
Morning opening: 11
Wethered Bitter, SPA, Winter Royal Ⓗ
Excellent village pub overlooking common ♠♫🅰️🅂

High Wycombe 16D9

10–2.30; 5.30–10.30 (11 F, S)
Beaconsfield Arms
110 Hughenden Road (A4128) ✆ 22820
Benskins Bitter Ⓗ
Outstanding location and hospitality, Disraeli connections ♠♪♣♫🅰️Ⓖ🕓🅂

Bell
Frogmoor (A4128) ✆ 21317
Saturday evening opening: 6
Fuller Chiswick Bitter, London Pride, ESB Ⓗ
Excellent town local with many bars
♠🎁♣♫🅲Ⓡ🅶🕓 (not Sun) 🍴🅂

Roundabout
Bridge Street (off A40)
✆ 29226
**Fuller London Pride, ESB
Morland Best Bitter
Morrell Bitter
Samuel Smith Old Brewery Bitter** Ⓗ
Town tavern with unusual decor ♪♣Ⓡ🅶 (Mon–Fri)🍴🅂

Wendover Arms
Desborough Avenue ✆ 26476
Morning opening: 10.30;
Saturday evening opening: 7
Brakspear Mild, Pale Ale, Special Bitter, Old Ⓗ
Large, friendly 1930s house
♠♪♣🎁♫🅰️Ⓡ🅶🕓🍴🅂♿

Holmer Green 16D9

10–2.30; 6–10.30 (11 F, S)
Earl Howe
Earl Howe Road (off A404)
✆ High Wycombe 713261
Courage Best Bitter, Directors Ⓗ
Gleaming, comfortable and friendly ♪♫🅰️Ⓖ🅂

Hughenden Valley 16D9

10.30–2.30; 5.30–10.30 (11 F, S)
Harrow
Warrendene Road
✆ Naphill 2382
Evening opening: 6
Courage Best Bitter, Directors Ⓖ
Comfortable country pub with oak-beamed public bar
♠♪♣♫🅰️Ⓖ🕓🅂

Iver 7H2

10.30–2.30; 5.30–10.30 (11 F, S)
Gurkha
Langley Park Road (B470)
✆ 654257
Courage Best Bitter, Directors Ⓗ
Large, comfortable and popular pub ♣♫🅰️Ⓖ🕓🅂♿

Iver Heath 7H2

10.30–2.30; 5.30–10.30 (11 F, S)
Black Horse
Slough Road

Benskins Bitter
Ind Coope Burton Ale [H]
Pleasant pub with popular pets' corner ♪♣▣℘🚗◔☾Ⓢ

Oddfellows Arms
☎ Iver 653684
Courage Best Bitter, Directors
Young Bitter, Special Bitter [H]
Congenial free house
♪♣℘🚗◔🍺

Lane End 7F1

10–2.30; 5.30–10.30 (11 F, S)

Clayton Arms
High Street (B482)
☎ High Wycombe 881269
Ruddle County
Watney Fined Stag Bitter
Webster Yorkshire Bitter [H]
Large 17th century pub, originally a manor house
🔥♪℘🚗[R]◔☾ (not Sun)Ⓢ

Little Hampden 16D9

10–2.30; 6–10.30 (11 F, S)

Rising Sun
Off Great Missenden-Princes Risborough Road OS 857040
☎ Hampden Row 393
Lunchtime opening: 12 noon
Adnams Bitter
Brakspear Special Bitter
Greene King Abbot
Samuel Smith Old Brewery Bitter [H]
Delightful country pub/restaurant in idyllic setting ♪♣℘🚗◔☾Ⓢ

Little Horwood 16D7

10.30–2.30; 6–11

Shoulder of Mutton
Church Street
☎ Winslow 2514
Aylesbury ABC Bitter
Morrell Light Mild [H]
Lively and improved 14th century village pub
🏠♪♣℘🚗◔☾ (Wed–Sun)Ⓢ

Little Missenden 16E9

10.30–2.30; 6–10.30 (11 F, S)

Crown
(Off A413)
☎ Great Missenden 2571
Ind Coope Bitter
Morrell Varsity
West Country Cider [H]
Deservedly popular village inn
🏠♣℘🚗◔

Littleworth Common 7G1

10.30–2.30; 5.30–10.30 (11 F, S)

Beech Tree
Dorney Wood Road
Wethered Bitter, SPA [H]
Small pub in the middle of the common ♣℘🚗◔

Blackwood Arms
Common Lane OS 934862
☎ Farnham Common 2169
Brakspear Pale Ale
Eldridge Pope Royal Oak
Fuller London Pride [H]
Friendly pub with good food, regular guest beers 🔥♪℘🚗◔☾

Long Crendon 16C8

10–2.30; 6–10.30 (11 F, S)

Chandos Arms
Bicester Road (B4011)
☎ 208659
Wethered Bitter, SPA [H]
Immaculate and friendly old thatched village pub
♣℘🚗◔☾ (not Sun)Ⓢ

Loudwater 16D9

10.30–2.30; 5.30–10.30 (11 F, S)

Happy Union
Boundary Road (A4094)
☎ Bourne End 20972
Evening opening: 6
Wethered Bitter, SPA, Winter Royal [H]
Friendly village pub, just off A40 🔥♪♣℘🚗◔ (not Sun)☾Ⓢ

Lye Green 16E9

11–2.30; 6–10.30 (11 F, S)

Black Cat
Lycrombe Road (off B4505) OS 982035
Benskins Bitter [H]
Pleasant pub on outskirts of Chesham ♣℘🚗[R]

Marlow 7G1

10.30–2.30; 5.30–10.30 (11 F, S)

Carpenters Arms
Spittal Street (A4155)
Wethered Bitter, SPA [H]
Lively pub with good bar snacks ♪♣▣℘Ⓢ♿

Clayton Arms
Quoiting Square (off A4155)
Evening opening: 6
Brakspear Mild, Pale Ale, Special Bitter [H] **Old** [G]
Friendly and unspoilt, excellent value ♣[R]🍺♿

Coach & Horses
West Street (A4155) ☎ 3013
Courage Best Bitter, Directors [H]
17th century pub with prize-winning garden
♪♣℘◔☾Ⓢ♿

All Marlow's 20 pubs sell real ale

Marsh Gibbon 16C7

10.30–2.30; 6–11

Greyhound
(Off A41)
☎ Stratton Audley 365
Closed Monday lunchtime
Phillips Heritage Bitter, Ailric Old Ale
Younger No 3 [H]
Superb 16th-century coaching inn with own brewery; occasional guest beers 🔥♣℘🚗[R]◔☾🍺Ⓢ

Marsworth 16E8

10–2.30; 6–10.30 (11 F, S)

Red Lion
Vicarage Road (off B489)
☎ Cheddington 668366
Aylesbury ABC Bitter
Draught Bass
Everard Tiger
Morrell Light Ale [H]
Excellent local near Grand Union canal 🏠♣🚗◔🍺Ⓢ

Milton Keynes 16D6

11–2.30; 6–11

Suffolk Punch
Heelands, Saxon Street
☎ 311166
Tolly Cobbold Mild, Bitter, Original, Old Strong [H]
Interesting new city pub with Suffolk theme
♪♣▣℘🚗◔☾🍺Ⓢ🚆

Newport Pagnell 16D6

10.30–2.30; 5.30–11

Cannon
50 High Street
☎ Milton Keynes 610042
Morning opening: 11
Aylesbury ABC Bitter
Everard Tiger [H]
Busy pub in town centre
🏠♪♣🚗▣[R]◔☾🍺Ⓢ

North Crawley 16E6

11–2.30; 6.30–11

Chequers
24 High Street ☎ 224
Greene King KK, IPA, Abbot [H]
Popular, friendly, unspoilt village local 🏠🔥♪♣℘🚗◔☾🍺Ⓢ

Try also: Cock (Wells)

Northend 7F1

10–2.30; 5.30–10.30 (11 F, S)

White Hart
(Off B480) OS 734923
☎ Turville Heath 353
Morning opening: 11
Brakspear Pale Ale, Special Bitter, Old [H]
Unspoilt little pub with extensive garden, in beautiful surroundings 🏠♪♣℘🚗▣◔Ⓢ

Old Bradwell 16D6

11–2.30; 6–11

Prince Albert
Vicarage Road
(Off H3 City Road)
☎ Milton Keynes 312080
Wells Eagle Bitter [H]
Modernised, friendly open-plan pub ♪♣℘🚗◔Ⓢ

Owlswick 16D8

10–2.30; 6–10.30 (11 F, S)

Shoulder Of Mutton
(Off B4009) OS 790062
☎ Princes Risborough 4304
Fuller London Pride, ESB
Marston Pedigree [E]
Owd Rodger [G]

Comfortable country inn, listed building
🔥♣🌿🚗🛏[R]◔🍽🍷Ⓢ

Princes Risborough 16D9

10–2.30; 6–10.30 (11 F, S)
Whiteleaf Cross
Market Square (A4010)
☎ 6834
Morland Mild, Bitter, Best Bitter [H]
Gleaming and comfortable town tavern ♪♣🌿◔🍽Ⓢ♿

Try also: Bell (Benskins)

Ravenstone 16D6

10.30–2; 5.30–10.30 (11 F, S)
Wheatsheaf
☎ Stoke Goldington 278
Wells Eagle Bitter
Bulmer Cider [G]
Genuine village pub, beer served from old bakery oven
🏠♪♣🌿🚗🍷Ⓢ⛺

Saunderton 16D9

10.30–2.30; 5.30–10.30 (11 F, S)
Rose & Crown
(A4010)
☎ Princes Risborough 5299
Opens at 11.30 am & 6 pm
Morland Bitter
Morrell Varsity
Young Special Bitter
Younger Scotch Bitter [H]
Comfortable country inn and restaurant 🏠🌿🚗🛏◔🍽Ⓢ♿

Seer Green 7G1

10.30–2.30; 5.30–10.30
Jolly Cricketers
Chalfont Road
Wethered Bitter, SPA [H]
Unchanged village pub of character ♣🚗🍷Ⓢ≷

Skirmett 16D9

10.30–2.30; 5.30–10.30 (11 F, S)
Old Crown
☎ Turville Heath 435
Brakspear Mild, Pale Ale, Special Bitter, Old [H]
Original and unspoilt village pub in attractive countryside
🏠♪♣◔🍽🍷Ⓢ

Stewkley 16D7

10–2.30; 6–10.30 (11 F,S)
Swan
Chapel Square ☎ 285
Courage Best Bitter, Dirctors [H]
Attractive beamed local catering for all tastes; inglenook fire 🏠♪♣🌿🚗◔🍽Ⓢ

Stoke Goldington 16D6

10.30–2.30; 5.30–10.30
White Hart
High Street (B526) ☎ 392
Evening opening: 6–11
Wells Eagle Bitter [H]
Attractive stone-built pub with skittles ♪♣🌿🚗◔🍷Ⓢ

Stoke Green 7G2

10.30–2.30; 5.30–10.30 (11 F, S)
Red Lion
(Off B416) ☎ Slough 21739
Charrington IPA
Draught Bass [H]
Excellent facilities for drinkers, non-smokers and children 🏠♪♣⊠🌿🚗◔🍽Ⓢ

Stoke Mandeville 16D8

10–2.30; 6–10.30 (11 F, S)
Woolpack
Risborough Road (A4010)
Morning opening: 11.30
Aylesbury ABC Bitter
Draught Bass [H]
Friendly half-thatched pub
🏠♪♣⊠🌿🚗🍷Ⓢ♿≷

Stoke Poges 7G2

10.30–2.30; 5.30–10.30 (11 F, S)
Plough
Wexham Street
Ind Coope Bitter, Burton Ale [H]
Popular and unspoilt ♪♣🌿🚗🍷

Stony Stratford 16D6

10.30–2.30; 5.30–11
Bull (Vaults Bar)
High Street
☎ Milton Keynes 567104
Lunchtime opening: 12 noon
Aylesbury ABC Bitter
Draught Bass
Everard Tiger
Morrell Light Mild [H]
Splendid Victorian bar adjoining historic coaching house 🏠🔥♪♣🌿🚗🛏[R]◔🍽🍷Ⓢ

The Lee 16D9

10.30–2.30; 6–10.30 (11 F, S)
Old Swan
Swan Bottom OS 902055
Adnams Bitter
Brakspear Special Bitter
Marston Pedigree
Morland Bitter [H]
Comfortable country pub, well worth finding 🌿🚗

Turville 16D9

10–2.30; 5.30–10.30 (11 F, S)
Bull & Butcher
☎ Turville Heath 283
Morning opening: 11
Brakspear Pale Ale, Special Bitter [H] **Old** [G]
Attractive, popular pub in superb countryside
🏠♪♣🌿🚗◔🍽🍷Ⓢ

Wavendon 16D6

11–2.30; 6–11
Plough
Walton Road
☎ Milton Keynes 584447
Benskins Bitter
Ind Coope Burton Ale [H]
Splendid pub with character
♪🌿🚗🍽Ⓢ

Wendover 16D8

10–2.30; 6–10.30 (11 F, S)
White Swan
18 High Stret
Aylesbury ABC Bitter
Ind Coope Burton Ale [H]
Weston Cider [G]
Welcoming, comfortable pub
♪♣🍷Ⓢ≷

Weston Turville 16D8

10.30–2.30; 6–10.30 (11 F, S)
Five Bells
Main Street
☎ Stoke Mandeville 3131
Morning opening: 11.30
Aylesbury ABC Bitter
Everard Tiger
Young Specal Bitter
Younger No 3 [H]
Imaginative transformation of old tied pub ♣🌿🚗🛏◔🍽🍷

Whaddon 16D7

10.30–2.30; 6–10.30 (11 F, S)
Lowndes Arms
High Street (off A5)
☎ Milton Keynes 501706
Morning opening: 11
Aylesbury ABC Bitter
Draught Bass
Everard Tiger [H]
Lively village local with pleasant atmosphere
🏠♪♣🌿🚗[R]◔🍽🍷Ⓢ

Whelpley Hill 17E9

10–2.30; 6–10.30 (11 F, S)
White Hart
(Off B4505) OS 000037
Benskins Bitter [H]
Boisterous country local with matching landlord 🏠♣🌿🚗Ⓢ

Wingrave 16D8

10.30–2.30; 6–10.30 (11 F, S)
Rose & Crown
The Green
Aylesbury ABC Bitter
Draught Bass [H]
Friendly three-bar village pub
🔥♪♣🌿🚗🍷

Winslow 16D7

10.30–2.30; 6–11
Nags Head
Sheep Street (A413) ☎ 2037
Aylesbury ABC Bitter
Draught Bass
Everard Tiger [H]
Attractive split-level pub, keen landlord 🏠🔥♪♣🌿🚗◔🍽Ⓢ

Worminghall 16C8

10–2.30; 6–10.30 (11 F, S)
Clifden Arms
OS 640083 ☎ Ickford 273
Halls Harvest Bitter
Ind Coope Burton Ale [H]
Picturesque 16th-century inn
♪♣🌿🚗◔🍷Ⓢ

Abbotsley 17G5

10.30–2.30; 6–11
Plough
High Green (B1046)
Paine XXX, EG [H]
Overlooking village green, hood skittles
🏠♪♣🚗◔◗🍺Ⓢ

Abington Piggotts 17G6

10–2.30; 6–11
Darby & Joan
☎ Steeple Morden 852273
Morning opening: 11.30
Adnams Bitter
Greene King XX, IPA, Abbot
Marston Pedigree
Ruddle County [H]
Large country pub, well worth finding
🏠♪♣✿🚗◗ (F,S) 🍺Ⓢ

Alwalton 17F3

10–2.30; 6–11
Wheatsheaf
Oundle Road (off A1)
Opens at 11 am & 7 pm
Ind Coope Burton Ale [G]
Popular village pub near showground 🏠♪♣✿🚗◔🍺

Barnack 17F2

10–2.30; 6–11
Millstone
Millstone Lane
☎ Stamford 740296
Everard Tiger, Old Original
Bulmer Cider [H]
Intimate limestone pub near hills and hollows
🏠⌈♪♣⊞✿🚗[R]◔◗Ⓢ♿⛺

Barrington 17H6

11.30–2.30; 6.30–11
Royal Oak
The Green (off A10)
☎ Cambridge 870791
Adnams Bitter
Greene King IPA, Abbot [H]
Attractive old pub; mind your head
🏠♪✿🚗◔◗Ⓢ

Bartlow 17J6

11.30–2.30; 6.30–11
Three Hills
Ashdon Road
☎ Cambridge 891259
Opens at 10.30 am and 6 pm
Greene King IPA, Abbot [H]
Beautiful pub in small village
♣✿🚗◔◗🍺Ⓢ

Bluntisham 17G4

10.30–2.30; 6–11
White Swan
High Street
Tolly Cobbold Bitter, Original, Old Strong [H]
Fenland village pub with jazz interest ⌈♪♣✿🚗🍺

Brampton 17F4

10.30–2.30; 6–11
Dragoon
Buckden Road (A141)
☎ Huntingdon 53510
Wells Eagle Bitter, Bombardier [H]
Contrasting bars, popular for food ♪♣✿🚗◔◗🍺Ⓢ

Buckden 17F5

10.30–2.30; 6–11
Falcon
Church Street (off A1)
Wells Eagle Bitter [H]
Village pub with separate games room 🏠♪♣⊞✿🚗Ⓢ

Burrough Green 17J5

11.30–2.30; 6.30–11
Bull
(B1061)
Opens 11–2; 7–11
Greene King XX, IPA [H]
Friendly village pub, busy on race days ♪♣✿🚗Ⓢ

Burwell 17J5

10.30–2.30; 6.30–11
Fox
The Causeway
Norwich Bullards Mild, Castle Bitter
Webster Yorkshire Bitter [H]
Old village community pub, carefully facelifted
🏠♪♣✿🚗[R]◔🍺Ⓢ

Cambridge 17H5

10–2.30; 6–11
Cambridge Arms
4 King Street ☎ 59650
Greene King XX, IPA, Abbot [H]
Old Scales' brewery incorporated into excellent pub ⌈♪♣✿◔◗🍺Ⓢ

County Arms
43 Castle Street (A604)
Adnams Bitter
Wethered Bitter
Whitbread Flowers Original Bitter [H]
Warm and welcoming three-bar pub 🏠♪♣✿◔🍺Ⓢ

Fleur de Lys
73 Humberstone Road
Opens 11–2.30; 7–11
Tolly Cobbold Mild, Bitter, Original, Old Strong [H]
Friendly and popular local
♪♣🚗🍺

Free Press
Prospect Row ☎ 68337
Greene King IPA, Abbot [H]
Hearty, friendly and busy, well renovated 🏠♣✿◔

Green Dragon
Water Street, Chesterton
Greene King XX, IPA, Abbot [H]
Popular 16th-century local
♪♣Ⓢ

Kingston Arms
Kingston Street
Greene King XX [G] **IPA, Abbot**
Rayment BBA [H]
Busy backstreet pub with friendly atmosphere ♪♣✿◔🍺Ⓢ

Oak
6 Lensfield Road ☎ 355566
Tolly Cobbold Bitter, Original, Old Strong [H]
Comfortable pub with good atmosphere ♪♣■[R]Ⓢ

Old Spring
Ferry Path (off Chesterton Road) ☎ 357228
Greene King XX [G] **IPA** [H]
Abbot [G]
Extensively de-modernised pub, complete with sawdust on floor ♪♣✿🚗◔◗Ⓢ

Red Lion
Mill End Road, Cherry Hinton
☎ 244826
Tolly Cobbold Mild, Bitter, Original, Old Strong [H]
Superbly renovated pub with witty landlord
🏠⌈♪♣✿🚗◔◗🍺Ⓢ♿

Royal Standard
292 Mill Road ☎ 247877
Morning opening: 11
Tolly Cobbold Bitter, Original, Old Strong [H]
Excellent community pub
⌈♪♣✿🚗■[R]🍺Ⓢ

Salisbury Arms
Tenison Road ☎ 60363
Free house with extensive range of beers – usually 12 real ales and draught scrumpy available ⌈♪♣◔🍺Ⓢ⇄

Spade & Becket
Thompsons Lane
☎ 311701
Tolly Cobbold Mild, Bitter, Original, Old Strong [H]
Riverside pub with pleasant garden ♪✿◔◗Ⓢ

Unicorn
High Street, Cherry Hinton
Greene King XX, IPA, Abbot [H]
Tastefully renovated; best mild in Cambridge
🏠♣✿🚗◔🍺Ⓢ

Zebra
Maids Causeway, Newmarket Road ☎ 59432
Opens 12 noon Saturdays
Greene King XX, IPA, Abbot [H]
Friendly pub with excellent food 🏠♪♣⊞◔◗🍺Ⓢ

Castor 17F3

10–2.30; 6–11
Royal Oak
24 Peterborough Road (A47)
Morning opening: 10.30

Ind Coope Bitter, Burton Ale [H]
Thatched listed building of character 🔥♣🍴🚗◔[S]

Chatteris 17H3

10–2.30; 6–11
Honest John
South Park Street ☎ 2698
Opens at 11 am & 7 pm
Adnams Bitter
Greene King IPA, Abbot [H]
Unusual town pub, formerly a labour exchange ♣🚗[R]♿

Cheveley 18C6

11.30–2.30; 6–11
Red Lion
High Street (off B1063)
☎ Newmarket 730233
Opens at 11 am and 7 pm
Greene King XX, IPA, Abbot [H]
Popular village local in horse-breeding country
🔥♪♣🚗🛏🍺

Clayhithe 17H5

11–2.30; 6–11
Bridge Hotel
(Off A10) OS 503644
☎ Cambridge 860252
Everard Tiger, Old Original [H]
Riverside hotel with suntrap garden 🔥♪♣🍴🚗🛏◔👪

Colne 17G4

10.30–2.30; 6–11
Green Man
Manns IPA, Bitter
Watney Fined Stag Bitter [H]
Superb fenland pub
🔥♪♣🍴🚗🍺[S]

Conington 17G5

10.30–2.30; 6–11
White Swan
(Off A604) ☎ Elsworth 251
Greene King XX, IPA, Abbot [H]
Excellent country pub with good selection of games
🔥⚐♪♣🍴🚗◔👪🍺[S]♿⛺

Coton 17H5

11.30–2.30; 6–11
John Barleycorn
High Street (Off A1303/M11)
Greene King XX, IPA, Abbot [H]
Friendly pub in quiet village
🔥♪♣🍴🚗◔🍺[S]♿⛺

Doddington 17H3

10–2.30; 6–11
Three Tuns
New Street (A141)
☎ March 740220
Norwich Castle Bitter
Webster Yorkshire Bitter [H]
Fine local with bowling green
🔥♪♣🍴🚗[R]◔👪🍺[S]♿

Dry Drayton 17H5

10.30–2.30; 6.30–11
Black Horse
35 Park Street (off A604)
☎ Crafts Hill 81055
Charrington IPA
Greene King IPA, Abbot
Tolly Cobbold Original
Bulmer Cider [H]
Friendly pub with real food
🔥♣🍴🚗◔👪[S]

Duxford 17H6

11.30–2.30; 6–11
Wheatsheaf
St Peters Street (off A505)
☎ Cambridge 832284
Greene King IPA, Abbot [H]
Excellent village pub/restaurant with bowling green ♪♣🍴🚗◔👪🍺[S]

Eaton Socon 17F5

10.30–2.30; 5.30–11
Bell
37 Great North Road (off A1)
Wells Eagle Bitter, Bombardier [H]
Pleasantly refurbished
🔥♪♣🍴🚗[S]

Old Sun
Great North Road (off A1)
Evening opening: 6
Greene King KK, IPA, Abbot [E]
Comfortable two-bar village pub ♪♣🚗◔👪🍺[S]

Elton 17F3

10.30–2.30; 6–11
Crown
8 Duck Street ☎ 232
Greene King IPA
Marston Pedigree
Ruddle County [H]
Old village green pub with atmosphere; regular guest beers 🔥♪♣🍴🚗[R]◔👪🍺[S]♿

Ely 17J4

10–2.30; 6–11
Prince Albert
Silver Street (off A10)
Opens at 11 am and 7 pm
Greene King XX [G] **IPA, Abbot** [H]
Small, intimate local, friendly mixed clientele ♪♣🍴[S]

West End
16 West End (off A10)
Norwich Castle Bitter
Webster Yorkshire Bitter [H]
Friendly pub, emphasis on games 🔥♪♣🍴[R]🍺

Fenstanton 17G5

10.30–2.30; 6–11
King William IV
High Street ☎ 62467
Tolly Cobbold Mild, Bitter, Original, Old Strong
Bulmer Cider [H]
Fine old pub with wealth of beams ♪♣🍴◔👪[S]

Fulbourn 17H5

11.30–2.30; 6–11
Six Bells
High Street
Tolly Cobbold Mild, Bitter, Original, Old Strong [H]
Interesting spacious local in village centre 🔥♪♣🍴🚗🍺[S]

Glatton 17F3

10–2.30; 6–11
Addison Arms
Sawtry Road
Opens at 10.30 am and 7 pm
Manns IPA, Bitter
Watney Fined Stag Bitter [H]
Collection of old carpenters' tools in bar 🔥♪♣🍴🚗◔👪🍺[S]

Godmanchester 17G4

10.30–2.30; 6–11
Black Bull
Post Street
☎ Huntingdon 53310
Morning opening: 11
Wethered Bitter
Bulmer Cider [H]
Beams and brasses in abundance; excellent food
🔥♪♣🎲🍴🚗🛏[R]◔👪🍺[S]

Great Eversden 18A6

11.30–2.30; 6–11
Hoops
(Off A603)
Morning opening: 11
Wells Eagle Bitter, Bombardier [H]
Lively local with Jacobean fireplace 🔥♪♣🍴🚗[S]♿

Great Gransden 17G5

10.30–2.30; 6–11
Crown & Cushion
☎ 214
Wells Eagle Bitter, Bombardier [H]
Enthusiastic landlord
♪🍴🚗◔👪[S]

Guyhirn 17H2

10.30–2.30; 6–11
Chequers
(A47)
Elgood Bitter [H]
Homely pub overlooked by the River Nene 🔥♪♣🍴🚗[R]🍺[S]

Hail Weston 17F5

10.30–2.30; 6–11
Royal Oak
(Off A45)
☎ Huntingdon 72527
Wells Eagle Bitter, Bombardier [H]
Village pub with prizewinning gardens ⚐♪♣🎲🍴🚗◔👪🍺[S]

Hartford 17G4

10.30–2.30; 6–11
Barley Mow
(A141) ☎ Huntingdon 50557
Wells Eagle Bitter, Bombardier [H]
Comfortable lounge-bar pub
♪♣🍴🚗◔[S]⛺

Helpston 17F2

10.30–2.30; 6–11
Blue Bell
Woodgate
✆ Peterborough 252394
Manns Bitter Ⓗ
The poet John Clare was once the pub's pot boy
🍴🎵🅿🏠🕮Ⓢ♿

Hemingford Abbots 17G4

10.30–2.30; 6–11
Axe & Compass
✆ Huntingdon 63605
Manns IPA, Bitter
Watney Fined Stag Bitter
Bulmer Cider Ⓗ
Thatched village pub with beams and inglenook fireplace
🍴🎵🅿🏠🕒🍺 (not Tue) Ⓢ 🏕

Heydon 17H6

11.30–2.30; 6.30–11
King William IV
(Off A505) ✆ Royston 838773
Adnams Bitter
Greene King XX, IPA, Abbot Ⓗ
An old curiosity shop of a pub
🎵🍺🅿🏠🕒🍺Ⓢ♿

Histon 17H5

10.30–2.30; 6.30–11
Red Lion
High Street (off B1049)
Adnams Bitter
Everard Tiger
Greene King IPA
Whitbread Flowers Original Bitter
Bulmer Cider Ⓗ
Excellent village free house, guest beers 🍴🎵🍺🅿🍺

Rose & Crown
2 Glebe Way ✆ 2448
Wethered Bitter
Whitbread Flowers Original Bitter Ⓗ
Fine 400-year-old pub in 'all real' village 🎵🍺🅿🕒🍺Ⓢ

Holywell 17G4

10.30–2.30; 6–11
Olde Ferryboat Inn
✆ Huntingdon 63227
Draught Bass
Greene King IPA, Abbot Ⓖ
Thatched riverside inn, reputedly haunted. In Guinness Book of Records as one of the oldest inns in England 🍴🎵🅿🏠🅁🕒🍺Ⓢ

Horningsea 17H5

10.30–2.30; 6.30–11
Plough & Fleece
High Street (off A45)
✆ Cambridge 860795
Greene King XX, IPA, Abbot Ⓗ
Friendly old pub with superb public bar and excellent food
🅿🕒🍺🍺

Huntingdon 17G4

10.30–2.30; 6–11
Victoria
Ouse Walk ✆ 53899
Paine XXX, EG Ⓗ
Country-style pub off town centre 🎵🅿🍺🕒🍺Ⓢ

Keyston 17E4

10.30–2.30; 6–11
Pheasant
(B663) ✆ Bythorn 241
Ruddle County
Tolly Cobbold Bitter Ⓗ
Large thatched pub with good range of food; hood skittles
🍴🍺🅿🏠🕒🍺Ⓢ

Kimbolton 17F5

10.30–2.30; 6–11
Half Moon
East Street (off A45)
Wells Eagle Bitter,
Bombardier Ⓗ
16th-century local in shadow of Kimbolton Castle
🎵🍺🅿🏠🍺

Kirtling 18C6

11–2.30; 6.30–11
Queens Head
Newmarket Road OS 691571
✆ Newmarket 730253
Tolly Cobbold Bitter,
Original Ⓗ
Fine Elizabethan pub with good food 🍴🎵🍺🅿🏠🕒🍺Ⓢ

Litlington 17G6

10.30–2.30; 6–11
Crown
Morning opening: 10.30
Greene King XX, IPA, Abbot Ⓗ
Village pub on one-way system; collection of hot cross buns on beams 🎵🍺🅿🏠Ⓢ

Lode 18C6

10–2.30; 6–11
Three Horseshoes
Lode Road
Greene King XX, IPA, Abbot Ⓗ
Friendly one-bar pub
🎵🍺🏠Ⓢ

March 17H3

10–2.30; 6–11
Ship
Nene Parade ✆ 56999
Evening opening: 6.30
Greene King XX, IPA, Abbot Ⓗ
17th century pub with carved beams 🎵🅁🕒🍺Ⓢ

White Horse
West End ✆ 3054
Opens at 10.30 am & 6.30 pm
Norwich Bullards Mild,
Castle Bitter
Webster Yorkshire Bitter Ⓗ
Thatched riverside pub with friendly atmosphere
🍴🎵🍺🅿🏠🅁🕒🍺Ⓢ♿⚓

Newton 17H6

10–2.30; 6–11
Queens Head
(Off A10)
Morning opening: 11
Adnams Bitter, Old Ⓖ
Idyllic, friendly 16th-century local 🍴🍺🏠🍺

Old Weston 17F4

10.30–2.30; 6–11
Swan
(B660) ✆ Winwick 400
Adnams Bitter
Greene King Abbot
Marston Pedigree Ⓗ
Large country village free house 🎵🍺🏠🕒🍺Ⓢ

Papworth Everard 17G5

10.30–2.30; 6–11
Kisby's Hut
Ermine Street North (A14)
✆ Huntingdon 88371
Tolly Cobbold Original Ⓗ
Popular village local near the settlement 🍴🎵🍺🍺🏠🕒🍺Ⓢ

Peterborough 17F3

10–2.30; 6–11
Blue Bell
Welland Road, Dogsthorpe
✆ 54890
Elgood Bitter Ⓗ
Peterborough's oldest pub; monkey's skull in cupboard
🎵🍺🍺🅿🏠🅁🕒Ⓢ

Blue Bell
6 The Green, Werrington
Elgood Bitter Ⓗ
Excellent pub on village green
🎵🍺🅿🍺

Botolph Arms
465 Oundle Road ✆ 234170
Charrington IPA
Draught Bass
Mitchells & Butlers Springfield Bitter
Ruddle County
Tolly Cobbold Original Ⓗ
Bulmer Cider Ⓖ
Converted farmhouse within city limits 🎵🍺🍺🅿🍺🕒🍺Ⓢ

Dragonfly
Herlington Centre, Orton Malborne ✆ 233130
Morning opening: 10.30
Tolly Cobbold Mild, Bitter, Original, Old Strong Ⓗ
Popular estate pub, interesting design 🎵🍺🅿🕒🍺🍺♿

Grain Barge
The Quayside, Embankment Road ✆ 311967
Draught Bass
Charrington IPA
Mitchells & Butlers Springfield Bitter Ⓗ
Excellently converted Humber keel on River Nene – interior a symphony in wood 🈺🅿🕒🍺Ⓢ

Lime Tree
Paston Lane, Paston
(off A15) ✆ 71813
Wethered Bitter Ⓗ
Good locals' pub, handpump
in lounge ⓕ♣🅰Ⓡ🅖🅘Ⓢ&

Peter Pan
Eastern Avenue, Dogsthorpe
(off A47) ✆ 41388
Morning opening: 10.30
Home Mild, Bitter Ⓔ
First class estate pub
ⓙ♣♫🅰Ⓖ🅘Ⓢ

Silver Jubilee
Heltwate, Bretton (off A47)
Greene King XX, IPA, Abbot Ⓖ
Opened in Jubilee year;
upstairs 'cellar'
ⓙ♫♣🏢♫🅰Ⓖ🅘Ⓢ&

Still
Cumbergate ✆ 68531
Closed Sundays and bank
holidays; closes 10.30 pm
Mon–Thu
Draught Bass
Elgood Bitter
Greene King Abbot
Marston Pedigree,
Owd Rodger Ⓖ
Oasis within Queensgate
shopping centre; guest beers
♫Ⓡ🅘

Woolpack
North Street, Stanground
Evening opening: 7
Whitbread Castle Eden Ale Ⓗ
Busy backstreet local with
own river moorings
🅰ⓙ♣♫🅘

Wortley Almshouses
Westgate ✆ 48839
Samuel Smith Old Brewery
Bitter Ⓗ
Excellent one-room town
centre pub ♫Ⓖ≋

Purls Bridge 18B4
10–2.30; 6–11
Ship
✆ Manea 578
Greene King XX (summer),
IPA, Abbot Ⓗ
Isolated riverside pub, popular
with anglers and birdwatchers
ⓙ♣♫Ⓡ� 🍴🅘

Rampton 17H5
10.30–2.30; 6.30–11
Black Horse
High Street
Greene King KK, IPA, Abbot Ⓗ
Classic example of a village
local 🅰ⓙ♣♫🅰🅘Ⓢ

Rings End 17H2
10.30–2.30; 6–11
Black Hart
(A141)
Elgood Bitter Ⓖ
Vintage fenland pub with
pre-decimal juke box 🅰ⓙ♣Ⓡ🅘Ⓢ

St Ives 17G4
10.30–2.30; 6–11
Oliver Cromwell
The Quay, Wellington Street
Greene King IPA
Ruddle County Ⓗ
Busy lounge bar; unusually
ornate pub sign ♫✍

Royal Oak
13 Crown Street
Morning opening: 10
Ind Coope Bitter, Burton Ale Ⓗ
16th-century hostelry with
wealth of beams and settles
🅰♫♣♫🅰Ⓖ🍴 (Mon–Sat) Ⓢ

St Neots 17F5
10–2.30; 6–11
Globe
Huntingdon Street (off
B1043) ✆ Huntingdon 72590
Wells Eagle Bitter,
Bombardier Ⓗ
Bulmer Cider Ⓖ
Low-beamed public bar and
comfortable lounge ♫♣✍Ⓖ🅘Ⓢ

Wheatsheaf
Church Street
Greene King XX, IPA, Abbot Ⓗ
Busy terraced town local 🅰♫♣

Saxon Street 18C6
11.30–2.30; 6.30–11
Reindeer
(Off B1063)
✆ Newmarket 730346
Opens at 11 am and 7 pm
Tolly Cobbold Bitter, Old
Strong Ⓖ
Totally unspoilt village local
🅰♫♣🅰Ⓡ&

Swaffham Bulbeck
17J5
10.30–2.30; 6.30–11
Black Horse
35 High Street (B1102)
Opens at 11.30 am and 7 pm
Adnams Bitter
Everard Beacon
Greene King IPA Ⓗ
Summer barbecues and
Thursday trad jazz
🅰ⓙ♣🅰Ⓖ🅘Ⓢ

Thorney Toll 17G2
10.30–2.30; 6–11
Black Horse
Wisbech Road (A47)
Opens 11 am & 7 pm in winter
Elgood Bitter Ⓗ
Friendly, no-frills pub on busy
road ♫♣♫🅰Ⓡ🅘Ⓢ

Thriplow 17H6
11.30–2.30; 6.30–11
Green Man
2 Lower Street (off A505)
Wells Eagle Bitter,
Bombardier Ⓗ
Pleasant village local
♫♣🅰Ⓖ🅘Ⓢ

Tilbrook 17F4
10.30–2.30; 6–11
Three Shuttles
(A45) ✆ Huntingdon 860244
Wells Eagle Bitter,
Bombardier Ⓗ
Pleasant family pub with
interesting collection of
animals 🅰ⓙ♣🏢♫🅰Ⓢ🄰

Turves 17G3
10–2.30; 6–11
Three Horseshoes
344 March Road ✆ 414
Morning opening: 11
Greene King IPA Ⓗ
Unusual isolated pub with
games room
🅰ⓙ♣🏢🅰Ⓖ🍴🅘&🄰

Ufford 17F2
10–2.30; 6–11
Olde White Hart
Home Bitter Ⓗ
Excellent stone-built pub with
contrasting bars ♣✍🅰🅘

Whittlesey 17G3
10.30–2.30; 6–11
Boat
2 Ramsey Road (B1040)
✆ Peterborough 202488
Elgood Bitter Ⓗ
Hats off to a fine pub
🅰ⓙ♣✍🅰Ⓡ🅘Ⓖ🍴🅘Ⓢ&

Willingham 17H5
10.30–2.30; 6–11
Three Tuns
Church Street (off B1050)
Greene King XX, IPA, Abbot Ⓖ
Straightforward village local;
ale fetched from back
ⓙⓙ♣✍🅰🅘&

Wisbech 17H2
10.30–2.30; 5.30–11
Hare & Hounds
North Brink (off A47) ✆ 3607
Evening opening: 6; open
until 3.30 pm Sat
Elgood Bitter Ⓗ
Tastefully modernised bar,
wood-panelled lounge
🅰♣🏢🅰Ⓡ🅘Ⓖ🍴🅘Ⓢ

Kings Head
Old Market (A47) ✆ 65402
Open until 3.30 pm Sat
Elgood Bitter Ⓗ
Two small rooms; keen
landlord ♫♣✍🅰Ⓖ🅘Ⓢ

Yaxley 17F3
10–2.30; 6–11
Three Horseshoes
179 Main Street (off A1)
Morning opening: 11
Manns Bitter
Watney Fined Stag Bitter Ⓗ
Welcoming thatched local
🅰ⓙ♣✍🅰Ⓖ🅘Ⓢ🄰

Acton Bridge 22C4

11–3; 5.30–10.30 (11 F, S)
Maypole
Station Road (off B5153)
Greenall Whitley Dark Mild, Bitter [H]
Warm welcome in excellent semi-modernised village pub
🔥ſ♪♣⚘🚗◔🍷Ⓢ🚉

Alderley Edge 23E4

11–3; 5.30–10.30 (11 F, S)
Moss Rose
Off Heyes Lane
Robinson Best Mild, Best Bitter [E] **Old Tom** [G]
Considerably extended and renovated old pub down a narrow lane. Known locally as Drumming Monkey ♪♣⚘🚗Ⓢ🚉

Alsager 22E5

11–3; 5.30–10.30 (11 F, S)
Mere
(B5077) ☎ 2019
Saturday evening opening: 6.30
Greenall Whitley Bitter [H]
Small, well-kept pub near town centre ♣⚘🚗◔🍷Ⓢ

Audlem 22D6

11–3; 6.30–10.30 (11 F, S)
Bridge
12 Shropshire Street (A525) OS 659435
Marston Merrie Monk, Pedigree [H] **Owd Rodger** [G]
Friendly canalside pub, mooring facilities nearby
🔥ſ♪♣🚗[R]🍷Ⓢ

Barthomley 22E5

11–3; 6–10.30 (11 F, S)
White Lion
Burtonwood Dark Mild, Bitter [H]
17th-century thatched pub in picturesque village 🔥♣⚘🚗🍷Ⓢ

Bickerton 22C5

11.30–3; 5.30–10.30 (11 F, S)
Bickerton Poacher
Wrexham Road (A534) OS 226313 ☎ 882922
Border Mild, Bitter [H]
Old country pub with bistro and barbecue park attached
🔥ſ♪♣⚘🚗[R]◔◗🍷Ⓢ♿⛺

Bollington 23F4

11–3; 5.30–10.30 (11 F, S)
Holly Bush
Palmerston Street (B5091)
☎ 73073
Robinson Best Mild, Best Bitter, Old Tom [H]
Pleasant terraced pub with wood-panelled lounge
🔥♪♣▣⚘◔◗Ⓢ

Vale
Adlington Road
(Off B5091) ☎ 75147
Tetley Walker Bitter
Thwaites Mild, Bitter [H]
Tastefully modernised stone terraced pub ♪◔Ⓢ

17 of the 19 pubs in Bollington serve real ale

Buglawton 23E4

11–3; 5.30–10.30 (11 F, S)
Robin Hood
Buxton Road (A54)
☎ Congleton 3616
Marston Burton Bitter, Pedigree [H]
Friendly, pleasant main road country pub 🔥♪♣⚘🚗◔◗Ⓢ

Burtonwood 22C3

11–3; 6–10.30 (11 F, S)
Elm Tree
Chapel Lane
Burtonwood Dark Mild, Bitter [E]
Small locals' pub ♪♣🚗🍷

Chester 22B4

11–3; 5.30–10.30 (11 F, S)
Albion
Park Street, near Newgate
Morning opening: 11.30
Greenall Whitley Dark Mild, Bitter [H]
Lively corner local, good lunchtime food 🔥ſ♪♣◔🍷Ⓢ

Marlborough Arms
3 St. Johns Street
Morning opening: 11
Whitbread Castle Eden Ale [H]
Small, comfortable and friendly ♪♣🍷Ⓢ

Olde Custom House
Watergate Street
Closes 10.30 pm F, S
Border Mild [E]
Exhibition Mild [H]
Bitter [E] **Old Master** [H]
Historic timbered building housing excellent local
🔥ſ♪♣[R]◔🍷

Spital Vaults
1 Alma Street, Boughton
Bass Mild, Cask Bitter [H]
Games pub with bagatelle table ♪♣🚗🍷Ⓢ

All Greenall Whitley pubs in the city centre serve real ale

Childer Thornton 22B4

11.30–3; 5.30–10.30 (11 F, S)
White Lion
New Road (off A41)
Thwaites Best Mild, Bitter [H]
Small, popular village pub
♪▣⚘🚗Ⓢ

Congleton 23E5

11–3; 5.30–10.30 (11 F, S)
Forresters Arms
Chapel Street ☎ 4320
Draught Bass
Mitchells & Butlers Springfield Bitter [E]
Comfortable local opposite church, recently modernised
ſ♪♣⚘[R]◔◗🍷Ⓢ♿

Crewe 22D5

11–3; 5.30–10.30 (11 F, S)
George
West Street (A532) ☎ 213462
Evening opening: 6.30
Peter Walker Best Bitter [H]
Smart pub, good garden for children
♪♣⚘🚗■◔◗🍷Ⓢ

Lion & Swan
215 West Street (A532)
Boddingtons Mild, Bitter [H]
Recently renovated, friendly locals' pub ♣🚗🍷

Rising Sun
130 Earle Street
Boddingtons Mild, Bitter [H]
Corner pub just off town centre ♪♣🍷Ⓢ

Croft 22D3

11.30–3; 5.30–10.30 (11 F, S)
Plough
Kenyon Lane
Evening opening: 6
Greenall Whitley Dark Mild, Bitter [E]
Small, popular local with excellent, homely bar 🔥♣⚘🚗🍷Ⓢ

Daresbury 22C3

11–3; 5.30–10.30 (11 F, S)
Ring o'Bells
Chester Road (off A56)
☎ Moore 256
Greenall Whitley Dark Mild, Bitter [H]
Unspoilt rural pub in village where Lewis Carroll lived
♪♣⚘🚗[R]◔◗🍷Ⓢ

Davenham 22D4

10.30–3; 5.30–10.30 (11 F, S)
Oddfellows
London Road
Greenall Whitley Mild, Bitter [E]
Four-roomed village pub
♣⚘🚗◔🍷

Disley 23F3

11–3; 5.30–10.30 (11 F, S)
Crescent
Buxton Road (A6)
Robinson Best Mild, Best Bitter [H]
Small and friendly terrace-end local 🔥♪♣▣⚘🚗🚉

Mousetrap
Buxton Old Road (off A6)
Wilsons Original Mild, Bitter [H]
Cosy pub near oldest part of village ♪⚘🚗🚉

Dunham-on-the-Hill 22C4

12–3; 7–10.30 (11 F, S)
Dunham Arms
(A56) ☎ Helsby 2107
Whitbread Castle Eden Ale Ⓗ
Friendly, quiet roadside local
♨♪♣♒🅿️🅰️🕒🍴🍷Ⓢ

Farndon 22B5

11–3; 5.30–10.30 (11 F, S)
Greyhound Hotel
(A534) ☎ 270244
Greenall Whitley Mild, Bitter Ⓗ
Specialises in Dee salmon; pottery attached
♨♪♣🆎♒🅰️🅱️🅲️🕒🍴🍷Ⓢ

Frodsham 22C4

11–3; 5.30–10.30 (11 F, S)
Bellemonte
Bellemonte Road, Overton (Off B5152)
Evening opening: 6
Samuel Smith Old Brewery Bitter Ⓗ
Friendly, lively pub with number of rooms and comfortable lounge
♨♪♣♒🅰️🍷

Golden Lion
Main Street (A56)
Samuel Smith Old Brewery Bitter Ⓗ
♨♪♣♒Ⓡ🕒⚡

Gawsworth 23E4

11–3; 5.30–10.30 (11 F, S)
Harrington Arms
Congleton Road (off A536)
Robinson Best Mild, Bitter, Best Bitter (occasional) Ⓗ
Unspoilt old pub, part of a farm ♣🆎♒🅰️🍷🅰️

Goostrey 22E4

11–3; 5.30–10.30 (11 F, S)
Crown
Main Road (off A535)
☎ Holmes Chapel 32128
Morning opening: 11.30
Marston Mercian Mild, Burton Bitter Ⓔ **Pedigree** Ⓗ
Comfortable country pub near Jodrell Bank ♪♣🆎♒🅰️🕒🍴🍷Ⓢ

Great Budworth 22D4

11–3; 5.30–10.30 (11 F, S)
George & Dragon
High Street (off A559)
☎ 891317
Tetley Walker Bitter Ⓗ
Attractive pub in picturesque village ♨♪♣🅰️Ⓡ🕒🍴🍷Ⓢ

Great Warford 22E4

11–3; 5.30–10.30 (11 F, S)
Stags Head
(Off A535) OS 814771
Boddingtons Mild, Bitter Ⓗ

Attractive country pub
♨♪♣♒🅰️🅱️Ⓢ

Higher Sutton 23F4

11–3; 5.30–10.30 (11 F, S)
Hanging Gate
Meg Lane OS 953695
☎ Sutton 2238
Opens at 12 noon & 7 pm
Chesters Best Bitter
Marston Burton Bitter, Pedigree, Owd Rodger Ⓗ
Old split-level stone-built pub with breathtaking views; known as Tommy Steel's
♨♪♣🅰️🕒🍴🍷

Holmes Chapel 22E4

11–3; 5.30–10.30 (11 F, S)
Swan Hotel
Station Road (A54)
☎ 32259
Samuel Smith Old Brewery Bitter Ⓔ
Large, comfortable village pub
♨♪♣🅰️🅱️Ⓒ🍴🍷Ⓢ⚡

All pubs in the town serve real ale

Huntington 22B5

11.30–3; 5.30–10.30 (11 F, S)
Red House
Sandy Lane ☎ Chester 24783
Evening opening: 6
Bass Mild, Draught Bass Ⓗ
Terraced riverside garden with beautiful views
♪♣♒🅰️Ⓑ🕒 (must book)🍷

Kettleshulme 23F4

11–3; 5.30–10.30 (11 F, S)
Bull's Head
Macclesfield Road (A5002)
Tetley Walker Mild, Bitter Ⓗ
Stone-built end-of-terrace inn in Peak National Park
♨♪♣♒🅰️🍷Ⓢ

Knutsford 22E4

11–3; 5.30–10.30 (11 F, S)
Builders Arms
Mobberley Road (off A537)
Marston Mercian Mild, Burton Bitter Ⓗ
Small, busy local ♣🍷⚡

Lach Dennis 22D4

11–3; 5.30–10.30 (11 F, S)
Duke o' Portland Arms
Holmes Chapel Road (off B5052)
Marston Burton Bitter Ⓗ
Friendly country local
♪♒🅰️🍷Ⓢ

Langley 23F4

11–3; 5.30–10.30 (11 F, S)
Leather Smithy
Clarke Lane ☎ Sutton 2313
Ansells Mild
Ind Coope Bitter, Burton Ale
Tetley Walker Bitter Ⓗ

Comfortable old country pub with delightful views across reservoir towards Macclesfield Forest ♨♪♣🆎♒🅰️🅱️🕒🍴🍷Ⓢ♿

Try also: St. Dunstan

Little Budworth 22C5

11–3; 5.30–10.30 (11 F, S)
Red Lion
Vicarage Lane ☎ 275
Robinson Best Mild, Best Bitter Ⓔ
Smart little pub with bowling green ♨♪♒🅰️🕒🍷

Little Leigh 22D4

11–3; 5.30–10.30 (11 F, S)
Hollybush
Runcorn Road (A49)
Greenall Whitley Dark Mild, Bitter Ⓗ
Friendly, unspoilt thatched farmhouse pub, Grade 2 listed building ♣🅰️🅰️🍷Ⓢ

Little Stanney 22B4

11.30–3; 5.30–10.30 (11 F, S)
Rake Hall
Rake Lane
☎ 051-355 9433
Burtonwood Dark Mild, Bitter Ⓗ
Large country house with spacious garden
🍴♣🆎♒🅰️🕒🍴🍷Ⓢ

Little Sutton 22B4

11.30–3; 5.30–10.30 (11 F, S)
Travellers Rest
14 Ledsham Road (off A41)
☎ 051-339 2176
Peter Walker Mild, Bitter, Best Bitter Ⓗ
Popular, tasteful, cosmopolitan old Walker's house ♪♣♒🅰️🕒🍴🍷Ⓢ♿

Lower Withington 22E4

12–3; 5.30–10.30 (11 F, S)
Black Swan
Trap Street, Gleadsmoss
OS 820682 ☎ 212
Tetley Walker Bitter Ⓗ
Comfortable little country pub tucked away in Cheshire lanes
♨♪♣♒🅰️🍷Ⓢ🅰️

Lymm 22D3

11–3; 5.30–10.30 (11 F, S)
Bulls Head
32 The Cross, Village Centre (B5158, off A56) ☎ 2831
Hydes Best Mild, Bitter Ⓔ
Friendly local pub, close to Bridgewater Canal ♪♣🍷

Railway
Mill Lane, Heatley (B5159, off A56) ☎ 2742
Boddingtons Bitter Ⓗ
Large, popular many-roomed pub ♪♣🅰️Ⓡ🍷Ⓢ

Macclesfield 23F4

1–3; 5.30–10.30 (11 F, S)
British Flag
42 Coare Street (off A523)
Robinson Best Mild, Best
Bitter H Old Tom G
Cosy, friendly local ♪♣

Jolly Sailor
Sunderland Street
Draught Bass H
An honest alehouse
♣♪≠

Nags Head
60 Waters Green ℰ 22468
Robinson Best Mild, Best
Bitter, Old Tom H
Large, roomy pub opposite
station
♨♪♣⊞®⅁♦®≠

Plough
1 Station Street (off Hibel
Road) ℰ 31167
Marston Mercian Mild,
Burton Bitter H
Friendly street corner pub,
with evidence of former
W. A. Smith's ownership
♪♣⊞®⅁➍ (Fri, Sat)≠

Puss in Boots
Buxton Road (A537)
Boddingtons Mild, Bitter H
Town local by canal bridge
♨♪♣

Railway View
Byrons Lane (A523)
Ansells Mild
Ind Coope Bitter
Tetley Walker Bitter H
Friendly and popular little
local ♪♣

Star
London Road (A523)
Marston Mercian Mild,
Burton Bitter, Pedigree H
Popular pub near football
ground ♨♣♪♠®®

Some 65 pubs in Macclesfield
serve real ale from 7 breweries

Middlewich 22D4

11–3; 5.30–10.30 (11 F, S)
Boar's Head
Kinderton Street (A54)
Robinson Best Mild, Best
Bitter H
Large town pub; Irish flavour
♪♣⊞♠®⅁♦®♦

Golden Lion
Chester Road (A54)
Greenall Whitley Bitter H
Cosy pub, staunchly
traditional
♪♣♠®⅁♦♦

Newton Brewery
Webbs Lane (off A54) ℰ 3502
Marston Mercian Mild,
Burton Bitter, Pedigree,
Merrie Monk H

Small friendly pub in quiet
side street by canal
♪♣♥♠⅁♦®

Mobberley 22E4

11–3; 5.30–10.30 (11 F, S)
Bird in Hand
Knolls Green (B5085)
Samuel Smith Old Brewery
Bitter H
Pleasant multi-roomed
roadside house
♨♪♣♠♠®®♦Å

Chapel House
Pepper Street OS 777819
Opens 11.30 am F, S
Boddingtons Bitter H
Friendly little country pub
♨♣♥♠®®≠

Try also: Roebuck; Church
Inn

Moulton 22D4

11–3; 5.30–10.30 (11 F, S)
Lion
Main Road (off A533)
ℰ Winsford 2451
Tetley Walker Bitter H
Large modernised red brick
Victorian pub ♪♣♥♠®⅁♦♦®

Mow Cop 23E5

11–3; 5.30–10.30 (11 F, S)
Cheshire View
Station Road
Evening opening: 6.30
Marston Burton Bitter,
Pedigree, Merrie Monk H
Lounge has superb views of
Cheshire Plains ♪♣♥♠®

Nantwich 22D5

11–3; 5.30–10.30 (11 F, S)
Oddfellows Arms
97 Welsh Row (A51)
Morning opening: 11.30;
Saturday evening opening: 7
Ind Coope Bitter H
Charming old pub with large
garden ♪♣♥®®

Red Cow
Beam Street ℰ 628581
Robinson Best Mild, Best
Bitter H Old Tom G
Near bus station; folk at
Festival time ♪♣♥♠⅁♦®®

Union
High Street ℰ 626046
Evening opening: 7
Marston Mercian Mild,
Burton Bitter, Pedigree H
Busy town-centre local
♪♣♠®®®

Neston 22B4

11.30–3; 5.30–10.30 (11 F, S)
Coach & Horses
11 Bridge Street (B5134)
Whitbread Castle Eden Ale H
Small, friendly local
♨♪♣♥®®≠

Newbold 23E5

11–3; 5.30–10.30 (11 F, S)
Horseshoe
OS 863602
Robinson Best Mild, Best
Bitter, Old Tom H
Small, comfortable country
pub ♪♣♥♠®®®

Northwich 22D4

11–3; 5.30–10.30 (11 F, S)
Freemasons Arms
Chester Road, Castle
Wilsons Original Mild,
Bitter E
Modernised friendly pub on
Castle Hill ♪♣⅁♦

Volunteer
London Road
Wilsons Original Mild,
Bitter H
Friendly locals' pub by football
ground ♪♣♥⅁♦

All pubs in Northwich town
centre serve real ale

Plumley 22D4

11–3; 5.30–10.30 (11 F, S)
Golden Pheasant
Plumley Moor Road (Off
A556) ℰ Lower Peover 2261
Lees GB Mild, Bitter E
Large, comfortable country
pub with restaurant
♨♪♣♥♠®⅁♦®®≠

Poynton 23F3

11–3; 5.30–10.30 (11 F, S)
Bull's Head
London Road North
(A523) ℰ 873099
Boddingtons Mild, Bitter E
Cosy roadside inn ♣⊞♠®®

Rainow 23F4

11–3; 5.30–10.30 (11 F, S)
Highwayman
(A5002)
ℰ Bollington 73245
Thwaites Bitter H
300-year-old pub with
magnificent view across hills
♨♪♣♥⅁➍®

Rode Heath 22E5

11–3; 5.30–10.30 (11 F, S)
Broughton Arms
Sandbach Road (A533)
Saturday evening opening: 6
Marston Burton Bitter,
Pedigree, Merrie Monk, Owd
Rodger H
Busy, friendly canalside pub
with canal bric-a-brac
♨♪♣♥♠⅁♦®

Runcorn 22C3

11.30–3; 5.30–10.30 (11 F, S)
Royal Oak
Heath Road South, Weston
Village

Marston Mercian Mild,
Burton Bitter Ⓗ
Friendly street-corner local
♪♣♦⑧

Wellington
Wellington Street, Old Town
Marston Mercian Mild,
Burton Bitter Ⓗ
Homely backstreet pub
♪♣⑧≉

Sandbach 22E5

11–3; 5.30–10.30 (11 F, S)

George
39 High Street (A533) ☎ 2039
Opens at 11.30 am & 7 pm
Wilsons Original Mild,
Bitter Ⓗ
Comfortable pub, folk on
Tuesday nights
♨♪♣♦♠Ⓡ♥⑧

Iron Grey
Middlewich Road ☎ 5988
Robinson Best Mild, Best
Bitter Ⓗ Old Tom Ⓖ
Unpretentious little pub
♨♣♠Ⓡ♥⑧

Sarn 22C6

11.30–3; 5.30–10.30 (11 F, S)

Queens Head
(Off B5069) OS 440447
Border Mild, Bitter Ⓗ
Lovely remote local by river
and watermill
♨♪♣♥♠♥

Saughall 22B4

11.30–3; 6–10.30

Egerton Arms
Hermitage Road
Bass Mild, Cask Bitter Ⓗ
Popular village local
♪♣♠♥

Sutton 23F4

11–3; 5.30–10.30 (11 F, S)

Church House
OS 932713 ☎ 2436
Boddingtons Bitter Ⓗ
Tastefully modernised village
local
♨♪♣♥♠Ⓖ♥♥⑧

Tarporley 22C5

11–3; 5.30–10.30 (11 F, S)

Rising Sun
High Street (A49)
Robinson Best Mild, Best
Bitter Ⓗ
Popular old pub, good bar
snacks ♨♠⑧

Tattenhall 22C5

11–3; 5.30–10.30 (11 F, S)

Aldersey Arms
Tattenhall Road
OS 495604 ☎ 70595
Evening opening: 7
McEwan 70/-
Marston Pedigree
Oak Aldersey Bitter Ⓗ

Large, popular pub with
restaurant, near canal
♨♪♣♥♠Ⓔ♠Ⓡ♥♥⑧♥Ⓐ

Sportsman's Arms
Burwardsley Road OS 487584
Thwaites Mild, Bitter Ⓗ
Popular village local with
bowling green
♨♪♣♥♠Ⓡ♥♣♠Ⓐ

Timbersbrook 23E5

11–3; 5.30–10.30 (11 F, S)

Coach & Horses
Dane in Shaw (off A527)
Evening opening: 6
Robinson Best Mild, Best
Bitter Ⓔ
Country pub with friendly
family atmosphere
♨♪♣♥♠♥⑧Ⓐ

Wardle 22D5

11–3; 5.30–10.30 (11 F, S)

Barbridge Inn
Chester Road (A51)
OS 616568
☎ Wettenhall 266
Opens at 12 noon; evening
opening: 7 (winter)
Boddingtons Mild, Bitter Ⓔ
Restaurant-orientated
canalside pub
♪♣♦♥♠Ⓖ♥⑧♣

Warrington 22D3

11–3; 5.30–10.30 (11 F, S)

Glassmakers Arms
Brick Street (off A57)
Wilsons Original Mild,
Bitter Ⓗ
Busy local with friendly
atmosphere ♪♣♦⑧≉

Manx Arms
31 School Brow (off A57)
Tetley Walker Mild, Bitter Ⓗ
Small, homely games pub
♪♣♦Ⓖ♥≉

Lower Angel
27 Buttermarket Street
Peter Walker Mild, Bitter, Best
Bitter Ⓗ
Drinkers' haven amidst keg
monopoly
♥♣♦⑧≉

Wheelock 22D5

11–3; 5.30–10.30 (11 F, S)

Commercial Hotel
Game Street (off A534)
Closed lunchtimes except
Sunday; evening opening: 8
Boddingtons Bitter
Marston Pedigree Ⓗ
Friendly village pub
♪♣♠Ⓡ♥⑧

Widnes 22C3

11.30–3; 5.30–10.30 (11 F, S)

Grapes
38 Widnes Road
Higsons Bitter Ⓗ
Traditional local ♥ (Sat) ♪♣♥

Griffin
Farnworth Street
Greenall Whitley Mild,
Bitter Ⓔ
Friendly street-corner local
♪♣♠♥

Willaston 22D5

11–3; 5.30–10.30 (11 F, S)

Nags Head
87 Wistaston Road
Opens at 12 noon & 6.30 pm
Boddingtons Mild, Bitter Ⓗ
Basic, tidy local ♣♠♥

Wilmslow 23E4

11–3; 5.30–10.30 (11 F, S)

Farmers Arms
Chapel Lane (off A34)
Boddingtons Mild, Bitter Ⓗ
Friendly and popular local
♨♪♣♥♠Ⓡ♥♥

New Inn
Alderley Road (A34)
☎ 523123
Hydes Best Mild, Bitter Ⓔ
Recently extended
town-centre pub ♥♪♣♠Ⓡ♥Ⓖ

Wincham 22D4

11–3; 5.30–10.30 (11 F, S)

Black Greyhound
Hall Lane (A559)
Greenall Whitley Dark Mild,
Bitter Ⓗ
Large, well-kept pub
♪♣♥♠Ⓡ♥Ⓖ⑧

Wincle 23F5

11–3; 5.30–10.30 (11 F, S)

Wild Boar
(A54) ☎ 219
Robinson Best Mild, Best
Bitter Ⓗ
Popular pub on the moors
♨♪♣♥♠Ⓖ♥⑧

Winsford 22D4

11–3; 5.30–10.30 (11 F, S)

Rifleman
Weaver Street (off A54)
Greenall Whitley Dark Mild,
Bitter Ⓔ
1930s-style pub with
attractive oak panelling
♪♣♠♥⑧

The ♨ symbol denotes a pub
with a real solid fuel fire

Billingham 30D3

-3; 5.30–10.30

Smiths Arms
The Green
Cameron Lion Bitter Ⓗ
Large, comfortable pub in
pleasant setting ♪♣♠

Three Horseshoes
Cowpen Bewley (off A689)
Morning opening: 11.30
Cameron Strongarm Ⓗ
Rural respite from industrial
area ♣Ⓖ♍Ⓢ

Crotton 30E3

-3; 7–10.30

Green Tree
High Street
Cameron Strongarm Ⓗ
Friendly, quiet, multi-roomed
local ┌♣Ⓡ♦

Egglescliffe 30C4

-3; 6–10.30

Pot & Glass
Church Road
Draught Bass Ⓗ
Charming village pub on
outskirts of Yarm
♣♫♠Ⓡ Ⓖ♦Ⓢ

Eston 30D3

-3; 5.30–10.30

Eston Hotel
Fabian Road (off A175)
Middlesbrough 453451
Samuel Smith Old Brewery
Bitter Ⓗ
Large, popular pub opposite
Langbaurgh Town Hall
♣♫♠Ⓛ♠Ⓡ Ⓖ♦Ⓢ

Queens Head
Guisborough Street
Cameron Strongarm Ⓗ
Small, friendly pub
♣♠Ⓢ

Guisborough 30E3

-3; 5.30–10.30

Anchor
Belmangate (off A171)
32715
Samuel Smith Old Brewery
Bitter Ⓗ
Small, busy cottage pub with
quoit club ♠♫♣♫Ⓖ♦

Globe
Northgate (A173)
Cameron Strongarm Ⓗ & Ⓔ
Busy public bar with large
modernised lounge
♣♦

Hartlepool 30D2

-3; 6–10.30

Causeway
Stranton ✆ 73954
Opens at 11.30 am & 7 pm
Cameron Strongarm Ⓗ
Busy pub close to Cameron's
Brewery ♣Ⓡ♦

Lion Hotel
Clarence Road
Opens 4.30 pm Friday
Cameron Lion Bitter Ⓗ
Large, pleasant pub near
football ground
♪♠♠Ⓡ♦Ⓢ♦

New Inn
Durham Street
Cameron Strongarm Ⓗ
Busy, friendly pub on the road
to the headland ♪♠♦Ⓢ

Lazenby 30D3

11–3; 6–10.30

Nags Head
Eston Road
Draught Bass Ⓗ
Unspoilt village local ♪♠♦

Loftus 31E3

11–3; 5.30–10.30

Angel
Market Place (A174)
Draught Bass Ⓔ
Quaint old one-room local ♪♠

Marske-by-the-Sea 30E3

11–3; 5.30–10.30

Clarendon
90 High Street (A1085)
Cameron Strongarm
Theakston Best Bitter, XB Ⓗ
Known as the 'Middle House'
♪♠Ⓖ≥

Middlesbrough 30D3

11–3; 5.30–10.30

Bodega Bar
Royal Exchange, Wilson Street
Closes 8 pm; closed Saturday
evenings and Sundays
Theakston Best Bitter, XB Ⓗ
Cosy cellar bar, popular with
businessmen and students
Ⓡ♦Ⓢ≥

Linthorpe Hotel
The Crescent, Linthorpe
Village ✆ 819287
Samuel Smith Old Brewery
Bitter Ⓗ
Real ale in pleasant public bar
♪♠♫♠Ⓡ♦

Princess Alice
Newport Road ✆ 243838
Draught Bass
Stones Best Bitter Ⓗ
Renovated in inter-war style,
near bus station
┌♪♠♫Ⓖ♦

Try also: Cambridge Hotel
(Sam Smith)

Redcar 30D3

11–3; 6–10.30

Lobster
Coatham Road (off A1085)
Samuel Smith Old
Brewery Bitter Ⓔ

Excellent atmosphere; snooker
table upstairs
┌♪♠♫♫♠Ⓡ Ⓖ♦Ⓢ

Saltburn 30E3

11–3; 5.30–10.30

New Marine Hotel
Marine Parade
✆ Guisborough 22695
Younger No. 3 Ⓗ
Large hotel on cliff-top
♪♠Ⓛ Ⓖ♦

Ship Inn
Old Saltburn
✆ Guisborough 22361
Drybrough Pentland Ⓐ
Old smugglers' haunt at
bottom of Saltburn Bank
♠♫♣♠♫♠Ⓡ Ⓖ♍♦Ⓢ

Victoria
East Dundas Street
Draught Bass
Cameron Lion Bitter,
Strongarm Ⓗ
Excellent recent conversion of
an old warehouse
♪♠♦Ⓢ≥

Stockton on Tees 30C3

11–3; 5.30–10.30

Cricketers Arms
Portrack Lane ✆ 65468
Theakston Best Bitter,
Old Peculier
Whitbread Castle Eden Ale
Bulmer Cider Ⓗ
Recently refurbished town
pub ♪♠♠Ⓖ Ⓢ

Lord Nelson
King Street
Cameron Strongarm Ⓗ
Comfortable pub in housing
estate ♪♠♠Ⓢ

Masham
Hartburn Village
Draught Bass Ⓗ
Cosy and deservedly popular
♪♠♠

Sun Inn
Knowle Street
Open until 4.30 pm Wed.
Draught Bass Ⓗ
Busy, 3 roomed town pub
♠┌♠♦

Wild Ox
136 Norton Road
Cameron Strongarm Ⓗ
Friendly and cosy pub with
four rooms ♪♠♠Ⓡ♦Ⓢ

Thornaby 30C4

11–3; 5.30–10.30

Collingwood
Trafalgar Street
Saturday evening opening: 7
Cameron Strongarm Ⓗ
Small, friendly and
well-modernised
┌♪♠Ⓡ♦Ⓢ≥

Cornwall

Albaston 3H6

10.30–2.30; 6–10.30 (11 F, S and summer)
Queens Head
Near Gunnislake (off A390)
Courage Heavy, Best Bitter, Directors H
Taunton Cider G
Lively local in old mining area
🏠🍴♣🛏R▣⊙&≢

Altarnun 3G5

11–2.30; 6–10.30 (11 F, S and summer)
Rising Sun
(Off A30/A395) OS 825215
Butcombe Bitter
Golden Hill Exmoor Ale
Martlet Brighton Special
Whitbread Bitter, Flowers Original Bitter H
Popular 16th-century country pub, frequent guest beers
🏠🍴♣🛏ℐR⊙&Å

Bodmin 3F6

10.30–2.30; 6–10.30 (11 F, S, and summer)
Hole in the Wall
Crockwell Street (off A30)
Closed Sundays
Draught Bass
Halls Harvest Bitter H
Popular pub, was a debtors' prison 🏠🍴♣ℐ⊙&

Boscastle 3F4

10.30–2.30; 5.30–10.30 (11 F, S and summer)
Cobweb
(B3263) ☎ 278
Butcombe Bitter
Cotleigh Tawny Bitter G
Wadworth 6X
Whitbread Bitter H
Flowers Original Bitter G
Ancient pub close to harbour
🏠🍴♣🛏ℐ🛏R🕒⊙Å

Camborne 2C8

10.30–2.30; 5.30–10.30 (11 F, S and summer)
Red Jackets
Trevenson Street
Devenish Bitter, Cornish Best Bitter H
Coates Cider (summer) G
Friendly town local 🏠🍴♣▣⊙≢

Cargreen 3H6

11–2.30; 6–10.30 (11 F, S and summer)
Spaniards
(Off A388) ☎ Saltash 2830
Draught Bass
St. Austell Tinners, Hicks Special
Wadworth 6X H
Hills Cider G
Fine pub in magnificent riverside position
🏠🍴♣♣🛏ℐ🛏R🕒⊙&

Chilsworthy 3H6

10.30–2.30; 6–10.30 (11 F, S and summer)
White Hart
(Off A390) OS 722416
Eldridge Pope Royal Oak
Fuller London Pride

Hook Norton Old Hookey
Wadworth 6X
Whitbread Flowers Original Bitter H
Countryman & Hills Cider G
Free house overlooking Tamar Valley, frequent guest beers
🏠🍴♣🛏ℐ🛏R⊙&≢

Chiverton Cross 2C7

11–2.30; 6–10.30 (11 F, S and summer)
Chiverton Arms
(A30) ☎ Truro 560240
Devenish Bitter,
Cornish Best Bitter H
Lively, popular country pub
🏠🍴♣ℐ🛏🕒⊙🍴⊙Å

Comford 2C8

10.30–2.30; 6–10.30 (11 F, S and summer)
Fox & Hounds
(A393) ☎ St. Day 820251
Draught Bass
St. Austell BB G
Comfortable roadside pub
🏠🍴♣ℐ🛏🕒⊙🍴⊙

Crantock 2D6

11–3; 6–11
Old Albion
☎ 830243
Courage Best Bitter H
400-year-old thatched pub
🏠ℐ🕒🍴⊙

Cremyll 3H7

10.30–2.30; 5.30–10.30 (11 F, S and summer)
Edgcumbe Arms
(B3247) OS 454535
Courage Best Bitter, Directors H
18th-century pub overlooking Plymouth Sound
ℐ♣🛏ℐR⊙Å

Cripplesease 2B8

10.30–2.30; 5.30–10.30 (11 F, S and summer)
Engine Inn
(B3311) OS 500368
☎ Cockwells 740204
Devenish Bitter, Cornish Best Bitter H
Taunton Cider G
Pleasant pub in rural area
🏠🍴♣🛏R🕒🍴⊙Å

Falmouth 2D8

10.30–2.30; 6–10.30 (11 F, S and summer)
Four Winds
Dracaena Avenue
St. Austell XXXX, BB, Tinners, Hicks Special H
Bulmer Cider G
Comfortable, refurbished house
ℐ♣🛏ℐ🛏⊙

Seven Stars
The Moor
Draught Bass
St. Austell Hicks Special
Whitbread Bitter G
Free house in same family for five generations
♣ℐ⊙≢

Fowey 3F7

11–2.30; 6–10.30 (11 F, S and summer)
King of Prussia
Town Quay (off A3082)
☎ 2450
St. Austell BB, Tinners, Hicks Special H
Situated on quay at water's edge
🏠ℐ♣🛏R🕒🍴⊙Å

Fraddon 2E7

11–3; 6–10.30 (11 F, S and summer)
Blue Anchor
☎ St. Austell 860352
St. Austell Tinners, Hicks Special H
Large, main road pub
ℐ♣🛏ℐ🛏R🕒🍴⊙

Golant 3F7

11–2.30; 6–10.30 (11 F, S and summer)
Fisherman's Arms
Fore Street, off Riverside
(Off B3269) ☎ 2453
Courage Best Bitter H
Taunton Cider G
Unspoilt riverside pub, popular with boating fraternity
🏠🍴♣🛏ℐ🛏R🕒⊙&Å

Goldsithney 2B8

10.30–2.30; 6–10.30 (11 F, S and summer)
Trevelyan Arms
(B3280) ☎ Penzance 710453
Devenish Bitter, Cornish Best Bitter H
Pleasantly modernised, large popular house
🏠🍴♣🛏R⊙Å

Gunwalloe 2C9

11–2.30; 6–10.30 (11 F, S and summer)
Halzephron
(Off A3085)
☎ Mullion 240406
Devenish Bitter, Cornish Best Bitter H
Comfortable old smugglers' haunt
🏠🍴♣🛏🛏🕒🍴⊙Å

Hayle 2B8

11–2.30; 6–10.30 (11 F, S and summer)
Bird in Hand
Bird Paradise, Trelissick Road (off A30) ☎ 753365
Paradise Bitter, Artists Ale, Victory Ale H
Converted coach house with own brewery; guest beers
ℐ♣🛏ℐ🛏R🕒🍴⊙Å

Helston 2C9

10.30–2.30; 6–10.30 (11 F, S and summer)
Blue Anchor
50 Coinagehall Street ☎ 6282
Blue Anchor Medium, Best, Special Bitter, Extra Special Bitter H
15th-century thatched house with own small brewery
🏠♣🛏R⊙Å

Kilkhampton 3G3

10.30–2.30; 5.30–10.30 (11 F, S and summer)
London Inn
(A39) ✆ 205
Draught Bass
Usher Best Bitter Ⓗ
Pleasant roadside pub
♪♣♠⚕🚼🚬Ⓡ☾🌑🍴⑤♿

Kingsand 3H7

10.30–2.30; 5.30–10.30 (11 F, S and summer)
Devonport Inn
The Cleave
Courage Best Bitter Ⓗ
Traditional pub overlooking
Plymouth Sound ♪♣⚕⑤≷

Landrake 3G6

10.30–2.30; 5.30–10.30 (11 F, S and summer)
Bullers Arms
(Off A38) ✆ 283
Courage Best Bitter Ⓖ
Unspoilt village local
♠♪♣🚼⚕🚬Ⓡ☾🌑⑤

Lanlivery 3F6

11–2.30; 6–10.30 (11 F, S and summer)
Crown
(Off A390) ✆ Bodmin 872707
Draught Bass
Welsh PA Ⓗ
Comfortable and popular
12th-century inn
♪♣🚼⚕🚬Ⓡ☾🌑🍴⑤♿ Å

Lanreath 3F7

10.30–2.30; 6–10.30 (11 F, S and summer)
Punch Bowl
(Off B3359) ✆ 20218
Draught Bass
St. Austell Tinners Ⓗ
Famous 400-year-old inn
♠♪♣🚼⚕🚬Ⓡ☾🌑🍴⑤♿ Å

Launceston 3G5

11–2.30; 5.30–10.30 (11 F, S and summer)
White Hart Hotel
The Square (off A30) ✆ 2013
Closes 5 pm Tuesdays,
re-opens 6
Halls Harvest Bitter
Ind Coope Burton Ale Ⓗ
Old coaching house in town
centre ♠♪♣🚼🚼⚕Ⓡ☾🌑🍴⑤

Lerryn 3F7

10.30–2.30; 5.30–10.30 (11 F, S and summer)
Ship
(Off A390) ✆ Bodmin 872374
Draught Bass
**Devenish Cornish Best
Bitter** Ⓗ
Old pub by River Lerryn
♪♣♠🚬Ⓡ🌑⑤♿

Liskeard 3G6

10.30–2.30; 5.30–10.30 (11 F, S and summer)
Barley Sheaf
Church Street (off A38)
**St. Austell BB, Tinners, Hicks
Special** Ⓗ
Old and friendly town pub
♠♪♣🚼🚼⚕Ⓟ🌑♿≷

Looe 3G7

10.30–2.30; 5.30–10.30 (11 F, S and summer)
Bullers Arms
East Looe ✆ 3558
Usher Best Bitter Ⓗ
Friendly pub with oak beams
♪♣☾🌑🍴 (summer) 🅿≷

Lostwithiel 3F6

11–2.30; 6–10.30 (11 F, S and summer)
Royal Oak
Duke Street (off A390)
✆ Bodmin 872552
Draught Bass
Eldridge Pope Royal Oak
Gibbs Mew Bishops Tipple
St. Austell Tinners
Wadworth 6X
Welsh PA
**Whitbread Flowers Original
Bitter** Ⓗ
Deservedly popular pub,
frequent guest beers
♪♣🚼🚬Ⓡ☾🌑🍴⑤≷

Mabe Burnthouse
2D8

11–2.30; 6–10.30 (11 F, S and summer)
New Inn
✆ Penryn 73428
**Devenish Bitter, Cornish Best
Bitter** Ⓗ
300-year-old pub, good food
♠♪♣🚼⚕🚬Ⓡ☾🌑🍴⑤ Å

Manaccan 2D9

11–2.30; 6–10.30 (11 F, S and summer)
New Inn
✆ 323
**Devenish Bitter, Cornish Best
Bitter** Ⓖ
Superb unspoilt thatched pub
♠♣🚬Ⓡ☾🌑

Metherell 3H6

11.30–2.30; 7–10.30 (11 F, S and summer)
Carpenters Arms
(Off A390) OS 409695
✆ St. Dominick 50242
Draught Bass Ⓖ
Courage Best Bitter Ⓗ
**Whitbread Flowers Original
Bitter** Ⓖ
14th-century inn off the
beaten track ♠♪♣⚕🚼Ⓗ🌑⑤♿ Å

Mevagissey 3E7

11–2.30; 6–10.30 (11 F, S and summer)
Kings Arms
17 Fore Street (off B3273)
**Courage Best Bitter, Directors
Taunton Cider** Ⓗ
Popular town-centre pub,
home-made food ♪♣☾🌑⑤ Å

Mullion 2C9

10.30–2.30; 6–10.30 (11 F, S and summer)
Old Inn
Churchtown (off A3083)
✆ 240240
**Devenish Bitter, Cornish Best
Bitter** Ⓗ
Historic inn on Lizard
peninsula ♠♪♣🚼⚕🚬Ⓡ☾🌑

Nancenoy 2D8

11–2.30; 6–10.30 (11 F, S and summer)
Trengilly Wartha
(Off B3291)
✆ Constantine 40631
**Devenish Bitter, Cornish Best
Bitter**
Trengilly Bitter Ⓗ
Comfortable hotel in splendid
countryside, with a 'house'
beer ♠♪♣🚼⚕🚬Ⓡ☾🌑⑤

Pendeen 2A8

10.30–2.30; 6–10.30 (11 F, S and summer)
Radjel
(B3306) ✆ Penzance 788446
St. Austell Tinners Ⓗ
Well-appointed, comfortable
inn ♠♪♣⚕🚼🚬Ⓗ🌑🍴⑤ Å

Pendoggett 3E5

10.30–2.30; 5.30–10.30 (11 F, S and summer)
Cornish Arms
(B3314) ✆ Port Isaac 263
Draught Bass
Butcombe Bitter Ⓖ
**Whitbread Flowers
Original Bitter** Ⓗ
16th-century ale-house with
exceptional food
♠♪🚼⚕🚬Ⓡ☾🌑🍴⑤♿

Penzance 2B8

10.30–2.30; 6–10.30 (11 F, S and summer)
Globe
Queen Square
**Devenish Bitter, Cornish Best
Bitter** Ⓗ
Friendly local in town centre
♠♪♣🍴⑤♿≷

Union Hotel
Chapel Street ✆ 2319
Evening opening: 5.30
Draught Bass Ⓖ
Hotel with traditional and
fashionable bars
♠♪⚕🚼🚬Ⓡ☾🌑🍴⑤≷

Perranwell 2D8

11–2.30; 6–10.30 (11 F, S and summer)
Royal Oak
✆ Truro 863175
**Devenish Bitter, Cornish Best
Bitter** Ⓗ
Pleasant village pub with good
food ♠♪♣⚕🚬Ⓡ☾🌑⑤ Å≷

Phillack 2B8

11–2.30; 6–10.30 (11 F, S and summer)
Bucket of Blood
Churchtown Road (off A30)
✆ Hayle 752378
**St. Austell BB, XXXX, Hicks
Special** Ⓗ
Lively village pub with a
fascinating history
♠♪♣🚼⚕♣Ⓡ☾🌑🍴⑤ Å≷

Philleigh 2D8

11–2.30; 7–10.30 (11 F, S and summer)
Roseland Inn
(Off A3078) ✆ Portscatho 254

Devenish Bitter, Cornish Best Bitter Ⓗ
17th-century pub, full of character ▥♪♣⬛♨⌂Ⓖ☺Å

Piece 2C8

11–2.30; 5.30–10.30 (11 F, S and summer)
Countryman Inn
✆ Redruth 215960
Usher Best Bitter Ⓗ
Friendly pub on Carn Brea
▥♪♣♨⬛Ⓡ☺🐕Ⓢ Å

Polgooth 3E7

10.30–2.30; 5.30–10.30 (11 F, S and summer)
Polgooth Inn
(Off A390) ✆ St. Austell 4089
St. Austell BB, Hicks Special Ⓗ
16th-century inn, formerly a counting house
▥♪♣⬛♨⬛Ⓡ Ⓢ♿Å

Polperro 3F7

10.30–2.30; 5.30–10.30 (11 F, S and summer)
Three Pilchards
Courage Best Bitter Ⓗ
Old pub by harbour ♪♣Ⓢ

Portscatho 2D8

11–2.30; 6–10.30 (11 F, S and summer)
Plume of Feathers
(Off A3078) ✆ 321
St. Austell BB, Tinners Ⓗ
Hicks Special Ⓖ
Friendly old village local
▥♪♣⬛⬛Ⓡ🐕🐕Ⓢ Å

Redruth 2C8

10.30–2.30; 6–10.30 (11 F, S and summer)
Mount Ambrose Inn
Mount Ambrose ✆ 215809
Supper licence till midnight
St. Austell XXXX, BB, Hicks Special Ⓗ
Pleasant old town local
▥♪♣♨⬛⬛Ⓖ🐕🐕Ⓢ

St. Agnes 2C7

11–2.30; 6–10.30 (11 F, S and summer)
Railway Inn
(B3277) ✆ 2310
Winter evening opening: 7
Devenish Bitter, Cornish Best Bitter Ⓗ
Quaint, popular village local
♣⬛♨Ⓡ Ⓢ Å

St. Austell 3E7

10.30–2.30; 5.30–10.30 (11 F, S and summer)
Queens Head
Fore Street (A390) ✆ 5452
Courage Heavy, Best Bitter, Directors Ⓗ
Friendly 14th-century hotel near church ♪♣⬛Ⓡ Ⓢ🐕≷

St. Blazey 3F7

10.30–2.30; 6–10.30 (11 F, S and summer)
Britannia
Tregrehan (A390) ✆ Par 2889
Draught Bass
Devenish Bitter, Cornish Best Bitter Ⓗ

16th-century inn, good food
▥♪♣⬛♨⬛Ⓡ Ⓖ🐕🐕Ⓢ Å

St. Columb 2D6

11–3; 6.30–10.30 (11 F, S and summer)
New Inn
✆ 880485
Devenish Bitter, Cornish Best Bitter Ⓗ
Pleasant town pub with keen and friendly landlord
▥♪♣⬛♨⬛Ⓡ Ⓖ🐕Ⓢ Å

St. Ives 2B8

10.30–2.30; 6–10.30 (11 F, S and summer)
Union
Fore Street
Courage Best Bitter Ⓖ
Lively pub in centre of busy resort ▥♣🐕Ⓢ Å≷

St. Just 2A8

11–2.30; 6–10.30 (11 F, S and summer)
Kings Arms
Market Square ✆ Penzance 788545
Winter evening opening: 7
St. Austell BB, Hicks Special
Bulmer Cider Ⓖ
Friendly family pub in lively village ▥♪♣⬛♨Ⓖ🐕🐕Ⓢ♿

St. Kew 3E5

10.30–2.30; 5.30–10.30 (11 F, S and summer)
St. Kew Inn
✆ St. Mabyn 259
St. Austell Tinners, Hicks Special Ⓖ
Delightful village pub
▥♨⬛Ⓖ🐕🐕Ⓢ Å

St. Mabyn 3E6

11–2.30; 6–11
St. Mabyn Inn
(Off A39) ✆ 266
Draught Bass
Whitbread Bitter, Flowers Original Bitter Ⓗ
Bulmer Cider Ⓖ
Typical friendly village pub
▥♪♣⬛♨⬛Ⓡ Ⓖ🐕Ⓢ♿Å

St. Mawgan 2D6

10.30–2.30; 6–10.30 (11 F, S and summer)
Falcon
✆ 225
Devenish Cornish Best Bitter
St. Austell BB, Tinners Ⓗ
Pleasant country pub in rural setting ⬛♨⬛Ⓖ🐕Ⓢ

St. Neot 3F6

10.30–2.30; 5.30–10.30 (11 F, S and summer)
London
(Off A38) ✆ Dobwalls 20263
Usher Best Bitter Ⓗ
Friendly village inn next to church ▥♪♣♨⬛⬛Ⓡ🐕Ⓢ

Stratton 3G3

10.30–2.30; 5.30–11
Kings Arms
Howls Road (A3072)
Courage Best Bitter Ⓗ

Old coaching house
♣⬛Ⓡ Ⓖ🐕Ⓢ♿

Torpoint 3H7

10.30–2.30; 6–10.30 (11 F, S and summer)
Kings Arms
37 Fore Street (A374)
✆ Plymouth 812882
Courage Heavy, Best Bitter Ⓗ
Pleasant local near Plymouth Ferry
♪♣♨Ⓡ Ⓖ🐕Ⓢ

Tregadillett 3G5

11–2.30; 6–10.30 (11 F, S and summer)
Eliot Arms
Square & Compass (A30)
✆ Launceston 2051
Devenish Cornish Best Bitter Ⓗ
Unspoilt 14th-century pub
▥♪♣⬛♨⬛Ⓡ Ⓖ🐕🐕Ⓢ Å

Tresillian 2D7

11–2.30; 6–10.30 (11 F, S and summer)
Wheel Inn
(A39) ✆ 293
Devenish Cornish Best Bitter Ⓗ
Coates Cider Ⓖ
Attractive thatched pub
♪♨⬛🐕Ⓢ

Truro 2D7

11–2.30; 5–10.30 (11 F, S and summer)
City Inn
Pydar Street
Courage Heavy, Best Bitter Ⓗ
Splendid local
♪⬛♨Ⓖ🐕Ⓢ

Wig & Pen
Castle Street ✆ 3028
St. Austell Tinners, Hicks Special Ⓗ
Comfortable pub, lintels were cathedral steps
▥♪♣⬛♨Ⓡ Ⓖ🐕Ⓢ≷

Tywardreath 3F7

11–2.30; 6–10.30 (11 F, S and summer)
New Inn
(Off A3082) ✆ Par 3901
Draught Bass
St. Austell BB, Tinners
Bulmer Cider Ⓖ
Popular and friendly village pub
♪♨⬛🐕Ⓢ♿Å≷

Upton Cross 3G6

10.30–2.30; 5.30–10.30 (11 F, S and summer)
Caradon Inn
(B3254)
Draught Bass Ⓗ
Bodmin Bell Bitter
Cotleigh Tawny Bitter Ⓖ
Whitbread Flowers Original Bitter Ⓗ
Hill Cider Ⓖ
Popular 18th-century country inn
▥♪♣♨⬛Ⓢ♿

Alston 29F2

11–3; 6–10.30 (11 F, S)
Swans Head Inn
Town Head (B6277) ✆ 81680
Drybrough Pentland Ⓗ
Friendly pub; the highest pub in the highest market town in England ♪♣🏠ℝⒺ🕒Ⓖ🅰

Ambleside 28D4

10.30–3; 6–10.30 (11 F, S)
Golden Rule
Smithy Brow (off A591) ✆ 2257
Hartley Mild, XB Ⓗ
Popular with all types
🏠♣🎱🍴Ⓢ

Try also: Royal Oak (Younger)

Appleby-in-Westmorland 29F3

11–3; 6–10.30 (11 F, S)
Crown & Cushion
Boroughgate
Vaux Sunderland Draught Bitter Ⓗ
The only Sunderland draught in the area 🏠♪♣🎱Ⓢ

Golden Ball
High Wiend ✆ 51493
Marston Burton Bitter, Pedigree (summer) Ⓗ
Small, friendly pub popular with enthusiastic drinkers
♪♣Ⓖ🍴Ⓢ🅱

Arnside 28E6

11–3; 6–10.30 (11 F, S)
Albion
Promenade (B5282)
Yates & Jackson Mild, Bitter Ⓔ
Busy, cosy pub 🏠♪♣🎱🍴🏠ℝ🤝

Askam-in-Furness 28C6

11–3; 6–10.30 (11 F, S)
Askam Hotel
Victoria Street (off A595)
Greenall Whitley Mild, Bitter Ⓗ
Refurbished free house on town outskirts
🏠♪♣🎱ℝⓈ🅱🅰🤝

Aspatria 28C2

11–3; 5.30–10.30 (11 F, S)
Fox & Hounds
King Street (A596)
Jennings Mild, Bitter Ⓗ
Pleasant and busy small hotel
♪♣ⒼⓈ

Barngates 28D4

11–3; 5.30–10.30 (11 F, S)
Drunken Duck
(Off B5286)
✆ Hawkshead 347
Jennings Bitter

Theakston XB, Old Peculier
Westmorland Slaters
Bitter Ⓗ
Cheerful crossroads pub in lovely setting; range of beers varies 🏠♣🎱🍴🏠ℝⓈ🅰

Barrow-in-Furness 28C6

11–3; 5.30–10.30 (11 F, S)
Crofters
Holbeck Park Drive
Thwaites Mild, Bitter Ⓗ
Converted farmhouse, very stylish ♪🎱🏠🤝Ⓢ

Crystal Palace
Dalkeith Street (off A590)
Jennings Mild, Bitter Ⓗ
Cosy, popular town-centre local ♪♣ℝⓈ🚼

Dominics (Wellington Inn)
Rawlinson Street (off A590)
Bass XXXX Mild, Toby Light Ⓔ
Stones Best Bitter Ⓗ
A beer house of the old tradition ♣ℝ🍴

Theatre Bar
Cavendish Street (off A590)
✆ 25272
Bass XXXX Mild, Toby Light, Draught Bass
Stones Best Bitter Ⓗ
Well-appointed town pub, busy lunchtimes ♪🎱ℝⒼ🍴🚼

Barrows Green 29E5

11–3; 6–10.30 (11 F, S)
Punch Bowl
(A65) ✆ Sedgwick 60267
Younger Scotch Bitter, No 3 Ⓗ
Roadhouse of character with oak settles ♪♣🎱🏠Ⓖ🍴🚼

Bassenthwaite 28C3

11–3; 5.30–10.30 (11 F, S)
Sun Inn
(Off A591) ✆ Bass Lake 439
Jennings Bitter Ⓗ
Comfortable village pub in picturesque surroundings
🏠♪🎱🏠ℝ🏠ℝⒼ🍴Ⓢ🅰

Baycliffe 28D6

10.30–3; 6–10.30 (11 F, S)
Farmers Arms
(Off A5087)
Hartley Mild, Bitter, XB Ⓗ
Popular, comfortable pub in picturesque village 🏠Ⓢ

Beckermet 28B4

11–3; 5.30–10.30 (11 F, S)
Royal Oak
(Off A595) ✆ 551
Hartley XB
Younger Scotch Bitter Ⓗ
Pleasant and friendly free house 🏠♣🎱🏠ℝⓈ🍴🏠ℝⒼ🍴Ⓢ

Bewcastle 32C8

11.30–3; 6–10.30 (11 F, S)
Limekiln Inn
OS 565745 ✆ Roadhead 229
Theakston Best Bitter Ⓗ
Modernised local in tourist area 🏠♣🅰🎱🏠ℝⓈ🍴Ⓢ🅱

Blencow 28E2

11–3; 6–10.30 (11 F, S)
Clickham Inn
(B5288) 3 miles south of village
Marston Mercian Mild, Burton Bitter, Pedigree Ⓗ
Attractive roadside inn, friendly welcome assured
🍴♣🅰🎱🏠Ⓖ🍴Ⓢ

Bolton Low Houses 28C2

11–3; 6–10.30 (11 F, S)
Oddfellows
(Off A595) ✆ Wigton 2049
Jennings Mild, Bitter Ⓗ
Welcoming country local of great character
🍴♣🏠ℝⒼ🍴🕒Ⓢ

Bowland Bridge 28E5

11–3; 6–10.30 (F, S)
Hare & Hounds
(Off A5074) OS 417895
✆ Crosthwaite 333
Tetley Walker Bitter Ⓗ
Large Lakeland inn, country and western on Wednesdays
🏠🍴♣🅰🎱🏠ℝⒼ🍴🕒Ⓢ

Bowness-on-Windermere 28E5

11–3; 5.30–10.30 (11 F, S)
Cabin
Lake Road ✆ 5678
Winter opening: 11.30 am & 6 pm
Hartley XB
Thwaites Bitter Ⓗ & Ⓔ
Live music every night, monthly guest beers in season 🍴♣🅰🎱🏠ℝⓈ🅰🤝

Hole in t'Wall (New Hall Inn)
Robinson Place
Hartley XB Ⓗ
Busy pub with bags of character 🏠🍴♣🅰🎱🤝🏠Ⓢ🅰🤝

Royal Oak Inn
Brantfell Road ✆ 3970
Whitbread Castle Eden Ale Ⓗ
Traditional small village pub, interesting matchbox collection ♪♣🤝🏠ℝ🅰Ⓢ🅰🤝

Brampton 29F3

11–3; 6–10.30 (11 F, S)
New Inn
(Off A66) ✆ Appleby 51231
Younger Scotch Bitter Ⓗ

Reputed to be the home of Appleby Fair
🏰♪♣✿🚗☾◗🍺[S]⛺

Brampton 29E1

11–3; 5.30–10.30 (11 F, S)

Scotch Arms
Main Street (A69) ☎ 2397
Evening opening: 6.30
McEwan 80/- [H]
Friendly, hospitable town-centre pub ♪♣✿🚗🍺[S]

Broadfield 28E2

11–3; 5.30–10.30 (11 F, S)

Crown
OS 409465 ☎ Southwaite 467
Matthew Brown Mild, Bitter [H]
Recently modernised country inn 🏰♪♣⊞✿🚗☾◗🍺[S]⛺

Brough 29G4

11–3; 6–10.30 (11 F, S)

Golden Fleece Hotel
(Off A66) ☎ 314
Whitbread Castle Eden Ale [H]
Village local proud of its reputation 🏰♪♣🚗▣☾◗🍺[S]♿

Broughton-in-Furness 28C5

11–3; 6–10.30 (11 F, S)

Black Cock
Princes Street (off A595)
Open all day Tuesdays
Matthew Brown John Peel Bitter [H]
16th century pub, full of character 🏰♣⊞✿☾◗[S]🚆

Burton-in-Kendal 29E6

11–3; 6–10.30 (11 F, S)

Kings Arms
Main Street (A6070)
☎ 781409
Mitchells Mild, Bitter, Extra Special Bitter [H]
Comfortable pub with small drinking areas 🏰♪♣⊞🚗▣[S]

Buttermere 28C3

11–3; 5.30–10.30 (11 F, S)

Bridge Hotel
(B5289) ☎ 252
Evening opening: 6; closed Nov–Feb
Theakston Mild, Best Bitter, Old Peculier
Bulmer Cider [H]
Friendly tourist hotel in beautiful valley ✿🚗▣☾◗🍺♿⛺

Cark-in-Cartmel 28D6

11–3; 6–10.30 (11 F, S)

Engine Inn
(B5278) ☎ Flookburgh 341
Bass XXXX Mild, Draught Bass [H]
Old up-market pub
♪♣⊞✿🚗▣☾◗🍺[S]🚆

Carlisle 28D1

11–3; 5.30–10.30 (11 F, S)

Crown Hotel
Botchergate (A6)
McEwan 70/- [H]
Convivial city-centre pub with superb Victorian bar
♪♣[R][S]🚆

Crown Inn
Scotland Road (A7)
McEwan 70/-
Younger No 3 [H]
Attractive roadside inn with wood-panelled smoking room
♪♣⊞✿[R]☾◗🍺[S]

Friars Tavern
Devonshire Street
Whitbread Castle Eden Ale [H]
Lively city-centre pub, real ale in downstairs bar ♪♣☾🍺[S]🚆

Theakston
London Road (A6)
Theakston Dark Mild, Best Bitter, XB, Old Peculier [H]
Tastefully renovated - only Theakstons in city
♪♣✿🚗▣[R]☾◗🍺[S]

Woolpack Inn
Milbourne Street (off A595)
☎ 32459
Jennings Mild, Bitter [H]
Popular, lively pub; beware of the dog ⌐♪♣▣☾◗[S]

Cartmel 28D6

10.30–3; 6–10.30 (11 F, S)

Pig & Whistle
Town End
Hartley XB [H]
The place to meet the Cartmel locals; landlord member of Magic Circle ♪♣✿🍺[S]

Royal Oak
Market Place ☎ 259
Duttons Bitter
Whitbread Castle Eden Ale [H]
Pleasant old pub with oak beams, brasses and local prints
🏰♪♣☾◗🍺[S]♿

Cleator Moor 28B4

11–3; 5.30–10.30 (11 F, S)

New Crown
Bowthorn Road (B5294/B5295)
Hartley Bitter, XB [H]
Bustling town local
⌐♪♣⊞[R]🍺[S]♿

Cockermouth 28C3

11–3; 5.30–10.30 (11 F, S)

Swan
Kirkgate
Evening opening: 6.30
Jennings Mild, Bitter [H]
Small, popular town pub ♪♣[S]

Tithe Barn Hotel
Station Street ☎ 822179
Open all day Monday
Jennings Mild, Bitter, Special Bitter (occasional) [H]
Comfortable town pub
♪♣[R]☾🍺[S]

Coniston 28D5

11–3; 5.30–10.30 (11 F, S)

Yewdale Hotel
(Off A593) ☎ 280
Hartley XB [E]
Smart, homely Lakeside house
🏰♪♣⊞✿🚗▣[R]☾◗[S]♿⛺

Crook 28E5

10.30–3; 6–10.30 (11 F, S and summer)

Sun Inn
(B5284) ☎ Stavely 821351
Opens 11.30 am & 6.30 pm in winter
Lorimer & Clark Best Scotch
Vaux Sunderland Draught Bitter, Samson [H]
Well-patronised roadside village local, good food, no jukebox 🏰♣⊞✿🚗[R]☾◗🍺[S]⛺

Crooklands 29E6

11–3; 6–10.30 (11 F, S)

Crooklands Hotel
(A65) ☎ 432
Marston Burton Bitter, Pedigree, Owd Rodger
Younger Scotch Bitter [H]
Excellent conversion of old buildings; beer range varies
🏰⌐♪♣⊞✿🚗▣[R]☾◗🍺[S]♿⛺

Crosby-on-Eden 28E1

11–3; 5.30–10.30 (11 F, S)

Stag Inn
(B6264)
Matthew Brown Mild, Bitter, John Peel Bitter [H]
Popular country local with low beams and narrow doors
🏰♪♣⊞✿🚗☾◗🍺[S]

Dalston 28D1

11–3; 5.30–10.30 (11 F, S)

Blue Bell
(B5299) ☎ Carlisle 710157
Younger No 3 [H]
Attractive village local
♪♣[R]☾🍺[S]🚆

Dalton-in-Furness 28C6

11–3; 5.30–10.30 (11 F, S)

Black Bull
Tudor Square (A590)
Hartley Mild, Bitter, XB [E]
Popular, central Whitbread pub ♪♣🍺

Red Lion
Market Street (A590)
☎ 62180
Tetley Mild, Bitter [H]
Comfortable and popular 16th-century inn, recently refurbished 🏰⌐♪♣✿▣[R][S]

Dent 29F5

11–3; 6–10.30 (11 Thu, F, S)
Sun
Main Street *C* 208
Younger Scotch
Bitter, No 3 Ⓗ & Ⓔ
Unspoilt 17th-century village
inn

Drigg 28B5

11–3; 5.30–10.30 (11 F, S)
Victoria Hotel
(Off B5344) *C* Holmrook 231
Jennings Mild, Bitter Ⓗ
Modernised pub by railway
station

Eaglesfield 28C3

11–3; 5.30–10.30 (11 F, S)
Black Cock
(Off A5086) OS 098282
Jennings Mild, Bitter Ⓗ
Friendly village local with
brasses and floral decorations

Egremont 28B4

11–3; 5.30–10.30 (11 F, S)
Blue Bell
Main Street (A595)
Hartley Mild, XB Ⓗ
Busy town-centre local

Kings Arms
Main Street (A595) *C* 820231
Bass XXXX Mild, Cask
Bitter, Draught Bass
Jennings Bitter Ⓗ
Smart, modern town-centre
pub

Elterwater 28D4

11–3; 5.30–10.30 (11 F, S)
Britannia Inn
(B5343) *C* Langdale 210
Bass Cask Bitter
Stones Best Bitter
Tetley Walker Mild, Bitter
Bulmer Cider Ⓗ
400-year-old village inn in
beautiful Langdale Valley

Embleton 28C3

11–3; 5.30–10.30 (11 F, S)
Olde Blue Bell
(B5291)
Jennings Mild, Bitter Ⓗ
One-room country local,
friendly landlady

Far Sawrey 28D5

11–3; 5.30–10.30 (11 F, S)
Sawrey Hotel
(B5285)
C Windermere 3425/4651
Jennings Bitter
Theakston Best Bitter,
Old Peculier Ⓗ
Converted stable with stalls
retained

Flookburgh 28D6

10.30–3; 6–10.30 (11 F, S)
Hope & Anchor
10 Market Street *C* 733
Hartley Mild, XB Ⓗ
Large local, welcoming
relaxed atmosphere

Glasson 28C1

11–3; 5.30–10.30 (11 F, S)
Highland Laddie
Opens at 12 noon & 7 pm
Matthew Brown Bitter Ⓗ
Friendly country inn, recently
refurbished

Glenridding 28D3

11–2.30; 6–10.30 (11 F, S)
Glenridding Hotel
(A592) *C* 228/224
Tetley Walker Mild, Bitter Ⓗ
Welcoming and comfortable
hotel overlooking Ullswater;
real ale in Ratchers Tavern

Goose Green 28D2

11–3; 6–10.30 (11 F, S)
String of Horses
(B5299)
Marston Mercian Mild,
Burton Bitter, Pedigree Ⓗ
Friendly, cosy country local

Gosforth 28B4

11–3; 5.30–10.30 (11 F, S)
Globe Hotel
(Off A595) *C* 235
McEwan 80/-
Younger No 3 Ⓗ
Friendly village local

Grasmere 28D4

11–3; 6–10.30 (11 F, S)
Travellers Rest
(A591) *C* 378
Lorimer Best Scotch
Vaux Sunderland Draught
Bitter Ⓗ
Pleasant roadside inn at foot
of Dunmail Raise

Great Broughton 28B3

11–3; 5.30–10.30 (11 F, S)
Punch Bowl
(Off A66)
Jennings Bitter Ⓗ
Excellent bar meals, cosy
atmosphere

Harrington 28B3

11–3; 5.30–10.30 (11 F, S)
Station Hotel
Grecian Terrace *C* 830351
Jennings Mild, Bitter Ⓗ
Friendly local near marina

Hawkshead 28D5

11–3; 5.30–10.30 (11 F, S)
Queens Head
Main Street
Hartley XB Ⓗ
Comfortable and enthusiastic
village pub, good food

Red Lion
Main Street (off B5286) *C* 213
Hartley Mild, XB
Whitbread Castle Eden Ale Ⓗ
Authentic old pub, lots of
black oak

Helton 29E3

12–3; 7–10.30 (11 F, S)
Helton Inn
(Off B5320)
C Hackthorpe 232
Closed Mon–Fri lunchtimes in
winter
Theakston Best Bitter, XB, Old
Peculier
Bulmer Cider Ⓗ
Attractive rural local

High Newton 28D6

11–3; 6–10.30 (11 F, S)
Crown
(Off A590) *C* Newby Bridge
31793/31351
Hartley XB Ⓗ
Roadside country pub with
jazz and folk club

Holme 29E6

11–3; 6–10.30 (11 F, S)
Smithy Inn
(B6384)
C Burton-in-Kendal 781302
Yates & Jackson Mild Ⓔ
Bitter Ⓗ
Rich in rural charm

Ireleth 28C6

12–3; 7–10.30 (11 F, S)
Bay Horse Inn
Ireleth Brow (A595)
Greenall Whitley Mild,
Bitter Ⓗ
Modernised house overlooking
Duddon estuary

Keekle 28B4

11–3; 5.30–10.30 (11 F, S)
Ewe & Lamb
High Padstow OS 005159
Matthew Brown Bitter, John
Peel Bitter Ⓗ
Well-modernised local with
busy lounge trade

Kendal 29E5

10.30–3; 6–10.30 (11 F, S)
Globe Inn
Market Place *C* 24042

Yates & Jackson Bitter E
Busy, comfortable pub with
split-level bar
🏮🍴🍺🔲🅮♿

Ring o'Bells
Kirkland
Vaux Mild
Lorimer Best Scotch H
Unspoilt cosy pub with waiter
service 🏮🍴🚲🍺🔲🎱♿

Sawyers Arms
Stricklandgate ℓ 29737
Hartley Mild, XB H
Town pub with local
entertainment at weekends
🎵🍴🍺🔲🅡♿

Shakespeare
Highgate
Younger Scotch Bitter, No 3 H
Town-centre pub with
theatrical background,
recently renovated 🎵🍺🔲🅢♿

Keswick 28D3

11–3; 5.30–10.30 (11 F, S)
Pack Horse Inn
Pack Horse Yard ℓ 72536
Jennings Mild, Bitter H
One of Keswick's oldest and
friendliest inns
🏮🍴🚲🍺🔲🅡🎱♿⛺

Twa Dogs
Penrith Road (A591) ℓ 72599
Jennings Mild, Bitter H
Friendly local with warm
atmosphere
🎵🍴🚲🍺🔲🅡🎱♿⛺

Kirkby Lonsdale
29F6

11–3; 6–10.30 (11 Thu, F, S)
Royal
Market Square (B6254)
ℓ 71217/71519
Tetley Bitter
Whitbread Castle Eden Ale
Younger Scotch Bitter, No 3 H
Large, well appointed
Georgian hotel
🏮🎵🚲🍺🔲🅡♿⛺

Lindal-in-Furness
28D6

10.30–3; 6–10.30 (11 F, S)
Railway
(Off A590)
Matthew Brown Mild, Bitter,
John Peel Bitter H
Excellent friendly village local
🏮🎵♿

Lorton 28C3

11–3; 5.30–10.30 (11 F, S)
Horseshoe
High Lorton OS 162257
Jennings Bitter, Special
Bitter H
Friendly village local,
originally the maltings for
Jennings brewery
🏮🍴🚲🍺🔲🅡♿🎱♿⛺

Try also: Wheatsheaf
(Jennings)

Lowick Green 28D5

10.30–3; 6–10.30 (11 F, S)
Farmers Arms
(A595) ℓ Greenodd 277
McEwan 80/-
Younger Scotch Bitter H
Comfortable, well-appointed
inn close to lakes
🏮🍴🚲🍺🔲🅡♿🎱♿

Maryport 28B2

11–3; 5.30–10.30 (11 F, S)
Crown
61 Senhouse Street
Jennings Mild, Bitter H
Small, friendly town pub,
recently modernised
🎵🍴🔲🅡♿

Melmerby 29F2

11–3; 5.30–10.30 (11 F, S)
Shepherds Inn
(A686) ℓ Langwathby 217
Marston Burton Bitter,
Pedigree H
Comfortable pub at foot of
fells, good food
🏮🍴🚲🍺🍴♿🎱♿

Monkhill 28D1

11–3; 5.30–10.30 (11 F, S)
Drovers Rest
OS 342586
Jennings Mild, Bitter H
Typically friendly Cumberland
village local 🚲🍴🚲🍺🔲🅡♿

Moota 28C2

11–3; 5.30–10.30 (11 F, S)
Laal Moota
(A595) ℓ Aspatria 20414
Jennings Bitter H
Friendly, comfortable pub,
guest beer 🏮🍴🚲🍴♿⛺

Morland 29F3

11–3; 6–10.30 (11 F, S)
Kings Arms
ℓ 328
Marston Burton Bitter,
Pedigree H
Lively pub in small village
🏮🎵🍴🚲🍴♿🎱♿

Nateby 29G4

11–3; 6–10.30 (11 F, S)
Black Bull
(B6259)
ℓ Kirkby Stephen 71588
Marston Burton Bitter H
At head of beautiful
Mallerstang Valley
🏮🎵🍴🚲🍺🔲♿🎱♿

Near Sawrey 28D5

11–3; 5.30–10.30 (11 F, S)
Tower Bank Arms
(B5285) ℓ Hawkshead 334
Hartley XB H

National Trust pub near
Beatrix Potter's house
🏮🍴🚲🚲🍺🔲🅡♿🎱♿

Nether Wasdale
28C4

11–3; 5.30–10.30 (11 F, S)
Strands Hotel
ℓ Wasdale 237 OS 125040
Jennings Bitter
Younger Scotch Bitter H
Popular country pub, visitors
made welcome
🏮🎵🍴🚲🚲🍺🔲🅡♿🎱♿⛺

Newton 28C6

11–3; 7–10.30 (11 F, S)
Farmers Arms
ℓ 62607
Thwaites Mild, Bitter H
Old-world country pub
🏮🎵🍴🚲🍺♿🎱♿

New Commercial
Matthew Brown Mild, Bitter,
John Peel Bitter H
Country local 🏮🎵🚲🍴♿

Outgate 28D5

11–3; 6–10.30 (11 F, S)
Outgate Inn
(B5286) ℓ Hawkshead 413
Hartley Mild, XB H
Excellent roadside country
pub 🏮🍴🚲🚲🍺🔲🅡♿🎱♿⛺

Penrith 29E3

11–3; 6–10.30 (11 F, S)
Carlton Hotel
Victoria Road (A6) ℓ 62691
Extra hour supper licence
every evening
Tetley Walker Bitter H
Friendly and comfortable
modernised hotel
🎵🍴🚲🍺🔲🅡♿🎱♿

Gloucester Arms
Great Dockray
Whitbread Castle Eden Ale H
Superb and genuine old-world
inn in town centre
🏮🍴🚲🚲🍺🅡♿🎱♿⛺

Salutation Hotel
Victoria Road ℓ 62637
Jennings Mild, Bitter E
Convivial pub, always a
friendly welcome
🎵🚲🚲🍺🔲🅡♿

Pooley Bridge 28E3

10.30–3; 6–10.30 (11 F, S)
Sun Hotel
(Off B5320) ℓ 205
Marston Pedigree H
16th century coaching inn at
north end of Ullswater
🏮🍴🚲🚲🍺🔲🅡♿🎱♿⛺

Ravenstonedale
29G4

11–3; 6–10.30 (11 F, S)
Kings Head
(Off A685)

Tetley Walker Mild, Bitter [H]
Comfortable local in picturesque village
🔥♪♣⊞✿🚗■◐◗🍺Ⓢ

Rockcliffe 32B8

11–3; 5.30–10.30 (11 F, S)

Crown & Thistle

(Off A74) ☎ 378
Younger IPA [H]
Hospitable modernised pub with friendly landlord
🔥Г♪♣⊞✿🚗◐◗🍺Ⓢ

Rowrah 28B3

11–3; 5.30–10.30 (11 F, S)

Stork Hotel

(A5086) ☎ Lamplugh 213
Jennings Mild, Bitter [H]
Friendly, relaxing country local 🔥♪♣⊞✿🚗■🍺

Rydal 28D4

11–3; 6–10.30 (11 F, S)

Glen Rothay Hotel

(A591) ☎ Ambleside 2524
Bass Cask Bitter
Hartley XB [H]
17th-century hotel facing picturesque Rydal Water
♪♣✿🚗■[R]◐◗🍺Ⓢ

St Bees 28B4

11–3; 5.30–10.30 (11 F, S)

Queens Hotel

Main Street (B5345)
☎ Egremont 822287
Theakston Best Bitter
Younger No 3 [H]
Friendly pub in popular seaside village
🔥Г♪♣⊞✿🚗■[R]◐◗🍺Ⓢ♿⛺⇌

Seascale 28B4

11–3; 5.30–10.30 (11 F, S)

Wansfell Hotel

Drigg Road (B5344) ☎ 28301
Bass Cask Bitter [H]
Friendly seaside hotel
♪⊞✿🚗■[R]◐◗🍺Ⓢ⛺⇌

Sedbergh 29F5

11–3; 6–10.30 (11 Thu, F, S)

Red Lion

Finkle Street (A683) ☎ 20433
Marston Mercian Mild, Burton Bitter [H]
Friendly local, tastefully renovated ♣⊞✿■◐◗Ⓢ⛺

Shap 29E4

11–3; 6–10.30 (11 F, S)

Greyhound Hotel

(A6) ☎ 474
Tetley Walker Mild, Bitter [H]
Large local with country and western nights
🔥Г♪♣⊞✿🚗■[R]◐◗🍺Ⓢ⛺

Silecroft 28C6

11–3; 6–11

Miners Arms

(Off A595) ☎ Millom 2325

Younger No 3 [H]
Large village pub
♪♣✿🚗■◐◗🍺Ⓢ♿⇌

Silloth 28C1

11–3; 5.30–10.30 (11 F, S)

Queens Hotel

Park Terrace (B5302)
☎ 31373
Tetley Walker Bitter [H]
Tastefully modernised Victorian seafront hotel
🔥♪♣⊞✿🚗■[R]◐◗🍺Ⓢ

Swinside 28C3

11–3; 5.30–10.30 (11 F, S)

Swinside Inn

OS 245218
☎ Braithwaite 253
Jennings Bitter [E] & [H]
Friendly inn in picturesque setting
🔥Г♪♣✿🚗■[R]◐◗🍺Ⓢ⛺

Talkin 29E1

12–2.30; 7–10.30 (11 F, S)

Hare & Hounds

☎ Brampton 3456
Closed weekday lunchtimes in winter except bank holidays
Theakston Best Bitter, XB, Old Peculier
Bulmer Cider [H]
Excellent country pub near Talkin Tarn
🔥♣⊞✿🚗■[R]◐◗🍺Ⓢ♿⛺⇌

Threlkeld 28D3

11–3; 5.30–10.30 (11 F, S)

Horse & Farrier

(Off A66)
Jennings Mild, Bitter [H]
Old-world pub at foot of Blencathra
🔥♣⊞✿🚗[R]🍺Ⓢ♿⛺

Ulverston 28D6

10.30–3; 6–10.30 (11 F, S, open all day Thursday)

Bay Horse Inn

Canal Foot (2 miles from town centre) ☎ 53972
Closed 3 pm–6 pm Thursdays
Mitchells Bitter [H]
Lively pub overlooking Morecambe Bay
🔥Г♪♣⊞✿🚗■◐◗Ⓢ

Devonshire Arms

Victoria Road
Thwaites Best Mild, Bitter [H]
Friendly, popular local near bus terminus
♪♣✿🚗🍺Ⓢ⇌

Hope & Anchor

Daltongate
Hartley Bitter, XB [H]
Excellent, popular town pub
Г♣◐◗

Kings Head

Queen Street ☎ 52892
Theakston Best Bitter [H]
Cosy, low-ceilinged free house
🔥♪✿■Ⓢ

Old Friends

Soutergate (B5281, off A590)
Closed 4 pm–7 pm Thursdays in winter
Hartley Bitter, XB [H]
Traditional local deserving of its name ♣🍺⇌

Wetheral 28E1

11–3; 5.30–10.30 (11 F, S)

Crown Hotel

(Off B6263) ☎ 208
Thwaites Best Mild, Bitter [H]
Well-appointed and popular, rare beers for area
♪♣⊞✿🚗■[R]◐◗Ⓢ⇌

Whitehaven 28B3

11–3; 5.30–10.30 (11 F, S)

Royal Standard

West Strand
Jennings Bitter [H]
Friendly dockside pub, popular with seamen ♣🚗🍺

Sun Inn

Hensingham (A595)
Jennings Mild, Bitter [H]
Popular locals' pub
♪♣🚗[R]🍺Ⓢ

Wigton 28D2

11–3; 5.30–10.30 (11 F, S)

Victoria

King Street (A596) ☎ 2672
Open till 4.30 pm Tuesdays
Jennings Mild, Bitter [H]
Basic and friendly town pub
♣⊞[R]🍺Ⓢ♿⇌

Winster 28E5

10.30–3; 6–10.30 (11 F, S)

Brown Horse

(A5074) ☎ Windermere 3443
Ruddle Bitter
Younger Scotch Bitter [H]
Popular hunting pub
♪♣⊞✿🚗[R]◐◗🍺Ⓢ♿

Winton 29G4

11.30–3; 6–10.30 (11 F, S)

Bay Horse Inn

(Off A685) OS 785105
Closed Monday lunchtimes
Younger Scotch Bitter, IPA [H]
Recently extended pub overlooking village green
🔥♪♣⊞✿◐◗🍺Ⓢ

Workington 28B3

11–3; 5.30–10.30 (11 F, S)

Appletree Inn

Finkle Street
Matthew Brown Mild, Bitter, John Peel Bitter [H]
Warm, friendly town-centre pub ♪♣Ⓢ♿

Commercial

Market Place
Jennings Mild, Bitter [H]
Friendly town-centre local
♣🍺

Keg Buster by Bill Tidy

Apperknowle 23J4

11–3; 6–10.30 (11 F, S)
Yellow Lion
High Street (off A61)
✆ Dronfield 413181
Tetley Bitter Ⓗ
Popular village pub with
restaurant ♪♣🅿♿🏠♦

Ashbourne 23G6

10.30–3; 6–11
White Hart Hotel
Church Street ✆ 44711
Marston Pedigree Ⓗ
Owd Rodger Ⓖ
Comfortable, modernised
corner house in historic street
♪♣🅰🔲🕒♦🏥

Ashford-in-the-Water 23G4

11–3; 6–11
Bulls Head
(Off A6) ✆ Bakewell 2931
Robinson Best Bitter Ⓗ
Warm, comfortable and
friendly ♪♪♣🅱🅿🏠♦🏥

Ashover 23H5

11–3; 5.30–10.30 (11 F, S)
Black Swan
Church Street (off A632)
✆ Chesterfield 590305
Draught Bass Ⓗ
Fine old coaching house in
picturesque village
🅰♪♣🅿🅰🔲🕒♦♿

Crispin
Church Street
Home Bitter Ⓗ
Old village inn rooted in
history 🅰♪♣🔲🅿🅰🏥♿

Bakewell 23G4

11–3; 6–11
Peacock
Market Place (off A6)
Open until 4 pm Mondays
except bank holidays
**Ward Best Mild, Sheffield Best
Bitter** Ⓔ
Pleasant, stone-built pub,
modernised internally
🅰♪♣🅿🅰♿♦

Bamford 23G3

11–3; 6–11
Derwent Hotel
(A6013) ✆ Hope Valley 51395
**Darley Thorne Best Bitter
Stones Best Bitter
Ward Sheffield Best Bitter** Ⓗ
Friendly pub with home
cooking
♪♣🅱🅿🅰🔲🅡🅖🕒♿🏥♦🅰🏥

Barlow 23H4

11–3; 5.30–10.30 (11 F, S)
Barlow Huntsman
Valley Road (B6051)
✆ Sheffield 899306
Darley Thorne Best Bitter

**Ward Sheffield Best Bitter
Vaux Samson** Ⓗ
Busy, friendly village-centre
local 🅰♪♣♿🅿🅰🔲🅡🅖🕒♦🏥

Beeley 23H4

11–3; 6–11
Devonshire Arms
(B6012) ✆ Darley Dale 3259
**Theakston Best Bitter, Old
Peculier** Ⓗ
400-year-old coaching inn
near Chatsworth House
🅰♪♣🅱🅿🅰🕒🏥♦🅰

Belper 23H6

10.30–2.30; 6–11
Old Kings Head
Brookside (A609) ✆ 2170
Marston Pedigree Ⓗ
Popular, friendly local ♪♣🅡♦♿

Birchover 23H5

11–3; 6–11
Red Lion
Main Street
(off B5056) ✆ Winster 229
**Tetley Bitter
Marston Burton Bitter,
Pedigree** Ⓗ
Classic village pub with
indoor well 🅰♪♣🅿🅰🅡🏥♦

Birch Vale 23F3

11–3; 5.30–11
Sycamore
Sycamore Road (off A6015)
✆ New Mills 42715
Lunchtime opening: 12 noon
**Boddingtons Bitter
Marston Burton Bitter
Winkle Birch Vale Mild,
Bitter** Ⓗ
Enterprising free house with
'house beers' from local
brewery ♪🅿🅰🔲🕒🏥♦

Bolehill 23H5

11–3; 6–11
Miners Standard
The Lanes OS 292551
Closed lunchtimes Mon–Fri,
evening opening: 8
Draught Bass Ⓖ
Basic rural local, worth
finding ♣🏥

Bonsall 23H5

11–3; 6–11
Barley Mow
The Dale (off A5012)
**Hardys & Hansons Best Mild,
Best Bitter** Ⓗ
Homely, friendly village local
with unique cellar behind bar
🅰♪♣🅿🅰🅡🏥♦🅰

Boylestone 23G6

10.30–2.30; 6–10.30 (11 F, S)
Rose & Crown
(Off A515) OS 177356
**Marston Pedigree, Merrie
Monk** Ⓗ
Bulmer Cider Ⓖ

Small country pub with low
beamed ceiling
🅰♪♣🅱🅿🅰🅡🏥♦♿

Brassington 23H5

10.30–3; 6–11
Olde Gate
(Off B5035)
Marston Pedigree Ⓗ
Built 1616; scrubbed tables in
bar and black-leaded fireplace.
Off High Peak Trail 🅰♣♦🅰🏥

Brimington 23J4

11–3; 5.30–10.30 (11 F, S)
Great Central
Station Road (off A61)
✆ Chesterfield 73807
Evening opening: 6.30
Shipstone Mild, Bitter Ⓔ
Friendly local near old canal
🅰♪♣🅰🔲🅡🏥♦

Buxton 23F4

11–3; 5.30–11
Bakers Arms
West Road (off A53)
Evening opening: 6
Draught Bass Ⓔ
Cottage pub with lots of
atmosphere ♪♣🅿🅰♦♿

Kings Head
Market Place ✆ 3469
**Marston Mercian Mild,
Burton Bitter, Pedigree** Ⓗ
Deceptively large pub in
corner of market
🅰♪♣🅱🅰🕒🏥♦🅰♿🍴

Railway
Bridge Street (off A6) ✆ 3402
Winter evening opening: 7
**Hardys & Hansons Best Mild,
Best Bitter** Ⓗ
Viaduct without and pictures
within reflect pub's name
♪♣🅿🅰🅡🕒🏥♦🅰♿🍴

Calow 23J4

11–3; 5.30–10.30 (11 F, S)
Somerset House
Top Road (A632)
Evening opening: 7
Ward Sheffield Best Bitter Ⓔ
Former farmhouse, converted
in 1950s ♪♣🅿🅰🏥♦

Castleton 23G3

11.30–3; 5.30–11
Bulls Head Hotel
Cross Street ✆ Hope Valley
20256
Robinson Best Bitter Ⓔ
Old Tom Ⓖ
Large, comfortable lounge
with log fire
🅰♪♣🅱🅿🅰🔲🅡🕒🏥♦♿🅰

Chapel-en-le-Frith 23G4

11–3; 5.30–11
New Inn
Manchester Road (A6)
✆ 812121

Robinson Best Mild, Best
Bitter Ⓗ Old Tom Ⓖ
Comfortable, stone-built
roadside pub
♠♪♣♥♠⊞Ⓖ↑◉♦♨

Old Pack Horse
Town End (A6) ℰ 812135
Robinsons Best Mild, Best
Bitter, Old Tom Ⓗ
Market town pub that serves
mild in light and dark form
♪♣♥♠⊞Ⓖ↑◉♦

Roebuck
Market Place (off A6)
ℰ 812274
Closes 4 pm Thursdays
Tetley Walker Mild, Bitter Ⓗ
Market pub of great character
near village stocks
♪♣♥♠⊞Ⓖ↑◉

Chesterfield 23J4
11–3; 5.30–10.30 (11 F, S)
Golden Fleece
9 High Street (off A61)
ℰ 32814
Closes 10.30 pm F, S
Tetley Bitter Ⓗ
Large town-centre pub with
two bars ♪♣♥Ⓖ◉♦

Grouse
Chatsworth Road, Brampton
(A619) ℰ 79632
Draught Bass
Stones Best Bitter Ⓗ
Friendly local ♪♣♠◉

Holme Hall
Linacre Road, Loundsey Green
ℰ 39995
Tetley Mild, Falstaff Best,
Bitter Ⓗ
♪♣♥♠⊞Ⓖ◉

Royal Oake
Shambles (off the Market)
Stones Best Bitter Ⓗ
Superb, half-timbered 13th
century inn, not to be missed
♪♣◉

Clay Cross 23J5
11–3; 6–10.30 (11 F, S)
Gardeners Arms
Market Street (off A61)
Hardys & Hansons Best Mild,
Best Bitter Ⓔ
Homely, two-roomed market
town pub ♪♣♠⊞◉

Crich 23H5
10.30–3; 6–11
Cliff Inn
Cromford Road, Cliff Side (off
B5035) ℰ Ambergate 2444
Hardys & Hansons Best Mild,
Best Bitter Ⓗ
Popular local near tramway
museum
♪♣♥♠⊞Ⓖ↑◉♦▲

Cutthorpe 23H4
11–3; 6–10.30 (11 F, S)
Gate Inn

(B6050) ℰ Chesterfield 76923
Lunchtime opening: 12 noon
Tetley Bitter Ⓗ
Free house with unusual
circular entrance
♠♪⊞♠⊞Ⓖ↑◉

Darley Bridge 23H5
11–3; 6–11
Three Stags Heads
(B5057) ℰ Darley Dale 2358
Hardys & Hansons Best Mild,
Best Bitter Ⓗ
250-year-old low-ceilinged
pub ♠♪♣♥♠⊞Ⓖ↑◉♦▲

Darley Dale 23H5
11–3; 6–11
Grouse
Dale Road North (A6) ℰ 2297
Hardys & Hansons Best Mild,
Best Bitter Ⓗ
Three-roomed pub with
friendly landlord
♪♣♥♠⊞◉♦▲

Derby 23H6
10.30–2.30; 6–10.30 (11 F, S)
Alexandra
Siddals Road
Shipstone Mild, Bitter Ⓗ
Renovated Victorian local,
birthplace of Derby CAMRA
♠♪♣♠◉≋

Exeter Arms
Exeter Place ℰ 46679
Marston Mercian Mild,
Burton Bitter, Pedigree Ⓗ
Lively little pub near market
place ♠♣Ⓖ◉

Ferrers Arms
Arleston Lane, Sinfin
ℰ 766003
Everard Burton Mild, Beacon,
Tiger, Old Original Ⓔ
Modern pub with period decor
in busy shopping complex
♪♣♥Ⓖ◉

Furnace
Duke Steet
Hardys & Hansons Best Mild,
Best Bitter Ⓗ & Ⓔ
Victorian foundryman's
slaker, recently renovated
↑♪♣♥◉

Great Northern
Junction Street
Ansells Mild
Ind Coope Burton Ale Ⓗ
Traditional side-street local ♣◉

Malt Shovel
Potter Street, Spondon (off
A52)
Draught Bass Ⓗ
Traditional village local of
character ♠♣♥♠◉

Maypole
Brook Street
Home Mild, Bitter Ⓔ
Friendly one-room pub in
shadow of mill ♪♣

Melbourne Bar
Normanton Road
Ansells Mild, Bitter
Ind Coope Bitter, Burton Ale Ⓗ
Corner local ♪◉

Smithfield
Meadow Road
Draught Bass Ⓔ
Town-centre pub isolated by
redevelopment ♠♪♣♥♠Ⓖ◉

Draycott 23J7
11–2.30; 6–10.30 (11 F, S)
Travellers Rest
Derby Road (A6005)
Marston Mercian Mild,
Pedigree Ⓗ
Victorian local ↑♣♠◉

Dronfield 23H4
11–3; 5.30–10.30 (11 F, S)
Old Sidings
91 Chesterfield Road (A61)
Lunchtime opening: 12 noon
Marston Pedigree, Owd
Rodger
Stones Best Bitter
Theakston Best Bitter, XB, Old
Peculier
Bulmer Cider Ⓗ
Long, narrow pub with
railway theme ♪♠◉≋

Duffield 23H6
10.30–2.30; 6–10.30 (11 F, S)
Bridge
Makeney Road (off A6)
Home Bitter Ⓔ
Smart pub with riverside
terrace ♪♣♥♠⊞◉

Earl Sterndale 23G4
11–3; 5.30–11
Quiet Woman
(B5053) ℰ Longnor 211
Marston Mercian Mild,
Burton Bitter Ⓗ
Superb example of village
green pub ♣♠⊞◉♦

Eckington 23J4
11–3; 5.30–10.30 (11 F, S)
White Hart
Church Street (off A616)
Evening opening: 7
Home Bitter Ⓔ
Pleasant village pub near
church ♪♣♠◉

Edale 23G3
11–3; 6.30–11
Nags Head
(Off A625) ℰ Hope Valley
70291
Morning opening: 11.30
Theakston Best Bitter
Wilsons Original Bitter Ⓗ
16th-century tourist pub at
start of Pennine Way
♠↑♣♥♠Ⓖ↑◉♦▲≋

Froggatt 23H4
11–3; 6–11
Chequers Inn

Froggatt Edge (B6054)
OS 761247
☎ Hope Valley 30231
Ward Sheffield Best Bitter Ⓗ
Country inn with local
character ▲Ⓔ♪⚲▲ⓖ♀Ⓢ♣Å

Glossop 23F3

11–3; 5.30–11
Grapes
High Street West ☎ 4147
**Boddingtons Best Mild,
Bitter** Ⓗ
Unspoilt pub, a gem of a
Northern local ♪♣Ⓡ♀≋

Prince of Wales
Mill Town (off A57) ☎ 64679
Opens at 11.30 am & 5 pm
**Marston Mercian Mild,
Burton Bitter, Pedigree,
Merrie Monk** Ⓗ
Cosy three-roomed free house
with original furnishings
▲♪♣Ⓔ▲Ⓡⓖ♀Ⓢ♣≋

Star
2 Howard Street off A57)
**Boddingtons Best Mild,
Bitter** Ⓗ
Good local near railway
station ♪♣Ⓢ≋

Hartshorne 23H7

10.30–3; 6–10.30 (11 F, S)
Chesterfield Arms
Repton Road (off A514)
☎ Burton-on-Trent 217267
Draught Bass Ⓗ
Pub with aviary in garden
▲♪♣Ⓔ⚲▲ⓖⓈ

Hassop 23H4

11–3; 6–11
Eyre Arms
(B6001)
Stones Best Bitter Ⓔ
Ivy-clad country pub with
contrasting rooms
▲♪♣Ⓔ⚲▲Ⓡ♀♣

Hathersage 23H4

11–3; 6–11
Plough
Leadmill Bridge (A622)
OS 805235
Opens at 12 noon & 7 pm or
later
Stones Best Bitter Ⓔ
Converted farm on the banks
of the Derwent ♪Ⓔ⚲▲♀Ⓢ♣Å≋

Hayfield 23F3

11–3; 5.30–11
George Inn
Church Street (off A624)
☎ New Mills 43691
Burtonwood Best Bitter Ⓗ
Low-beamed 16th century
pub, modernised (in 1750)
♪♣⚲▲▲Ⓡ♣Å

Lantern Pike
(A624) Little Hayfield village
☎ New Mills 44102

Wilsons Original Mild,
Bitter Ⓗ
Comfortable 18th century inn
overlooked by Pennine hills
▲♣Ⓔ⚲▲Ⓔ▲Ⓡⓖ♀♣Ⓢ♣

Heage 23H6

10.30–2.30; 6–11
White Hart
(B6013) ☎ Ambergate 2302
Opens at 11 am & 7 pm
Draught Bass Ⓔ & Ⓖ
Large, many-roomed pub at
crossroads
▲♪♪♣Ⓔ⚲▲Ⓡⓖ♀Ⓢ♣

Heanor 23J6

11–3; 6.30–10.30 (11 F, S)
Jolly Colliers
Derby Road (A608) ☎ Langley
Mill 4771
Ind Coope Bitter Ⓗ
L-shaped bar and lounge
▲♪♣ⓖ♀Ⓢ♣Å

Holmesfield 23H4

11–3; 5.30–10.30 (11 F, S)
Travellers
20 Main Road (B6054)
Evening opening: 6
Home Bitter Ⓔ
Friendly village local ♣⚲♀

Hope 23G3

11–3; 5.30–11
Old Hall
(A625)
Evening opening: 6
Stones Best Bitter Ⓔ
Popular oak-panelled
roadhouse with grand piano
▲♪♪♣⚲▲Ⓡⓖ♀Ⓢ♣Å≋

Horsley 23J6

11–2.30; 6–10.30 (11 F, S)
Coach & Horses
47 Church Street OS 381445
☎ Derby 880581
**Marston Pedigree, Merrie
Monk** Ⓗ **Owd Rodger** Ⓖ
Popular village pub with
passing trade ♪♣♣▲ⓖⓈ

Horsley Woodhouse 23J6

11–3; 6–11
Jolly Colliers
Main Street (A609)
Evening opening: 7
**Ward Best Mild, Sheffield Best
Bitter** Ⓔ
Friendly village local with
weekend singalongs
♪♪♣⚲▲Ⓢ

Ilkeston 23J6

11–3; 6–10.30 (11 F, S)
Durham Ox
Durham Street (off A6007)
**Ward Best Mild, Sheffield Best
Bitter** Ⓔ
A friendly, popular backstreet
local ▲♪♣⚲▲ⓖ♀Ⓢ♣

Ingleby 23H7

10.30–2.30; 7–10.30 (11 F, S)
John Thompson Inn
(Off A514) ☎ Melbourne 2469
**John Thompson JTS XXX
Bitter
Marston Pedigree** Ⓗ
Tastefully converted
farmhouse overlooking River
Trent ♪⚲▲ⓖⓈ

Kilburn 23J6

11–3; 6–11
Hunter Arms
Church Street (A609)
☎ Derby 882907
**Draught Bass
Mitchells & Butlers Mild,
Springfield Bitter** Ⓗ
Interesting local, rare outlet
for M & B mild
▲♪♣⚲▲Ⓡⓖ♀Ⓢ♣

Knockerdown 23H5

11–3; 6–10.30 (11 F, S)
Knockerdown Inn
(B5035)
**Marston Pedigree,
Merrie Monk** Ⓖ
Small, steep-roofed roadhouse
in quiet isolation ▲▲ⓖ♀

Linton 23H8

11–3; 6–10.30 (11 F, S)
Square & Compass
Caldwell Road
Marston Pedigree Ⓗ
Lively village pub, used
mainly by locals ♪♣⚲▲♀Ⓢ

Little Hucklow 23G4

11–3; 7–11
Old Bulls Head
(Off A6049)
**Winkle Saxon Cross Bitter,
Ivanhoe Bitter** Ⓗ
Connoisseurs' pub, part of
Peakland's unchanging
character ▲♪♣Ⓔ⚲▲♀Ⓢ♣Å

Long Eaton 26A8

11–3; 6–10.30 (11 F, S)
Tiger
Tamworth Road (A453)
**Marston Burton Bitter,
Pedigree** Ⓔ
Popular town pub
♪♣⚲▲Ⓡⓖ♀Ⓢ

Longlane 23H6

10.30–2.30; 6–10.30 (11 F, S)
Three Horseshoes
OS 250381
Ind Coope Burton Ale Ⓗ
Cosy old-world atmosphere
▲♪♣⚲▲♀

Lower Hartshay 23J5

11–3; 6–11
Gate
(Off A610)
Shipstone Mild, Bitter Ⓗ

Characterful pub in pleasant
setting ♨♪♣✿🅰🅸⑧♿

Makeney 23H6

10.30–2.30; 6–10.30 (11 F, S)

Hollybush

(Off A6)
**Marston Pedigree, Owd
Rodger**
Ruddle County 🅖 & 🅗
Excellent pub with original
timbers ♨♣✿🅰🅸

Marehay 23J6

11–3; 6–11

Hollybush

Brook Lane (off A61)
✆ Ripley 42558
Evening opening: 6.30
Shipstone Mild, Bitter
Bulmer Cider 🅗
Tastefully modernised with
excellent view of cricket field
♨♪♣✿🅰🅸🅻🅖♥ (must book)
🅸⑧♿

Matlock 23H5

10.30–3; 6–11

Sycamore

Sycamore Road (off A6)
Evening opening: 7
Draught Bass 🅗
Traditional comfortable pub
♪♣✿🅰🅻⑧

Melbourne 23J7

10.30–2.30; 6–10.30 (11 F, S)

Sir Francis Burdett

Derby Road (A514) *✆ 2105*
Draught Bass
**Mitchells & Butlers Mild,
Springfield Bitter 🅗**
Popular roadhouse outside
village 🄵♪♣✿🅰🅸🅻♥🅸⑧

Middle Handley 23J4

11–3; 5.30–10.30 (11 F, S)

Devonshire Arms

Westfield Lane (off B6052)
Stones Best Bitter 🅗
Lively village local ♨♣✿🅰🅸

Millthorpe 23H4

11–3; 5.30–10.30 (11 F, S)

Royal Oak

(B6051) *✆ Sheffield 890870*
Darley Thorne Best Bitter
Ward Sheffield Best Bitter 🅗
300-year-old village pub
with excellent fare ♨♣🅰🅸⑧

Milton 23H7

10.30–2.30; 6–10.30 (11 F, S)

Swan

(Off B5008)
Marston Pedigree 🅗
Modernised country pub with
friendly atmosphere
♨🄵♪♣✿🅰🅸🅸⑧

New Mills 23F3

11–3; 5.30–11

Crescent

Market Street (off A6015)

Tetley Walker Mild, Bitter 🅗
Recently extended, attractive
pub in crescent-shaped,
stonebuilt terrace ♪♣🅻♥🅸⑧≋

Pack Horse

Mellor Road *✆ 42365*
Opens at 12 noon and 7 pm
Tetley Walker Bitter 🅗 & 🅖
Moorside pub with spectacular
view towards Kinder Scout
♨♪♣✿🅻♥⑧

Rock Tavern

Wirksmoor Road (off A6015)
✆ 42885
**Robinson Best Mild, Best
Bitter 🄴**
Modernised backstreet local
overlooking the Torrs
🄵♪♣🗺✿🅰🅻♥⑧≋

Oakerthorpe 23J5

11–3; 6–11

Butchers Arms

Four Lanes End (B6013)
✆ Alfreton 832369
**Hardys & Hansons Best
Bitter 🄴**
Popular eating house at busy
crossroads ♨♪✿🅰🅸⑧

Ockbrook 23J6

10.30–2.30; 6–10.30 (11 F, S)

Royal Oak

(Off A52) *✆ Derby 662378*
Evening opening: 7
Draught Bass
**Mitchells & Butlers Mild,
Springfield Bitter 🅗**
Interesting, popular pub with
small rooms ♨♣✿🅰🅸⑧♿

Over Haddon 23G5

11–3; 6–11

Lathkil Hotel

(Off B5055) *✆ Bakewell 2501*
Darley Thorne Best Bitter
**Ward Best Mild, Sheffield Best
Bitter 🅗**
Welcoming stone hostelry
with fine views over Lathkil
Dale ♨♣🗺✿🅰🅻♥⑧🏕

Peak Forest 23G4

11–3; 5.30–11

Devonshire

(A623) *✆ Buxton 3875*
**Ward Best Mild, Sheffield Best
Bitter 🄴**
Pleasant, welcoming roadside
inn ♨♣🗺✿🅰🅻🅸🅻♥🅸⑧♿🏕

Pinxton 23J5

11–3; 6–11

Three Horseshoes

Town Street (B6019)
**Hardys & Hansons Best
Bitter 🄴**
Many-roomed local
♨♣✿🅰🅸🅸⑧♿

Repton 23H7

10.30–2.30; 6–10.30 (11 F, S)

Shakespeare

Main Street

**Everard Burton Mild, Beacon,
Old Original 🅗**
Large comfortable lounge and
friendly bar 🄵♪♣✿🅰🅻🅖♥🅸⑧

Ridgeway 23J4

11–3; 6–10.30 (11 F, S)

Phoenix

High Lane (B6054)
✆ Sheffield 486440
Ward Sheffield Best Bitter 🄴
17th-century coaching inn
♪✿🅰🅻🅖 (Mon–Fri) 🍴

Rosliston 23H8

11–3; 6–10.30 (11 F, S)

Plough

Main Street
✆ Burton-on-Trent 761354
**Marston Mercian Mild,
Pedigree 🅗 Owd Rodger 🅖**
Popular village pub
♨♣✿🅰🅸🅻🅸⑧♿

Sawley 23J7

11–3; 6–10.30 (11 F, S)

Bell Hotel

Tamworth Road (B6540)
Shipstone Mild, Bitter 🅗
Good local with games room
♪♣✿🅰🅸⑧

Scarcliffe 23J4

11–3; 5.30–10.30 (11 F, S)

Horse & Groom

(B6417)
✆ Chesterfield 823152
Evening opening: 7
Home Bitter 🅗
Low-beamed old coaching inn
♨🄵♪♣🗺✿🅰🅻🅖🍴

Shardlow 23J7

10.30–2.30; 6–10.30 (11 F, S)

Dog & Duck

London Road (A6)
✆ Derby 792224
**Marston Pedigree, Merrie
Monk 🅗 Owd Rodger 🅖**
Cruck-built original, much
extended
♨🄵♪♣🗺✿🅰🅻🅖🅸⑧♿🏕

Shakespeare

London Road (A6)
Home Mild, Bitter 🄴
Popular roadhouse, old but
much modernised
♪♣🗺✿🅰🅻🅸⑧

Shirebrook 23J4

11–3; 5.30–10.30 (11 F, S)

Station Hotel

Station Road (B6407)
✆ Mansfield 742210
Evening opening: 7
Shipstone Mild, Bitter 🄴
Recently modernised hotel
built in 1896 ♪♣✿🅰🅻🅖♥🅸⑧

Shirland 23J5

11–3; 6–10.30 (11 F, S)

Duke of Wellington

Main Road (A61)

Home Mild, Bitter Ⓔ
Roadside pub with good
atmosphere 🏨🍴♣�Ⓡ🍽️Ⓢ

Smalley 23J6

11–3; 6–10.30 (11 F, S)
Nag's Head
Main Road (A608)
**Marston Mercian Mild,
Burton Bitter, Pedigree** Ⓗ
Comfortable roadside pub
🍴♣�Ⓢ

Somercotes 23J5

11–3; 6–11
Horse & Jockey
Leabrooks Road (B6016)
Home Mild, Bitter Ⓗ
Deservedly popular local,
recently refurbished
🏨🍴♣Ⓡ🍽️Ⓢ♿

South Wingfield
23J5

11–3; 6–11
Yew Tree
Manor Road (B5035)
Opens at 12 noon & 7 pm
**Marston Pedigree
Ruddle County** Ⓗ
Small friendly pub near
Wingfield Manor 🏨♣🚙🍽️Ⓢ

Stanton 23H7

11–3; 6–10.30 (11 F, S)
Gate
Woodlands Road (A444)
✆ Burton-on-Trent 216818
Marston Pedigree Ⓗ
Main road pub with pleasant
beer garden 🍴♣🚙�ⓉⓈ

Stanton-by-Dale
23J6

11–3; 7–10.30 (11 F, S)
Stanhope Arms
Shipstone Bitter Ⓔ
Cosy, popular, well-kept
village pub 🍴♣🚙🏨Ⓢ

Stone Edge 23H5

11–3; 5.30–10.30 (11 F, S)
Red Lion
(B5057) ✆ Chesterfield
566142
**Darley Thorne Best Bitter
Ward Best Mild, Sheffield Best
Bitter** Ⓗ
Extensively renovated pub,
real ale in main bars only
🏨🍴🎲🚙🏨Ⓡ�ⓉⓈ♿🍸

Stoney Middleton
23H4

11–3; 7–11
Royal Oak
The Dale (A623)
✆ Hope Valley 31392
Morning opening: 12 noon
**Marston Pedigree
Tetley Bitter** Ⓗ
16th-century pub built of
local limestone
🍴♣🚙�ⓉⓈ♿🍸

Sutton-cum-
Duckmanton 23J4

11–3; 6–10.30 (11 F, S)
Arkwright Arms
Bolsover Road (A632)
✆ Chesterfield 32053
**Marston Burton Bitter,
Pedigree
Whitbread Castle Eden Ale** Ⓗ
Convivial roadside pub with
beer garden and donkeys;
guest beers 🏨🍴♣🎲🚙🏨ⓉⓈ

Swadlincote 23H7

11–3; 6–10.30 (11 F, S)
Angel
Church Street (B586)
✆ Burton 214260
Marston Pedigree Ⓗ
Friendly local, tastefully
modernised 🍴♣🚙🏨ⓉⓈ

Tideswell 23G4

11–3; 6–11
Anchor Inn
Four Lane Ends (A623)
✆ 871371
**Robinson Best Mild, Best
Bitter** Ⓔ **Old Tom** Ⓖ
Friendly, 500-year-old
crossroads pub
🏨🍴♣🏨Ⓔ🏨Ⓡ�ⓉⓈ♿🍸

George Hotel
Commercial Road (B6049)
✆ 871382
**Hardys & Hansons Best Mild,
Best Bitter** Ⓗ
17th-century village inn, near
church
🏨🍴♣🏨🎲🚙🏨ⒺⒶⓇ�ⓉⓈ♿🍸

Tintwhistle 23F3

11–3; 5.30–10.30 (11 F, S)
Old Oak
Manchester Road (A628)
Tetley Walker Bitter Ⓗ
Smart, comfortable pub in
Pennine Valley village 🍴♣Ⓢ

Turnditch 23H6

10.30–2.30; 6–10.30 (11 F, S)
Tiger
Belper Road (A517)
Ind Coope Bitter, Burton Ale Ⓗ
Smart, modernised country
pub 🏨🍴🚙🏨Ⓢ♿

Wardlow Mires 23G4

11–3; 6–11
Three Stags Heads
(A623) ✆ Tideswell 871251
Younger Scotch Bitter Ⓗ
Unspoilt small country pub
🏨🏨🍽️🍸

Whaley Bridge 23F4

11–3; 5.30–11
Board Inn
62 Chapel Road (A6)
Morning opening: 11.30
**Robinson Best Mild, Best
Bitter** Ⓗ

Single bar, comfortable pub
with good views
🏨🍴♣🏨ⓇⓊⓈ

Navigation Inn
Johnson Street (off A6)
✆ 2308
Saturday evening opening: 6
Boddingtons Bitter Ⓗ
Small, renovated pub near
Peak Forest canal terminus
🍴♣🚙ⒸⓊⒸ♣🍸

Shepherd's Arms
Old Road (A6)
**Marston Mercian Mild,
Burton Bitter, Pedigree** Ⓗ
Excellent local with good vault
and garden
🏨🍴🎲🚙ⒸⓉ🍽️Ⓢ♿

Willington 23H7

10.30–2.30; 6–10.30 (11 F, S)
Green Man
(B5008)
Draught Bass Ⓔ
Newly modernised, but
retaining pleasant atmosphere
🍴♣🚙🏨ⓇⒶⓈ

Windley 23H6

10.30–3; 6–10.30 (11 F, S)
Puss in Boots
Nether Lane (B5023)
Draught Bass Ⓗ
Isolated roadhouse with
pleasant beer garden 🏨♣🚙🏨Ⓢ

Winster 23H5

11–3; 6–11
Miners Standard
✆ 279
**Marston Pedigree
Ruddle County** Ⓗ
Many-roomed country pub in
lovely setting
🏨🍴♣🏨🚙🏨ⓇⒸ�ⓉⓈ🍸

Wirksworth 23H5

11–3 (4 Tues); 6–11
Black's Head
Market Place (B5035)
**Hardys & Hansons Best Mild,
Best Bitter** Ⓗ
Neat, comfortable little pub in
interesting small town
🏨♣🚙Ⓢ♿

Hope & Anchor
Market Place (B5023) ✆ 2694
Home Mild, Bitter Ⓔ
Roomy local with splendid
fireplace
🏨♣🏨ⒺⓇ🍽️Ⓢ🍸

Youlgreave 23G5

10.30–3; 6.30–11
Bulls Head Hotel
Church Street (A524)
✆ 307
**Marston Mercian Mild,
Burton Bitter, Pedigree** Ⓗ
Friendly 16th century
coaching inn
🍴♣🚙🏨ⒺⓇⒸ�ⓉⓈ🍸

Devon

Appledore 3H2

11–2.30; 6–11
Beaver
Irsha Street (off A39)
✆ Bideford 4822
Whitbread Flowers Original Bitter
Taunton Cider Ⓗ
Waterfront pub with nautical flavour ♪♣❀🅿🚗🅰Ⓡ🅿Ⓢ

Ashburton 4A6

11–2.30; 5–10.30 (11 F, S and summer)
London Hotel
West Street (off A38) ✆ 52478
Cotleigh Tawny Bitter
Thompsons Aysheberton Mild, Bitter, IPA Ⓗ
Hills Cider Ⓖ
Old coaching house with its own brewery 🅰♪♣🅰Ⓡ🅖🚬Ⓢ

Axminster 4E5

10.30–2.30; 5.30–10.30 (11 F, S and summer)
Millway
Chard Road (A358) ✆ 32774
Palmer BB, IPA
Gaymer Cider Ⓖ
Large post-war pub; excellent bar snacks ♪♣🅰🅿Ⓡ🅖🚬Ⓢ

Axmouth 4E5

10.30–2.30; 5.30–10.30 (11 F, S and summer)
Ship
Church Street (B3172)
✆ Seaton 21838
John Devenish Bitter, Wessex Best Bitter Ⓗ
Taunton Cider Ⓖ
Welcoming old inn on picturesque Axe estuary; excellent food
♣❀🅰Ⓡ🅖🚬Ⓢ🅰

Aylesbeare 4C5

10.30–2.30; 6–10.30 (11 F, S)
Halfway Inn
(A3052/B3180)
✆ Woodbury 32273
Devenish Wessex Best Bitter Ⓗ
Recently improved crossroads pub ♪♣❀🅰Ⓡ🅖🚗🚬Ⓢ🅰

Barnstaple 3J2

11–2.30; 5–11
Barnstaple Inn
Trinity Street (off A361)
Courage Best Bitter Ⓖ
Friendly, traditional pub near large public car park ♪♣🅖🚬Ⓢ

Corner House
Joy Street
Draught Bass
Welsh Hancocks Bitter Ⓗ
Interesting, friendly locals' pub ♣🅰Ⓢ

Rolle Quay
Rolle Street (A39) ✆ 5182
Morning opening:
11.30–2.30
Usher Best Bitter, Founders Ale Ⓗ
Popular town-centre pub
♣🅰🚬🚬Ⓢ

Bideford 3H2

11–2.30; 6–11
Portobello
Silver Street (A39) ✆ 2991
Courage Best Bitter, Directors Ⓗ
Taunton Cider Ⓖ
Corner local with intimate lounge bar ♪♣🅴🅿🚗🚬Ⓢ♿

Blackawton 4B8

10.30–2.30; 5.30–10.30 (11 F, S and summer)
Normandy Arms
(Off B3207) ✆ 316
Draught Bass
Blackawton Bitter Ⓗ
Headstrong Ⓖ
Comfortable 15th-century village pub
🅰♪♣🅴🅿🅰Ⓖ🚬Ⓢ

Branscombe 4D5

10.30–2.30; 5.30–10.30 (11 F, S and summer)
Three Horseshoes
(A3052) ✆ 251
Evening opening: 6
Draught Bass
Hall & Woodhouse
Badger Best Bitter
Halls Harvest Bitter
Wadworth 6X
Hills Cider Ⓗ
Large roadside inn
♪♣❀🅰🅿🚬🚬Ⓢ

Brixham 4B7

10.30–2.30; 5.30–10.30 (11 F, S and summer)
Burton Hotel
23 Burton Street ✆ 2805
Courage Best Bitter, Directors Ⓖ
Friendly pub without frills
♪♣🅰🚬🚬Ⓢ

Ernie Lister Bar
49 King Street ✆ 55751
Opens at 11 am & 6 pm
Draught Bass
Blackawton Bitter Ⓗ
Victorian-style bar in quayside hotel, named after local pilot
♪🚗🅰Ⓖ🚬Ⓢ

Broadhembury 4D4

10.30–2.30; 6–10.30 (11 F, S and summer)
Drewe Arms
(Off A373) ✆ 267
Draught Bass
Bulmer Cider Ⓖ
Picturesque thatched pub
🅰♪♣🅴❀🅰Ⓡ🅖🚬 (not Mon) 🚬Ⓢ

Broadhempston 4B7

11–2.30; 6–10.30 (11 F, S and summer)
Monks Retreat
(Off A381)
✆ Ipplepen 812203
Courage Directors
Hall & Woodhouse
Badger Best Bitter
Whitbread Bitter Ⓗ
Hills Cider Ⓖ
Friendly pub off the beaten track ♪♣🅰🅖🚬Ⓢ

Chagford 4A5

10.30–2.30; 6–10.30 (11 F, S and summer)
Bullers Arms
Mill Street ✆ 2438
Morning opening: 11
Devenish Wessex Best Bitter
Usher Best Bitter, Founders Ale
Bulmer Cider Ⓗ
Traditional, unspoilt local with keen landlord
♪♣🅴🅿Ⓡ🚬Ⓢ

Challacombe 4A2

11–2.30; 6–10.30 (11 F, S and summer)
Black Venus
(B3358) ✆ Parracombe 251
Whitbread Bitter Ⓖ
Low-beamed, traditional country inn 🅰♪♣❀🅰🅿🅖🚬🚬Ⓢ

Cheriton Fitzpaine 4B4

11–2.30; 5.30–10.30 (11 F, S and summer)
Half Moon
Evening opening: 6.30
Whitbread Bitter Ⓗ
Homely village pub with cosy lounge ♪♣🅰Ⓡ🚬Ⓢ

Chittlehampton 3J2

10.30–2.30; 6–10.30 (11 F, S and summer)
Bell
The Square (off B3227)
Hall & Woodhouse
Badger Best Bitter Ⓗ
Stone-built pub opposite magnificent church tower
🅰♪♣❀🚬Ⓢ

Colyton 4E5

11–2.30; 6–10.30 (11 F, S and summer)
Kingfisher
Dolphin Street ✆ 52476
Eldridge Pope Dorchester Bitter, Royal Oak
Hall & Woodhouse
Badger Best Bitter
Wadworth 6X Ⓗ
Bulmer Cider Ⓖ
Delightful stone-walled pub
♪♣🅴🅿Ⓡ🅖🚬🚬Ⓢ

Cornwood 3J6

10.30–2.30; 5.30–10.30 (11 F, S and summer)
Cornwood Inn
Draught Bass
Blackawton Bitter Ⓗ
Headstrong
Ind Coope Burton Ale
Welsh Hancocks Pale Ale Ⓗ
Enthusiastic landlord, frequent guest beers
♪♣❀🅰🚬Ⓢ

Crediton 4B5

10.30–2.30; 5.30–10.30 (11 F, S)
Duke of York
High Street ✆ 2655
Draught Bass
Welsh Hancocks Bitter Ⓗ
Cosy pub with good home-cooked food ♪🅖🚬🚬Ⓢ

Devon

Croyde 3H1

10.30–2.30; 5–11

Thatched Barn Inn
Off A361) ℰ 890349
Draught Bass
Whitbread Flowers Original
Bitter Ⓗ
Delightful 15th-century inn
♪♣☷ℰ🅿️🅰️🔲Ⓡ🅶🍴🕙Ⓢ🅰️

Cullompton 4C4

11–2.30; 5–10.30 (11 F, S and summer)

White Hart
ℰ 2646
Evening opening: 6
Whitbread Bitter, Flowers
Original Bitter Ⓗ
Friendly old town-centre pub
with comfortable lounge
♣🅰️🔲Ⓡ🅶🍴🕙Ⓢ≷

Dartmouth 4B8

11–2.30; 6–10.30 (11 F, S and summer)

George & Dragon
Mayors Avenue ℰ 2523
Evening opening: 6.30
Draught Bass
Whitbread Bitter, Flowers
Original Bitter
Mills Cider Ⓖ
Cosy pub with friendly
atmosphere ♪♣🅿️🅰️🔲Ⓢ

Dawlish 4C6

11–2.30; 5–10.30 (11 F, S and summer)

Prince Albert
28 The Strand
Draught Bass
Eldridge Pope Royal Oak
Whitbread Bitter Ⓔ
Warm, convivial and beery Ⓢ

Dittisham 4B7

11–2.30; 6–10.30 (11 F, S and summer)

Red Lion
Off B3207) ℰ 235
Blackawton Bitter
Usher Best Bitter Ⓗ
Mills Cider Ⓖ
Popular pub near the River
Dart ♪♣🅰️🔲🅶🍴Ⓢ

Doddiscombsleigh 4B5

11–2.30; 6–10.30 (11 F, S)

Nobody Inn
Off B3193)
ℰ Christow 52394
Draught Bass
Hall & Woodhouse
Badger Best Bitter Ⓖ
Ancient pub/restaurant with
guest beers 🅰️🅿️🅰️🅶🍴Ⓢ

Drewsteignton 4A5

10.30–2.30; 6–10.30 (11 F, S and summer)

Drewe Arms
Off A382)
Whitbread Bitter
Bulmer Cider Ⓖ
Classic Devon village pub
🅰️♣🅿️🍴Ⓢ

Ermington 3J7

11–2.30; 6–10.30 (11 F, S and summer)

First & Last
(B3210) ℰ Modbury 830671
Halls Harvest Bitter
Ind Coope Burton Ale Ⓗ
Country inn with charm and
character
🍴♪♣☷🅿️🅰️🔲🅶🍴🕙Ⓢ🅰️🅰️

Exeter 4B5

11–2.30; 5–10.30 (11 F, S)

Bystock Hotel
(Stocks Bar)
Bystock Terrace ℰ 72709
Evening opening: 6
Draught Bass
Courage Directors Ⓗ
Pleasant hotel bar with
adjoining restaurant
♪♣🅿️🔲Ⓡ🅶🍴🕙Ⓢ≷

Poltimore Arms
Pinhoe (B3181)
John Devenish Bitter, Wessex
Best Bitter
Taunton Cider Ⓗ
Lively local in the outskirts
🍴♪♣🅿️🅰️🕙Ⓢ≷

Ropemakers Arms
30 Blackboy Road (B3181)
John Devenish Bitter, Wessex
Best Bitter
Taunton Cider Ⓗ
Contrasting two-bar local
near town centre 🍴♪♣🅰️🕙Ⓢ≷

Seven Stars
Alphington Road ℰ 59567
Closes 3 pm Fridays
Draught Bass Ⓔ
Popular modern pub near
cattle market ♪♣🅿️🅰️🅶🕙Ⓢ

Ship
Martins Lane ℰ 72040
Draught Bass
Whitbread Bitter Ⓗ
Sir Francis Drake's other ship
♪🅶🍴🕙Ⓢ≷

Exmouth 4C6

10.30–2.30; 5.30–11

Clinton Arms
Littleham Village
(Off A376) ℰ 4054
Evening opening: 6
Usher Best Bitter, Founders
Ale Ⓗ
Bulmer Cider Ⓖ
Modern village pub
🅰️♪♣🅿️🅰️🔲🕙Ⓢ🅰️

Royal Oak
31 Exeter Road (A377)
ℰ 72932
John Devenish Bitter, Wessex
Best Bitter Ⓗ
Traditional town local
♪🅰️🅶🕙Ⓢ≷

Great Torrington 3H3

10.30–2.30; 6–10.30 (11 F, S and summer)

Black Horse
The Square (A386)

ℰ Torrington 2121
Usher Best Bitter Ⓗ
Ancient coaching house
🍴♪♣🔲🕙Ⓢ

Hartland 3G2

10.30–2.30; 6–10.30 (11 F, S and summer)

Anchor
Fore Street (off A39) ℰ 414
Winter evening opening: 6.30
St Austell Tinners
Usher Best Bitter
Taunton Cider Ⓗ
Thoughtfully modernised pub
♪♣🅿️🅰️🔲Ⓡ🅶🍴🕙Ⓢ🅰️

Haytor Vale 4B6

11–2.30; 6–10.30 (11 F, S and summer)

Rock Inn
ℰ 205
Draught Bass
Whitbread Bitter, Flowers
Original Bitter Ⓗ
Superb 17th-century
Dartmoor village inn
🅰️♣☷🅿️🅶🍴🕙Ⓢ

Hemerdon 3J7

11–2.30; 5.30–10.30 (11 F, S and summer)

Miners Arms
(Off A374)
Draught Bass Ⓖ & Ⓗ
Countryman Cider Ⓖ
Old tin miners' pub with low
ceiling
♪♣🅿️🅰️🕙Ⓢ

Holbeton 3J7

10.30–2.30; 6–11

Mildmay Colours
ℰ 248
Blackawton Bitter
Ind Coope Burton Ale
Palmer IPA
Summerskills Bigbury Best
Bitter Ⓖ
Usher Best Bitter Ⓗ
Friendly village pub with
carvery; good value
♪♣🅿️🅶🍴🕙Ⓢ🅰️

Holcombe 4C6

11–2.30; 6–10.30 (11 F, S and summer)

Smugglers Inn
(A379) ℰ Dawlish 862301
Courage Best Bitter,
Directors Ⓗ
Large roadside pub with
panoramic views
🍴♪♣🅿️🅰️Ⓡ🅶🕙Ⓢ

Horndon 3H5

10.30–2.30; 5.30–10.30 (11 F, S and summer)

Elephant's Nest
(Off A386) OS 518801
Opens at 11.30 am & 6.30 pm
Palmer IPA
St Austell Tinners, Hicks
Special
Usher Best Bitter, Founders
Ale Ⓗ
16th-century pub in
Dartmoor National Park
🅰️♪♣🅿️Ⓢ🅰️

Devon

Horsebridge 3H5

12–2; 7–10.30 (11 F, S and summer)
Royal Inn
OS 401709
☎ Milton Abbot 214
Winter evening opening:
7.30; closed Mon lunchtimes
Courage Best Bitter
Royal Inn Tamar Ale,
Horsebridge Best Bitter, Heller
Wadworth 6X H
Interesting old pub by
pack-horse bridge, brewing its
own beer
🅿🎵♣🛏🅿🏪🕓🍴🍽⑧🅱Å

Ide 4B5

11–2.30; 5.30–10.30 (11 F, S)
Huntsman
High Street (off A30)
John Devenish Bitter, Wessex
Best Bitter H
Taunton Cider G
Ancient pub with longest sign
in Devon 🅿🎵♣🛏🅿🏪🕓🍴⑧

Ilfracombe 3H1

11–2.30; 5–11
Wellington Arms
High Street (A361) ☎ 62206
Courage Best Bitter H
Beamed pub with 'Iron Duke'
theme 🍴🎵♣🛏🅿🏪🕓🍴🍽Å

Kenton 4C6

10.30–2.30; 5.30–10.30 (11 F, S)
Devon Arms
(A379) ☎ Starcross 890213
Hall & Woodhouse
Badger Best Bitter H
Taunton Cider E
Pleasantly renovated
18th-century inn
🎵♣🛏🅿🏪🔲🅁🕓🍴🍽⑧

Kilmington 4E5

10.30–2.30; 5.30–10.30 (11 F, S and summer)
New Inn
The Hill (off A35)
☎ Axminster 33376
Palmer BB, IPA G
Attractive thatched village
pub 🅿🎵♣🛏🅿🏪🔲🅁🕓🍴⑧

Kingsbridge 4A8

10.30–2.30; 5.30–10.30 (11 F, S and summer)
Hermitage Bar
3 Mill Street ☎ 3234
Draught Bass
Whitbread Bitter H
Friendly town pub
🎵🕓🍴⑧

Kingsteignton 4B6

11–2.30; 5–10.30 (11 F, S and summer)
Old Rydon
Rydon Lane ☎ 4626
Evening opening: 6
Draught Bass
Cotleigh Tawny Bitter
Wadworth 6X H
Attractive old-world inn
🅿🎵🅿🏪🕓🍴⑧

Landscove 4B7

11–2.30; 6–10.30 (11 F, S and summer)
Live & Let Live
Near Ashburton
☎ Staverton 663
Courage Best Bitter
Wadworth 6X H
Hills Cider G
Lively, well-kept country inn
🅿♣🛏🅿🏪🕓🍴🍽⑧

Lapford 4A4

10.30–2.30; 5.30–10.30 (11 F, S)
Old Maltscoop
(Off A377) ☎ 330
Cotleigh Tawny Bitter
Wadworth 6X, Old Timer
Inch Cider G
16th-century pub, formerly a
brewery
🅿🎵♣🛏🅿🏠🔲🅁🕓🍴🍽⑧≷

Liverton 4B6

11–2.30; 5.30–10.30 (11 F, S and summer)
Star
(Off A38)
Courage Best Bitter,
Directors H
Taunton Cider G
Old and unspoilt inn 🎵♣🅿🏪⑧

Luton 4B6

10.30–2.30; 6–10.30 (11 F, S and summer)
Elizabethan Inn
(Off A380) ☎ Teignmouth 5425
Draught Bass
John Devenish Bitter, Wessex
Best Bitter H
Hills Cider G
400-year-old building, licence
granted by royal decree
🎵♣🅿🏪🕓🍴🍽⑧

Lutton 3J6

10.30–2.30; 6–10.30 (11 F, S and summer)
Mountain
(Off A38) OS 596594
Cotleigh Tawny Bitter,
Nutcracker
Golden Hill Exmoor Ale H
Wadworth 6X G
Peaceful country inn with
beautiful view ♣🅿🏪🕓

Lynton 4A1

11–2.30; 6–11
Crown
Sinai Hill (A39) ☎ 2253
Draught Bass
Whitbread Flowers Original
Bitter H
Old-style hotel 🎵♣🛏🅿🏠🕓🍴🍽⑧

Merrivale 3J5

11–2.30; 6–10.30 (11 F, S and summer)
Dartmoor Inn
(Off B3357)
☎ Princetown 340
Cotleigh Tawny Bitter
Golden Hill Exmoor Ale
St Austell Tinners
Wadworth 6X G
Lovely Dartmoor pub, ideal for
hikers 🅿🎵🅿🏪🕓🍴⑧Å

Milton Abbot 3H5

10.30–2.30; 6–10.30 (11 F, S and summer)
Edgcumbe
(A384) ☎ 229
Usher Best Bitter
Wadworth 6X
Whitbread Flowers
Original Bitter H
Typical country inn,
handpumps in lounge
🅿🎵♣🅿🏪⑧

Milton Coombe 3H6

10.30–2.30; 6–10.30 (11 F, S and summer)
**Who'd Have
Thought it**
(Off A386)
Draught Bass
Eldridge Pope Royal Oak
Golden Hill Exmoor Ale
Usher Best Bitter
Wadworth 6X H
16th-century pub in wooded
valley 🍴🅿🏪⑧

Newton Abbot 4B6

11–2.30; 5–10.30 (11 F, S and summer)
Queens Hotel
Queen Street ☎ 5216
Draught Bass
Courage Directors
Halls Harvest Bitter H
Comfortable hotel
🍴🔲🅿🏠🔲🅁🕓🍴⑧≷

Two Mile Oak
Totnes Road, Abbotskerswell
Evening opening; 6
Draught Bass H
Eldridge Pope Royal Oak G
Whitbread Bitter H
Attractive 15th-century inn,
two miles from town
🅿🎵🎵♣🅿🏪🕓🍴⑧

Wolborough

55 Wolborough Street
Evening opening: 5.30
Whitbread Bitter G
Small and friendly 🎵♣⑧

Newton St Cyres 4B5

11–2.30; 6–10.30 (11 F, S)
**Beer Engine
(formerly Barn Owl)**
Sweetham (off A377) ☎ 282
Beer Engine Piston Bitter, Rail
Ale
Golden Hill Exmoor Ale
Halls Harvest Bitter H
New home-brew pub with
railway connections
🅿🎵♣🛏🅿🏪🅁🕓🍽⑧≷

Ottery St. Mary 4D5

10.30–2.30; 5.30–10.30 (11 F, S)
Half Moon
North Street ☎ 2793
Devenish Wessex Best Bitter H
Taunton Cider G
Cheerful one-bar local on
outskirts of town 🎵♣🔲🕓🍴⑧

Paignton 4B7

10.30–2.30; 5.30–10.30 (11 F, S and summer)

Ship
Manor Road ☎ 551416
Draught Bass [H]
Large, nautical-style pub and restaurant ♪🚗☾☛[S]

Parkham 3H3

11–2.30; 6–10.30 (11 F, S and summer)

Bell
(Off A39) ☎ Horns Cross 201
Draught Bass [G]
Whitbread Bitter, Flowers Original Bitter [H]
A well-furnished pub
♪♣✿🚗[R]☾☛[S]⛺

Parracombe 4A2

11–2.30; 5.30–10.30 (11 F, S and summer)

Hunters
Heddons Mouth (off A39)
☎ 230
Draught Bass
Whitbread Flowers Original Bitter [H]
Impressive gardens in lovely Exmoor setting
Γ♪♣⊞✿🚗▣[R]☾☛🍷[S]⛺

Pennymoor 4B4

11–2.30; 6–10.30 (11 F, S and summer)

Cruwys Arms
(Off A373)
☎ Cheriton Fitzpaine 347
Whitbread Bitter [G]
Unspoilt country pub with splendid open fire
🏠♣⊞✿🚗☾☛🍷[S]

Plymouth 3H7

10–2.30; 6–10.30 (11 Th, F, S)

Berni Grand
The Hoe, Elliot Street
☎ 661195
Morning opening: 11
Draught Bass
Eldridge Pope Royal Oak
Usher Best Bitter, Founders Ale [H]
Grand Victorian hotel on seafront; good value pint in cellar bar ♪♣▣☾☛🍷

Clifton Hotel
Clifton Place, North Hill
Whitbread Bitter [H]
Friendly local ♪♣🍷[S]

Ferry House
888 Wolseley Road (off A38)
Courage Best Bitter [H]
Riverside pub by Tamar Bridge
♪♣⊞🍷[S]

Pennycomequick
Alma Road ☎ 61412
Halls Harvest Bitter
Ind Coope Burton Ale [H]
Large pub, two minutes from station ♪♣✿☾☛🍷[S]🚉

Pym Arms
Pym Street, Stoke
Morning opening: 11
Eldridge Pope IPA, Royal Oak
Halls Harvest Bitter
St Austell Hicks Special
Usher Best Bitter
Wadworth 6X [G]
See the only water-cooled beer in Plymouth ♪♣🍷[S]

Royal Marine
Torridge Way, Efford
Morning opening: 10.30
Courage Heavy, Best Bitter [H]
Spacious pub on housing estate 🏠Γ♪♣✿🚗🍷[S]

St Levan
St Levans Road, Ford
Halls Harvest Bitter [H]
Friendly locals' pub ♪♣⊞✿🍷[S]

Shipwrights
13 Sutton Road, Coxside
Courage Best Bitter, Directors [H]
Pleasant pub near city centre and Barbican ♪♣✿🍷[S]

Stopford Arms
172 Devonport Road
Morning opening: 10.30
Courage Heavy, Best Bitter, Directors [H]
Good regular trade in both bars Γ♪♣✿🍷[S]♿

Swan Hotel
6 Cornwall Beach, Devonport (off A374)
Morning opening: 11.30
Eldridge Pope Dorchester Bitter, Royal Oak
Golden Hill Exmoor Ale
Hook Norton Old Hookey
Marston Owd Rodger
St Austell Hicks Special
Usher Best Bitter, Founders Ale
Wadworth 6X [H]
Good atmosphere, great beer
🏠Γ♪♣🍷[S]

Terminus
Paradise Place, Stoke
Morning opening: 11
Courage Heavy, Best Bitter [H]
Friendly neo-Victorian locals' pub near college
Γ♪♣⊞✿[R]☾☛🍷[S]

Thistle Park Tavern
1 Sutton Road, Coxside
Morning opening: 11.30
Eldridge Pope Royal Oak
St Austell Hicks Special
Usher Best Bitter
Wadworth 6X [H]
For tipplers only – no beer bores please 🏠♪♣🍷[S]

Three Crowns
The Parade, Barbican
Courage Heavy, Best Bitter, Directors [H]
In pleasant surroundings in the historic Barbican ♪♣✿🍷[S]

Woodland Fort
Butt Park Road, Crownhill (off A38)
Morning opening: 11
Courage Best Bitter [H]
Busy local near old fort
♪♣✿🍷[S]

Plymtree 4C4

10.30–2.30; 5.30–10.30 (11 F, S)

Blacksmiths Arms
☎ 322
Opens 12–2; 7–10.30 (11 F, S)
Cotleigh Tawny Bitter
Golden Hill Exmoor Ale [H]
Wadworth 6X [G]
Unspoilt country pub
♪♣✿▣[R]☾☛[S]

Poundsgate 4A6

11–2.30; 6–10.30 (11 F, S and summer)

Tavistock Inn
(A384) ☎ 251
Courage Heavy, Best Bitter [H]
Hills Cider [G]
Old pub with 14th-century staircase ♣✿🚗🍷[S]

Princetown 3J6

11–2.30; 6–10.30 (11 F, S and summer)

Plume of Feathers
☎ 240
Draught Bass
St Austell Hicks Special [H]
Hills Cider [G]
A must for moor walkers and folk fans; guest beer in summer 🏠Γ♪♣⊞✿🚗▣🍷[S]⛺

Prince of Wales
Tavistock Road (B3357)
☎ 219
Wadworth 6X
Whitbread Flowers Original Bitter [H]
Hills Cider [G]
Warm, friendly inn, good base for walkers 🏠♣✿🚗☾☛🍷[S]⛺

Putts Corner 4D5

10.30–2.30; 5.30–10.30 (11 F, S)

Hare & Hounds
(A375/B3174) OS 146962
Courage Directors
Usher Founders Ale [H]
Wadworth 6X [G]
Large garden with facilities for children; selection of beers varies ⊞✿🚗☾☛[S]

Rockbeare 4C5

10.30–2.30; 5.30–10.30 (11 F, S)

Bidgood Arms
(A30) ☎ Whimple 822262
Whitbread Bitter, Flowers Original Bitter [H]
Large roadside pub with camping/caravan park attached
🏠♪♣✿🚗▣☾☛🍷[S]⛺

Salcombe 4A8

10.30–2.30; 5.30–10.30 (11 F, S and summer)

Burner's Victoria
Fore Street
Draught Bass
Hills Cider [G]
Old yachting pub ♣⊞✿🍷[S]

Sampford Courtenay 3J4

10.30–2.30; 6–10.30 (11 F, S and summer)
New Inn
(A3072)
☎ North Tawton 247
Whitbread Bitter G
Ancient inn of character

Shaugh Prior 3J6

11–2.30; 6–10.30 (11 Th, F, S and summer)
White Thorn
☎ Plymouth 839245
Courage Best Bitter H
Friendly country pub on edge of Dartmoor

Sidford 4D5

10.30–2.30; 5.30–10.30 (11 F, S)
Blue Ball
(A3052) ☎ Sidmouth 4062
John Devenish Bitter, Wessex Best Bitter H
Taunton Cider G
14th-century thatched pub

Sidmouth 4D5

10.30–2.30; 5.30–10.30 (11 F, S)
Anchor
Old Fore Street ☎ 4129
John Devenish Bitter, Wessex Best Bitter H
Taunton Cider G
Busy pub near seafront

Silverton 4C4

11–2.30; 6–10.30 (11 F, S and summer)
Three Tuns
Tuns Lane ☎ Exeter 860352
Draught Bass
Eldridge Pope Royal Oak
Wadworth 6X
Welsh Hancocks Bitter H
Low-beamed pub with collection of keys and antiques

Slapton 4B8

11.30–2.30; 6–10.30 (11 F, S and summer)
Tower Inn
(Off A379)
☎ Kingsbridge 580216
Blackawton Bitter
Cotleigh Tawny Bitter
Wadworth 6X H
Comfortable 14th-century free house; guest beers always available

South Brent 4A7

10.30–2.30; 5.30–10.30 (11 F, S and summer)
Royal Oak
Station Road (off A38)
☎ 2133
Draught Bass
Hall & Woodhouse Badger Best Bitter
Whitbread Flowers Original Bitter H
Hills & Taunton Cider G
Friendly village pub

South Molton 4A3

11–2.30; 5.30–10.30 (11 F, S and summer)
Goose & Gander
Queen Street (A361) ☎ 2526
Usher Best Bitter H
Comfortable hotel bar

Sticklepath 3J4

10.30–2.30; 6–10.30 (11 F, S and summer)
Devonshire
(A30) ☎ 626
Courage Best Bitter
Usher Best Bitter H
Gray Cider G
Friendly village pub

Tavistock 3H6

10.30–2.30; 5.30–10.30 (11 F, S and summer)
Cornish Arms
West Street (A390)
Open till 4 pm Wed, 4.30 Fri
Courage Heavy, Best Bitter H
Relatively expensive pub, rare outlet for Heavy

Teignmouth 4C6

11–2.30; 5–10.30 (11 F, S and summer)
Kings Arms
French Street ☎ 5268
Courage Best Bitter, Directors H
Large pub with 1940s atmosphere

Tiverton 4C4

11–2.30; 5–10.30 (11 F, S and summer)
Four in Hand
Fore Street
Draught Bass
Hall & Woodhouse Badger Best Bitter H
Busy saloon bar next door to old cinema

Racehorse
Wellbeck Street ☎ 252606
Usher PA, Best Bitter
Bulmer Cider H
Popular, renovated local near town centre

Topsham 4C5

11–2.30; 5–10.30 (11 F, S)
Bridge
Exmouth Road (A377)
Closes 2 pm, re-opens 6
Golden Hill Exmoor Ale
Hall & Woodhouse Badger Best Bitter
Wadworth 6X H
Rambling and ancient pub of great character

Try also: Kings Arms, Higher Shapter Street

Torquay 4C7

10.30–2.30; 5.30–10.30 (11 F, S and summer)
Clarence Hotel
Newton Road, Torre ☎ 24417
Halls Harvest Bitter
Ind Coope Burton Ale H
Warm and friendly pub

Crown & Sceptre
2 Petitor Road ☎ 38290
Courage Heavy, Best Bitter, Directors H
Popular local, worth a visit

Pullman Bar
Sea Front ☎ 25234
Draught Bass
Halls Harvest Bitter H
Part of new Grand Hotel, railway decor

Totnes 4B7

10.30–2.30; 5.30–10.30 (11 F, S and summer)
Dartmouth Inn
28 Warlands
Courage Best Bitter, Directors H
Hills & Taunton Cider G
Lively, popular town pub

Uplowman 4C4

11–2.30; 5–10.30 (11 F, S and summer)
Redwoods
☎ Sampford Peverell 820418
Cotleigh Tawny Bitter G
Comfortable lounge with open fire, lively public bar

Upottery 4D4

11–2.30; 6–10.30 (11 F, S and summer)
Sidmouth Arms
(Off A30) ☎ 252
Whitbread Bitter H
Large village centre pub, popular for meals

Westleigh 3H2

10.30–2; 5–10.30 (winter)
11–2.30; 5.30–11 (summer)
Westleigh Inn
(Off A39) ☎ Instow 860867
Usher Best Bitter, Founders Ale H
16th-century inn in unspoilt village

Yelverton 3H6

10.30–2.30; 6–10.30 (11 F, S and summer)
Rock Inn
(A386) ☎ 852022
Draught Bass
St Austell Hicks Special
Whitbread Flowers Original Bitter H
Countryman Cider G
Ancient, rambling, multi-bar hotel

Dorset

General opening hours: 10.30–2.30; 6–10.30 (11 F, S and summer)

Askerswell 5F5

Spyway Inn
(Off A35) *C* Powerstock 250
Poole Dolphin Best Bitter
Usher PA, Best Bitter Ⓗ
Bulmer Cider Ⓖ
Beautiful old pub with
marvellous views
🅰🆎🍽🏠🔲Ⓡ🅶🍷🟡Ⓢ🅰

Beaminster 5F4

Greyhound
The Square (A3066)
C 862496
Palmer BB, IPA Ⓗ
Friendly pub in small town
🅰🍹🔲Ⓡ🅶🍷🟡Ⓢ

Blandford Forum 5J4

Badger Hotel
Salisbury Road (A354)
C 52166
Hall & Woodhouse Hector's
Bitter, Badger Best Bitter Ⓗ
Popular town pub
🍹🅰🆎🍽🏠🔲Ⓡ🅶🍷🟡Ⓢ

Bournemouth 6B7

Beaufort Bar
2 Queens Road, Westbourne
C 763333
Ringwood Bitter, Fortyniner,
4X Porter
Wadworth 6X Ⓗ
Smart lounge bar with relaxed
atmosphere 🍹🏠🅶🟡�Ⓣ

Brunswick Hotel
199 Malmesbury Park Road,
Springbourne *C* 20197
Whitbread Strong Country
Bitter, Pompey Royal Ⓗ
Friendly backstreet local
🅰🍹🍽🆎Ⓡ🟡Ⓢ

Cricketers Arms
Windham Road,
Springbourne *C* 21589
Whitbread Strong Country
Bitter, Flowers Original
Bitter Ⓗ
Victorian pub
🍹🍽🏠Ⓡ🟡Ⓢ🔔

Bourton 5H3

Red Lion
(A303) *C* 840241
Hall & Woodhouse Hector's
Bitter, Badger Best Bitter Ⓗ
Fine village pub
🅰🍹🍽🅶🏠🟡Ⓢ

Bridport 5F5

Bull Hotel
East Street (A35) *C* 22878
Draught Bass
Eldridge Pope Royal Oak
Hall & Woodhouse

Badger Best Bitter
Welsh Hancocks Bitter Ⓗ
Comfortable old coaching inn
🅰🆎🍽🏠🔲Ⓡ🅶🟡Ⓢ🅰

Broadwey 5G6

Railway
Dorchester Road (A354)
John Devenish Bitter, Wessex
Best Bitter Ⓖ
Friendly roadside local
🍹🍽🏠Ⓡ🟡Ⓢ🔺🔔

Cattistock 5F5

Fox & Hounds
C Maiden Newton 20444
Opens at 11 am & 7 pm
John Devenish Bitter
Taunton Cider Ⓗ
Typical friendly village local
🅰🍹🍽🆎🍽🏠Ⓡ🟡Ⓢ

Cerne Abbas 5G5

Red Lion
24 Long Street (off A352)
C 441
Devenish Wessex Best Bitter Ⓗ
Eldridge Pope IPA Ⓖ
Tisbury Local Bitter Ⓗ
Wadworth 6X (summer) Ⓖ
Bulmer Cider Ⓖ
Convivial one-bar pub with
stained glass windows
🅰🍹🍽🆎🍽🏠🔲Ⓡ🅶🟡Ⓢ🅰

Charmouth 5E5

Coach & Horses
(A35) *C* 60321
Palmer BB, IPA, Tally Ho Ⓗ
Excellent main road village
pub 🍹🍽🆎🍽🏠🟡🟡Ⓢ🅰

Chickerell 5G6

Fisherman's Arms
Lower Putton Lane
(off B3157) OS 650805
C Weymouth 785136
Devenish Wessex Best Bitter Ⓖ
Friendly local off the beaten
track 🅰🍹🍽🆎🍽🏠Ⓡ🅶🟡🟡Ⓢ🅰🅰

Christchurch 6B7

Castle Tavern
7 Church Street *C* 485199
Draught Bass
Ringwood Bitter, Fortyniner Ⓗ
Old Thumper Ⓖ
Busy pub near town centre
🍹🍽🔲Ⓡ🅶🟡Ⓢ🔺

Corfe Mullen 6A7

Coventry Arms
(A31) *C* Sturminster Marshall
857284
Opens at 11 am & 6.30 pm
John Devenish Bitter, Wessex
Best Bitter Ⓖ
Interesting old low-beamed
local 🅰🍹🍽🅶🟡🟡Ⓢ🅰

Holme Bush

(Off A350)
Whitbread Strong Country
Bitter Ⓖ
Cosy and jolly country inn
🍷🅰🍹🍽🅰Ⓢ

Dorchester 5G5

Bulls Head
92 High Street, Fordington
C 64874
Opens at 11 am & 6.30 pm
Hall & Woodhouse
Badger Best Bitter Ⓗ
Unassuming town local
🍷🍹🍽🆎🍽🏠🅶🟡🟡Ⓢ🔺

Kings Arms
High East Street
C 65353
John Devenish Bitter, Wessex
Best Bitter Ⓗ
Handsome old coaching inn,
featured in Hardy's 'Mayor of
Casterbridge'
🅰🆎🅰🏠🔲Ⓡ🅶🟡🟡Ⓢ🔺

Evershot 5G4

Acorn
Fore Street (off A37)
C 228
Opens at 11 am & 7 pm
Draught Bass
Devenish Wessex Best Bitter
Hardington Best Bitter Ⓗ
Lively village pub
🅰🍹🍽🆎🍽🏠🔲Ⓡ🅶🟡🟡Ⓢ🅰

Godmanstone 5G5

Smiths Arms
(A352) OS 668974
C Cerne Abbas 236
John Devenish Bitter, Wessex
Best Bitter Ⓖ
15th-century thatched
smithy – claims to be the
smallest pub in England
🅰🍹🍽🅰🅶🟡Ⓢ

Hazelbury Bryan 5H4

Antelope
(Off A357) OS 746090
Hall & Woodhouse
Hector's Bitter
Taunton Cider Ⓖ
Jolly village inn
🍷🍽🅰🟡Ⓢ

King Stag 5H4

Green Man
(B3143)
C Hazelbury Bryan 338
Opens at 11 am & 7 pm
Everard Tiger Ⓖ
Golden Hill Exmoor Ale Ⓗ
Wadworth 6X Ⓖ
Renovated pub with good ale
and food
🅰🍹🍽🆎🍽🏠🔲Ⓡ🅶🟡Ⓢ🅰

Dorset

Langton Herring
5G6

Elm Tree
(Off B3157) OS 615824
✆ Abbotsbury 257
Devenish Wessex Best Bitter Ⓗ
Large pub in tiny village, full
in summer ♨♪⚲🅿️Ⓡ🅖🌙Ⓢ♿

Langton Matravers
6A8

Kings Arms
(B3069) ✆ Swanage 422979
Whitbread Strong Country Bitter Ⓗ
Bulmer Cider Ⓖ
Excellent village local with
Purbeck longboard
♨♣🎲⚲🍴Ⓡ🅘Ⓢ

Ship
(B3069) ✆ Swanage 422884
Whitbread Strong Country Bitter Ⓗ
Bulmer Cider Ⓖ
Interesting pub with morbid
history ♨♣🎲⚲🍴Ⓡ🅘Ⓢ

Litton Cheney
5G5

White Horse
(Off A35) OS 549901
✆ Long Bredy 539
Palmer BB, IPA, Tally Ho Ⓗ
Friendly village local by small
stream ♨♪♣⚲🅖🌙Ⓢ🅐

Lyme Regis
5E5

Angel
Mill Green ✆ 3267
Palmer BB, IPA, Tally Ho
Gaymer Cider Ⓖ
Good pub down by the river
♨♪♣🎲⚲🍴🅘Ⓢ🅐

Lytchett Minster
5J5

St Peters Finger
(Off A35) ✆ 622275
Draught Bass
Hall & Woodhouse Badger Best Bitter Ⓗ
Cheerful and historic inn with
contrasting bars
♨♪♣⚲🅖🌙Ⓢ

Milton Abbas
5H5

Hambro Arms
(Off A354) ✆ 880233
Devenish Wessex Best Bitter Ⓗ
Thatched pub in unspoilt
model village
♨♪♣⚲🍴Ⓡ🅖🌙Ⓢ

Morden
5J5

Cock & Bottle
(Off B3075) ✆ 238
Hall & Woodhouse Badger Best Bitter Ⓗ
Pleasant rural pub
♪♣⚲🅖🌙Ⓢ

Poole
6A7

Brewers Arms

Dear Hay Lane (off A350)
Evening opening: 6.30
Whitbread Strong Country Bitter Ⓗ
Small town pub and listed
building ♪♣🅗🅘Ⓢ♿

Bulls Head
Parr Street, (off A35)
Whitbread Strong Country Bitter Ⓖ
Charming small pub in lower
Parkstone ♪♣🅐🅘Ⓢ♿

Dorset Knob
164 Alder Road, Parkstone
Hall & Woodhouse Hector's Bitter, Badger Best Bitter Ⓗ
Friendly pub in residential
area ♪⚲🌙Ⓢ

Inn in the Park
26 Pinewood Road,
Branksome Park ✆ 761318
Poole Dolphin Best Bitter
Wadworth 6X Ⓗ
Plush, comfortable pub near
the sea ♪♣🎲⚲🅐Ⓡ🌙Ⓢ

King Charles
Thames Street ✆ 674950
Whitbread Strong Country Bitter
Bulmer Cider Ⓗ
Small, lively pub near the
quay ♪♣🎲⚲🅘Ⓢ

Lord Nelson
The Quay ✆ 673774
Hall & Woodhouse
Badger Best Bitter Ⓗ
Popular pub with folk music
♨♪♣⚲🅘🌙Ⓢ

Pure Drop
East Street ✆ 675312
Eldridge Pope IPA Ⓗ
Town local with a warm
welcome ♪♣⚲🅘🌙Ⓢ

Sweet Home
25 Ringwood Road (A348)
Morning opening: 11
Hall & Woodhouse
Badger Best Bitter
Bulmer Cider Ⓗ
Excellent local with Saturday
night singsongs ♪♣⚲🅐🌙Ⓢ

Victoria Cross
Ashley Road, Parkstone
✆ 736130
Eldridge Pope Dorchester Bitter, IPA Ⓗ **Royal Oak** Ⓖ
Pleasant and spacious single
bar ♪⚲🅐🌙Ⓢ

Portesham
5G5

Half Moon
Front Street (off B3157)
✆ Abbotsbury 227
John Devenish Bitter, Wessex Best Bitter Ⓖ
Locally popular timbered
village pub ♨♣⚲🅗🌙Ⓢ

Portland
5G6

Britannia

17 Fortuneswell ✆ 820159
Eldridge Pope Dorchester Bitter, IPA Ⓗ
Typical English pub, warm
and friendly atmosphere
♪♣⚲🌙Ⓢ♿

Clifton Hotel
Grove Road, Easton ✆ 820473
Morning opening: 11
John Devenish Bitter, Wessex Best Bitter Ⓗ
Lively, welcoming pub with
skittle alley ♨♪♣⚲🅐Ⓡ🌙Ⓢ

Shaftesbury
5H3

Ship
Bleke Street (top of Tout Hill,
off A30) ✆ 3219
Hall and Woodhouse Hector's Bitter, Badger Best Bitter Ⓗ
Superb 17th-century local
♨🅘♪♣⚲🌙Ⓢ

Shave Cross
5F5

Shave Cross Inn
Marshwood Vale (off B3162)
OS 415980
✆ Broadwindsor 68358
Opens at 11 am & 7 pm;
closed Mondays except bank
holidays
Draught Bass
Devenish Wessex Best Bitter
Eldridge Pope Royal Oak
Hall & Woodhouse
Badger Best Bitter
Taunton Cider (summer) Ⓖ
Marvellous 14th-century free
house ♨♣🅐🌙Ⓢ🅐

Shillingstone
5H4

Seymer Arms
(A357)
✆ Child Okeford 860488
Hall & Woodhouse
Hector's Bitter, Badger Best Bitter (summer) Ⓗ
Popular roadside local
♪⚲🅐🅗Ⓖ🌙Ⓢ

Spetisbury
5J4

Drax Arms
High Street (A350)
✆ Blandford 52658
Hall & Woodhouse Hector's Bitter, Badger Best Bitter Ⓗ
Lively and jolly
♪⚲🅐🅖🌙Ⓢ

Stoke Abbott
5F5

New Inn
(Off B3162) OS 455008
✆ Broadwindsor 68333
Palmer BB, IPA Ⓗ
Pleasant one-bar village inn
♨♪♣⚲🅐🅖🌙Ⓢ🅐

Sturminster Newton
5H4

Bull
(A357) ✆ 72435

Open until 4 pm Mondays
Hall & Woodhouse Hector's
Bitter, Badger Best Bitter Ⓗ
Convivial hostelry with skittle
alley ♪♣♨🅿🏠ₗⒼ🐾🕯Ⓢ

Swanage 6A8

Red Lion
High Street ☎ 423533
Whitbread Strong Country
Bitter, Pompey Royal
Bulmer Cider Ⓖ
Popular town-centre local;
handpumps decorative only
♠♪♣♨🅿🏠🅁ₗⒼ🐾🕯Ⓢ

Tarrant Hinton 5J4

Crown
(A354) ☎ 369
Hall & Woodhouse
Hector's Bitter Ⓗ
Cheerful roadside pub
♠♪♣♨🅿🏠Ⓖ🐾🕯Ⓢ

Thornford 5G4

Kings Arms
☎ Yetminster 872294
Opens at 11 am & 7 pm
Hall & Woodhouse Hector's
Bitter, Badger Best Bitter Ⓗ
Comfortable country ale
house with glass-fronted beer
engines ♪♣♠🅁Ⓖ🐾🕯Ⓢ

Trent 5G3

Rose & Crown
(Off A30)
Draught Bass
Eldridge Pope Dorchester
Bitter Ⓗ
Traditional village pub♣🏠ₗⒼⓈₖ

Wareham 5J5

Railway Tavern
Northport
Morning opening: 11
John Devenish Bitter, Wessex
Best Bitter Ⓗ
Two good bars; railway theme
in lounge ♪♣🏠♨🅿ₗⒸ🕯Ⓢ≋

West Bay 5H5

Haddon House
(B3157) ☎ Bridport 23626
Courage Best Bitter
Eldridge Pope Royal Oak Ⓗ
Small friendly hotel
🏠🅿🏠🅁ₗⒼ🐾Ⓢ🅰

West Bexington 5F5

Manor Hotel
(Off B3157) OS 534868
☎ Burton Bradstock 897785
EldridgePopeDorchesterBitter,
IPA, Royal Oak Ⓗ
Beamed cellar bar with open
fire ♠♪♨🅿🏠🅁ₗⒼ🐾Ⓢ🅰

West Stafford 5H5

Wise Man Inn
☎ Dorchester 63694

Opens at 11 am & 6.30 pm in
winter
John Devenish Bitter, Wessex
Best Bitter Ⓗ
Taunton Cider Ⓖ
Small, unspoilt pub, winter
haunt of Frome Valley Morris
men ♠♪♣♨🅿🏠ₗⒼ🐾🕯Ⓢₖ🅰

Weymouth 5G6

Albion
St Thomas Street
Opens at 11 am and 6.30 pm
John Devenish Bitter, Wessex
Best Bitter Ⓗ
Popular one-bar pub opposite
GPO ♪♣🐾Ⓢ

Golden Lion Hotel
St Edmund Street ☎ 786778
John Devenish Bitter, Wessex
Best Bitter Ⓗ
Roomy old coaching inn
♪🎱🅁Ⓖ🐾Ⓢ

Kings Arms
Trinity Road
John Devenish Bitter, Wessex
Best Bitter Ⓗ
Colourful harbourside pub full
of nautical bric-a-brac ♪♣Ⓢ

Nothe Tavern
Barrack Road, The Nothe
☎ 70935
Opens 6.30 pm in winter
Eldridge Pope IPA, Royal Oak Ⓗ
Excellent spacious tavern
overlooking harbour
ₗ♪♣♨🏠Ⓖ🐾Ⓢ

Portland Railway
20 King Street ☎ 783411
Draught Bass
Hall & Woodhouse
Hector's Bitter Ⓗ
Reliable one-bar pub
♪♣🎱Ⓢ≋

Weatherbury Hotel
Carlton Road North ☎ 786040
Ringwood Bitter
Welsh Hancocks Bitter
Whitbread Strong Country
Bitter, Pompey Royal Younger
IPA Ⓗ
Out-of-town hotel; guest beers
ₗ♪♣♨🅿🏠🅁ₗⒼ🐾Ⓢ

Wimborne 6A7

Rising Sun
38 East Street ☎ 883464
Morning opening: 11
Hall & Woodhouse Hector's
Bitter, Badger Best Bitter Ⓗ
Modernised riverside pub
♪♨Ⓖ🐾Ⓢ

Winkton 6B7

Fisherman's Haunt
Salisbury Road (B3347)
☎ Christchurch 484071
Draught Bass
Courage Directors Ⓗ
Popular free house
overlooking River Avon
♠♪🏠♨🅿🅁ₗⒼ🐾Ⓢₖ

Lamb Inn
Burley Road (off B3347)
☎ Bransgore 72427
Hall & Woodhouse
Badger Best Bitter
Ind Coope Burton Ale
Tisbury Local Bitter
Wadworth 6X Ⓗ
Friendly rural local in green
fields ♪♣♨🅿Ⓖ🐾🕯Ⓢ

Winterborne Kingston 5H5

Greyhound
(Off A31) ☎ Bere Regis 332
Hall & Woodhouse Hector's
Bitter, Badger Best Bitter Ⓗ
Cheerful village pub
ₗ♪♣♨🅿🏠Ⓖ🐾🕯Ⓢ

Winterborne Stickland 5H4

Crown
(Off A354)
John Devenish Bitter Ⓖ
18th-century village inn
♠♪♣♨🅿🏠Ⓢ

Worth Matravers 6A8

Square & Compass
(Off B3069)
Whitbread Strong Country
Bitter, Pompey Royal
Bulmer Cider Ⓖ
A real bastion of the Purbecks,
with extensive coastal views
♠ₗ♣♨🅿🏠🅁Ⓢ

Wyke Regis 5G6

Mermaid Inn
64 High Street (off A354)
John Devenish Bitter, Wessex
Best Bitter Ⓗ
Excellent lively pub ♠♪♣🐾Ⓢ

Yetminster 5G4

White Hart
(Off A37) ☎ 872338
Opens at 11 am & 7 pm
Draught Bass
Welsh Hancock's Bitter Ⓗ
Pleasant atmosphere in
ancient building
♠♪♣♨🅿🏠🅁ₗⒼ🐾🕯Ⓢₖ≋

WARMEST WELCOME

♦ A REAL FIRE PUB ♦

The ♠ symbol denotes a pub
with a real solid fuel fire

Aycliffe 30B3

11–3; 6–10.30
North Briton
Aycliffe Village (A167)
☎ 312281
Evening opening: 5.30
Vaux Samson [H]
Popular large roadside pub; ask for cask ♪♣🚗[R]◷❥🍷Ⓢ

Barnard Castle 29J3

11–3; 6–10.30
Cricketers Arms
Galgate (A67)
Saturday evening opening: 6.30
Cameron Strongarm [H]
Popular, basic local ♪♣[R]🍷Ⓢ

Old Well
21 The Bank (A67)
☎ Teesdale 38871
McEwan 80/-
Theakston Best Bitter, XB [H]
Friendly pub near Buttermarket
♪♣℘■[R]◷❥🍷

Three Horseshoes
Galgate (A67)
☎ Teesdale 38774
Open all day Wednesdays
Draught Bass [E]
Popular town-centre pub
♪♣⊞℘◷❥🍷Ⓢ

Beamish Burn 30B1

11–3; 6–10.30
Shepherd & Shepherdess
☎ Durham 700349
Vaux Sunderland Draught Bitter, Samson [H]
Comfortable, traditional pub beside Beamish Museum
♪℘🚗◷❥Ⓢ⛺

Billy Row 30B2

11–3; 6–10.30
Dun Cow
Old White Lea (off B6293)
OS 149372
Cameron Lion Bitter
Theakston Best Bitter [H]
Isolated, ancient free house, unchanged in fifty years ♣🚗🍷

Bishop Auckland 30B3

11–3; 6–10.30 (11 S)
Newton Cap
Newton Cap Bank (A689)
Cameron Strongarm [H]
Basic local, high above the river Wear ♪♣[R]🍷🚉

Sportsmans
Market Square ☎ 603478
Theakston Old Peculier
Whitbread Durham Ale, Castle Eden Ale
Bulmer Cider [H]
Often crowded town-centre pub 🔥♪♣◷🍷Ⓢ🚉

Bishop Middleham 30C2

11–3; 6–10.30
Red Lion
3 Bank Top (off A177)
☎ Ferryhill 51298
Whitbread Castle Eden Ale [H]
Friendly local overlooking village green 🔥♪♣℘🚗◷❥Ⓢ

Bishopton 30C3

11–3; 6–10.30
Talbot
The Green
☎ Sedgefield 30371
Evening opening 5.30 pm
Cameron Lion Bitter, Strongarm [H]
Popular country pub in small village 🔥♪♣℘🚗[R]Ⓢ♿

Brandon 30B2

11–3; 6–10.30
Brawns Den
Winchester Drive, Dere Park
☎ Durham 781687
Tetley Bitter [H]
Smart new pub on the edge of private housing estate
♪♣℘🚗◷❥Ⓢ

Canney Hill 30B3

11–3; 6–10.30 (11 S)
Sportsman
(A689) near Bishop Auckland
Cameron Lion Bitter, Strongarm [H]
Justifiably popular, well-run roadside inn 🔥♪♣℘🚗[R]◷🍷Ⓢ

Cockfield 30A3

11–3; 6–10.30
Queens Head
Front Street (off A698) ☎ 364
Cameron Lion Bitter, Strongarm [H]
Busy village local ♪♣🚗[R]🍷Ⓢ

Consett 30A1

11–3; 6–10.30
Park
Newmarket Street (off A692)
☎ 502369
Cameron Lion Bitter [H]
Plain town pub with resident minah bird ſ♣[R]❥🍷

Cornsay Colliery 30B2

11–3; 6.30–10.30
Fir Tree
Hedley Hill Lane (B6301)
☎ Esh Winning 418
Lorimer Best Scotch [H]
Isolated, old-fashioned and unspoilt; known locally as 'The Monkey' 🔥ſ♣⊞℘🚗[R]🍷♿

Cowshill 29G2

11–3; 6–10.40
Cowshill Hotel
(B6293) ☎ Wearhead 236
Theakston Best Bitter, XB [H]
Congenial country pub in Upper Weardale
🔥♣🚗■◷❥🍷Ⓢ

Coxhoe 30C2

11–3; 6–10.30
Cricketers
Cornforth Lane
☎ Durham 770510
Vaux Sunderland Draught Bitter [H]
Friendly village local with lively atmosphere
🔥ſ♪♣⊞℘[R]◷❥🍷Ⓢ

Crook 30B2

11–3; 6–10.30
Travellers Rest
97 Wheatbottom (A690)
☎ 2184
Cameron Lion Bitter, Strongarm [E]
Congenial local on outskirts of town ♣🚗[R]🍷

Croxdale 30B2

11–3; 6–10.30
Coach & Horses
Butchers Race (A167)
☎ Spennymoor 814484
Lorimer Best Scotch
Vaux Samson [H]
Convivial coaching inn with homely atmosphere
🔥♪♣⊞℘🚗[R]◷❥Ⓢ♿⛺

Darlington 30B4

11–3; 5.30–10.30
Britannia
Archer Street (off A68)
Morning opening: 11.30
Cameron Strongarm [H]
Historic and homely, facing inner ring road ♣🚗[R]

Collectors Arms
Richardsons Yard, Houndgate
☎ 286008
Evening opening: 6; closed Sunday lunchtimes
Cameron Lion Bitter, Strongarm
Samuel Smith Old Brewery Bitter
Theakston Old Peculier
Younger No. 3 [H]
Central pub, busy at weekends
♪◷

Highland Laddie
The Green, Haughton-le-Skerne (A66)
Cameron Strongarm [E]
Large suburban pub in former village ♪♣🚗🍷

Durham 30B2

11–3; 6–10.30
Dun Cow
Old Elvet
Whitbread Castle Eden Ale [H]
Attractive, congenial old city pub near the gaol
♣🍷Ⓢ🚉

Durham

Garden House
North Road ☎ 42460
Vaux Samson 🅷
Well-appointed pub to suit all
tastes ♪♣♨🅰❶⑩≷

Half Moon
New Elvet ☎ 64528
Draught Bass 🅷
Busy city-centre pub ♣❶⑩≷

New Inn
Church Street Head ☎ 47209
Bass Extra Light 🅷
Caters for all tastes
♣♨🅰🅲❶⑩≷

Shakespeare
Saddler Street ☎ 69709
McEwan 80/-
Younger No. 3 🅷
Small, quaint inn on the way
to the cathedral ❶⑩≷

Stonebridge Inn
Stonebridge (A690) ☎ 69591
Whitbread Castle Eden Ale 🅷
Comfortable, congenial local
on road to Crook ♪♣♨🅰🅲❶⑩

Travellers Rest
72/73 Claypath ☎ 65370
Theakston Best Bitter, XB, Old
Peculier 🅷
City-centre pub with wine bar
♣🅲❶⑩≷

Victoria
6 Hallgarth Street (A177)
☎ 65269
McEwan 80/-
Younger No. 3
Bulmer Cider 🅷
Friendly Victorian local
🅰🅳🅁❶⑩≷

Ebchester
30A1

-3; 6–10.30
Chelmsford
Front Street ☎ 560213
Vaux Samson 🅷
Tasteful pub overlooking
Derwent Valley
♣♨🅰🅲❶⑩

Edmondsley
30B1

-3; 6–10.30
Fleece
Drybrough Pentland 🅷
Friendly village local, lively
atmosphere ♪♣❶

Esh
30B2

-3; 6–10.30
Cross Keys
Front Street
☎ Durham 731279
Whitbread Castle Eden Ale 🅷
Delightful village local
♨🅰🅲❶⑩

Ravenwood
30B3

-3; 6–10.30
Bay Horse Inn
(off A688)
☎ Bishop Auckland 832697

Whitbread Castle Eden Ale 🅷
Friendly family pub
♪♣♨🅳♨🅰🅳🅁🅲❶⑩⑤

Ferryhill
30B2

11–3; 6–10.30
Black Bull
(Off A167) ☎ 51676
McEwan 80/-
Younger No. 3
Bulmer Cider 🅷
Large, lively local in busy
village ♪♣🅰🅁❶⑩⑤

Framwellgate Moor
30B2

11–3; 6–10.30
Happy Wanderer
Beech Road ☎ Durham 64580
Draught Bass
Stones Best Bitter 🅷
Comfortable estate pub with
full catering facilities
♪♪♣🅷♨🅰🅲🅁🅲❶⑩⑤♿≷

Marquis of Granby
Front Street (off A167)
☎ Durham 69382
Samuel Smith Old Brewery
Bitter 🅷
Community-conscious,
homely pub with folk club
♪♪♣🅷♨🅰🅳🅁🅲❶⑩⑤♿≷

Gilesgate Moor
30B2

11–3; 6–10.30
Lord Seaham
Rennys Lane
Cameron Strongarm 🅷
Friendly old pub
♪♣🅰🅁❶⑩

Queens Head
2 Sherburn Road (A181)
☎ Durham 65649
Tetley Bitter 🅷
Thriving inn, just outside
Durham city centre
♪♪♣♨🅰❶⑩

Three Horseshoes
Sunderland Road ☎ Durham
69818
Whitbread Castle Eden Ale 🅷
Attractive, popular and
friendly village local
♪♪♣♨🅰🅲♥⑩

Great Stainton
30C3

11–3; 5.30–10.30
Kings Arms
☎ Sedgefield 30361
Opens at 12 noon & 7 pm
Whitbread Castle Eden Ale 🅷
Unspoilt small bar, large
lounge and restaurant
♨♣🅲♥⑩

Greta Bridge
30A4

11–3; 6–10.30
Morritt Arms Hotel
(A66) ☎ Teesdale 27232
Theakston Best Bitter 🅷
Smart hotel with fascinating
murals in bar ♨♣🅷♨🅰🅳🅁🅲♥

Haswell
30C2

11–3; 6–10.30
Oddfellows Arms
86 Front Street (B1280)
Bass Extra Light 🅷
Friendly, unspoilt village local
🅰♪♣🅰❶⑩

Holwick
29H3

11–3; 6–10.30
Strathmore Arms
(Off B6276)
☎ Middleton-in-Teesdale 362
Theakston Best Bitter 🅷
Isolated, friendly pub, popular
with walkers and campers
🅰♪♣🅷♨🅰🅳🅁🅲♥⑩🄰

Howden-le-Wear
30B2

11–3; 6–10.30
Surtees
(A698)
Open until 11 pm Saturdays
Cameron Strongarm 🅷
Popular local on outskirts of
village 🅰♪🅰🅳🅁❶

Hunwick
30B2

11–3; 6–10.30
Wheatsheaf
(B6286)
Open until 11 pm Saturdays
Cameron Lion Bitter,
Strongarm 🅷
Small, friendly bar and large
games room ♪♣🅁❶

Lanchester
30B1

11–2.30; 6–10.30
Blue Bell
Front Street (off A691)
☎ 520433
Vaux Samson 🅷
Quiet village pub with friendly
atmosphere ♪♣🅲♥❶⑩

Langley Park
30B2

11–3; 6–10.30
Centurion
Wall Nook Lane
☎ Durham 731323
Opens at 11.30 am & 7 pm
Vaux Samson 🅷
Country pub on river bank,
Roman theme ♪♨🅰🅲♥⑩

Medomsley
30A1

11–3; 6–10.30
Miners Arms
Manor Road (B6310)
☎ Ebchester 560428
Vaux Sunderland Draught
Bitter 🅷
Smart, cosy village pub
♪♣♨🅰🅲♥❶⑩⑤

Neasham
30C4

11–3; 5.30–10.30
Fox & Hounds
24 Teesway
☎ Darlington 720350
Evening opening: 6.30 pm

Durham

Vaux Samson H
Excellent village local in
riverside setting
♪♣🏠🏃🍴♿👥🅿👥

Newton Hall 30B2

11–3; 6–10.30
Jovial Monk
Canterbury Road
☎ Durham 64689
Tetley Bitter H
Smart estate pub with
catering facilities ♪🏃🏠♿👥

Piercebridge 30B3

11–3; 5.30–10.30
Wheatsheaf Hotel
(Off A67)
Morning opening: 11.30
Cameron Strongarm H
Popular local in attractive
village with Roman remains
🛏♪🏃🏠👥

Pity Me 30B2

11–3; 6–10.30
Lambton Hounds
62 Front Street (off A167)
☎ Durham 64742
Lorimer Best Scotch H
Small, friendly village pub
🛏♪🏃🏠🅿👥

Romaldkirk 29H3

11–3; 6–10.30
Rose & Crown
(B6277) ☎ Teesdale 50213
Open until 11 pm Saturdays
Cameron Lion Bitter
Theakston Best Bitter H
Excellent country hotel and
village inn ♪♣🏠🅿🍴♿👥

Seaton 30C1

11–3; 6–10.30
Seaton Lane Inn
Seaton Lane
Opens at 12 noon & 6.30 pm
Matthew Brown John Peel
Bitter
Samuel Smith Old Brewery
Bitter
Theakston Best Bitter, XB, Old
Peculier H
Friendly old village inn, guest
beers on gravity 🛏♪♣🏃🏠👥

Sedgefield 30C3

11–3; 6–10.30
Nags Head
8 West End ☎ 20234
Draught Bass E
Refurbished 300-year old inn
near village green, good food
♪🏠🅿🍴♿👥🅿👥♿

Shildon 30B3

11–3; 6–10.30
Cross Keys
Cheapside (off A6072)
☎ Bishop Auckland 772485
Cameron Strongarm H
Small and friendly, oldest pub
in town 🛏♪♣🅿👥

King William
Eldon Road (off A6072)
☎ Bishop Auckland 772405
Cameron Strongarm H
Pleasant street-corner local
♪♣♿👥👥

Shincliffe 30B2

11–3; 6–10.30
Seven Stars
(A177) ☎ Durham 48454
Lorimer Best Scotch
Vaux Sunderland Draught
Bitter H
Cosy, friendly pub with
interesting decoration
🛏♪🏃🏠♿👥👥

Spennymoor 30B2

11–3; 6–10.30
Crown
Whitworth Terrace (A6074)
Vaux Samson H
Large, friendly town pub
♪🏠♿

Staindrop 30A3

11–3; 6–10.30
Black Swan
40 Front Street ☎ 60214
Cameron Lion Bitter,
Strongarm H
Active local near Raby Castle
🏃♣🅿👥

Stanhope 29H2

11–3; 6–10.30
Phoenix
Market Place (A689)
☎ 214
Cameron Best Bitter,
Strongarm H
Small, old-fashioned hotel
♪♣🏠🅿🍴♿👥🛏

Summerhouse 30B3

11–3; 5.30–10.30
Raby Hunt Inn
(B6279) OS 202191
☎ Piercebridge 604
Evening opening: 6.30
Cameron Strongarm
Theakston Best Bitter H
Pleasant country village pub
🛏♪🏃🏠♿👥♿

Tanfield 30B1

11–3; 6–10.30
Peacock
(Off A692)
Lorimer Best Scotch
Vaux Samson E
Friendly village local with
strong cricketing connections
♪♣🏠👥

Tantobie 30B1

11–3; 6–10.30
Bird Inn
White-le-Head (B6311)
☎ Stanley 32416
Opens at 12 noon & 7 pm
Belhaven 80/-, Strong
Cameron Strongarm

Marston Pedigree, Merrie
Monk H
A pub for all tastes; frequent
guest beers ♪♣🏠👥🍴

Commercial

Front Street
Whitbread Castle Eden Ale H
Pleasant, busy village local
♪♣🏃🏠👥🍴♿

Tow Law 30A

11–3; 6–10.30
Surtees
Hill Terrace (A68)
Lorimer Best Scotch
Vaux Samson H
Cosy village local 🍴♪♣🏠♿

West Auckland 30B

11–3; 6–10.30
Prince of Wales
Front Street (A688)
Open until 11 pm Saturdays
Cameron Lion Bitter,
Strongarm H
Bustling, friendly local on
village green ♪♣🏠👥🍴

West Cornforth 30C

11–3; 6–10.30
Square & Compass
The Green (off B6291)
☎ Ferryhill 54606
Bass Extra Light
Stones Best Bitter H
Lively local on secluded village
green ♪♣🏃🏠👥🍴♿

Witton Gilbert 30B

11–3; 6–10.30
Glendenning Arms
Front Street (A691)
Vaux Samson H
Friendly village pub with
strong horse-racing
connections 🛏♣🏃🏠👥

Travellers Rest

Front Street (A691)
☎ Durham 710458
Cameron Lion Bitter,
Strongarm
McEwan 70/-
Younger No. 3 H
Traditional, friendly village
pub 🛏♪♣🏃🏠🅿♿🍴👥

Wolsingham 30A

11–3; 6–10.30
Black Lion
Meadhope Street
(Off B6296)
Cameron Lion Bitter H
Modernised old back-street
pub 🍴♪♣🍴👥🛏

Woodhouses 30B

11–3; 6–10.30
Bay Horse
(Off A6073) OS 189281
Closed Mon–Fri lunchtimes
Cameron Lion Bitter H
Tiny country pub with
horse-racing decor ♣🏃🏠

Althorne 11F2

0–2.30; 6–11
Huntsman & Hounds
Green Lane (off B1010)
Morning opening: 10.30
Greene King IPA, Abbot [G]
Attractive thatched pub in rural Essex 👪♣🌿🚗🍷[S]⛺

Arkesden 18B8

1.30–2.30; 6–10.30 (11 F, S)
Axe & Compasses
(Off B1038) OS 483344
☎ Clavering 272
Greene King Abbot
Rayment BBA [H]
17th century pub in pretty village ♪♣🌿🚗☽◗🍷

Bannister Green 18C9

10.30–2.30; 6–11
Three Horseshoes
(Off A120)
☎ Great Dunmow 820467
Ridley Bitter [E] & [H]
Delightful pub facing village green 👪♪♣🌿🚗☽◗🍷[S]

Bardfield End Green 18C8

10.30–2.30; 6–10.30 (11 F, S)
Butchers Arms
Near Thaxted
Greene King Abbot
Rayment BBA [H]
Picturesque thatched pub on cricket green 👪🔥♪♣🌿🚗[S]

Basildon 10D2

10–2.30; 6–10.30 (11 F, S)
Jolly Cricketers
Arterial Road, Nevedon (A127) ☎ 726231
Ind Coope Bitter, Burton Ale [H]
Busy weekday lunchtime trade ♪♣🌿🚗☽🍷[S]

Battlesbridge 10E2

10–2.30; 6–11
Barge
Hawk Hill (off A130)
☎ Wickford 2622
Ind Coope Bitter, Burton Ale [H]
Bulmer Cider [G]
Popular riverside inn near antique centre
👪🔥♪♣🌿🚗☽◗[S]🚉

Baythorn End 18D7

10.30–2.30; 6–11
Swan
(A604)
Greene King IPA, Abbot [H]
Tastefully refurbished old pub
♪♣🌿🚗🍷[S]

Belchamp St Paul 18D7

10.30–2.30; 6–11
Plough
OS 790421
Greene King IPA [H] **Abbot** [G]
Unspoilt old-style village local
👪♣⊞🌿🚗🍷[S]

Billericay 10D2

10–2.30; 6–10.30 (11 F, S)
White Hart
138 High Street (B1007)
Charrington IPA
Mitchells & Butlers Springfield Bitter [H]
Well-run pub in real ale town
♪♣🌿🚗[R]☽[S]

Blackmore End 18D8

10.30–2.30; 6.30–11
Red Cow
Near Braintree
☎ Great Dunmow 850337
Ridley Bitter [G]
Fine, comfortable village pub
👪♣🌿🚗☽◗[S]

Boreham 18D9

10–2.30; 6–11
Six Bells
Main Road
Morning opening: 11
Greene King XX, IPA, Abbot [H]
Large, tastefully renovated pub with children's playground ♪♣🌿🚗☽🍷[S]

Try also: Cock (Ridley); **Queens Head** (Greene King)

Bradfield 19F8

10.30–2.30; 6–11
Strangers Home
The Street (B1352)
Norwich Bullards Mild, Castle Bitter
Webster Yorkshire Bitter [H]
Spacious, friendly village inn
🔥♪♣⊞🌿🚗🍷[S]⛺

Braintree 18D8

10.30–2.30; 6–11
Kings Head
Coggeshall Road (A120)
Evening opening: 6.30
Ridley Bitter [H]
Friendly local, petanque played 👪♪♣🌿🚗☽🍷[S]♿

Brentwood 10C2

10–2.30; 6–10.30 (11 F, S)
Victoria
Ongar Road (A128) ☎ 223371
Greene King IPA, Abbot
Ridley Mild
Bulmer Cider [H]
Friendly, popular one-bar local 👪♪♣🌿☽♿

Broads Green 18C9

10.30–2.30; 6–10.30 (11 F, S and summer)
Walnut Tree
(Off A130)
Evening opening: 6.30
Ridley Bitter [G] & [H]
Victorian pub of character on village green 👪♪♣🌿🚗🍷[S]

Buckhurst Hill 10B2

10.30–2.30; 6–10.30 (11 F, S)
Roebuck Hotel (Connaught Bar)
North End (off A121)
☎ 01-505 4636
Draught Bass
Courage Best Bitter
Rayment BBA
Bulmer Cider [H]
THF hotel in pleasant surroundings with smart bar
👪♣⊞🌿🚗■[R]☽◗[S]

Warren Wood House
Epping New Road (A104)
☎ 01-504 0244
Charrington IPA
Ruddle Bitter, County
Young Special Bitter [H]
Pleasant Webster's house on edge of Epping Forest
♪🌿🚗☽◗[S]♿

Bulmer Tye 18D7

10.30–2; 6.30–11
Fox
(A131) OS 849388
☎ Sudbury 77505
Greene King IPA, Abbot [H]
Friendly village inn
👪♣🌿☽◗[S]

Burnham-on-Crouch 11F2

10–2.30; 6–11
New Welcome Sailor
74 Station Road
Greene King IPA, Abbot [H]
Basic in the very best fashion
♪♣🚗[R]🚉

All pubs in Burnham sell real ale

Burton End 18B8

10.30–2.30; 6–10.30 (11 F, S)
Ash
Near Stansted Airport
OS 532237
☎ Bishop's Stortford 814841
Greene King Abbot
Rayment BBA [H]
Charming 17th century thatched pub 👪♪♣🌿🚗☽◗🍷[S]

Canvey Island 10E3

10–2.30; 6–10.30 (11 F, S)
Admiral Jellicoe
283 High Street ☎ 68370
Charrington IPA [H]
Busy seasonal pub
🔥♪♣🚗■[R]☽🍷[S]

Castle Hedingham 18D8

10.30–2.30; 6–11

Bell
(B1058) ☎ Hedingham 60350
Greene King IPA, Abbot [G]
Superb old timbered pub in ancient village
🔥♪♣⊞⚘🚗[R]◔☾🍷[S]

Chappel 18E8

10.30–2.30; 5.30–11
Swan
(Off A604) ☎ Earls Colne 2353
Brightlingsea Bitter
Greene King IPA, Abbot [H]
Popular old inn close to Stour Valley railway ⚘🚗◔☾🍷[S]♿

Chelmsford 10D1

10–2.30; 6–11
Golden Fleece
Duke Street ☎ 56752
Truman Prize Mild, Bitter, Best Bitter, Sampson
Hanbury's Extra Strong [H]
Large, noisy and popular; flagship of Eagle Taverns
♪⚘◔[S]🚆

Orange Tree
Lower Anchor Street
Greene King IPA, Abbot [H]
Popular town pub
♪♣⚘🚗◔🍷[S]♿

Rising Sun
232 New London Road (A122) ☎ 352782
Morning opening: 11
Charrington IPA
Mitchells & Butlers Springfield Bitter [H]
Comfortable town pub
🔥♪♣🚗◔☾ (Mon–Thu) 🍷[S]♿

Star & Garter
159 Moulsham Street
Morning opening: 11
Truman Prize Mild, Bitter [H]
Pleasant refurbished pub in interesting street
⌈♪♣⚘[R]◔

Cock Clarks 10E2

10–2.30; 6–11
Fox & Hounds
(Off B1010) OS 816028
Ridley Bitter [G]
Quiet Essex village pub
♪♣⚘🚗🍷[S]

Coggeshall 18D8

10.30–2.30; 6–10.30 (11 F, S)
Fleece
27 West Street (A120)
☎ 61412
Greene King IPA, Abbot [H]
Modernised comfortable Tudor house with large garden, adjoining Paycocke's
🔥⚘🚗■◔☾[S]

Colchester 19E8

10.30–2.30; 5.30–11
Artilleryman
54–56 Artillery Street
Greene King XX, IPA, Abbot [H]
Friendly corner local, basic public bar and smooth lounge
♪♣⚘🍷[S]

Bugle Horn
30 Barrack Street ☎ 575843
Tolly Cobbold Mild, Bitter, Original [H]
Friendly, tastefully refurbished local ♪♣⚘■🍷[S]♿

Hospital Arms
Crouch Street ☎ 73572
Tolly Cobbold Bitter, Original, Old Strong [H]
Modernised popular town pub with rugby theme ♪◔

Live & Let Live
Millers Lane, Stanway (Off A120)
Ridley Bitter
Truman Prize Mild, Bitter [H]
♪♣⚘🚗☾🍷[S]

Rose & Crown Hotel
East Street ☎ 86677
Tolly Cobbold Bitter [H]
Rambling medieval inn of character; wine bar in cellar
♪⊞⚘🚗■[R]◔☾[S]🚆

Coopersale 10C2

10.30–2.30; 6–10.30 (11 F, S)
Garnon Bushes
Coopersale Common (off B181) ☎ Epping 73069
Charrington IPA
Draught Bass [H]
Popular pub comprising two terraced cottages
🔥♪♣⚘🚗◔[S]

Copford 18E8

10.30–2.30; 6–11
Alma
Copford Green (off A120)
☎ Colchester 210607
Greene King IPA, Abbot [H]
Rural local, minimally modernized and enduringly popular 🔥⌈♣⚘🚗■[S]🚆

Coxtie Green 10C2

10.30–2.30; 6–10.30 (11 F, S)
White Horse
(Off A128)
Ind Coope Burton Ale
Romford Brewers Bitter [H]
Traditional country local
♪♣⚘🚗🍷[S]

Dedham 19F8

10.30–2.30; 6–10.30 (11 F, S)
Lamb
Lamb Corner (off B1029)
Tolly Cobbold Bitter, Original
Bulmer Cider [G]
Well-preserved 15th-century monks' house ⚘🚗◔🍷[S]

Duton Hill 18C8

10.30–2.30; 6–10.30 (11 F, S)
Rising Sun
(Off B184) OS 269602
☎ Great Easton 204
Ridley Bitter [H]
Tastefully altered small villag
pub ♣⊞⚘🚗■◔☾[S]

Earls Colne 18E

10.30–2.30; 6–11
Bird in Hand
Coggeshall Road (B1024)
Opens at 11 am & 7 pm
Ridley Bitter [E]
Quiet rural 19th-century loca
🔥♪♣⚘🚗🍷[S]

Epping 10C

10.30–2.30; 6–10.30 (11 F, S)
Forest Gate
Bell Common (off B1393)
Adnams Bitter
Rayment BBA
Bulmer Cider [H]
Old free house on edge of Epping Forest 🔥♣⚘🚗[S]

Feering 18E

10.30–2.30; 6–10.30 (11 F, S and summer)
Bell
The Street (off A12)
Greene King IPA, Abbot [H]
14th-century rural inn and shop ♪♣⚘🚗[R]🍷[S]

Finchingfield 18C

10–2.30; 6–11
Red Lion
Church Hill (B1053)
☎ Great Dunmow 810400
Ridley Bitter [H]
Traditional pub in lovely village
♪♣⚘🚗■◔☾🍷[S]

Fingringhoe 19F

10.30–2.30; 5.30–11
Whalebone
☎ Rowhedge 307
Ind Coope Bitter, Burton Ale [H]
Attractive village inn; spectacular view from garden
⚘🚗[R]◔ (not Mon) ☾[S]♿

Fobbing 10D

10–2.30; 6–10.30 (11 F, S)
White Lion
Fobbing Road (off B1420)
Ind Coope Bitter, Burton Ale [H]
Fine village local, connections with Anne Boleyn. Guest beers from Allied group
♣⚘🚗[R]◔🍷[S]

Fyfield 10C

10.30–2.30; 6–10.30 (11 F, S)
Black Bull
Dunmow Road (B184)
☎ 225
Morning opening: 11
Charrington IPA
Draught Bass [H]
Old building with new dining room 🔥♪♣⚘🚗☾[S]

Good Easter 18C9

10.30–2.30; 6–11
Star
The Endway (off A1060)
Benskins Bitter
Ind Coope Burton Ale Ⓗ
Pleasant, friendly village local
🅰♪♣🖤🏠Ⓡ🕯Ⓢ

Grays 10D3

10.30–2.30; 5.30–10.30 (11 F, S)
Wharf
London Road (off A126)
Evening opening: 6
Ind Coope Bitter,
Burton Ale Ⓗ
Fine old riverfront inn
🦶♣🖤🏠Ⓖ🕯Ⓢ

Great Burstead 10D2

10.30–2.30; 6–10.30 (11 F, S)
Kings Head
Southend Road (A129)
✆ Billericay 58785
Draught Bass
Charrington IPA
Mitchells & Butlers Springfield
Bitter Ⓗ
Recently renovated pub with
restaurant
🅰♪♣🅗🖤🏠Ⓖ🕯🍴Ⓢ

Great Chesterford 18B7

10.30–2.30; 6–10.30 (11 F, S)
Plough
(Off B1383)
Greene King IPA, Abbot Ⓖ
Superb 18th-century village
pub ♣🖤🏠Ⓢ≈

Great Dunmow 18C8

10–2.30; 6–10.30 (11 F, S)
Boars Head
High Street (B184) ✆ 3630
Benskins Bitter Ⓗ
Splendid old beamed pub;
guest beers
🖤🏠ⒶⓇ🕯Ⓖ🕯

Try also: Cricketers (Ridley)

Great Easton 18C8

10–2.30; 6–10.30 (11 F, S)
Swan
Off B184) OS 606255 ✆ 359
Charrington IPA Ⓗ
Comfortable village local
♣🖤🏠Ⓖ🕯🕯Ⓢ

Great Leighs 18D9

10–2.30; 6–11
Dog & Partridge
Main Road (A131) ✆ 331
Ridley Bitter Ⓗ & Ⓔ
Popular two-bar pub
♣🖤🖤🏠Ⓖ🕯🕯Ⓢ⚘

Great Saling 18D8

11–2.30; 6–11
White Hart
(Off A120)
✆ Great Dunmow 850341

Ridley Bitter Ⓔ
Superb Tudor pub with
galleried saloon bar
♪♣🖤🏠Ⓖ🕯🕯Ⓢ

Great Sampford 18C8

10.30–2.30; 6–10.30 (11 F, S)
Red Lion
(B1053)
Ridley Bitter Ⓗ
Excellent pub, carefully rebuilt
after fire ♣🖤🏠Ⓔ🅰Ⓢ

Harlow 10C1

10.30–2.30; 6–10.30 (11 F, S)
White Admiral
Mowbray Place, Mark Hall
Moors (off A414)
Charrington IPA Ⓗ
Pleasantly matured new town
pub of the 50s ♪♣🕯

Harwich 19G8

10.30–2.30; 6–11
Alma
Kings Head Street ✆ 3474
Tolly Cobbold Mild, Original Ⓗ
Unpretentious fishermen's
haunt ♪♣🖤🖤Ⓡ🕯≈

Hatfield Broad

Oak 18C9

10.30–2.30; 6.30–10.30 (11 F, S)
Dukes Head
High Street (B183) ✆ 283
Courage Best Bitter,
Directors Ⓗ
Comfortable village local
🅰♪♣🖤🏠Ⓖ🕯Ⓢ

Hatfield Heath 18B9

10.30–2.30; 5.30–10.30 (11 F, S)
White Horse
(A414)
✆ Bishops Stortford 730351
Greene King Abbot
Rayment BBA Ⓗ
Timbered pub on village green
♣🖤🏠Ⓖ🕯🕯Ⓢ

*All pubs in Hatfield Heath
serve real ale*

Hazeleigh 11E2

10.30–2.30; 6–11
Royal Oak
Fambridge Road, Maldon
OS 849047
Greene King IPA, Abbot Ⓖ
Tasefully modernised country
pub one mile south of Maldon
♪♣🖤🏠Ⓢ

Helions

Bumpstead 18C7

11–2.30; 6.30–11
Three Horseshoes
(Off B1054) OS 650414
✆ Steeple Bumpstead 298
Greene King IPA, Abbot Ⓗ
Superb remote old pub, worth
finding 🅰♪♣🖤🏠Ⓖ🕯🕯Ⓢ

Henny Street 18E7

10.30–2.30; 6–11
Swan
(Off A131) ✆ Twinstead 238
Greene King XX, IPA, Abbot Ⓗ
Fine riverside pub with
fishing rights ♪♣🖤🏠Ⓖ🕯🕯Ⓢ

High Beech 10B2

10.30–2.30; 6–10.30 (11 F, S)
Duke of Wellington
Wellington Hill (off A104)
Ind Coope Bitter,
Burton Ale Ⓗ
Pleasant pub near Epping
Forest beauty spot ♪♣🖤🏠Ⓖ

Leigh-on-Sea 11E3

10–2.30; 6–11
Grand Hotel
131 The Broadway
Courage Best Bitter,
Directors Ⓗ
Large multi-roomed pub with
live music every night
🅰Ⓡ♪♣🖤🖤🏠Ⓡ🕯

Smack Inn
High Street, Old Leigh Town
✆ Southend 76765
Crouch Vale Best Bitter, SAS
Manns IPA
Watney Fined Stag Bitter
Webster Yorkshire Bitter Ⓗ
Family pub near cockle sheds
🅰♪♣🖤🖤Ⓖ🕯Ⓢ♿⚘

Little Baddow 10E1

10.30–2.30; 6–11
General's Arms
The Ridge ✆ Danbury 2069
Morning opening: 11
Charrington IPA
Mitchells & Butlers Springfield
Bitter Ⓗ
Friendly three-bar pub
🅰♣🖤🏠Ⓡ🕯Ⓖ🕯Ⓢ

Little Bromley 19F8

11–2.30; 6–11
Wheatsheaf
(Off A121)
Adnams Bitter
Greene King IPA Ⓗ
Small, weatherboarded
cottage-style local ♪♣🖤🖤🏠Ⓢ

Little Walden 18C7

11–2.30; 6–10.30 (11 F, S)
Crown
(B1052)
✆ Saffron Walden 27175
Adnams Bitter
Ruddle County
Webster Yorkshire Bitter Ⓗ
Thriving village local
🅰♣🖤🏠Ⓖ🕯Ⓢ

Littley Green 18D9

10–2.30; 6–11
Compasses
(Off A131) OS 698172
Ridley Bitter Ⓖ

Old-style country pub near brewery ♠♪♣♀🏠

Maldon 11E1

10.30–2.30; 6–11
Carpenter's Arms
33 Gate Street ✆ 53833
Greene King IPA, Abbot Ⓗ
Cosy backstreet pub ♪♣Ꮺ♀🗡Ⓢ

Manningtree 19F8

11–2.30; 6–11
Station Buffet
Manningtree Station
(Off A317) ✆ 4140
Closed Sunday evenings
Adnams Mild, Bitter Ⓗ
Brightlingsea Bitter Ⓖ
Greene King IPA, Abbot Ⓗ
Bulmer Cider Ⓖ
Attractively eccentric;
magnificent bar and food
♠♪♣🖾♀Ⓡ🅖♪🥄⇌

Margaretting 10D2

10–2.30; 6–11
Red Lion
Roman Road (B1002)
Morning opening: 11
Ridley Mild, Bitter Ⓖ
Fine old pub with regular live
jazz ♠♪♣♀🏠Ⓢ🗡

Mashbury 18C9

11–2.30; 6–10.30 (11 F, S and summer)
Fox
Fox Road OS 650127
Ridley Mild, Bitter Ⓖ
Delightful isolated old country
pub ♠♪♣♀🏠Ⓢ🗡

Messing 18E9

10.30–2.30; 5.30–11
Old Crown
(Off A12) ✆ Tiptree 815575
Ridley Bitter Ⓗ
In pleasant village setting,
good food 🗡🖾♀🏠Ⓡ🅖🥄Ⓢ

Mill Green 10D2

10–2.30; 6–11
Viper
(Off A12)
Truman Prize Mild, Bitter,
Best Bitter Ⓗ
Unspoilt country pub in
woodland setting ♠♣♀🏠Ⓢ

Monk Street 18C8

11–2.30; 6–10.30 (11 F, S)
Greyhound
(Off B184) OS 614288
✆ Thaxted 830864
Adnams Mild
Ridley Bitter Ⓗ
Tastefully refurbished, with
cosy public bar
♠♣♀🏠Ⓒ🥄Ⓢ

Moreton 10C1

10–2.30; 6–10.30 (11 F, S)
White Hart
Ind Coope Bitter, Burton Ale Ⓗ

Excellent old village pub with
four bars
♠🏁♣♀🏠🅡Ⓖ (Tue–Fri)🥄Ⓢ

Mount Bures 18E8

10.30–2.30; 6–11
Thatchers Arms
(Off A604) OS 905318
✆ Bures 227460
Greene King XX, IPA, Abbot
Mauldon Bitter Ⓗ
Original tap room and fine
new restaurant
🏁♣♀🅖Ⓒ🥄Ⓢ🥄🗡⇌

Mountnessing 10D2

10–2.30; 6–10.30 (11 F, S)
Plough
Roman Road (B1002)
Truman Bitter, Best Bitter Ⓗ
Pleasant two-bar pub, ask for
handpumped beer
♪♣♀🏠Ⓢ

Mundon 11E2

10–2.30; 6–10.30 (11 F, S)
Round Bush
Purleigh Road (B1010)
Greene King IPA, Abbot Ⓖ
Off the beaten track,
interesting stillage ♪♣🏠🥄

Nazeing 10B1

11–2.30; 6–10.30 (11 F, S)
Coach & Horses
Waltham Road (B194) ✆ 3151
Ind Coope Bitter Ⓗ
Pleasant pub with 'Christies'
window ♪♣♀🏠Ⓒ🥄Ⓢ

Orsett 10D3

10.30–2.30; 6–10.30 (11 F, S)
Foxhound
High Road (off A13/A128)
Courage Best Bitter,
Directors Ⓗ
Popular village local
♠♪♣♀🏠🥄Ⓢ

Pleshey 10D1

10–2.30; 6–11
Leather Bottle
The Street (off A130)
Ridley Bitter Ⓖ & Ⓗ
Excellent unspoilt pub in
attractive village ♠♪♣♀🏠🥄Ⓢ

Purleigh 11E2

10–2.30; 6–11
Bell
(Off B1010) ✆ Maldon 828348
Ind Coope Bitter Ⓗ
Old pub on hill by the church
♠♣♀🏠🅡Ⓒ🥄

Rayleigh 10E2

10–2.30; 6–10.30 (11 F, S)
Paul Pry
14 High Road (A129)
✆ 742859
Manns IPA
Watney London Bitter, Fined
Stag Bitter Ⓗ

Split-level ex-Luker's house
♪♀🏠🅡Ⓒ🥄Ⓢ

Rayleigh Lodge
The Chase (off A1015)
✆ 732149
Ridley Bitter
Truman Bitter,
Sampson Hanbury's Extra
Strong
Bulmer Cider Ⓗ
Good family pub with
landscaped garden
♪♣♀🏠Ⓒ🥄Ⓢ

Rettendon 10E.

10–2.30; 6–10.30 (11 F, S)
Wheatsheaf
Rettendon Common (A130)
Ridley Bitter Ⓖ
Superb weatherboarded inn
♪♣🏠Ⓢ

Rochford 11E.

10–2.30; 6–10.30 (11 F, S)
Golden Lion
North Street
Adnams Bitter
Greene King Abbot
Young Special Bitter Ⓗ
Small, cosy free house with
guest beer ♪♣Ⓒ Ⓢ

Saffron Walden 18B7

10.30–2.30; 6–10.30 (11 F, S)
Sun
Gold Street (off B1052)
Ridley Mild, Bitter Ⓗ
Welcoming old town pub off
High Street ♪♣♀🏠🅡Ⓢ

Victory
Little Walden Road (B1052)
Greene King IPA, Abbot Ⓗ
Cheerful and popular town
local ♪♣♀Ⓒ🥄Ⓢ

Try also: Railway Arms
(Benskins)

South Benfleet 10E3

10–2.30; 6–10.30 (11 F, S)
Half Crown
27 High Street
Charrington IPA Ⓗ
Popular local with Toby jug
collection ♪♣🏠🥄Ⓢ⇌

Southend-on-Sea 11E3

10–2.30; 6–10.30 (11 F, S)
Esplanade
Western Esplanade ✆ 46658
Truman Bitter, Best
Bitter, Sampson Hanbury's
Extra Strong
Excellent estuary views
♪♣🖾♀🅡Ⓒ Ⓢ

Liberty Belle
10 Marine Parade ✆ 66936
Courage Best Bitter,
Directors Ⓗ
Comfortable seafront house,
nautical flavour ♪♣Ⓒ🥄Ⓢ

ry also: Railway Hotel

outhminster 11F2

–2.30; 6–10.30 (11 F, S)
Railway
ation Road
reene King IPA, Abbot G
ictorian pub spared from
odernisation ♣☎🅰Ⓡ📶≋

outh Woodham errers 10E2

–2.30; 6–10.30 (11 F, S)
own Crier
handlers Way
Chelmsford 329774
d Coope Bitter, Burton Ale H
ters from Allied group
♣🖼🅰🅿Ⓖ📶🅧🅰

tanford-le-Hope 10D3

–2.30; 6–10.30 (11 F, S)
Rising Sun
hurch Hill (B1420)
**ourage Best Bitter,
irectors** H
opular pub near the church
♣🅰Ⓡ📶🅧

tanford Rivers 10C2

–2.30; 6–10.30 (11 F, S)
White Bear
ondon Road (A113)
Ongar 362185
d Coope Bitter,
urton Ale H
mall, traditional country pub
♣🅿🅰Ⓡ🅖📶🅧

tansted Mountfitchet 18B8

.30–2.30; 6–10.30 (11 F, S)
Queens Head
ower Street (B1051)
Bishop's Stortford 812458
olly Cobbold Bitter, Original,
ld Strong H
omfortable and hospitable
illage local ♣🅿📶🅧🅰≋

ry also: Dog & Duck
Rayment); Cock (Rayment)

tisted 18D8

.30–3; 6–11
Dolphin
A120) ✆ Braintree 21143
Morning opening: 11
Ridley Mild, Bitter G
ine old inn 🅰♣🅿🅿🅰🅖📶🅧🅰

tock 10D2

–2.30; 6–11
Bear
he Square (off B1007)
840232
d Coope Bitter,
urton Ale H
ine old English hostelry
♣🅿🅰Ⓡ🅖📶

Thaxted 18C8

10.30–2.30; 6–10.30 (11 F, S)
Star
(B184)
**Ind Coope Bitter,
Burton Ale** H
Excellent pub in historic
village ☞♣🅿🅰📶🅧

Try also: **Bull** (Benskins);
Swan (free)

Toppesfield 18D8

10.30–2.30; 6.30–11
Green Man
(Off A604) OS 739374
✆ Great Yeldham 237418
Greene King IPA, Abbot H
Delightful friendly pub in
remote village ♪♣🅿🅰Ⓡ🅖📶🅧

Waltham Abbey 10B2

10.30–2.30; 6–10.30 (11 F, S)
Coach & Horses
Green Yard (off A121)
**McMullen AK, Country
Bitter** H
Basic locals' pub opposite
Abbey ♪♣Ⓡ🅖📶

Walton-on-the-Naze 19G8

10.30–2.30; 6–10.30 (11 F, S)
Royal Marine
Old Pier Street (off B1034)
**Adnams Bitter
Everard Tiger
Ruddle County
Samuel Smith Old Brewery
Bitter
Worthington Best Bitter** G
Distinctive and friendly inn,
unusual gravity dispense
♣🅧≋

West Thurrock 10C3

10.30–2.30; 5.30–10.30 (11 F, S)
Ship
470 London Road (A126)
**Charrington IPA
Mitchells & Butlers Springfield
Bitter** H
Deservedly popular
workingmen's local ♪♣🅰🅖📶

White Notley 18D9

10.30–2.30; 6.30–11
Cross Keys
The Street (off B1018)
Ridley Mild, Bitter H
Excellent 14th-century village
inn 🅰♣🅿🅰📶🅧≋

White Roding 18C9

10–2.30; 6–10.30 (11 F, S)
Black Horse
(A1060) ✆ 322
Ridley Mild, Bitter E
Pleasant old roadside pub,
excellent home cooking
🅰♪♣🅿🅖📶🅧🅰

Wickham Bishops 11E1

10.30–2.30; 6–11
Mitre
2 The Street ✆ Maldon 891378
Ridley Mild H **Bitter** G
Bulmer Cider H
Deservedly popular, wide
range of snacks 🅰♪♣🅿🅰🅖📶🅧

Widdington 18B8

10.30–2.30; 6–10.30 (11 F, S)
Fleur de Lys
(Off B1383)
✆ Saffron Walden 40659
**Adnams Bitter
Greene King IPA, Abbot
Webster Yorkshire Bitter** H
Excellent pub in lovely village
🅰♪♣🅿🅰Ⓡ🅖📶🅧

Widford 10D1

10–2.30; 6–11
Sir Evelyn Wood
56 Widford Road (off A12)
Greene King IPA, Abbot H
Lovely, simple town pub
🅰♣🅿📶🅧

Witham 18D9

10–2.30; 6–11
George
36 Newland Street ✆ 511098
Ridley Mild, Bitter E & H
Large town-centre pub,
recently refurbished
♪♣🖼🅰🅖📶🅧🅰≋

Victoria
Powers Hall End (off B1389)
✆ 511809
Ridley Mild, Bitter G
Spacious, renovated old
country pub ♪♣🖼🅿🅰🅖📶🅧

Wivenhoe 19F8

11–2.30; 6–11
Rose & Crown
The Quay
Ind Coope Bitter H
Harbourside local in scenic
setting; comfortable and
popular ♣🅿🅧≋

Wix 19F8

11–2.30; 7–11
Waggon
Rectory Hill (off A604) ✆ 279
**Adnams Bitter
Brightlingsea Bitter
Tolly Cobbold Mild** H
Old Strong G
Lively country pub
🅰♪♣🅿🅰🅖📶🅧

Writtle 18C9

10–2.30; 6–11
Wheatsheaf
The Green (off A122)
Opens at 11 am & 6.30 pm;
closes 10.30 pm Mon–Thu
Greene King IPA, Abbot G
Excellent, friendly pub ♪♣🅰📶

Aldsworth 15H6

10.30–2.30; 6–10.30 (11 F, S)

Sherbourne Arms
(A433)
Cirencester Bitter
Morland Bitter
Wadworth 6X [H]
One-bar pub just outside village 🏠♣℘🚗🕒🍽[S]

Ampney Crucis 15H7

10.30–2.30; 6–10.30 (11 F.S)

Butchers Arms
(Off A417) ☎ Poulton 486
Whitbread WCPA, Bitter, Flowers Original Bitter [H]
Weston Cider [G]
Popular village pub
♪♣℘🕒🍽🍺[S]

Arlingham 15E6

10.30–2.30; 6–10.30 (11 F. S and summer)

Old Passage Inn
(Off B4071) OS 696113
☎ Gloucester 740547
Wadworth IPA, 6X [H]
Popular riverside pub with restaurant
♪♣℘🚗🍽(Tues–Sat)[S]

Ashleworth 15F5

10.30–2.30; 6–10.30 (11 F, S)

Arkle
(Off A417)
Donnington BB, SBA
Wadworth Devizes Bitter [H]
Small, one-bar free house
🏠♪♣▣℘🚗[S]

Bishops Cleeve 15G5

10.30–2.30; 6–10.30 (11 F, S)

Farmers Arms
Evesham Road (A435)
Whitbread WCPA, Bitter, Flowers Original Bitter
Bulmer Cider [H]
A rarity – main road pub that caters for locals 🔥♣℘🚗🍺[S]⛺

Royal Oak
Church Road (off A435)
☎ 2664
Halls Harvest Bitter
Ind Coope Burton Ale [H]
Thatched village pub near parish church ♪♣℘🚗[R]🕒🍽🍺[S]

Blockley 15H5

11–2.30; 7–10.30 (11 F, S)

Crown
High Street (off B4479)
☎ 700245
Hook Norton Best Bitter
Wadworth 6X
Whitbread Bitter [H]
18th-century coaching inn with occasional guest beers
♪♣℘🚗■[R]🕒🍽🍺[S]

Bream 14E7

10.30–2.30; 6–10.30 (11 F, S)

Olde Winding Wheel
(B4231) ☎ Dean 562856
Marston Pedigree
Whitbread Flowers Original Bitter [H]
Carefully restored roadside inn 🏠♪♣℘🚗🕒🍽🍺[S]

Broadwell 15H5

10.30–2.30; 6–10.30 (11 F, S)

Fox Inn
(Off A429) ☎ Stow 30212
Donnington BB, SBA
Weston Cider [H]
Small pub in lovely village; good food ♣℘🚗■🕒🍽[S]⛺

Brockweir 14D7

11–2.30; 6–10.30 (11 F, S and summer)

Brockweir Inn
(Off A466) ☎ Tintern 548
Hook Norton Best Bitter
Wadworth 6X
Whitbread WCPA, Bitter, Flowers Original Bitter
Bulmer Cider [H]
Tastefully restored Wye Valley inn. Whitbread Bitter sold as 'Brockweir Best Bitter'
🔥♪♣℘🚗■🕒🍽🍺[S]

Chedworth 15H6

10.30–2.30; 6.30–11

Seven Tuns
(Off A429) ☎ Fossebridge 242
Opens at 11 am and 6 pm
Courage Best Bitter, Directors [H]
Traditional Cotswold country pub 🔥♣▣℘🚗[R]🕒🍽🍺[S]

Cheltenham 15G5

10.30–2.30; 6–10.30 (11 F, S)

Beaufort Arms
London Road (A40)
Wadworth IPA, 6X, Old Timer [H]
Popular pub on outskirts of town
♪♣℘🚗🕒🍺[S]

Fountain Inn
North Place (off A435)
Donnington BB, SBA
Hook Norton Best Bitter, Old Hookey
Usher Best Bitter, Founders Ale [H]
Large town-centre pub in converted Regency building
🔥♪♣℘🕒[S]

Haymaker
Windyridge Road, Wymans Brook
Courage Bitter, Best Bitter, Directors [H]
Split-level pub on modern housing estate
♪♣℘🚗🕒[S]

Rotunda
Montpellier Walk ☎ 522994
Halls Harvest Bitter
Ind Coope Burton Ale [H]
Lively pub with pavement drinking area
♪℘🕒[S]🚆

Chipping Campden 15H

10.30–2.30; 6.30–10.30 (11 F, S)

Eight Bells
(B4035) ☎ Evesham 840371
Whitbread WCPA, Flowers Original Bitter [H]
15th century inn with cobble courtyard 🔥♪♣℘[R][S]

Cirencester 15G

10–2.30; 6–10.30 (11 F, S and summer)

Brewers Arms
Cricklade Street ☎ 3763
Evening opening: 6.30
Arkell BB, BBB, Kingsdown Ale [H]
Good town pub – friendly landlord ♪♣[R]🕒🍽🍺[S]

Drillmans Arms
Ermine Street (A417) ☎ 3892
Archer Village Bitter, Best Bitter, Golden [H]
Archer tied house on outskirt of town ♪♣▣℘🚗■🕒🍽🍺[S]

Woodbine
Chesterton Lane (off A419)
Courage Bitter, Best Bitter, Directors [H]
Suburban Courage 'Ale House' ♪♣℘🚗🕒🍺[S]

Cranham 15F

10.30–2.30; 6–10.30 (11 F, S)

Black Horse
(Off A46)
☎ Gloucester 812217
Whitbread Flowers Original Bitter
Bulmer Cider [G]
Friendly, popular village-centre pub
🔥♣℘🚗[R]🕒🍽🍺[S]⛺

Elkstone 15G

10.30–2.30; 6–10.30 (11 F, S)

Highwayman Inn
Beech Pike (A417)
☎ Miserden 221
Arkell BB, BBB, Kingsdown Ale [H]
Comfortable, stone-built pub
🏠♣▣℘🚗🕒🍽[S]♿

Fairford 15H

10–2.30; 6–10.30 (11 F, S and summer)

Bull Hotel
The Square (off A417)
☎ Cirencester 712566
Opens at 12 noon and 6.30 p
Arkell BB, BBB, Kingsdown Ale [H]
Fine hotel of character
♪♣℘🚗■🕒🍽[S]

Marlborough Arms
(A417)
Archer Best Bitter
Usher Best Bitter
Wadworth 6X [H] **Old Timer** [G]
Handpumps in the public bar
♪♣🚗🍺[S]

Glasshouse 15E6

10.30–2.30; 6–10.30 (11 F, S)
Glasshouse Inn
May Hill, Longhope (off A40)
Whitbread WCPA, Bitter
Bulmer and Symonds Cider G
Unspoilt pub at foot of May
Hill ♣⚲🏠①⑤

Gloucester 15F6

10.30–2.30; 6–10.30 (11 F, S)
Cross Keys
Cross Keys Lane, off Southgate
Street ☎ 23358
Whitbread WCPA, Bitter,
Flowers Original Bitter H
15th-century wooden-beamed
exterior
♪♣①⑤≷

Crown & Thistle
Barton Street ☎ 34314
Hook Norton Best Bitter
Marston Pedigree
Usher Best Bitter
Wadworth 6X H
Newly extended ale bar with
restaurant
♪①➐⑤≷

Deans Walk Inn
St Catherine Street ☎ 22853
Draught Bass
Halls Harvest Bitter
Hook Norton Best Bitter
Wadworth 6X H
Popular local close to the
cathedral
♪♣⚲🏠①⑤

Northend Vaults
Northgate Street ☎ 23560
Whitbread WCPA, Flowers
Original, Pompey Royal H
Friendly town-centre pub with
bric-a-brac
①⑤≷

Great Barrington 15H6

10.30–2.30; 6.30–10.30 (11 F, S)
Fox Inn
(Off A40) ☎ Windrush 385
Donnington XXX, BB, SBA H
Old country pub with skittle
alley ♣⚲🏠🔲①⑤

Great Rissington 15H6

10.30–2.30; 6–10.30 (11 F, S)
Lamb Inn
OS 200174 ☎ Bourton on the
Water 20388
Opens at 11 am and 6.30 pm
Wadworth 6X G
Welsh Worthington Pale Ale
Whitbread Flowers Original
Bitter
Taunton Cider H
Well-balanced atmosphere for
locals and visitors
♪♣🔲⚲🏠🅐🆁①⑤➐⑤🅰

Guiting Power 15H5

10.30–2.30; 6–10.30 (11 F, S)

Olde Inn
(Off B4068) ☎ 392
Courage Best Bitter,
Directors
Hook Norton Best Bitter H
Comfortable free house in
unspoilt village ♣⚲①➐①⑤

Haresfield 15F6

10.30–2.30; 6–10–30 (11 F, S)
Beacon Hotel
(Off B4008)
☎ Gloucester 728884
Welsh Fussells Best Bitter H
Lively village pub alongside
railway line ♪♣⚲🏠🆁①➐①⑤

Hartpury 15F5

10.30–2.30; 6–10.30 (11 F, S)
Royal Exchange
(A417)
Halls Harvest Bitter H
Well-kept village local
🅰♪♣🔲⚲🏠①➐①⑤

Joyford 14D6

10.30–2.30; 6–10.30 (11 F, S)
Dog & Muffler
(Off B4432) OS 579132
Samuel Smith Old Brewery
Bitter
Bulmer Cider H
Warm, cosy pub, handy for
Symonds Yat ♪♣🔲⚲🏠①⑤

Kempsford 15H7

10.30–2.30; 6–10.30 (11 F, S)
George
(Off A419)
Arkell BB, BBB, Kingsdown
Ale H
Attractive pub near USAF base
♪♣⚲🏠①➐①⑤

Kineton 15H5

10.30–2.30; 6–10.30 (11 F, S)
Halfway House
(Off B4068)
☎ Guiting Power 344
Donnington BB, SBA H
Beautiful country pub, handy
for Cotswold Farm Park
🅰♣⚲🏠①⑤

Lechlade 15J7

10.30–2.30; 6–10.30 (11 F, S)
Crown
(A361) ☎ 52218
Archer Best Bitter, Golden
Devenish Wessex Best Bitter
Hook Norton Mild (summer),
Best Bitter
Morland Bitter, Best Bitter
Weston Cider H
Old coaching inn with good
food ♪♣⚲🔲①➐①⑤

Longborough 15H5

10.30–2.30; 6–10.30 (11 F, S)
Coach & Horses
(Off A424)
Donnington XXX, BB, SBA H
Friendly pub in quiet Cotswold
village ①♪♣⚲⑤

Lower Swell 15H5

10.30–2.30; 6–10.30 (11 F, S)
Golden Ball
(B4068) ☎ Stow 30247
Donnington XXX, BB, SBA H
Lovely stone pub ♪➐⚲🏠🔲⑤

Lydbrook 14E6

10.30–2.30; 6–10.30 (11 F, S)
Forge Hammer
(B4234) ☎ Dean 60310
Marston Pedigree H
Symond Cider G
Fine, comfortable inn with
iron-making and railway
mementoes ♪♣⚲🏠①⑤

Mickleton 15H4

10.30–2.30; 6–10.30 (11 F, S)
Butchers Arms
(A46) ☎ 285
Whitbread Bitter,
Flowers Original Bitter
Bulmer Cider H
Tastefully modernised
16th-century pub
♣⚲🏠①➐①⑤

Moreton in Marsh 15H5

10.30–2.30; 6–10.30 (11 F, S)
Wellington
London Road (A44)
Hook Norton Mild, Best
Bitter H
Bulmer Cider E
Friendly local on edge of town
♪♣⚲⑤

Nailsworth 15F7

10.30–2.30; 6–10.30 (11 F, S)
Tipputs Inn
Tiltups End, Horsley (A46)
☎ 2466
Morning opening: 10
Archer Golden
Draught Bass
Hook Norton Best Bitter
Robinson Best Bitter H
Modernised country pub with
extensive menu
①♪♣⚲🏠①➐⑤🅰

Naunton 15H5

10.30–2.30; 6–10.30 (11 F, S)
Black Horse Inn
(Off B4068)
☎ Guiting Power 378
Donnington BB, SBA H
Typical Cotswold pub
①♪♣⚲🏠🔲①➐①⑤🅰

Newent 15E5

11–2.30; 7–10.30 (11 F, S)
Red Lion
Broad Street (B4216)
☎ 820215
Whitbread WCPA,
Flowers Original Bitter H
Lively town-centre locals' pub
①♪♣🔲⚲🏠🆁①➐①⑤

North Nibley 15E7

10.30–2.30; 6–10.30 (11 F, S and summer)

New Inn
Waterley Bottom OS 758953
✆ Dursley 3659
Summer morning opening:
11; winter opening 12 noon
and 7 pm
Cotleigh Tawny Bitter
Greene King Abbot
Tolly Cobbold Original
Smiles Best Bitter ⓗ
Whitbread Flowers Original
Bitter
Inch Cider ⓖ
Unspoilt country pub in quiet
valley; guest beers
♪🚲✿🏠🅁Ⓖ🍴🕯Ⓢ

Paxford 15H5

10–2.30; 6–10.30 (11 F, S)
Churchill
(B4479) ✆ 203
Hook Norton Mild, Best
Bitter, Old Hookey ⓗ
Bulmer Cider ⓖ
Well-kept country local
♪🚲✿🔲🕯Ⓢ▲

Poulton 15H7

10.30–2.30; 6–10.30 (11 F, S)
Falcon
(A417) ✆ Paxford 392
Closed Tuesday lunchtimes
Wadworth IPA, 6X ⓗ
Cotswold stone pub, easy to
miss 🚲✿🏠🅁Ⓖ🍴🕯Ⓢ♿

Prestbury 15G5

10.30–2.30; 6–10.30 (11 F, S)
Royal Oak
The Burgage (off A46)
Whitbread WCPA, Bitter,
Flowers Original Bitter ⓗ
Bulmer Cider Ⓔ
Attractive village pub near
Cheltenham
🏠🚲✿🏠ⒼⓈ

Purton 15E7

10.30–2.30; 7–10.30 (11 F, S)
Berkeley Hunt
(Off A38)
Nailsea Jacobs Best Bitter
Theakston Best Bitter
Wadworth 6X
Bulmer Cider ⓖ
Country local on banks of
Sharpness canal
♪🚲✿✿🕯Ⓢ

St Briavels 14D7

10.30–2.30; 6–10.30 (11 F, S and summer)
George
(Off B4228) ✆ 228
Marston Pedigree
Wadworth IPA, 6X ⓗ
Bulmer Cider ⓖ
Old hotel outside castle moat
🏠♪🚲✿🏠🅁Ⓖ🍴Ⓢ

Sapperton 15G7

10.30–2.30; 6–10.30 (11 F, S)
Bell
(Off A419)
✆ Frampton Mansell 298
Archer Village Bitter, Golden

Wadworth 6X
Whitbread WCPA,
Flowers Original Bitter ⓗ
Weston Cider ⓖ
A convivial, go-ahead village
local 🚲✿🏠🅁Ⓖ🍴🕯Ⓢ▲

Sheepscombe 15F6

10.30–2.30; 6–10.30 (11 F, S)
Butchers Arms
(Off A46)
✆ Gloucester 812113
Whitbread WCPA,
Flowers Original Bitter ⓗ
Bulmer Cider Ⓔ
Popular pub with interesting
sign ♪🚲✿🏠🔲Ⓢ

Shurdington 15G6

10.30–2.30; 6–10.30 (11 F, S)
Bell Inn
Shurdington Road (A46)
✆ Cheltenham 862245
Whitbread WCPA,
Flowers Original Bitter
Bulmer Cider ⓗ
Friendly roadside local,
recently extended
🚲✿🏠Ⓖ🍴🕯Ⓢ

Slimbridge 15F7

10.30–2.30; 6–10.30 (11 F, S and summer)
Tudor Arms
Shepherd's Patch (off A38)
✆ Cambridge 306
Davenports Bitter
Smiles Best Bitter
Whitbread WCPA,
Flowers Original Bitter ⓗ
Farmhouse cider ⓖ
Canalside free house
♪🚲✿🎦🏠🅁Ⓖ🍴🕯Ⓢ▲

Staverton 15F5

10.30–2.30; 6–10.30 (11 F, S)
House in the Tree
Haydens Elm (B4063)
Whitbread WCPA,
Flowers Original Bitter ⓗ
Bulmer Cider Ⓔ
Small, cosy country pub
🚲🏠🕯Ⓢ

Stow-on-the-Wold 15H5

10.30–2.30; 6–10.30 (11 F, S)
Queens Head
The Square (off A429)
✆ 30563
Donnington XXX (winter), BB,
SBA ⓗ
Bulmer Cider ⓖ
Comfortable Cotswold
town-centre pub
♪🚲✿🔲Ⓖ🍴🕯Ⓢ

Stroud 15F7

10.30–2.30; 6–10.30 (11 F, S and summer)
Duke of York
Nelson Street ✆ 78715
Butcombe Bitter
Halls Harvest Bitter
Wadworth 6X ⓗ
Pleasantly modernised lounge
bar ♪ⒼⓉ

Tetbury 15F

10.30–2.30; 6–10.30 (11 F, S)
Crown
Gumstool Hill (off A433)
✆ 52469
Whitbread WCPA,
Flowers Original Bitter ⓗ
Friendly town-centre pub
♪🍴🚲✿🏠Ⓖ🍴Ⓢ

Tewkesbury 15F

10–2.30; 6–10.30 (11 F, S and summer)
Berkeley Arms
Church Street (A38)
✆ 293034
Morning opening: 10.30
Wadworth Devizes Bitter, 6X,
Old Timer ⓗ
Bulmer Cider ⓖ
Interesting 17th-century pub
🍴✿🔲🅁🕯Ⓢ▲

Britannia
High Street (A38)
Davenports Bitter ⓗ
One-bar town pub ♪🚲🕯Ⓢ▲

Uley 15F

10–2.30; 6–10.30 (11, F, S)
Kings Head
The Street (B4066)
✆ Dursley 860282
Wadworth Devizes Bitter,
6X ⓗ
Bulmer & Taunton Cider ⓖ
Friendly roadside hotel
♪🚲✿🏠🔲🍴🕯Ⓢ

Winchcombe 15G

10.30–2.30; 5.30–10.30 (11 F, S)
Corner Cupboard
Gloucester Street (A46)
✆ 602303
Whitbread WCPA, Bitter,
Flowers Original Bitter ⓗ
Bulmer Cider Ⓔ
Excellent old-fashioned pub
with holiday flat
🚲✿🏠🔲Ⓖ

Woodchester 15F

10.30–2.30; 6–10.30 (11 F, S)
Ram
South Woodchester (off A46)
✆ Amberley 3329
Archer Village Bitter ⓗ
Holden Bitter
Hook Norton Best Bitter
Usher PA, Best Bitter ⓗ
Refurbished village inn;
regular guest beers
♪🚲✿🏠Ⓖ🍴🕯Ⓢ

Woolaston Common 14E

10.30–2.30; 6–10.30 (11 F, S and summer)
Rising Sun
(Off A48) OS 590009
Closed Wednesday lunchtime
Butcombe Bitter ⓖ
Hook Norton Best Bitter
Theakston Best Bitter ⓗ
Lovely country pub with
superb view 🏠🚲🎦🚲🏠Ⓢ

Aldershot   7G4

10.30–2.20; 5.30–10.30 (11 F, S and summer)

Albion
Waterloo Road ✆ 319286
Evening opening: 6
Gale Dark Mild, BBB, HSB,
XXXXX Ⓗ
Friendly retreat ♪♣ⒼⓈ≉

Lord Campbell
Alexandra Road ✆ 23059
Courage Best Bitter,
Directors Ⓗ
Comfortable, spacious town
pub, enthusiastically run
🏠♪♣⚲Ⓒ🅿Ⓢ♿≉

White Swan
161 North Lane ✆ 20528
Gale HSB
Tamplins Bitter
Usher Best Bitter
Watney Fined Stag Bitter Ⓗ
Impressive beerhouse
🏠♪♣⚲🅿🅰ⒷⓇⒼ🅿Ⓢ♿

Alresford   6E5

10.30–2.20; 6–10.30 (11 F, S and summer)

Horse & Groom
Broad Street (A31) ✆ 2583
Whitbread Strong Country
Bitter, Pompey Royal Ⓗ
Large, cosy pub, plenty of oak
beams ♪⚲Ⓒ🅿Ⓢ

Alton   7F4

10.30–2.20; 6–10.30 (11 F, S and summer)

Kings Head
Market Street ✆ 82313
Open till 3.30 pm Tuesdays
Courage Best Bitter, Directors Ⓗ
Friendly country pub in town
centre 🏠♣⚲🅿ⓇⒼⓈ≉

Andover   6C4

10–2.30; 6–10.30 (11 F, S)

Angel
High Street ✆ 52086
Weekday opening: 10.30
Marston Mercian Mild,
Burton Bitter, Pedigree Ⓗ
15th-century inn, oldest
building in town 🏠♪♣⚲ⒼⓈ≉

Lardicake
Adelaide Road ✆ 3447
Morning opening: 11.30
Bourne Valley Weavers Bitter,
Andover Ale, Wallop
Bulmer Cider Ⓗ
Tastefully converted Victorian
local; regular guest beers
🏠♪♣🅰⚲Ⓡ🅿🅿

Merrie Monk
New Street ✆ 52675
Marston Mercian Mild,
Burton Bitter, Pedigree,
Merrie Monk, Owd Rodger Ⓗ
Lively, busy local with
reputation for excellent food
♪♣⚲🅰ⒷⒼ🅿🅿

Avon   6B7

10.30–2.30; 6–10.30 (11 F, S and summer)

Tyrrells Ford Hotel
(B3347) ✆ Bransgore 72646
Evening opening: 7
Courage Directors
Marston Pedigree Ⓗ
Ringwood Best Bitter Ⓖ
Wadworth 6X Ⓗ
Converted country house in
large grounds ♪⚲🅰🅰ⒷⓇⒼ🅿Ⓢ

Barton-on-Sea   6C7

10.30–2.30; 6–10.30 (11 F, S and summer)

Marine
24 Marine Drive East (off
A337) ✆ New Milton 614782
Wadworth Devizes Bitter, 6X,
Old Timer Ⓗ
Comfortable free house on sea
front ♪♣🅱⚲🅰🅰Ⓒ🅿Ⓢ♿🅰≉

Basing   7E3

10.30–2.30; 5.30–10.30 (11 F, S)

Crown
The Street (off A30)
✆ Basingstoke 21424
Courage Best Bitter,
Directors Ⓗ
Three bars and children's
room ♪♣🅱⚲🅰ⒷⒸ🅿🅿Ⓢ

Basingstoke   7E4

10.30–2.30; 5.30–10.30 (11 F, S)

Hopleaf
Upper Church Street ✆ 65538
Draught Bass Ⓗ
Roomy town pub 🅿♪♣Ⓒ🅿Ⓢ

Queens Arms
Bunnian Place ✆ 65488
Courage Best Bitter,
Directors Ⓗ
Small town local
♪♣🅿ⒷⓇⒼ🅿Ⓢ♿≉

Three Barrels
Winklebury Centre ✆ 54180
Opens at 11 am & 6 pm
Marston Burton Bitter,
Pedigree, Owd Rodger Ⓗ
Large, comfortable estate pub
♪♣🅰🅰Ⓢ

Bighton   7E5

10.30–2.30; 6–10.30 (11 F, S and summer)

Three Horseshoes
(Off A31/B3046)
Gale Light Mild, BBB, HSB Ⓗ
Unspoilt traditional local, a
'collectors' pub 🅿🅿♣⚲🅰🅰Ⓢ

Bishopstoke   6D6

10–2.30; 6–10.30 (11 F, S)

Longmead Arms
Longmead Avenue (off
B3037)
Morning opening: 11
Marston Mercian Mild,
Burton Bitter, Pedigree Ⓗ
Owd Rodger Ⓖ
Post-war pub with a good
local trade 🏠♪♣⚲🅰🅰Ⓢ

Bishop's Waltham   6E6

10–2.30; 6–10.30 (11 F, S and summer)

Bunch of Grapes
St Peter's Street (off A333)
✆ 2935
Closes 2 pm weekdays
Courage Best Bitter Ⓖ
Unspoilt tavern in narrow
medieval street 🅿♣⚲🅿🅰🅰

Mafeking Hero
Bank Street (off A333)
Whitbread Strong Country
Bitter, Pompey Royal Ⓗ
Good village pub with own
fish and chip shop 🏠♪⚲🅰Ⓢ

Botley   6D6

10–2.30; 6–10.30 (11 F, S)

Brewery Bar
10 Winchester Street (A3051)
Marston Mercian Mild,
Burton Bitter, Pedigree Ⓗ
Owd Rodger Ⓖ
Popular village pub,
deceptively large
🏠♪♣🅰Ⓢ≉

Braishfield   6D5

10–2.30; 6–10.30 (11 F, S)

Dog & Crook
Crook Hill ✆ 68530
Morning opening: 11
Whitbread Strong Country
Bitter, Pompey Royal Ⓖ
Small friendly village pub
🏠🅿♣⚲🅰Ⓒ🅿🅿

Brimpton Common   6E3

10–2.30; 5.30–10.30 (11 F, S)

Pineapple
(B3051) ✆ Tadley 4376
Evening opening: 6
Wethered Bitter, SPA,
Winter Royal Ⓗ
Superb thatched, oak-beamed
pub 🅿♪♣⚲🅰ⓇⒼ🅿🅿

Broughton   6C5

10–2.30; 6–10.30 (11 F, S)

Greyhound
High Street (off B3084) ✆ 464
Marston Mercian Mild,
Burton Bitter, Pedigree,
Merrie Monk (summer), Owd
Rodger Ⓗ
Lively village pub, Cunard
liner theme in lounge
🏠♪♣Ⓒ🅿🅿 (not Mon)🅿Ⓢ🅰

Burghclere   6D3

10–2.30; 6–10.30 (11 F, S)

Queen
(Off A34)
Marston Mercian Mild,
Pedigree
Wadworth 6X Ⓗ
Pleasant, roomy open-plan
village pub ♪♣🅱⚲🅿Ⓢ

Catherington   7F6

10.30–2.30; 6–10.30 (11 F, S and summer)

Farmers Inn
Catherington Lane (off A3)
✆ Horndean 592402

Morning opening: 11
Gale Dark Mild, BBB, HSB [E]
Lively, sociable rural pub
♪♣🌳🚗🕒◗🍺[S]

Charlton 7F6

10.30–2.30; 6–10.30 (11 F, S and summer)
Red Lion
(Off A3)
Gale Dark Mild, BBB, HSB, XXXXX [H]
Busy 12th-century pub with inglenooks 🏨♪🌳🚗[R]🕒🍺[S]

Cheriton 6E5

10.30–2.30; 6–10.30 (11 F, S and summer)
Flowerpots
(Off A272) ☎ Bramdean 318
Whitbread Strong Country Bitter, Pompey Royal [G]
Cosy and unspoilt village local
🏨♪♣🌳🚗■[R]🍺[S]⛺

Chilbolton 6D4

10–2.30; 6–10.30 (11 F, S)
Abbots Mitre
☎ 348
Whitbread Strong Country Bitter, Pompey Royal [H]
Welcoming pub with excellent food ♪♣🌳🚗■[R]🕒◗🍺[S]

Church Crookham 7F3

10.30–2.30; 5.30–10.30 (11 F, S)
North Horns
Beacon Hill Road (B3013)
☎ Fleet 3976
Opens at 11 am & 6 pm
Friary Meux Bitter
Ind Coope Burton Ale [H]
Welcoming pub with worldwide bottle collection
👪♪♣🌳🚗🕒🍺[S]♿⛺

Cowplain 7F6

10–2.30; 6–10.30 (11 F, S)
Rainbow
244 Milton Road (off B2150)
Tamplins Bitter [A]
Usher Best Bitter
Watney Fined Stag Bitter
Webster Yorkshire Bitter
Bulmer Cider [H]
Friendly, popular estate pub
♪♣🌳🚗🕒🍺[S]

Crawley 6D5

10.30–2.30; 6–10.30 (11 F, S and summer)
Rack & Manger
Stockbridge Road (A272)
☎ Sparsholt 281
Marston Mercian Mild, Burton Bitter, Pedigree, Merrie Monk, Owd Rodger [H]
Large quiet lounge, public bar with many games
🏨♪♣🌳🚗🕒◗🍺[S]

Crondall 7F4

10.30–2.30; 5.30–10.30 (11 F, S and summer)
Hampshire Arms
Pankridge Street (off A287)
☎ Aldershot 850418
Courage Best Bitter, Directors [H]
Most welcoming modernised village pub ♣▣🌳🚗🕒◗[S]♿

Denmead 7E6

10–2.30; 6–10.30 (11 F, S and summer)
Harvest Home
Southwick Road (off B2150)
Gale BBB, HSB, XXXXX [E]
Smart, comfortable and popular rural pub ♪🌳🚗[S]

Droxford 7E6

10–2.30; 6–10.30 (11 F, S and summer)
White Horse
High Street (A32) ☎ 490
Draught Bass
Courage Directors
Gale BBB, HSB
Gibbs Mew Bishops Tipple
Hall & Woodhouse Badger Best Bitter
Ringwood Best Bitter, Old Thumper
Wadworth 6X [H]
Excellent country inn
🏨♪♣🌳🚗■[R]🕒◗🍺[S]⛺

Dundridge 6E6

10.30–2.30; 6–10.30 (11 F, S and summer)
Hampshire Bowman
Dundridge Lane (1 mile off B3035) OS 579185
☎ Bishop's Waltham 2940
Opens at 11 am and 6.30 pm
Gale BBB, HSB, XXXXX [G]
Remote but popular ♪♣🌳🚗[S]⛺

East End 6D3

10–2.30; 6–10.30 (11 F, S)
Axe & Compasses
(Off A343)
☎ Highclere 253403
Wadworth 6X [H]
Rural delight, worth finding
👪♪♣▣🌳🚗[R]🕒◗[S]⛺

East Worldham 7F4

10.30–2.30; 6–10.30 (11 F, S and summer)
Three Horseshoes
(B3004) ☎ Alton 83211
Gale Light Mild, BBB, HSB, XXXXX [H]
Imposing country pub near village pottery
🏨👪♪♣🌳🚗🕒◗ (Wed–Sun)[S]♿

Eling 6D6

10–2.30; 6–10.30 (11 F, S and summer)
Village Bells
Eling Hill
Opens at 10.30 am & 6.30 pm
Gale HSB
Tamplins Bitter
Usher Best Bitter [H]
Comfortable village local near working tidal mill 👪♪♣🌳🚗🍺[S]

Ellisfield 7E4

10.30–2.30; 6–10.30 (11 F, S)
Fox
Green Lane (off A339)
☎ Herriard 210
Eldridge Pope Dorchester Bitter, Royal Oak
Marston Pedigree, Merrie Monk [H] **Owd Rodger** [G]
Busy country inn; guest beers
🏨♣🌳🚗🕒◗🍺[S]

Emsworth 7F6

10–2.30; 6–10.30 (11 F, S)
Lord Raglan
Queen Street (off A27) ☎ 2587
Gale Light Mild, BBB, HSB, XXXXX [H]
Cheerful pub on Sussex border
🏨👪♪♣🌳🕒🍺🚆

Try also: Ship (Bass), or any Gales house

Ewshot 7F4

10.30–2.30; 5.30–10.30 (11 F, S)
Windmill
Church Lane
☎ Aldershot 850439
Friary Meux Bitter
Ind Coope Burton Ale [H]
Village pub with 18-hole pitch-and-putt course
🏨♣🌳🚗🕒[S]♿

Fareham 6E6

10–2.30; 6–10.30 (11 F, S and summer)
Golden Lion
High Street (A32) ☎ 234061
Gale BBB, HSB, XXXXX [H]
Lively pub in historic street
♪♣🚗🕒[S]

Farnborough 7G3

10.30–2.30; 5.30–10.30 (11 F, S)
Prince of Wales
Rectory Road (off A325)
Opens at 11.30 am & 6 pm
Eldridge Pope Royal Oak
Hall & Woodhouse Badger Best Bitter
King & Barnes Sussex Bitter
Shepherd Neame Bitter
Wethered Bitter, SPA [H]
Regular guest beers ♪🚗🚆

Squirrel
Park Road (off A3011)
☎ 542982
Evening opening: 6
Friary Meux Bitter
Ind Coope Burton Ale [H]
Comfortable lounge, darts-orientated public bar
👪♪♣🌳🚗🕒◗🍺[S]🚆

Fritham 6C6

10–2.30; 6–10.30 (11 F, S and summer)
Royal Oak
Whitbread Strong Country Bitter, Pompey Royal [G]
Rustic thatched cottage
🏨♣🌳🍺⛺

Froyle 7F4

11–2.30; 6–10.30 (11 F, S and summer)
Hen & Chicken
Lower Froyle (A31)
☎ Bentley 72115

Ballard Best Bitter
Brakspear Special Bitter
Gale HSB
Hall & Woodhouse Badger Best Bitter, Tanglefoot
Whitbread Strong Country Bitter
Bulmer Cider [H]
Busy roadside pub
⌂⚐♪❦🚗◷☽[S]

Funtley 6E6

10–2.30; 6–10.30 (11 F, S and summer)

Miners Arms
112 Funtley Road
☎ Fareham 232065
Gale BBB, HSB [H] **XXXXX** [G]
Popular village pub with pleasant atmosphere
♪♣❦🚗◷☽ (not Sun)🍷[S]⛺

Golden Pot 7F4

11–2.30; 6–10.30 (11 F, S and summer)

Golden Pot
(A32) ☎ Alton 84130
Courage Best Bitter, Directors [G] & [H]
Friendly roadside pub
♪♣❦🚗[R]◷🍷

Gosport 7E7

10–2.30; 6–10.30 (11 F, S and summer)

Railway Inn
Forton Road (A32) ☎ 80980
Draught Bass
Eldridge Pope IPA, Royal Oak
Whitbread Strong Country Bitter [H]
Popular friendly free house
⚐♪♣🚗[R]◷☽🍷[S]

Vine Hotel
64 Stokes Road ☎ 84121
Whitbread Flowers Original Bitter, Strong Country Bitter, Pompey Royal [H]
Friendly pub attracting passing trade
⚐♪♣▦❦🚗[R]◷☽🍷[S]

Hamble 6D6

10–2.30; 6–10.30 (11 F, S)

Olde Whyte Harte
High Street (B3397)
☎ 452108
Gale Light Mild, BBB, HSB, XXXXX [H]
Popular 16th-century pub
⌂♣❦◷☽[S]

Hambledon 7E6

10.30–2.30; 6–10.30 (11 F, S and summer)

Bat & Ball
Broadhalfpenny Down (off B2150) ☎ 692
Friary Meux Bitter
Ind Coope Burton Ale [H]
Famous for the origins of cricket; good food ♪❦🚗◷☽[S]

Vine
West Street (off B2150) ☎ 419
Courage Directors
Gale BBB, HSB, XXXXX
Hermitage Best
Marston Pedigree [H]
400-year-old pub in historic brewing village
⌂⚐♪♣❦[R]◷☽ (not Mon)🍷[S]

Hammer Vale 7G5

11–2.30; 6–10.30 (11 F, S)

Prince of Wales
(Off B2131)
☎ Haslemere 52600
Gale Light Mild, BBB, HSB, XXXXX [G]
Refurbished but retaining character ⌂⚐♪❦🚗◷☽🍷[S]

Hannington 6E3

10–2.30; 5.30–10.30 (11 F, S)

Vine
(Off A339)
☎ Kingsclere 298525
Eldridge Pope Dorchester Bitter, IPA, Royal Oak
Fuller ESB
Gibbs Mew Bishops Tipple
Usher Best Bitter
Bulmer Cider [H]
Popular village pub and restaurant ⌂♪♣▦❦🚗[R]◷☽[S]

Havant 7F6

10–2.30; 6–10.30 (11 F, S)

Old House at Home
South Street (off A27)
☎ 483464
Gale BBB, HSB, XXXXX [H]
Busy 14th-century town-centre pub ⌂♪♣◷🍷[S]≹

Robin Hood
6 Homewell
Gale Light Mild, BBB, HSB, XXXXX [G]
Unspoilt pub, full of character
⌂♪♣❦🍷≹

Hawkley 7F5

10–2.30; 6–10.30 (11 F, S and summer)

Hawkley Inn
OS 746292 ☎ 205
Opens at 11 am or later
Ballard Best Bitter [H]
Eldridge Pope Dorchester Bitter [E] **IPA**
Hall & Woodhouse Badger Best Bitter
Marston Pedigree [H]
Convivial pub in peaceful village ⌂❦🚗[R][S]

Hayling Island 7F7

10–2.30; 6–10.30 (11 F, S)

Maypole
9 Havant Road (A3023)
☎ 3670
Gale Light Mild, BBB, HSB [H]
Friendly main road local
♪♣❦🚗◷🍷[S]♿⛺

Headley 7F5

11–2.30; 6–10.30 (11 F, S)

Holly Bush
(B3002)
☎ Headley Down 712211
Opens 12–2; 7–10.30
Courage Best Bitter [H]
Sturdy Victorian village local
♪♣▦❦🚗▣[R]◷🍷[S]♿

Hedge End 6D6

10–2.30; 6–10.30 (11 F, S)

Barleycorn
Lower Northam Road (off A334) ☎ Botley 4171
Marston Mercian Mild, Burton Bitter, Pedigree [H]
Popular friendly local
♪♣❦🚗▣◷🍷[S]

Try also: Fountain, St Johns Road (Marston)

Horndean 7F6

11–2.30; 6–10.30 (11 F, S and summer)

Brewers Arms
Five Heads Road (off A3)
☎ 592404
Gale Dark Mild, BBB, HSB, XXXXX [H]
Busy, friendly village local
♪♣🚗◷🍷[S]

Horton Heath 6D6

10–2.30; 6–10.30 (11 F, S)

Rising Sun
Botley Road (A3057)
☎ Southampton 692377
Whitbread Strong Country Bitter, Pompey Royal [H]
Busy roadside pub
⚐♪♣▦❦🚗◷[S]⛺

Hythe 6D6

10.30–2.30; 6–10.30 (11 F, S and summer)

Lord Nelson
High Street
Whitbread Strong Country Bitter [H] **Pompey Royal** (winter)
Bulmer Cider [G]
Waterfront pub with quaint bars ♪♣❦🍷[S]♿

Kingsclere 6E3

10.30–2.30; 5.30–10.30 (11 F, S)

Crown
(A339) ☎ 298865
Opens at 11 am & 6 pm
Courage Best Bitter, Directors [H]
Comfortable pub with good food ♪♣❦🚗▣[R]◷☽🍷[S]♿

King's Somborne 6C5

10–2.30; 6–10.30 (11 F, S)

Crown
(A3057)
Whitbread Strong Country Bitter [G]
Friendly, homely 15th-century inn ♪♣❦🚗🍷[S]♿

Leckford 6D4

10–2.30; 6.30–10.30 (11 F, S)

Leckford Hutt
(A30) ☎ Andover 810738
Marston Mercian Mild, Burton Bitter, Pedigree,

Merrie Monk, Owd Rodger H
Cosy, isolated roadside inn
🏨🍴🎵♿🅿🚗🚌🕐🌳⑨&Å

Longparish 6D4

10–2.30; 6–10.30 (11 F, S)
Buck
(A303) ✆ 407
Gale HSB
Gibbs Mew Premium Bitter H
Tastefully modernised main
road inn 🏨🍴🎵♿🅿🚗🚌🕐⑨

Longstock 6C4

10–2.30; 6–10.30 (11 F, S)
Peat Spade
(Off A30) ✆ Andover 810612
Gale Light Mild, BBB, HSB H
Friendly village pub near
River Test 🏨♣🅿🍴🔲Ⓡ🚌🕐🍽⑨&

Lyde Green 7F3

10.30–2.30; 5.30–10.30 (11 F, S)
Fox
✆ Basingstoke 882279
Draught Bass
Hall & Woodhouse Badger
Best Bitter
Morland Mild, Bitter, Best
Bitter
Ruddle County
Theakston Best Bitter H
Lively single-bar village local
♣🅿🚌⑨

Lymington 6C7

10–2.30; 6–10.30 (11 F, S and summer)
King's Arms
St Thomas Street (off A337)
✆ 72594
Whitbread Strong Country
Bitter, Pompey Royal H
Town pub with good local
trade 🎵♣🅿🔲Ⓡ🚌🕐🍽⑨≷

Olde English
Gentleman

Queen Street (A37) ✆ 72139
Morning opening: 11
Devenish Bitter, Wessex Best
Bitter
Taunton Cider H
Popular pub, good value beer
and food 🏨🎵♣🅿🚗🅿Ⓡ
🕐 (not Tue)🍽⑨≷

Lyndhurst 6C6

10.30–2.30; 6–10.30 (11 F, S and summer)
Mailmans Arms
71 High Street
Morning opening: 11
Marston Mercian Mild,
Burton Bitter, Pedigree H
Friendly locals' pub, no
electronics 🏨♣🅿🍽⑨

Michelmersh 6C5

10–2.30; 6–10.30 (11 F, S)
Bear & Ragged Staff
Stockbridge Road (A3057)
✆ Braishfield 68682
Whitbread Strong Country
Bitter, Pompey Royal H
Spacious country inn with

---

good garden
🏨🍴🎵♣🅿🔲🚌🕐🍽⑨&

Minstead 6C6

10.30–2.30; 6–10.30 (11 F, S and summer)
Trusty Servant
✆ Cadnam 2137
Whitbead Flowers Original
Bitter, Pompey Royal H
New Forest pub by the village
green 🍴🅿🚗🔲Ⓡ⑨Å

Monk Sherborne 7E3

10.30–2.30; 5.30–10.30 (11 F, S)
Mole
(Off A340)
✆ Basingstoke 850033
Morland Mild, Bitter, Best
Bitter H
Remote but popular village
local ♣🅿🚌Ⓒ🍽⑨

Mortimer West
End 7E3

10.30–2.30; 5.30–10.30 (11 F, S)
Olde Turners Arms
(Off A340) ✆ Reading 332961
Brakspear Pale Ale, Special
Bitter, Old H
Country inn, emphasis on
food 🏨🅿🚗🔲Ⓡ🕐🍽

Nether Wallop 6C5

10–2.30; 6–10.30 (11 F, S)
Five Bells
(Off A343)
✆ Andover 781572
Marston Mercian Mild,
Burton Bitter, Pedigree, Owd
Rodger H
Village pub with skittle alley
♣🅿🚗🔲Ⓡ🕐⑨

Newton Valence
7F5

11–2.30; 6–10.30 (11 F, S and summer)
Horse & Groom
(A32) ✆ Tisted 220
Gale HSB
Usher Best Bitter
Tamplins Bitter
Watney Fined Stag Bitter H
Petanque played in garden
🎵🅿🚗🔲Ⓡ🕐⑨Å

Oakhanger 7F5

10.30–2.30; 6–10.30 (11 F, S and summer)
Red Lion
(Off B3004)
Courage Best Bitter, Directors H
Classic village local
🎵♣🅿🚗⑨&Å

Oakley 6E4

10–2.30; 5.30–10.30 (11 F, S)
Beech Arms Hotel
Andover Road (B3400)
✆ Basingstoke 780210
Halls Harvest Bitter
Ind Coope Burton Ale H
Former motel, regaining
'local' image 🎵🅿🔲Ⓡ🕐🍽⑨

Owslebury 6D5

11–2.30; 6–10.30 (11 F, S and summer)
Shearers Arms
Owslebury Bottom
(Off A333) OS 514242 ✆ 296
Gale BBB, HSB, XXXXX
Hall & Woodhouse
Badger Best Bitter
Wadworth 6X H
Peaceful rural setting
🏨🎵♣🅿🚌🕐⑨&Å

Passfield 7F5

10.30–2.30; 6–10.30 (11 F, S and summer)
Passfield Oak
Passfield Common (B3006)
✆ 205
Ballard Best Bitter
Gale BBB, HSB
Marston Pedigree
Younger IPA H
Modernised family pub
🏨🍴🎵🅿🔲🚌Ⓒ🕐⑨&Å

Pennington 6C7

10–2.30; 6–10.30 (11 F, S and summer)
Musketeer
26 North Street (off A337)
✆ Lymington 76527
Morning opening: 11
Gale BBB, HSB
Ringwood Best Bitter H
Friendly, comfortable village
pub, guest beers
🏨🍴♣🅿🔲🚌🕐⑨≷

Petersfield 7F5

10–2.30; 6–10.30 (11 F, S and summer)
Square Brewery
The Square (off A3) ✆ 64291
Gale BBB, HSB, XXXXX H
Busy pub in market square
🎵♣🅿🚌🕐🍽⑨≷

Portsmouth 7E7

10.30–2.30; 6–10.30 (11 F, S and summer)
Artillery
1 Hester Road, Milton,
Southsea
Friary Meux Bitter
Ind Coope Burton Ale H
Traditional backstreet pub
🎵♣🅿🕐⑨

Brewer's Arms
170 Milton Road, Milton
(Off A2030)
Gale Light Mild, BBB, HSB,
XXXXX G
Friendly local with keen
landlord
🏨🎵♣🅿🍽⑨&

Castle Tavern
119 Somers Road, Southsea
Whitbread Strong Country
Bitter, Pompey Royal H
Country pub in the city
🎵♣🅿🍽⑨≷

Electric Arms
192 Fratton Road ✆ 823293
Friary Meux Bitter H
Fine friendly local on main
road 🎵♣🚌🕐🍽⑨≷

Fifth Hants Volunteer Arms
Albert Road, Southsea
Gale Light Mild, BBB, HSB Ⓗ
XXXXX Ⓖ
Popular local, birthplace of
local CAMRA branch ▲♣♚♟

George
84 Queens Street, Portsea
☎ 821041
Courage Directors
Southsea Admirals Ale
Whitbread Strong Country
Bitter, Pompey Royal Ⓗ
Listed building with well in
centre of bar ♪♣Ⓓ®Ⓖ◎♚⬇≢

Old House at Home
104 Locksway Road, Milton,
Southsea
Whitbread Flowers Original
Bitter, Strong Country Bitter,
Pompey Royal Ⓗ
Unusual pub with murals and
paintings by landlord
▲♪♣Ⓔ♚♟Ⓢ⬇

Phoenix
13 Duncan Road, Southsea
☎ 821189
Whitbread Strong Country
Bitter, Pompey Royal Ⓗ
Stage door bar for Kings
Theatre ♪♣♚®Ⓖ♟◎Ⓢ

Portland Hotel
Kent Road, Southsea
☎ 825126
Courage Best Bitter,
Directors Ⓗ
Large hotel with contrasting
bars, near shopping precinct
♪♣♚♟♟®Ⓖ◎Ⓢ

Red, White & Blue
150 Fawcett Road
Evening opening: 6.30
Gale BBB, HSB Ⓗ
One-bar local, interesting red,
white and blue cocktails
♣♟≢

R.M.A. Tavern
58 Cromwell Road, Eastney,
Southsea ☎ 820896
Gale Dark Mild, BBB, HSB,
XXXXX Ⓗ
Friendly local with wine bar
♣Ⓔ♚®Ⓖ♟◎Ⓢ⬇

Scotts Bar
Eldon Street, Southsea
☎ 826018
Morning opening: 11
Courage Directors
Fuller London Pride
Marston Pedigree
Southsea Captains Bitter,
Admirals Ale Ⓗ
Superb city free house; guest
beers ♪®Ⓖ♟◎Ⓢ≢

Sir Loin of Beef
152 Highland Road, Southsea
☎ 820115
Eldridge Pope IPA, Royal
Oak Ⓗ

Friendly, comfortable
street-corner local ♪♣Ⓖ♟Ⓢ

Swan
100 Copnor Road,
Copnor ☎ 662445
Draught Bass
Welsh Hancocks Bitter Ⓗ
Recently refurbished,
comfortable local ♪♣♚♟ⒶⒼ♟Ⓢ

Wellington
62 High Street, Old
Portsmouth ☎ 818965
Friary Meux Bitter
Ind Coope Burton Ale Ⓗ
Pleasant pub in historic area
♪♣Ⓖ♟Ⓢ

Prior's Dean   7F5
11–2.30; 6–10.30 (11 F, S and summer)
White Horse
OS 714290 ☎ Tisted 387
Ballard Bitter
Draught Bass
Eldridge Pope Dorchester
Bitter, Royal Oak Ⓗ
Gale HSB
Marston Burton Bitter Ⓖ
Pedigree, Merrie Monk
Ringwood Fortyniner, Old
Thumper
Wadworth 6X, Old Timer Ⓗ
Worth finding ▲♚♟Ⓖ◎Ⓢ

Romsey   6C6
10–2.30; 6–10.30 (11 F, S)
Tudor Rose
Cornmarket ☎ 512126
Courage Best Bitter,
Directors Ⓗ
Small, friendly 15th-century
pub ▲♪♣♚♟Ⓖ◎Ⓢ≢

St Mary Bourne   6D4
10–2.30; 6–10.30 (11 F, S)
Coronation Arms
(B3048) ☎ 432
Morning opening: 10.30
Marston Mercian Mild,
Burton Bitter, Pedigree Ⓗ
Lively focal point of village life
♪♣♚♟Ⓢ

Selborne   7F5
10.30–2.30; 6–10.30 (11 F, S and summer)
Selborne Arms
The Street (B3006) ☎ 247
Courage Best Bitter,
Directors Ⓖ
Pub with strong sporting and
jazz connections
▲♪♣♚♟Ⓖ♟◎Ⓢ⬇

Setley   6C7
11–2.30; 6–10.30 (11 F, S and summer)
Filly Inn
(A337) near Brockenhurst
☎ Lymington 23449
New Forest Real Ale Ⓗ
Ringwood Old Thumper Ⓖ
Wadworth 6X Ⓗ
Genuine horse brasses and
low beams
♪♚♟Ⓖ♟◎⬇▲≢

Soberton   7E6
11–2.30; 6–10.30 (11 F, S and summer)
White Lion
School Hill (off A32) OS
610168 ☎ Droxford 346
Winter evening opening: 7
Friary Meux Bitter
Gale HSB Ⓗ
Southsea Admirals Ale Ⓖ
Usher Best Bitter Ⓗ
17th century country pub
with a la carte restaurant
▲♣♚♟♟Ⓖ♟◎Ⓢ

Southampton   6D6
10–2.30; 6–10.30 (11 F, S)
Brook
446 Portswood Road
Marston Mercian Mild,
Burton Bitter, Pedigree Ⓗ
Traditional street-corner local
♪♣♟Ⓢ◎≢

Freemantle Arms
33 Albany Road , Freemantle
Marston Mercian Mild,
Burton Bitter Ⓗ
Back-street local,
mild-drinkers' outpost ♪♣♚♟

Mason's Arms
St Mary Street
Opens at 11 am & 7 pm
Gale Dark Mild, BBB, HSB,
XXXXX Ⓗ
Excellent small pub ▲♪♟♟

New Inn
Bevois Valley Road (A335)
Gale Dark Mild (summer),
BBB, HSB, XXXXX Ⓗ
A beer-drinkers' pub
♪♣Ⓖ (Mon–Fri)

Osborne Hotel
54 Shirley Road ☎ 21589
Marston Mercian Mild,
Pedigree, Owd Rodger Ⓗ
Victorian pub with notable
engraved windows ♪♣Ⓖ♟≢

Park Inn
37 Carlisle Road, Shirley
Wadworth IPA, 6X, Old
Timer Ⓗ
Small, friendly sidestreet local
♪♣♟

Salisbury Arms
126 Shirley High Street
Marston Mercian Mild,
Burton Bitter, Pedigree Ⓗ
Straightforward local with
central bar ♪♣♟

Sloan's Wine Bar
21 Oxford Street ☎ 20785
Closed Sunday lunchtimes
Devenish Wessex Best Bitter Ⓗ
Popular bar in old town
♪♟♚Ⓖ♟Ⓢ

Southwick   7E6
10.30–2.30; 6–10.30 (11 F, S)
Red Lion
High Street (off A333)

Hampshire

Cosham 377223
Gale Light Mild, BBB, HSB ⊞
XXXXX Ⓖ
Taunton Cider ⊞
Pleasantly modernised village
local ♪♣⚲🚗🚍Ⓖ🎵🍴Ⓢ

Steep 7F5

10.30–2.30; 6–10.30 (11 F, S and summer)
Cricketers
1 Church Road
Gale Dark Mild, BBB, HSB ⊞
XXXXX Ⓖ
1930s-style roadhouse, now a
lively local
♪♣⚲🚗Ⓢ

Stockbridge 6C5

10–2.30; 6–10.30 (11 F, S)
White Hart
(A30/A272)
Andover 810475
Morning opening: 10.30
Draught Bass
Gale HSB
Wadworth 6X
Welsh Hancocks Bitter
Taunton Cider ⊞
Welcoming old inn with
restaurant
🎵♪♣⚲🅿🚗⊞Ⓡ🅶🎵🍴Ⓢ🔥🅐

Stratfield Saye 7F3

10.30–2.30; 6–10.30 (11 F, S)
New Inn
(Off A33) *Mortimer 332255*
Winter evening opening: 7
Bourne Valley Andover Ale
Gale XXXD
Hall & Woodhouse Badger
Best Bitter, Tanglefoot ⊞
Remote and friendly boozer,
worth finding; regular guest
beers
🅐♣⚲🚗Ⓢ🅐

Swanwick 6E6

10–2.30; 6–10.30 (11 F, S and summer)
Old Ship
Bridge Road (A27)
Locks Heath 5646
Gale BBB, HSB ⊞ & Ⓔ
Original low beams and
unusual nautical features;
separate restaurant
♪⚲🚗🍴Ⓢ🅐≷

Twyford 6D5

11–2.30; 6–10.30 (11 F, S and summer)
Phoenix
High Street (A333) *713322*
Marston Mercian Mild,
Burton Bitter, Pedigree ⊞
Welcoming inn, excellent food
🅐♪♣⚲🚗Ⓡ🅶🎵Ⓢ

Vernham Dean 6C3

10–2.30; 6–10.30 (11 F, S)
George
(Off A343) *Linkenholt 279*
Opens at 12 noon and 7 pm
Marston Burton Bitter,
Pedigree ⊞
Excellent pub in every way
🅐♪🈂♣🔁⚲🚗Ⓡ🎵Ⓢ🅐

Waltham Chase 6E6

10–2.30; 6–10.30 (11 F, S and summer)
Black Dog
Winchester Road (A333)
Wickham 832316
Marston Mercian Mild,
Burton Bitter, Pedigree ⊞
Friendly roadside inn
🅐♪⚲🚗🅶🎵Ⓢ

West Dean 6C5

10–2.30; 6–10.30 (11 F, S)
Red Lion
(Off A27) *Lockerley 40469*
Whitbread Flowers Original
Bitter, Strong Country Bitter,
Pompey Royal ⊞
Friendly village pub straddling
two counties 🅐♪♣⚲🚗Ⓖ🎵Ⓢ≷

West Wellow 6C6

10.30–2.30; 6–10.30 (11 F, S and summer)
Rockingham Arms
Canada Road (off A36)
22473
Courage Best Bitter
Gale HSB
Wadworth 6X, Old Timer ⊞
Popular local, good value
🅐♪♣⚲🚗🅶🎵Ⓢ

Weyhill 6C4

10–2.30; 6–10.30 (11 F, S)
Star
(A303) *2356*
Gale Light Mild, BBB, HSB,
XXXXX Ⓔ
Well-patronised, comfortable
roadside pub ♪♣⚲🚗🅶🎵Ⓢ

Wherwell 6D4

10–2.30; 6–10.30 (11 F, S)
White Lion
(B3420) *Chilbolton 317*
Whitbread Strong Country
Bitter, Pompey Royal ⊞
Renovated old coaching inn in
lovely village
🅐♪♣⚲🚗⊞Ⓡ🅶 (not Sun) 🎵Ⓢ

Whitchurch 6D4

10–2.30; 6–10.30 (11 F, S)
Bell
Bell Street (off B3400) *2671*
Courage Best Bitter
Fuller ESB
Gibbs New Premium Bitter
500-year-old small town
local; lively but romantic
🅐♪🈂♣🚗Ⓡ🅶🎵Ⓢ≷

Red House
London Street (B3400) *2066*
Halls Harvest Bitter
Ind Coope Burton Ale ⊞
16th-century inn with folk
club Mondays
🅐♪🈂♣🅱⚲🚗🅶🎵Ⓢ🅐

Whitsbury 6B6

11–2.30; 6–11
Cartwheel
Rockbourne 362
Halls Harvest Bitter

Ind Coope Burton Ale ⊞
Friendly and popular country
pub 🅐♪♣⚲🅿🚗🅐Ⓢ

Wickham 6E6

10–2.30; 6–10.30 (11 F, S and summer)
Roebuck
Kingsmead (A32) *832150*
Gale BBB, HSB ⊞ XXXXX
Bulmer Cider Ⓖ
Pleasant country pub north of
village, excellent food
♪♣⚲🅶🎵Ⓢ🅐

Winchester 6D5

10.30–2.30; 6–10.30 (11 F, S and summer)
Bell
83 St Cross Road (A333)
Marston Mercian Mild,
Burton Bitter, Pedigree ⊞
First-class pub in historic St
Cross 🅐♪♣⚲🚗Ⓢ

Exchange
9 Southgate Street *54718*
Courage Best Bitter, Directors ⊞
Active city-centre pub
🎵♪♣⚲Ⓖ🎵Ⓢ≷

Green Man
53 Southgate Street *65429*
Morning opening: 11
Marston Mercian Mild,
Burton Bitter, Pedigree ⊞
Honest, friendly local close to
city centre ♪♣🅶Ⓖ🎵Ⓢ≷

King Alfred
8 Saxon Road, Hyde *54370*
Marston Mercian Mild,
Burton Bitter, Pedigree ⊞
Lively back-street Victorian
local ♪♣⚲🅿Ⓡ🅶Ⓢ🅐≷

Old Market Inn
The Square *52585*
Closes 10.30 pm Mon–Thu in
summer
Whitbread Strong Country
Bitter, Flowers Original
Bitter ⊞
Tourist haunt in lee of
cathedral ♪🅶Ⓢ≷

Theatre Pub
Jewry Street
Gale Dark Mild (summer),
BBB, HSB, XXXXX
Bulmer Cider ⊞
Lively, tiny bar attached to the
theatre 🎵♪♣Ⓢ🅐≷

The 🅐 symbol denotes a pub
with a real solid fuel fire

Astwood Bank 15G3

11–2.30; 6–10.30 (11 F, S)
Oddfellows Arms
Foregate Street (off A441,
access via Retreat Street)
Mitchells & Butlers Mild Ⓗ
Springfield Bitter Ⓔ Brew XI Ⓗ
Friendly and popular
backstreet local ♣🅿🍴

Aymestrey 14C3

11.30–2.30; 6.30–10.30 (11 F, S)
Crown
(A4110) ☎ Kingsland 440
Malvern Chase Ale
Mitchells & Butlers
Springfield Bitter Ⓗ
Friendly riverside free house
🍴♣🅿🏨🕒🍴🛏️🅂

Bartestree 14D4

10.30–2.30; 6–10.30 (11 F, S)
New Inn
Hereford Road (A438)
Marston Capital, Burton
Bitter, Pedigree Ⓗ
Imposing Victorian 'Gothic'
roadhouse ♪🅿🏨Ⓡ🅂

Belbroughton 15F2

10.30–2.30; 6–10.30 (11 F, S)
Queens
Queens Hill (B4188)
☎ 730276
Morning opening: 11
Marston Burton Bitter,
Pedigree, Merrie Monk Ⓔ
Popular, well-appointed
village pub ♪🏨Ⓡ🕒🍴🅂

Bewdley 15F2

11–2.30; 7–10.30 (11 F, S)
Great Western
Kidderminster Road (A456)
Hanson Mild, Bitter Ⓔ
Rambling old pub next to
Severn Valley railway
🏨♣🏨Ⓡ🍴

Hop Pole
Cleobury Road (A456)
Marston Mercian Mild,
Burton Bitter, Pedigree Ⓗ
Friendly pub on hill above
town 🍴♣🅿🏨Ⓡ🍴🅂

Horn & Trumpet
Dog Lane
Courage Directors Ⓗ
Cosy, welcoming friendly pub
♪♣🍴🅂🄰

Pack Horse
High Street
Ansells Bitter
Ind Coope Burton Ale Ⓗ
Small, cosy pub in narrow side
street 🏨♪♣🍴🅂

Birtsmorton 15F5

10–2.30; 6–10.30 (11 F, S)
Farmer's Arms
Birts Street (off B4208)
Hook Norton Best Bitter

Malvern Chase Ale
Ruddle County
Simpkiss Bitter Ⓗ
16th-century village inn
♣🅿🏨🍴🅂

Bishops Frome 14E4

10.30–2.30; 6–10.30 (11 F, S)
Green Dragon
(Off B4124)
☎ Munderfield 607
Opens at 12 noon & 7 pm
Bailey BB
Hook Norton Best Bitter
Malvern Chase Ale
Robinson Best Bitter, Old Tom
Taylor Landlord
Wadworth 6X
Woods Special Bitter Ⓗ & Ⓖ
Excellent country pub with
home cooking; frequent guest
beers 🏨🍴♣🏨🅿🕒🍴🍴

Bliss Gate 15F2

11–2.30; 7–10.30 (11 F, S)
Bliss Gate
(Off A456) OS 747725
Marston Burton Bitter,
Pedigree Ⓗ
Pleasant village inn, aero
theme in bar 🏨🍴♣🏨Ⓡ🅂

Bournheath 15G2

10.30–2.30; 6–10.30 (11 F, S)
New Inn
Doctor's Hill
Evening opening: 7
Mitchells & Butlers Mild,
Springfield Bitter Ⓗ
Friendly old local
♪♣🅿🏨

Bransford 15F4

10.30–2.30; 6–10.30 (11 F, S)
Fox
Hereford Road (A4103)
Davenports Bitter Ⓗ
Comfortable roadside country
inn ♪♣🅿🏨🅂

Bretforton 15H4

10.30–2.30; 6–10.30 (11 F, S)
Fleece
The Square (off B4035)
Donnington SBA
Hook Norton Best Bitter
Malvern Chase Ale
Marston Pedigree Ⓗ
Beautiful old village inn,
restored by the National Trust
🏨♣🅿🏨🅂

Broad Marston 15H4

10–2; 6–10.30 (11 F, S)
Shoulder of Mutton
OS 139463
Whitbread Bitter
Local cider Ⓖ
Homely, thatched local 🏨♣🍴

Broadwas 15F3

10.30–2.30; 6–10.30 (11 F, S)
Royal Oak
(A44)

Marston Mercian Mild,
Burton Bitter, Pedigree Ⓗ
Welcoming wayside tavern
with fine views ♪♣🅿🍴🅂

Bromsgrove 15G2

10.30–2.30; 6–10.30 (11 F, S)
Britannia
Worcester Road
Opens at 11 am & 7 pm
Mitchells & Butlers Mild, Brew
XI Ⓔ
Cosy, friendly little pub
🍴♣🏨🅿🅂🍺

Red Lion
High Street
Banks Mild, Bitter Ⓔ
Small, busy main road bar
♪♣🅿🏨🅂🍺

Bromyard 14E3

10.30–2.30; 6–10.30 (11 F, S)
Bay Horse
High Street
Mitchells & Butlers Mild,
Brew XI Ⓗ
Town-centre local in
traditional style ♣🄳🍴

Hop Pole Hotel
Market Square ☎ 82449
Marston Mercian Mild,
Burton Bitter, Pedigree Ⓗ
Comfortable market town
hotel 🏨♪♣🏨🏨Ⓡ🕒🍴🅂

Canon Pyon 14D4

10.30–2.30; 6–10.30 (11 F, S)
Nag's Head
(A4110) ☎ 252
Ansells Bitter
Bailey BB
Hook Norton Best Bitter
Wem Best Bitter
Fleming Cider Ⓖ
Appealing village free house
🏨🍴♣🄳♪🏨Ⓡ🕒🍴🅂🅟

Carey 14D5

11.30–2.30; 6.30–11
Cottage of Content
☎ 242
Hook Norton Best Bitter, Old
Hookey
Whitbread Flowers
Original Bitter Ⓗ
Idyllic country pub
🏨🍴♣🅿🏨Ⓔ🕒🍴🅂

Castlemorton 15F4

10.30–2.30; 6–10.30 (11 F, S)
Plume of Feathers
(B4208)
Evening opening: 7; closed
Mon–Fri lunchtimes
Hook Norton Best Bitter Ⓗ
Extraordinary agricultural
local ♣🅿🏨🍴

Clifton-upon-Teme 15E3

10.30–2.30; 6–10.30 (11 F, S)
Lion Hotel
(A4204)

Draught Bass
Simpkiss Bitter
Woods Special Bitter H
Friendly old village pub
🍴♣♠🚪🍷ⓢ

Colwall 15E4

11–2.30; 5.30–10.30 (11 F, S)

Chase
Chase Road, Upper Colwall
Bailey BB H
Banks Mild, Bitter E
Donnington BB, SBA
Malvern Chase Ale H
Friendly roadside tavern on
hillside 🍴♣🅿ⓢ

Dodford 15G2

10.30–2.30; 6–10.30 (11 F, S)

Dodford Inn
Whinfield Road (off A448) OS
939729 ✆ Bromsgrove 32470
Davenports Mild, Bitter H
Comfortable pub in superb
countryside ♣🅿🚪🍴🍷ⓢ

Droitwich 15F3

11–2.30; 6–10.30 (11 F, S)

Eagle & Sun
Hanbury Wharf (B4090)
Draught Bass
Mitchells & Butlers
Springfield Bitter H
Attractive canalside pub,
excellent food 🅿🚪🍷ⓢ

Railway
Hampton Road ✆ 770056
Marston Mercian Mild,
Burton Bitter E
Pleasant and popular local
🍴♣🚪🍷⚲

Dulas 14C5

10–2.30; 6–10.30 (11 Mon, F, S)

Trout
(Off B4347)
✆ Golden Valley 240356
Woods Special Bitter
Bulmer Cider H
Known as the 'Found
Out' – in beautiful valley
♣♠🅿🚪🍷ⓢ

Eldersfield 15F5

10–2.30; 6–10.30 (11 F, S)

Greyhound
Lime Street OS 814305
Donnington SBA
Whitbread WCPA G
Unspoilt pub on Gloucester-
shire border 🍴♣🅿🚪🍷ⓢ

Elmley Castle 15G4

10.30–2.30; 6.30–10.30 (11 F, S)

Queen Elizabeth
Marston Burton Bitter H
Popular 16th-century inn
🍴♣🅿🚪🍷

Ewyas Harold 14C5

11–2.30; 6.30–10.30 (11 Mon, F, S)

Dog
(Off B4347)

✆ Golden Valley 240598
Ansells Bitter H
Robinson Best Bitter, Old
Tom G
Bulmer Cider H
Small, welcoming pub with
antique shop ♠🍴♣🚪🍷ⓢ

Fownhope 14D5

10.30–2.30; 6–10.30 (11 F, S)

Forge & Ferry
Ferry Lane (off B4224) ✆ 391
Banks Mild, Bitter
Davenports Bitter
Marston Pedigree, Merrie
Monk
Usher Best Bitter H
Weston Cider G
Lively village pub, occasional
guest beers
♠🍴♣🚪🅿🚪🍷ⓢ

Green Man
(B4224) ✆ 243
Hook Norton Best Bitter
Samuel Smith Old Brewery
Bitter
Wadworth 6X H
Weston Cider G
Splendid old timbered historic
inn ♠🍴🅿🚪🚪🍷ⓢ

Grimley 15F3

10.30–2.30; 6.30–10.30 (11 F, S)

Camp House Inn
Camp Lane (off A443)
Whitbread WCPA, Bitter H
Bulmer Cider G
Cosy old Severnside inn
🍴♣🅿🚪🍷ⓢ

Hereford 14D4

10.30–2.30; 6–10.30 (11 F, S)

Bay Horse
Kings Acre Road (A438)
Whitbread WCPA, Bitter,
Flowers Original Bitter H
Popular and convivial pub on
outskirts of town 🍴♣🅿🚪🍷ⓢ

Britannia
Cotterill Street, Brecon Road
Whitbread WCPA, Flowers
Original Bitter
Weston Cider H
Unspoilt backstreet local ♣ⓢ

Saracen's Head
St Martin's Street (off A49)
Courage Directors
Malvern Chase Ale
Marston Burton Bitter,
Pedigree H
Dunkerton Cider G
Popular riverside pub
🍴♣🅿🚪🍷ⓢ

Himbleton 15G3

10.30–2.30; 6–10.30 (11 F, S)

Galton Arms
Banks Mild, Bitter H
Country pub cum village local
🍴♣🚪ⓢ

Holy Cross 15G2

10.30–2.30; 6–10.30 (11 F, S)

Bell & Cross
(Off A491)
Mitchells & Butlers Mild, Brew
XI H
A step back in time into this
village local ♠🍴♣🍷

Ismere 15F2

11–2.30; 7–10.30 (11 F, S)

Waggon & Horses
(A451) 2½ miles north-west of
Kidderminster OS 870801
Hanson Mild, Bitter H
Fine roadside inn, traditional
jazz ♠🍴♣🅿🚪🍷ⓢ

Kidderminster 15F2

11–2.30; 7–10.30 (11 F, S)

Hare & Hounds
Stourbridge Road,
Broadwaters (A449)
Batham Mild, Bitter H
Spartan bar, split-level lounge
🍴♣🚪🍷ⓢ

King William
St. John's Street, off Ring Road
Banks Mild, Bitter E
Small side-street local
🍴♣🅿🍷ⓢ

Old Tumbling
Sailors
Mill Lane
Mitchells & Butlers Highgate
Mild, Brew XI H
Small, friendly sidestreet local
♠🍴♣🍷

Parkers Arms
Park Lane
Banks Mild, Bitter E
Out-of-the-way pub backing
onto canal 🍴♣🅿🚪🍷

Railway Train
Offmore Road
Mitchells & Butlers Highgate
Mild, Brew XI E
Sidestreet pub 🍴♣🅿🍷⚲

Station Inn
Fairfield (off A448)
Davenports Bitter H
Sidestreet local with large
garden 🍴♣🚪🅿🍷ⓢ⚲

Kington 14C3

10.30–2.30; 5.30–10.30 (11 F, S)

Olde Tavern
(Railway Tavern)
Victoria Road (off A44)
No lunchtime opening;
Opens 7.30 pm (Mon–Sat)
Ansells Bitter H
Superb old inn, unspoilt by
progress ♠🚪🍷

Ledbury 15E4

10.30–2.30; 6–10.30 (11 F, S)

Feathers
High Street (A417) ✆ 2600
Open until 4 pm Wednesdays
Draught Bass
Mitchells & Butlers Brew XI E
Highgate Old Ale

Weston Cider G
Historic coaching inn with
smart lounge bars
♨☰🚃Ⓡ🅖🖐🎁🚲

Royal Oak Hotel
The Southend ☎ 2110
Banks Mild
Malvern Chase Ale
Marston Pedigree Ⓗ
Owd Rodger
Weston Cider G
Friendly hotel with
comfortable lounge bars
♨🍴🍺📶☰Ⓡ🅖🖐🎁

Seven Stars
The Homend (A417) ☎ 2824
Evening opening: 6.30
Whitbread WCPA, Bitter Ⓗ
Weston Cider G
Cosy, traditional pub with
beer garden ♨🚗♪🍺📶🗐🅖🖐🎁🚲

Leintwardine 14C2
10.30–2.30; 6–10.30 (11 F, S)

Sun Inn
(Off A4110)
May open late evenings
Ansells Mild, Bitter G
Amazing old pub – a remnant
of the past 🍴🎁

Leominster 14D3
10.30–2.30; 6–10.30 (11 F, S)

Royal Oak
South Street (A44) ☎ 2610
Hook Norton Best Bitter
Woods Special Bitter
Bulmer Cider Ⓗ
Market town hotel with guest
beers ♨♪🗐📶☰Ⓡ🅖🖐🎁

Lingen 14C3
11.30–2.30; 6.30–10.30 (11 F, S)

Royal George
(Off B4362)
Evening opening: 7.30
Mon–Thu
Three Tuns XXX, Castle
Steamer
Weston Cider Ⓗ
Superb village focal point;
post office attached ♨♪🍴☰🍺

Long Green 15F5
10–2.30; 6–10.30 (11 F, S)

Hunters Inn
(B4211) near Longdon
Wadworth IPA, 6X Ⓗ
Modernised country pub
♪🍴📶🅖🖐🎁

Lulsley 15E3
10–2.30; 6–10.30 (11 F, S)

Fox & Hounds
(Off A44) OS 739546
Banks Mild, Bitter Ⓔ
Smart country pub 🍴☰🖐🎁

Lyonshall 14C3
10.30–2.30; 6.30–10.30 (11 F, S)

Royal George
(A480) ☎ 210

Whitbread Bitter, Flowers
Original Bitter Ⓗ
Smart black and white village
inn ♨♪🍴📶☰🍺🅖🖐🎁🚲♿

Malvern 15F4
10–2.30; 6–10.30 (11 F, S)

Brewers Arms
West Malvern (B4232)
Marston Burton Bitter Ⓗ
Friendly pub on Malvern hills
♪🍺🖐🎁

Martley 15E3
10–2.30; 6–10.30 (11 F, S)

Crown
(B4197)
Banks Mild, Bitter Ⓔ
Friendly village pub ♪🍴☰Ⓡ🎁

Michaelchurch
Escley 14C5
11–2.30; 6–10.30 (11 Mon, F, S)

Bridge Inn
OS 332236 ☎ 646
Winter evening opening: 7
Hook Norton Best Bitter
Mitchells & Butlers
Springfield Bitter
Robinson Best Bitter
Wadworth 6X
Bulmer & Weston Cider Ⓗ
16th-century inn with lawned
gardens and trout stream
♨♪🍴🗐📶☰Ⓡ🅖🖐🎁🚲⛺

Newbridge Green
15F4
10–2.30; 6–10.30 (11 F, S)

Drum & Monkey
(B4211)
Banks Mild, Bitter
Draught Bass
Donnington BB, SBA Ⓗ
Tastefully enlarged country
pub with excellent restaurant
♪🍴📶☰🅖🖐🎁

Newnham Bridge
14E3
10–2.30; 6–10.30 (11 F, S)

Tavern
Tavern Lane (off A456)
Bartlett Mild, Bitter Ⓔ
Modern village pub brewing its
own beer 🍴🍺☰📶🖐🎁

Norton 15G4
10.30–2.30; 7–10.30 (11 F, S)

Norton Grange
(A435/A439)
☎ Evesham 870215
Marston Burton Bitter,
Pedigree Ⓗ
Rural family-run hotel
♨☰♪🍴📶☰🚃Ⓡ🅖🖐🎁🚲⛺

Ombersley 15F3
10.30–2.30; 6–10.30 (11 F, S)

Cross Keys
(Off A449)
Marston Mercian Mild,
Burton Bitter

Theakston Best Bitter Ⓗ
Friendly village pub with
guest beers ♨♪🍴📶🅖🖐🎁

Pembridge 14C3
11–2.30; 6.30–10.30 (11 F, S)

New Inn
(Off A44) ☎ 427
Whitbread Bitter
Bulmer Cider Ⓗ
Idyllic village inn – a real gem
♨♪🍴📶☰🍺Ⓡ🅖🖐🎁

Pershore 15G4
11–2.30; 5.30–10.30 (11 F, S)

Millers Arms
Bridge Street (A44)
Davenports Bitter
Hook Norton Best Bitter
Malvern Chase Ale
Wadworth 6X Ⓗ
Popular town-centre tavern
🖐♪🍴🖐🎁

Redditch 15G3
10.30–2.30; 6–10.30 (11 F, S)

Golden Cross
Unicorn Hill ☎ 63711
Closes 10.30 pm F, S
Banks Mild, Bitter Ⓔ
Modern, well-designed town
pub ♪🍴📶🅖🍺🖐🎁🚲

Queens Head
Bromsgrove Road ☎ 63966
Mitchells & Butlers Mild,
Springfield Bitter Ⓔ
Cosy, jovial pub ♨🍴🍺📶🅖🖐🎁

Richards Castle 14D3
10.30–2.30; 6–10.30 (11 F, S)

Castle
(B4361) ☎ 678
Wem Mild, Best Bitter Ⓗ
Pleasant country pub
♨♪🍴📶☰🅖🖐🎁

Ross-on-Wye 14E5
10–2.30; 6–11

King Charles II
Broad Street ☎ 62039
Open until 4 pm Thursdays
Marston Capital, Burton
Bitter, Pedigree Ⓗ
Pleasant town-centre pub
♨♪🍴🗐📶Ⓡ🅖🖐🎁

Sedgeberrow 15G4
11.30–2.30; 7–10.30 (11 F, S)

Queen's Head
(Off A435)
Malvern Chase Ale
Marston Pedigree Ⓗ
Village pub with good
atmosphere ♨🗐📶Ⓡ🅖🖐⛺

Sellack 14D5
10.30–2.30; 6–11

Love Pool
Hoarwithy Road
Morning opening: 11.30;
winter evening opening: 7
Wadworth Devizes Bitter,
6X Ⓗ

Picturesque country inn
🏠🌳🅿🍴🚾♿

Shenstone 15F2

10.30–2.30; 6–10.30 (11 F, S)
Plough
(Off A450)
Opens at 10 am and 7 pm
Batham Mild, Bitter, Delph Strong Ale Ⓗ
Splendid country pub 🏠🅿🚗🍴

Shrawley 15F3

10.30–2.30; 6.30–10.30 (11 F, S)
Rose & Crown
(B4196, off A451/A443)
Opens at 11 am & 7 pm
Marston Burton Bitter, Pedigree Ⓗ
Pleasant village pub with large garden; excellent food
🍴🅓🚗🅿🚾🍴Ⓢ⛺

Stoke Works 15G3

10.30–2.30; 6.30–10.30 (11 F, S and summer)
Boat & Railway
Shaw Lane (1½ miles from M5 Junction 5)
Hanson Mild, Bitter Ⓔ
Popular canalside local in quaint setting 🏠🌳🅿🍴

Bowling Green

Shaw Lane (1 mile from M5 Junction 5)
Banks Mild, Bitter Ⓔ
Small, friendly pub
🍴🌳🅿🍴Ⓡ🍴Ⓢ

Stourport-on-Severn 15F2

11–2.30; 7–10.30 (11 F, S)
Bird in Hand
Holly Bush
Whitbread Bitter Ⓗ
Old canalside pub with bowling green 🏠🍴🌳🅿🍴

Suckley 15E4

11–2.30; 6–10.30 (11 F, S)
Nelson
Hook Norton Best Bitter Ⓗ
Hostelry with pleasant atmosphere 🍴🌳🅿🚾🍴Ⓢ

Tedstone Wafre 15E3

10–2.30; 6–10.30 (11 F, S)
Gate Hangs Well
High Lane, Lower Sapey (B4214)
Marston Pedigree
Mitchells & Butlers
Springfield Bitter Ⓗ
Isolated country inn
🏠🍴🌳🅿Ⓡ🍴Ⓢ

Tenbury Wells 14E3

10–2.30; 6–10.30 (11 F, S)
Pembroke House
Cross Street (B4214)
Wem Mild, Best Bitter Ⓔ
Substantial old pub
🍴🌳🅿🍴Ⓢ

Titley 14C3

10.30–2.30; 6–10.30 (11 F, S)
Stagg
(B4355) ☎ Kington 230221
Mitchells & Butlers Mild, Brew XI Ⓗ
Friendly country inn
🏠🌳🅿Ⓡ🍴

Upper Welland 15F4

11–2.30; 5.30–10.30 (11 F, S)
Hawthorn
Near Welland
Banks Mild
Hook Norton Best Bitter
Marston Burton Bitter
Younger IPA Ⓗ
Pleasant, friendly hostelry; occasional guest beers
🍴🎵🌳🚾🍴🍴Ⓢ

Upton-on-Severn 15F4

10–2.30; 6–10.30 (11 F, S)
Olde Anchor Inn
High Street
Hook Norton Best Bitter Ⓗ **Old Hookey** Ⓖ
Jolly Roger Bitter, Severn Bore Special, Anchor Old Ale
Whitbread Flowers Original Bitter Ⓗ
Home-brew pub, ex-bodysnatchers haunt
🎵🍴🚾🍴Ⓢ

Weobley 14C4

10.30–2.30; 6–10.30 (11 F, S)
Red Lion
(Off A4112) ☎ 220
Wadworth 6X
Whitbread Bitter Ⓗ
Famed for its food, setting and welcome 🌳🍴🅓🚾🍴Ⓢ

Whitney-on-Wye 14B4

10.30–2.30; 6–10.30 (11 F, S)
Rhydspence
(A438) ☎ Clifford 262
Opens at 11 am & 7 pm; closed Mondays in winter
Draught Bass
Robinson Best Bitter Ⓗ
Old Tom
Fleming Cider Ⓖ
14th-century inn with lovely garden, overlooking Wye valley; renowned for food 🏠🍴🌳🅓🚾🍴Ⓢ

Whittington 15F4

10–2.30; 6–10.30 (11 F, S)
Swan
(A44, off M5 Junction 7)
Banks Mild, Bitter Ⓔ
Basic bar, plush lounge
🎵🌳🅓🅿🍴

Woolhope 14E5

10.30–2.30; 6–10.30 (11 F, S)
Butchers Arms
(Off B4224) ☎ Fownhope 281

Opens at 11.30 am & 7 pm (winter)
Hook Norton Best Bitter
Marston Pedigree
Woods Special Bitter Ⓗ
Weston Cider Ⓖ
14th-century low-beamed inn
🏠🍴🌳🅓🚾🍴

Worcester 15F3

11–2.30; 5.30–10.30 (11 F, S)
Bedwardine
Bromyard Road (A44)
Davenports Mild, Bitter Ⓗ
Large, friendly hostelry
🏠🍴🌳🅿🚾🍴Ⓢ

Farriers Arms

Fish Street ☎ 27569
Courage Directors Ⓗ
Extended old inn with famous cold table 🍴🍴🅓🚾🍴Ⓢ

Herefordshire House

Bransford Road (A4103)
Mitchells & Butlers
Highgate Mild, Springfield Bitter Ⓗ
Lively, cheerful local
🎵🍴🅓🚾🍴Ⓢ

Lamb & Flag

30 The Tything (A38)
Marston Burton Bitter, Pedigree Ⓗ
Lively and welcoming
🍴🎵🍴🌳Ⓢ

Mount Pleasant

London Road
Whitbread WCPA, Bitter, Flowers Original Bitter Ⓗ
Friendly hostelry on main road 🎵Ⓡ🅓🚾🍴Ⓢ

West Midland Tavern

Lowesmoor Place
Donnington BB
Holden Bitter
Whitbread Flowers Original Bitter Ⓗ
Cleverly modernised, stylish ale house 🎵🍴🅓Ⓡ🍴Ⓢ

General opening hours: 10.30–2.30; 5.30–10.30 (11 F, S)

Abbots Langley 17F9

Royal Oak
Kitters Green ✆ 65163
Evening opening: 6
Benskins Bitter Ⓗ
Large public bar, comfortable
lounge
♪♣☻🅿🅰Ⓖↂ

Aldbury 16E8

Valiant Trooper
(Off A41)
Open at 10 am & 6 pm
Adnams Mild, Bitter
Fuller ESB
Marston Pedigree Ⓗ
Fine inn in picturesque village
♣🅿🅰

Ardeley 17G7

Jolly Waggoner
OS 310272
✆ Walkern 350
Greene King KK, IPA,
Abbot Ⓖ
Picturesque village pub
🅰♣🅿🅰Ⓖ🐾⑱Ⓢ

Aspenden 17G7

Fox
(Off A10) ✆ Royston 71886
Greene King KK, IPA,
Abbot Ⓔ
Lively local in quiet backwater
♪♣🅿🅰ⓇⒼ⑱Ⓢ

Aston End 17G7

Crown
Long Lane ✆ Shephall 263
Ind Coope Bitter, Burton Ale Ⓗ
Rural retreat on edge of new
town ♣🅿🅰Ⓢ

Ayot Green 17G8

Waggoners
Brickwall Close
✆ Welwyn GC 24241
(Off A1(M)) OS 222139
Opens 7 pm Sats in winter
Wethered Bitter Ⓗ
Welcoming and rural
🅰♣🅿🅰Ⓖ🐾Ⓢ

Ayot St. Lawrence 17F8

Brocket Arms
Shaw's Corner
✆ Stevenage 820250
Opens at 11 am & 6 pm
Everard Old Original
Greene King IPA, Abbot
Victoria Special Bitter
Wadworth 6X Ⓗ
Blands Cider Ⓖ
Beautiful 15th century pub,
understandably popular
🅰♣🅿Ⓖ🐾⑱

Baldock 17G7

George IV
London Road (A6141)
Greene King XX, IPA, Abbot Ⓗ
Excellent pub at southern edge
of town ♪♣🅿🅰Ⓖ🐾⑱Ⓢ

Barley 17H6

Fox & Hounds
High Street (B1368)
Fox & Hounds Nathaniel
Special, Nog, Hogshead, Old
Pharaoh
Bulmer Cider Ⓗ
Exceptional home-brew pub
with gallows sign; guest beers
🅰♪♣🅿🅰Ⓖ⑱Ⓢↂ

Berkhamsted 17E8

Rising Sun
George Street
Benskins Bitter Ⓗ
Splendid canalside local,
perilous for the over-indulgent
♣≷

Bishop's Stortford 17H7

Fox
Rye Street (B1004) ✆ 51623
Opens at 11 am & 6 pm
Courage Best Bitter, Directors
Rayment BBA Ⓗ
Unspoilt locals' pub with
riverside garden; horseshoes
played 🅰♣🅿🅰Ⓖ🐾⑱Ⓢ

Three Tuns
36 London Road (A1184)
Greene King Abbot
Rayment BBA Ⓗ
Congenial pub close to station
🅰♪♣🅰Ⓖ⑱Ⓢↂ

Bourne End 17E8

White Horse
London Road (A41)
Adnams Bitter
Young Bitter, Special Bitter Ⓗ
Small, popular pub 🅿🅰Ⓖ

Briden's Camp 17E8

Crown & Sceptre
Red Lion Hill (off A4146)
Adnams Bitter
Courage Directors
Greene King IPA, Abbot
Marston Pedigree Ⓗ
Outstanding, popular free
house 🅰♣🅿🅰Ⓖ

Broxbourne 17G8

Crown
Old Nazeing Road (off B194)
Charrington IPA
Draught Bass Ⓗ
Riverside pub with large
garden 🅰♣🆇🅰Ⓖ🐾⑱Ⓢ≷

Burnham Green 17G8

White Horse
1 White Horse Lane
✆ Bulls Green 416
Evening opening: 6
Benskins Bitter
Ind Coope Burton Ale Ⓗ
Traditional village pub on
green 🅰♣🅿🅰Ⓖ⑱ↂ🅰

Bushey 17F9

Swan
Park Road (off A411)
Benskins Bitter Ⓗ
Unique, untouched public
bar-only boozer 🅰♣🅿Ⓢ

Carpenders Park 17F9

Partridge
St Georges Drive, Oxhey
Evening opening: 5
Truman Prize Mild, Bitter,
Best Bitter, Sampson
Hanbury's Extra Strong
Bulmer Cider Ⓗ
Efficient local with good
atmosphere ℓ♣🅿🅰ⒼↂⓈↂ≷

Chapmore End 17G8

Woodman
(Off B158) OS 328163
Opens at 12 noon and 6 pm
Greene King XX, IPA,
Abbot Ⓖ
Rural cottage pub with
children's play area
🅰♣🅿🅰⑱Ⓢↂ🅰

Charlton 17F7

Windmill
(Off A505) ✆ Hitchin 2096
Wells Eagle Bitter,
Bombardier Ⓗ
Streamside village pub in
idyllic setting ℓ♣🅿🅰Ⓖ⑱Ⓢ

Cheshunt 17G9

Red Cow
198 Windmill Lane
Charrington Crown, IPA Ⓗ
Friendly pub with collection of
hats 🅰♪♣🅰Ⓖↂ⑱≷

Chipperfield 17E9

Royal Oak
The Street
Benskins Bitter
Ind Coope Burton Ale Ⓗ
Comfortable pub in attractive
village 🅿🅰ⓇⒼ

Chipping 17G7

Countryman
(A10) ✆ Royston 72616
Morning opening: 11

Greene King IPA
Ruddle County, Yokel Bitter [H]
Excellent free house with 'house' beer 🏠♪▣⚘🚗☾❥[S]

Codicote 17F8

Goat
High Street (B656)
Benskins Bitter
Ind Coope Burton Ale [H]
Cosy 16th-century pub with split-level lounge
♪♣⚘🚗☾❥🍷[S]

Colney Heath 17F8

Crooked Billet
88 High Street (B6426)
Adnams Bitter
Greene King Abbot
Marston Pedigree
Victoria Special Bitter
Wethered Bitter [H]
Bulmer Cider [G]
Friendly cottage-style family pub ♣⚘🚗☾🍷[S]♿⛺

Queens Head
(B6426)
Wethered Bitter, Winter Royal
Whitbread Flowers Original Bitter [H]
Friendly unspoilt 18th century pub
🏠♪♣⚘🚗[R]☾🍷[S]♿

Croxley Green 17F9

Artichoke
The Green OS 069956
Truman Prize Mild, Bitter, Best Bitter [H]
Attractive pub on village green
♣▣⚘🚗☾[S]

Datchworth 17G8

Plough
5 Datchworth Green
OS 268183
Greene King KK, XX, IPA, Abbot [H]
One-bar village local
🏠♣⚘🚗☾🍷

Essendon 17G8

Rose & Crown
22 High Street (B158)
Opens at 11 am and 6 pm
Ind Coope Bitter, Burton Ale [H]
Popular, easy-going village pub 🏠♣⚘🚗🍷

Flamstead 17F8

Three Blackbirds
2 High Street (off A5)
☎ Luton 840330
Evening opening: 6
Ruddle County
Watney London Bitter, Fined Stag Bitter
Webster Yorkshire Bitter [H]
A pub for all seasons
🏠♣⚘🚗☾❥[S]

Flaunden 17E9

Green Dragon
Morning opening: 11.30
Ind Coope Bitter
Marston Pedigree [G]
Renovated inn with unspoilt bar ♣⚘🚗[R]☾🍷

Frithsden 17E8

Alford Arms
OS 017098
Opens at 10 am & 6 pm
Cherrypickers Bitter
Wethered Bitter
Whitbread Flowers Original Bitter
Bulmer Cider [H]
Whitbread's first home-brew house 🏠♣⚘🚗☾❥[S]

Furneux Pelham 17H7

Star
The Causeway OS 431278
☎ Brent Pelham 227
Opens at 11 am & 6 pm
Greene King KK, Abbot
Rayment BBA [H]
Welcoming old pub in picturesque brewery village
🏠♪♣⚘🚗[R]☾❥ (not Sun) [S]

Great Offley 17F7

Bull
High Street (off A505)
OS 144270
Watney London Bitter, Fined Stag Bitter [H]
Genuine local in village dominated by restaurants
♪♣⚘🚗🍷[S]

Harpenden 17F8

Old Cock Inn
58 High Street (A1081)
☎ 2649
Truman Bitter, Best Bitter, Sampson Hanbury's Extra Strong [H]
Bulmer Cider [G]
Popular old pub; jazz Sunday lunchtimes
🏠🔥♪⚘🚗☾❥🚉

Hatfield 17G8

Wrestlers
89 Great North Road
(Off A414) ☎ 62116
Ind Coope Bitter, Burton Ale [H]
Modernised old pub with plenty of brass
🏠♪⚘🚗☾♿🚉

Haultwick 17G7

Rest & Welcome
OS 339230
Opens at 12 noon and 6 pm
McMullen AK, Country Bitter [H]
The name says it all
🏠♪♣⚘🚗

Hemel Hempstead 17E8

Marchmont Arms
Piccotts End (off A4146)
☎ 54320
Charrington IPA
Draught Bass
Mitchells & Butlers Springfield Bitter [H]
Converted Victorian mansion
♪♣🚗▣☾❥

Hertford 17G8

Bell & Crown
29 Cowbridge (B158)
Saturday evening opening: 7
McMullen AK, Country Bitter [H]
Small, popular local ♪♣🍷[S]

Great Eastern Tavern
29 Railway Place
Opens at 11 am & 6 pm Sats
McMullen AK, Country Bitter [H]
Lively local ♪♣▣⚘🚗[R]🍷[S]♿🚉

Unicorn
Hartham Lane (off B158)
McMullen AK [H]
Uncluttered cottage pub, a must for pub enthusiasts
♪♣⚘🍷♿

Hexton 17F7

Raven
(Off B655) ☎ Luton 881209
Opens at 11 am and 6 pm
Wethered Bitter
Whitbread Castle Eden Ale, Flowers Original Bitter
Early 20th century village estate pub 🏠🔥♪♣⚘🚗[R]☾❥🍷[S]

High Wych 17H8

Rising Sun
Courage Best Bitter, Directors [H]
Basic, friendly locals' pub
🏠♣🚗🍷

Hoddesdon 17G8

Rose & Crown
90 Amwell Street (A1170)
Lunchtime opening: 12 noon
Wethered Bitter
Whitbread Flowers Original Bitter [H]
Popular town local ♪♣🚗🍷[S]

Ickleford 17F7

Cricketers
107 Arlesey Road (off A600)
☎ 31747
Adnams Bitter
Everard Old Original
Paine EG
Samuel Smith Old Brewery Bitter
Whitbread Flowers Original Bitter [H]

Enthusiastically run pub; guest beers include local brews
🔥♪♣✿🚗🛏[R]◔ (not Sat) ◗

Kings Langley 17F9

Old Palace
Langley Road (off A41)
Benskins Bitter [H]
Small local ♣✿🍺

Langley 17F7

Farmers Boy
Homefield Lane (off B656)
☎ Stevenage 820436
Opens at 11 am and 6 pm
Greene King IPA, Abbot [H]
Comfortable village pub with keen landlord
♪♣✿🚗◔◗ (not Sun) 🍺[S]

Leavesden 17F9

Swan
College Road
Opens at 11 am and 6 pm
Greene King KK, IPA, Abbot [H]
Modernised in traditional pub style ♪♣✿🚗◔🍺[S]♿

Ley Green 17F7

Plough
Plough Lane OS 162243
Greene King XX, IPA, Abbot [H]
Homely rural local with unusual fruit tree 🔥♪♣✿🚗🍺

Little Hadham 17H7

Nags Head
Hadham Ford (off A120)
Evening opening: 6
Greene King KK, Abbot
Rayment BBA [G]
Attractive 400-year-old pub
🔥♪♣✿◔◗🍺[S]

Little Wymondley 17F7

Bucks Head
Stevenage Road (A602)
Wethered Bitter, Winter Royal
Whitbread Flowers Original Bitter [H]
Old-world decor
✿🚗[R]◔ (Mon–Fri) [S]

Long Marston 16D8

Queens Head
38 Tring Road
Morning Opening: 10
Aylesbury ABC Bitter
Draught Bass
Everard Tiger
Morrell Light Ale
West Country Cider [G]
Excellent village local
♪♣✿🚗[R]◔

Much Hadham 17H8

Bull
High Street (B1004) ☎ 2668
Opens at 11 am and 6 pm
Benskins Bitter
Ind Coope Burton Ale [H]
Caters for all ages
🔥♪♣🛏✿🚗[R]◔◗🍺[S]

All pubs in Much Hadham sell real ale

Old Bricket Wood 17F9

Old Fox
School Lane OS 125002
Evening opening: 6
Benskins Bitter
Ind Coope Burton Ale [H]
Coates Cider [G]
Cosy old pub at end of long wooded lane 🔥♣✿🚗🍺

Oxhey 17F9

Villiers Arms
108 Villiers Road (off A4008)
Morning opening: 11
Saturday evening opening: 7
Benskins Bitter
Ind Coope Burton Ale [H]
Attractive small street corner local ♪♣✿◔[S]

Pimlico 17F8

Swan
Bedmond Road OS 093054
Wethered Bitter
Whitbread Flowers Original Bitter [H]
Small and friendly ♣✿🚗

Potters Bar 17G9

Green Dragon
St Albans Road, Near Trotters Bottom (A1081)
Wethered Bitter, Winter Royal
Whitbread Castle Eden Ale, Flowers Original Bitter
Bulmer Cider [H]
Refurbished coaching inn with horseshoe pitch
🔥┌♪♣✿🚗◔🍺[S]

Puckeridge 17H7

Buffalo's Head
High Street (off A10)
☎ Ware 821949
Benskins Bitter
Victoria Bitter [H]
Well-run pub, unusual guest beers 🔥♪♣✿🚗◔◗🍺[S]

Redbourn 17F8

Cricketers
East Common (off A5183)
Benskins Bitter
Ind Coope Burton Ale [H]
Pleasant pub by the common
♪♣✿🚗[R]◔🍺[S]

Rickmansworth 17E9

Feathers
Church Street
Benskins Bitter
Ind Coope Burton Ale [H]
Boisterous public bar, sedate lounge ♪♣✿🚗🍺

Fox & Hounds
High Street
Courage Best Bitter, Directors [H]
Pleasant lounge, friendly darts bar ♪♣✿🚗[R]◔🍺[S]

Ridge 17F9

Old Guinea
Crossoaks Lane OS 215004
☎ Potters Bar 42126
Ind Coope Bitter, Burton Ale [H]
Out-of-the-way pub, worth finding; keg fire in summer
🔥┌♣✿🚗◔◗🍺[S]

Royston 17G6

Jockey
Baldock Street (off A505)
☎ 43377
Wethered Bitter
Whitbread Castle Eden Ale, Flowers Original Bitter [H]
Well-run town local
♪♣✿🚗🛏◔◗🍺[S]🚉

St Albans 17F8

Farriers Arms
Lower Dagnall Street
McMullen AK, Country Bitter [H]
Deservedly popular, busy boozer ♣◔🍺[S]

Goat
37 Sopwell Lane ☎ 60881
Hook Norton Best Bitter, Old Hookey
Morrell Dark Mild
Wadworth 6X [H]
Deservedly popular old coaching inn: guest beers always available ┌♣✿[R]◔[S]

Rose & Crown
10 St Michaels Street (off A414)
Benskins Bitter
Ind Coope Burton Ale [H]
Pleasant old pub near two museums; guest beer
🔥┌♪♣✿🚗🍺[S]

White Lion
91 Sopwell Lane ☎ 50540
Ind Coope Bitter, Burton Ale [H]
Everything a good local should be 🔥♣✿◔🍺

Sarratt 17E9

Cock
Church Lane (off A404)
Morning opening: 11
Benskins Bitter
Ind Coope Burton Ale [H]
Fine old country pub 🔥✿🚗[R]◔

Sawbridgeworth 17H8

King William IV
Vantorts Road (off A1184)

Courage Best Bitter, Directors [H]
17th-century village pub with unusual handpumps
🔥♣❀◷🍷[S]

Shenley 17F9

Black Lion
142 London Road
☎ Radlett 5728
Benskins Bitter
Ind Coope Burton Ale [H]
Well-kept village pub
♪♣❀🚗◷☽🍷[S]

Stevenage 17G7

Red Lion
High Street, Old Town
Opens at 11 am & 6 pm
Greene King XX, IPA, Abbot [H]
Old coaching inn
🔥⚐♪♣❀🚗[R]◷🍷

Two Diamonds
High Street, Old Town
Evening opening: 6
McMullen AK, Country Bitter [H]
Untouched by modern times
♣◷🍷

Therfield 17G6

Bell
Near Royston OS 333374
Evening opening: 6
Greene King IPA, Abbot [H]
More than just a village pub
♣❀🚗[S]⛺

Fox & Duck
Old Village Green
☎ Kelshall 246
Adnams Bitter
Banks & Taylor Shefford Bitter
Samuel Smith Old Brewery Bitter
Tolly Cobbold Mild [H]
Fine pub with church pews in bar and aviary in garden
🔥♪♣❀🚗[R]◷☽🍷[S]

Tring 16E8

Kings Arms
King Street (off A41) ☎ 3318
Fuller ESB
Phillips Heritage Bitter
Wells Eagle Bitter, Bombardier [H]
Good local with unique interior ♪♣❀◷☽

Tyttenhanger 17F8

Barley Mow
Barley Mow Lane (off A405)
OS 189060
Selection from: **Adnams, Brakspear, Courage, Everard, Fuller, Greene King, Marston, Ruddle, Samuel Smith, Victoria, Wadworth, Webster, Young**
A permanent beer exhibition with 17 handpumps
🔥♪♣❀🚗[R]◷[S]♿

Waltham Cross 17G9

Queens Head
55 Eleanor Cross Road (A121)
Morning opening: 11
Charrington Crown, IPA [H]
Old town-centre pub, isolated by new junction ♣❀🚗🍷[S]

Ware 17G8

Spread Eagle
37 Amwell End ☎ 2784
McMullen AK, Country Bitter [H]
Friendly local with sporting public bar
♪♣❀🚗◷☽🍷[S]♿🚆

Wareside 17H8

Chequers
(B1004) ☎ Ware 67010
Opens at 11 am & 6.45 pm
Adnams Bitter
Mickles Birch Bitter
Tolly Cobbold Original
Victoria Bitter [H]
Comfortable, friendly free house 🔥♪♣🚗◷☽[S]

Watford 17F9

Tantivy
91 Queens Road ☎ 27624
Morning opening: 11
Benskins Bitter
Ind Coope Burton Ale [H]
Excellent local town pub
🔥♪♣❀◷🍷[S]

Watton-at-Stone 17G8

Bull
113 High Street (A602)
☎ Ware 830388
Benskins Bitter [H]
Rambling, ancient village local ♪♣❀🚗[R]◷☽🍷[S]🚆

Welwyn 17G8

Baron of Beef
11 Mill Lane ☎ 4739
Opens at 11 am & 6 pm
McMullen AK, Country Bitter [H]
Characters both sides of the bar 🔥♪♣🚗◷🍷[S]♿

White Hart
2 Prospect Place (off B197)
Morning opening: 11
Wethered Bitter
Whitbread Flowers Original Bitter [H]
Fine old building: well run and lively 🔥♪♣❀🚗[R]◷🍷

West Hyde 17E9

Royal Oak
Old Uxbridge Road (off A412)
Wethered Bitter, SPA, Winter Royal [H]
Bright public bar, comfortable saloon 🔥♪♣❀🚗◷🍷

Wheathampstead 17F8

Cherry Trees
261 Lower Luton Road (A6129) ☎ 2342
Benskins Bitter
Ind Coope Burton Ale [H]
180-year-old pub with children's play area
♪♣❀🚗◷♿

John Bunyan
Coleman Green OS 190127 (off A6129) ☎ 2037
Opens at 11 am and 6 pm
McMullen AK, Country Bitter [H]
Tastefully refurbished pub, large jug collection
🔥♪♣❀🚗◷☽[S]♿

Wicked Lady
Nomansland Common (B651)
OS 176127 ☎ 2128
Everard Old Original
Gale HSB
Marston Pedigree, Owd Rodger
Robinson Best Bitter
Wadworth 6X [G]
Bulmer & Zum Cider [H] & [G]
Enterprising beer exhibition with good food
🔥♪❀🚗◷☽[S]

Whitwell 17F7

Maidens Head
High Street (B651) ☎ 392
McMullen AK, Country Bitter [H]
Attractive pub near watercress beds
🔥♣❀🚗◷🍷[S]

Willian 17F7

Fox
(Off A6141) OS 224307
☎ Letchworth 5289
Charrington IPA [H]
Busy, comfortable pub overlooking duckpond
♪♣❀🚗◷☽🍷[S]

Wilstone 16D8

Half Moon
(Off B489) ☎ Tring 6410
Aylesbury ABC Bitter
Morrell Light Ale [H]
Attractive exterior, well-modernised interior
🔥♣❀🚗◷

Wormley West End 17G8

Woodman
OS 339059
☎ Hoddesdon 463719
McMullen AK, Country Bitter [H]
16th century coaching house, retaining horsey flavour
🔥♪♣❀🚗◷☽🍷[S]♿

Barton-upon-Humber
26E3

10.30–2.30; 6–10.30 (11 F, S and summer)

Coach & Horses
High Street ☎ 32161
Opens 11–3 in summer
Tetley Mild, Bitter Ⓗ
Large, busy pub; try the
sandwiches ♪♣Ⓡ🄸Ⓢ

Volunteer Arms
13 Whitecross Street (off
A1077)
North Country Riding Bitter Ⓗ
Small inn, nicely furnished
🅰♪♣Ⓖ (not Mon) 🄸

Wheatsheaf
Holy Dyke (A1077) ☎ 33175
Evening opening: 7
**Ward Best Mild, Sheffield Best
Bitter** Ⓔ
Popular, modernised old pub
♪♣🄿Ⓖ🄸≠

Beverley
31G8

11–3; 6–10.30 (11 F, S)

Moulders Arms
32 Wilbert Lane, Butcher Row
Evening opening: 7
Bass Mild
Stones Best Bitter Ⓗ
Busy street-corner local
♪♣🄿🄸≠

Rose & Crown
North Bar Without
(A164/A1035) ☎ 862532
Evening opening: 7
**Darley Dark, Thorne Best
Bitter**
Ward Sheffield Best Bitter Ⓗ
Large, friendly pub near
racecourse 🅰♪♣🄿🅰Ⓡ🄶🄾🄸Ⓢ

Royal Standard
North Bar Within
**Darley Dark, Thorne Best
Bitter** Ⓗ
Hospitable, unchanging local
of character ♣🄸

White Horse (Nellie's)
Hengate ☎ 861973
Closes 4 pm Wed, 5 pm Sat
**Samuel Smith Old Brewery
Bitter** Ⓗ
Many-roomed gas-lit hostelry
🅰🄵♣🄴🅰🄶Ⓖ🄸Ⓢ≠

Woolpack
37 Westwood Road
Opens at 12 noon and 7 pm
North Country Riding Bitter Ⓗ
Well-renovated local near
Westwood ♪♣🄿Ⓖ Ⓢ

Bridlington
31H7

10.30–3; 6–10.30 (11 F, S and summer)

Bull & Sun
Baylegate ☎ 76105
**Darley Dark, Thorne Best
Bitter** Ⓗ
Roomy pub set in the old town
♪♣🄴🄿🄸Ⓢ

Friendly Forester
Marton Road ☎ 75515
Tetley Mild, Best Bitter Ⓗ
Comfortable and modern,
specialising in breakfasts
(but no accommodation)
♪🄰Ⓖ🄿Ⓢ

Hilderthorpe
Hilderthorpe Road (near
harbour) ☎ 72205
Bass Mild
Draught Bass Ⓗ
Large, busy, unassuming local
🅰♪♣🄴🄶Ⓢ

Brigg
26E4

10.30–3 (4 Thu); 6–11

Dying Gladiator
Bigby Street (A15)
Opens at 11 am & 6.30 pm
**Webster Yorkshire Mild,
Bitter** Ⓗ
Cosy, down-to-earth free
house
🅰♪♣🄿🄸Ⓢ

White Horse
Wrawby Street (A15)
☎ 52242
Closes 2.30 pm
**Ward Best Mild,
Sheffield Best Bitter** Ⓗ & Ⓔ
Popular and welcoming old
inn ♪♣🄴🄶Ⓢ

Woolpack
Market Place (A15)
Tetley Mild Ⓔ **Bitter** Ⓗ
Busy town-centre local with
quiet lounge
♪♣🄰🄸Ⓢ

Cleethorpes
27G4

11–3; 6–10.30 (11 F, S in summer)

Crows Nest
Balmoral Road ☎ 698867
**Samuel Smith Old
Brewery Bitter** Ⓗ
Large, popular local
♪♣🄰Ⓡ🄸

Darley's Hotel
Grimsby Road ☎ 691530
**Darley Dark, Thorne Best
Bitter**
Ward Sheffield Best Bitter Ⓗ
Large, main road hotel with
several bars and a bistro
🄵♪♣🄴🄿🅰Ⓡ🄶🄾🄸Ⓢ⅄

No. 2 Refreshment Room
Cleethorpes Station
Darley Thorne Best Bitter
Ward Sheffield Best Bitter
Younger No 3 Ⓗ
Excellent basic boozer
♣🄿🄰🄸≠

Nottingham
7 Sea View Street
Evening opening: 7
Tetley Mild, Bitter Ⓗ
Traditional without being
basic ♪♣🄿🄸🄸Ⓢ

Queens Hotel
28 Sea View Street
Evening opening: 5.30
Tetley Mild, Bitter Ⓗ
Large pub with a room to suit
every taste 🄵♪♣🄿Ⓡ🄸

Cottingham
26E2

11–3; 6–10.30

Tiger
King Street
Bass Mild, Draught Bass Ⓗ
Near village square, often
crowded ♪♣🄸Ⓢ

Driffield
31G7

11–2.30; 7–10.30 (11 F, S and summer)

Old Falcon
57 Market Place
**Cameron Lion Bitter,
Strongarm**
Tetley Mild, Bitter
Younger IPA Ⓗ
Ex-John Smiths' pub, now a
thriving free house 🄵♪♣🄰Ⓖ Ⓢ

Dunswell
27E2

11–3; 6–10.30 (11 F, S and summer)

Ship
(A1174)
Bass Mild
Stones Best Bitter Ⓗ
Externally attractive roadside
pub 🄵♪♣🄿🄰

Eastoft
26C3

10.30–3; 6–10.30 (11 F, S)

Haywain
Samson Street (A161)
Morning opening: 11
Cameron Lion Bitter
(summer), **Strongarm**
(winter) Ⓗ
Single-storey, single-room pub
with haywain in car park;
weekly guest beers
🄵♪♣🄿🄰🄸Ⓢ♿

Epworth
26C4

10.30–3; 6–10.30 (11 F, S)

Epworth Tap
9–11 Market Place (off A161)
☎ 873333
Evening opening: 7
Closed lunchtimes; supper
licence until midnight
Darley Thorne Best Bitter Ⓗ
Friendly wine bar and bistro
♪⅄

Etton
31G8

11–3; 7–10.30 (11 F, S)

Light Dragoon
Main Street
Younger IPA, No 3 Ⓗ
Busy, attractive pub
🄵♪♣🄿Ⓖ🄸Ⓢ

Flamborough
31H6

10.30–3; 5.30–10.30 (11 F, S & summer)

Rose & Crown
High Street ☎ 850455
**Cameron Lion Bitter,
Strongarm** Ⓗ

Unspoilt locals' pub away
from the town centre
♪♣🏚🚭♥🚲Ⓢ

Goole 26C3

10.30–3; 6–10.30 (11 F, S)
North Eastern
Boothferry Road
(A161/A614)
**Darley Dark, Thorne Best
Bitter**
Ward Sheffield Best Bitter Ⓗ
Plush lounge, huge
games-orientated taproom
♪♣Ⓡ🚲🚭♥Ⓢ≷

Railway Tavern
Boothferry Road ☎ 2959
Open until 5 pm Wednesdays
Tetley Mild, Bitter Ⓗ
Lively three-roomed town
alehouse ☏♪♣🚭Ⓡ🚭Ⓢ≷

Vermuyden
Bridge Street (A161)
Tetley Bitter Ⓗ
Basic dockland boozer ♪♣🚲♥Ⓢ

Grimsby 27F4

11–3; 6–10.30
Corporation
88 Freeman Street
Evening opening: 7
Bass Mild, Draught Bass Ⓗ
Town pub, cosy comfortable
lounge, basic bar ♪♣♥

Freemans Arms
132 Freeman Street
Bass Mild, Draught Bass Ⓗ
A basic local near the docks
♪♣♥

Granary
Restaurant
Haven Mill, Garth Lane
☎ 46338
Evening opening:
7.30–11.30
Bateman XB Ⓗ
Symonds Cider Ⓖ
Real beer and real food in old
grain mill ☏♪🏚Ⓡ🚲🚭♥Ⓢ≷

Tivoli Tavern
14 Old Market Place
Bass Mild, Draught Bass Ⓗ
Cosy, one-roomed
Edwardian-style lounge ♪🚭≷

White Bear
137 Freeman Street
Evening opening: 7
**Darley Dark, Thorne Best
Bitter** Ⓗ
Pleasant atmosphere;
sing-songs at weekends
☏♪♣♥

Gunness 26D3

11.30–3; 5–10.30 (11 F, S)
Jolly Sailor
Station Road (A18)
**Bass Brew Ten, Draught
Bass** Ⓗ
Large wharfside pub on trunk
road ♪♣🏚♥≷

Hedon 27F2

11–3; 6–10.30 (11 F, S and summer)
Shakespeare
Baxtergate (off A1033)
Evening opening: 7
**Darley Dark, Thorne Best
Bitter** Ⓗ
An attractive old local ♪♣♥🏚

Hessle 26E2

11–3; 6–10.30
George (Tophouse)
Prestongate
Bass Mild
Stones Best Bitter Ⓗ
Friendly local near the square
♪♣🚭♥Ⓢ

Hibaldstow 26D4

11–3; 6–11
Wheatsheaf
Station Road (A15)
☎ Brigg 54056
**Ward Sheffield Best Mild, Best
Bitter** Ⓔ
Popular pub with dining
facilities 🏚♪♣🏚Ⓡ🚲🚭♥Ⓢ

Hollym 27G3

11–3; 6–10.30 (11 F, S)
Plough
Main Street (off A1033)
Tetley Mild, Bitter Ⓗ
Cheerful village pub
🏚♪♣🚭♥Ⓢ

Hornsea 31H8

11–3; 6.30–10.30 (11 F, S and summer)
Victoria
Market Place ☎ 3133
Bass Mild
Stones Best Bitter Ⓔ
Comfortable pub, friendly and
well-run ♣🚭♥🚲🚭Ⓢ🚹

Hull 27E2

11–3; 6–10.30
Black Boy
150 High Street, Old Town
Tetley Mild, Bitter Ⓗ
Historic and interesting,
complete with ghost
🏚☏♪♣Ⓡ♥Ⓢ

Blacksmiths Arms
Naylors Row, Clarence Street
**Darley Dark, Thorne Best
Bitter** Ⓗ
Popular streetcorner local
🏚♪♣🏚Ⓡ♥

City
Lowgate
Bass Mild, Draught Bass Ⓗ
Comfortable town pub
opposite Guildhall ♪♣Ⓢ

Clarence
Charles Street
Saturday evening opening:
5.30
Tetley Mild, Bitter Ⓗ
Excellent down-to-earth
drinkers' pub ♪♣♥

County
Charles Street ☎ 224593
North Country Riding Bitter Ⓗ
Basic local escaping brewery
refurbishment scheme
♪♣Ⓡ♥Ⓢ

King Edward VII
1 Anlaby Road
☎ 25811/28944
Evening opening: 7.30 (7 F, S)
**Darley Dark, Thorne Best
Bitter**
Ward Sheffield Best Bitter Ⓗ
City-centre pub with weekly
guest beer; full range upstairs
♪♣Ⓡ🚲♥Ⓢ≷

New Inn
Hedon Road, Marfleet
(A1033) ☎ 74141
Evening opening: 5.30
Tetley Mild, Bitter Ⓗ
Busy dockland pub
♪♣🚭🏚Ⓡ♥Ⓢ

Oberon
Queen Street, Old Town
Weekday opening: 5.30
Bass Mild, Draught Bass
Stones Best Bitter Ⓗ
Excellent pub with friendly,
relaxed atmosphere
☏♣🏚Ⓡ♥🚹

Olde White Hart
Silver Street, Old Town
☎ 26363
Saturday evening opening: 7
Younger IPA, No 3
Well-preserved inn, involved
in the Civil War 🚭🚲Ⓢ

Providence
St Stephens Square, Spring
Street
North Country Riding Bitter Ⓗ
Busy corner local, darts
predominate ☏♪♣♥≷

Victoria Dock
Tavern
Great Union Street
Bass Mild
Stones Best Bitter Ⓗ
Small, cosy dockland pub
♪♣♥

Wellington
Peel Street/Wellington Lane
Evening opening: 7
Tetley Mild, Bitter Ⓗ
Street-corner local of
character ♣♥

Whalebone
165 Wincolmlee
Weekday evening opening:
5.30
Tetley Mild, Bitter Ⓗ
Gem in an industrial area ♪♣♥

Immingham 27F3

11–3; 6–10.30 (11 F, S)
Bluestone
Bluestone Lane ☎ 76594
Saturday evening opening: 7
Bass Mild, Draught Bass Ⓗ

Modern pub with plush lounge ♪♣♥🅰🕒 (Mon–Fri) 🛈Ⓢ

Keadby 26D3

11–3; 6.30–10.30 (11 F, S)
South Yorkshire
(B1392, off A18)
Tetley Mild, Bitter Ⓗ
Village local by canal and River Trent
🚶♪♣🅰🛈

Kirton in Lindsey 26D4

11–3; 6–11
Royal Oak
Church Street (off B1400)
✆ 648407
Evening opening: 6.30
Whitbread Castle Eden Ale Ⓗ
Refurbished, cheerful pub
🏠♪♣🅱♥🅰🔲🕒🛈Ⓢ

Langtoft 31G7

10.30–2.30; 6–10.30 (11 F, S & summer)
Ship
Front Street (B1249)
✆ Driffield 87243
Opens at 11 am & 6.30 pm
Cameron Lion Bitter Ⓗ
Excellent village pub
🏠♪♣🅱♥🅰🔲🅁🕒🛈Ⓢ♿

Leven 27E1

11–3; 6.30–10.30 (11 F, S and summer)
Hare & Hounds
North Street ✆ 42523
Tetley Mild, Bitter Ⓗ
Youthful, busy local
♪♣♥🅰🕒Ⓢ

Little Driffield 31G7

10.30–2.30; 6–10.30 (11 F, S and summer)
Downe Arms
York Road (off A163)
✆ Driffield 42243
Opens at 12 noon & 7 pm
Cameron Lion Bitter, Strongarm Ⓗ
17th-century inn just off the by-pass ♪♣🅱♥🅰🔲🅁Ⓢ🅰

Low Catton 31E7

10.30–3; 6–10.30 (11 F, S)
Gold Cup
(Off A166)
✆ Stamford Bridge 71354
Cameron Lion Bitter
Theakston Best Bitter
Younger Scotch Bitter Ⓗ
Popular free house in sleepy village 🏠♪♣🅰🕒🛈Ⓢ

Newport 26D2

11–3; 6–10.30 (11 F, S)
King's Arms
Main Street (A63) ✆ Howden 40289
Evening opening: 7
Tetley Mild, Bitter Ⓗ
Well kept, comfortable main road pub
♪♣🅰🕐 (Thu–Sat) 🛈Ⓢ

Owston Ferry 26C4

10.30–3; 6–10.30 (11 F, S)
Crooked Billet
Silver Street OS 813998
Darley Dark, Thorne Best Bitter Ⓗ
Charming Isle riverside pub, hospitable local atmosphere
🚶♪♣♥🅰🅁Ⓢ

Paull 27F2

11–3; 6–10.30 (11 F, S)
Humber Tavern
Main Street ✆ Hull 899347
Evening opening: 7
Bass Mild, Draught Bass
Stones Best Bitter Ⓗ
Many-roomed local with river views ♪♣🅁Ⓢ

Royal Oak
42 Main Street ✆ Hull 897678
Evening opening: 6.30
Darley Dark, Thorne Best Bitter Ⓗ
Friendly local with impressive vista of estuary and bridge
🏠♪♣🅱♥🅰🅁🕒🕐Ⓢ

Pocklington 26C1

10.30–3; 6.30–10.30 (11 F, S)
Wellington Oak
Canal Head (A1079) ✆ 3854
Tetley Bitter Ⓗ
Revitalised roadside free house, close to Pocklington Canal terminus
♪🅰🕒🕐Ⓢ

Rawcliffe 26C3

10.30–3; 6–10.30 (11 F, S)
Royal
Bridge Lane (off A614)
Tetley Bitter Ⓗ
Fine old fashioned local
🚶♣🅰🛈Ⓢ

Rudston 31H7

10.30–3; 6–10.30 (11 F, S)
Bosville Arms
(B1253)
Bass Mild, Extra Light Ⓗ
Interesting roadside pub with brass curios 🅰🛈🅰

Ryehill 27F3

11–3; 7–10.30 (11 F, S)
Crooked Billet
Pit Lane (off A1033)
Tetley Mild, Bitter Ⓗ
Busy, out-of-the-way country inn 🏠♪♣🅰🛈Ⓢ

Sandtoft 26C4

10.30–3; 6–10.30 (11 F, S)
Reindeer
Thorne (off A18, M180)
✆ Scunthorpe 710774
Closed Mon–Thu lunchtimes; opens late evenings
Tetley Bitter Ⓗ
Popular Isle free house near trolleybus museum
🏠🚶♪♣♥🅰🔲🕒🕐Ⓢ🅰

Scawby Brook 26D4

10.30–3; 6–11
King William IV
(A15) ✆ Brigg 53147
Ward Sheffield Best Bitter Ⓔ
Horsey country pub
🏠♣🅱🕒🕐Ⓢ

Scunthorpe 26D3

11.30–3; 5–10.30 (11 F, S)
Queen Bess
Derwent Road (off A18)
Evening opening: 6
Samuel Smith Old Brewery Bitter Ⓗ
Large and lively, country and western Thursdays ♪♣🅰🛈🅰Ⓢ

Skerne 31G7

11–2.30; 6.30–10.30 (11 F, S and summer)
Eagle
Wansford Road
Cameron Lion Bitter Ⓗ
Friendly, cosy pub with unusual Victorian handpumps 🏠♣🅰🅰

Sledmere 31G7

10.30–3; 6–10.30 (11 F, S and summer)
Triton
(B1251) ✆ Driffield 86644
Younger Scotch Bitter Ⓗ
Fine, friendly old free house
♪🅰🅰🅁

Stamford Bridge 31E7

10.30–3; 6–10.30 (11 F, S)
Bay Horse
(A166)
Cameron Lion Bitter Ⓗ
Village local overlooking summer tourist trap ♪♣♥🅰🅰

Sutton-upon-Derwent 31E8

12–2.30; 7–10.30 (11 F, S)
St. Vincent Arms
(B1228) ✆ Elvington 349
Cameron Lion Bitter
Theakston Best Bitter, Old Peculier
Younger IPA, Scotch Bitter Ⓗ
Good-looking country inn
♪♣🅱♥🅰🔲🅁🕒🕐Ⓢ🅰

Walkington 31G8

11–3; 6–10.30 (11 F, S)
Barrel
East End (A1230)
Cameron Lion Bitter Ⓗ
Old village pub with convivial atmosphere 🏠♣♥🅰

Winteringham 26D3

10–2.30; 6–10.30 (11 F, S)
Bay Horse
Silver Street (off A1077)
Evening opening: 7
Bass Mild, Brew Ten Ⓗ
Unspoilt pub frequented by all ages ♪♣♥🅰🅰

General opening hours: 10.30–3, 6–11

Arreton
6E8

White Lion
Newport Road (A3056)
Whitbread Strong Country Bitter, Pompey Royal G
Well-appointed old pub
🏠♣☂🅿️🏮🍴Ⓢ

Binstead
6E7

Fleming Arms
Binstead Road ✆ 63415
Whitbread Strong Country Bitter H
Popular, renovated village pub
♪♣☂🅿️🏮Ⓖ🍴🐶Ⓢ▲

Chale
6D8

Wight Mouse
(Off A3055) ✆ Niton 730431
Burt VPA
Whitbread Strong Country Bitter, Pompey Royal H
Free house of character
♪♪♣🎫☂🏮🍴Ⓛ🐶Ⓢ

Cowes
6D7

Duke of York
York Street ✆ 295171
Whitbread Strong Country Bitter, Pompey Royal H
Popular with locals ♪♣Ⓖ🐶Ⓢ

Horseshoe
Northwood (A3020)
Whitbread Strong Country Bitter, Pompey Royal H
Popular pub at busy road
junction ♪♣🏮🍴Ⓢ

East Cowes
6D7

Victoria Tavern
62 Clarence Road
Burt VPA H
Well-modernised town pub
♪♣🍴Ⓢ

Fishbourne
6E7

Fishbourne Inn
Fishbourne Lane (off A3054)
✆ 882823
Whitbread Strong Country Bitter, Pompey Royal Bulmer Cider H
Turn left off Pompey car ferry
♪🎫☂🏮🐶🍴🐶🍴

Freshwater
6C8

Prince of Wales
Whitbread Strong Country Bitter, Pompey Royal H
Deservedly popular local
♪♪♣🏮🍴Ⓢ

Freshwater Bay
6C8

Starkes
Whitbread Strong Country Bitter, Pompey Royal H
Popular village pub ♪♪♣☂🏮🍴Ⓢ

Godshill
6E8

Griffin
Newport Road
Whitbread Strong Country Bitter, Pompey Royal H
Old, friendly village pub
♪♣🎫☂🏮🍴Ⓢ

Try also: **Taverners** (free)

Gurnard
6D7

Woodvale
Woodvale Road
Whitbread Strong Country Bitter, Pompey Royal H
Seashore Victorian pub with
fine views ♪♪🎫☂🅿️Ⓢ

Haven Street
6E7

White Hart
Whitbread Strong Country Bitter, Pompey Royal H
Village pub near the steam
railway ♪♪♣🎫☂🏮Ⓖ🐶🍴

Hulverstone
6D8

Sun
(B3399)
Whitbread Strong Country Bitter G
Genuine roadside inn, 300
years old ♣☂🏮🍴

Lake
6E8

Manor House
Sandown Road (A3055)
Draught Bass H
Large village pub ♪♣☂🏮Ⓢ

Newchurch
6E8

Pointers
Whitbread Strong Country Bitter G
Unspoilt 18th-century village
pub ♣☂🏮🍴

Newport
6D8

Barley Mow
57 Shide Road (A3056)
✆ 523318
Whitbread Strong Country Bitter, Pompey Royal H
Comfortable pub in pleasant
location ♪♪♣☂🏮Ⓖ🐶🍴

St. Crispin
8 Carisbrooke Road
Whitbread Strong Country Bitter G
Homely, two-bar town pub
♪♣Ⓖ🐶🍴🐶Ⓢ

Wheatsheaf
St. Thomas Square ✆ 523865
Whitbread Strong Country Bitter, Pompey Royal Bulmer Cider H
18th-century hotel, tastefully
renovated ♪♪🎫🏮Ⓖ🐶🍴Ⓢ

Try also: **Calverts Hotel** (free)

Niton
6D8

Royal Sandrock
Sandrock Road
Burt VPA G
Rambling pub of character
♪♪♣🎫☂🏮Ⓢ▲

Pondwell
7E7

Wishing Well
✆ Seaview 3222
Burt VPA H
Popular free house with
self-catering chalets
♪♪♣🎫☂🏮Ⓢ▲

Porchfield
6D7

Sportsman's Rest
Whitbread Strong Country Bitter, Pompey Royal G
Popular country pub
♪♣🏮🍴Ⓢ

Ryde
6E7

Castle
164 High Street
Evening opening: 7
Gale Light Mild, BBB, HSB, XXXXX H
Busy central pub ♪♣☂Ⓢ

Esplanade Bars
Esplanade ✆ 62549
Closes 2.30 pm; closed in
winter
Burt VPA
Courage Directors H
Comfortable hotel bar
♪🎫🏮Ⓖ🐶🍴

Railway
68 St. John's Road
Whitbread Strong Country Bitter, Pompey Royal Bulmer Cider H
Friendly local away from
seafront ♪♣☂Ⓢ≠

Royal Squadron
High Street
Burt VPA
Gale HSB
Usher Best Bitter H
Large, refurbished
town-centre bar ♪Ⓖ🐶Ⓢ≠

Yelf's Hotel
Union Street ✆ 64062
Draught Bass
Burt VPA H
Comfortable THF hotel bar
♪🎫☂🏮🅿️Ⓖ🐶

St. Helens
7E7

Vine Inn
Upper Green Road
Whitbread Strong Country Bitter, Pompey Royal H
Popular pub overlooking
village green ♪♪♣🎫☂Ⓢ▲

Sandown 7E8

Castle
Fitzroy Street ☎ 404164
Burt VPA Ⓗ
Smart town pub ♪♣☞Ⓡ🕒🍴🍷Ⓢ

Commercial
15 St. John's Road
Gale Light Mild, BBB, HSB Ⓗ
Excellent, tastefully improved
old town-centre pub ♪♣☰☞🍷Ⓢ

York
Wilkes Road
Whitbread Strong Country
Bitter, Pompey Royal Ⓗ
Well-modernised and
comfortable ♪♣Ⓢ

Seaview 7E7

Seaview Hotel
High Street ☎ 2278
Burt VPA Ⓗ
Popular seafront hotel
♪♣☰☞🏠Ⓡ🕒🍷Ⓢ&

Shalfleet 6D7

New Inn
(A3054) ☎ Calbourne 314
Whitbread Strong Country
Bitter, Pompey Royal Ⓗ
Popular with farmers and
yachtsmen 🏠🕒🍷Ⓢ

Shanklin 6E8

Crab
Old Village
Whitbread Strong Country
Bitter, Pompey Royal Ⓗ
Reputedly the island's most
photographed pub
🕯♪♣☰☞🏠🕒🍴🍷Ⓢ

Shorwell 6D8

Crown
Whitbread Strong Country
Bitter, Pompey Royal Ⓖ
Popular old pub with
delightful garden
☞🏠🍷Ⓢ

Totland 6C8

Broadway
The Broadway
Whitbread Strong Country
Bitter, Pompey Royal Ⓗ
Friendly village local ♪♣🍴Ⓢ

Ventnor 6E8

Bonchurch Inn
The Shute
Whitbread Strong Country
Bitter, Pompey Royal Ⓖ
Old stone pub with cobbled
courtyard ♪♣☞🏠Ⓢ

Blenheim
High Street
Whitbread Strong Country
Bitter, Pompey Royal Ⓔ
Converted off-licence in
central position ♪♣🍴Ⓢ

Mill Bay
Esplanade
Burt BMA, VPA Ⓗ
Seafront pub with glass-
fronted beer engines
♪♣🍴Ⓢ

Volunteer
Albert Street
Burt BMA, VPA Ⓗ
Superb town local ♣🍴Ⓢ

Whitwell 6E8

White Horse
OS 521780
Whitbread Strong Country
Bitter, Pompey Royal Ⓗ
Attractive outside and inside
♣🏠Ⓢ

Wootton 6E7

Woodman's Arms
Station Road
Whitbread Strong Country
Bitter Ⓗ
Country pub, tastefully
modernised ♪♣☰🏠Ⓢ

Wroxall 6E8

Star
Burt BMA, VPA Ⓗ
Tastefully rebuilt after a
serious fire ♪♣☞🏠🕒🍴🍷Ⓢ

Yarmouth 6C7

Bugle
The Square ☎ 760272
Whitbread Strong Country
Bitter Ⓗ
Cosy and comfortable, with
character ☞🏠🕒🍴

Hop Scotched?

The hop gardens of Kent are under attack. Disease, the recession, foreign competition and technical improvements threaten to wipe out the already shrunken acreage of hop gardens in this country. A familiar and apparently timeless part of the national scene could be lost for ever.

Hop growing is a highly risky business at the best of times. There is a three year cycle between planting and harvesting, and a considerable investment in the pole and wirework systems over which the hops grow, the machines to pick them and the oast houses in which to dry them.

A poor summer – an all-too-common occurrence in England – poses an additional threat to these vulnerable plants. One of the worst problems, however, is the fungal disease verticillium wilt,

which has no known cure. Newer strains of hops are being developed which are more resistant to the disease, but these are only a small part of the present crop.

For the past 50 years, the Hops Marketing Board has helped to ensure a reasonable stability of price and demand for the growers, but the present situation will test their ability to protect them to the limit.

It is ironic that the hop growers themselves have helped to develop the technology that now enables brewers to extract twice as much of the "business" ingredients – from the same quantity of hops, thus halving demand. In 20 years, the number of English growers has halved; If the trend continues, one day the Kent hop fields will be just a bitter memory.

Appledore 11F6

0–2.30; 6–10.30 (11 F, S and summer)
Railway Inn
Appledore Station
(B2080) ℓ 253
Felinfoel Double Dragon
Fremlins Bitter
Marston Pedigree
Young Bitter
Younger No. 3 Ⓗ
Weston Cider Ⓖ
Friendly, enterprising haven;
range varies
♨♪♠⊞♨🅁Ⓖ🌂⑩◑

Ash 11H4

0–2.30; 6–10.30 (11 F, S and summer)
Lion Hotel
The Street ℓ Dover 812234
Fremlins Bitter Ⓗ
Former staging post with two
interesting bars
♨♪♠🅁Ⓖ🌂⑩◑

All four pubs in the village
sell real ale

Ashford 11F5

0–2.30; 6–10.30 (11 F, S and summer)
Beaver
Beaver Road (B2070)
Shepherd Neame Mild,
Bitter Ⓗ Stock Ale (winter) Ⓖ
Pleasant pub on edge of town
♠🅰⑩

Prince Albert
New Street
Ind Coope Bitter, Burton Ale Ⓗ
Small, lively local ♪♠⑩

Smiths Arms
Rugby Gardens
Tamplins Bitter Ⓗ
Recently modernised riverside
local ♪♠♨🅰≷

Bapchild 11F4

0–2.30; 6–11
Fox & Goose
2 Fox Hill (A2)
Courage Directors Ⓗ
Popular village local with
aviary in garden
♠⊞♨🅰⑩

Benenden 10E6

0–2.30; 6–11
King William IV
The Street (B2086)
Morning opening: 11.30
Shepherd Neame Mild Ⓖ
Bitter Ⓗ
Excellent village local catering
for all tastes ♨♪♠♨🅰Ⓖ◑⑩

Benover 10D5

0–2.30; 6–11
Woolpack Inn
(B2162) ℓ Collier Street 356
Shepherd Neame Mild, Bitter,
Stock Ale Ⓗ
Splendid country pub in fine
setting ♨♪♠⊞♨🅰Ⓖ◑⑩

Birchington 11H4

11–2.30; 5.30–11
Acorn
6 Park Lane ℓ 41196
Shepherd Neame Mild, Bitter Ⓗ
Small, friendly pub
♪♠⊞♨🅰Ⓖ◑⑩

Bishopsbourne 11G5

10.30–2.30; 6–10.30 (11 F, S and summer)
Mermaid
(Off A2)
Shepherd Neame Mild,
Bitter Ⓗ
Very attractive, worth a
detour ♠♣♨Ⓖ

Boughton 11F4

11–3; 6–11
Three Horseshoes
Staple Street
Shepherd Neame Mild, Bitter,
Stock Ale Ⓖ
Genuine country pub with
collection of stone bottles;
many games ♠♣🅰⑩◑

Broadstairs 11J4

10.30–2.30; 6–11
Lord Nelson
Nelson Place
Fremlins Bitter Ⓗ
One-bar local ♠♪♠🅰⑩

Neptune's Hall
Harbour Street
Shepherd Neame Bitter, Stock
Ale Ⓗ
Large Victorian town pub
♨♪♨🅁⑩

Royal Albion Hotel
Albion Street ℓ Thanet 68071
Fremlins Bitter
Fuller ESB
Shepherd Neame Mild,
Bitter Ⓗ
Friendly hotel bar
♨♪♨🅰🅁Ⓖ◑⑩

Burham 10D4

10.30–2.30; 6.30–11
Toastmasters
Church Street ℓ 61299
Fuller ESB
Ruddle County
Young Special Ⓗ
Attractive village pub, several
guest beers ♠Ⓖ◑⑩

Canterbury 11G4

10–2.30; 6–10.30 (11 F, S and summer)
Gentil Knyght
Shipman Avenue, London
Road Estate (off A2)
Shepherd Neame Mild,
Bitter Ⓗ
Friendly estate pub with bat
and trap ♪♨🅰⑩◑

Kentish Cricketers
14 St. Peters Street ℓ 64227
Shepherd Neame Mild,
Bitter Ⓗ

Comfortable high street pub
with cricketing connections
♪♪🅁Ⓖ◑♨≷

Prince of Wales
51 King Street ℓ 63650
Fremlins Bitter Ⓗ
Near cathedral; inexpensive
food ♪♠🅁Ⓖ⑩♨

Dragoon
100 Military Road (off A28)
Opens at 10.30 am & 6.30 pm
Shepherd Neame Mild,
Bitter Ⓗ
Pleasant local with outdoor
drinking in old graveyard
♪♪♠Ⓖ♨≷

Charing 11F5

10–2.30; 6–10.30 (11 F, S and summer)
Royal Oak
High Street (off A20) ℓ 2307
Fremlins Bitter Ⓗ Tusker Ⓖ
Biddenden Cider Ⓗ
Live music on Saturdays
♪♪♠♨🅰Ⓖ◑♨≷

Chartham 11G5

10–2.30; 6–10.30 (11 F, S and summer)
Artichoke Inn
Rattington Street (off A28)
ℓ 316
Evening opening: 6.30
Shepherd Neame Mild,
Bitter Ⓗ
Originally an ancient hall
house ♨♪♠♨🅰⊞⑩◑♨≷

Chatham 10E4

10.30–2.30; 6–11
Constitution Castle
Constitution Hill
Shepherd Neame Mild,
Bitter Ⓗ
Pleasant little local ♪♠♨⑩

Chiddingstone 10C5

10–2.30; 6–10.30 (11 F, S)
Castle Inn
(B2027) ℓ Penshurst 870247
Shepherd Neame Bitter, Best
Bitter
Young Special Bitter Ⓗ
Taunton Cider Ⓖ
Old, attractive building in
National Trust village ♠♣
⊞♨Ⓖ◑ (Thu–Mon)⑩♨♣

Chilham 11G5

10.30–2.30; 6–10.30 (11 F, S and summer)
Alma
Canterbury Road (off A28)
Courage Directors
Shepherd Neame Bitter, Stock
Ale Ⓗ
Pleasant, renovated free
house, other beers available
occasionally ♨♪♠🅁Ⓖ◑⑩♨≷

Chillenden 11H5

10–2.30; 6–10.30 (11 F, S and summer)
Griffins Head
OS 271535
Shepherd Neame Mild, Bitter Ⓗ

Kent

Rural pub with friendly welcome ♪♣☒♠☎☜

Conyer 11F4

10.30–3; 6–11
Ship
Conyer Quay
Fremlins Bitter, Tusker ⊞
Full of character and nautical curios ♠♪♣♠⌂☜⌐☜

Cranbrook 10E6

10–2.30; 6–11
Duke of York
High Street (B2189)
Shepherd Neame Mild, Best Bitter, Stock Ale ⊡
Small, friendly one-bar pub, worth a visit ♠♪♣☞⌂☜

Dargate 11G4

11–3; 6–11
Dove Inn
(Off A229)
Shepherd Neame Mild, Bitter ⊞
Attractive interior and lovely garden ♠♪♣☒☞♠⊞⌂☜⌐♨

Dartford 10C3

10–2.30; 6–11
Malt Shovel
3 Darenth Road (off A226)
Morning opening: 11
Fuller London Pride
Shepherd Neame Bitter
Young Bitter, Special Bitter, Winter Warmer ⊞
17th-century inn near town centre ☞♠☎☜

Tiger
28 St. Albans Road
(Off A226) ☎ 24391
Courage Best Bitter, Directors ⊞
Workingmen's local, excellent lunchtime meals ♪♣☞⌂☜

Victory
26 East Hill (A226)
Shepherd Neame Mild, Bitter, Best Bitter, Stock Ale (winter) ⊞
Small, friendly corner local
⌐♪♣☞⌂☜

Deal 11H5

10–2.30; 6–10.30 (11 F, S and summer)
Admiral Penn
Beach Street
Fremlins Bitter ⊞
Nautical mementoes; fine view of Straits of Dover ♪♣☎☜≷

Kings Head
9 Beach Street
Shepherd Neame Bitter
Webster Yorkshire Bitter ⊞
Popular with younger drinkers, modernised and comfortable ♪≷

Yew Tree
Mill Hill
Fremlins Tusker ⊞

Large pub, popular with miners ♪♣♠☎☜≷

Doddington 11F4

10.30–3; 6–11
Chequers
The Street
Shepherd Neame Mild, Bitter ⊞
Picturesque country inn
♠♪♣☎☜

Dover 11H5

10–2.30; 6–10.30 (11 F, S and summer)
Dublin Man o' War
Lower Road, Kearnsey
Fremlins Bitter ⊞
Two-bar pub near Kearnsey Abbey gardens ♪♣☎☜≷

Fountain
238 London Road
Fremlins Bitter ⊞
Unpretentious local with uphill skittle alley ♪♣☞☜

Malvern Inn
19 Clarendon Road
Shepherd Neame Mild, Bitter ⊞
Friendly local, popular with mining fraternity ♪♣☞☜≷

White Lion
Tower Street
Shepherd Neame Mild, Bitter ⊞
Pleasant local in turn-of-the-century residential area ♪♣☎≷

East Farleigh 10D5

10–2.30; 6–10.30 (11 Thu, F, S)
Walnut Tree
Forge Lane OS 743531
Shepherd Neame Mild, Bitter, Stock Ale ⊞
Sought-after, unspoilt country pub ♠♠

East Malling 10D4

10–2.30; 6–11
Rising Sun
Mill Street
☎ West Malling 843284
Shepherd Neame Mild, Bitter ⊞ **Stock Ale** (winter) ⊡
Friendly local with excellent home-made food
♪♣☒☞⊞⌂☜♨≷

East Peckham 10D5

10–2.30; 6–11
Bush, Blackbird & Thrush
Peckham Bush OS 664498
Morning opening: 11
Fremlins Bitter ⊞
Fine pub in rural setting amongst orchards
♠♪♣♠☎☜♨♭

Edenbridge 10B5

10–2.30; 6–10.30 (11 F, S)
Star
132 High Street

Shepherd Neame Bitter, Best Bitter ⊞
Busy town local ⌐♪♣☞⌂☜

Try also: Old Eden Inn
(Fremlins)

Elham 11G5

10–2.30; 6–10.30 (11 F, S)
Kings Arms
The Square ☎ 242
Fremlins Bitter ⊞
Excellent village inn with Elham Valley Railway photographs ♣⌂☜

Faversham 11F4

10.30–3; 6–11
Albion
Front Brents ☎ 533897
Fremlins Bitter ⊞
Comfortable inn on edge of creek ♪♣☒☞♠⊞⌂☜⌐☜

Mechanics Arms
44 West Street
Shepherd Neame Mild, Bitter ⊞
Splendid unspoilt local ♪♣☎☜

Folkestone 11G6

10–2.30; 6–10.30 (11 F, S and summer)
Lifeboat
North Street
Courage Directors
Fremlins Bitter
Shepherd Neame Bitter, Best Bitter ⊞
Enterprising free house near fishmarket ♪♣☜

Pullman Wine Bar
Church Street ☎ 52524
Opens at 11 am and 6.30 pm
Watney Fined Stag Bitter
Webster Yorkshire Bitter ⊞
A must for railway enthusiasts ♪♣☞⌐☜

Raglan
104 Dover Road
Evening opening: 7
Fremlins Bitter ⊞
Martlet Old Devil ⊡
Comfortable, friendly free house, always a guest beer ♪♣☜

Richmond Tavern
1 Margaret Street
Shepherd Neame Mild, Bitter ⊞ **Stock Ale** (winter) ⊡
Excellent pub, worth seeking out ♪♣☎☜

Gillingham 10E4

10.30–2.30; 6.30–11
Falcon
Marlborough Road ☎ 50614
Truman Prize Mild, Bitter, Best Bitter ⊞
Well-kept town pub ♪♣☞⌂☜

United Services
27 Arden Street ☎ 52004
Shepherd Neame Bitter ⊞
Well-kept, friendly town pub
♪♣☎⌂☜

Gravesend 10D3

0–2.30; 6–11
Jolly Drayman
Wellington Street (off 226)
Charrington IPA H
Attractive low-ceilinged pub,
once part of Wellington
Brewery ♣♪✿🅰🅸◉≷

New Inn
4 Milton Road (A226)
Fremlins Bitter, Tusker H
Popular and original local in
town centre ♪♣🅸≷

Pier Hotel
Town Pier (A226) ✆ 67193
Hilton Clipper, Gravedigger,
Buccaneer, Lifebuoy H
West Country Cider G
Renovated pub near river with
brewery in cellar ♪✿🅶◉◉≷

Station
Stone Street (A227) ✆ 52290
Truman Prize Mild, Bitter,
Best Bitter H
Quiet, comfortable pub near
town centre ♪♣✿🅶🅸◉◉♿≷

Hadlow 10D5

0–2.30; 6–11
Harrow
Maidstone Road (A26)
Courage Best Bitter,
Directors H
Smart country pub with
cricketing theme
♣♪♣✿🅰🅶◉♿

Halling 10D4

0–2.30; 6–11
Homeward Bound
72 High Street (A228)
Shepherd Neame Mild,
Bitter H
Friendly village pub ♪♣🅰≷

Harrietsham 11E5

0–2.30; 6–11
Ringlestone Inn
OS 879558
Opens at 11.30 am & 6.30 pm
Everard Tiger, Old Original
Fremlins Bitter, Tusker
Goacher's Maidstone Ale
Tolly Cobbold Original G
Unspoilt 17th-century pub;
range of beers may vary
♣🅰🅶♿🅰

Harvel 10D4

0–2.30; 6–11
Amazon & Tiger
Off A227)
Everard Tiger, Old Original
Fremlins Bitter
Shepherd Neame Bitter H & G
Small and popular village local
♣♪♣✿🅰🅶♿🅸◉♿

Hastingleigh 11G5

0–2.30; 6–10.30 (11 F, S and summer)
Bowl Inn
OS 448096 ✆ Elmstead 332

Opens at 11.30 am & 7 pm;
closed Wed lunchtimes in
winter
Canterbury Ale
Everard Tiger
Fremlins Bitter H
Friendly, unspoilt country
pub, range may vary
♣♪✿♪🅰🅸◉

Hawkenbury 10E5

10.30–2.30; 6–11
Hare & Hounds
Headcorn Road (off A229)
Closed Mon/Tue lunchtimes;
opens 12 noon Wed–Sat
Fremlins Bitter
Young Bitter H
Friendly and lively free house
♪♣♪🅰♿ (Wed–Sun)

Herne Bay 11G4

10–2.30; 6–10.30 (11 F, S and summer)
Prince of Wales
Mortimer Street
Shepherd Neame Bitter H
Friendly Victorian house near
seafront ♪♣🅸◉

Hook Green 10D6

10–2.30; 6–11
Elephants Head
(B2169) OS 655358
Morning opening: 11
Draught Bass H
Butcombe Bitter G
Cotleigh Tawny Bitter H
Nutcracker, Old Buzzard G
Golden Hill Exmoor Ale
Harvey BB H XXXX G
Excellent rural pub; guest
beers ♣♪♣✿🅰🅶♿

Hythe 11G6

10.30–2.30; 6–10.30 (11 F, S and summer)
Bell Inn
Seabrook Road (A259)
Fremlins Bitter, Tusker H
Traditional 16th-century inn
with character ♪♣✿🅰🅶🅸◉

Kilndown 10D6

10–2.30; 6–11
Globe & Rainbow
Rogers Rogh Road (off A21)
OS 700353
✆ Lamberhurst 890283
Morning opening: 11
Fremlins Bitter
Young Bitter, Special Bitter H
Large inn with restaurant
♣♪♣✿♪🅰🅱🅶♿◉♿

Leigh 10C5

10–2.30; 6–11
Bat & Ball
High Street (B2027)
Closes 10.30 pm Mon–Thu in
winter
Fremlins Bitter H
Excellent village local
♣♪♣🅸◉🅰≷

Lenham 11E5

10–2.30; 6–10.30 (11 F, S)

Dog & Bear
The Square (off A20)
✆ Maidstone 858219
Shepherd Neame Mild, Bitter H
Genuine public bar and
comfortable lounge in old
coaching inn ♣♪♣✿🅱🅸🅸◉≷

Lordswood 10E4

10–2.30; 6–11
Victoria Cross
Lordswood Lane, near
Chatham ✆ Medway 63417
Courage Directors H
Comfortable, modern pub
with restaurant ♪✿🅰♿◉

Lower Higham 10D3

10.30–2.30; 6–11
Railway Tavern
Chequers Street (A226)
Shepherd Neame Mild,
Bitter H
First class village pub
♪♣🅰🅶🅸◉

Luddenham 11F4

10.30–3; 6–11
Mounted Rifleman
OS 981627
Fremlins Bitter G
Beer is carried up from the
cellar ♣♣♪✿♪

Luddesdown 10D4

10.30–2.30; 6–11
Golden Lion
OS 673666
Morning opening: 11.30
Truman Prize Mild, Bitter,
Best Bitter H
Welcoming village local in
Downland setting ♣♪♪✿♪

Maidstone 10E5

10–2.30; 6–11
Dog & Gun
213 Boxley Road
Morning opening: 11
Shepherd Neame Mild, Bitter,
Best Bitter (summer), Stock
Ale (winter) H
Popular town local with two
contrasting bars ♪♣♪♣✿🅱🅸◉

Dragoon
40 Sandling Road (A229, off
M20) ✆ 52620
Shepherd Neame Mild, Bitter,
Stock Ale H
Friendly pub near the barracks
♪♣🅱🅶🅸◉≷

Drakes Crab &
Oyster House
Fairmeadow ✆ 52531
Fremlins Bitter, Tusker
Wethered Bitter H
Busy pub, near river and town
centre ♪✿🅶♿◉≷

First & Last
40 Bower Place OS 752551
Fremlins Bitter H
Cosy street corner local ♣🅸◉

Kent

Wheelers Arms
1 Perry Street (off A229)
Opens at 11 am & 6.30 pm
**Shepherd Neame Mild,
Bitter** Ⓗ
Stock Ale (winter) Ⓗ & Ⓖ
Small, friendly local ♪♣♨Ⓡ☺Ⓖ

Margate 11H4

11–2.30; 5.30–11
Orb Inn
243 Ramsgate Road
**Shepherd Neame Mild, Bitter,
Best Bitter, Stock Ale**
(winter) Ⓗ
Friendly traditional pub
♠♪♣♨♠☺♪☺

Spread Eagle
25 Victoria Road
☎ Thanet 293396
Opens at 11 am & 5.30 pm
**Courage Directors
Ruddle County
Shepherd Neame Best Bitter
Spread Eagle Bitter
Young Special Bitter** Ⓗ
Splendid corner pub with
restaurant and 'house' beer;
range of beers varies ♪♨☺♪☺

Mark Beech 10C5

10–2.30; 6–10.30 (1 F, S and summer)
Kentish Horse
(Off B2026) OS 475427
Fremlins Bitter Ⓗ
Small, rural local with family
garden, children's playground
and aviary ♠♣♨♠♪☺Å

Marshside 11G4

10.30–2.30; 6–10.30 (11 F, S and summer)
Gate
(Off A28)
**Shepherd Neame Mild, Bitter,
Best Bitter, Stock Ale** Ⓖ
Lively country pub, superb
value ♠♪♣♨♠♪☺♭Å

Mereworth 10D5

10–2.30; 6–11
Queens Head
Butchers Lane (off A26)
Shepherd Neame Bitter Ⓗ
Traditional pub in the heart of
hop country ♣♠♪☺

Mersham 11F6

10–2.30; 6–10.30 (11 F, S)
Royal Oak
The Street ☎ Ashford 24218
**Shepherd Neame Mild,
Bitter** Ⓗ
Excellent three-bar village
local ♪♣♨Ⓡ♪

Milton Regis 11E4

10–2.30; 6–11
White Hart
High Street (off B2005)
**Truman Prize Mild, Bitter,
Best Bitter, Sampson
Hanbury's Extra Strong**
Large, thriving friendly pub
♪♣♨Ⓡ♪☺

Minster (Sheppey) 11F4

10–2.30; 6–11
British Queen
Chequers Road, Sheppey
(B2008)
Shepherd Neame Bitter Ⓗ
Popular refurbished local
♪♣♠♪☺

Newchurch 11G6

10–2.30; 6–10.30 (11 F, S and summer)
Black Bull
**Shepherd Neame Mild,
Bitter** Ⓖ
Pleasant, tasteful old pub
♠♣♫♪♠Ⓡ☺♭

New Romney 11F6

10–2.30; 6–10.30 (11 F, S and summer)
Warren Inn
Dymchurch Road (A259)
☎ 2090
**Shepherd Neame Mild, Bitter,
Stock Ale** Ⓗ
Friendly, renovated pub
♪♪♣♨♠♠♪☺♭

Oad Street 11E4

10–2.30; 6–11
Plough & Harrow
(Off A249) OS 870621
Opens at 11 am & 6.30 pm;
closed Monday lunchtimes
**Hook Norton Mild
Shepherd Neame Bitter** Ⓗ
Popular rural free house with
guest beers ♠♪♣♫♨♠♪

Ospringe 11F4

10.30–3; 6–11
Anchor
33 Ospringe Street (A2)
☎ Faversham 532085
Shepherd Neame Mild, Bitter Ⓗ
Popular village local
♠♪♣♨♠♪☺

Plaxtol 10D5

10–2.30; 6–11
Papermakers Arms
The Street (off A227)
Fremlins Bitter, Tusker Ⓗ
Improved, friendly village
local ♪♪♣♨♠♪☺♭

Rainham 10E4

10–2.30; 6–11
Rose
249 High Street (A2)
**Shepherd Neame Mild, Best
Bitter** Ⓗ
Lively pub, tastefully
decorated bars ♪♣♠♪☺

Ramsgate 11H4

11–2.30; 5.30–11
Blazing Donkey
St. Luke's Avenue
**Shepherd Neame Mild,
Bitter** Ⓗ
Darts local outside town
centre ♪♪♣♨♪☺

Falstaff
Addington Street
Shepherd Neame Mild, Bitter Ⓗ
Large backstreet local
♠♪♪♣♨Ⓡ♪☺

Red Lion
1 King Street ☎ Thanet 52659
Truman Bitter, Best Bitter Ⓗ
Popular corner local in town
centre ♪♣♫♪♭♪☺

Rochester 10D4

10–2.30; 6.30–11
Bell
21 Cossack Street ☎ 45461
**Shepherd Neame Bitter, Stock
Ale** Ⓗ
Welcoming, friendly local
♪♣♪♭≉

Roebuck
47 St. Margarets Street
**Courage Best Bitter,
Directors** Ⓗ
Spacious public bar, cosy
lounge ♪♣♭♪♭♭

Try also: Greyhound
(Shepherd Neame)

St. Margarets-at-Cliffe 11H5

10–2.30; 6–10.30 (11 F, S and summer)
Cliffe Tavern
High Street ☎ Dover 852400
Morning opening: 11
**Courage Directors
Fremlins Bitter
Shepherd Neame Best Bitter** Ⓗ
Comfortable weatherboarded
pub opposite Norman church
♨♠♭♪♭☺

All four pubs in the village sell
real ale

St. Nicholas-at-Wade 11H4

10.30–2.30; 6–11
Bell
The Street (off A28)
Fremlins Bitter, Tusker Ⓗ
Excellent old country pub
♠♪♣♨♠Ⓡ☺

Sandwich 11H4

10–2.30; 6–10.30 (11 F, S and summer)
Market Inn
7 Cattle Market ☎ 611133
**Shepherd Neame Mild, Bitter,
Stock Ale** Ⓗ
Popular pub near ancient
guildhall ♠♪♭☺≉

New Inn
**Truman Bitter, Best Bitter,
Sampson Hanbury's Extra
Strong** Ⓗ
Modernised and comfortable,
emphasis on evening meals
♪♨♠♭♪☺≉

Selling 11F5

10.30–3; 6–11

White Lion
he Street ✆ 211
hepherd Neame Mild,
itter Ⓗ
mart country inn renowned
r home cooking
♫Ⓓ♨⌂ℝⓒ♍⊛

Sevenoaks 10C5

–2.30; 6–10.30 (11 F, S)
Dorset Arms
ondon Road (A2028)
remlins Bitter, Tusker Ⓗ
opular Victorian town-centre
ub with mock-Edwardian
ecor ♫♣Ⓔℝⓒ

Chatterling 11H4

–2.30; 6–10.30 (11 F, S and summer)
Green Man
edding Hill (A257) OS
68584 ✆ Dover 812525
oung Bitter, Special Bitter,
Vinter Warmer Ⓗ
omfortable free house with
estaurant ♨♫♨Ⓑⓒ♍⊛

heerness 11F3

–2.30; 6–11
Red Lion
igh Street, Bluetown
ff A249) ✆ 663165
orning opening: 11.30
raught Bass
remlins Bitter Ⓗ
eal ale mecca close to the
ocks; guest beers ♫♣♍⊛

horeham 10C4

–2.30; 6–10.30 (11 F, S)
Royal Oak
igh Street (off A225)
remlins Bitter, Tusker Ⓗ
ocal involved in village life
♣♍⊛

outhborough 10C5

–2.30; 6–11
Royal Oak
eldhurst Road (off A26)
Tunbridge Wells 20444
hepherd Neame Mild,
tter, Best Bitter Ⓗ
ood honest house with
omfortable saloon
♣♨Ⓑⓒ♍♍⊛

outhfleet 10D4

–2.30; 6–11
Black Lion
ed Street ✆ 2386
ruman Bitter, Best Bitter Ⓗ
omfortable thatched pub in
uiet village ♫♨♨Ⓑⓒ♍⊛ⓢ

tanford 11G6

0–2.30; 6–10.30 (11 F, S)
rum
ne Street, North Stanford
ff B2068) OS 129384
orning opening: 11
urage Best Bitter, Directors
ary Meux Bitter
d Coope Burton Ale
hepherd Neame Bitter Ⓗ

Refurbished Kentish coaching
inn ♨♫♣Ⓔ♨Ⓑⓒ♍⊛ⓢ♈♋≷

Stansted 10D4

10–2.30; 6–11
Black Horse
Tumblefield Road (off A20)
Winter evening opening: 7
Fremlins Bitter, Tusker Ⓗ
Popular and cheerful rural
pub ♨♫♣Ⓔ♨♨ⓒ♍♍⊛

Stone-in-Oxney 11F6

10–2.30; 6–10.30 (11 F, S and summer)
Crown
The Street OS 939277
Beard BB
Fremlins Bitter
Shepherd Neame Bitter Ⓗ
Biddenden Cider Ⓖ
Thriving country pub; guest
beers ♨♫♣Ⓔ♨ⓒ♍♍ (not Sun)⊛

Stone Street 10C5

10–2.30; 6–10.30 (11 F, S)
Rose & Crown
OS 576546 ✆ Plaxtol 810233
Fremlins Bitter Ⓗ
Welcoming country pub with
large garden
♨♫♣♨♨Ⓑℝⓒ♍♍⊛♋

Strood 10D4

10–2.30; 6–11
Cobham Inn
17 Frindsbury Road (A228)
Courage Best Bitter,
Directors Ⓗ
Welcoming and friendly local
♫♣ℝⓒ♍⊛

Tilmanstone 11H5

10–2.30; 6–10.30 (11 F, S and summer)
Plough & Harrow
Dover Road (A256) ✆ 611424
Gale HSB
Harvey XX, BB, XXXX Ⓖ
Usher Best Bitter Ⓗ
Pleasantly renovated
♫♨♨Ⓑⓒ♍⊛

Tonbridge 10C5

10–2.30; 6–11
Primrose
112 Pembury Road (off A21)
Morning opening: 11
Fremlins Bitter Ⓗ
Small, friendly two-bar
weatherboarded pub
♨♫♣♨♨Ⓑⓒ♍⊛ⓢ≷

Try also: Rose & Crown (free)

Tunbridge Wells 10C6

10–2.30; 6–10.30 (11 F, S and summer)
Bruins
5 London Road (A26) ✆ 35757
Everard Tiger, Old Original
Friary Meux Bitter
Shepherd Neame Bitter Ⓗ
Festooned with teddy bears;
Italian restaurant en suite
♫♫♣ⓒ♍⊛≷

Sussex Arms
Sussex Mews, Nevill Street
(Off A267)
Harvey PA Ⓗ XXXX
Royal Tunbridge Wells
Bitter Ⓖ
Legendary place of
refreshment; collection of pots
♨♣♨♨Ⓡ⊛≷

Upper Upnor 10E4

10–2.30; 6–11
Tudor Rose
29 High Street
Gale BBB
Young Bitter, Special Bitter Ⓗ
Superb free house near castle
♫♣Ⓔ♨♨⊛

Try also: Kings Arms
(Courage)

West Farleigh 10D5

11–2.30; 6.30–11
Chequers Inn
(B2010) ✆ Maidstone 812589
Fremlins Bitter Ⓗ
Country pub with reading
matter on all walls and
ceilings ♍♣♨♨Ⓑ♨⊛

West Cliffe 11H5

10–2.30; 6–10.30 (11 F, S and summer)
Swingate
Dover Road (A258) OS
Draught Bass Ⓗ
Pleasant roadside pub near
A2/A258 roundabout
♨♫♨♨Ⓑ⊛

Westerham 10C5

10–2.30; 6–10.30 (11 F, S)
General Wolfe
High Street (A25)
Friary Meux Bitter
Ind Coope Burton Ale Ⓗ
Well-renovated old pub near
former Black Eagle Brewery
♨♫♣♨♨⊛

Whitstable 11G4

10–2.30; 6–10.30 (11 F, S and summer)
Coach & Horses
Oxford Street ✆ 264732
Shepherd Neame Mild, Bitter,
Stock Ale (winter) Ⓗ
Refurbished pub with
bring-and-buy bookshelves
♫♣♨Ⓒ♨⊛ⓢ≷

Golden Lion
Belmont Road
Fremlins Bitter Ⓗ
Pleasant, refurbished local
with snooker table ♫♣♨ℝ⊛≷

Wickhambreaux 11G4

10–2.30; 6–10.30 (11 F, S and summer)
Rose
The Green (off A257)
Fremlins Bitter, Tusker Ⓗ
Charming 13th-century
house ♨♫♣♨♨Ⓑℝ⊛ⓢ

ccrington 29G9

.30–3; 6–11

delphi

venue Parade (off A680)
hwaites Mild, Best Mild, itter [E]
usy town pub with friendly tmosphere ♪♣✿🚗[R]◔Ⓢ

lston 29F9

.30–3; 6–11

Vhite Bull

etween Longridge & rimsargh (B6243)
hwaites Best Mild, Bitter [E]
nusual pub layout inside ♣🚗Ⓢ

ltham 29G9

.30–3; 6–11

reyhound

Vhalley Road (A680)
amuel Smith Old rewery Bitter [H]
lush main road pub, warm nd inviting 🔥♪♣✿🚗🍺Ⓢ

ughton 22B2

–3; 5.30–10.30 (11 F, S)

og & Gun

ong Lane (off B5197)
urtonwood Light Mild, Dark ild, Bitter [H]
ural pub on edge of town 🚗🍺🚆

alderstone 29F9

–3; 6–11

Iyerscough

59)
obinson Best Mild, Best itter [H]
ld inn near airfield ♪✿🚗Ⓢ

arnoldswick 29H8

–3; 5.30–11

ross Keys

hurch Street (B6251)
3330
atthew Brown Mild, Bitter [H]
easant town centre pub ✿🚗[R]◔

artle 29E9

.30–3; 6–10.30 (11 F, S)

itting Goose

S 486329
hwaites Mild, Bitter [E]
leasant location near Bartle all ♪♣✿🚗◔◗Ⓢ

axenden 29G9

.30–3; 6–11

lma

anchester Road (A680)
vening opening: 7.30
atthew Brown Mild, Bitter [H]
osy old pub on two levels; arts date back to 16th entury ♣[R]🍺Ⓢ

elmont 22D1

–3; 6–11

Black Dog

Bolton Road (A675)
☎ Belmont Village 218
Holt Mild, Bitter [H]
Old village pub and climbers' haunt 🔥♣🚗[R]◔◗Ⓢ

Bickerstaffe 22C2

11–3; 5.30–10.30 (11 F, S)

Stanley Gate

Liverpool Road (A570)
Greenall Whitley Mild, Bitter [E]
Inviting hostelry standing guard at a lonely crossroads ♪♣🚗🍺Ⓢ

Bilsborrow 29E8

10.30–3; 6–11

White Bull

Garstang Road (A6)
☎ Brock 40324
Matthew Brown Mild, Bitter [H]
Small friendly canalside pub 🔥♪♣⊞✿🚗[R]🍺Ⓢ

Blackburn 29F9

10.30–3; 6–11

Corporation Park

Revidge Road (off A677)
Thwaites Best Mild, Bitter [H]
Highest pub in town ♪♣Ⓢ

Fountain

Accrington Road (A679)
Bass XXXX Mild Draught Bass [H]
Busy main road pub, rare outlet for Draught Bass ♪🍺

Havelock

Havelock Street
Thwaites Mild, Bitter [H]
Friendly locals' pub ɾ♪♣✿🍺Ⓢ

Prince of Wales

97 Montague Street (off A677)
Matthew Brown Mild, Bitter [H]
Lively town pub ♪♣🍺

Blackpool 28D9

10.30–3; 6–11

Bispham Hotel

Red Bank Road (off A584)
☎ 51752
Samuel Smith Old Brewery Bitter [H]
Popular with locals and holidaymakers ɾ♪♣🚗[R]◔🍺Ⓢ

Criterion

Topping Street
Tetley Mild, Bitter [H]
Town-centre pub with character ♪◔Ⓢ

Empress

Exchange Street, North Shore
☎ 20413
Thwaites Mild, Bitter [H]
Victorian hotel
🔥ɾ♪♣🛏[R]◔🍺Ⓢ🚆

Kings Arms

Talbot Road ☎ 25522
Draught Bass
Higsons Mild, Bitter [H]
Popular town-centre local opposite station ɾ♪♣🚗[R]🍺Ⓢ🚆

Saddle

286 Whitegate Drive, Marton (A587)
Morning opening: 11.30
Bass XXXX Mild, Cask Bitter Draught Bass [H]
Old inn of character with collection of antique photographs 🔥🚗

Bolton-le-Sands 29E7

10.45–3; 5.45–10.30 (11 F, S and summer)

Blue Anchor

Main Road (off A6)
☎ Hest Bank 823241
Mitchells Mild, Bitter [H]
Comfortable village local 'twixt two churches
🔥♪♣⊞✿[R]🍺

All pubs in Bolton-le-Sands serve real ale

Briercliffe 29H9

11–3; 5.30–11

Roggerham Gate

Todmorden Road OS 884337
☎ Burnley 22039
Younger No 3, IPA [H]
Remote pub in attractive setting ♣🚗[R]◔◗🍺Ⓢ

Brookhouse 29E7

10.45–3; 5.45–10.30 (11 F, S and summer)

Black Bull

Brookhouse Road ☎ Caton 770329
Yates & Jackson Mild, Bitter [E]
Country pub with plush lounge and lively vault
🔥ɾ♪♣⊞✿🚗🛏[R]◔◗🍺♿⛺

Burnley 29G9

11–3; 5.30–11

Old Duke

56 Briercliffe Road (off A56)
☎ 26136
Bass Cask Bitter [E]
Large open-plan pub ♪♣🚗[R]Ⓢ

Prince Albert

41 Curzon Street (off A679)
☎ 24788
Jennings Bitter
Taylor Best Bitter, Landlord, Ram Tam
Thwaites Best Mild, Bitter
Younger IPA [H]
Busy open-plan free house
ɾ♪♣◔Ⓢ🚆

White Hart

45 Church Street (A56)
Evening opening: 6.30
Thwaites Bitter [E]
Post-war pub with three bars
♪♣🚗[R]🍺Ⓢ

Carnforth 29E6

10.45–3; 5.45–10.30 (11 F, S and summer)

Shovel

North Road (B6254)
Boddingtons Bitter [E]
Busy pub with several rooms
♪♣✿🚗

Lancashire

Catforth 29E9

10.30–3; 6–10.30 (11 F, S)
Running Pump
(Off B5269) ☎ 690265
Robinson Best Mild, Best Bitter Ⓗ
Excellent country inn
♪🏠🅰️Ⓡ🅶🍺🕯️Ⓢ

Caton 29E7

10.45–3; 5.45–10.30 (11 F, S and summer)
Station
2 Hornby Road (A683)
☎ 770323
Mitchells Mild, Bitter, Extra Special Bitter Ⓔ
Large locals' pub with small dining room 🅰️♣🏬♪🏠🍺➔Ⓢ

Try also: Ship (Yates & Jackson)

Charnock Richard 22C1

11–3; 5.30–10.30 (11 F, S)
Hinds Head
(A49)
Burtonwood Dark Mild Ⓗ
Bitter Ⓔ
Handy for Park Hall leisure centre ♪♣🏠Ⓢ

Chatburn 29G8

11–3; 6–11
Black Bull
Bridge Road (off A59)
☎ 41200
Duttons Bitter
Whitbread Castle Eden Ale Ⓗ
Friendly village pub with enthusiastic landlord 🅰️♪♣🅰️♀

Chipping 29F8

10.30–3; 6–11
Sun
Windy Street
Boddingtons Best Mild, Bitter Ⓗ
Haunted pub with stream running through cellar
🅰️♪♪🅶🍺Ⓢ🅰️

Talbot
Boddingtons Best Mild, Bitter Ⓗ
Busy village pub near Trough of Bowland 🅰️♪♣🏬Ⓢ🅰️

Chorley 22C1

11–3; 5.30–10.30 (11 F, S)
Albion
Bolton Street
Tetley Mild, Bitter Ⓗ
Small pub with wood panelled bar ♪♣♀

Black Horse
Long Lane, Limbrick
Matthew Brown Mild, Bitter Ⓔ
John Peel Bitter Ⓗ
Popular country pub south-east of town
♪♣🏬🅶🍺Ⓢ

Jackson Arms
Cunliffe Street

Thwaites Best Mild, Bitter Ⓗ
Spartan two-roomed pub ♪♣♀🍺

Queens
Preston Road (A6)
Duttons Bitter
Hartley XB
Whitbread Castle Eden Ale Ⓗ
Plastic frogs and vine leaves abound ♪♣Ⓢ

Church 29G9

10.30–3; 5.30–11
Bridge
Henry Street ☎ Accrington 32166
Evening opening: 6
Bass XXXX Mild, Cask Bitter
Jennings Bitter Ⓗ
Friendly, small local next to sports centre
♪♣🏬🅰️Ⓡ🅶🍺Ⓢ🍺

Clayton-le-Moors 29G9

10.30–3; 5.30–11
Old England Forever
13 Church Street
Opens at 11 am & 7 pm
Matthew Brown Mild, Bitter Ⓗ
Small, locals' pub with rare tiled bar ♪♣♀Ⓢ

Cleveleys 28D8

10.30–3; 6–11
Royal Hotel
North Promenade ☎ 852143
Boddingtons Bitter
Hartley XB
Marston Pedigree Ⓗ
Lively two-bar, seafront pub
♪♣🏬🅰️Ⓡ🅶Ⓢ🅰️

Tap House (off licence)
32 Cumberland Avenue
☎ 854578
Opens: 9.30–3; 6–10
(12 noon–10 Sat)
Hartley XB
Marston Pedigree, Owd Rodger
Mitchell ESB
Theakston XB
Symonds Cider Ⓗ
Guest beers: discount to card-carrying CAMRA members

Victoria
Victoria Road West (B5412)
☎ 853306
Morning opening: 11
Samuel Smith Old Brewery Bitter Ⓗ
Large tied house, no real ale in public bar ♪♣🏬🅰️Ⓡ🅶🍺Ⓢ

Clitheroe 29G8

11–2; 6–11
Buck
Lowergate (off A671)
☎ 23299
Thwaites Best Mild, Bitter Ⓗ
Busy, central, young person's pub ♪♣Ⓡ Ⓢ

Cloughfold 29G9

11.30–3; 5–11
Ashworth Arms
Bacup Road (A681)
Bass XXXX Mild, Cask Bitter Ⓔ
Tastefully modernised local with small rooms ♪♣Ⓢ

Colne 29H8

11–3; 5.30–11
Crown
Albert Road (A56) ☎ 863580
Evening opening: 7.15
Bass XXXX Mild, Cask Bitter
Jennings Bitter
Stones Best Bitter Ⓗ
Excellent hotel with steak bar; only draught Stones in this area 🅰️♪♣🅰️🏬🅶🍺Ⓢ🍺

Golden Ball
Burnley Road (A56)
☎ 861862
Tetley Mild, Bitter Ⓗ
Pleasant, main road pub with a prize winning cellar
♪♣♀🅶🍺Ⓢ

Hole i' th' Wall
8 Market Street (A56)
Bass XXXX Mild, Cask Bitter Ⓔ
Old, unchanged pub 🅰️♣🏬Ⓢ

Red Lion
31 Market Street (A56)
☎ 863743
Taylor Dark Mild, Best Bitter Ⓔ
Popular town-centre pub catering for all tastes ♪♣🅰️Ⓡ Ⓢ

Coppull Moor 22C1

11–3; 5.30–10.30 (11 F, S)
Plough & Harrow
Preston Road (A49) ☎ 791349
Thwaites Best Mild, Bitter Ⓔ
Compact roadside pub with rare brew for area ♪♣Ⓡ🅶🍺Ⓢ

Cowpe 23E1

11.30–3; 5–11
Buck
Cowpe Road (off A681)
Evening opening: 7
Taylor Dark Mild, Best Bitter, Landlord
Thwaites Best Mild, Bitter Ⓗ
Classic terraced village local, worth finding ♪♣🅰️♀Ⓢ

Croston 22C1

11–3; 5.30–10.30 (11 F, S)
Lord Nelson
Out Lane
Higsons Mild, Bitter Ⓗ
Popular village pub ♪♣♀🅰️♀

Dalton 22C2

11–3; 5.30–10.30 (11 F, S)
Prince William
Beacon Lane ☎ Upholland 623989
Burtonwood Dark Mild, Bitter Ⓔ

easantly situated inn
ljoining cricket field, handy
r Ashurst Beacon
⊞✿🚗[R]◷❥Ⓢ

arwen 22D1

-3; 6–11

olden Cup
ackburn Road (A666)
hwaites Mild, Bitter [H]
efurbished pub retaining
omely atmosphere ♪⊞🚗[R]Ⓢ

l Thwaites' pubs in Darwen
rve real ale

olphinholme 29E7

.45–3; 5.45–10.30 (11 F, S and summer)

leece
ay Horse, near Lancaster
S 509532
itchells Mild, Bitter, Extra
pecial Bitter [H]
nspoilt country pub on
olated crossroads
♣⊞✿🚗🍷Ⓢ

denfield 22E1

.30–3; 5–11

oach & Horses
arket Street (off A56/A680)
ilsons Original Mild,
itter [H]
leasant village local ⌐♪♣🚗🍷

lswick 28E8

.30–3; 6–11

oot & Shoe
eech Road (off B2569)
Great Eccleston 70206
hwaites Best Mild, Bitter [H]
odernised village pub
♪♣✿🚗◷Ⓢ

hip
igh Street (B2569)
oddingtons Best Mild,
itter [H]
leasant village inn due for
odernisation 🏛♪♣✿🚗🍷

ntwistle 22D1

-3; 5.30–11

trawbury Duck
vershores Road (off B6213)
Turton 852013
vening opening: 7
artley XB
oorhouse Pendle Witches
rew
uddle County
aylor Dark Mild, Best Bitter,
andlord
hitbread Castle Eden Ale [H]
harming, rural free house;
hoice of beer varies
⌐♪♣✿🚗⊟❥🍷Ⓢ⇄

uxton 22C1

-3; 5.30–10.30 (11 F, S)

uxton Mills
igan Road (A49)
urtonwood Dark Mild,
itter [E]
ell-kept village pub 🏛♪♣🚗🍷Ⓢ

Fleetwood 28D8

10.30–3; 6–11

Fleetwood Arms
188 Dockstreet
Higsons Mild, Bitter [H]
Dockside tavern of great
character ♪♣🍷Ⓢ

Prince Arthur
46–48 Lord Street (A585)
Winter evening opening: 6.30
Duttons Bitter
Whitbread Castle Eden Ale [H]
Centrally situated pub with
lively, friendly atmosphere
♪♣⊞[R]🍷Ⓢ

Forton 29E8

11–3; 6–11

New Holly
(A6) OS 492505 ☎ 791568
Thwaites Best Mild, Bitter [E]
Busy, plush roadside hotel
♪♣⊞✿🚗⊟[R]◷❥🍷Ⓢ♿⛺

Freckleton 28E9

10.30–3; 6–11

Coach & Horses
Preston Old Road (off A584)
Boddingtons Best Mild,
Bitter [E]
Popular, village centre pub
♣✿🚗🍷Ⓢ

Garstang 29E8

11–3; 6–11

Eagle & Child
High Street (B6430) ☎ 2139
Matthew Brown Mild, Bitter [H]
Large, friendly pub
🏛⌐♪♣🚗⊟Ⓢ

Glasson Dock 28E7

10.45–3; 5.45–10.30 (11, F, S and summer)

Caribou
Victoria Terrace (B5290)
☎ Galgate 751356
Thwaites Mild, Bitter [H]
Large, modernised hotel
overlooking harbour
♪♣⊞⊟[R]Ⓢ⛺

All three pubs in Glasson Dock
serve real ale

Great Harwood 29G9

11–3; 6.30–11

Wellington
Town Gate (A6064)
Bass XXXX Mild, Cask Bitter
Jennings Bitter [H]
Excellent pub with thriving
tap room; opposite town
square ⌐♪♣🍷Ⓢ

Halton 29E7

10.45–3; 5.45–10.30 (11 F, S and summer)

White Lion
Church Brow
☎ Halton-on-Lune 811210
Mitchells Mild, Bitter [H]
Comfortable village local
🏛♣⊞🚗◷

Hambleton 28D8

10.30–3; 6–11

Shard Bridge
Shard Lane ☎ Blackpool
700208
McEwan 70/-
Younger No 3 [H]
Popular inn and restaurant by
toll bridge 🏛♪✿🚗[R]◷❥Ⓢ♿⛺

Helmshore 22E1

11.30–3; 5–11

Robin Hood
Holcombe Road (B6235)
Wilsons Original Mild,
Bitter [H]
A charming small pub near
textile museum ⌐♪♣Ⓢ

Hest Bank 28E7

10.45–3; 5.45–10.30 (11 F, S and summer)

Hest Bank
2 Hest Bank Lane (off A6 and
A5105) ☎ 822226
Boddingtons Best Mild,
Bitter [E]
Old coaching inn turned busy
local 🏛♪♣✿🚗⊟[R]◷🍷Ⓢ

Heysham 28E7

10.45–3; 5.45–10.30 (11 F, S and summer)

Royal
7 Main Street ☎ 51475
Mitchells Mild, Bitter [H]
Old pub in narrow street
♪♣⊞✿🚗◷

Hoghton 29F9

10.30–3; 6–10.30 (11 F, S)

Boars Head
(A675)
Whitbread Castle Eden Ale [H]
Bucolic interior with attached
restaurant 🏛♪🚗◷❥Ⓢ

Holme Chapel 29H9

11–3; 5.30–11

Queens
Burnley Road (A646)
Burtonwood Dark Mild,
Bitter [H]
Grand village local ♪♣🍷Ⓢ

Try also: Gordon Lennox
(Bass)

Hornby 29F6

10.45–3; 5.45–10.30 (11 F, S and summer)

Royal Oak
Main Street (A683) ☎ 21228
Yates & Jackson Mild, Bitter [E]
Plush country pub
♪♣⊞🚗◷❥Ⓢ

Huncoat 29G9

10.30–3; 6–11

White Lion
1 Highergate Road
☎ Accrington 33581
Matthew Brown Mild, Bitter [E]
John Peel Bitter [H]
Friendly local opposite village
stocks ♪♣✿🚗◷Ⓢ⇄

Lancashire

Lancaster 29E7

10.45–3; 5.45–10.30 (11 F, S and summer)

Farmers Arms
Penny Street (A6) ℰ 36368
Yates & Jackson Mild, Bitter E
Renovated up-market town
hotel ♪✦🅿️📠🅁🅖🅘●⑧&⚅

Freeholders Arms
49 Ullswater Road
Yates & Jackson Mild, Bitter E
Lively old-fashioned local
⚅♪✦🅿️

Moorlands
Quarry Road
Evening opening: 6.30
Mitchells Mild, Bitter H
Large, thriving
turn-of-the-century local
⚅♪✦🅗🅁🅘⑧

Water Witch
Aldcliffe Road (off A6)
**Westmorland Slaters Bitter,
Cumberland Strong**
Yates & Jackson Mild H
Canalside stables attractively
converted; moorings available
⚅♪✦🅿️🅖●⑧&

All Mitchells' and Yates &
Jackson pubs in Lancaster
serve real ale

Leyland 22C1

11–3; 5.30–10.30 (11 F, S)

Crofters
Leyland Lane
**Matthew Brown Mild, Bitter,
John Peel Bitter** H
Well-renovated local ♪✦🅰️⑧

Eagle & Child
Church Road
**Burtonwood Dark Mild,
Bitter** H
Ancient inn, much altered
inside ♪✦🅰️⑧

Little Eccleston 28E8

10.30–3; 6–11

Cartford Hotel
Cartford Lane (off A586)
ℰ Great Eccleston 70166
Wilsons Original Bitter H
Modernised country pub by
toll bridge 🅰️♪✦🅰️🅁🅖●⑧Å

Longridge 29F8

11–3; 5.30–11

Alston Arms
Matthew Brown Mild, Bitter H
Spacious pub on road to
Chipping ♪✦🅰️🅘

Townley Arms
Berry Lane
Tetley Walker Mild, Bitter E
Adjacent to former railway
station 🅰️♪✦🅰️🅘

Longton 29E9

10.30–3; 5.30–10.30 (11 F, S)

Dolphin (Flying Fish)
Marsh Lane

Often closed lunchtimes
midweek
Thwaites Best Mild, Bitter H
Pub-cum-farmhouse on
Longton Marsh, to be
extended 🅰️✦🅿️🅰️🅘

Lytham 28D9

10.30–3; 6–11

Captains Cabin
Henry Street (off A584)
ℰ 736226
Whitbread Castle Eden Ale H
Busy pub with view of stillage
♪✦🅿️🅖🅘⑧⚅

Hole in One
Forest Drive ℰ 739968
Thwaites Mild, Bitter H
Tastefully designed pub in
new residential area
♪✦🅿️🅰️🅖🅘&⚅

Queens
Central Beach ℰ 737316
**Matthew Brown Bitter, John
Peel Bitter**
Bulmer Cider H
Popular, spacious sea front
pub ♪✦🅗🅿️🅰️🅁🅖●🅘⑧⚅

Mawdesley 22C1

11–3; 5.30–10.30 (11 F, S)

Black Bull
Hall Lane
**Greenall Whitley Mild,
Bitter** E
700-year-old pub, once
nicknamed Hell's Hob
⚅♪✦🅿️🅰️⑧

Morecambe 28E7

10.45–3; 5.45–10.30 (11 F, S and summer)

Midland
Marine Road West (A589)
ℰ 417180
**Moorhouse Premier Bitter,
Pendle Witches Brew** H
Huge plush hotel ⚅♪🅗🅖●⚅

Pier Hotel
285 Marine Road (A589)
ℰ 417928
**Matthew Brown Mild, Bitter,
John Peel Bitter** H
Cosy, traditional local on
promenade ♪✦🅖

Victoria
14 Victoria Street ℰ 420690
**Yates & Jackson Mild,
Bitter** E & H
One large, comfortable bar
⚅♪✦🅗🅖

York Hotel
Lancaster Road (B5274)
ℰ 418226
Mitchells Mild H **Bitter** H & G
Large, busy pub
♪✦🅗🅿️🅰️🅗🅁🅖●&

Newchurch-in-
Rossendale 29G9

11.30–3; 5–11

Boars Head

69 Church Street (off B6238)
Bass XXXX Mild, Cask Bitter
Jennings Bitter H
Lively village local built in
1674 ♪✦

Ormskirk 22F

11–3 (4 Thu); 5.30–10.30 (11 F, S)

Greyhound
Aughton Street (B5197)
Peter Walker Mild, Bitter H
Popular town local 🅰️✦🅰️🅁🅘⚅

Horsehoe
Southport Road (A570)
**Tetley Walker Mild, Best
Bitter** H
Friendly and lively alehouse
♪✦🅘⚅

Kicking Donkey
Narrow Moss Lane
OS 411101 ℰ 72657
Closes 3 pm Thursdays
Ind Coope Burton Ale
Tetley Walker Mild, Bitter H
Popular and attractive
country pub 🅰️✦🅱️🅿️🅰️🅖

Queen Inn
Aughton Street
**Vaux Sunderland Draught
Bitter, Samson** H
Handsome town pub with
attractive bar 🅰️♪✦🅗🅁🅘⚅

Snigs Foot
Church Street
**Burtonwood Light Mild, Dark
Mild, Bitter** E
Unassuming facade hides
popular local of character
⚅♪✦🅗🅁🅘⚅

Yew Tree
Grimshaw Lane (off A59)
Closes 3 pm Thursdays
Higsons Mild, Bitter H
Modern pub on town's
outskirts ♪✦🅰️🅘⚅

Osbaldeston 29F

11–3; 6–11

Bay Horse
Longsight Road (A59)
Thwaites Mild, Bitter H
Compact rural pub on main
road ✦🅰️🅘

Overton 28E

10.45–3; 5.45–10.30 (11 F, S and summer)

Ship
Main Street OS 435579 ℰ 23
Yates & Jackson Mild, Bitter E
Genuine late Victorian pub
🅰️✦🅿️🅰️🅁🅘Å

Padiham 29G

11–3; 5.30–11

Kings Arms
2 Mill Street, off Burnley Road
(A671) ℰ 71493
**Taylor Dark Mild, Best Bitter
Landlord**
Thwaites Mild, Bitter H
Modernised pub, very popula
with the younger set ♪✦🅖⑧

arbold 22C2
3; 5.30–10.30
tocks Tavern
der Road (A5209) ☎ 2902
tley Walker Mild, Bitter H
omfortable village local with
tractive lounge bar, crowded
weekends ♪♣♠♿❶Ⓢ≷

enwortham 29E9
30–3; 6–10.300 (11 F, S)
lack Bull
pe Lane
eenall Whitley Mild,
tter E
nall, well-heeled local
♣♠❶Ⓢ

illing 28E8
30–3; 6–11
olden Ball
hool Lane (off A588) ☎ 212
waites Best Mild, Bitter H
pular village pub with
wling greens
♣⌘♿♠❶Ⓢ♿Å

easington 29F9
30–3; 6–11
utlers Arms
ff A674)
atthews Brown Mild,
tter H
iendly village pub with
wling green ♪♣⌘❶Ⓢ≷

y also: Railway (Wilsons)

oulton 28D8
30–3; 6–11
astle Gardens
rleton ☎ 882861
ens at 11.30 am & 7 pm
ss XXXX Mild, Cask Bitter H
pular, modernised pub on
tskirts of Poulton
♪♣♠♿♿

hatched House
ll Street (off A586)
orning opening: 11
ddingtons Bitter E
sy town-centre pub ♠❶Ⓢ≷

reesall 28D8
30–3; 6–11
aracen's Head
rk Lane (off A588)
Knott End 810346
waites Best Mild, Bitter H
odernised, friendly village
cal ♠♪♣♠♿❶Ⓢ≷

reston 29E9
30–3; 6–10.30 (11 F, S)
ox & Grapes
x Street
atthew Brown Mild,
hn Peel Bitter H
nall, dimly-lit town-centre
b ♪≷

eorge
hurch Street

Thwaites Mild, Best Mild,
Bitter E
First-class pub ♪♣♿Ⓡ♿Ⓢ

Greyhound
London Road (A6)
Boddingtons Best Mild,
Bitter H
Basic pub with lively tap room
♣❶

Maguires Tavern
30 Avenham Street
McEwan 80/- H
Large split-level free house
♪♿≷

Maudland
1 Pedder Street
Matthew Brown Mild, Bitter H
Small street-corner local
♪♣❶Ⓢ

Mitre Tavern
90 Moor Lane
Vaux Sunderland Draught
Bitter, Samson H
Modern, friendly two-bar local
♪♣♠♿Ⓢ

Moorbrook
North Road
Thwaites Best Mild, Bitter H
Popular pub awaiting
modification ♠♪♣♿Ⓢ

New Britannia
Heatly Street
Duttons Bitter
Whitbread Castle Eden Ale H
Small, often-packed pub near
polytechnic ♪♣♿Ⓢ≷

New Welcome Inn
15 Cambridge Street
Thwaites Best Mild, Bitter H
Small pub in development
area ♪♣Ⓢ

Old Blue Bell
Church Street
Small Smith Old Brewery
Bitter H
Attractive town centre pub
♪♿≷

Old Dog
Church Street
Matthew Brown Mild, Bitter E
Town pub dating back to
Cromwellian times ♪♣♿Ⓢ≷

Royal Consort
Meadow Street
Boddingtons Best Mild,
Bitter E
Popular pub near infirmary
♪♣❶

Royal Garrison
Watling Street Road
Matthew Brown Mild, Bitter,
John Peel Bitter H
Large pub opposite Fulwood
Barracks ♪♣♠♿❶Ⓢ

Sun
Friargate
Thwaites Mild, Bitter E

Comfortable town pub
♪♣♿❶≷

Theatre
Fishergate
Boddingtons Best Mild,
Bitter H
Busy pub with tiled frontage
♪♣❶Ⓢ≷

All Boddingtons' and
Thwaites' pubs in Preston
serve real ale

Rufford 22C1
10.30–3; 6–10.30 (11 F, S)
New Fermor Arms
(Off A59)
Blezards Bitter
Tetley Walker Mild, Bitter H
Modern pub, popular with
young people; Blezards
brewed on the premises
♪♣♠♿Ⓢ≷

St. Anne's-on-Sea 28D9
10.30–3; 6–11
Queensway
Whitbread Castle Eden Ale H
Modern Beefeater eating
house ♪♿♿♣♿Å

Victoria
Church Road ☎ 727786
Boddingtons Best Mild, Bitter
Oldham Mild, Bitter H
Popular pub, modernised in
Victorian style ♪♣♿♿❶Ⓢ≷

Scarisbrick 22B2
11–3; 5.30–10.30 (11 F, S)
Heatons Bridge
2 Heatons Bridge Road
(B5242) OS 404118
Tetley Walker Mild, Walker
Best Bitter H
Basic but welcoming Victorian
canalside pub ♣♠♿♣❶

Silverdale 28E6
10.45–3; 5.45–10.30 (11 F, S and summer)
Silverdale
Shore Road ☎ 701206
Boddingtons Bitter E
Popular free house in
charming village
♠♪♣⌘♿♠❶Ⓡ❶Ⓢ

Skelmersdale 22C2
11–3; 5.30–10.30 (11 F, S)
Victoria
Sandy Lane
Peter Walker Mild, Best
Bitter H
Homely local ♪♣❶

Slyne 29E7
10.45–3; 5.45–10.30 (11 F, S and summer)
Slyne Lodge
Main Road (A6) ☎ Hest Bank
823389
Lunchtime opening: 12 noon
Hartley XB
Ruddle Bitter

Tetley Bitter
Theakston Best Bitter Ⓗ
Popular pub, formerly a
private club
♪♣🏠♨🏠▣Ⓡ🕙🕭Ⓢ

Snatchems 28E7

10.45–3; 5.45–10.30 (11 F, S and summer)
Golden Ball
Lancaster Road (off B5273)
OS 448616
Closes 10.30 pm Mon–Thu in
summer
Mitchells Mild, Bitter Ⓗ
Bulmer Cider Ⓖ
On bank of River Lune, cut off
by highest tides
🏠♪♣♨🏠♟

Stacksteads 23E1

11.30–3; 5–11
Beehive
468 Newchurch Road (A681)
**Wilsons Original Mild,
Bitter** Ⓗ
Small and friendly with
convivial atmosphere ♪♣

Torrisholme 28E7

10.45–3; 5.45–10.30 (11 F, S and summer)
George
302 Lancaster Road (B5321)
✆ Morecambe 418477
Yates & Jackson Mild, Bitter Ⓔ
Large 1930s local with
panelling in lounge bar
♪♣Ⓡ♟

Turn 22E1

11.30–3; 5–11
Plane Tree
300 Rochdale Road (A680)
Bass XXXX Mild, Cask Bitter Ⓗ
Comfortable, friendly village
pub; afternoon teas in
summer
🏠♪♣♨🏠🕙🕭Ⓢ

Ulnes Walton 22C1

10.30–3; 6–10.30 (11 F, S)
Rose & Crown
Southport Road (A581)
**Burtonwood Dark Mild,
Bitter** Ⓗ
Old inn between Croston and
Euxton ♪♣♨🏠♟Ⓢ

Upholland 22C2

11–3; 5.30–10.30 (11 F, S)
Plough & Harrow
Old Ormskirk Road (off
A577), ✆ 622338
**Boddingtons Best Mild,
Bitter** Ⓗ
Listed building with pleasantly
modernised interior
♪♣♨🏠🕙🕭Ⓢ

White Lion
10 Church Street (off A577)
✆ 622593
Tetley Walker Mild, Bitter Ⓗ
Plush and comfortable village
pub ♪🏠🕙🕭Ⓢ

Waddington 29G8

10.30–3; 6–11
Higher Buck
The Square
✆ Clitheroe 23226
Thwaites Best Mild Ⓔ **Bitter** Ⓗ
Well-furnished local in
picturesque village
♪♣♨🏠🕙🕭Ⓢ

Walton-le-Dale 29E9

10.30–3; 6–10.30 (11 F, S)
Bridge
Victoria Road (A6)
**Matthew Brown Mild, Bitter,
John Peel Bitter** Ⓗ
Pleasant pub on banks of
Ribble ♪♣♨🏠🕙🕭Ⓢ

Victoria
Higher Walton Road (A675)
**Boddingtons Best Mild,
Bitter** Ⓔ
Small, red brick Victorian pub
♪♣♨🏠♟

Wesham 28E9

10.30–3; 6–11
Lane Ends
Weeton Road (off A585)
**Boddingtons Best Mild,
Bitter** Ⓔ
Friendly locals' pub
♪♣♨🏠Ⓡ🕭Ⓢ🅰🚆

Whalley 29G8

11–3; 6–11
Swan
King Street (off A59)
✆ 2195
Whitbread Castle Eden Ale Ⓗ
Comfortable, central pub near
the abbey ♪🎱🏠🕙🕭Ⓢ

Wheatley Lane 29G8

11–3; 5.30–11
Sparrow Hawk
Wheatley Lane Road (off
A6068)
✆ Nelson 64126
Bass XXXX Mild Ⓔ **Cask Bitter
Draught Bass** Ⓗ
Popular pub in rural setting
♨🏠🕙🕭Ⓢ

Try also: White Swan (free)

White Coppice 22D1

11–3; 5.30–10.30 (11 F, S)
Railway
Coppice Lane OS 611198
Matthew Brown Mild, Bitter Ⓗ
Isolated but popular country
pub 🏠♪♣♨🏠Ⓢ

Whittington 29F6

10.45–3; 5.45–10.30 (11 F, S and summer)
Dragon's Head
Main Street (B6254)
✆ Kirkby Lonsdale 71545
Mitchells Mild, Bitter Ⓗ
Friendly village inn
🏠♪🎱♨🏠🕙Ⓢ

Whittle-le-Woods 22C

11–3; 5.30–10.30 (11 F, S)
Lord Nelson
Brindle Road (B5256)
**Matthew Brown Mild, Bitter,
John Peel Bitter** Ⓗ
Ancient low-ceilinged inn,
tastefully modernised ♪🏠🕙

Royal Oak
Chorley Old Road
Matthew Brown Mild, Bitter Ⓗ
Small, friendly village pub ♪♣

Worsthorne 29H

11–3; 5.30–11
Crooked Billet
Smith Street
Tetley Mild, Bitter Ⓗ
Cosy village pub, well worth a
visit 🏠♪♣♨🏠Ⓢ

Wray 29F

10.45–3; 5.45–10.30 (11 F, S and summer)
George & Dragon
Main Street (off B6480)
✆ Hornby 21403
Mitchells Mild, Bitter Ⓗ
Popular, congenial country
pub 🏠♣♨▣Ⓢ

Wrightington 22C

11–3; 5.30–10.30 (11 F, S)
Tudor
Mossy Lea Road (B5250)
**Greenall Whitley Mild,
Bitter** Ⓗ
Modernised roadside inn ♪🏠Ⓢ

*The 🅰 symbol denotes a pub
with a real solid fuel fire*

Ashby-de-la-Zouch
16A1

10.30–2.30; 5.30–10.30 (11 F, S)
Shoulder of Mutton
Market Street (A453)
✆ 415540
Evening opening: 6.30
Draught Bass
Mitchells & Butlers Mild Ⓗ
Splendid town-centre pub
with old signs and prints
✶♪♣🅟🅰🗎Ⓡ🅖🌳💷Ⓢ🌜

Ashby Folville
16C2

10.30–2.30; 6–10.30 (11 F, S)
Carington Arms
(B674) ✆ Gaddesby 228
Winter evening opening: 7
Everard Beacon, Tiger, Old Original
Bulmer Cider Ⓗ
Large, imposing Tudor-style
country pub, petanque played
🅰♪♣🅟🅰🖵Ⓡ🅖 (not Sun)
🌳 (Sun–Thu) Ⓢ🌜

Bardon Hill
16B2

10.30–2.30; 5.30–10.30 (11 F, S)
Birch Tree
(A50) ✆ Coalville 32134
Everard Burton Mild, Tiger, Old Original Ⓗ
Friendly and busy roadside
inn ✶♪♣🅰🅖💷Ⓢ🌜

Barrow-on-Soar
16B1

10.30–2; 6–10.30 (11 F, S)
Lime Kiln
North Street (B675)
Ansells Mild
Ind Coope Bitter Ⓗ
Small, friendly village local
known as the 'Trap'
🅰♪♣🅟🅰💷Ⓢ🅰

Barwell
16B3

10–2.30; 5.30–10.30 (11 F, S)
Blacksmiths Arms
Chapel Street ✆ Earl Shilton
43252
Marston Mercian Mild, Burton Bitter, Pedigree Ⓗ
Popular half-timbered pub
with large bar ♪♣🅰Ⓡ
🅖 (weekdays) 🌳Ⓢ

Try also: Queens Head
(Marston)

Birstall
16C2

11–2; 6–10.30 (11 F, S)
White Horse
White Horse Lane (off A6)
Ansells Mild, Bitter
Ind Coope Burton Ale Ⓗ
Canalside pub with large
lounge and cosy bar
✶ (Tue) ♣🅟🅰🅖🌳Ⓢ

Bitteswell
16B3

10.30–2.30; 5.30–11
Olde Royal Oak

✆ Lutterworth 2406
Opens 11–2.30; 7–12
(1 am F, S)
Davenports Bitter Ⓗ
Renovated 400-year-old
coaching inn
✶♪♣🅟🅰🅰Ⓡ🅖🌳💷Ⓢ🅰

Blaby
16B3

10–2; 5.30–10.30 (11 F, S)
Black Horse
Sycamore Street (off A426)
✆ Leicester 771209
Shipstone Mild, Bitter Ⓗ
Friendly pub with lively
weekend singalongs
✶♪♣🅰🅖 (Mon–Fri) 🌳

Blackfordby
16A1

10.30–2.30; 6–10.30 (11 F, S)
Blue Bell
✆ Burton 216737
Marston Pedigree, Merrie Monk Ⓗ
Bulmer Cider Ⓖ
Pleasant village inn adjoining
garden centre 🅰♪🅟🅰🅖Ⓢ

Bottesford
26C8

10–2.30; 6–10.30 (11 F, S)
Red Lion
Grantham Road (A52)
Opens at 11 am & 7 pm
Hardys & Hansons Best Mild, Best Bitter Ⓔ
Welcoming pub with relaxed
atmosphere ♪♣🅰🅖Ⓢ

Try also: Bull; Rutland Arms

Clipsham
16E2

12–2.30; 7–11
Olive Branch
(Off A1) ✆ Castle Bytham 355
Ruddle Bitter, County
Samuel Smith Old Brewery Bitter Ⓗ
Pleasant rural pub with
restaurant 🅟🅰Ⓡ🅖🌳Ⓢ🅰

Coalville
16A2

10.30–2.30; 5.30–10.30 (11 F, S)
Victoria
Whitwick Road (B5329)
✆ 32216
Opens at 11 am & 6.30 pm
Shipstone Mild, Bitter Ⓗ & Ⓔ
Popular pub with live music at
weekends
✶♪♣🅰🅟🅰🅖💷Ⓢ🅰

Cottesmore
16E2

11–2.30; 6.30–11
Sun Inn
Main Street (B668)
✆ Oakham 812321
Everard Beacon, Tiger, Old Original Ⓗ
Popular 18th century
thatched pub ♣🅰🅟🅰Ⓡ🅖🌳

Cropston
16B2

10.30–2; 5.30–10.30 (11 F, S)
Bradgate Arms

Station Road
✆ Leicester 362120
Ind Coope Burton Ale Ⓗ
Mitchells & Butlers Mild
Ruddle Bitter, County
Samuel Smith Old Brewery Bitter Ⓗ
Old free house of character;
guest beer on Tuesdays
🅰♣🅟🅰🅖🌳Ⓢ

Desford
16B2

11–2; 6–10.30 (11 F, S)
Olde Lancaster Inn
Station Road (B5380) ✆ 2589
Everard Beacon, Tiger, Old Original Ⓗ
Attractive 18th-century pub
with two rooms and
restaurant 🅰♪♣🅟🅰🅖🌳Ⓢ

Dunton Bassett
16B3

11–2.30; 6–11
Merrie Monk
Station Road (off A426)
Marston Mercian Mild, Pedigree Ⓗ
Busy country pub
🅰♪🌳♣🅰🌳Ⓢ

Earl Shilton
16B3

10–2; 5.30–10.30 (11 F, S)
Dog & Gun
Keats Lane (off A47) ✆ 42425
Marston Mercian Mild, Burton Bitter, Pedigree Ⓔ
Large locals' bar and quieter
comfortable lounge ♪♣🅰
🅖 (Mon–Fri)🌳 (Tue–Sat)🌳Ⓢ

Red Lion
High Street (A47) ✆ 43356
Morning opening: 10.30
Draught Bass
Mitchells & Butlers Mild Ⓗ
Popular three-roomed village
centre local ♪♣🅟🅰Ⓡ🌳Ⓢ

Gaddesby
16C2

10.30–2.30; 6–10.30 (11 F, S)
Cheney Arms
Rearsby Lane (B674) ✆ 260
Everard Beacon, Old Original Ⓗ
Fine old country pub, formerly
a dower house 🅰♣🅟🅰🅟🅰🖵Ⓡ🌳Ⓢ🅰

Gilmorton
16B3

10.30–2.30; 5.30–11
Talbot Inn
Lutterworth Road
Opens at 11.30 am & 7 pm
Banks Mild, Bitter Ⓔ
Quiet village local ♪♣🅟🅰🌳Ⓢ🅰

Groby
16B2

11–2; 6–10.30 (11 F, S)
Earl of Stamford
Leicester Road (off A50)
✆ Leicester 875616
Everard Burton Mild, Beacon, Tiger, Old Original Ⓔ
Well-run large village pub
♪♣🅟🅰🅖🌳

Harby 26C8

11–2.30; 6–10.30 (11 F, S)

Nags Head
☎ 60209
Home Bitter [E]
Traditional, friendly half-timbered pub 🔥♣⚘🚗◔🍴[S]

Hinckley 16A3

10–2; 5.30–10.30 (11 F, S)

Black Horse
Upper Bond Street (A447)
☎ 637613
Opens at 11 am & 6 pm
Marston Mercian Mild, Burton Bitter, Pedigree [H]
Bulmer Cider [G]
Cosy, timbered local with several small rooms
🔥♣⊞🚗[R]🍴[S]

Greyhound
New Buildings ☎ 615235
Morning opening: 11;
Saturday evening opening: 7
Marston Mercian Mild, Burton Bitter, Pedigree [H]
Many-roomed, lively town-centre pub
🔥⌐♪♣[R]◔🍴[S]

Weavers Arms
Derby Road (B580)
Morning opening: 11
Marston Mercian Mild, Burton Bitter, Pedigree [E]
Owd Rodger [G]
Bustling, lively three-roomed town pub 🔥♪♣⚘🍴[S]

Hose 26C9

10.30–2.30; 6–10.30 (11 F, S)

Black Horse
Bolton Lane
Opens at 11 am & 7 pm
Home Mild, Bitter [H]
Friendly three-roomed village local 🔥⌐♪♣🚗🍴[S]

Huncote 16B3

11–2; 6–10.30 (11 F, S)

Red Lion
☎ Leicester 862233
Everard Burton Mild, Beacon, Tiger, Old Original [H]
Quiet, cosy village pub; long alley skittles
🔥⌐♪♣⚘🚗[R]◔🍴[S]⛺

Hungarton 16C2

10–2; 6–10.30 (11 F, S)

Black Boy
☎ 601
Opens 11 am & 6.30 or 7pm
Mitchells & Butlers Mild, Brew XI [H]
Excellent country pub
🔥♪♣⚘🚗[R]◔🍴[S]♿

Illston-on-the-Hill 16C3

10–2; 6.30–11

Fox & Goose
(Off B6047)
Everard Tiger, Old Original [H]
Small, unspoilt country pub
🔥♪♣⚘🍴[S]

Kegworth 16B1

10–2; 6–10.30 (11 F, S)

Cap & Stocking
Borough Street (off A6)
Mitchells & Butlers Mild, Springfield Bitter [G]
Classic village pub; ale served from jugs
🔥♪♣⚘[S]

Try also: Fosters Arms (Whitbread)

Leicester 16C2

10.30–2.30; 5.30–10.30

Abbey Hotel
St Margarets Way ☎ 222103
Morning opening: 11
Ansells Mild, Bitter [H]
Pool bar and quieter cosy lounge
⌐♪♣⊞⚘[R]◔🌙 (Wed–Sun) 🍴[S]

Blackbird
Blackbird Road (A5125 Ring Road) ☎ 22678
Saturday evening opening: 6
Everard Burton Mild, Beacon, Tiger, Old Original [H]
Many-roomed pre-war suburban local
♪♣⊞⚘🚗[R]◔[S]♿

Bricklayers Arms
78 Welford Road (A50)
☎ 540687
Shipstone Mild, Bitter [H] & [E]
Bulmer Cider [H]
Tastefully modernised, former Beeston Brewery house
⌐♪♣⚘[R]◔🍴[S]

Empire Hotel
217 Fosse Road North
☎ 21602
Evening opening: 6
Ansells Mild, Bitter [H]
Large Victorian hotel with comfortable, spacious lounge and small public bar
⌐♪♣⚘🚗⊞[R]◔🌙🍴[S]♿

Gipsy Lane Hotel
Gipsy Lane (off A46) ☎ 62799
Evening opening: 6
Home Mild, Bitter [E]
Large three-roomed 1930s pub
♪♣⚘🚗[R]◔🍴[S]

Globe
Silver Street ☎ 29819
Everard Burton Mild, Beacon, Tiger, Old Original
Bulmer Cider [H]
Popular, unspoilt 19th century pub, slightly modernised ♪♣[R]◔🍴[S]

Joiners Arms
Sanveygate ☎ 26420
Banks Mild, Bitter [E]
Comfortable town-centre pub
♪♣🚗[R]◔🍴[S]♿

Magazine
Newarks Street ☎ 540523
Morning opening: 11
Draught Bass
Mitchells & Butlers Mild, Springfield Bitter [H]
Popular city-centre pub near polytechnic ⌐♪♣⚘[R]🍴[S]

Richmond Arms
Hinckley Road (A47) ☎ 29608
Opens at 11 am & 6 pm
Draught Bass
Mitchells & Butlers Mild, Springfield Bitter [E]
Pleasant new town pub
♪♣⚘🚗◔🍴[S]♿

Salmon Inn
Butts Close Lane, near St Margarets bus station
☎ 50239
Banks Mild, Bitter [E]
Small, friendly, down-to-earth local ♪♣⚘[R]◔🌙🍴[S]♿

Sir Robert Peel
Jarrom Street (off A50)
☎ 540893
Morning opening: 11
Everard Burton Mild, Beacon, Tiger, Old Original
Bulmer Cider [H]
Victorian pub behind infirmary; cosy lounge
♪♣⚘◔ (Mon–Fri) 🍴[S]♿

Stirrup Cup
Thurncourt Road (off A47)
Evening opening: 6
Shipstone Mild, Bitter [H]
Large estate pub 🔥♪♣⚘🚗🍴

Tudor
100 Tudor Road
Opens at 11 am & 6 pm
Everard Burton Mild, Beacon, Old Original [H]
Comfortable modernised pub
♪♣⊞⚘🍴[S]♿

Littlethorpe 16B3

10.30–2; 5.30–10.30 (11 F, S)

Plough
Station Road
Opens at 11 am & 6 pm
Everard Burton Mild, Beacon, Tiger, Old Original [H]
Cosy thatched local
⌐♪♣⚘🚗[R]🍴[S]🚆

Long Whatton 16B1

10.30–2; 5.30–10.30 (11 F, S)

Royal Oak
26 The Green
Marston Burton Bitter, Pedigree [H]
Friendly village local
⌐♪♣⚘🚗🍴[S]

Loughborough 16B1

10.30–2; 5.30–10.30 (11 F, S)

Gate
Meadow Lane (B679)
Marston Mercian Mild, Pedigree [H]
Small, friendly and pleasantly modernised town pub 🔥♪♣⚘🍴

Old Pack Horse
Woodgate (off A6) ☎ 214590
Hardys & Hansons Best Mild,
Best Bitter Ⓗ
Small, popular pub
♪♣♨🅿🏠Ⓖ🕙⑧

Paget Arms
41 Oxford Street ☎ 239712
Everard Burton Mild, Beacon,
Tiger, Old Original
Bulmer Cider Ⓗ
Back street local, popular with
students ☂♪♣🅗♨Ⓖ🕙⑧

Peacock Inn
Factory Street (off A6)
Mitchells & Butlers Mild,
Springfield Bitter Ⓗ
One of a disappearing breed of
town pubs ♪♣🅡🕙⑧

Windmill
Sparrow Hill ☎ 216314
Opens at 11 am & 7 pm
Ansells Mild
Ind Coope Bitter,
Burton Ale Ⓗ
Oldest pub in town, near the
church 🏠♪♣🅡🕙⑧

Try also: **Blacksmiths Arms**
(Home); **Boat** (Marston)

Lyddington
16D3

12–2.30; 6.30–11
Marquis of Exeter
(Off A6003)
☎ Uppingham 2477
Bateman XXXB
Litchborough
Northamptonshire Bitter,
Tudor Ale
Ruddle Bitter, County Ⓗ
Smart, up-market pub/hotel
♪♨🅿🏠🅡Ⓖ➐⑧♨

Old White Hart
(Off A6003)
☎ Uppingham 3810
Opens 12–2; 7–11; closed
Mon & Tue lunchtimes except
bank holidays
Greene King XX, IPA, Abbot Ⓗ
Intimate old inn of character
♪♣♨🅡⑧

Market Harborough
16C3

11–2.30; 6–11
Cherry Tree
Kettering Road (A6)
Everard Burton Mild, Beacon,
Tiger, Old Original
Bulmer Cider Ⓗ
Pleasant thatched pub ♣♨🅡🕙⑧

Red Cow
High Street (A6)
Marston Burton Bitter,
Pedigree Ⓗ
Locals' pub with fine frontage
♣🕙⑧

Medbourne
16D3

11–2.30; 6–11
Neville Arms

Opens at 12 noon & 7 pm
Adnams Bitter
Hook Norton Best Bitter
Marston Pedigree
Ruddle Bitter, County Ⓗ
Impressive pub by stream
♣♨🅡Ⓖ➐⑧

Melton Mowbray
16D1

11–2.30; 6.30–10.30 (11 F, S)
Noels Arms
31 Burton Street ☎ 62363
Ansells Mild
Ind Coope Bitter, Burton Ale Ⓗ
Young, lively and friendly pub
🏠♪♣♨🅗🅡Ⓖ🕙⑧≋

Moira
16A2

10.30–2.30; 5.30–10.30 (11 F, S)
Ashby Woulds
Blackfordby Lane (Off B5003)
Everard Burton Mild, Beacon,
Tiger, Old Original Ⓗ
Modern pub on eastern edge
of village ♪♣🅿🏠Ⓖ♨

Mountsorrel
16B2

10–2; 5.30–10.30 (11 F, S)
Bull & Mouth
61 Leicester Road (A6)
☎ Leicester 374834
Opens at 10.30 am & 6 pm
Ansells Mild
Ind Coope Bitter Ⓗ
Pleasant old coaching inn
🏠♪♣♨🅡Ⓖ➐🕙⑧

Waterside Inn
Sileby Road (off A6)
☎ Leicester 302758
Opens at 10.30 am & 6 pm
Everard Old Original Ⓗ
Canalside pub and restaurant
in pleasant setting
♪♣♨🅡Ⓖ➐🕙⑧♨

Muston
26C8

10.30–2.30; 6–10.30 (11 F, S)
The Gap
Muston Gap (A52)
Marston Pedigree Ⓗ
Interesting, friendly
300-year-old pub 🏠♪♣🏠⑧♨

Nanpantan
16B1

10–2; 5.30–10.30 (11 F, S)
Priory
(B5350) ☎ Loughborough
216333
Home Mild, Bitter Ⓔ
Comfortable three-bar pub,
good service ♣🅗♨🅿🏠Ⓖ🕙⑧

North Luffenham
16E2

10.30–2.30; 6–11
Horse & Panniers
☎ Stamford 720091
Opens at 11.30 am & 7 pm
Everard Burton Mild, Beacon,
Tiger, Old Original Ⓗ
Excellent, refurbished village
local 🏠♪♣♨🅿🏠Ⓖ🕙⑧♨

Oadby
16C2

10–2; 5.30–10.30 (11 F, S)
Black Dog
London Road (A50)
☎ Leicester 712233
Banks Mild, Bitter Ⓔ
Friendly town local in
comfortable lounge
♪♣🅗♨🅿🏠Ⓖ🕙⑧

Oakham
16D2

10.30–2.30; 6–11
Wheatsheaf
Northgate (off A606) ☎ 3458
Everard Burton Mild, Beacon,
Tiger, Old Original
Bulmer Cider Ⓗ
Friendly local, well worth
finding ♪♣♨Ⓖ🕙⑧≋

Osgathorpe
16B1

10.30–2.30; 5.30–10.30 (11 F, S)
Royal Oak
Opens at 12 noon & 7 pm
Mitchells & Butlers Mild Ⓗ
Cosy, popular village inn
🏠♪♣♨🅿🅡

Packington
23H8

10.30–2.30; 5.30–10.30 (11 F, S)
Bull & Lion
☎ Ashby 413882
Marston Pedigree Ⓗ Owd
Rodger (winter) Ⓖ
Old coaching inn with real
atmosphere ♪♣♨🅿🏠🅡Ⓖ➐⑧♨♨

Peggs Green
16A1

10.30–2.30; 5.30–10.30 (11 F, S)
New Inn
(B587) ☎ Coalville 222293
Draught Bass
Mitchells & Butlers Mild Ⓗ
Country inn of character
🏠♪♣♨🅿🅡⑧♨

Plungar
26C8

10.30–2.30; 6–10.30 (11 F, S)
Anchor
(Off A52) ☎ Harby 60589
Opens at 11 am & 7 pm
Home Bitter Ⓗ
Locals' pub with collection of
cigarette cards and photos
♣🅗♨🅿Ⓖ➐🕙⑧

Preston
16D2

11–2.30; 6–11
Kingfisher
(A6003) ☎ Manton 256
Bateman XB
Marston Pedigree
Ruddle County Ⓗ
Smart travellers' pub with
games area 🏠♪♣♨🅿Ⓖ➐⑧

Quorn
16B2

10–2; 5.30–10.30 (11 F, S)
Blacksmiths Arms
Meeting Street (off A6)
Morning opening: 11
Marston Pedigree Ⓗ
Owd Rodger Ⓖ

Busy village pub with homely atmosphere 🔥Γ♪♣🛏✿🚗[R]🍺Ⓢ♿

Ryhall 17E2

10.30–2.30; 6–11

Green Dragon

(Off A6121) ☎ Stamford 53081
Evening opening: 7
Samuel Smith Old Brewery Bitter [H]
Pleasant pub in village square 🔥♪♣✿◔🍽 (not Sun)🍺Ⓢ

Saltby 26D9

11–2; 6–10.30 (11 F, S)

Nags Head

☎ Grantham 860491
Greene King IPA, Abbot [H]
Tastefully modernised free house 🔥♪♣🚗[R]🍽🍺Ⓢ

Shepshed 16B1

10–2; 5.30–10.30 (11 F, S)

Bull & Bush

61 Sullington Road
Opens at 10.30 am & 6.45 pm
Marston Mercian Mild, Pedigree, Merrie Monk, Owd Rodger [H]
Popular and friendly, a real community pub Γ♪♣✿🚗Ⓢ

Richmond Arms

Forest Street (off B5330)
Morning opening: 11.30
Draught Bass
Mitchells & Butlers Mild [H]
Friendly pub, renowned among mild drinkers Γ♪♣✿🍺Ⓢ

Sileby 16C2

10.30–2; 5.30–10.30 (11 F, S)

Free Trade Inn

Cossington Road ☎ 4494
Everard Burton Mild, Beacon, Tiger, Old Original
Bulmer Cider [H]
Thatched cottage pub 🔥♪♣✿🚗◔Ⓢ

Skeffington 16C2

10–2; 6–10.30 (11 F, S)

Fox & Hounds

(A47) ☎ Billesdon 250
Davenports Mild, Bitter [H]
Busy main-road pub, good food 🔥♣✿🚗[R]◔🍽 (not Sun)🍺Ⓢ♿

South Wigston 16C3

10–2; 5.30–10.30 (11 F, S)

Grand Hotel

Canal Street ☎ Leicester 782561
Opens 10.30 am & 5.45 pm
Shipstone Mild, Bitter [H]
Large, down-to-earth Victorian local ♪♣🚗[R]🍺

Stathern 16D1

10.30–2.30; 6–10.30 (11 F, S)

Red Lion

(Off A52/A607)
Opens at 11 am & 7 pm
Home Mild, Bitter [E]
Friendly backstreet village pub 🔥Γ♪♣🚗🍺Ⓢ

Swithland 16B2

11–2; 6–10.30 (11 F, S)

Griffin

☎ Woodhouse Eaves 890535
Everard Burton Mild, Beacon, Tiger, Old Original [H]
Pleasant village inn, friendly reception ♪♣🛏✿🚗[R]◔Ⓢ

Thrussington 16C2

10.30–2; 5.30–10.30 (11 F, S)

Blue Lion

Rearsby Road (off A46)
☎ Rearsby 266
Opens at 11 am & 6.30 pm
Ind Coope Bitter, Burton Ale [H]
Friendly pub packed full of curios ♪♣✿🚗◔ (not Sun) 🍽 (not Tue)🍺Ⓢ⛺

Thurmaston 16C2

10–2; 5.30–10.30 (11 F, S)

Harrow

635 Melton Road (off A47)
☎ 69679
Shipstone Mild, Bitter [H]
Refurbished local retaining excellent public bar Γ♪♣🚗[R]◔🍺Ⓢ

Tinwell 17E2

10.30–2.30; 6–11

Crown

☎ Stamford 2492
Opens at 11.30 am & 7 pm
Samuel Smith Old Brewery Bitter
Bulmer Cider [H]
Jovial landlord in popular village pub 🔥♪♣✿🚗◔🍽🍺Ⓢ

Tugby 16D2

10–2; 5.30–10.30

Fox & Hounds

Hallaton Road (off A47) ☎ 282
Morning opening: 11
Greene King XX, Abbot
Samuel Smith Old Brewery Bitter
Bulmer Cider [H]
Popular country free house with good restaurant; guest beer 🔥♪🚗[R]◔🍽🍺Ⓢ⛺

Tur Langton 16C3

10.30–2.30; 6–11

Bulls Head

(B6047) ☎ East Langton 373
Marston Pedigree
Ruddle Bitter, County [H]
Small, cosy village pub 🔥♪♣🛏✿🚗[R]◔🍽🍺Ⓢ♿⛺

Uppingham 16D3

11–2.30; 6–11

Exeter Arms

Leicester Road (off A47)
☎ 822900
Everard Beacon, Tiger, Old Original [H]
Low-ceilinged, multi-roomed pub with good atmosphere Γ♪♣✿[R]◔🍽🍺Ⓢ

Walcote 16B4

10.30–2.30; 5.30–11

Black Horse

(A427) ☎ Lutterworth 2684
Burton Bridge Bitter
Hook Norton Best Bitter
Hoskins Bitter
Whitbread Flowers Original Bitter [H]
Popular free house; guest beers 🔥♪♣🛏🚗[R]◔🍽

Whetstone 16B3

10.30–2; 5.30–10.30 (11 F, S)

Wheatsheaf

High Street ☎ Leicester 86491
Evening opening: 6
Ansells Mild
Ind Coope Bitter [H]
Locals' bar and comfortable lounge ♪♣✿🚗[R]◔ (Mon–Fri)🍺

Whissendine 16D2

10.30–2.30; 6–11

White Lion

Main Street (off A606) ☎ 233
Everard Beacon, Tiger, Old Original [H]
Welcoming pub in pleasant village Γ♪♣✿🚗■[R]◔Ⓢ

Whitwell 16E2

11–2.30; 6–11

Noel Arms

(A606) ☎ Empingham 334
Morning opening: 11
Marston Pedigree
Ruddle County
Samuel Smith Old Brewery Bitter [H]
Near Rutland Water 🔥✿🚗■[R]◔🍽🍺Ⓢ

Whitwick 16B2

10.30–2.30; 5.30–10.30 (11 F, S)

Waggon & Horses

Church Lane (B587)
Marston Pedigree [H]
Basic two-room boozer ♪♣🍺Ⓢ

Wymeswold 16C1

10.30–2; 6–10.30 (11 F, S)

Windmill

Brook Street ☎ 881074
Home Bitter [H]
Friendly country pub, boules popular 🔥Γ♣🛏✿🚗[R]◔🍽🍺Ⓢ♿

The 🔥 symbol denotes a pub with a real solid fuel fire

Alford 27G6

0–2.30; 6–10.30 (11 F, S)
Windmill
Market Place
Bass Mild, Brew Ten Ⓔ
Comfortable hotel in market
square ♪♣⚅🅰🅱Ⓡ🅘Ⓢ

Aswarby 26E8

0–2.30; 6.30–11
Tally Ho
(A15) ☎ Culverthorpe 205
Bateman XB
Hereward Bitter
Bulmer Cider Ⓗ
Friendly roadhouse;
accommodation in converted
outhouses ♠♪⚆🅰🅱Ⓖ🅘Ⓢ

Aubourn 26D6

0–2.30; 6–11
Royal Oak
☎ Bassingham 291
Bateman XB, XXXB
Samuel Smith Old
Brewery Bitter Ⓗ
Modernised local with good
atmosphere ♪♣⚆🅰Ⓖ🅘Ⓢ

Belchford 27F6

0.30–2.30; 6.30–11
Blue Bell
(Off A153) ☎ Tetford 602
Opens at 11 am & 7 pm;
closed Monday lunchtimes
Ind Coope Burton Ale Ⓗ
Comfortable village pub with
collection of old rural
implements
♠♪♣⚆🅰Ⓡ Ⓖ🅣 (not Mon)Ⓢ

Billingborough 27E8

10.30–2; 6.30–11
Fortescue Arms
27 High Street (B1177)
☎ Sleaford 240228
Ind Coope Bitter Ⓗ
Popular with young people;
ask for 'traditional'
🅰♪♣⚆🅰Ⓡ Ⓖ🅘Ⓢ

Billinghay 27F7

10–2.30; 6–11
Coach & Horses
Tattershall Road (A153)
☎ 860250
Home Mild, Bitter Ⓔ
Cheerful, friendly large
roadside pub 🅣♣⚅🅰♯⚆Ⓖ🅘Ⓢ

Binbrook 27F4

10.30–2.30; 6–10.30 (11 F, S)
Plough
Market Place (off B1203)
Bass Mild, Brew Ten Ⓗ
Comfortable, friendly village
local, renovated in open-plan
style ♪♣🅰🅘Ⓢ

Blyton 26D4

10.30–2.30; 6–10.30 (11 F, S)
Black Horse
High Street (A159)

Morning opening: 11
Bass Mild, Brew Ten Ⓗ
Comfortable village local
♪♣🅰🅰Ⓖ🅘Ⓢ

Boston 27G8

10.30–3; 6.30–11
Britannia
Church Street ☎ 65178
Opens at 11 am & 7 pm; open
until 4 pm Wednesdays
Bateman Mild, XB Ⓗ
Small and attractive old
town-centre pub ♪♣⚆Ⓖ🅘Ⓢ

Carpenters Arms
Witham Street ☎ 62840
Bateman Mild, XB Ⓗ
Small bustling backstreet local
🅰♪♣⚅🅰⚆🅰Ⓡ Ⓖ🅘Ⓢ

Duke of York
Lincoln Lane ☎ 63120
Opens at 11 am & 7 pm
Bateman Mild, XB Ⓗ
Popular old pub next to police
station 🅣♪♣⚆🅰ⒼⓈ

King William IV
Horncastle Road ☎ 61640
Evening opening: 6
Bateman Mild, XB Ⓗ XXXB Ⓖ
Popular and friendly local for
all ages 🅰♪♣⚆🅰Ⓖ🅘Ⓢ

New Inn
Pen Street ☎ 62835
Home Bitter Ⓔ
Mock-Tudor pub with
eccentric atmosphere
♪♣🅰Ⓖ🅘

Ship Tavern
Custom House Lane ☎ 62992
Bateman XB Ⓗ
Popular old town pub
♪♣⚆🅰Ⓖ🅘Ⓢ

Still
Market Place
Open until 4 pm Wednesdays
Shipstone Mild, Bitter
Bulmer Cider Ⓗ
Busy market pub ♪♣

Bourne 27E9

10–2; 5.30–11
Golden Lion
West Street ☎ 424591
Samuel Smith Old
Brewery Bitter Ⓗ
Popular town local with good
atmosphere 🅰♪♣⚆🅰Ⓖ🅘Ⓢ

Nags Head
Market Place ☎ 422095
Evening opening: 7
Ind Coope Bitter, Burton Ale Ⓗ
Friendly, multi-roomed town
pub 🅰♪♣⚆🅰Ⓡ🅘Ⓢ

Burgh le Marsh 27H6

10.30–2.30 (3 summer); 6–11
White Hart
(A158) ☎ Skegness 810321
Younger Scotch Bitter, IPA Ⓗ

Smart and friendly pub
🅰♪♣⚆🅰Ⓔ🅘Ⓢ

Castle Bytham 26D9

11–2; 6–11
Fox & Hounds
High Street (off A1)
Ind Coope Burton Ale Ⓗ
Small, friendly local known as
the 'Rathole' ♣🅰

Caythorpe 26D7

10.30–3; 6–11
Red Lion
High Street
Priory Pride, Ned Belcher
Bitter Ⓗ
Pleasant 17th-century pub
♣🅰⚆🅰🅘Ⓢ

Chapel St. Leonards 27H6

10.30–2.30 (3 summer); 6–11
Ship
Sea Road
Bateman Mild, XB, XXXB Ⓗ
Friendly atmosphere for locals
and tourists 🅰🅣♣🅰🅰

Coleby 26D7

10–2.30; 6–11
Bell
Fair Lane (off A607)
☎ Lincoln 810240
Samuel Smith Old
Brewery Bitter
Bulmer Cider Ⓗ
Modernised village pub with
excellent meals
🅰♪♣⚆🅰Ⓖ🅘Ⓢ

Tempest Arms
High Street
☎ Lincoln 810287
Ind Coope Burton Ale Ⓗ
Well-appointed village local
with fine views over Trent
valley ♪♣⚆🅰Ⓖ🅘Ⓢ

Coningsby 27F7

10–2.30; 6.30–11
Leagate Inn
Boston Road (B1192)
☎ 42370
Adnams Bitter
Greene King Abbot
Ruddle County
Shipstone Bitter Ⓗ
Old coaching inn with
secluded garden; guest beers
🅰♪♣⚆🅰Ⓖ🅘Ⓢ

White Bull
High Street (A153) ☎ 42439
Hardys & Hansons Best
Bitter Ⓔ
Busy, popular local with large
riverside garden
♪♣⚆🅰Ⓖ🅘Ⓢ

Corby Glen 26E9

10.30–2.30; 6.30–11
Woodhouse Arms
(A151)

Bateman Mild, XB, XXXB [H]
Roadside inn with attractive interior; occasional guest beers ♪♣✿🚗◔🍖🍷Ⓢ

Croft 27H7

10.30–2.30 (3 summer); 6–11
Old Chequers
Lymn Bank
Bateman Mild, XB, XXXB [H]
Quaint pub with large open-range fire 🔥👪♣✿🚗🍷⛺

East Ferry 26C4

10.30–2.30; 6.30–10.30 (11 F, S)
Emerald Arms
High Street (A159)
☎ Laughton 522
Opens at 12 noon & 7 pm
Manns Bitter [H]
Only pub in this remote Trentside village
👪♪♣⊞✿🚗◔🍖🍷Ⓢ♿

Edenham 26E9

11–2.30; 6–11
Five Bells
Main Street (A151) ☎ 235
Samuel Smith Old Brewery Bitter [H]
Pleasant village pub with restaurant ♪♣✿🚗[R]◔🍖🍷Ⓢ

Folkingham 27E8

11.30–2; 6.30–11
New Inn
West Street (off A15) ☎ 371
Hardys & Hansons Best Mild, Best Bitter [H]
Pleasant renovated inn
🔥♪♣✿🚗[R]◔🍖🍷

Fosdyke 27G8

10.30–3; 7–11
Ship
Main Road (A17) ☎ 628
Bateman Mild, XB [H]
Popular roadside pub with nautical decor ♪♣✿🚗◔🍖Ⓢ

Freiston 27G8

10.30–3; 6.30–11
Kings Head
Church Road (off A52)
Bateman Mild, XB [H]
Unspoilt village local
🔥♪♣✿🚗◔🍖🍷Ⓢ

Fulbeck 26D7

11–2.30; 7–11
Hare & Hounds
(A607) ☎ Loveden 72441
Bateman XB, XXXB [G]
Old stone-built coaching inn
♪♣✿🚗🛏[R]🍖🍷Ⓢ

Gainsborough 26C5

10–2.30; 6–10.30 (11 F, S)
Horse & Groom
1 Beaumont Street ☎ 3388
Open until 4 pm Tuesdays
Tetley Mild, Bitter [H]
Large hotel with enthusiastic landlord 🔥👪♪♣🚗🛏[R]Ⓢ🚉

Grantham 26D8

11–3; 6.30–11
Angel & Royal
High Street ☎ 5816
Evening opening: 6
Draught Bass
Ruddle County [H]
Historic coaching inn; note fireplace and masonry
✿🚗🛏[R]◔🍖🍷Ⓢ

Chequers
Butchers Row, Market Place
☎ 76383
Evening opening: 6
Everard Tiger, Old Original
Marston Burton Bitter, Pedigree, Owd Rodger
Younger No. 3
Bulmer Cider [H]
Busy town pub, popular with young people; regular guest beers 🔥♪♣[R]🍷Ⓢ

Granby
Market Place
Evening opening: 6; open until 4 pm Sats
Home Mild, Bitter [E]
Popular market-place pub
♪♣🚗🍷

Shirley Croft Hotel
Harrowby Road (off A52)
☎ 3260
Evening opening: 6
Bateman XB, XXXB [H]
Interesting Victorian hotel in own grounds, comfortable lounge 👪♪♣✿🚗🛏[R]◔🍖Ⓢ

Try also: Cherry Tree; Five Bells; Kings Hotel; Nags Head

Harlaxton 26D8

10.30–3; 6–11
Gregory Arms
Grantham Road (A607)
☎ Grantham 4587
Home Mild, Bitter [E]
Welcoming roadside pub
♪♣✿🚗[R]◔🍷Ⓢ

Heckington 27E8

10.30–2.30; 6.30–11
Royal Oak
Boston Road (A17)
Samuel Smith Old Brewery Bitter [H]
Pleasant and comfortable village pub 🔥♪♣✿🚗[R]🍷Ⓢ♿

Heighington 26E6

10–2.30; 6–11
Butcher & Beast
Fen Road
Opens at 11 am & 7 pm
Bateman XB [H]
Modernised 19th-century village local ♪♣[R]🍷Ⓢ

Hemingby 27F6

10.30–2.30; 6.30–11
Coach & Horses
(Off A158)
Bateman Mild, XB [H]
Smart one-bar pub
🔥♪♣✿🚗Ⓢ

Holbeach 27G

10.30–3; 6–11
Bell
High Street (A151)
☎ 23223
Open until 4 pm Thursdays
Elgood Bitter [H]
Welcoming town-centre hote
♪♣🛏◔🍖 (not Wed) Ⓢ

Holdingham 26E

10–2.30; 6–11
Jolly Scotchman
(A15) ☎ Sleaford 304864
Manns Bitter [H]
Friendly country pub
🔥👪♪♣✿🚗◔🍖Ⓢ

Horncastle 27F

10–2.30; 6.30–11
Bull Hotel
Bull Ring ☎ 3331
Bass Mild, Draught Bass [H]
Market town hotel, popular with locals
♪🚗🛏[R]🍖Ⓢ

Fighting Cocks
West Street
Darley Dark, Thorne Best Bitter [H]
Colourful and unpretentious local; rare brew for the count
🔥👪♪♣✿🚗[R]🍷Ⓢ

Ingham 26D

10–2.30; 5.30–11
Black Horse
The Green (off B1398)
☎ Lincoln 730214
Samuel Smith Old Brewery Bitter [H]
Typical village local with comfortable lounge
♪♣✿🚗◔🍖🍷Ⓢ

Windmill
(B1398)
Bass Mild, Brew Ten, Draught Bass [H]
Unpretentious and relaxed; starting point for Burton Hun
🔥♪♣✿🚗🍷Ⓢ⛺

Keelby 27F

11–2.30; 7–10.30 (11 F, S)
Kings Head
(Off A18)
Bass Mild, Draught Bass [H]
Village local with caring landlord
♣🚗🍷

Kirton 27F

10.30–3; 6.30–11
Peacock
High Street (A16)
☎ Boston 722427
Manns Bitter [H]
Cosy lounge and bustling bar
🔥👪♪♣⊞✿[R]◔🍖🍷Ⓢ

Lincolnshire

Langrick 27F7

10–2.30; 6.30–11

Ferry Boat
Ferry Road (B1192) ☎ 273
Home Bitter Ⓔ
Smart old inn near River
Witham ♪♣♨🅰
🌂 (not Mon, Tue, Thu)🍴

Leadenham 26D7

10–2.30; 6–10.30 (11 F, S)

George
(A17) ☎ Loveden 72251
Ruddle Bitter, County Ⓗ
Large hotel with more than
400 whiskies
♪♣🅷♨🅰🅻🆁🅖✆🛇

Lincoln 26D6

11–3; 5.30–11

City Vaults
Alfred Street
Ward Best Mild, Sheffield Best
Bitter Ⓗ
Genuine old-fashioned ale
house off the High Street ⌜♣⒳🍴

Cornhill Vaults
Cornhill (off High Street)
☎ 35113
Open until 4 pm Fridays
Samuel Smith Old
Brewery Bitter Ⓗ
Old corn cellar serving good
food ♪🅷🆁🅖🌂🍴≉

Golden Eagle
21 High Street ☎ 21058
Opens at 12 noon (11
summer) & 6.30 pm
Bateman Mild, XB, XXXB Ⓗ
Bateman's only tied house in
the city ♪♣♨🅰🆁🅸🛇🅻≉

Jolly Brewer
Broadgate
Evening opening: 7; closed
Sunday lunchtimes
Bateman XB
Draught Bass
Everard Tiger
Hardys & Hansons Best Bitter
Bulmer Cider Ⓗ
1930s-style free house with
Wurlitzer and murals
🅰♪♣🅖≉

Lindum Hotel
Broadgate ☎ 24081
Bateman XXXB
Ward Sheffield Best Bitter Ⓗ
Small, pleasant city-centre
hotel ♪♣🔲🍴≉

Queen in the West
Moor Street (off A57)
Ward Best Mild, Sheffield Best
Bitter
Bulmer Cider Ⓗ
Tastefully modernised street
corner local ♪♣🅸≉

Roebuck
310 High Street ☎ 28400
Shipstone Mild, Bitter Ⓗ
City-centre pub with friendly
atmosphere ♪♣🅷🆁🅖🛇≉

Small Beer
(off-licence)
91 Newland Street West
(Off A57) ☎ 28628
Opens 12 noon (10.30 am
Sat)–10.30 pm
Bateman XXXB
Everard Old Original
Taylor Landlord
Ward Sheffield Best Bitter Ⓗ
Symond Cider Ⓖ
Guest beers at all times

Stags Head
68 Newport (A15) ☎ 34495
Evening opening: 6
Home Mild, Bitter Ⓔ
Large, straightforward pub
♣🅰🆁🅖🛇🍴

Strugglers
83 Westgate
Bass Mild, Draught Bass Ⓗ
Busy, basic and bursting with
people ♣🍴

Treaty of Commerce
High Street
Evening opening: 6.30
Ind Coope Bitter, Burton Ale
Paine XXX, St. Neots Bitter,
EG Ⓗ
Welcoming pub with
discounts Wednesday
evenings; one Paine beer
available at a time ♪♣🅖🍴≉

White Hart
(Orangery)
Bailgate ☎ 26222
Bateman XB, XXXB
Samuel Smith Old Brewery
Bitter Ⓗ
Casablanca with an
astrodome, attached to THF
hotel ⌜🔲🆁🅖🌂

White Horse
21 Hungate
Manns Bitter
Watney Fined Stag Bitter Ⓗ
Popular city pub with sporting
connections ♪♣🅖🛇≉

Long Bennington 26D8

11.30–3; 6 (7 S)–11

Royal Oak
High Street (off A1)
☎ Loveden 81733
Marston Pedigree Ⓖ
Friendly, popular local
♪♣♨🅰🆁🛇🌂

Long Sutton 27G9

10.30–3; 7–11

Bull
Market Place (A17)
☎ Holbeach 362258
Open until 4 pm Fridays
Draught Bass Ⓗ
Superb, rambling old hotel;
delightful anachronism from
an earlier age
🅷🅰🔲🆁🅖🌂🍴🛇

Louth 27G5

11–3; 6.30–11

Malt Shovel
Northgate
Open until 4 pm Wed & Fri
Bateman Mild, XB Ⓗ
Unpretentious pub 🅰♪♣🍴

Turks Head
Aswell Street
Open until 4 pm Wed & Fri
Ward Best Mild, Sheffield Best
Bitter Ⓔ
Quiet, straightforward pub 🆁🍴

Wheatsheaf
Westgate
Draught Bass Ⓗ
Fine 17th-century inn near
historic church
♨🅰🅖🛇

Maltby-le-Marsh 27H5

11–2.30; 6–11

Crown
(A1104)
Evening opening: 7
Bateman Mild Ⓔ XB,
XXXB Ⓔ & Ⓗ
Cosy, ivy-covered pub with
nautical decor
🅰♣♨🅰🛇🅰

Mareham-le-Fen 27F7

10–2.30; 6.30–11

Royal Oak
Main Street (A115) ☎ 203
Bateman Mild, XB, XXXB Ⓗ
Attractive thatched country
pub, good food
♪♨🅰🅖🛇

Market Deeping 17F2

10–2; 5.30–11

Bull
Market Place ☎ 343320
Opens at 11 am & 6 pm
Everard Tiger, Old Original Ⓗ
A gem – voted 1980 pub of
the year by local CAMRA
branch 🅰🔲🆁🅸🛇

Market Rasen 27E5

10.30–2.30 (4 Tue); 6.30–11

Red Lion
King Street ☎ 842424
Younger Scotch Bitter, IPA,
No. 3 Ⓗ
Tasteful pub with friendly
service
♪♣🅰🅖🛇🅸🛇≉

Marshchapel 27G4

10–2.30; 6–10.30 (11 F, S and summer)

Greyhound
Seadyke Way (A1031)
☎ 267
Bateman Mild, XB, XXXB Ⓔ
Small and comfortable
♪♣🅰🅖🛇🛇

Moulton Marsh

27G9

10.30–3; 6–11
Hare & Hounds
Red Cow Drove (off A17)
Home Mild, Bitter Ⓗ
Isolated old local on marshes
🅰♪♣🅟🅐

Nettleham

26E6

10–2.30; 5.30–11
Plough
The Green ✆ Lincoln 750275
Evening opening: 6
Bateman Mild, XB Ⓗ
Comfortable, welcoming
village pub ♪♣🅟♪🅟🅖Ⓢ

North Hykeham

26D6

11–2.30; 6–11
Lincoln Green
Lincoln Road (off A46)
✆ Lincoln 688258
Home Mild, Bitter Ⓔ
Large, popular pub with
comfortable lounge
♪♣🅟🅖🅐

North Thoresby 27F4

10–2.30; 6–10.30 (11 F, S and summer)
New Inn
Station Road (off A16)
Bass Mild, Draught Bass Ⓗ
Friendly village local catering
for all tastes ♣🅟🅐

Old Bolingbroke

27G6

10.30–2.30; 6–11
Black Horse
Mill Lane ✆ East Kirkby 300
Bateman Mild, XB Ⓗ
Friendly village pub opposite
castle ruins 🅰♪♣🅟🅐🅟Ⓢ

Old Leake

27G7

10.30–3; 6.30–11
White Hart
Church Road (B1184)
✆ Boston 870286
Bateman Mild, XB Ⓗ
Attractive, friendly village pub
🅰♪♣🅟🅐🅡🅖🅐Ⓢ🅐

Rippingale

27E9

11–2; 7–11
Bull
High Street (off A15)
✆ Dowsby 652
**Samuel Smith Old Brewery
Bitter** Ⓗ
Comfortable, friendly village
pub 🅰♪♣🅟🅐🅡🅖🅐Ⓢ🅐

Rothwell

27F4

10.30–2.30; 6–10.30 (11 F, S)
Nickerson Arms
Near Caistor (off A46)
✆ Swallow 300
**Adnams Bitter
Bateman XXXB**

Everard Beacon, Tiger, Old
Original
Taylor Landlord
Tetley Mild, Bitter Ⓗ
Popular village pub, 6 real ales
always available
♪♣🅐🅟🅟🅐🅡🅖🅐Ⓢ

Ruskington

27E7

10.30–2.30; 6–11
Black Bull
Rectory Road (B1188)
✆ 832270
Bateman XB Ⓗ
Friendly village local;
excellent meals ♪♣🅐🅐

Saracen's Head 27G9

10.30–3; 6–11
New Saracen's Head
Washway Road (A17)
Greene King Abbot Ⓗ
Welcoming roadside inn
🅰♪♣🅗🅟🅐Ⓢ

Scamblesby

27F5

10.30–2.30; 6.30–11
Green Man
Old Main Road (off A153)
✆ Stenigot 282
Bateman Mild, XB, XXXB Ⓗ
Old pub near Cadwell Park,
interesting handpumps
🅰♪♣🅐🅡🅖🅐Ⓢ🅐🅐

Scotton

26D4

10.30–2.30; 6–10.30 (11 F, S)
Three Horseshoes
Westgate (off A159)
Bass Mild, Brew Ten Ⓗ
Sensitively renovated village
local 🅰♪♣🅟🅐

Skegness

27H6

10.30–3 (2.30 winter); 6–11
Shades
Lumley Road
Shipstone Mild, Bitter Ⓔ
Traditional town local ♪♪♣🅟♪

Vine
Vine Road, off Drummond
Road ✆ 3018
Bateman Mild, XB Ⓗ
Comfortable hotel with
Tennyson connections
🅰♪🅐🅐🅖🅐Ⓢ

Skendleby

27G6

10.30–2.30; 6–11
Blacksmiths Arms
Spilsby Road
Bateman XB Ⓗ
Gem of a pub – picturesque
and welcoming 🅐🅐

Sleaford

26E7

10–2.30; 6–11
Waggon & Horses
Eastgate ✆ 303388
Opens at 10.30 am & 6.30 pm
Draught Bass Ⓗ

Busy open-plan pub
♪♣🅟🅖Ⓢ

South Kyme

27F7

10.30–2.30; 6.30–11
Hume Arms
(B1395)
✆ Billinghay 860620
Opens at 11 am & 7 pm
Bateman XB Ⓗ
Attractive, friendly village pub
♪♣🅟🅖🅐♪

South Rauceby 26E8

10.30–2.30; 6.30–11
Bustard Arms
Tom Lane (off A153)
**Draught Bass
Ruddle County** Ⓗ
Village pub with genuine
Italian food; regular guest
beers ♪🅟🅐🅡🅖♪Ⓢ

Spalding

27F9

10.30–3 (4 Tue); 6–11
Bull
Churchgate ✆ 67749
Evening opening: 7
Home Mild, Bitter Ⓗ
Large, modern pub facing
River Welland ♪♣🅟🅐🅖🅐Ⓢ
🅐 (overnight only)

Olde White Horse
Churchgate ✆ 3529
**Samuel Smith Old
Brewery Bitter** Ⓔ
Thatched, 15th-century pub
near High Bridge 🅰♪♣🅐🅖♪Ⓢ

White Hart
Market Place ✆ 5668
Evening opening: 7
**Bateman XB
Greene King Abbot** Ⓗ
Large old THF hotel
♪🅟🅐🅡🅖♪Ⓢ

Spilsby

27G6

10–2.30 (3 summer); 6–11
Bull
Halton Road (B1195)
✆ 52240
Bateman Mild, XB, XXXB Ⓗ
Large, comfortable pub with
snooker table; beer sometimes
on gravity ♪♣🅐🅖🅐♪Ⓢ🅐

George Hotel
Market Place ✆ 52528
Home Mild, Bitter Ⓗ & Ⓔ
Pleasant hotel, popular with
locals ♪♣🅗🅐🅡🅖♪🅐Ⓢ

Stamford

17E2

10–2.30; 6–11
Hurdler
93 Newcross Road ✆ 63428
Opens at 11 am & 6.30 pm
**Everard Burton Mild, Beacon,
Tiger, Old Original** Ⓔ
Good estate pub near fire
station ♪♣🅟🅖🅐♪🅐Ⓢ

Jolly Brewer
Foundry Road

Samuel Smith Old Brewery Bitter
Bulmer Cider Ⓗ
One-room pub, known locally
as 'the brewery' ♠♪♣✦♠Ⓖ☺Ⓢ

Northfields
Drift Road ☎ 2689
Morning opening: 11
Home Bitter Ⓔ
Estate pub with long alley
skittles ♠♪♣✦♠ⓇⓁⓈ

Scotgate Inn
Scotgate ☎ 52901
Opens at 11 am & 7 pm
**Samuel Smith Old
Brewery Bitter**
Bulmer Cider Ⓗ
Melbourn's showpiece, live
jazz Wednesdays
ⓕ♪♣♠Ⓖ☺Ⓢ♦

Victoria
Ryhall Road
**Samuel Smith Old Brewery
Bitter** Ⓗ
Victorian free house near
hospital ♪♣✦♠Ⓢ♦

Stickford 27G7
10–2.30; 6–11
Red Lion
Main Road (A16)
☎ Stickney 488
Home Bitter Ⓗ
Attractive, pleasant village
pub ♠♪♣✦♠Ⓐ Ⓖ☺Ⓢ

Stow 26D5
10.30–2.30; 7.30–11
Cross Keys
Lunchtime opening: 11–2
**Theakston Best Bitter, Old
Peculier**
Ward Sheffield Best Bitter Ⓗ
Pleasant, popular country
local ♠♪♣✦♠ⓇⒾⓈ

Surfleet 27F9
10.30–3; 6.30–11
Crown
Gosberton Road (A16) ☎ 466
Bateman XB Ⓗ
Pleasant village local with
cosy snug ♠♪♣✦♠ⒶⒾⓇⓈ

Swineshead
Bridge 27F8
10.30–3; 6.30–11
Barge
(A17/A1121)
☎ Boston 820267
Home Bitter Ⓗ
Smart, popular hotel
♪♣♠✦♠Ⓖ☺ⓉⒾⒶ⚡

Tetford 27G6
10–2; 6.30–11
White Hart
East Street ☎ 255
Morning opening: 12 noon
Bateman XXXB
Ind Coope Bitter Ⓗ

Friendly, rural hotel in heart
of Tennyson country
♠♪♣✦♠ⓇⒼⓉⒾⓈ

Thorpe St. Peter 27H7

10.30–2.30; 6–11
Three Tuns
Culvert Road
Bateman Mild Ⓗ
Friendly fishermen's pub
♠♣✦♠Ⓐ⚡

Throckenholt 17G2

10–2.30; 6–11
Four Horseshoes
South Eau Bank
(B1166, off A47)
Closes 1 pm lunchtimes,
re-opens 7
Elgood Bitter Ⓖ
Totally unspoilt local with
post office in shed ♠♠♠⚡

Uffington 17F2

10–2; 5.30–11
Gainsborough Lady
Main Street (A16) ☎ Stamford
52540
Opens at 10.30 am & 6 pm
**Samuel Smith Old
Brewery Bitter** Ⓗ
Comfortable pub catering for
all ages ♪♣✦♠ⓇⒼⓉⒾⓈ

Waddingham 26D4

11–2.30; 6–10.30 (11 F. S)
Marquis of Granby
High Street (B1205, off A15)
**Ward Best Mild, Sheffield Best
Bitter** Ⓗ & Ⓔ
Small, friendly country pub
♠♪♣✦♠Ⓡ⚡

Wainfleet 27H7

10.30–3 (2.30 winter); 6–11
Royal Oak
High Street
☎ Skegness 880328
Bateman XB Ⓗ
Attractive and friendly, once
part of Bethlehem Hospital for
the insane ♠♪♣✦♠Ⓖ⚡

Washingborough 26E6

10–2.30; 6.30–11
Washingborough
Hall
Church Hill ☎ Lincoln 790340
Adnams Bitter
Bateman Mild, XB Ⓗ
Friendly hotel with regular
guest beers
♠♣✦♠ⒶⒾⓇⒼⓉⓈ

Welby 26D8

10.30–3; 7–11
Crown & Anchor
(Off B6403) ☎ Loveden 30307
Ind Coope Bitter Ⓗ
Cosy pub in picturesque
village ♪♣✦♠ⓇⒼ⚡Ⓢ

Welton 26E5

10–2.30; 6.30–11
Black Bull
The Green ☎ 60220
Ind Coope Bitter Ⓗ
Old coaching inn with
excellent meals
♣✦♠ⒼⓉⒾⓈ

Wigtoft 27F8

10.30–3; 6.30–11
Golden Fleece
Main Road (A17)
☎ Sutterton 484
Bateman Mild, XB Ⓗ
Comfortable and friendly
village local ♪♣✦♠ⓇⒼⒾⓈ

Wilsford 26E8

11–3; 6–11
Plough
Main Road (A153)
☎ Loveden 30304
Opens 12–2.30, re-opens 7
Bass Mild, Draught Bass Ⓗ
Small, friendly village pub
♠♪♣✦♠Ⓖ⚡ⒾⓈⒶ

Witham on the
Hill 26E9

11–2.30; 6–11
Six Bells
(Off A6121) ☎ 246
**Samuel Smith Old Brewery
Bitter** Ⓗ
Pleasant country local
♪♣✦♠⚡Ⓢ

Withern 27G5

11–2.30; 6–11
Red Lion Hotel
Vyner Road (A157) ☎ 50365
Winter evening opening: 6.45
Home Mild, Bitter Ⓗ
Large pub, ideal for families
ⓕ♪♣✦♠ⒶⒾⓇⒼ⚡Ⓢ

Woodhall Spa 27F6

10–2.30, 6.30–11
Gamecock
Stanhope Avenue (off B1151)
Bateman XB Ⓗ
Friendly, mock-Tudor local
ⓕ♣⚡Ⓐ

Wragby 27E5

10–2.30; 6–11
Adam & Eve
Market Place (A158)
☎ 858207
Younger Scotch Bitter Ⓗ
Friendly old pub with pleasant
bar ♠♪♣✦♠ⓇⒼ⚡Ⓢ

Wrangle 27G7

10.30–3; 6.30–11
Coach & Horses
Main Road (A52)
☎ Boston 870901
Bateman Mild, XB Ⓗ
Welcoming, comfortable
country pub
♠♪♣✦♠Ⓖ⚡Ⓢ

As the map above shows, Greater London is divided into clear geographical regions: Central (consisting of the postal districts EC1, EC2, EC3, EC4, WC1, WC2, W1 & SW1), East, North, North West, South East, South West and West. Within each region areas are arranged in ascending order of postal districts (E1, E2, etc), followed by the outlying areas that do not have postal numbers. Visitors to London should note that adjacent postal districts away from the centre rarely have adjacent numbers. To walk from N1 to N2, for example, would take up a major part of the evening's drinking time.

The second thing that the visitor should beware of is the overpricing of beer in some pubs. London prices are higher than in the rest of the country anyway, but it is not impossible to pay 20 pence above the normal price of a pint in certain pubs, with free houses usually being the worst offenders. Your only effective course of action in such a case is to vote with your feet and choose another pub where the landlord is not quite so avaricious. There are around 3000 real beer pubs in London, so you shouldn't have too far to walk.

From being one of the worst areas in which to get a decent pint during the depths of the Red Revolution, London has become among the best. For those who wish to make an exhaustive investigation of London pubs, the local guide *Real Beer in London* and its 1983 supplement provide details on enough pubs to keep even the most hardened pub crawler occupied for at least twelve months. *Real Beer in London* and guides to real beer in many other parts of the country can be obtained direct from CAMRA, details on page 321.

Central London

EC1: City

11.30–3; 5.30–11
Hand & Shears
1 Middle Street 9H2
Courage Best Bitter, Directors [H]
Small, friendly historic pub
♪♣[R]◔🍷[S]

Olde Mitre
Ely Court, Ely Place 9G2
Closes at 10.30 pm except Fridays, closed weekends
Friary Meux Bitter
Ind Coope Burton Ale [H]
400-year-old pub hidden behind Hatton Garden ⚘🍷[S]

EC3: City

11.30–3; 5–11
Lamb Tavern
10 Leadenhall Market 9J2
Closes at 7.30 pm Mon–Fri; closed weekends
Draught Bass
Wethered Bitter
Young Bitter, Special Bitter, Winter Warmer [H]
Victorian Market pub ♣🍷[S]

EC4: City

11.30–3; 5–11
Olde Cheshire Cheese
Wine Office Court
145 Fleet Street 9G2
Closes at 9 pm; closed weekends
Marston Pedigree, Merrie Monk [H]
Busy historic pub ⚘[R]◔◗

WC1: Bloomsbury 8C2

11–3; 5.30–11
Lamb
94 Lamb's Conduit Street
Young John's Ale, Bitter, Special Bitter, Winter Warmer [H]
Historic pub with snob screens
⚘◔◗[S]

WC1: Kings Cross 8C1

11–3; 5.30–11
Prince Albert
2 Acton Street
Truman Prize Mild, Bitter, Best Bitter, Sampson Hanbury's Extra Strong [H]
Large, comfortable award-winning pub ♪♣⚘◔◗[S]♿🚉

WC2: Charing Cross 8E5

11–3; 5.30–11
Ship & Shovel
2 Craven Passage
Adnams Bitter
Brakspear Special Bitter
Ruddle Bitter, County
Young Bitter [H]
Popular free house; occasional discount beers ⚘◔[S]🚉

WC2: Covent Garden 8C2

11–3; 5.30–11
Marquess of Anglesey
39 Bow Street
Closed Sundays
Young John's Ale, Bitter, Special Bitter, Winter Warmer [H]
Busy corner pub ◔◗[S]

WC2: St. Giles 8C2

11–3; 5.30–11
Angel
61 St. Giles High Street
Courage Best Bitter, Directors [H]
Historic pub with reputedly haunted cellar ♣⚘◔[S]

W1: Marylebone 8B2

11–3; 5.30–11
Angel
37 Thayer Street
Samuel Smith Old Brewery Bitter [H]
Popular pub with upstairs bar
♪♣⚘[R]◔◗[S]

Devonshire Arms
21a Devonshire Street
Friary Meux Bitter
Ind Coope Burton Ale [H]
Friendly local ♪♣◔[S]

Prince Regent
71 Marylebone High Street (off A501) ☎ 01-935 2018
Charrington IPA
Mitchells & Butlers Springfield Bitter [H]
Festooned with bric-a-brac
◔◗ (Mon–Fri)

W1: Mayfair 8D5

Red Lion
1 Waverton Street
Manns IPA
Ruddle County
Watney London Bitter, Fined Stag Bitter
Webster Yorkshire Bitter [H]
Historic pub in quiet side street; Mayfair prices ⚘◔◗[S]

W1: Soho 8B2

Star & Garter
62 Poland Street
Courage Best Bitter, Directors [H]
Small, busy pub off Oxford Street [R]◔[S]

SW1: Belgravia 8D5

11–3; 5.30–11
Antelope
22 Eaton Terrace (off A3217)
Benskins Bitter
Ind Coope Burton Ale
Taylor Walker Mainline [H]
Unspoilt haven in select area
◔ (Mon–Sat) ◗ (Mon–Fri)

Star Tavern
6 Belgrave Mews West
Fuller Chiswick Bitter, London Pride, ESB [H]
Popular unpretentious mews pub 🏠♣◔[S]

SW1: Chelsea 8D5

11–3; 5.30–11
Royal Court Tavern
8 Sloane Square (A3217)
☎ 01-730 9191
Ruddle Bitter
Samuel Smith Old Brewery Bitter
Wadworth 6X
Wethered Bitter [H]
Plush, dimly-lit bar attached to hotel ♪⚘■[R]◔[S]

SW1: Pimlico 8D5

11–3; 5.30–11
Fox & Hounds
29 Passmore Street
Saturday evening opening: 6
Charrington IPA
Draught Bass [H]
Small, lively one bar local; beer and wine licence only ♣[S]

Rising Sun
44 Ebury Ridge Road
Young John's Ale, Bitter, Special Bitter, Winter Warmer [H]
Busy local near Victoria Coach Station ♣⚘◔🍷[S]

SW1: Westminster 8E5

11–3; 5.30–11
Buckingham Arms
62 Petty France
Saturday evening opening: 7
Young John's Ale, Bitter, Special Bitter, Winter Warmer [H]
Popular pub with one long bar, near passport office ◔◗[S]

Red Lion
48 Parliament Street
Ind Coope Burton Ale
Taylor Walker Bitter, Mainline [H]
Ornate pub with cellar bar and upstairs restaurant ♪[R]◔◗[S]

East London

E1: Stepney Green 9F5

11–2.30; 5–11
Fish & Ring
141a White Horse Road
Fuller London Pride
Wells Bombardier
Samuel Smith Old Brewery Bitter [H]

Comfortable and friendly corner local ♪♫♣♠⑧

E1: Whitechapel
9E5

11–2.30; 5–11
Lord Nelson
230 Commercial Road
Charrington IPA
Draught Bass
Mitchells & Butlers Springfield Bitter Ⓗ
Friendly pub with restored Victorian interior ♫♪♣♥Ⓖ♥⑧

E2: Bethnal Green
9E5

11–2.30; 5–11
Approach Tavern
47 Approach Road
Courage Directors
Everard Old Original
Webster Yorkshire Bitter Ⓗ
Lively, friendly local; range may vary ♠♣Ⓡ⑧≋

Marksman
254 Hackney Road (A1208)
Everard Tiger, Old Original
Godson Best Bitter Ⓗ
Welcome respite from keg and disco pubs, guest beers ♪Ⓖ

E3: Bromley-by-Bow
9F5

11–2.30; 5–11
Pearly King
94 Bromley High Street
Beach Pearly Bitter, Best Bitter
Greene King Abbot
Samuel Smith Old Brewery Bitter
Young Bitter Ⓗ
Renovated pub in traditional style ♫♪Ⓡ

E4: Chingford
9F3

11–3; 5.30–10.30 (11 F, S)
Larkshall
Larkshall Road (B160, south of New Road) ✆ 01-524 6026
Courage Best Bitter,
Directors Ⓗ
Interesting mix of styles in renovated pub ♪♠Ⓔ♥♠⑧≋

E5: Clapton
9E4

11–2.30; 5–11
Anchor & Hope
5 High Hill Ferry
Fuller London Pride, ESB Ⓗ
Small and busy riverside pub ♠Å

E7: Forest Gate
9F4

11–3; 5.30–10.30 (11 F, S)
Railway Tavern
73 Forest Lane
Ind Coope Burton Ale
Taylor Walker Bitter,
Mainline Ⓗ
Small, quiet lunchtime pub Ⓖ⑧≋

Travellers Rest
12 Cemetery Road
Charrington IPA Ⓗ
Isolated graveyard pub with characterful clientele ♫♪♣♠

E8: London Fields
9E4

11–2.30; 5–11
Lady Diana
95 Forest Road
Adnams Bitter
Fuller London Pride
Greene King Abbot
Samuel Smith Old Brewery Bitter
Young Bitter, Special Bitter Ⓗ
Friendly, plush one-bar pub in up-and-coming suburb ♪♠♥⑧

E9: Homerton
9E4

11–2.30; 5–11
Chesham Arms
15 Mehetabel Road
Fuller London Pride
Pitfield Hoxton Heavy
Samuel Smith Old Brewery Bitter
Wethered Bitter Ⓗ
Lively youngsters' boozer ♪

Tiger
245 Wick Road
Young John's Ale, Bitter,
Special Bitter, Winter Warmer Ⓗ
Large, friendly, renovated pub ♪♠Ⓖ♥⑧

White Lion
331 Wick Road
Truman Prize Mild, Best Bitter, Sampson Hanbury's Extra Strong Ⓗ
Three-bar pub with unusual pre-war decor ♠♠Ⓖ

E10: Leyton
9F4

11–3; 5.30–10.30 (11 F, S)
Holly Bush
32 Grange Road
Ind Coope Burton Ale
Taylor Walker Bitter,
Mainline Ⓗ
Friendly pub with excellent public bar ♪♠♥⑧⑧

E11: Leytonstone
9F4

11–3; 5.30–10.30 (11 F, S)
Colegrave Arms
145 Cann Hall Road (A11)
Charrington IPA Ⓗ
Friendly pub with saloon, private and public bars ♪♠♥

E11: Wanstead
9F4

11–3; 5.30–10.30 (11 F, S)
Nightingale
51 Nightingale Lane
Courage Best Bitter,
Directors Ⓗ
Small, interesting two-bar pub off the high street ♪♥♥

E12: Manor Park
9F4

11–3; 5.30–10.30 (11 F, S)
Avenue Hotel
90 Church Road
Charrington IPA Ⓗ
Large, traditional pub ♪♠♥

E13: Canning Town
9F5

11–3; 5.30–10.30 (11 F, S)
Red House
299 Barking Road
Truman Prize Mild, Bitter, Best Bitter, Sampson Hanbury's Extra Strong Ⓗ
Busy establishment with varied bars ♫♪♠♥

E14: Limehouse
9F5

11–2.30; 5.30–11
Grapes
76 Narrow Street
Ind Coope Burton Ale
Taylor Walker Bitter,
Mainline Ⓗ
Historic riverside pub ♥Ⓖ

E14: Poplar
9F5

11–2.30; 5.30–11
Falcon
202a East India Dock Road
Saturday evening opening: 7
Truman Best Bitter, Sampson Hanbury's Extra Strong Ⓗ
Small, friendly pub with original exterior ♪♠Ⓖ♥⑧

E14: Stepney
9F5

11–2.30; 5.30–11
Queens Head
8 Flamborough Street
(off A13)
Evening opening: 5
Young John's Ale, Bitter,
Special Bitter, Winter Warmer Ⓗ
Popular local ♪♠Ⓖ♥⑧

E15: Stratford
9F4

11–3; 5.30–10.30 (11 F, S)
Princess of Wales
25 West Ham Lane
Ind Coope Burton Ale
Taylor Walker Bitter,
Mainline Ⓗ
Quiet sidestreet pub ♪♠♥≋

Railway Tavern
131 Angel Lane
Opens 6 am–8 am Mon–Sat
Charrington IPA
Draught Bass Ⓗ
Friendly, local with breakfast session for early risers and night workers ♪♠Ⓖ⑧≋

E16: North Woolwich
9G5

11–3; 5.30–10.30 (11 F, S)
Ram Tavern

26 North Woolwich Road
Truman Bitter, Best Bitter Ⓗ
Full-blooded East End local ♪♣

E17:
Walthamstow 9F4

11–3; 5.30–10.30 (11 F, S)
Flowerpot
128 Wood Street
Draught Bass Ⓗ
Friendly local with good mix
of regulars ♪♣≉

Barking 9G4

11–3; 5.30–10.30 (11 F, S)
Crooked Billet
River Road, Creekmouth (off
A13) ℰ 01-594 2623
Charrington IPA Ⓗ
Friendly local ♨♪♣♫♠Ⓖ♥Ⓢ

Barkingside 9G4

11–3; 5.30–10.30 (11 F, S)
Doctor Johnson
175 Longwood Gardens
(Off A406/A123)
**Courage Best Bitter,
Directors** Ⓗ
Large, straightforward
suburban local ♪♣♫♠Ⓘ♥♥

Cranham 9J4

10–2.30; 6–10.30 (11 F, S)
Thatched House
384 St Mary's Lane (B187)
Morning opening: 10.30
**Charrington IPA
Draught Bass** Ⓗ
Unusual, friendly 1930's
country pub ♨♪♣♫♠ⒾⒼ

Hornchurch 9H4

10–2.30; 6–10.30 (11 F, S)
Harrow
130 Hornchurch Road
(A124)
Romford Brewers Bitter Ⓗ
Cosy, friendly pub with large
garden ♪♣♫♠Ⓘ♥Ⓢ

Rainham 9H5

10.30–2.30; 6–10.30 (11 F, S)
Bell
The Broadway (B1337)
**Ind Coope Burton Ale
Romford Brewers Bitter** Ⓗ
Stylish local with restaurant
♪♣♫♠ⒾⒼ♥Ⓢ♠≉

Romford 9H4

10–2.30; 6–10.30 (11 F, S)
Royal Oak
90 Victoria Road (off A125)
**Charrington IPA
Draught Bass
Mitchells & Butlers Springfield
Bitter** Ⓗ
Friendly local threatened by
road development ♪♣♠Ⓢ≉

Upminster 9H4

10–2.30; 6–10.30 (11 F, S)
White Hart

Hacton Lane (off A124)
**Charrington IPA
Draught Bass
Mitchells & Butlers Springfield
Bitter** Ⓗ
Popular and friendly country
pub ♨♪♣♫♠Ⓖ♥ (Sat only)

Woodford Bridge
9F3

11–3; 5.30–10.30 (11 F, S)
Crown and Crooked
Billet
13 Cross Road (B173)
**Charrington IPA
Mitchells & Butlers Springfield
Bitter** Ⓗ
Friendly pub facing a pleasant
green ♪♣♠Ⓢ

Woodford Green 9F3

11–3; 5.30–10.30 (11 F, S)
Castle
393 High Road (A104)
**Truman Bitter, Best Bitter,
Sampson Hanbury's Extra
Strong
Bulmer Cider** Ⓗ
Well-appointed house in
Georgian style ♪♣♫Ⓖ♥Ⓢ

Travellers Friend
496 High Road (A104)
**Draught Bass
Ridley Bitter
Young Special Bitter** Ⓗ
Delightful pub with snob
screens Ⓖ

North London

N1 : Canonbury 8E4

11–3; 5.30–11
Marquess Tavern
32 Canonbury Street
**Young John's Ale, Bitter,
Special Bitter, Winter
Warmer** Ⓗ
Pleasant pub near new River
Walk ♨♣Ⓖ♥Ⓢ♠≉

N1 : Hoxton 9E5

11–3; 5.30–11
Prince Arthur
49 Brunswick Place
Saturday evening opening: 8
Shepherd Neame Bitter Ⓗ
Friendly backstreet pub ♪♣Ⓢ≉

N1 : Islington 8E4

11–3; 5.30–11
Malt & Hops
33 Caledonian Road (A5203)
**Boddingtons Bitter
Felinfoel Double Dragon
Gibbs Mew Wiltshire Bitter,
Premium Bitter, Bishops
Tipple
Marston Pedigree
Samuel Smith Old Brewery
Bitter
Wadworth 6X** Ⓗ
Wedge-shaped pub with dark
interior ♪Ⓢ≉

Swan Tavern
125 Caledonian Road (A5203
**Charrington IPA
Draught Bass** Ⓗ
Interesting bric-a-brac in both
bars ♪♣ⓇⒼ♥♠≉

N2 : East Finchley
8D4

11–3; 5.30–11
Five Bells
165 East End Road (A504,
off A1000) ℰ 01-883 1714
**Truman Bitter, Best Bitter,
Sampson Hanbury's Extra
Strong** Ⓗ
Friendly, welcoming pub with
large garden
♪♣♫♠Ⓖ♥

Welch Brothers
130 High Road (A1000)
**Greene King Abbot
Wadworth 6X
Young Special Bitter
Bulmer Cider** Ⓗ
Twelve handpumps serve ever
changing range ♪♣ⒼⓈ♠

N2 : Fortis Green
8D4

11–3; 5.30–11
Clissold Arms
**Courage Best Bitter,
Directors** Ⓗ
Quiet pre-war pub ♣♠Ⓡ♥

N6 : Highgate 8E4

11–3; 5.30–11
Duke's Head
16 Highgate High Street
(B519)
**Charrington IPA
Draught Bass** Ⓗ
Quiet and cosy ♪Ⓢ

Victoria
28 North Hill (off A1)
**Wethered Bitter, Special
Bitter, Winter Royal
Whitbread Flowers
Original Bitter** Ⓗ
Pleasant local ♫ⒼⓈ

N7 : Holloway 8E4

11–3; 5.30–11
Leighton Arms
101 Brecknock Road (A5200)
**Taylor Walker Bitter,
Mainline** Ⓗ
Large, one-bar pub with spiral
staircase ♪♣♫ⓇⒼ♥Ⓢ♠

N8 : Hornsey 8E4

11–3; 5.30–11
Princess Alexandra
Park Road
**Ruddle County
Watney London Bitter, Fined
Stag Bitter
Webster Yorkshire Bitter** Ⓗ
Ornamented country pub with
two gardens
♪♫♠Ⓖ♥Ⓢ♠

N9: Lower Edmonton 9E3

10.30–2.30; 5.30–10.30 (11 F, S)
Rising Sun
240 Winchester Road (off A10)
Taylor Walker Bitter ⊞
Large, out-of-the-way pub
♣♫�''♠♪

N16: Stoke Newington 9E4

11–3; 5.30–11
Rose & Crown
199 Church Street (B104)
Truman Prize Mild, Bitter,
Best Bitter, Sampson
Hanbury's Extra Strong ⊞
Bulmer Cider Ⓖ
Attractive wood-panelled pub
by Clissold Park ♣☺Ⓢ

N17: Tottenham 9E4

10.30–2.30; 5.30–10.30 (11 F, S)
Chequers
641 High Road (A10)
Charrington IPA
Draught Bass ⊞
Plush one-bar local near
Spurs FC ♪♣♫☺Ⓢ≉

N22: Wood Green 8E4

10.30–2.30; 5.30–10.30 (11 F, S)
Nags Head
203 High Road
Charrington IPA
Draught Bass ⊞
Large, roomy lounge,
collection of racehorse
paintings ♪Ⓡ☺♫Ⓢ≉

Barnet 8D3

10.30–2.30; 5.30–10.30 (11 F, S)
Alexandra
35 Wood Street,
Chipping Barnet (A411)
Morning opening: 11
Truman Prize Mild, Bitter,
Best Bitter, Sampson
Hanbury's Extra Strong ⊞
Always full of life ♠♫☺Ⓢ

Sebright Arms
Alston Road, Chipping
Barnet (A471)
McMullen AK, Country
Bitter ⊞
Cheerful local ♣♠🚻Ⓢ

Enfield 8E3

10.30–2.30; 5.30–10.30 (11 F, S)
Cricketers
9 Chase Side Place (off A110)
McMullen Country Bitter ⊞
Tucked-away lively pub
♣♫🚻☺♫🚹

New Barnet 8D3

10.30–2.30; 5.30–10.30 (11 F, S)
Builders Arms

---

3 Albert Road (A110)
Greene King KK, IPA, Abbot ⊞
Rebuilt and doubled in size –
well worth finding ♣♫☺🚹≉

Ponders End 9E3

10.30–2.30; 5.30–10.30 (11 F, S)
Falcon
115 South Street (off A1010)
Draught Bass
Mitchells & Butlers Springfield
Bitter ⊞
Entrance guarded by
25-pounder gun ♪♣

Whitewebbs 9E2

10.30–2.30; 5.30–10.30 (11 F, S)
King & Tinker
Whitewebbs Lane (off A10)
Taylor Walker Bitter,
Mainline ⊞
Popular, historic pub
♣♫🚹🅰

North-west London

NW1: Camden Town 8D5

11–3; 5.30–11
Victoria
2 Mornington Terrace
Adnams Bitter
Fuller London Pride
Greene King Abbot
Hall & Woodhouse
Badger Best Bitter
Samuel Smith Old
Brewery Bitter
Whitbread Castle Eden Ale ⊞
Busy backstreet Whitbread
free house ♪♣♫Ⓡ☺♫Ⓢ

NW1: Marylebone 8B2

11–3; 5.30–11
Gloucester Arms
5 Ivor Place
Ind Coope Burton Ale
Taylor Walker Bitter,
Mainline ⊞
♣≉

NW3: Hampstead 8D4

11–3; 5.30–11
Rosslyn Arms
48 Rosslyn Hill (A502)
Courage Best Bitter,
Directors ⊞
Down-to-earth local, unusual
for Hampstead ♣Ⓢ

Wells Hotel
Well Walk (off A502)
Fremlins Tusker
Wethered Bitter
Whitbread Castle Eden Ale,
Flowers Original Bitter
Bulmer Cider ⊞
Busy old pub, completely
revamped ♫♣♫☺

NW5: Kentish Town 8D4

11–3; 5.30–11
Pineapple
51 Leverton Street (off A400)
Ind Coope Burton Ale
Taylor Walker Bitter,
Mainline ⊞
Traditional local ♫♣♠≉

NW6: Kilburn 8D5

11–3; 5.30–11
Coopers Arms
164 Kilburn High Road (A5)
Closes 10.30 pm
Charrington IPA
Draught Bass ⊞
Unique character for area
♪♣♫≉

NW7: Mill Hill 8C3

10.30–2.30; 5.30–10.30 (11 F, S)
Railway Tavern
129 Hale Lane (off A5109)
Truman Prize Mild, Bitter,
Best Bitter, Sampson
Hanbury's Extra Strong ⊞
Well-run, busy local, miles
from railway
♪♣♫🚻☺🚹

NW8: St. John's Wood 8D5

11–3; 5.30–11
Princess Royal
11 Circus Road (off A41)
Charrington IPA ⊞
Handy for Lords ♣♫

Rossetti
23 Queen's Grove
Fuller London Pride, ESB ⊞
Pre-Raphaelite 'trattoria'
with restaurant ♫🚹☺♫

Pinner 8B4

10.30–2.30; 5.30–10.30 (11 F, S)
Oddfellows Arms
2 Maxwell Lane (off A404)
Ind Coope Burton Ale
Benskins Bitter ⊞
Comfortable one-bar pub
♣☺Ⓢ

Rayners Lane 8B4

10.30–2.30; 5.30–10.30 (11 F, S)
Rayners Hotel
Village Way East (A4090)
Truman Prize Mild, Bitter,
Best Bitter, Sampson
Hanbury's Extra Strong ⊞
Pleasant three-bar local
♫♣♠Ⓡ🚻🅸Ⓢ

Sudbury Hill 8C4

10.30–2.30; 5.30–10.30 (11 F, S)
Black Horse
1018 Harrow Road (A4008)
Ind Coope Burton Ale
Taylor Walker Bitter,
Mainline ⊞
Friendly pub ♫♣♫🚹☺🅸≉

South-east London

SE1: Bermondsey
9E5

11–3; 5.30–11
Sultan
238 St. James's Road
Evening opening: 6 (7.45 Sat)
Shepherd Neame Bitter, Special Bitter, Stock Ale [H]
Friendly local ♪♣[R]◔Ⓢ

SE1: London Bridge
8E5

11–3; 5.30–11
Globe
8 Bedale Street
Saturday opening: 6.30–8.30 pm; closed rest of weekend
Brakspear Special Bitter
Ruddle County [H]
Basic pub in Borough Market ſ♪♣[R]◔🍺Ⓢ🚆

Leather Exchange Tavern
15 Leather Market Street
Fuller Chiswick Bitter, London Pride, ESB [H]
Happy hour in mid-evening session ♪[R]◔Ⓢ

SE1: Southwark
8E5

11–3; 5.30–11
Founders Arms
52 Hopton Street
Young John's Ale, Bitter, Special Bitter [H]
New, comfortable pub on riverside development 🌹◔◗Ⓢ

SE1: Waterloo
8E5

11–3; 5.30–11
Anchor & Hope
39 The Cut
Saturday evening opening: 7
Wells Eagle Bitter, Bombardier [H]
Friendly local pub, recently extended ♪♣◔🍺Ⓢ🚆

Kings Arms
25 Roupell Street
Saturday evening opening: 8
Ind Coope Burton Ale
Taylor Walker Bitter, Mainline [H]
Friendly backstreet pub with bottle collection ♪♣◔🍺Ⓢ🚆

SE3: Blackheath
9F6

11–3; 5.30–11
British Oak
109 Old Dover Road (off A2/A207)
Courage Best Bitter, Directors [H]
Spacious two-bar pub ♣🌹◔◗🍺Ⓢ

Railway Tavern
16 Blackheath Village
Friary Meux Bitter
Ind Coope Burton Ale
Taylor Walker Mainline [H]
Stylishly modernised pub 🌹[R]◔◗ (summer) 🍺Ⓢ🚆

SE5: Camberwell
8E5

11–3; 5.30–11
Station Tavern
18 John Ruskin Street (off A215)
Charrington IPA [H]
Quiet (station closed 1916), unspoilt 3-bar pub 🔥ſ♪♣[R]🍺Ⓢ

SE10: Greenwich
9F5

11–3; 5.30–11
Cricketers
22 King William Walk (A206)
Charrington IPA [H]
Cricket memorabilia ♪♣🍺Ⓢ

North Pole
131 Greenwich High Road (A206) ☎ 01-858 0815
Saturday opening: 12 and 7
Adnams Bitter
Arkell BBB
Godson Black Horse
Greene King Abbot [H]
Busy pub, guest beers ♪♣[R]◔Ⓢ🚆

Richard I (Tolly)
52/54 Royal Hill (off A206)
Saturday evening opening: 7
Young John's Ale, Bitter, Special Bitter, Winter Warmer [H]
Small, popular local ♣🌹◔🍺Ⓢ

Royal George
2 Blissett Street (off A2211)
Saturday evening opening: 7
Shepherd Neame Best Bitter [H]
One-bar pub with collection of bric-a-brac ♪◔

SE13: Ladywell
9F6

11–3; 5.30–11
Jolly Farmers
354 Lewisham High Street (A21)
Fremlins Bitter, Tusker
Wethered Bitter
Whitbread Flowers Original Bitter [H]
Lively Whitbread free house ♪♣🌹◔Ⓢ🚆

SE15: Nunhead
9E6

11–3; 5.30–11
Man of Kent
2 Nunhead Green
Truman Bitter, Best Bitter [H]
Popular local with interesting bric-a-brac ♪♣🍺Ⓢ

Old Nun's Head
15 Nunhead Green (Off A2214)
Saturday evening opening: 7
Charrington IPA
Draught Bass [H]
Tudor exterior hides warm, friendly pub ♪♣[R]◔🍺Ⓢ

SE16: Rotherhithe
9F5

11–3; 5.30–11
Blacksmiths Arms
257 Rotherhithe Street
OS 366802 ☎ 01-237 1249
Fuller Chiswick Bitter, London Pride, ESB [H]
Large, three-bar gem ſ♪♣◔🍺Ⓢ

Ship
39 St. Marychurch Street
Adnams Bitter
Arkell BBB
Courage Directors
Marston Pedigree
Moorhouse Premier Bitter [H]
Friendly, backstreet free house; guest beers ſ♪♣🌹Ⓢ

SE16: Surrey Docks
9E5

11–3; 5.30–11
Prince of Orange
118 Lower Road (A200)
Opens 12.30–3; 7–12
Truman Prize Mild, Bitter, Best Bitter, Sampson
Hanbury's Extra Strong [H]
One of London's leading jazz venues – nightly ſ♪🌹[R]◔◗Ⓢ

SE18: Woolwich
9G5

11–3; 5.30–11
Lord Derby
89 Walmer Terrace
Saturday evening opening: 7
Courage Best Bitter, Directors [H]
Homely, well-run three-bar pub ♪♣🌹[R]◔🍺Ⓢ🚆

Princess of Wales
18 Wilmount Street
Saturday evening opening: 6
Wethered Bitter [H]
Friendly family local in centre of Woolwich 🔥ſ♪♣▦[R]Ⓢ🚆

SE19: Upper Norwood
9E6

10.30–2.30; 5.30–10.30 (11 F, S)
Royal Albert
42 Weston Hill
Charrington IPA
Draught Bass [H]
Splendid array of jugs in saloon bar ♪♣🌹◔🍺Ⓢ

SE20: Penge
9E6

10.30–2.30; 5.30–10.30 (11 F, S)
Golden Lion
61 Maple Road (off A213)
Fuller London Pride, ESB
Young Bitter, Special Bitter [H]
Busy free house popular with young; guest beers ♪♣🌹◔Ⓢ

SE22: East Dulwich
9E6

11–3; 5.30–11
Crystal Palace Tavern
193 Crystal Palace Road
**Ind Coope Burton Ale
Taylor Walker Bitter** H
Busy local with contrasting
bars ♪♣♦☺

SE25: South Norwood
9E7

10.30–2.30; 5.30–10.30 (11 F, S)
Albert Tavern
65 Harrington Road
**Courage Best Bitter,
Directors** H
Tastefully refurbished local
♪♣♦☺☺≢

Goathouse
2 Penge Road ✆ 01-778 5752
**Fuller Chiswick Bitter, London
Pride, ESB** H
Lively house with occasional
modern jazz ♪♣♦♠☺♠☺

SE25: Woodside
9E7

10.30–2.30; 5.30–10.30 (11 F, S)
Joiners Arms
50 Woodside Green (B243)
Ind Coope Bitter H
Aladdin's cave of ornamental
brasses in saloon ♪♣♦♠☺☺≢

SE26: Sydenham
9E6

11–3; 5.30–11
Bricklayers Arms
189 Dartmouth Road (A2216)
**Young John's Ale, Bitter,
Special Bitter, Winter
Warmer** H
Basic, friendly local ♪♣♦

Dulwich Wood House
39 Sydenham Hill (off A212)
**Young John's Ale, Bitter,
Special Bitter, Winter
Warmer** H
Popular pub near Crystal
Palace Park; garden bar with
electric pump ♠♣♦♠☺♠☺♠♠

Addiscombe
9E7

10.30–2.30; 5.30–10.30 (11 F, S)
Cricketers
47 Shirley Road
**Courage Best Bitter,
Directors** H
Large, popular pub ♦♠☺☺

Beckenham
9F7

10.30–2.30; 5.30–10.30 (11 F, S)
Olde George Inn
High Street (A232)
**Ind Coope Burton Ale
Taylor Walker Bitter,
Mainline** H

Weatherboarded pub with
open-plan bar ♠♠☺☺

Belvedere
9G5

10–2.30; 6–11
Victoria
2 Victoria Street (of A206)
**Charrington IPA
Draught Bass** H
Corner pub with a warm
welcome ♪♠☺

Bexley
8G6

10.30–2.30; 6–11
Black Horse
63 Albert Road (off A222)
**Courage Best Bitter,
Directors** H
Cosy friendly local ♪♣♦♠☺≢

Bexleyheath
9G6

10.30–2.30; 6–11
Kings Head
5 Market Place
**Courage Best Bitter,
Directors** H
Old and popular ♪♣♦♠

Bromley
9F7

10.30–2.30; 5.30–10.30 (11 F, S)
Bricklayers Arms
143 Masons Hill (A21)
Shepherd Neame Bitter H
Recently refurbished
street-corner pub ♣♠☺

Freelands Tavern
31 Freelands Road
**Courage Best Bitter,
Directors** H
Excellent suburban local
♪♣♦☺

Chelsfield
9G7

10.30–2.30; 6–10.30 (11 F, S)
Five Bells
Church Road (off A224)
**Courage Best Bitter,
Directors** H
Traditional weatherboarded
Kent pub ♣♦♠☺

Chislehurst
9G6

10.30–2.30; 5.30–10.30 (11 F, S)
Bull's Head
Royal Parade (A208)
**Young John's Ale, Bitter,
Special Bitter** H
Winter Warmer H & G
Large ivy-clad pub with
restaurant ♠♠♠♠☺☺

Imperial Arms
Old Hill (off A223)
**Courage Best Bitter,
Directors** H
Welcoming hillside pub ♪♣♦

Croydon
8E7

10.30–2.30; 5.30–10.30 (11 F, S)
Dog & Bull
24 Surrey Street (off A23)
**Young John's Ale, Bitter,
Special Bitter, Winter
Warmer** H
Street market pub ♪☺

Duke of Cambridge
7 Holmesdale Road
Charrington IPA H
Friendly back street local,
strong darts following ♪♣☺

Royal Standard
1 Sheldon Street (off A23)
Fuller London Pride H **ESB**
Bulmer Cider G
Oasis of tradition in Croydon's
office desert ♠♣♦♠♠☺♠≢

Downe
9F8

10.30–2.30; 5.30–10.30 (11 F, S)
George & Dragon
High Street
**Charrington IPA
Draught Bass** H
The natural selection; Charles
Darwin lived nearby ♣♦♠♠

Erith
9H5

10–2.30; 6–11
Brewers Arms
22 Brook Street ✆ 38292
Morning opening: 11
Truman Bitter, Best Bitter H
Small pub with live music
most nights ♪♣♦♠

Footscray
9G6

10–2.30; 6–11
Seven Stars
High Street (A211)
**Charrington IPA
Mitchells & Butlers Springfield
Bitter** H
Interesting historic pub,
varied clientele ♪♣♦♠♠♠♠♠

Sidcup
9G6

10–2.30; 6–11
Alma
Alma Road (off A222)
**Courage Best Bitter,
Directors** H
Deservedly popular suburban
pub ♪♣♦♠♠☺≢

Thornton Heath
8E7

10.30–2.30; 5.30–10.30 (11 F, S)
Prince of Wales
2 Parchmore Road
**Ind Coope Burton Ale
Taylor Walker Bitter,
Mainline** H
Blue-painted jazz pub near
clocktower ♠♪♣♠♠☺☺≢

South-west London

SW4: Clapham
8B6

11–3; 5.30–11
Jolly Gardeners
115 St. Alphonsus Road
(off A2217)
Saturday evening opening: 6
**Charrington IPA
Draught Bass** H
Small pub; well worth finding
♠♪♣♠♠♠☺♠

Tim Bobbin

1 Lillieshall Road
Manns IPA
Watney London Bitter, Fined
Stag Bitter
Webster Yorkshire Bitter Ⓗ
Highly decorated outside,
comfortable within ♪♣

SW5: Earls Court
8D5

11–3; 5.30–11
Great British Beer Factory

148 Old Brompton Road
Adnams Bitter
Boddingtons Bitter
Everard Tiger, Old Original
Godson Black Horse
Ruddle County
Truman Best Bitter, Sampson
Hanbury's Extra Strong
Bulmer Cider Ⓗ
Specialises in discount pints ♪Ⓖ

SW6: Parsons Green
8D6

11–3; 5.30–11
Duke of Cumberland

235 New Kings Road
Young John's Ale, Bitter,
Special Bitter, Winter
Warmer Ⓗ
Popular Edwardian pub ♣ⒼⓎⓈ

White Horse

1 Parsons Green
Charrington IPA
Draught Bass
Mitchells & Butlers Springfield
Bitter Ⓗ
Large, friendly pub facing
green ♪♪♣ⓎⓇⒼ♈Ⓢ

SW6: West Brompton
8D5

11–3; 5.30–11
Atlas

16 Seagrave Road (off A3218)
Truman Bitter, Best Bitter Ⓗ
Popular local behind Earls
Court exhibition hall ♨♪♣ⓇⓎ

SW7: South Kensington
8D5

11–3; 5.30–11
Anglesea Arms

15 Selwood Terrace (off A308)
Saturday evening
opening: 6.30 (winter)
Adnams Bitter
Brakspear Special Bitter
Greene King Abbot
Ruddle County
Young Special Bitter Ⓗ
Busy drinking establishment,
bank of 6 handpumps ⓎⒼⓈ

SW8: South Lambeth
8E6

11–3; 5.30–11
Surprise

Southville
Young John's Ale, Bitter,
Special Bitter Ⓗ
Lovely little pub ♪♣Ⓨ

SW9: Brixton
8E6

11–3; 5.30–11
Railway Hotel

20 Atlantic Road (off A23)
Manns IPA
Ruddle County
Webster Yorkshire Bitter Ⓗ
Busy backstreet three-bar
local ♪♪♣ⒼⓎⓈ♉♈≩

SW11: Clapham Junction
8D6

11–3; 5.30–11
Beehive

197 St. Johns Hill (A3036)
Fuller London Pride, ESB Ⓗ
Small and busy; but friendly
and welcoming ♪♣ⒼⓈ≩

SW12: Balham
8D6

11–3; 5.30–11
Duke of Devonshire

39 Balham High Road
Saturday evening opening: 7
Young John's Ale, Bitter,
Special Bitter, Winter
Warmer Ⓗ
Expensively redecorated, but
retaining atmosphere
♣ⓎⓇⒼⓎⓈ

SW15: Putney
8D6

11–3; 5.30–11
Bricklayers Arms

32 Waterman Street
Ruddle County
Watney London Bitter, Fined
Stag Bitter
Webster Yorkshire Bitter Ⓗ
Unchanged, young persons'
pub of great character ♪♣ⓎⓈ

Jolly Gardeners

61 Lacy Road (off A219)
Fuller London Pride, ESB Ⓗ
Well-run pub off the beaten
track ♨♪♣Ⓨ ⓖⓎⓈ

SW16: Streatham
8E6

11–3; 5.30–11
Leigham Arms

1 Wellfield Road (off A23)
Charrington IPA Ⓗ
Popular busy 'village' local
♪♣ⓎⓈ

Pied Bull

498 Streatham High Road
(Off A23) ℂ 01-764 4003
Young John's Ale, Bitter,
Special Bitter, Winter
Warmer Ⓗ
Well-run pub with five bars
♣Ⓨ♉ⒼⓎ≩

SW17: Earlsfield
8D6

11–3; 5.30–11
Leather Bottle

538 Garratt Lane (A217)
Young John's Ale, Bitter,
Special Bitter Ⓗ
Traditional bar and busy
saloon ♣Ⓨ♉Ⓢ

SW17: Tooting
8D6

11–3; 5.30–11
Prince of Wales

646 Garratt Lane (A217)
Young John's Ale, Bitter,
Special Bitter Ⓗ
Boisterous pub ♪♣ⓇⓎⓎ♉ⓇⓈ

SW18: Wandsworth
8D6

11–3; 5.30–11
Brewery Tap

68 High Street ℂ 01-870 2894
Saturday evening opening: 7
Young John's Ale, Bitter,
Special Bitter Ⓗ
Good beer as it should be
♪♣ⓇⒼ♈Ⓢ

SW19: Merton
8D6

11–2.30; 5.30–11
Princess Royal

25 Abbey Road (off A24)
Saturday evening opening:
6.30 (winter)
Courage Best Bitter,
Directors Ⓗ
Tastefully refurbished, well
managed local ♪♣ⓎⒼⓎ♉

Trafalgar

23 High Path
Closes 10.30 pm Mon–Thu,
Saturday evening opening: 7
Charrington IPA
Fuller London Pride
Gale HSB
Mitchells & Butlers Springfield
Bitter Ⓗ
Two tiny, contrasting bars
♪♣♉Ⓢ

SW19: Wimbledon
8D6

11–3; 5.30–11
Alexandra

33 Wimbledon Hill Road
(A219)
Young John's Ale, Bitter,
Special Bitter, Winter
Warmer Ⓗ
Popular pub, recently saved
from demolition ♣♈Ⓖ♉Ⓢ

Carshalton
8D?

10.30–2.30; 5.30–10.30 (11 F, S)
Greyhound

2 High Street (A232)
ℂ 01-647 1511
Young John's Ale, Bitter,
Special Bitter, Winter
Warmer Ⓗ
Large 18th-century house
♣Ⓨ♈ⒾⓇⒼ♈Ⓢ♉≩

Sun

4 North Street (off A232)
Ind Coope Bitter, Burton Ale Ⓗ
Outstanding value for both
beer and food ♣ⓇⒼⓎⓈ♉≩

Cheam 8D7

10.30–2.30; 6.30–10.30 (11 F, S)
Prince of Wales
28 Malden Road (off A232)
Friary Meux Bitter
Ind Coope Burton Ale H
Popular two-bar pub, good
lunchtime food ♪♣♀☺♿&

Kingston 8C7

10.30–2.30; 5.30–10.30 (11 F, S)
Kingston Mill
High Street (A307)
Arkell BBB, Kingsdown Ale
Gibbs Mew Premium Bitter,
Bishops Tipple H
Riverside free house, fine range
of real bottled beers ♪♪♣☺

Norbiton
16 Clifton Road (off A308)
Manns IPA
Ruddle County
Watney London Bitter, Fined
Stag Bitter
Webster Yorkshire Bitter
Bulmer Cider H
Comfortable lounge and lively
bar; good food ♪♣♀☺♿➊☺

Ram
34 High Street (A307)
Courage Best Bitter,
Directors H
Comfortable pub near
riverside ♪♣♀☺☺&

Wych Elm
93 Elm Road
Fuller Chiswick Bitter, London
Pride, ESB H
Refurbished backstreet local
♪♣♀➊☺

Mitcham 8D7

11–3; 5.30–11
Windmill
Commonside West (A236)
Ind Coope Burton Ale
Taylor Walker Bitter H
Small friendly pub on
Mitcham Common ♪♀&

New Malden 8C7

10.30–2.30; 5.30–10.30 (11 F, S)
Woodies
Thetford Road (off A3)
Fuller London Pride
Greene King IPA, Abbot
Samuel Smith Old Brewery
Bitter H
Taunton Cider G
Pleasant free house set in its
own grounds ♨♪♣♀♿☺☺

Richmond 8C6

11–3; 5.30–11
Angel & Crown
5 Church Court
Fuller Chiswick Bitter, London
Pride, ESB H
In one of Richmond's
delightful alleys ♪♪☺☺➎

White Cross Hotel
Water Lane ✆ 01-940 0909
Evening opening: 6
Young John's Ale, Bitter,
Special Bitter, Winter
Warmer H
Attractive riverside pub
☒♀☺☺➊☺

Surbiton 8C7

10.30–2.30; 5.30–10.30 (11 F, S)
Railway Tavern
1 Ewell Road (A240)
Draught Bass
Brakspear Bitter, Special Bitter
King & Barnes Festive
Oak Best Bitter, Old Oak
Samuel Smith Old
Brewery Bitter H
Free house with wide range,
cheap for the area ♪♀☺☺➎

Sutton 8D7

10.30–2.30; 5.30–10.30 (11 F, S)
New Town
7 Lind Road ✆ 01-642 0032
Young John's Ale, Bitter,
Special Bitter, Winter
Warmer H
Plush multi-level lounge;
popular, traditional bar ♣☺➊☺

West London

W2: Paddington
8D5

11–3; 5.30–11
Queens Railway
Tavern
15 Chilworth Street (off
A4206) ✆ 01-723 5918
Friary Meux Bitter
Ind Cooper Burton Ale H
Comfortable pub, in side street
♪♣☺☺➎

W3: Acton 8C5

11–3; 5.30–10.30 (11 F, S)
Red Lion &
Pineapple
281 High Street (A4020)
Fuller Chiswick Bitter, London
Pride, ESB H
Three-bar pub with tree in
saloon ♣♀☺☺

W4: Acton Green
8C5

11–3; 5.30–10.30 (11 F, S)
Swan
119 Acton Lane (off B490)
Sat evening opening: 6.30
Charrington IPA
Draught Bass H
Busy corner local with village
atmosphere ♣♀☺➊

W4: Chiswick 8C5

11–3; 5.30–10.30 (11 F, S)
George IV
185 Chiswick High Road
(A315) ✆ 01-994 4624
Fuller London Pride, ESB H

Large two-bar house
♨♪♣♀♀☺☺➊☺

W5: Ealing 8C5

11–3; 5.30–10.30 (11 F, S)
Red Lion
13 St. Mary's Road (A3001)
Closes 2.30 pm Mon–Fri
Fuller Chiswick Bitter, London
Pride, ESB H
Lively and busy one-bar local
opposite Ealing Studios ♀☺☺

W6:
Hammersmith 8D5

11–3; 5.30–11
Brook Green
170 Shepherds Bush Road
(A219) ✆ 01-603 9233
Young John's Ale, Bitter,
Special Bitter, Winter
Warmer H
Grand imposing pub of
character ♣®☺ (not Sun) ➊☺

Cross Keys
57 Black Lion Lane (off A315)
Fuller Chiswick Bitter, London
Pride, ESB H
A well-run local; live music
most evenings ♪♣♀®☺☺

Thatched House
115 Dalling Road (off A315)
Young John's Ale, Bitter,
Special Bitter, Winter
Warmer H
Friendly pub, often crowded
♣♀♿☺➊☺

W8: Kensington
8D5

11–3; 5.30–11
Britannia
1 Allen Street (off A315)
Young John's Ale, Bitter,
Special Bitter H
Winter Warmer G
Busy pub with large wood
panelled saloon and small
public bar ♣♀☺➊ (Mon–Fri)➊

W8: Notting Hill
Gate 8D5

11–3; 5.30–11
Uxbridge Arms
13 Uxbridge Street
Fremlins Tusker
Wethered Bitter
Whitbread Flowers Original
Bitter H
Small, lively up-market local
♀☺

W9: Maida Vale
8D5

11–3; 5.30–11
Truscott Arms
55 Shirland Road
Arkell BBB
Fuller ESB
Shepherd Neame Bitter
Samuel Smith Old
Brewery Bitter
Wells Eagle Bitter H

Pleasantly decorated pub with unique row of 10 handpumps, guest beers; jazz Tues and Wed evenings ⌐♪♣℘[R]◔[S]

W10: North Kensington 8D5

11–3; 5.30–11
Narrow Boat
346 Ladbroke Grove (off A404)
Fuller London Pride, ESB [H]
Small, friendly one bar local by canalside ♪℘[S]

W11: Holland Park 8D5

11–3; 5.30–11
Duke of Clarence
203 Holland Park Avenue (A40) ☎ 01-603 5431
Charrington IPA
Draught Bass [H]
Spacious pub with large garden ♪♣℘◔◗[S]

W11: Westbourne Park 8D5

11–3; 5.30–11
Frog & Firkin
41 Tavistock Crescent
Bruce Tavistock Bitter, Bullfrog Bitter, Dogbolter [H]
Popular home-brew pub with pianist and hat collection: guest beers ⌐♪℘◔◗(not Sun)[S]

W12: Shepherds Bush 8D5

11–3; 5.30–11
Crown & Sceptre
57 Melina Road
Fuller London Pride, ESB [H]
Popular local in side street ⌐♪♣℘[R]◔🍷

W14: West Kensington 8D5

11–3; 5.30–11
Radnor Arms
247 Warwick Road (A3220)
Adnams Bitter
Eldridge Pope Royal Oak
Everard Tiger
West Country Cider [H]
Small, reasonably-priced free house; guest beers ⌐♪♣℘◔[S]🚆

Bedfont 8B6

10.30–2.30; 5.30–10.30 (11 F, S and summer)
Beehive
333 Staines Road (A315)
Fuller London Pride, ESB [H]
Pub with lovely rose garden, close to airport ⌐♪♣℘🚗◔🍷

Brentford 8C5

11–3; 5.30–10.30 (11 F, S)
Griffin
57 Brook Road (off A4)
Fuller Chiswick Bitter, London Pride, ESB [H]
Opposite Brentford football club; lively atmosphere ♪♣℘[R]◔🍷[S]🚆

Magpie & Crown
128 High Street (A315)
☎ 01-560 5658
Ruddle County
Watney London Bitter
Webster Yorkshire Bitter [H]
Comfortable high street local; good food ⌐♪℘▣[R]◔◗[S]🚆

Cowley 8AS

10.30–2.30; 5.30–10.30 (11 F, S)
Royal Oak
High Street (A408)
Benskins Bitter
Taylor Walker Mainline [H]
Pleasant family pub in rural setting ⌐♪♣℘🚗[R]◔🍷🚆

Cranford 8B5

11–3; 5.30–10.30 (11 F, S)
Queens Head
123 High Street (off A312)
Fuller Chiswick Bitter, London Pride, ESB [H]
1930s mock-Tudor with three real fires 🏠♪♣℘🚗◔[S]

Greenford 8B5

11–3; 5.30–10.30 (11 F, S)
Black Horse
425 Oldfield Lane North (off A4127) ☎ 01-578 1384
Fuller London Pride, ESB [H]
Cosy canalside pub ♪♣℘🚗◔🍷[S]⛺

Hampton Court 8C7

11–3; 5.30–11
Cardinal Wolsey
The Green, Hampton Court Road (A308) ☎ 01-941 3781
Fuller London Pride, ESB [H]
Smart pub with royal connections ♪♣℘🚗▣[R]◔◗[S]

Hampton Hill 8B6

11–3; 5.30–11
Windmill
80 Windmill Road (off A312)
Charrington IPA
Draught Bass
Mitchells & Butlers Springfield Bitter [H]
Small and popular ♪♣℘🚗◔🍷

Hillingdon 8A5

10.30–2.30; 5.30–10.30 (11 F, S)
Red Lion
Uxbridge Road, Hillingdon Hill (A4020) ☎ Uxbridge 34474
Fuller London Pride, ESB [H]
Built 1465, excellent woody pub ▦℘🚗◔[S]

Star
Uxbridge Road, Hillingdon Heath (A4020)
Charrington IPA
Draught Bass [H]
Friendly, main road local ♪♣℘◔🍷[S]

Hounslow 8B6

11–3; 5.30–10.30 (11 F, S)
Earl Russell
274 Hanworth Road (A314)
Saturday evening opening: 7
Fuller London Pride, ESB [H]
Excellent pub with good public bar ♪♣℘🚗◔🍷[S]🚆

Queen Victoria
121 Bath Road (A3006)
Fuller Chiswick Bitter, London Pride, ESB [H]
Cosy, busy and friendly local ♪℘🚗◔[S]

Isleworth 8C6

11–3; 5.30–10.30 (11 F, S)
Swan Inn
1 Swan Street (off A3004)
Fuller Chiswick Bitter, London Pride, ESB [H]
Home-made food a speciality 🏠♪♣℘[R]◔◗🍷[S]

Southall 8B5

11–3; 5.30–10.30 (11 F, S)
Lord Wolseley
48 Dudley Road
Fuller London Pride, ESB [H]
Excellent friendly pub with geese in garden ℘🚗[R]◔🍷[S]🚆

Northcote Arms
Northcote Avenue (off A4020)
Fuller London Pride, ESB [H]
Friendly pub, ⌐♪♣℘🚗[R]◔🍷[S]🚆

Teddington 8C6

10.30–2.30; 5.30–11
Abercorn Arms
76 Church Road (off A313)
Young John's Ale, Bitter, Special Bitter, Winter Warmer [H]
Comfortable, Victorian pub, live jazz Mondays ⌐♪♣℘◔🍷[S]

Twickenham 8C6

11–3; 5.30–11
Eel Pie
9 Church Street (off A305)
Adnams Bitter
Everard Tiger
Hall & Woodhouse
Hector's Bitter, Tanglefoot
Webster Yorkshire Bitter
Wethered Bitter, SPA [H]
Compact, lively free house with restaurant ♣[R]◔◗[S]

Prince Albert
30 Hampton Road (A311)
Fuller Chiswick Bitter, London Pride, ESB [H]
Excellent old pub, often crowded ♣℘◔[S]

Uxbridge 8A5

10.30–2.30; 5.30–10.30 (11 F, S)
Crown & Olde Treaty House
90 Oxford Road (A4020)
Wethered Bitter, SPA, Winter Royal [H]
Large pub dating back to Civil War ♪♣℘🚗[R]◔🍷[S]♿

Affetside   25F1

11.30–3; 5–10.30 (11 F, S)

Pack Horse Inn
52 Watling Street (off A676)
OS 760140
☎ Tottington 3802
Evening opening: 7
Hydes Best Mild, Bitter E
Rural pub of historical interest
on roman road
♠♩✻♫♪⌂R✿☺♿⚘

Altrincham   25F4

11–3; 5.30–10.30 (11 F, S)

Bakers Arms
Pownall Road
Hydes Mild, Bitter E
Lively modern pub, built back
to front; worth finding
♩♪✿☺

Faulkners Arms
57 Stamford New Road
**Wilsons Original Mild,
Bitter** H
Narrow-fronted, comfortable
one-bar pub; chess played
♠☺≉

Malt Shovels
Stamford Street
☎ 061-928 2053
Morning opening: 11.30;
Saturday evening opening: 7
**Samuel Smith Old Brewery
Bitter** H
Comfortable pub with live
music most evenings
♩♪✿⌂R✿☺⚘☺

Victoria Tavern
29 Stamford Street
**Bass XXXX Mild
Draught Bass** E
Brightly renovated pub ♩♠✿☺≉

Ashton-in-Makerfield   24D3

11.30–3.30; 5.30–10.30 (11 F, S)

Kings Arms
Warrington Road (A49/A58)
**Peter Walker Mild, Best
Bitter** H
Excellent lively pub ♠♩♪♠R♫

Red Lion
Gerrard Street (A58)
**Greenall Whitley Mild,
Bitter** H
Unspoilt town-centre pub
known locally as Mary's or
Nutter Arms ♩♠♫

Ashton-under-Lyne   25H3

11–3; 5–10.30 (11 F, S)

Oddfellows Arms
Kings Road
**Robinson Best Mild, Best
Bitter** H & E
Comfortable, friendly
suburban pub ♩♠⌂

Station
Warrington Street

**Boddingtons Bitter
Marston Pedigree, Merrie
Monk
Ruddle County** H
Comfortable, welcoming free
house, abounding in
railwayana ♠R✿☺

Aspull   24E2

11.30–3; 5.30–10.30 (11 F, S)

Kirkless Hall
Albion Drive, off Cale Lane
☎ Wigan 42871
**Burtonwood Dark Mild,
Bitter** H
Canalside pub at Wigan's 'top
lock' ♩♠♫⌂R✿☺⚘☺

Queens Head
2 Lucas Nook, Fingerpost
(B5238)
May open late evenings
**Tetley Walker Mild
Peter Walker Best Bitter** H
Excellent corner pub with two
lounges ♩♠⌂R✿

Astley   25E3

11.30–3.30; 5.30–10.30 (11 F, S)

Cart & Horses
Manchester Road (A572)
Holt Mild, Bitter H
Fine, rambling pub with
Bennet-style murals ♩♠♫

Atherton   25E2

11.30–3.30; 5.30–10.30 (11 F, S)

Station
Bolton Road (A579)
**Greenall Whitley Mild,
Bitter** E
Large and comfortable
open-plan pub ♩♠♫⌂R✿☺≉

Bamfurlong   24D2

11.30–3.30; 5.30–10.30 (11 F, S)

Bamfurlong Hotel
71 Lily Lane (A58)
**Tetley Walker Mild
Peter Walker Best Bitter** H
Large, roomy pub with
traditional long vault ♩♠♫☺

Billinge   24D3

11.30–3.30; 5.30–10.30 (11 F, S)

Holts Arms (Foot o' the Causeway)
Crank Road (off B5206)
Evening opening: 7
**Burtonwood Dark Mild,
Bitter** H
Excellent, unspoilt old inn
with bowling green
♠♩♠♫⌂R✿☺
(County boundary runs
through Billinge – see also
under Merseyside)

Blackley   25G2

11–3; 5.30–10.30 (11 F, S)

Old House at Home
Bottomley Side, Manchester 9
(off A664)
Evening opening: 7
Wilsons Original Mild, Bitter H

Homely local tucked away by
ICI ♩♠✻♫⌂R✿☺

Blackrod   24E2

11–3; 5.30–10.30 (11 F, S)

Poacher
1/3 Scot Lane (off A6)
☎ Wigan 832741
**Burtonwood Dark Mild,
Bitter** H
Homely pub with good-value
food ♩♠☺⚘☺

Bolton   25F2

11–3; 5.30–10.30 (11 F, S)

Alma Inn
152 Bradshawgate (A575)
**Burtonwood Dark Mild,
Bitter** H
Pleasant town-centre pub,
recently extended
♠♩♠R☺⚘☺≉

Falcon
Kay Street (A673) ☎ 27352
**Peter Walker Best Bitter
Tetley Mild** H
Traditional local with
interesting tiles and Tong's
Brewery windows
♩♠✻♠R☺

George
92 Great Moor Street
**Wilsons Original Mild,
Bitter** E
Hospitable town-centre pub
near bus station and open
market ♩♠♫≉

Gibralter Rock
224 Deane Road (A676)
Evening opening: 7
**Greenall Whitley Mild,
Bitter** E
Well-run two-roomed local
♩♠♫☺

Howcroft
36 Pool Street (off A673)
**Peter Walker Mild, Best
Bitter** H
Thriving pub with a bowling
green ♠♩♠♫♠

York Hotel
Newport Street (off A579)
**Burtonwood Dark Mild,
Bitter** E
Town-centre local
♩♠✿R☺≉

Boothstown   25F3

11–3; 5.30–10.30 (11 F, S)

Royal Oak
20 Leigh Road (A572)
**Wilsons Original Mild,
Bitter** H
Recent alterations but retains
village atmosphere ♩♠R♫☺

Bredbury   25H3

11–3; 5.30–10.30 (11 F, S)

Rising Sun
Stockport Road (A560)
Wilsons Original Mild, Bitter H

Comfortable, friendly pub
♪♣℘◷🚆

Burnage 25G3

11–3; 5.30–10.30 (11 F, S)
Victoria Inn
196 Burnage Lane (off A34)
Boddingtons Mild, Bitter [E]
Large, popular and friendly pub 🔥♣🚗◷♀🚆

Bury 25G2

11.30–3; 5–10.30 (11 F, S)
Help Me Thro'
Crostons Road (B6214)
Thwaites Mild, Bitter [H]
Basic welcoming pub just outside town centre 🔥♪♣🚗♀

Carrington 25F3

11–3; 5.30–10.30 (11 F, S)
Windmill
Manchester Road (A6144)
Samuel Smith Old Brewery Bitter [H]
300-year-old semi-rural local
🔥♪♣℘🚗◷♀

Cheadle 25G4

11–3; 5.30–10.30 (11 F, S)
Old Star
High Street (A560)
Saturday evening opening: 6.45
Hydes Mild, Bitter [E]
Comfortable, busy local on main road ♣♀Ⓢ

Printers Arms
220 Stockport Road (A560)
Robinson Best Mild, Best Bitter [E]
Thriving local ♪♣℘🚗♀Ⓢ

Cheetham 25G3

11–3; 5.30–10.30 (11 F, S)
Derby Brewery Arms
95 Cheetham Hill Road, Manchester 8 (A665)
Holt Mild, Bitter [H]
Modernised brewery tap with accent on tradition and comfort ♪♣◷♀Ⓢ

Chorlton-on-Medlock 25G3

11–3; 5.30–10.30 (11 F, S)
Grafton
Grafton Street (off A34)
Holt Mild, Bitter [H]
Unassuming local near the university, mixed clientele
♪♣◷Ⓢ

Compstall 25H4

11–3; 5.30–10.30 (11 F, S)
Andrew Arms
George Street
Robinson Best Mild, Best Bitter [H]
Friendly pub near Etherow nature reserve 🔥♪♣🚗[R]◷♀Ⓢ

Daisy Hill 25E2

11–3; 5.30–10.30 (11 F, S)
Three Crowns
152 Lower Leigh Road (B5325)
Tetley Walker Mild
Peter Walker Best Bitter [H]
Friendly roadside local
♪♣℘🚗♀Ⓢ♿🚆

Delph 25H2

11.30–3; 5–10.30 (11 F, S)
Horse & Jockey
Standedge (A62)
Evening opening: 7; closed weekday lunchtimes
Taylor Best Bitter, Landlord
Theakston Dark Mild, Best Bitter, Old Peculier [H]
Comfortable moorland pub with '40s atmosphere 🔥♪🚗

Denshaw 25H2

11.30–3; 5.30–10.30 (11 F, S)
Rams Head (Old Tupps)
Ripponden Road (A672)
Sunday lunchtime only; evening opening: 6:30
Theakston Dark Mild, Best Bitter, Old Peculier [G]
Neat moorland pub with fine views 🔥♪🚗

All five pubs in the village serve real ale

Denton 25H3

11–3; 5.30–10.30 (11 F, S)
Dog & Partridge
Ashton Road (A6017)
Robinson Best Mild, Bitter [H]
Small and friendly terraced local ♪♣♀

White House
Ashton Road (A6017)
Samuel Smith Old Brewery Bitter [H]
Local pub catering for all tastes 🛏♪♣🚗♀Ⓢ

Didsbury 25G3

11–3; 5.30–10.30 (11 F, S)
Crown
770 Wilmslow Road, Manchester 20 (A5145)
Greenall Whitley Mild, Bitter [E]
Typical Manchester vault, homely atmosphere ♣℘♀

Gateway
882 Wilmslow Road, Manchester 20 (A34)
Hydes Mild, Bitter [E]
Large, traditional and hospitable pub
🔥🛏♪♣🚗[R]◷♀Ⓢ🚆

Dukinfield 25H3

11–3; 5–10.30 (11 F, S)
Gardeners Arms
153 Astley Street

Robinson Best Mild, Best Bitter [H] **Old Tom** [G]
Street corner local – friendly with no frills ♪♣

Eccles 25F

11–3; 5.30–10.30 (11 F, S)
Duke of York
89 Church Street (A57)
☎ 061-707 5409
Chesters Best Mild, Best Bitter
Marston Pedigree
Taylor Golden Best, Landlord, Ram Tam
Thwaites Bitter [H]
Bulmer Cider [G]
Basic, busy pub maintaining CAMRA ideals
🔥🛏♪♣⊞℘■[R]◷♀Ⓢ🚆

Grapes
439 Liverpool Road, Peel Green (A57)
Holt Mild, Bitter [H]
Splendidly preserved Edwardian interior 🛏♪♣🚗[R]♀

Park Hotel
142 Monton Road, Monton (B5229)
Holt Mild, Bitter [E]
Strong canal theme in unusual snug ♪♣🚗[R]♀

Queens Arms
Green Lane, Patricroft (B5231, off A57)
Boddingtons Mild, Bitter [E]
Cosy retreat by early railway line ♪♣⊞℘[R]♀Ⓢ🚆

White Lion
133 Liverpool Road (A57)
Holt Mild, Bitter [H]
Pre-war atmosphere persists in classic corner house 🔥🛏♪♣

Failsworth 25G

11.30–3; 5.30–10.30 (11 F, S)
Cotton Tree
96 Ashton Road East (off A62)
Marston Mercian Mild, Burton Bitter [H]
Well-kept local ♪🚗[R]◷Ⓢ

Pack Horse
481 Oldham Road, Wrigley Head (A62)
Saturday evening opening: 7
Marston Mercian Mild, Burton Bitter [H]
Listed building with pleasant atmosphere ♪♣℘🚗Ⓢ

Farnworth 25F

11–3; 5.30–10.30 (11 F, S)
Bradford Arms
47 Buckley Lane (A5082)
Boddingtons Best Mild, Bitter [E]
Busy, modern two-roomed pub ♣🚗♀Ⓢ

Bridgewater
27 Buckley Lane (A5082)
☎ 73760

Samuel Smith Old Brewery Bitter Ⓗ
Comfortable pub with good lunchtime meals ♪🏠Ⓡ🅶Ⓢ

Gatley 24G4

11–3; 5.30–10.30 (11 F, S)
Horse & Farrier
Gatley Road (A560)
Hydes Best Mild, Bitter Ⓔ
Anvil Strong Ale Ⓖ
Busy, interesting village centre local 🏠♣🏠Ⓡ🅶≷

Gorton 25G3

11–3; 5.30–10.30 (11 F, S)
Suburban Hotel
Middlewich Street, off Hyde Road (off A57)
Lees GB Mild, Bitter Ⓗ
Skilfully modernised multi-roomed local ♪♣🏠Ⓡ🅶≷

Heaton Mersey 25G3

11–3; 5.30–10.30 (11 F, S)
Griffin Hotel
553 Didsbury Road (off A5145)
Holt Mild, Bitter Ⓗ
Classic Victorian pub with superb interior, saved from demolition 🏠♣🏠Ⓢ

Heaton Norris 25G3

11–3; 5.30–10.30 (11 F, S)
Nursery
Green Lane (off A6)
Hydes Mild, Bitter Ⓔ
Roomy local with superb bowling green ♣🏠🏠🅶Ⓢ

High Lane 24H4

11–3; 5.30–10.30 (11 F, S)
Bulls Head
Buxton Road (A6)
Boddingtons Bitter Ⓗ
Comfortable pub close to canal bridge ♪♣🏠🏠

Royal Oak
Buxton Road (A6)
✆ Disley 2380
Burtonwood Dark Mild, Bitter Ⓗ
Comfortable roadside pub ♪♣🏠🅶Ⓢ

Hindley 24E2

11.30–3.30; 5.30–10.30 (11 F, S)
Cumberland Arms
Chapel Green
Tetley Walker Mild
Peter Walker Best Bitter Ⓔ
Deservedly popular local with fine vault atmosphere ♣Ⓡ≷

Worthington
Market Street (A58)
✆ Wigan 53294
Burtonwood Dark Mild, Bitter Ⓗ
Well-run central pub with good-value food
🏠♪♣🅶➔ (Wed–Sun) 🏠Ⓢ≷

Hollinwood 25G2

11.30–3; 5–10.30 (11 F, S)
Old Post Office
Manchester Road (A62)
Oldham Mild, Bitter Ⓗ
Traditional drinking house ♪♣🏠Ⓢ≷

Woodman
Manchester Road (A62)
Lees GB Mild, Bitter Ⓗ
Moonraker Ⓔ
Welcoming local in good drinking area ♪♣Ⓢ≷

Hulme 23G3

11–3; 5.30–10.30 (11 F, S)
Manchester Regiment
Chester Road
Greenall Whitley Mild, Bitter Ⓔ
Large, modern pub ♪♣🏠Ⓢ

Hyde 25H3

11–3; 5.30–10.30 (11 F, S)
Cheshire Ring
Manchester Road (A57)
Evening opening: 7 (approx)
Matthew Brown Bitter
Darley Thorne Best Bitter
Taylor Landlord
Thwaites Mild, Bitter
Vaux Sunderland Draught Bitter, Samson
Ward Sheffield Best Bitter
**Winkle Saxon Cross Bitter,
Cheshire Ring Bitter** Ⓗ
Enterprising free house with 'house' beer
♪🏠Ⓡ🅶Ⓢ≷

Cotton Tree
Markham Street, Newton
Wilsons Original Mild, Bitter Ⓗ
Genial pub in suburb of Hyde ♪♣🏠Ⓢ

Moulders Arms
Mottram Road (A57)
Tetley Walker Mild, Bitter Ⓗ
Comfortable pub close to football ground ♪♣🏠

White Gates
Manchester Road (A57)
Samuel Smith Old Brewery Bitter Ⓗ
Comfortable northern local with superb traditional vault ♪♣🏠🅶Ⓢ≷

Ince-in-Makerfield 24D2

11.30–3.30; 5.30–10.30 (11 F, S)
Park
Manchester Road (A577)
Wilsons Original Mild, Bitter Ⓔ
Popular modern pub with bowling green ♪♣🏠🏠Ⓢ

Irlam & Cadishead 25F3

11–3; 5.30–10.30 (11 F, S)
White Horse
575 Liverpool Road (A57)
✆ 061-775 2820
Evening opening: 7
Tetley Walker Mild, Bitter Ⓗ
Large, comfortable lounge, traditional vault
🏠♪♣🏠🅶Ⓢ≷

Leigh 25E3

11.30–3.30; 5.30–10.30 (11 F, S)
Bridgewater Arms
St. Helen's Road
Greenall Whitley Mild, Bitter Ⓔ
Friendly central pub ♪♣🏠Ⓢ

Railway
Twist Lane ✆ 673916
Tetley Walker Mild
Peter Walker Best Bitter Ⓗ
Run by same family for many years ♪♣Ⓡ🏠

Littleborough 25H1

11.30–3; 5–10.30 (11 F, S)
Railway
Inghams Lane (B6225)
✆ Rochdale 76250
**Bass XXXX Mild, Cask Bitter,
Draught Bass** Ⓔ
Village local atmosphere, just out of town centre
♪♣🏠🏠Ⓡ🅶Ⓢ≷

Little Lever 25F2

11–3; 5.30–10.30 (11 F, S)
Horseshoe
71 Lever Street (B6209)
Hydes Best Mild, Bitter Ⓔ
Comfortable two-roomed pub ♪♣🏠Ⓢ

Longsight 25G3

11–3; 5.30–10.30 (11 F, S)
Waggon & Horses
438 Stockport Road,
Manchester 15 (A6)
✆ 061-224 2649
Evening opening: 6
Wilsons Original Mild, Bitter
Bulmer Cider Ⓗ
Large Tudor-style pub ♪♣🏠🏠Ⓡ🏠

Manchester City Centre 25G3

11–3; 5.30–10.30 (11 F, S)
Britons Protection
Great Bridgewater Street
Tetley Walker Mild, Bitter Ⓗ
Superb Victorian tiling and woodwork ♪🏠Ⓡ🅶Ⓢ≷

Bulls Head
84 London Road, Piccadilly, 1 (A6) ✆ 061-236 1724
Saturday evening opening: 7
Burtonwood Dark Mild, Bitter Ⓗ

Hospitable and friendly, serving excellent lunchtime meals ♪♣☺🅟Ⓢ

Castle & Falcon
19 Bradshaw Street, 4 (off A664) ☎ 061-832 2975
Burtonwood Dark Mild, Bitter Ⓗ
Small, hidden pub, often crowded; reputedly a former gaol ♪♣☺🅟Ⓢ⇄

Coach & Horses
London Road, Piccadilly, 1 (A6)
Saturday evening opening: 7
Tetley Walker Mild Winkle Saxon Cross Bitter Ⓗ
Basic free house ♪♣🅟⇄

Crown
321 Deansgate (A56) ☎ 061-834 1930
Wilsons Original Mild, Bitter Ⓗ
Basic Victorian pub ♪♣🎫🅡Ⓡ Ⓢ⇄

Grey Horse Inn
80 Portland Street (off A6)
Morning opening: 11:30; Saturday evening opening: 7
Hydes Mild, Bitter Ⓔ
Tiny, friendly city-centre pub ♪Ⓢ

Harp & Shamrock
36 New Mount Street, 4 (off A664)
Marston Mercian Mild, Burton Bitter, Pedigree Ⓗ
Finding it is a challenge amply rewarded ♪♣🅟⇄

Jolly Angler
47 Ducie Street (off A665)
Hydes Best Mild, Bitter Ⓗ
Unique backwater with fiercely loyal customers 🅰♪♣🎫🅡☺🅟Ⓢ⇄

Peveril of the Peak
127 Great Bridgewater Street
Wilsons Original Mild, Bitter Ⓗ
Traditional tiled pub with stained glass windows ♪♣🅟Ⓢ⇄

Sinclair's Oyster Bar
Shambles Square (off A56) ☎ 061-834 0430
Saturday evening opening: 6
Samuel Smith Old Brewery Bitter Ⓗ
Two-storey renovation evokes Victorian era ♪♣🅿🅡☺Ⓢ⇄

Square Albert
14 Albert Square ☎ 061-835 1000
Evening opening: 8 (wine bar)
Tetley Walker Mild, Bitter Ⓗ
Modern interior in old Memorial Hall ♪☺Ⓢ

Unicorn
26 Church Street, 4 (off A62)

Bass Mild, Toby Light Draught Bass Stones Best Bitter Ⓗ
Extensive wooden panelling; HQ of Honourable Order of Bass Drinkers ♪♣🎫🅡Ⓡ☺Ⓢ⇄

Marple 25H4
11–3; 5.30–10.30 (11 F, S)

Hatters Arms
Church Lane
Robinson Best Mild, Best Bitter Ⓗ
Traditional small, cosy local with good vault ♪♣☺&

Mellor 25H4
11–3; 5.30–10.30 (11 F, S)

Royal Oak
Longhurst Lane
Robinson Best Mild, Best Bitter Ⓔ
Busy pub, popular with local sportsmen ♪♣Ⓢ

Middleton 25G2
10.30–3; 5–10.30 (11 F, S)

Dog & Partridge
42 Spring Vale (off A669)
Boddingtons Bitter Oldham Mild, Bitter Ⓔ
Renovated pub with interesting window ♪🅿🅰Ⓢ

Ring O'Bells
St. Leonard's Square (via New Lane, off A664)
Lees GB Mild, Bitter Ⓔ
Busy young persons' pub of historical interest ♪♣🅡🅟

White Hart
86 Rochdale Road (A664)
Lees GB Mild, Bitter Ⓔ
Traditional local with busy tap room ♪♣🅿🅰🅡🅟

Mosley Common 25F2
11.30–3.30; 5.30–10.30 (11 F, S)

Colliers Arms
Manchester Road (A577)
Wilsons Original Mild, Bitter Ⓗ
Pleasant old pub with comfortable lounge ♪♣🅰🅟

Mossley 25H2
11–3; 5.30–10.30 (11 F, S)

Tollemache Arms
Manchester Road (A635)
Robinson Best Mild, Best Bitter Ⓗ **Old Tom** Ⓖ
Fine small local, cosy and welcoming ♪♣🅰Ⓢ

Moss Nook 25G4
11–3; 5.30–10.30 (11 F, S)

Tatton Arms
Trenchard Road (off Ringway Road, B5166)
Robinson Best Mild, Best Bitter Ⓔ
350-year-old pub, once a farmhouse 🅰♣🅿☺🅟

Moston 25G2
11–3; 5.30–10.30 (11 F, S)

Blue Bell
Moston Lane (off A664/A6104) ☎ 061-681 4053
Holt Mild, Bitter Ⓗ
Spacious Edwardian local with busy public bar ♪♣🅰🅡🅟Ⓢ

Dean Brook
94 St. Mary's Road, 10 (off A62) ☎ 061-681 2348
Marston Mercian Mild, Burton Bitter Ⓗ
Central bar kept busy by four rooms ♪♣🅰🅟Ⓢ⇄

New Hey 25H1
11.30–3; 5–10.30 (11 F, S)

Bird in the Hand (Top Bird)
113 Huddersfield Road (A640, off M62) ☎ Shaw 847978
Samuel Smith Old Brewery Bitter Ⓗ
Pleasant village local ♪♣🅰☺🅟🅟Ⓢ⇄

Newton Heath 25H3
11–3; 5.30–10.30 (11 F, S)

Prince of Wales
838 Oldham Road, 10 (A62)
Wilsons Original Mild, Bitter Ⓗ
Eccentric local known as the 'Dead House' ♣🅟

Northenden 25G4
11–3; 5.30–10.30 (11 F, S)

Crown Inn
Ford Lane, Manchester 22 (off B5167)
Boddingtons Best Mild, Bitter Ⓔ
Small and popular ♪♣🅿☺Ⓢ

Oldham 25H2
11.30–3; 5–10.30 (11 F, S)

Clarksfield Hotel
Ronald Street (via Balfour Street, off A669)
Boddingtons Bitter Oldham Mild, Bitter Ⓗ
Spacious and popular backstreet local ♪♣🅟⇄

Crown
113 Huddersfield Road, Hill Stores (A62)
Boddingtons Bitter Oldham Mild, Bitter Ⓗ
Recently renovated local retaining original bar ♪♣🅟Ⓢ⇄

Dog & Partridge
Constantine Street (off Greenacres Road, A62)
Matthew Brown Mild, Bitter, John Peel Bitter Ⓗ
Friendly village local, worth finding 🅰♣🅰🅟Ⓢ

Friendship
495 Lees Road, Salem (A669)
Wilsons Original Mild, Bitter Ⓗ

vely local near Medlock
alley ⌐♪♣🍺Ⓢ

y also: Hope, Greenacres
oad (free)

rrell 24D2

30–3.30; 5.30–11.30 (11 F, S)

iner's Lamp
rell Road (A574)
Wigan 224876
waites Best Mild, Bitter [H]
easant and popular local
♣🚗◔☛🍺Ⓢ

ose & Crown
urch Street
Upholland 625569
tley Walker Mild, Bitter [H]
nall, comfortable local,
ndy for Orrell RUFC
♣🌷🚗◔🍺Ⓢ⇌

artington 25F3

3; 5.30–10.30 (11 F, S)

ing William IV
anchester Road (A6144)
arston Mercian Mild,
rton Bitter, Pedigree [E]
l, comfortable village pub in
odern surroundings ♪🚗[R]🍺

restwich 25G2

0–3; 5–10.30 (11 F, S)

ed Lion
8 Bury New Road (A56, off
52)
lt Mild, Bitter [E]
rge pub with many rooms
♣🌷🚗🍺Ⓢ

adcliffe 25F2

0–3; 5–10.30 (11 F, S)

asons Arms
on Street (off A665)
061-723 3159
ening opening: 7 (Mon–Fri)
waites Mild, Bitter [H]
dernised but retaining
aracter 🏠♪♣⊞🌷🚗◔🍺Ⓢ

amsbottom 25F1

3; 5–10.30 (11 F, S)

oyal Oak
idge Street (off A676)
ening opening: 7
waites Mild, Bitter [E]
rraced town-centre pub
🍺Ⓢ

eddish 25G3

3; 5.30–10.30 (11 F, S)

nion
Broadstone Road (B5169)
binson Best Mild, Best
ter [E]
od local pub ♪♣🌷🚗[R]🍺Ⓢ♿

ochdale 25G1

0–3; 5–10.30 (11 F, S)

lbert
otland Road (A680)
ilsons Original Mild, Bitter [H]
ngenial street-corner
cal ♪♣🍺

Cemetery
470 Bury Road (B6222)
☎ 43214
Boddingtons Bitter
Oldham Mild
Ruddle County
Taylor Best Bitter, Landlord [H]
Symonds Cider [G]
Renovated four-roomed pub
with restaurant; guest beers
🏠♪♣🚗[R]◔☛🍺Ⓢ

Cross Yates
69 Whitworth Road (A671)
Holt Mild, Bitter [H]
Carefully renovated local
⌐♪♣🍺

Healey
172 Shawclough Road,
Shawclough (B6377)
Evening opening: 6
Robinson Best Mild, Best
Bitter [H] **Old Tom** [G]
Tiled lounge bar with serving
hatch to vault ♣[R]🍺

Royton 25H2

11.30–3; 5–10.30 (11 F, S)

Angel
230 Shaw Road (A663)
Lees GB Mild, Bitter [E]
Lively pub with a welcoming
atmosphere ♪♣🚗[R]🍺Ⓢ

Greyhound
Elly Clough, Holden Fold (off
A663) ☎ 061-624 4504
Evening opening: 7
Lees GB Mild, Bitter [E]
Country pub atmosphere
♪♣🌷🚗◔Ⓢ

Sale 25F3

11–3; 5.30–10.30 (11 F, S)

Woodcourt
Brooklands Road (off A560)
☎ 061-973 1849
Wilsons Original Mild, Bitter [E]
Magnificent mansion house in
own grounds ⌐♪♣🌷🚗[R]◔☛Ⓢ

Sale Moor 25F3

11–3; 5.30–10.30 (11 F, S)

Legh Arms
Northenden Road (B5166)
Holt Mild, Bitter [E]
Large drinking man's
Edwardian pub ⌐♣🚗[R]🍺

Salford 25G3

11–3; 5.30–10.30 (11 F, S)

Bricklayers Arms
146 Ordsall Lane, 5 (off
A5066/A57)
Holt Mild, Bitter [H]
Extended and modernised, yet
retaining many original
features ♪♣🚗🍺Ⓢ

Eagle
Collier Street (off Greengate,
A6/A56)
Holt Mild, Bitter [H]
Unsigned exterior hides
archetypal real pub ♪♣🍺⇌

Horseshoe
Back Hope Street, Higher
Broughton, 7 (off A56)
Bass XXXX Mild, Cask Bitter [H]
Comfortable backwater with
old bottle collection ♪♣🌷🚗

Spinners Arms
Oldfield Road, 5 (A5066, off
A6)
Marston Mercian Mild,
Burton Bitter [H]
Hectic community pub ⌐♪♣🍺Ⓢ

Union Tavern
105 Liverpool Street, 5 (off
A5066/A6053)
Holt Mild, Bitter [H]
Local character retained in
recent improvements
⌐♪♣🚗🍺Ⓢ

Waggon & Horses
Bolton Road, 6 (A6)
Holt Mild, Bitter [H]
First-rate 1980s pub
♪♣🚗◔🍺♿

Shaw 25H2

11.30–3; 5–10.30 (11 F, S)

Morning Star
Grains Road (off A663)
Lees GB Mild, Bitter [H]
Large, refurbished local
♪♣🌷🚗🍺⇌

Springhead 25H2

11.30–3; 5–10.30 (11 F, S)

Spinners
Woodbrook, off Cooper Street
(Between A669 & A62)
Lees GB Mild, Bitter [E]
Lively local, worth finding
⌐♪♣🚗◔🍺Ⓢ

Stalybridge 25H3

11–3; 5.30–10.30 (11 F, S)

Old Hunters Tavern
Acres Lane
Robinson Best Mild, Best
Bitter [H]
Small, comfortable pub with
character ♣Ⓢ

Stamford Arms
Stamford Street
Usually opens 7 pm evenings
Burtonwood Dark Mild,
Bitter [H]
Comfortably renovated pub,
close to bus and railway
stations ♪♣🚗◔Ⓢ⇌

Standish 24D2

11.30–3.30; 5.30–10.30 (11 F, S)

Black Horse
Church Street (off A49)
Wilsons Original Mild,
Bitter [H]
Well-run locals' pub by the
church ♪♣🌷🚗

New Seven Stars
Preston Road (A49)
Burtonwood Dark Mild,
Bitter [H]

Isolated, homely pub with keen landlord ♪♣🚗❥Ⓢ

Stockport 25G4

11–3; 5.30–10.30 (11 F, S)

Arden Arms
23 Millgate (off A626)
Robinson Best Mild, Best Bitter [H]
Fine pub with collection of grandfather clocks ♣✿🚗[R]🍺Ⓢ

Armoury
Greek Street, Shaw Heath (off A6)
Robinson Best Mild, Best Bitter [E] **Old Tom** [G]
Multi-roomed traditional pub ♪♣[R]🍺Ⓢ🚉

Blossoms
Buxton Road, Heaviley (A6)
Robinson Best Mild, Best Bitter, Old Tom [H]
Pleasant and popular local ♪♣🚗🍺Ⓢ🚉

George
15 Wellington Road North (A6) ☎ 061-480 5996
Saturday evening opening: 7
Draught Bass
Higsons Mild, Bitter [H]
Plush and interesting town-centre pub; rare brew for the area ⌐♪♣◷❥♿🚉

Royal Oak
High Street ☎ 061-480 5633
Robinson Best Mild, Best Bitter [H] **Old Tom** [G]
Multi-roomed old pub near brewery
🛏♪♣[R]🍺Ⓢ🚉

Swan with Two Necks
36 Princes Street (off A6)
Robinson Best Mild, Best Bitter [E]
Unspoilt pub in city-centre shopping precinct
♪♣⊞✿[R]◷🍺Ⓢ

Stretford 25F3

11–3; 5.30–10.30 (11 F, S)

Melville
Barton Road (off A5181)
Evening opening: 6.30 (Wed & Sat)
Holt Mild, Bitter [E]
Busy 1930s estate pub
♪♣✿🚗[R]◷🍺Ⓢ

Swinton & Pendlebury 25F2

11–3; 5.30–10.30 (11 F, S)

White Lion
242 Manchester Road, Swinton (A6, off A572)
Robinson Best Mild, Best Bitter, Old Tom [E]
200-year-old pub, extensively altered in the 60s
♪♣⊞🚗[R]🍺

White Swan
Worsley Road, Swinton (A572, off A580)
☎ 061-794 1504
Holt Mild, Bitter [H]
Five distinctive rooms with wood panelling and bric-a-brac ♪♣◷🍺

Windmill
690 Bolton Road, Pendlebury (A666, off B5231)
☎ 061-794 1609
Samuel Smith Old Brewery Bitter [H]
Victorian shell hides much-altered interior
♪♣✿🚗◷🍺

Tottington 25F1

11.30–3; 5–10.30 (11 F, S)

Hark to Towler
48 Market Street (B6213)
Thwaites Mild, Bitter [H]
Busy village local of character
♪♣🚗🍺Ⓢ♿

Tyldesley 25E2

11.30–3.30; 5.30–10.30 (11 F, S)

Mort Arms
Elliot Street (A577)
Holt Mild, Bitter [H]
Unspoilt, ultra-traditional town pub ♪♣🍺

Union
Castle Street
Thwaites Best Mild, Bitter [H]
Enjoying a revitalisation since its Greenall days ♪♣🍺

Uppermill 25H2

11.30–3; 5.30–10.30 (11 F, S)

Cross Keys
Running Hill Gate, via Church Road (off A670)
☎ Saddleworth 4626
Evening opening: 7
Lees GB Mild, Bitter [H]
Old moorland pub in picturesque setting
🛏⌐♪♣✿🚗[R]◷🍺Ⓢ

Try also: Church Inn, Church Road (free)

Walkden 25F2

11–3; 5.30–10.30 (11 F, S)

Morning Star
Manchester Road, Swinton (A6, off M62) ☎ 061-794 4927
Holt Mild, Bitter [E]
Popular pub with lively weekend sing-songs
⌐♪♣🚗◷🍺Ⓢ🚉

Walshaw 25F1

11.30–3; 5.30–10.30 (11 F, S)

White Horse
18 Hall Street (off B6213)
Thwaites Mild, Bitter [E]
Warm, cheerful pub with enthusiastic landlord
♪♣🚗🍺Ⓢ♿

West Gorton 25G

11–3; 5.30–10.30 (11 F, S)

Dolphin Inn
9 Clowes Street, Manchester 12 (off A57)
Marston Mercian Mild, Burton Bitter [H]
Homely pub, all welcome
♪♣🍺Ⓢ

Westhoughton 25F

11–3; 5.30–10.30 (11 F, S)

White Lion
2 Market Street (A58)
Holt Mild, Bitter [H]
Modernised pub retaining character ♪♣🚗🍺Ⓢ

Whitefield 25G

11.30–3; 5–10.30 (11 F, S)

Coach & Horses
71 Bury Old Road, Besses o' th' Barn (A665, off M62)
Saturday evening opening: 6
Holt Mild, Bitter [H]
Wonderfully traditional four-roomed local ♪♣🚗🍺🚉

Eagle & Child
Higher Lane (A665, off M62)
☎ 061-766 3024
Holt Mild, Bitter [H]
Large, well-appointed pub with bowling green
⌐♪♣⊞✿🚗[R]◷🍺Ⓢ🚉

Wigan 24D

11–3; 5.30 (or 7)–10.30 (11 F, S)

Bird i' th' Hand
Gidlow Lane
Tetley Walker Mild, Bitter [H]
Small, popular local, known as Th' 'Enhole ♪♣🍺

Old Pear Tree
44 Frog Lane ☎ 43677
Burtonwood Dark Mild, Bitter [H]
Friendly pub with good lunches 🛏♪♣🚗◷🍺Ⓢ🚉

Park
Hope Street (opposite bus station) ☎ 42315
Draught Bass
Peter Walker Mild, Bitter, Be Bitter [H]
Best choice of real ale in Wigan, threatened with demolition 🛏♪♣[R]🍺Ⓢ🚉

Silverwell
Darlington Street
Peter Walker Mild, Best Bitter [H]
Large, lively drinking house
⌐♪♣🚗🍺

Whitesmiths Arms
88 Standishgate (A49)
Boddingtons Best Mild, Bitter
Small, popular town-centre pub near Wigan RLFC ♪Ⓢ

Try also: Market Tavern (Younger)

Bebington 24B4
.30–3; 5.30–10.30

Cleveland Arms
1 Bebington Road (off A41)
051-645 2847
Saturday evening opening: 7
Thwaites Best Mild, Bitter ⊞
Archetypal friendly local, built
1859 ♪♣☺🅟≷

Rose & Crown
7 The Village
051-6455024
Thwaites Mild, Bitter ⊞
Boisterous, friendly local, built
1732 ♪♣🏢☺🅟

Billinge 24D3
.30–3.30; 5.30–10.30 (11 F, S)

Forresters Arms
Main Street (A571)
Burtonwood Dark Mild,
Bitter ⊞
Small friendly local ♪♣🅟
(County boundary runs
through Billinge; see also
under Greater Manchester)

Birkenhead 24B4
.30–3; 5.30–10.30

Angel
Beckwith Street (off A553)
Opens at 11 am & 5 pm
Boddingtons Mild, Bitter
Marston Pedigree, Merrie
Monk, Owd Rodger ⊞
Superbly restored, very
popular free house
♪♣☺🍺🅟≷

Blossoms
47 Cleveland Street (A5030)
Evening opening: 5
Bass Cask Bitter Ⓔ
Small and friendly dockland
pub ♪♣🅟

Crown Hotel
28 Conway Street
Evening opening: 5
Higsons Mild, Bitter ⊞
Lively local opposite
Birkenhead Market 🏢♪♣🅟🍺≷

Fireman's Arms
Oliver Street (off A552)
Evening opening: 5
Wilsons Original Bitter ⊞
Busy town-centre pub
♪♣🍺≷

Victoria Lodge
1–83 Victoria Road
Hartley XB
Whitbread Castle Eden Ale
Bulmer Cider ⊞
Comfortable, modernised
back-street local
♣🎱💈🍺☺🅟🍺🍺

Vittoria Vaults
6 Vittoria Street (off A553)
Opens at 11 am & 5 pm
Higsons Mild, Bitter ⊞
True local, a legend in its
lifetime 🏢♪♣☺🍺🍺≷

Windsor Castle
44 Oxton Road
Evening opening: 5 (5.30 Sat)
Wilsons Original Mild,
Bitter ⊞
Friendly town local with
superb etched windows ♪🍺

Bootle 24B3
11.30–3; 5.30–10.30

Merton Arms
2 Irlam Road, Liverpool 20
Higsons Mild, Bitter ⊞
Well-kept local ♪♣Ⓡ🍺🍺≷

Greasby 24A4
11.30–3; 5.30–10.30

Irby Mill
Mill Lane (off B5139)
Higsons Mild, Bitter ⊞
Pleasant stone-built country
pub 🏢♪🏢🍺

Heswall 24A4
11.30–3; 5.30–10.30

Black Horse
Lower Village (off A540)
℡ 051-342 2254
Evening opening: 5
Bass Mild, Cask Bitter
Draught Bass ⊞
Social centre of Lower Village
🏢♣🏢☺🍺🍺

Hoylake 24A4
11.30–3; 5.30–10.30

Plasterers Arms
Back Seaview Road
Evening opening: 5
Whitbread Castle Eden Ale ⊞
Traditional small local ♪♣🍺

Liverpool City Centre 24B3
11.30–3; 5–10.30

Baltic Fleet
33a Wapping, 1
Higsons Mild, Bitter
Younger Scotch Bitter,
No. 3 ⊞
Old dockside pub, now a free
house 🏢🏢☺🍺🍺

Caledonia
22 Caledonia Street,
Edge Hill, 7
Higsons Mild, Bitter ⊞
Musicians pub 🍺🍺

Cambridge
51 Mulberry Street,
Edge Hill, 7
Burtonwood Dark Mild,
Bitter ⊞
Immediately behind maternity
hospital ♪☺

Carnarvon Castle
5 Tarleton Street, 1
Closed Sundays
Draught Bass
Higsons Bitter ⊞
Attractive interior
🏢♪🍺≷

Corn Market
Old Ropery, Fenwick Street, 1
Wilsons Original Mild,
Bitter ⊞
Unusual woodcarvings
♪☺🍺🍺≷

Dart
31 Gildart Street, 3
Tetley Walker Mild, Bitter ⊞
Friendly local, recently
redecorated ♪♣🍺

Excelsior
121 Dale Street, 2
Opening hours vary; closed
Sat evening and all day
Sunday
Higsons Mild, Bitter ⊞
Head office tap ☺🍺

Falkland Arms
191 London Road, 3
Peter Walker Mild, Bitter ⊞
Justifiably popular Irish pub
🏢♪🍺🍺

Furnace
112 St James Street, 1
Peter Walker Mild, Bitter ⊞
Interesting Falstaff mirror ♪♣🍺

Globe
17 Cases Street, 1
Higsons Mild, Bitter ⊞
Incredible sloping floor 🍺≷

Grapes
25 Mathew Street, 2
Closed Sundays
Higsons Mild, Bitter ⊞
World-famous pub near
Cavern Club site Ⓡ☺

Lion
67 Moorfields, 2
Peter Walker Mild, Bitter ⊞
Ornate tiling ♪☺🍺≷

Midland
25 Ranelagh Street, 1
Peter Walker Mild, Bitter ⊞
Heavy with etched glass 🍺≷

Poste House
Cumberland Street, 1
Closed Sunday
Higsons Bitter ⊞
Small, busy pub Ⓡ☺🍺≷

Roscoe Head
24 Roscoe Street, 1
Tetley Walker Mild, Bitter ⊞
For connoisseurs 🍺🍺

Saddle
Dale Street, 2
Closes 9 pm; closed Sundays
Bass Mild, Cask Bitter
Draught Bass ⊞
Refurbished and pricey ☺🍺🍺≷

Villiers
(Ma Shepherds)
6 Elliot Street, 1
Higsons Mild, Bitter ⊞
Interesting pub steeped in
tradition 🍺≷

Merseyside

White House
185 Duke Street, 1
Peter Walker Mild, Bitter Ⓗ
Close to Chinatown ♠♀

White Star
(Quinn's)
2 Rainford Gardens, 2
Bass Cask Bitter
Draught Bass Ⓗ
'Mecca' ♀Ⓢ

Yates' Wine Lodge
37 Moorfields, 2
Boddingtons Bitter Ⓔ
Real sardines and
stone-ground flour ♪♀Ⓢ⇌

Ye Cracke
13 Rice Street, 1
Boddingtons Bitter
Marston Pedigree, Merrie
Monk Ⓗ
Musicians, artists and poets
♪♪♠♫♀

Liverpool: East

Bay Horse
14 Grinfield Street,
Edge Hill, 7
Thwaites Mild, Bitter Ⓗ
Large but spartan alehouse
♠♪♠♀

Clock
110 High Street,
Wavertree, 15
Higsons Mild, Bitter Ⓗ
Small and crowded ♪

Clubmoor
119 Townsend Lane,
Clubmoor, 6
Higsons Mild, Bitter Ⓗ
Large, comfortable suburban
local ♪♀Ⓢ

Earl Marshall
107 Earle Road, Edge Hill, 7
Peter Walker Mild, Bitter,
Best Bitter Ⓗ
Unpretentious local ♪♪♠♀

Flat House
583 West Derby Road
Tetley Walker Mild, Bitter Ⓗ
Real ale oasis in Tuebrook
♪♪♠♀

Gregsons Well
2 West Derby Road,
Kensington, 6
Higsons Mild, Bitter Ⓗ
Two public bars
♠♪♪♠♀Ⓢ

Grosvenor
123 Bishopsgate Street,
Wavertree, 15
Tetley Walker Mild, Bitter Ⓗ
Renovated local ♪♠♀

Halton Castle
86 Mill Lane, West Derby, 12
Higsons Mild, Bitter Ⓗ
Comfortable village local
♠♠♀Ⓢ

Newsham Park
108 Boaler Street,
Kensington, 6
Tetley Walker Mild, Bitter Ⓗ
Small, friendly local ♪Ⓡ♀

Oxford
67 Oxford Street, Edge Hill, 7
Higsons Mild, Bitter Ⓗ
Small and genial ♪♠Ⓖ♀

Prince Alfred
77 High Street, 15
Higsons Mild, Bitter Ⓗ
Small corner pub ♠♪♠♀

Royal Standard
West Derby Road,
Kensington, 6
Draught Bass
Higsons Mild, Bitter Ⓗ
Locals' pub ♪♪♠♀

Salisbury
40 Albany Road,
Old Swan, 13
Higsons Mild, Bitter Ⓗ
Well hidden ♪♀Ⓢ

Wheatsheaf
186 East Prescot Road, Knotty
Ash, 14
Higsons Mild, Bitter Ⓗ
Large suburban local with
waitress service ♠♀

Willowbank
329 Smithdown Road,
Wavertree, 15
Peter Walker Mild, Bitter Ⓗ
Busy pub ♪♠♀Ⓢ

Woodcroft
279 Smithdown Road,
Wavertree, 15
Bass Mild, Cask Bitter
Draught Bass Ⓗ
Unpretentious pub ♪♀

Liverpool: North

Breckside
377 Walton Breck Road, 4
Tetley Walker Mild, Bitter Ⓗ
'Flat-iron' shaped local near
Liverpool FC ♠♪♪♠♀

Breeze
66 Lancaster Street, Walton, 9
Higsons Mild, Bitter Ⓗ
Thriving local, renowned for
mild ♪♀

Bull
2 Dublin Street, 3
Tetley Walker Mild,
Walker Best Bitter Ⓗ
Irish atmosphere ♪♪♀

Clock
167 Walton Road, 4 (A59)
Peter Walker Mild, Bitter Ⓗ
Popular locals' pub ♪♪♀Ⓢ

Crescent Vaults
37 Everton Brow, Everton, 5
Higsons Mild, Bitter Ⓗ
Near old Everton 'lock-up'
♪♪♠♀

Feathers
Vauxhall Road, 3
Tetley Walker Mild,
Walker Best Bitter Ⓗ
Large local ♪♪♠♀Ⓢ

Grove
147 Breckfield Road North,
Anfield, 5
Higsons Mild, Bitter Ⓗ
Courteous, efficient service in
comfortable surroundings ♪♠

Old Barn
38 Old Barn Road, Anfield, 4
Higsons Mild Ⓗ
Small, well-hidden
mild-drinkers' local ♪♪♠♀

St Hilda
County Road, Kirkdale, 5
Evening opening: 5
Thwaites Mild, Bitter Ⓔ
Popular pub, threatened with
demolition ♪♪♠♀Ⓢ

Stanley Arms
48 Thirlmere Road, Anfield, 5
Burtonwood Dark Mild,
Bitter Ⓗ
Former Whitbread pub, now
thriving ♪♪♠♀

Stanley Bar
99 Stanley Road, 5
Peter Walker Mild, Bitter Ⓗ
Thriving, solidly-built local
♪♀Ⓢ

Thistle
33 Heyworth Street, 5
Peter Walker Mild, Bitter Ⓗ
Survived redevelopment to
serve new community ♪♀

Union
81 Commercial Road,
Sandhills, 5
Tetley Walker Mild, Bitter Ⓗ
Near Sandhills station ♪♠♀⇌

Walton (Top House)
122 Walton Village, 4
Higsons Mild, Bitter Ⓗ
Popular village local near
Everton FC ♠ ♀

Liverpool: South

Bleak House
131 Park Hill Road, 8
Higsons Mild, Bitter Ⓗ
Small local ♪♪♠♀

Coburg (The Devils)
1 Stanhope Street, 8
Tetley Walker Mild, Bitter Ⓗ
Fine stained-glass windows
♪♪♠Ⓡ♀Ⓢ

Empress
93 High Park Street, 8
Tetley Walker Mild, Bitter Ⓗ
Friendly local ♪♪♠♀

King Street Vaults
74 King Street, Garston, 19
Peter Walker Mild, Bitter Ⓗ
In Garston's dockland ♪♠♀Ⓢ⇌

asonic
Lark Lane, Aigburth, 17
ter Walker Mild, Bitter Ⓗ
sy pub in 'arty' area
🛈Ⓢ≷

oxteth (Collins's)
1 Park Street, 8
ter Walker Mild, Bitter Ⓗ
xing memorabilia ♪♣🛈

ellington Butts
Windsor Street, 8
gsons Mild, Bitter Ⓗ
aracterful pub near
glican cathedral 🅰♪♣🛈

ew Brighton 24B3

0–3; 5.30–10.30

ommercial
Hope Street (off A554)
ening opening: 5
ter Walker Mild, Bitter, Best
ter Ⓗ
all, friendly local, table
vice in lounge ♪♣🛈Ⓢ≷

agazine Hotel
agazine Brow
051-639 3381
ens at 12 noon & 5 pm
aught Bass Ⓗ
easant multi-roomed pub
erlooking Mersey 🅰🅰Ⓡ🄶

ewton-le-Willows
24D3

0–3.30; 5.30–10.30 (11 F, S)

ills Head
uthworth Road (A572)
028
Coope Burton Ale
tley Walker Mild, Bitter Ⓗ
odernised pub, popular for
eals 🄴♪🅰🄶🍴Ⓢ

ld Crow
8 Crow Lane East (A572)
tley Walker Mild, Bitter,
alker Best Bitter Ⓔ
endly local with
mfortable lounge and
larged vault ♪♣🅰🛈Ⓢ

ainhill 24C3

–3.30; 5.30–10.30 (11 F, S)

ach & Horses
herup Lane
gsons Bitter Ⓗ
ourban local ♪♣🅰Ⓢ

. Helens 24D3

0–3.30; 5.30–10.30 (11 F, S)

ngel
rrow Street
eenall Whitley Mild,
ter Ⓔ
wn-centre pub in
destrian precinct ♪♣🛈≷

ope & Anchor
y Road, Gerards Bridge
tley Walker Mild, Bitter Ⓗ
ch-improved local, only
ndpumped Tetleys for miles
🛈

Phoenix
Canal Street
Boddingtons Mild, Bitter Ⓔ
Refurbished local in industrial
setting ♪♣🛈

Swan
Corporation Street
Greenall Whitley Mild, Bitter Ⓔ
Busy town-centre pub ♪♣🛈≷

Wheatsheaf
Mill Lane, Sutton Leach
**Greenall Whitley Mild,
Bitter** Ⓔ
Many-roomed pub with
bowling green ♣🅰🛈Ⓢ

Southport 24B1

11.30–3; 5.30–10.30 (11 F, S)

Bold Arms
Botanic Road, Churchtown
Tetley Walker Mild, Bitter Ⓗ
Popular old pub
🅰♪♣🄰🅰🄶🍴Ⓢ

Old Ship
43 Eastbank Street
Evening opening: 5
**Ind Coope Burton Ale
Peter Walker Mild, Bitter, Best
Bitter** Ⓗ
Recently renovated ♪♣🄰Ⓡ🄶≷

Windmill
Seabank Road
**Matthew Brown Mild, Bitter,
John Peel Bitter** Ⓗ
Mid-terrace pub 🅰♪♫🄴🄰🄶

Zetland Hotel
Zetland Street
Evening opening: 6
**Burtonwood Dark Mild,
Bitter** Ⓔ
Suburban pub with bowling
green ♪♣🄰🅰Ⓡ

Try also: Scarisbrick Hotel,
Lord Street (free)

Thatto Heath 24D3

11.30–3.30; 5.30–10.30 (11 F, S)

Vine
Elephant Lane

Boddingtons Mild, Bitter Ⓔ
Popular locals' pub, recently
modernised ♪♣🛈≷

Thornton Hough
24B4

11.30–3; 5.30–10.30

Seven Stars
Church Road (B3156)
Whitbread Castle Eden Ale Ⓗ
Refurbished one-bar pub in
model village 🅰♪♫🄰🄶🍴Ⓢ

Wallasey 24B3

11.30–3; 5.30–10.30

Egremont Ferry
48 Tobin Street (off A554)
☎ 051-639 1753
Higsons Mild, Bitter Ⓗ
Popular riverside local
♪♣🄰Ⓡ🛈Ⓢ

McCulloch's
212 Rake Lane (B5143)
**Draught Bass
McEwan 70/-** Ⓗ
Tastefully renovated free
house ♪♣Ⓢ

Mona Castle
161 Wheatland Lane
(Off B5145)
Evening opening: 5
Tetley Walker Mild, Bitter Ⓗ
Lively town local ♪♣🅰🛈Ⓢ

Waterloo 24B3

11.30–3; 5.30–10.30 (11 F, S)

Marine
South Road, Liverpool 22
Higsons Mild, Bitter Ⓗ
Near Crosby paddling pool
♣🛈≷

Victoria Hotel
27 Bath Street, Liverpool 22
Peter Walker Mild, Bitter Ⓗ
Close to Crosby marina
♪♣🄶🍴≷

Volunteer Canteen
45 East Street, Liverpool 22
Higsons Mild, Bitter Ⓗ
Crowded backstreet pub ♣🛈≷

There's a certain honesty that I like about this place.

ttleborough 19F4

#0–2.30; 6–11
riffin
urch Street (A11)
452149
eene King Abbot
lly Cobbold Bitter,
iginal H
mfortable hotel; guest beers
⚬⌐♣⚘🅰🅴🅲⚬🍷🆗⚬&🅰⚄

illingford 19F2

2.30; 7–11
orge
1145)
nams Bitter, Old
eene King Abbot G
stefully converted former
ithy
⌐♣🅰⚘🅴🅲⚬🆗⚬⚙

inham 19E1

#0–2.30; 6–11
hequers
ont Street (B1388)
982397
ens at 11 am & 7 pm
oodforde Wherry Best
tter, Norfolk Porter H
cellent locals' pub; guest
er⌐♣⚘🅰

ickling 19G2

0–2.30; 6–11
**uckinghamshire
rms**
1354) ℰ Aylsham 2133
nams Bitter
eene King Abbot
d Coope Burton Ale
lly Cobbold Original H
th-century N.T. property
th fine food
⚘🅰🅴🅱🅲⚬🆗⚬

ofield 19H3

0–2.30; 5.30–11
ings Head
47) ℰ Norwich 715456
ethered Bitter H
nter Royal G
furbished local with
memade food and a ghost
⌐♣⚘🅰🅲⚬🆗⚙⚄&

radwell 19J3

0–2.30; 6–11
n
4 Beccles Road (A143)
ening opening: 6.30
rwich Bullards Mild
ebster Yorkshire Bitter H
aditional public bar with
parate 'upmarket' lounge
ilding
♣⚘🅰🅱🅲⚬🆗⚙⚄&

rundall 19G3

0–2.30; 6–11
are
ation Road (off A47)
nams Bitter, Old
urage Best Bitter, Directors
lly Cobbold Original H

Large pub catering for boating
tourists and locals
⚬⌐♣⚘🅴🅱🅰🅱🅲⚬🆗⚙⚄&⚄

Burnham Thorpe 18E1

11–2.30; 6–11
Lord Nelson
(Off A149)
Greene King XX, IPA, Abbot G
Traditional pub with jug
service⌐♣⚘🅰⚙🅰

Castle Acre 18D3

11–2.30; 6–11
Ostrich
Stocks Green (off A1065)
ℰ 398
Greene King XX, IPA, Abbot H
Popular pub on green
⚬⌐♣⚘🅴⚘🅰🅱🅲⚬🆗⚙⚄🅰

Chedgrave 19H4

10.30–2.30; 6–11
White Horse
Norwich Road (off A146)
**Norwich Bullards Mild, Castle
Bitter** H
Excellent unspoilt country pub
near River Chet ♣🅱🆗⚄&

Clenchwarton 18C2

10–2.30; 6–11
Victory
243 Main Road (A17)
ℰ King's Lynn 2377
Elgood Bitter H
Friendly roadside inn
⚬♣⚘🅰🅱⚙⚄

Cley 19F1

10.30–2.30; 6–11
**George & Dragon
Hotel**
High Street (A149) ℰ 740652
Opens at 11 am & 7 pm
**Woodforde Wherry Best
Bitter** H
Tourist hotel and village social
centre; good food
⚬⌐♣⚘🅰🅴🅱🅲⚬🆗⚙⚄&🅰

Cockley Cley 18D3

10.30–2.30; 6–11
**Twenty
Churchwardens**
Swaffham Road (off A1065)
Opens at 11 am & 6.30 pm
**Adnams Bitter
Burton Bridge Bitter
Samuel Smith Old Brewery
Bitter** H
Former schoolhouse; guest
beer⚬⌐♣⚘🅴⚘🅰🅲⚬🆗⚙⚄🅰

Coltishall 19G2

11–2.30; 6–11
Red Lion
Church Street (B1354)
Wethered Bitter H
Winter Royal G
16th-century pub close to
River Bure ♣⚘🅰🅲⚙⚄

Cromer 19G1

11–2.30; 7–11
Red Lion Hotel
Tucker Street (off A149)
ℰ 512737
Opens at 10 am & 6 pm
**Adnams Bitter
Greene King Abbot
Norwich Bullards Mild** H
Clifftop hotel with genuine
public bar; many guest beers
⚬⌐♣🅴🅱⚘🅰🅱🅲⚬🆗⚙⚄&🅰⚄

Deopham 19F4

10.30–2.30; 5.30–11
Victoria
(Off B1108) OS 051008
Opens at 12 noon & 7 pm;
closed Monday lunchtimes
**Adnams Bitter
Greene King Abbot
Ind Coope Bitter, Burton Ale** H
Beamed country pub with
restaurant and barbecues
⚬⌐♣⚘🅰🅲⚬🆗⚙⚄🅰

Diss 19F5

10–2.30; 6–11
Sun Inn
Mere Street (off A1066)
ℰ 3828
Open until 4 pm Fridays
**Adnams Bitter, Old
Courage Best Bitter
Greene King Abbot** G
Mereside drinkers' pub
⚬⌐♣⚘🅱🅲⚙⚄🅰⚄

Downham
Market 18C3

10.30–2.30; 6–11
Castle Hotel
Paradise Road (off A10)
ℰ 382157
**Adnams Bitter
Downham Bitter
Greene King Abbot** H
Hotel with own brewhouse
⚬⌐♣🅱⚘🅰🅱🅲⚬🆗⚙⚄⚙⚄

Live & Let Live
London Road (A10) ℰ 383933
**Adnams Bitter
Everard Old Original
Greene King IPA, Abbot** H
Popular split-level pub
⚙♣⚘🅲⚙🆗⚙⚄⚄

East Dereham 19E3

10–2.30; 6–11
Phoenix Hotel
Church Street ℰ 2276
Opens at 11 am & 6.30 pm
**Adnams Bitter
Greene King Abbot** H
Modern hotel, real ale in Otter
bar⌐♣⚘🅱🅴🅱🅲⚬🆗⚙⚄&🅰

Eccles 19E4

11–2.30; 5.30–11
**Old Railway Tavern
(Eccles Tap)**
Station Road (off A11)
Evening opening: 7

Adnams Bitter
Greene King IPA, Abbot
Samuel Smith Old
Brewery Bitter ⊞
Off the beaten track but worth
a visit ♪♣⊞♯⋒⊛≉

Erpingham 19G2

11–2.30; 6.30–11
Spread Eagle
(Off A140) ☎ Cromer 761591
Adnams Bitter
Everard Old Original
Greene King Abbot
Samuel Smith Old
Brewery Bitter
Woodforde Spread Eagle
Bitter, Norfolk Porter, Golden
Eye ⊞
Friendly country free house,
occasional guest beers
♣♪♣♯⋒⊞Ⓖ⋒⊛♂

Gayton 18D2

10.30–2.30; 6–11
Crown
(B1145) ☎ 252
Greene King XX, IPA, Abbot ⊞
Busy village local
♪♣♯⋒⊞Ⓖ⋒Ⓘ⊛

Gorleston 19J3

10.30–2.30; 6–11
Lord Nelson
33 Trafalgar Road West (off
A12)
Norwich Bullards Mild
Webster Yorkshire Bitter ⊞
Bright and pleasant, a
traditional local
♪♣♯⋒Ⓘ

Short Blue
High Street
Adnams Bitter
Courage Best Bitter
Woodforde Wherry Best
Bitter ⊞
Tastefully modernised free
house ♪♯Ⓖ

Great Bircham 18D2

10.30–2.30; 6.30–11
Kings Head
Lynn Road (B1153)
☎ Syderstone 265
Adnams Bitter
Draught Bass ⊞
Country hotel
♣⊞♯⋒⊞Ⓖ⋒Ⓘ⊛

Great Moulton 19G4

11.30–2; 6.30–11
Fox & Hounds
Frith Way (off A140)
Wethered Bitter Ⓖ
15th century pub with oil
lamps, dining room upstairs
♣Ⓘ⊞♯⋒⋒Ⓘ⊛Å

Great Ryburgh 19E2

10.30–2.30; 6–11
Boar Inn
31 Station Road (off A1067)
☎ 212

Tolly Cobbold Mild, Bitter,
Original ⊞
Large, modernised village free
house ♣♪♣♯⋒⊞Ⓡ⋒⊛♂

Great Yarmouth 19J3

10.30–2.30; 5.30–11
Crystal
Northgate Street (A12)
Evening opening: 6
Adnams Bitter, Old
Draught Bass
Mitchells & Butlers Springfield
Bitter ⊞
Traditional corner pub near
market place ♪♣♯Ⓘ⊛♂≉

Talbot
Howard Street North (off
A12)
Adnams Bitter, Old
Draught Bass ⊞
Busy single-bar free house
near market place ♪♣Ⓘ⊛♂≉

Happisburgh 19H2

10.30–2.30; 6–11
Victoria
Lower Street
Adnams Bitter
Greene King IPA, Abbot
Samuel Smith Old
Brewery Bitter ⊞
Excellent seaside retreat
☞♪♣♯⋒⊞Ⓖ⋒⊛♂Å

Harleston 19G5

10–2.30; 6–11
Cherry Tree
London Road (off A143)
Adnams Mild, Bitter, Old Ⓖ
Excellent pub ♣♪♣♯⋒Ⓘ⊛♂

Hethersett 19F3

10.30–2.30; 6–11
Kings Head
Norwich Road (off A11)
Norwich Bullards Mild, Castle
Bitter
Webster Yorkshire Bitter ⊞
Cottage-style 16th-century
pub ♣♪♣♯⋒⊞Ⓖ⋒Ⓘ⊛

Heydon 19F2

11–2.30; 6.30–11
Earle Arms
(Off B1149) ☎ Saxthorpe 376
Closes 2 pm Mon–Fri
Adnams Bitter Ⓖ
Traditional country pub in
idyllic setting
♪♯⋒⊞Ⓘ⊛

Hilborough 18D4

10.30–2.30; 6–11
Swan
Near Swaffham (A1065)
☎ Great Cressingham 380
Greene King IPA, Abbot
Ind Coope Burton Ale
Tolly Cobbold Original ⊞
Delightful country inn
♣♪☞♯⋒⊞Ⓡ⋒Ⓖ⊛Å

Horsham St Faith 19G

10.30–2.30; 7–11
Kings Head
Back Street (off A140)
Webster Yorkshire Bitter ⊞
Friendly and caring single-bar
local ♣♪♣♯⋒⊞Ⓡ⋒Ⓖ⊛♂

Hunworth 19F

10.30–2.30; 6–11
Blue Bell
The Green (off B1149)
Adnams Bitter
Ruddle County
Woodforde Wherry Best
Bitter ⊞
Popular country pub
♣Ⓘ♣♯⋒⊞Ⓡ⋒Ⓖ⊛♂

Itteringham 19F

10.30–2.30; 6–11
Walpole Arms
(Off B1354)
Tolly Cobbold Original Ⓖ
Excellent unspoilt pub with
rural atmosphere ♣♪♣♯⋒Ⓘ

King's Lynn 18C

10.30–2.30; 6–11
Lattice House
Chapel Street
Bateman XB
Everard Tiger, Old Original
Greene King IPA
Marston Pedigree ⊞
Excellently restored 15th-
century pub ☞♣♯Ⓡ⋒Ⓘ⊛≉

London Porter House
London Road
Greene King IPA, Abbot Ⓖ
Small, quaint, popular pub on
street corner Ⓗ♯⊛Å≉

Martham 19H

10.30–2.30; 6–11
Victoria Inn
Repps Road
☎ Great Yarmouth 740774
Webster Yorkshire Bitter ⊞
Friendly village local, excellent
food ♣♪♣♯⋒⊞Ⓡ⋒Ⓖ⋒Ⓘ⊛

Mundesley 19G

10.30–2.30; 6–11
Royal
Paston Road (off B1159)
☎ 720096
Adnams Bitter
Charrington IPA
Greene King Abbot ⊞
Fascinating hotel bar with
Nelsonian associations
♣Ⓘ♣⊞♯⋒⊞Ⓡ⋒Ⓖ⋒Ⓘ⊛Å

New Buckenham 19F

10.30–2.30; 5.30–11
Kings Head
Market Place (B1113)
Opens at 11.30 am & 7 pm
Wethered Bitter Ⓖ

Unspoilt, well-run village local
🅰♪♣🌿🍴🅁🅖🍷🍴🅢🅰

North Walsham
19G2

10.30–2.30; 6–11
Wheelwrights Arms
Bacton Road, White Horse
Common (B1150)
Adnams Bitter
Greene King IPA, Abbot Ⓗ
Converted barn with cosy
atmosphere ♪♣🌿🅰🅖🍴♣

North Wootton 18C2

10.30–2.30; 6–11
Red Cat Hotel
(Off A149)
☎ Castle Rising 244
Adnams Bitter Ⓗ Old Ⓖ
Greene King Abbot
Marston Pedigree Ⓗ
Sporting country hotel
🅰🅗🌿🅿🔲🅁🅖🍷🍴🅢

Norwich
19G3

10.30–2.30; 5.30–11
Beehive
30 Leopold Road (off Norwich
Ring Road)☎ 51628
Courage Best Bitter,
Directors Ⓗ
Keen suburban local
♪♣🌿🅰🅁🅖🍴🅢♣

Constitution
Constitution Hill (B1150)
Saturday evening opening: 7
Norwich Castle Bitter
Webster Yorkshire Bitter Ⓗ
Popular 1930's pub
🅰♪♣🌿🅰🅖🍴♣

Horse & Dray
137 Ber Street ☎ 24741
Adnams Bitter, Old
Bulmer Cider Ⓗ
Comfortable friendly Adnams'
tied house 🅰♪♣🌿🅖🍷🍴🅢♣

Kings Arms
22 Hall Road
Greene King XX, IPA, Abbot Ⓗ
Traditional friendly local
♪♣🍴🅢

Lion & Castle
73 West Pottergate ☎ 27974
Norwich Bullards Mild, Castle
Bitter Ⓗ
Lively two-bar old-world pub
♪♣🌿🍷🍴🅢

Micawbers Tavern
92 Pottergate ☎ 26627
Adnams Bitter
Draught Bass
Norwich Bullards Mild
Tolly Cobbold Original
Webster Yorkshire Bitter
Woodforde Broadsman Bitter Ⓗ
Popular, refurbished old
corner pub ♪🍴🅢

Mill Tavern
Angel Road (2 Millers Lane)
Evening opening: 6

Adnams Mild, Bitter, Old Ⓗ
Excellent pub near park
♪♣🌿🅰♣

Pickwick
41 Earlham Road
Tolly Cobbold Mild, Bitter,
Original, Old Strong Ⓗ
Victorian-style pub, Tolly's
Norwich flagship ♪♣🌿🅰🅖🍴♣

Plasterers Arms
43 Cowgate ☎ 613089
Opens at 11 am & 7 pm
Adnams Bitter, Old
Everard Old Original
Greene King Abbot
Ind Coope Burton Ale
Ruddle County
Samuel Smith Old
Brewery Bitter
Tolly Cobbold Original
Gaymer Cider Ⓗ
Dark and popular ♪♣🍴

Plough
58 St Benedicts Street
Courage Best Bitter,
Directors Ⓗ
Basic off-beat young persons'
pub ♪♣🍴🅢

Rose Tavern
88 Rupert Street ☎ 25339
Wethered Bitter Ⓗ
Winter Royal Ⓖ
Colourful local
♪♣🅗🌿🅰🅖🍷🍴🅢♣

Ten Bells
78 St Benedicts
Adnams Bitter
Greene King Abbot
Home Bitter
Samuel Smith Old
Brewery Bitter Ⓗ
Small and popular; nine beers
always available ♪🅢

White Lion
73 Oak Street ☎ 20630
Adnams Bitter
Greene King XX, IPA, Abbot
Samuel Smith Old Brewery
Bitter
Woodforde White Lion Bitter,
Broadsman Bitter, Norfolk
Porter Ⓗ
Busy, friendly and unspoilt
free house ♪♣🍴♣🅢

White Lion
St Martins, Palace Plain
Courage Best Bitter,
Directors Ⓗ
Small, comfortable two-bar
pub ♪♣🌿🅁🅖♣≋

Windmill
Plumstead Road
Evening opening: 6
Greene King XX, IPA, Abbot Ⓗ
Excellent roadside pub
♪♣🌿🅰🅖♣🅢

Outwell
18B3

10.30–2.30; 6–11
Red Lion
Wisbech Road (A1122, off
A1101)

Elgood Bitter Ⓗ
Village pub on waterway
🅰♪♣🅰🅁🍷🅢

Overstrand
19G1

10.30–2.30; 6–11
Overstrand Court
5 High Street (off B1159)
☎ 282
Greene King IPA, Abbot Ⓗ
Country hotel in coastal
village 🅰♪🅗🌿🅿🅰🅁🅖🍷🍴🅢🅰

Oxborough
18D3

10.30–2.30; 6–11
Bedingfeld Arms
(Off A134) ☎ Gooderstone 300
Greene King XX, IPA, Abbot Ⓗ
Popular pub by Oxborough
Hall 🅰♪♣🌿🅰🅁🅖🍷🍴🅢🅰

Poringland
19G4

10.30–2.30; 5.30–11
Swan
119 The Street (B1332)
Opens at 11 am & 6 pm
Norwich Bullards Mild
Webster Yorkshire Bitter Ⓗ
Modern two-bar village local
♪♣🌿🅰🅁🅖🍷🍴🅢♣

Reedham
19H3

10.30–2.30; 6–11
Reedham Ferry
(B1140)
Opens at 11 am & 6.30 pm
Adnams Bitter Ⓗ Old Ⓖ
Tolly Cobbold Original Ⓗ
Old ferryside family pub
♪♣🅗🌿🅰🍷♣🅢🅰

Reepham
19F2

10.30–2.30; 6–11
Old Brewery House
Market Square (off B1145)
☎ 8181
Adnams Bitter, Old
Burton Bridge Bitter
Greene King Abbot
Samuel Smith Old
Brewery Bitter Ⓗ
Small hotel with good leisure
facilities ♪🅰🔲🅁🅖🍷🍴🅰

Ringstead
18D1

11–2.30; 6–11
Gin Trap
High Street, near Hunstanton
(off A149)
Adnams Bitter Ⓗ Old Ⓖ
Country inn, French bowls
played ♪♣🌿🅰🍷🍴♣

Roydon
19F5

10.30–2.30; 6–11
White Hart
High Road (A1066)
☎ Diss 3597
Norwich Bullards Mild
Webster Yorkshire Bitter Ⓗ
Beams and horse brasses
♪♣🌿🅰🔲🅁🍷🍴

Salhouse
19G3

10.30–2.30; 6–11

Lodge
Vicarage Road
Courage Best Bitter, Directors
Greene King IPA, Abbot
Tolly Cobbold Original H
Converted Georgian vicarage,
smart and busy ♪♣♨🅿🚗Ⓡℂ🌙♦

Sea Palling 19H2
10.30–2.30; 6–11
Hall Inn
Waxham Road (B1159)
☎ Hickling 323
Opens at 12 noon & 7 pm in
winter
Adnams Bitter H Old Ⓖ
Courage Directors
Greene King Abbot
Samuel Smith Old Brewery
Bitter H
Centuries-old, occasional
guest beers
🛏♪♣🍴🚗🅿🚗🈂Ⓡℂ🌙🕚Ⓢ▲

Sheringham 19F1
10–2.30; 6–11
Lobster
13 High Street ☎ 822716
Evening opening: 6.30
Norwich Castle Bitter H
Unspoilt two-bar seafront inn
🛏🍴♣🍴🅿🚗🅰Ⓡℂ🌙🕚Ⓢ≢

Skeyton 19G2
10.30–2.30; 5.30–11
Goat
Evening opening: 6.30
Norwich Bullards Mild
Webster Yorkshire Bitter H
Old thatched inn, skilfully
refurbished ♪♣♨🅿🚗ℂ🌙🕚Ⓢ

Snettisham 18C1
10.30–2.30; 6–11
Rose & Crown
Old Church Lane (off A149)
Adnams Bitter H Old Ⓖ
Greene King IPA, Abbot H
Attractive 14th-century pub
🛏▲🈂🅿🚗Ⓡℂ🌙🕚Ⓢ

Stanhoe 18D1
10.30–2.30; 6–11
Crown
Burnham Road (B1155)
Elgood Bitter H
Friendly country pub
♪♣🅿🚗🕚Ⓢ▲

Thetford 18E5
10–2.30; 6–11
Norfolk Terrier
Croxton Road (B1110)
Morning opening: 10.30
Tolly Cobbold Mild, Bitter,
Original H
Excellent modern tied house
🕚♪♣🅿🚗ℂ🌙🕚Ⓢ

Thomas Paine Hotel
White Hart Street (off A11)
Adnams Bitter
Tolly Cobbold Original Ⓔ
Historic free house
♪🈂🚗🅰Ⓡℂ🌙🕚Ⓢ≢

Thompson 18E4
10.30–2.30; 6–11
Chequers
Near Watton (off A1075)
Evening opening: 6.30
Adnams Bitter
Greene King Abbot H
16th-century pub with guest
beers 🈂🅿🚗ℂ🌙🕚Ⓢ

Thornham 18D1
10.30–2.30; 6–11
Lifeboat
Ship Lane (off A149) ☎ 236
Adnams Bitter Ⓖ & H
Greene King XX Ⓖ **IPA, Abbot**
Tolly Cobbold Original H
Traditional ex-smugglers pub
🛏🍴♪♣🈂🅿🚗🅰Ⓡℂ🌙🕚Ⓢ♦▲

Thorpe St Andrew 19G3
10.30–2.30; 5.30–11
Buck
Yarmouth Road (A47)
Evening opening: 6
Norwich Bullards Mild
Webster Yorkshire Bitter H
Listed building by River Green
🍴♣🈂🅿🚗ℂⓈ

Tibenham 19F4
10.30–2.30; 6–11
Greyhound
(Off B1134) ☎ Tivetshall 676
Opens 12–2 & 7–11; closed
Mon, Tue lunchtimes
Adnams Bitter, Old H & Ⓖ
Worth finding; good food
🛏🍴♪♣🈂🅿🚗🅰Ⓡ🌙🕚Ⓢ▲

Toft Monks 19H4
10.30–2.30; 6–11
Toft Lion
The Street (A143)
Opens at 11 am & 7 pm
Adnams Bitter H Old Ⓖ
Courage Best Bitter H
Friendly roadside inn, good
food 🛏🍴♪♣🈂🅿🚗🅰Ⓡ🌙▲

Trowse 19G3
10.30–2.30; 5.30–11
Crown Point
(A146) ☎ Norwich 25689
Morning opening: 11
Wethered Bitter H
Unspoilt village pub with plate
collection ♪♣♨🚗ℂ🌙🕚Ⓢ

Walpole Cross Keys 18B2
10.30–2.30; 6–11
Woolpack
Main Road (A17)
Evening opening: 7
Adnams Bitter
Greene King IPA, Abbot H
Old country pub just off new
by-pass
🛏♪♣🈂🅿🚗🅰Ⓡℂ🌙🕚Ⓢ

Walsingham 19E1
10.30–2.30; 6–11
Bull
Shirehall Plain (B1105) ☎ 333
Webster Yorkshire Bitter H
Unspoilt village pub
🛏♪♣🈂🅿🚗Ⓡ🅹Ⓢ♦

Wells-next-the Sea 18E1
10.30–2.30; 6–11
Edinburgh
Station Road (A149)
☎ Fakenham 710120
Charrington IPA
Draught Bass
Greene King XX, IPA, Abbot H
Excellent free house
🛏♪♣🈂🈁🅿🚗Ⓡℂ🌙🕚Ⓢ♦▲

Winterton-on-Sea 19J2
10.30–2.30; 6–11
Fishermans Return
The Lane (off B1159) ☎ 305
Winter evening opening: 7
Norwich Bullards Mild, Castle
Bitter
Webster Yorkshire Bitter H
Excellent old inn, good food
🍴♪♣🅿🚗🅰Ⓡℂ🌙🕚Ⓢ♦

Wolterton 19F2
10.30–2.30; 6–11
Saracens Head
(Off A140) ☎ Matlaske 287
Evening opening: 7
Adnams Bitter
Greene King Abbot H
Isolated but popular
🛏🍴♪♣🈂🅿🚗🅰Ⓡℂ🌙Ⓢ▲

Wroxham 19G3
10–2.30; 6–11
Hotel Wroxham
The Bridge (off A1151) ☎ 206
Evening opening: 5.30
Courage Best Bitter, Directors
Woodforde Broadsman Bitter,
Wherry Best Bitter, Norfolk
Porter H **Festive Strong Ale** Ⓖ
Popular modern hotel
🍴♪♣🈂🅿🚗🅰Ⓡℂ🌙🕚Ⓢ♦≢

Wymondham 19F4
10.30–2.30; 5.30–11
Cross Keys Inn
Market Place ☎ 602152
Norwich Bullards Mild, Castle
Bitter
Webster Yorkshire Bitter H
Market inn with welcoming
atmosphere ♪🈁🅿🚗🌙🕚Ⓢ≢

Feathers
Town Green ☎ 605675
Opens at 11 am & 7 pm
Adnams Bitter, Old
Greene King Abbot
Marston Pedigree
Woodforde Wherry Best
Bitter H
Modernised old pub
🍴♪♣🈂🅿🚗🌙🕚Ⓢ♦

Abthorpe 16C6

10.30–2.30; 7–11
New Inn
Silver Street (A43)
Hook Norton Best Bitter [H]
Country local ⌂♪♣✿🚗🍷Ⓢ

Ashton 17F3

10–2.30; 6–11
Chequered Skipper
(Off A605) ☎ Oundle 73494
Opens at 11 am & 6.30 pm
Adnams Bitter
Paine Skipper, EG [H]
Exciting village pub
⌂Γ♪♣✿🚗◷☾🍷Ⓢ

Badby 16B5

10.30–2.30; 6–11
Windmill
Main Street (off A361)
☎ Daventry 702363
Courage Directors
Everard Tiger
Hook Norton Best Bitter [H]
Refurbished village pub
⌂♪♣⊞✿🚗▣◷☾🍷Ⓢ⛺

Barnwell 17E4

11–2.30; 6–11
Montague Arms
(Off A605) ☎ Oundle 73726
Evening opening: 6.30
Adnams Bitter
Marston Pedigree
Wells Eagle Bitter,
Bombardier [H]
500-year-old stone-built pub
⌂Γ♪♣✿🚗◷☾Ⓢ⛺

Blakesley 16C6

11–2.30; 7–11
Bartholomew Arms
High Street ☎ 860292
Marston Pedigree
Younger Scotch Bitter [H]
Enlarged village pub
⌂♪♣✿▣[R]◷Ⓢ

Braunston 16B5

10.30–2.30; 6–11
Old Plough
High Street (off A45)
Opens at 11 am & 6.30 pm
Ansells Mild, Bitter
Ind Coope Burton Ale [H]
Popular canal-village pub
⌂♪♣⊞✿🚗[R]◷☾🍷Ⓢ♿⛺

Brixworth 16C4

10.30–2.30; 5.30–11
George
(A508)
Wells Eagle Bitter,
Bombardier [H]
Popular modern pub behind old frontage ♪♣✿🚗[R]◷🍷

Buckby Wharf 16C5

10.30–2.30; 6–11
New Inn
(A5) ☎ Long Buckby 842540
Marston Pedigree [H]
Popular canalside free house
♪♣✿🚗◷☾🍷Ⓢ♿

Bulwick 16E3

11–2.30; 6–11
Queen's Head
(A43) ☎ 272
Bateman XXXB
Greene King IPA
Marston Pedigree [H]
Comfortable 17th-century free house ⌂♪✿🚗[R]◷☾Ⓢ

Burton Latimer 16D4

11–2.30; 6.30–11
Olde Victoria
Bakehouse Lane (off A6)
Opens at 12 noon & 7 pm
Adnams Bitter
Greene King IPA, Abbot
Ruddle County
Tolly Cobbold Original [H]
Smart pub with bric-a-brac ✿🚗

Charlton 16B7

10–2.30; 6–11
Rose & Crown
Main Street
Draught Bass
Mitchells & Butlers Springfield Bitter, Brew XI [H]
Small, friendly pub in rural conservation area ⌂Γ♣✿🚗[R]🍷

Corby 16D3

10.30–2.30; 6–11
Knights Lodge
Tower Hill Road (off A6003)
Everard Beacon, Tiger, Old Original [H]
Listed 17th-century pub in a clearing in Rockingham Forest
⌂♪✿🚗[R]◷Ⓢ♿

Cottingham 16D3

10.30–2.30; 6–11
Royal George
Blind Lane (off B670)
Marston Capital, Pedigree,
Owd Rodger [H]
Small, busy pub
⌂♪♣✿🚗[R]◷☾🍷Ⓢ

Crick 16C4

10.30–2.30; 6–11
Red Lion
Main Road (A428, off M1)
Lunchtime opening: 11.30–2
Manns IPA [H]
Watney Fined Stag Bitter [E]
Busy, food-orientated coaching inn near canal
Γ♣🚗◷☾ (not Sun) Ⓢ

Daventry 16B5

10.30–2.30; 5.30–11
Dun Cow
Brook Street (A361) ☎ 71545
Davenports Bitter [H]
Modernised 17th-century coaching inn ⌂Γ♪♣🚗[R]🍷Ⓢ♿

Deanshanger 16D6

10.30–2.30; 6–11
Fox & Hounds
High Street (off A422)
Aylesbury ABC Bitter
Draught Bass
Weston Cider [H]
Old fashioned, family-run pub
⌂Γ♣✿🚗◷☾🍷Ⓢ

Desborough 16D4

11–2.30; 7–11
George
High Street (off A6)
Everard Tiger [H]
Modernised ironstone pub
♪♣✿🚗[R]🍷Ⓢ♿

Eastcote 16C5

12–2.30; 6–10.30 (11 F, S)
Eastcote Arms
(Off A5) near Towcester
Closed Monday lunchtimes
Marston Pedigree
Samuel Smith Old Brewery Bitter [H]
Welcoming, attractive village pub; guest beer ⌂♪✿🚗Ⓢ♿

Eydon 16B6

11–2.30; 6.30–11
Royal Oak
Lime Avenue (off A361)
Everard Burton Mild, Tiger, Old Original
Litchborough Tudor Ale [H]
Many-roomed village pub with ship's boiler; guest beers
⌂♪♣⊞✿🚗[R]◷☾🍷Ⓢ

Finedon 16E4

11–2.30; 7–11
Prince of Wales
Well Street (off A510/A6)
Marston Capital, Pedigree [H]
Backstreet local with plush lounge ♪♣🚗[R]🍷Ⓢ♿

Fotheringhay 17E3

10–2.30; 6–11
Falcon
(Off A605) ☎ Cotterstock 254
Elgood Bitter
Greene King IPA, Abbot
Hereward Bitter
Litchborough Tudor Ale [H]
Good restaurant pub
⌂♣✿🚗[R]◷☾🍷Ⓢ

Gayton 16C5

10.30–2.30; 6–11
Queen Victoria
High Street (off A43)
Ansells Bitter
Everard Old Original
Hook Norton Best Bitter
Ruddle County [H]
Versatile village pub
⌂♪♣🚗[R]◷☾🍷Ⓢ

Great Cransley 16D4

11–2.30; 7–11
Three Cranes
Loddington Road (off A43)
Marston Capital, Pedigree [H]
Splendid local with good garden
⌂♣✿🚗[R]🍷♿

Great Houghton
16D5

10.30–2.30; 5.30–10.30 (11 F, S)
Old Cherry Tree
(Off A428)
**Wells Eagle Bitter,
Bombardier** 🅷
Hard-to-find village pub
🏠♣🅿🍴🅖🕒

Greatworth
16B6

11–2.30; 7–11
The Inn
Chapel Road (off A422)
**Hook Norton Mild, Best
Bitter** 🅷
Bulmer Cider 🅖
Real village pub with
restaurant
🏠♪🍴♣🅴🅿🍴🅿🕒🍷🛈🅢

Grendon
16D5

10.30–2.30; 6–11
Crown
34 Manor Road
**Marston Pedigree
Samuel Smith Old Brewery
Bitter** 🅷
Ex-Watney free house; guest
beers 🏠♪♣🅿🍴🅿🕒🍷🛈🅢♿

Hargrave
17E4

10.30–2.30; 6–11
Nags Head
Church Street (A45)
Wells Eagle Bitter 🅷
Bombardier 🅖
Picturesque village local
🏠♪♣🅿🍴🅢▲

Harringworth
16E3

11–2.30; 6.30–11
White Swan
Seaton Road ☎ Morcott 543
**Marston Pedigree
Ruddle Country** 🅷
Young persons' bar, diners'
lounge 🏠♪♣🅒🍷🛈🅢

Helmdon
16B6

11–2.30; 6–11
Bell
Church Street ☎ Sulgrave 315
Hook Norton Best Bitter 🅷
Busy village pub with
old adverts 🏠♪♣🅿🍴🅱🛈

Higham Ferrers
16E5

10.30–2.30; 6–11
Queens Head
High Street (A6)
**Draught Bass
Mitchells & Butlers Springfield
Bitter** 🅷
Busy, friendly one-room
corner local ♪♣🅢

Islip
17E4

11–2.30; 6–11
Woolpack
Kettering Road (A604)
**Greene King IPA, Abbot
Tolly Cobbold Bitter,
Original** 🅷

12th-century former wool
merchants hostelry
♪♣🅿🅖🕒↩ (not Sun, Mon)🛈🅢

Kettering
16D4

10.30–2.30; 5.30–11
Alexandra Arms
Victoria Street ☎ 512253
Opens at 11 am & 7 pm
Manns IPA, Bitter 🅷
Friendly backstreet local with
attractive facade ♪♣🅿🅁🛈🅢♿

Cherry Tree
Market Square ☎ 514706
**Wells Eagle Bitter,
Bombardier** 🅷
Unspoilt town-centre local
🏠♣🅁🛈🅢♿↩

Three Cocks Inn
48 Lower Street (off A6)
Opens at 11 am & 5.30 pm
Marston Capital, Pedigree 🅷
Quiet local near town centre
♪♣🅱🛈🅢

Woolcomber
St Johns Road
Morning opening: 11
Home Bitter 🅔
Flourishing modern estate
local ⌐♪♣🅿🅱🛈🅢

Marston St. Lawrence
16B6

11–2.30; 7–11
Marston Inn
Main Street (off A422)
Hook Norton Best Bitter 🅖
Idyllic village local 🏠♣🅿🅱🛈

Middleton Cheney
16B6

10.30–2.30; 6.30–11
Red Lion
High Street (off A422)
**Mitchells & Butlers Mild,
Springfield Bitter** 🅷
Happy-go-lucky local with
cartoon sign 🏠♪♣🅱🅁🛈🅢

Northampton
16D5

11–2.30; 6–10.30 (11 F, S)
Bat & Wickets
Bailiff Street ☎ 38277
Evening opening: 6.30
**Courage Best Bitter,
Directors** 🅷
Popular, friendly local
⌐♪♣🅒🅢🛈🅢

Bull & Butcher
Bridge Street (off A508)
☎ 35904
Opens at 10.30 am & 5.30 pm
**Manns IPA, Bitter
Bulmer Cider** 🅷
Friendly town-centre local,
good games pub ♣🅱🅁🛈🅢↩

Garibaldi
Bailiff Street
**Draught Bass
Mitchells & Butlers Springfield
Bitter** 🅷
Renovated Victorian local,
popular lunchtimes ♣🛈

King William IV
Commercial Street ☎ 21307
Morning opening: 10.30
**Everard Tiger, Old Original
Greene King Abbot
Hook Norton Best Bitter, Old
Hookey
Marston Pedigree
Samuel Smith Old Brewery
Bitter
Weston Cider** 🅷
Busy town-centre free house
♪♣🅒🛈🅢↩

Pig & Whistle
Blackthorn Bridge Court,
Blackthorn (off A4500)
**Everard Beacon, Tiger, Old
Original** 🅷
Comfortable estate pub
⌐♪♣🅿🅱🛈🅢

Saddlers Arms
Bridge Street ☎ 32940
Morning opening: 10.30
Davenports Mild, Bitter 🅷
Locals' bar, young persons'
lounge ⌐♪♣🅱🅁🅒🕒↩

Silver Horse
Goldings Road (off A4500)
**Ansells Mild
Ind Coope Bitter, Burton Ale** 🅷
Comfortable estate pub, keen
darts players ⌐♪♣🅿🅱🛈

Tanners
Billingbrook Road, Thorplands
(Off A43) ☎ 45835
Home Bitter 🅔
Imposing three-storey estate
pub with steps ⌐♪♣🅱🅁🛈🅢

Norton
16C5

11–2.30; 6–11
White Horse
Daventry Road (off A5)
**Wells Eagle Bitter,
Bombardier** 🅷
Excellent modernised village
pub ♪♣🅿🅒🕒🍷🛈🅢♿

Orlingbury
16D4

10.30–2.30; 5.30–11
Queens Arms
Isham Road
Manns IPA, Bitter 🅷
Village pub with friendly,
relaxed atmosphere ♪♣🅿🅿🅒🛈

Oundle
17E3

10–2.30; 6–11
Ship
West Street (A605) ☎ 73918
**Marston Capital,
Burton Bitter, Owd Rodger
Wethered Bitter
Bulmer Cider** 🅷
17th-century, stone-built pub
🅿🅱🅁🅒🕒🍷🛈🅢

Raunds
17E4

10.30–2.30; 5.30–11
World Upside Down
Marshalls Road (off A605)
Opens at 11 am & 7 pm

Marston Capital, Pedigree [H]
Small town local near the square ♪♣🍴🚗👪Ⓢ

Rockingham 16D3

10.30–2.30; 6–11
Sondes Arms
Main Street (A6003)
Whitbread Castle Eden Ale [H]
Large, ivy-covered pub below Castle 🔥♪♣🛏🍴🚗[R]◔☾👪Ⓢ

Rothwell 16D4

10.30–2.30; 6–11
Rowell Charter
Sun Hill (A6)
Morning opening: 11.30
Adnams Bitter
McEwan 70/-
Younger IPA [H]
Comfortable old pub 🔥♪🚗◔☾

Rushden 16E5

10.30–2.30; 6–11
King Edward VII
Queen Street (off A6)
Evening opening: 6.30
Wells Eagle Bitter [H]
Street-corner local; former off-licence ♪♣👪Ⓢ

Rose & Crown
High Street (A6)
Marston Capital, Burton Bitter, Pedigree, Merrie Monk [H] **Owd Rodger** [G]
Traditional retreat in the main street ♪♣[R]👪Ⓢ

Shutlanger 16C6

10.30–2.30; 6.30–11
Plough
Main Road (off A5)
Wells Eagle Bitter, Bombardier [H]
Lively pub which has recorded a singalong LP 🎯♣🍴🚗👪Ⓢ⛺

Southwick 17E3

10–2.30; 6–11
Shuckburgh Arms
Morning opening: 10.30
Adnams Bitter
Litchborough Northamptonshire Bitter
Ruddle County [H]
Old thatched pub in heart of village 🔥♪♣🍴🚗◔☾👪Ⓢ

Stoke Doyle 17E3

10.30–2.30; 6–11
Shuckburgh Arms
☎ Oundle 72339
Ruddle County
Samuel Smith Old Brewery Bitter [H]
Spacious village local, TV in children's room
🔥♪♣🛏🍴🚗▣[R]◔☾Ⓢ

Sulgrave 16B6

11–2.30; 7–11
Star
Manor Road (off B4525)
Hook Norton Best Bitter, Old Hookey [H]
Old flagstoned pub 🔥♣👪

Thornby 16C4

12–2.30; 6.30–11
Red Lion
Main Road (A50)
Adnams Bitter
Marston Capital, Pedigree [H]
Bulmer Cider [G]
Smart, value-for-money pub; guest beer 🔥♣🍴🚗Ⓢ♿

Towcester 16C6

10.30–2.30; 5.30–11
Saracens Head
Watling Street (A5/A43)
☎ 50414
Wells Eagle Bitter, Bombardier [H]
Coaching inn with Dickensian connections 🔥♪🚗▣[R]◔☾Ⓢ

Twywell 16E4

10.30–2.30; 6–11
Old Friar
Lower Street (off A604)
Manns IPA, Bitter
Watney Fined Stag Bitter [H]
Unpretentious rural pub
🔥♪♣🍴🚗◔☾👪Ⓢ♿

Wadenhoe 17E4

11–2.30; 7–11
King's Head
Church Street
Marston Pedigree [H]
Hidden-away, thatched village pub 🔥♣🍴🚗[R]👪Ⓢ

Wakerley 16E3

10–2.30; 6–11
Exeter Arms
(Off A43) ☎ Morcott 817
Morning opening: 11
Ind Coope Burton Ale
Samuel Smith Old Brewery Bitter [H]
Modernised, friendly rural free house 🔥♪♣🍴🚗[R]
◔☾ (Thu–Sun) 👪Ⓢ⛺

Weedon 16C5

10.30–2.30; 6–11
Crossroads Hotel
Watling Street (A5/A45)
☎ 40354
Evening opening: 5.30
Adnams Bitter
Draught Bass
Litchborough Northamptonshire Bitter, Tudor Ale [H]
Famous for its clocks and 'chemist's shop' bar
♪🛏🍴🚗▣[R]◔☾Ⓢ

Narrowboat
Stowe Hill (A5) ☎ 40536
Wells Eagle Bitter, Bombardier [H]
Bulmer Cider [G]
Bright, popular canalside pub
♪♣🛏🍴🚗[R]◔☾Ⓢ♿

Welford 16C4

11–2.30; 6–11
Swan
High Street (A50) ☎ 481
Marston Burton Bitter, Pedigree [H]
Smart village pub
🔥🎯♪♣🛏◔☾Ⓢ♿

Wellingborough 16D5

10.30–2.30; 5.30–11
Vivian Arms
Knox Road (off B571)
Opens 11–2 (Mon–Fri); evening opening: 6 (Sat)
Wells Eagle Bitter [H]
Splendid backstreet local
♪♣🍴🚗👪Ⓢ♿🚆

Volunteer
69 Midland Road ☎ 22228
Evening opening: 7
Mitchells & Butlers Springfield Bitter, Brew XI [H]
Basic town local 🎯♪♣👪Ⓢ🚆

Weston 16B6

11–2.30; 6.30–11
Crown
OS 589469 ☎ Sulgrave 382
Fuller ESB
Hook Norton Best Bitter
Marston Pedigree [H] **Owd Rodger** [G]
Whitbread Flowers Original Bitter [H]
Weston Cider [G]
Stone-flagged country pub; guest beers
🔥🎯♪♣🛏🍴🚗[R]☾👪Ⓢ

Whitfield 16C6

11–2.30; 6–11
Sun
(Off A43) ☎ Syresham 232
Banks & Taylor Shefford Bitter
Hook Norton Best Bitter, Old Hookey
Theakston Old Peculiar
Whitbread Flowers Original Bitter [H]
Excellent food; guest beers
🔥♪♣🛏🍴🚗▣[R]◔☾Ⓢ

Wollaston 16E5

10.30–2.30; 6–11
Cuckoo
Bell End
Morning opening: 11
Wells Eagle Bitter, Bombardier [H]
Friendly village pub near church 🔥♪♣🍴◔☾👪Ⓢ

Yarwell 17F3

10–2.30; 6–11
Angel
Main Street
Greene King IPA
Tolly Cobbold Original [H]
Refurbished stone-built village pub 🔥♪♣🛏🍴◔☾👪Ⓢ⛺

Use it or lose it is not just a motto for post offices, it seems. Pubs throughout the country run the risk of closure through redevelopment or brewery rationalisation schemes. What looks rational to a brewery can look more like rationing to its customers, however, and the study and analysis of pub closures throughout the British Isles has left CAMRA's Pub Preservation Group sadder and wiser.

> "Villagers are to hold an ale supping siege to stop a brewery calling time on their local. When the bailiffs arrive to throw them out, it will be all hands to the pumps. The landlord, the ladies' and men's darts teams, the pigeon club, dominoes team, Royal British Legion branch and two soccer sides will be locked inside."
>
> – Press cutting about the threatened closure by Bass Worthington of The Bank House, Hixon, Staffs.

There are countless stories of decaying town centres; pub-less villages; and once-thriving communities left without a choice of pleasant places for drinking, relaxation and enjoyment. Local Councils press blindly on with 1960s-style comprehensive development plans, totally insensitive to those elements which make up a true community. Monopolistic and greedy breweries would rather sell unwanted pubs delicensed than allow a competitor a small share of the local market. Pubs have been closed simply because their lavatories were not up to standard.

Many of our breweries, especially the big ones, do not like people to know too much about the pubs which they are closing down, and it is difficult to obtain any information from them. So CAMRA's Lost Locals List, first published in 1983 and reproduced in part in the book "Time Gentlemen, Please" is a noteworthy, if depressing achievement.

Pubs are used by people, and people love their pubs. CAMRA concerns itself with pub closures as the only consumer organisation speaking on behalf of pub users. Closures inspired by Council plans can be fought through the democratic process of raising objections at the right time and the right place. Some we win, some we lose. The breweries who decide, at their own instigation, to close a pub are answerable to no democratic process, and very often would prefer not to answer for themselves at all.

To obtain a licence to open a new public house is extremely difficult. Consultations must be carried out with council, police and fire authorities, and all sorts of vested interests have an opportunity to object. To close a pub, a brewery need consult with no-one. One day it's open; next day it's shut, leaving a gaping hole in the life of the local community.

> "Alas, the doors were closed on 2 November 1982 and the village is virtually dead in the evenings and at weekends. The teams have temporarily, we hope, moved out to neighbouring villages. The last buses are at 6 pm and the pensioners now have nowhere to go in the evening."
>
> – Letter to CAMRA from a regular at the Swan Inn, Braybrooke, Northants.

The brewers will argue that their decisions are made on purely financial grounds, of course, but it is strange that the companies which are getting rid of the most pubs are those which are the largest and the most remote from their customers. The smaller breweries such as Batemans or Jennings seem to be able to maintain the tiniest pubs in the most remote rural locations. Might the enormous amounts spent by the biggest breweries on hierarchical management structures, nonsensical transport routes and pointless media advertising, not be better spent on maintaining and cherishing ordinary pubs?

Of course, CAMRA has no intention of opposing all pub closures. They are inevitable in areas of genuine population or economic decline; and some places must be considered to be over-pubbed. A pub should be

> "The Villiers is a small, unpretentious town centre pub in Elliot Street, Central Liverpool. It is one of the last remaining city centre locals that hasn't been tarted-up or "improved" and its clientele reflects the fact. It is a pub which bridges generations and is patronised by all ages and trades: market-traders and market-users, theatre-goers, shoppers etc. After nearly a century's contribution to the famous "Scouse spirit" it would be demolished to make way for a multi-million pound shopping development."
>
> – Press release: Save The Villiers Co-ordinating Committee.

able to provide its licensee with a decent living, but there are many alternatives to closure. A pub can be sold to a more local brewery who can run it in a different style with less overheads, or to a free trade entrepreneur who will devote much personal attention to making the pub a success, or the licensee can be allowed and encouraged to diversify his trade.

While the diverse and characterful pubs of north-west England have suffered much from the recent round of pub closures, perhaps the area to suffer the worst is Norfolk. The cause of the trouble was the brewery take-over boom of the 1960s which left Watneys as by far the major pub-owners of the county, having inherited the pubs of four major Norwich breweries.

Large numbers of pubs were closed and whole communities were left dry and publess.

When CAMRA asked a senior Watney executive in 1980

> "I believe the Buck Inn is much more than a museum piece, although its quaint fixtures and fittings undoubtedly make it an interesting and intriguing pub to visit. It is, in my opinion, an essential part of the village. It has had a unique connection with our mediaeval Priory Church, founded in 1064".
>
> – letter to CAMRA about the threatened closure of The Buck, from the Rector of Rumburgh, Suffolk.

whether any further closures were planned, we were told that there were to be none, except in very special cases.

Since then things have gone from bad to worse. 35 Watney (now Norwich Brewery) pubs have been closed in recent months. The Green Man at Briston and White Hart at Diss are now private houses. The Ship at Cromer, Royal Standard at East Dereham and Old Crome at Norwich are to be shops. Many others stand empty, future unknown, and it is believed that the final number to be closed could reach 200. Norwich Brewery pubs are rarely, if ever, sold in Norfolk with a licence, so the opportunity for some new blood and a choice of beers is forever denied the unlucky Norfolk drinking public.

CAMRA's Pub Preservation Group wants to know about all lost, or potentially lost locals, preferably before they close, so that we may be able to help your fight to save them. Please contact us c/o 34 Alma Road, St Albans, Herts AL1 3BW.

Allerdean 33F3

11–3; 6–11
Plough
(B6354) OS 966465
Evening opening: 7
Belhaven 80/-
Younger No. 3 Ⓗ
Well-modernised, isolated
pub, enthusiastic landlady
♠♪♣🖳♯🅿️Ⓡ🅖♟️☺ⓢ♿

Alnmouth 33H5

11–3; 6–10.30 (11 in summer)
Red Lion
(A1068) ✆ 830584
McEwan 80/-
Younger No. 3 Ⓗ
Popular, cosy pub in coastal
village ♠♣♯Ⓢ

Alnwick 33G5

11 3; 6.30 11
Oddfellows Arms
Narrowgate (off A1)
✆ 602695
Vaux Samson Ⓗ
Comfortable pub next to
castle, excellent food
♠♣🖳Ⓡ🅖♟️

Queens Head Hotel
Market Street ✆ 602442
Drybrough Pentland Ⓗ
Friendly town pub with over
150 whiskies ♣♠🖳Ⓡⓢ

Tanners Arms
2 Hotspur Place
Opens at 12 noon & 7 pm
Belhaven 80/- Ⓗ
Small, lively town pub, guest
beers ♪Ⓢ

Amble 33H6

11–3; 6–10.30
Masons Arms
McEwan 70/- Ⓗ
Plain, friendly pub, real
ale in bar only ♪♣♟️

Bamburgh 33G4

11–3; 6–10.30 (11 F, S)
Castle Hotel
(B1341, off B1342)
✆ 351
Lorimer Best Scotch Ⓗ
Sun lounge great for kids, bar
good for drinkers
♠♪♣🖳♯🅿️Ⓡ🅖♟️☺Å

Bedlington 33H7

11–3; 6–10.30 (11 F, S)
Northumberland Arms
East Front Street
Drybrough Pentland, Eighty Ⓗ
Comfortable pub with
excellent meals and mini-beer
festivals ♪♣♠Ⓡ🅖Ⓢ

Sun
Front Street
Cameron Lion Bitter,
Strongarm Ⓗ

Lively, friendly local with
popular landlord
♪♣♠Ⓡ🅖☺

Belford 33G4

11–3; 6–10.30 (11 F, S)
Salmon Inn
(Old A1) ✆ 245
Lorimer Best Scotch Ⓗ
Inspect real ale drinkers'
register – and sign it ♪♣♠Ⓡ♟️

Berwick upon Tweed 33F3

11–3; 6–10.30 (11 F, S)
Brewers Arms
Marygate (old A1)
McEwan 80/- Ⓐ
Town-centre pub with
remarkable glass frontage
♪♣♠🖽♟️Ⓢ Å

Free Trade
Castlegate (old A1)
Opens at 12 noon & 7 pm
Lorimer Best Scotch Ⓗ
Unspoilt, characterful bar
♪♣♟️≈

Hen & Chickens Hotel
Sandgate (off old A1)
Evening opening: 7
Lorimer Best Scotch Ⓗ
18th-century hotel near
Elizabethan walls and river
♪♣🖽♯🅿️Ⓡ🅖♟️☺♿

Meadow House
North Road (old A1)
✆ 304173
Lorimer Best Scotch Ⓗ
England's northernmost pub
offering a friendly hail or
farewell
♠♪♣♯🅿️🅖♟️☺Å

Old Angel
Marygate (old A1) ✆ 306674
Lorimer Best Scotch Ⓗ
Good, cheerful, commonsense
central pub ♠♪♣Ⓡ♟️Ⓢ

White Horse
Castlegate (A1) ✆ 306157
Lorimer Best Scotch Ⓗ
Busy, friendly pub
♪♣Ⓡ🅖♟️☺≈

Blyth 33H7

11–3; 6–10.30 (11 F, S)
Royal Tavern
Beaconsfield Street
Vaux Samson Ⓗ
Friendly town pub
♪♣🅖♟️Ⓢ

Bowsden 33F3

11–3; 6–10.30 (11 F, S)
Black Bull
(Off B6525) OS 991418
McEwan 70/- Ⓗ
Cosy, friendly village pub,
worth a detour
♠♪♣♠Ⓡ♟️Ⓢ♿Å

Corbridge 33F8

11–3; 6–10.30
Lion of Corbridge Hotel
Bridge End ✆ 2504
Open until 11 pm F, S and
summer
McEwan 80/-
Theakston Best Bitter Ⓗ
Large, friendly hotel with
excellent restaurant
♪♣♠🖳Ⓡ🅖♟️☺≈

Tynedale Hotel
Market Place (off A68)
Jennings Bitter Ⓗ
Friendly small hotel,
take-away meals
♠♪♣🖳🅖♟️☺≈

Wheatsheaf
Watling Street (off A68)
✆ 2020
Open until 11 pm F, S and
summer
Vaux Sunderland Draught
Bitter Ⓗ
Excellent local in historic
village ♪♣🖽♯🅿️🖳Ⓡ🅖♟️☺≈

Dipton Mill 33E8

11–3; 6–10.30
Dipton Mill Inn
2 miles south of Hexham on
Whitley Chapel road
OS 930610
Closed weekday lunchtimes
McEwan 70/- Ⓗ
Theakston Best Bitter Ⓖ
Cosy, well-kept isolated inn;
occasional guest beers ♠♯♠

Eglingham 33G5

11–3; 7–11
Tankerville Arms
15 The Village (B6436)
Jennings Mild Ⓗ
Basic village pub with friendly
atmosphere ♠♣🖽♠♟️

Etal 33E3

11–3; 6–10.30 (11 F, S)
Black Bull
(Off B6354)
✆ Crookham 200
Lorimer Best Scotch
Vaux Samson Ⓗ
Thatched pub in idyllic setting
♠♪♣🖽♠🅖♟️☺Å

Falstone 33D7

11–3; 6–10.30
Black Cock
OS 726875
Vaux Samson Ⓗ
Friendly village local, popular
with tourists to Kielder Water
♪♣♯🅖♟️Ⓢ

Featherstone 32D8

11–3; 6–10.30
Wallace Arms Hotel
OS 684608 ✆ Haltwhistle
20375

)rybrough Pentland [H]
;ecluded country inn with
ıigh class restaurant
🔥♪♣🛏⚘🚗■◷🎯🍷[S]🚉

Greystead 32D7

1–3; 6–10.30
Moorcock Inn
)S 768868 ☎ Bellingham
40269
)rybrough Pentland [H]
;olitary inn on Kielder road,
:een landlord
🔥♪♣🛏🚗[R]◷🎯🍷[S]

Haltwhistle 32D8

1–3; 6–10.30
Grey Bull Hotel
Main Street (A69)
☎ 20298
Theakston Best Bitter, XB [H]
Pleasant old town hotel
♪♣🛏🚗■[R]◷🍷[S]🚉

New Inn
Vest Road (off A69)
Lorimer Best Scotch [E]
Friendly local with occasional
ive music ↱♣🍷♿🚉

Hedley on the Hill 33F9

1–3; 6–10.30
Feathers
(Off B3609) OS 078591
Drybrough Pentland
Theakston Best Bitter, XB [H]
Isolated inn on rise of steep
ıill 🔥♪♣🚗🍷

Hexham 33F8

1–3; 6–10.30
Coach & Horses
Priestpopple ☎ 603132
Tetley Bitter [H]
Friendly, comfortable hotel in
historic town ♪♣⚘[R]◷🎯🍷[S]🚉

Horsley 33G8

1–3; 6–10.30 (11 F, S and summer)
Crown & Anchor
(B5628, off A69) OS 094660
☎ Wylam 3105
Lorimer Best Scotch
Vaux Sunderland Draught
Bitter, Samson [H]
Stone-built village pub
overlooking the valley
🔥♪♣🚗◷🎯🍷[S]

Lowick 33F3

1–3; 6–10.30 (11 F, S)
Black Bull
(B6353) ☎ Berwick 88228
Drybrough Pentland
McEwan 70/-, 80/- [H]
Holiday cottage to let; guest
beers 🔥↱♪♣⚘🚗■[R]◷🎯🍷[S]⛺

Morpeth 33G7

1–3; 6–10.30 (11 F, S)
Wansbeck
Kirkhill Estate ☎ 512575

Stones Best Bitter [H]
Comfortable, spacious modern
estate pub ♪♣🚗[R]◷🎯🍷[S]♿

Netherton 33F5

11–3; 6–10.30
Star
OS 989077
Opening hours may vary
Whitbread Castle Eden Ale [G]
Unspoilt gem in isolated
village, knock if closed 🔥🍷

Norham-on-Tweed 33E3

11–3; 6–10.30 (11 F, S)
Mason's Arms
(B6470) ☎ 82326
Lorimer Best Scotch [H]
Small, friendly border hotel in
anglers' paradise
🔥♪♣🛏■[R]🍷[S]⛺

Ponteland 33G8

11–3; 6–10.30 (11 F, S and summer)
Olde Waggon
Higham Dykes (A696)
OS 130758 ☎ Belsay 696
Draught Bass [H]
Friendly, comfortable wayside
inn with small bar and
extended lounge
🔥♪♣🛏⚘🚗◷🍷[S]♿

Riding Mill 33F8

11–3; 6–10.30
Broomhaugh Hotel
Broomhaugh House (off A68)
☎ 256
Theakston Best Bitter, XB [H]
Converted Victorian manor
house in extensive grounds
♪♣🛏⚘🚗■[R]🎯🍷[S]🚉

Seahouses 33G4

11–3; 6.30–11
Black Swan
Union Street ☎ 720227
Lorimer Best Scotch
Vaux Samson [H]
Holiday harbour hostelry,
highly commended
🔥↱♪♣🛏■[R]🍷[S]

Seaton Sluice 33H7

11–3; 6–10.30
Waterford Arms
(Off A193)
☎ Seaton Delaval 480450
Vaux Sunderland Draught
Bitter [H]
Large, comfortable hotel just
off seafront
↱♪♣🚗■[R]◷🎯🍷[S]

Shoreswood 33F3

11–3; 6–10.30 (11 F, S)
Salutation Inn
(A698) OS 924466
☎ Norham 82291
Lorimer Best Scotch [H]
Enthusiastic landlord, good
food 🔥♪♣⚘🚗[R]◷🎯🍷[S]⛺

Stagshaw 33F8

11–3; 6–10.30
Errington Arms
(B6318) OS 986687
☎ Great Whittington 250
Lorimer Best Scotch
Vaux Samson [H]
Comfortable pub near
Hadrian's Wall
🔥♪♣⚘🚗◷🎯[S]

Stannersburn 32D7

11–3; 6–10.30
Crown
Near Falstone
OS 722867
☎ Bellingham 40382
McEwan 80/- [H]
Cosy inn near Kielder Water
🔥♪♣⚘🚗■◷🎯🍷[S]

Tweedmouth 33F3

11–3; 6–10.30 (11 F, S)
Harrow
Main Street (off old A1)
Lorimer Best Scotch [H]
Highly convivial pub used by
truckers, seafarers and locals
🔥↱♪♣🛏⚘[R]◷🎯🍷[S]⛺

Queens Head
42 Church Road (old A1)
Lorimer Best Scotch
Vaux Samson [H]
Small, well-run unspoilt pub
🔥♪♣[R]🍷[S]

Thatch House
West End (under old A1)
Lorimer Best Scotch [H]
Cheerful pub in shadow of
Royal Tweed Bridge
♪♣[R]🍷[S]

Wooler 33F4

11–3; 6–10.30 (11 F, S)
Anchor Inn
Cheviot Street (off A697)
☎ 81412
Vaux Samson [H]
Well-run, friendly pub
↱♪♣■[R]◷🎯🍷[S]⛺

Ryecroft Hotel
Ryecroft Way (A697)
☎ 81459
Evening opening: 5.30
Lorimer 70/-, 80/-
Marston Burton Bitter [H]
Friendly, family-run hostelry
with pioneering landlord
🔥♪♣🛏⚘🚗■[R]🎯[S]⛺

Wylam 33G8

11–3; 6–10.30
Fox & Hounds
Main Street
☎ 3246
Lorimer Best Scotch
Vaux Sunderland Draught
Bitter [H]
Excellent village pub in George
Stephenson's village
↱♪♣🚗◷🎯🍷[S]🚉

Arnold 26B8

10.30–2.30; 6–10.30 (11 F, S)
Cross Keys
Front Street (off A60)
Shipstone Mild, Bitter E
Traditional pub in centre of
town ♪♣♏⌂Ⓡ⦿Ⓢ

Druids Tavern
High Street (off A60)
**Hardys & Hansons Best Mild,
Best Bitter** E
Down-to-earth pub
♪♣⦿⦿

Aslockton 26C8

10.30–2.30; 6–10.30 (11 F, S)
Old Greyhound
Main Street (off A52)
Home Bitter H
Unspoilt country pub near
station ♣⚑♏⌂Ⓖ⦿⦿⇌

Awsworth 26A8

10.30–2.30; 6–10.30 (11 F, S)
Gate Inn
**Hardys & Hansons Best Mild,
Best Bitter** E
Pleasant three-roomed local
♪♣⦿Ⓡ⦿Ⓢ

Bagthorpe 26A7

10.30–2.30; 6–10.30 (11 F, S)
Dixies Arms
School Lane (off B600)
Home Mild, Bitter H
A local's pub. A footpath
connects with the Miners
Arms at Selston
♏♪♣♏⦿Ⓡ⦿⦿

Shepherds Rest
Lower Bagthorpe (off B600)
Home Mild, Bitter E
Pretty whitewashed alehouse
♣♏⦿⦿

Beeston 26B8

10.30–2.30; 6–10.30 (11 F, S)
Boat & Horses
Trent Road
Home Mild, Bitter E
Fine, traditional pub close to
canal ♪♏⦿⦿Ⓢ

Crown
Church Street
**Hardys & Hansons Best Mild,
Best Bitter** H
Quaint, atmospheric pub; top
pressure in lounge
♪♣⦿⦿

Try also: **Prince of Wales;
Queens; Royal Oak**
(Shipstones)

Bingham 26C8

10.30–2.30; 6–10.30 (11 F, S)
Wheatsheaf
Long Acre (A52) ℰ 38358
Shipstone Bitter E
Fine old coaching inn
⦿♪♏Ⓖ⦿(Sat)⦿Ⓢ

Blidworth 26B7

10.30–3; 6–10.30 (11 F, S)
Black Bull
Field Lane (B6020)
Shipstone Mild, Bitter
Bulmer Cider H
Pleasant mock-Tudor
alehouse in mining village
♏♏♣♏⌂Ⓖ⦿⦿Ⓢ

Blidworth Bottoms 26B7

10.30–2.30; 6–10.30 (11 F, S)
Fox & Hounds
Fishpool
**Hardys & Hansons Best Mild,
Best Bitter** E
Friendly pub in picturesque
setting
♪♣♏⦿⦿Ⓢ

Blyth 28B5

11–3; 6–10.30 (11 F, S)
Angel
(Off A1 & A634) ℰ 213
Evening opening: 7
**Hardys & Hansons Best Mild,
Best Bitter** E
Fine old coaching inn with
huge fires
♏♪♣♏♏⌂Ⓡ⌂Ⓖ⦿⦿Ⓢ

Burton Joyce 26B8

10.30–2.30; 6–10.30 (11 F, S)
Wheatsheaf
(A612) ℰ 3298
Home Mild, Bitter E
Large popular pub with
separate restaurant
⦿♪♣♏⌂Ⓡ⌂Ⓖ⦿⦿Ⓢ

Calverton 26B7

10.30–2.30; 6–10.30 (11 F, S)
Admiral Rodney
Home Mild, Bitter E
Comfortable old pub in mining
village ♪♣♏⦿⦿Ⓢ

Caythorpe 26C8

10.30–2.30; 6–10.30 (11 F, S)
Black Horse
ℰ Lowdham 3520
Shipstone Bitter H
Reputed hiding-place of Dick
Turpin
♣♏⌂Ⓖ⦿ (must book)⦿Ⓢ

Old Volunteer
ℰ Lowdham 3205
**Hardys & Hansons Best Mild,
Best Bitter** E
Tastefully modernised,
traditional country pub
♪♣♏⦿Ⓡ⦿Ⓢ

Coddington 26D7

10.30–2.30; 6–10.30 (11 F, S)
Inn on the Green
Main Street (off A17)
Whitbread Castle Eden Ale H
Large inn for all the family
♪⚑♏⌂Ⓖ⦿Ⓢ

Colston Bassett 26C8

10.30–2.30; 6–10.30 (11 F, S)
Martins Arms
Closed Sundays
Draught Bass
Ruddle County H
Delightful village pub with
characterful clientele ♣⦿⦿

Cotgrave 26B8

10.30–2.30; 6–10.30 (11 F, S)
Manvers Arms
Shipstone Mild, Bitter H
Popular, attractive,
many-roomed pub ♪♣⦿⦿Ⓢ

Cropwell Bishop 26C8

10.30–2.30; 6–10.30 (11 F, S)
Wheatsheaf
Nottingham Road (off A46)
Home Mild, Bitter E
Good old-fashioned village
local ♏♪♣⦿Ⓡ⦿Ⓢ

Drakeholes 26C5

12–3; 7–11
Griff Inn
(Off A631) ℰ Retford 817206
Closed Monday lunchtimes
Draught Bass
Webster Yorkshire Bitter H
Modernised pub overlooking
canal, previously named the
White Swan ♪♏⌂Ⓖ⦿⦿Ⓢ♿

East Leake 26B8

10.30–2.30; 6–10.30 (11 F, S)
Bulls Head
Main Street
Home Mild, Bitter E
Popular pub, extensively
rebuilt ⦿♪♣♏⦿⦿Ⓢ

Eastwood 26A8

10.30–2.30; 6–10.30 (11 F, S)
Greasley Castle
Hill Top (A610)
**Hardys & Hansons Best Mild,
Best Bitter** E
Late Victorian pub with
modernised interior ♪♣⦿Ⓢ

Great Northern
Derby Road (A610)
**Hardys & Hansons Best Mild,
Best Bitter** E
Splendid canalside local, full
of bric-a-brac ♪♣♏⦿♿

Old Wine Vaults
Church Street (A610)
Shipstone Mild, Bitter E
A pub of character in
D. H. Lawrence country
♪♣⦿Ⓢ

Edwinstowe 26B7

11–3; 6.30–10.30 (11 F, S)
Manvers Arms
Welbeck Drive ℰ Mansfield
823561
Shipstone Mild, Bitter H

Smart estate pub near
Sherwood Forest
♪♣♥♠₧Ⓡ❶◑♿▲

Epperstone 26B7

10.30–2.30; 6–10.30 (11 F, S)
Cross Keys
Main Street (off A6197)
**Hardys & Hansons Best Mild,
Best Bitter** Ⓔ
Picturesque village inn with
keen landlord ♪♣♥♠₧Ⓡ❶◑

Fiskerton 26C7

10.30–2.30; 6–10.30 (11 F, S)
Bromley Arms
Fiskerton Wharf
Hardys & Hansons Best Mild Ⓔ
Best Bitter Ⓗ & Ⓔ
Attractive riverside pub
♪♣♥♠₧Ⓡ❶◑

Flintham 26C8

10.30–2.30; 6–10.30 (11 F, S)
Boot & Shoe
(Off A46)
Home Bitter Ⓗ
Friendly country local,
comfortable lounge with open
fire ♠♪♣♠❶

Forest Town 26B8

10.30–3; 6–10.30 (11 F, S)
White Gates
Clipstone Road (B6030)
✆ Mansfield 24689
**Samuel Smith Old Brewery
Bitter** Ⓗ
Imposing road house with
lively vaults, keen landlord
♪♣♥♠₧Ⓡ❶◑❶◑

Gotham 26B8

10.30–2.30; 6–10.30 (11 F, S)
Sun
**Everard Burton Mild, Beacon,
Tiger, Old Original** Ⓗ
Fine village inn ♪♣♠❶

Harworth 26B5

11–3; 6–10.30 (11 F, S)
Galway Arms
Scrooby Road
**Hardys & Hansons Best Mild,
Best Bitter** Ⓔ
Lively miners' local with large
games room ♠♪♣♠₧Ⓡ❶◑

Hayton 26C5

1–3; 7–11
Boat Inn
Main Street (B1403) ✆ Retford
700158
**Draught Bass
Cameron Lion Bitter,
Strongarm** Ⓗ
Pleasantly situated by
Chesterfield Canal
♠♪♣♥₧♠₧Ⓡ❶◑

Hickling 26C9

0.30–2.30; 6–10.30 (11 F, S)
Plough
Off A606)

Home Bitter Ⓗ
Splendid village inn, haunt of
fishermen ♪♣♥₧Ⓡ◑❶◑

Hoveringham 26C7

10.30–2.30; 6–10.30 (11 F, S)
Marquis of Granby
Main Street
Draught Bass Ⓔ
**Marston Pedigree
Ruddle County** Ⓗ
Small, popular village pub
♪♣♠◑❶◑

Hucknall 26B7

10.30–2.30; 6–10.30 (11 F, S)
Red Lion
High Street
Home Mild, Bitter Ⓔ
Old town pub with many
small rooms ♠♣♠❶

Huthwaite 26A7

11–3; 6–10.30 (11 F, S)
Miners Arms
(B6026)
Home Bitter Ⓗ
Small, friendly pub ♣♠❶◑

Workpeople's
(Off A615)
Home Mild, Bitter Ⓔ
Lively pub, once a coaching
inn ♪♣❶

Kimberley 26A8

10.30–2.30; 6–10.30 (11 F, S)
Lord Clyde
**Hardys & Hansons Best Mild,
Best Bitter** Ⓗ
Superb friendly pub opposite
war memorial ♠♪♣❶◑

Nelson & Railway
Station Road ✆ Nottingham
382177
**Hardys & Hansons Best Mild,
Best Bitter** Ⓔ
Brewery tap with cheerful
landlord ♪♣♥♠₧Ⓖ❶◑

Lambley 26B8

10.30–2.30; 6–10.30 (11 F, S)
Woodlark
Church Street
Home Bitter Ⓔ
Excellent village local with
skittle alley ♪♣♠₧♠₧Ⓡ❶◑

Linby 26B7

10.30–2.30; 6–10.30 (11 F, S)
Horse & Groom
Main Street (B6011)
Home Mild, Bitter Ⓔ
Spacious pub handy for
Newstead Abbey ♪♥♠Ⓖ❶◑

Lowdham 26B7

10.30–2.30; 6–10.30 (11 F, S)
World's End
Plough Lane (off A6097)
**Marston Burton Bitter,
Pedigree** Ⓗ
Cheery pub with a nautical
flavour ♪♣♥♠₧Ⓖ❶◑

Mansfield 26B7

10.30–3; 6–10.30 (11 F, S)
Crown & Anchor
Exchange Row
**Hardys & Hansons Best Mild,
Best Bitter** Ⓔ
Pleasant town-centre drinking
house ♪♣❶◑

Talbot
Nottingham Road (A60)
Shipstone Bitter Ⓔ
Tastefully decorated pub near
football ground ♪♣♠Ⓖ❶❶

Mansfield Woodhouse 26B6

10.30–3; 6–10.30 (11 F, S)
Greyhound
Home Mild, Bitter Ⓔ
Deservedly popular pub in
town centre ♪♥♠❶

Maplebeck 26C7

10.30–2.30; 6.30–10.30 (11 F, S)
Beehive
(Off A616)
**Shipstone Bitter
Bulmer Cider** Ⓗ
Smallest pub in the county,
idyllic setting ♪♣♥♠❶

Nether Langwith 26B6

10.30–3; 6–10.30 (11 F, S)
Jug & Glass
Queens Walk (A632)
Morning opening: 11
**Hardys & Hansons Best Mild,
Best Bitter** Ⓔ
Stone-built local ♪♣♥♠❶

Newark 26C7

10.30–2.30; 6–10.30 (11 F, S)
Kirrages
Middlegate
**Draught Bass
Ruddle Bitter, County** Ⓗ
Town-centre pub popular
with all ages ♪♣♠Ⓖ❶◑≢

Newcastle Arms
Appletongate (off A17)
Evening opening: 7
Home Mild, Bitter Ⓔ
Excellent local near Priory
Brewery ♠♪♣❶≢

Old Kings Arms
Kirkgate (off A46) ✆ 703416
**Everard Tiger, Old Original
Marston Burton Bitter,
Pedigree** Ⓗ
Popular with young people;
occasional guest beers ♪♪Ⓖ❶≢

Nottingham 26B8

10.30–2.30; 5.30–10.30
Belle Vue
Woodborough Road
Shipstone Mild, Bitter Ⓔ
Popular, comfortable
surburban pub ♪♣♠❶♿

Cooper's Arms
Porchester Road (off A612)
Home Mild, Bitter E
Excellent local near Carlton
Hill ♪♣🅰️®🎵

Fox
17 Dale Street, Sneinton
Ind Coope Burton Ale H
Comfortable old pub,
tastefully refurbished ♪♣🎵®

Framesmiths Arms
Main Street, Bulwell
Shipstone Mild, Bitter E
Redecorated, simple local
known as the 'Monkey' ♣🎵

Golden Fleece
Mansfield Road (A60)
Shipstone Mild, Bitter E
Traditional street-corner local,
full of curios 🅰️♪♣🅿️🕒®

Johnson Arms
Abbey Street, Dunkirk
Shipstone Mild, Bitter
Bulmer Cider H
Pleasant pub named after its
builder ♪♣🎵🕒®

Loggerheads
Cliff Road
Home Mild, Bitter E
Quaint old pub under cliffs
♪♣🎵🕒®

Lord Nelson
Lord Nelson Street, Sneinton
📞 55207
**Hardys & Hansons Best
Bitter** E
Pleasant up-market pub
known as the White House
♪🎵🕒®

Magpie
Meadow Lane
Home Mild, Bitter E
Deservedly popular pub near
Notts County FC ♪♣🅰️®

Narrow Boat
Canal Street 📞 51947
Shipstone Mild, Bitter
Bulmer Cider H
Deservedly popular pub,
always a hive of activity
🎵♪♣®🕒🎵®⧖

Newcastle Arms
Nuthall Road (A610)
Home Mild, Bitter E
Large, popular pub on road to
motorway ♪♣🅰️🎵

Newmarket
Lower Parliament Street
📞 411532
Home Mild, Bitter H & E
Pub full of character, very low
prices ♪♣®🕒🎵®

Nottingham Castle
Lower Parliament Street
📞 54601
Ansells Mild
Ind Coope Bitter, Burton Ale H
Brick box hides a pleasant
interior ♪♣🎵🅰️®🕒⊗⧖

Old Angel
Stoney Street
Home Mild, Bitter E
Unspoilt Victorian pub in lace
market area ♪♣®🎵🕒

Old Pear Tree
Bulwell Lane, Basford
Home Mild, Bitter E
Old, unspoilt small-roomed
pub ♪♣🎵®

Peacock
Mansfield Road (A60) 📞 42152
Home Mild, Bitter E
Pleasant table service in
lounge, basic vaults ♣®🕒🎵®

Pheasant
Prospect Street, Radford
Shipstone Mild, Bitter E
Fine pub tucked away behind
cigarette factory ♪♣🅿️®🎵®

Quorn
Hucknall Road, Sherwood
(B683)
Home Mild, Bitter E
Busy suburban local, keen
landlord ♪♣🅰️🎵

Real Thing
(off-licence)
Mansfield Road (A60)
Opens 4.30–8.30 evenings;
closed Sundays
Burton Bridge Bitter
Everard Beacon, Tiger
Marston Pedigree
Theakston Old Peculier G
Containers supplied or take a
jug; casks to order; frequent
guest beers

Running Horse
Alfreton Road (A610)
Shipstone Mild, Bitter
Bulmer Cider H
The pick of the bunch in a
popular drinking area 🎵♪🕒®

Trip to Jerusalem
Castle Road
Draught Bass
**Marston Pedigree, Owd
Rodger**
Ruddle County
**Samuel Smith Old Brewery
Bitter**
Whitbread Castle Eden Ale H
Reputedly oldest inn in
England, with rooms hewn
out of Castle Rock 🅰️♪®®

Turf Tavern
Upper Parliament Street
Shipstone Mild, Bitter
Bulmer Cider H
One-room lounge bar, busy
and friendly ♪🕒®

Nuncargate 26A7
10.30–2.30; 6–10.30 (11 F, S)
Cricketer's Arms
(Off A611)
Home Mild, Bitter E
A cosy retreat from the
surrounding mining belt
♪♣🅰️🎵®

Ollerton 26B6
10.30–3; 6–10.30 (11 F, S)
White Hart
Market Place (off A614)
**Samuel Smith Old Brewery
Bitter** E
Busy pub in the old part of the
village ♪♣🅰️🎵®

Redhill 26B8
10.30–2.30; 6–10.30 (11 F, S)
Waggon & Horses
Mansfield Road (A60)
Home Mild, Bitter H
Friendly pub run by
ex-Nottingham Forest player
♪♣🅰️🎵®

Retford 26C5
10.30–3; 6–11
Albert Hotel
Albert Road 📞 708694
Morning opening: 11; open
until 4 pm Thu, Sat
Webster Yorkshire Bitter
Whitbread Castle Eden Ale H
Smart, friendly town pub
serving excellent food
♪♣🅰️®🕒🍴🎵⊗⧖

Market Hotel
West Carr Road, Ordsall
📞 703278
Abbey Quail
**Cameron Lion Bitter,
Strongarm**
Tetley Bitter
Whitbread Castle Eden Ale
Younger No. 3 H
Pleasant pub popular
with businessmen
♪♣🅿️♪®🅰️®🕒🎵®⧖

New Sun
Spital Hill
Open until 4 pm Sat
Darley Thorne Best Bitter E
Welcoming pub with cosy
atmosphere, just off town
centre ♪♣🅰️🎵

Ship Inn
Wharf Road 📞 704412
Open until 4 pm Thu & Sat;
evening opening: 7
Home Mild, Bitter E
Renowned local, unspoilt and
friendly ♪♣🅿️🎵®

Turks Head
Grove Street 📞 702742
Lunchtime opening: 11–3
(4 Sat); evening opening: 7
**Ward Mild, Sheffield Best
Bitter** E
Popular town centre pub
🅰️♪♣🅰️🔲

Rolleston 26C7
11–2.30; 6.30–10.30 (11 F, S)
Crown
Main Street
Marston Pedigree H
Quiet, unassuming local in
rural village 🅰️♣🅿️🅰️🎵

uddington 26B8
.30–2.30; 6–10.30 (11 F, S)
ed Heart
asthorpe Street (off A60)
hipstone Mild, Bitter [E]
xcellent village inn with
vely bar ♪♣🚗🍺[S]

caftworth 26B5
–3; 7–11
ing William
Off A631) ☎ Doncaster
10292
losed lunchtimes Mon–Thu
Vhitbread Castle Eden Ale
ulmer Cider [H]
Velcoming village pub, good
ood 🏠♪♣⊞🌿🚗[R]☾🍴[S]♿⛺

elston 26A7
.30–3; 6–10.30 (11 F, S)
Horse & Jockey
hurch Lane
hipstone Bitter [H]
ld free house of considerable
haracter ♪♣🚗🍺

White Lion
B600)
hipstone Mild, Bitter [H]
omfortable and popular local
♣🌿☾🍺[S]

outh Clifton 26C6
–2.30; 6.30–10.30 (11 F, S)
ed Lion
ain Street
ome Bitter [E]
riendly local in quiet village
♣🌿🚗🍺

outhwell 26C7
.30–2.30; 6–10.30 (11 F, S)
ewcastle Arms
ockerton Road
hipstone Mild, Bitter [E]
riendly local on edge of
outhwell ♪♣🌿🚗🍺[S]

tapleford 26A8
.30–2.30; 6–10.30 (11 F, S)
ld Cross
hurch Street
hipstone Mild, Bitter [E]
raditional local, 150 years
ld ♪♣🌿🚗🍺[S]

utton Bonington 26A9
.30–2.30; 6–10.30 (11 F, S)
ld Plough
Off A6006)
hipstone Mild, Bitter [H]
leasant modern pub ♪♣🚗🍺

utton-in-Ashfield 26A7
.30–2.30; 6–10.30 (11 F, S)
enmans Head
arket Place
ome Mild, Bitter [E]
vely, down-to-earth pub
♣■[R]🍺

Duke of Sussex
Alfreton Road ☎ 52560
Hardys & Hansons Best Mild, Best Bitter [E]
Lively and convivial pub
♪♣🚗☾🍴🍺[S]

Teversal 26A6
10.30–3; 6–10.30 (11 F, S)
Carnarvon Arms
Fackley Road
Hardys & Hansons Best Mild, Best Bitter [E]
Roadside inn with wood-panelled lounge, good meals ♣🌿🚗☾🍴🍺[S]

Thurgarton 26C7
10.30–2.30; 6–10.30 (11 F, S)
Coach & Horses
(A612)
Home Mild, Bitter [E]
Excellent village local ♪♣🚗🍺[S]

Tuxford 26C6
11–3; 6–11
Royal Oak
Sibthorpe Hill (off A1)
☎ 870375
Tetley Bitter
Whitbread Castle Eden Ale, Durham Ale [H]
Lively pub with cosy atmosphere 🏠♪♣🌿🚗[R]☾🍴[S]⛺

Walkeringham 26C5
11.30–2.30; 6.30–10.30 (11 F, S)
Brickmakers Arms
(Off A161) ☎ Gainsborough 890375
Closed Sat lunchtimes
Tetley Bitter
Younger Scotch Bitter [H]
Comfortable village pub
🏠♪♣🌿🚗■[R]☾🍴[S]♿

Warsop 26B8
11–3; 6–10.30 (11 F, S)
Hare & Hounds
Church Street (B6035)
☎ Mansfield 842440
Hardys & Hansons Best Mild, Best Bitter [H]
Comfortable town-centre pub with restaurant
↱♪♣🌿🚗[R]☾🍴🍺[S]♿

Watnall 26A7
10.30–2.30; 6–10.30 (11 F, S)
Queens Head
(B600)
Home Mild, Bitter [E]
Old pub with unusual wood panelled walls and ceiling in bar 🏠↱♣🌿🚗🍺[S]

West Leake 26B9
10.30–2.30; 6–10.30 (11 F, S)
Star (Pit House)
☎ East Leake 2233
Draught Bass
Mitchells & Butlers Springfield Bitter [H]
Fine old coaching inn 🏠♣■☾🍺

Weston 26C6
11–2.30; 6.30–10.30 (11 F, S)
Boot & Shoe
Old Great North Road (off A1)
Cameron Lion Bitter, Strongarm [H]
Prominent pub, rooms to suit all tastes ♪♣🌿🚗☾🍴🍺[S]

Westwood 26A7
10.30–2.30; 6–10.30 (11 F, S)
Gate
Main Road
Hardys & Hansons Best Mild, Best Bitter [H]
Pleasant, cheerful pub
🏠♣🚗🍺[S]

Wilford 26B8
10.30–2.30; 6–10.30
Ferry
Main Road
Shipstone Mild, Bitter [H]
Picturesque pub, access by footbridge over Trent from Nottingham ♪♣🌿🚗[R]☾🍺[S]

Woodborough 26B7
10.30–2.30; 6–10.30 (11 F, S)
Nags Head
Main Street
Hardys & Hansons Best Mild, Best Bitter [E]
Attractive village pub ♣🌿🚗🍺[S]

Worksop 26B5
11–3; 6–10.30 (11 F, S)
Fishermans Arms
Church Walk ☎ 472806
Evening opening: 7
Home Bitter [E]
Small modernised local near Victoria Square ♪♣🚗[R]🍺[S]🚉

French Horn
Potter Street ☎ 472958
Open until 4 pm Wednesdays
Stones Best Bitter [E]
Fine pub by Town Hall, jostling bar and quiet snug
♪♣[R]🍺

Greendale Oak
Norfolk Street
Stones Best Bitter [E]
Small backstreet house, pleasantly warm and cosy ♣🌿🍺

Lion
Bridge Street ☎ 477925
Webster Yorkshire Dark, Bitter [H]
Renovated old coaching inn with popular lounge and restaurant ↱♪♣⊞🌿🚗[R]☾🍴🍺[S]

Wysall 26B9
10.30–2.30; 6–10.30 (11 F, S)
Plough
(Off A60)
McEwan 70/-
Shipstone Mild, Bitter [H]
Splendid country pub in quiet village ♪♣🌿

Oxfordshire

Abingdon 16B9

10–2.30; 6–10.30 (11 F, S)
Old Anchor
St Helens Wharf
Morland Mild, Bitter ⊞
A gem of a pub in
a splendid setting ♣♨♙

Ox Inn
15 Oxford Road (A4183)
Morning opening: 10.30
**Morland Mild, Bitter, Best
Bitter** ⊞
Busy friendly pub ♪♣♨🚗🄲♪

Appleton 16A9

10–2.30; 6–10.30 (11 F, S)
Plough
Eaton Road (off A420)
Morning opening: 10.30
**Morland Mild, Bitter, Best
Bitter** ⊞
Bulmer Cider 🄶
Friendly village pub with
doctor's surgery
🅿♪♣🄱♨🚗🅁🄲♙Å

Balscote 16A6

10–2.30; 6–11
Butchers Arms
Near Banbury (off A422)
Winter opening hours vary
Hook Norton Mild 🄶 **Best
Bitter** ⊞
A gem of a local, formerly the
local abbatoir 🄵♣♨🚗🄲

Banbury 16B6

10–2.30; 6–11
Bell
Middleton Road (A361)
**Mitchells & Butlers Mild,
Springfield Bitter** ⊞
Friendly workingmen's local
🅿♣🄱🄲≢

Coach & Horses
4 Butchers Row 📞 3043
**Hook Norton Mild, Best
Bitter** ⊞
Underrated town centre pub
🄵♣🄳🄲🅂♿

Duke of Wellington
101 Warwick Road (A41)
Morning opening: 11 Mon–Wed
Morrell Dark Mild, Bitter ⊞
♪♣🄱🄲🅂♿

Wheatsheaf
65 George Street
**Mitchells & Butlers Mild,
Springfield Bitter** ⊞
Former coaching inn with
warm atmosphere, noted for
mild 🅿🄵♣♨🄿🅁♙

Benson 16C9

10–2.30; 6–10.30 (11 F, S)
Crown
52 High Street (off B4009)
**Morland Mild, Bitter, Best
Bitter** ⊞
Straightforward, tidy two-bar
local 🅿♪♣♨🄱🅁🄲🅂

Binfield Heath 7F2

10–2.30; 6–10.30 (11 F, S)
Bottle & Glass
Harpsden Road
**Brakspear Mild, Pale Ale,
Special Bitter, Old** ⊞
Gaymer Cider 🄶
The classic country pub with
good food 🅿♨🄱🄲♪🅂

Bletchingdon 16B8

10–2.30; 6–10.30 (11 F, S)
Rock of Gibraltar
Enslow Bridge (A4095)
**Usher Best Bitter, Founders
Ale** ⊞
Popular 18th-century pub by
canal 🅿🄵♣🄱♨🚗🅁🄲♪🅂Å

Blewbury 6E1

10.30–2.30; 6–10.30 (11 F, S)
Red Lion
Nottingham Fee (off A417)
Opens at 11 am & 6.30 pm
**Brakspear Pale Ale, Special
Bitter, Old** ⊞
Small and inviting village pub
🅿♨🚗🄲♪🅂

Bodicote 16B6

10–2.30; 6–11
Plough
May open late
Bodicote Jim's Brew, No 9 ⊞
Curious pub just outside
Banbury, now brewing its
own beer ♪♨🚗🅁🄲♿🅂

Britwell Salome 7E1

10.30–2.30; 6–10.30 (11 F, S)
Red Lion
(B4009) 📞 Watlington 2304
**Brakspear Mild, Pale Ale,
Special Bitter** ⊞
Pleasant village local,
excellent food ♪♨🚗🄱🄲♿♪🅂

Burford 15J6

10–2.30; 6–10.30 (11 F, S)
Lamb Inn
Sheep Street (off A361)
📞 3155
Morning opening: 11
Wadworth IPA, 6X ⊞
Old Timer 🄶
Superb and traditional
Cotswold inn 🅿♨🚗🄱🅁🄲♪♙

Royal Oak
Witney Street (off High Street,
A361) 📞 3278
Opens 10.30 am & 6.30 pm
**Wadworth IPA, 6X, Old
Timer** 🄶
Unpretentious backstreet local
🅿🄵♣♨🄱🅁🄲♪🅂

Chesterton 16B7

10–2.30; 6–10.30 (11 F, S)
Red Cow
📞 Bicester 41337
Usher Best Bitter ⊞
Tastefully updated village pub
♪♣♨🚗🄲♪♙

Chipping Norton 15

10–2.30; 6–10.30 (11 F, S and summer)
Red Lion
Albion Street
Morning opening: 10.30
**Hook Norton Best Bitter, Old
Hookey**
Bulmer Cider ⊞
Laughing, joking local, due f♦
renovation 🄵♪♣♨🄱♿

Claydon 16▮

10–2.30; 6–11
Sun Rising
(Off A423) 📞 Farnborough 3♦
Winter opening hours vary
**Hook Norton Best Bitter
Whitbread WCPA, Flowers
Original Bitter**
Bulmer Cider ⊞
Popular and friendly village
local near canal ♪♣♨🚗🄲♪♙

Clifton 16▮

10–2.30; 6–11
**Duke of
Cumberland's Hea▮**
📞 Deddington 38534
**Halls Harvest Bitter
Ind Coope Burton Ale** ⊞
Sporting country pub
🅿♪♨🄱🅁🄲♿🅂

Crowell 16

10–2.30; 6–10.30 (11 F, S)
Catherine Wheel
(Off B4009)
**Aylesbury ABC Bitter
Draught Bass** ⊞
Old drovers' hostelry circa
1730, 🅿♪♣♨🚗🄲

Deddington 16

10–2.30; 6–10.30 (11 F, S)
Crown & Tuns
New Street (A423) 📞 38343
**Hook Norton Mild, Best
Bitter** ⊞
Friendly, unpretentious old
coaching inn ♣♨🄳🅁♿🅂

Faringdon 1♦

10–2.30; 6–10.30 (11 F, S)
Folly
54 London Street (off A420▮
Morrell Bitter 🄶
Charming little town pub
🅿♨🅁🄲♿

Fifield 1▮

10–2.30; 6–10.30 (11 F, S)
Merrymouth Inn
Burford Road (A424)
📞 Shipton-under-Wychwoo▮
830759
Donnington BB, SBA ⊞
Historic inn mentioned in
Domesday Book
🅿♪♣♨🄱🄲♪🅂Å

Forest Hill 16

10–2.30; 6–10.30 (11 F, S)

White Horse
Near Wheatley (B4027)
Morrell Light Ale Ⓗ
Quiet, unassuming local ♠♣▩☗

Fulbrook
15J6

12–2.30; 6–10.30 (11 F, S)

Masons Arms
Shipton Road (A361)
Morning opening: 11
Hook Norton Best Bitter
Wadworth 6X Ⓖ
Popular 400-year-old
Cotswold village pub
♣☷⅊ⓇⒼ☗⅂⑤&

Garsington
16B9

12–2.30; 6–10.30 (11 F, S)

Plough
Oxford Road (off B480)
Open at 10.30 am & 6.30 pm
Courage Best Bitter,
Directors Ⓗ
Busy, friendly pub with large
enclosed garden ♠⅃♣⅊▩Ⓖ⑤

Goring
6E2

11.30–2.30; 6–10.30 (11 F, S)

John Barleycorn
Manor Road (off B4009)
⅁ 872509
Brakspear Pale Ale, Special
Bitter Ⓗ
Attractive beamed pub, meals
always available ♣▣Ⓖ☗⅂⑤≷

Goring Heath
7E2

12–2.30; 6–10.30 (11 F, S)

King Charles Head
Reading Road (off B4526)
Fuller London Pride, ESB
Wethered Bitter, SPA Ⓗ
Ivy-clad pub tucked away in
the woods ♠⅃♣⅊▩Ⓖ☗⅂⑤

Great Tew
16A7

12–2.30; 6–10.30 (11 F, S and summer)

Falkland Arms
(Off B4022)
Morning opening: 11; closed
on lunchtimes except bank
holidays
Donnington BB
Hook Norton Best Bitter
McMullen Country Bitter
Wadworth 6X Ⓗ
Interesting old inn in
preserved village; frequent
guest beers
⅂♣⅊▩Ⓖ⅂ (not Mon) ⑤ A

Henley-on-Thames
7F2

12–2.30; 6–10.30 (11 F, S)

Bull
Bell Street (A423) ⅁ 4821
Brakspear Mild, Pale Ale,
Special Bitter, Old Ⓗ
Oldest pub in Henley; recently
extended ♠⅃♣⅊▩Ⓡ Ⓖ☗⅂⑤

Old White Hart
Hart Street (A423) ⅁ 3103
Brakspear Pale Ale, Special
Bitter, Old Ⓗ

Comfortable pub with
restaurant ♠⅃☗⅊▩Ⓡ Ⓖ☗⅂⑤

Royal Hotel
51 Station Road (off A4155)
⅁ 77526
Morning opening: 10.30
Brakspear Mild, Pale Ale Ⓗ
Friendly local in former hotel
near river ⅃☗⅊▩◨Ⓡ Ⓖ☗≷

Saracens Head
Greys Road (off A4155)
Brakspear Mild, Pale Ale Ⓗ
Friendly local out of town
centre ♠⅃♣▩Ⓡ☗⑤

Three Tuns
5 Market Place (off A423)
⅁ 3260
Brakspear Mild, Pale Ale,
Special Bitter Ⓗ Old Ⓖ
Excellent town pub ⅃♣⅊Ⓖ☗⅂⑤

Hook Norton
16A7

10–2.30; 6–11

Pear Tree
Scotland End
Hook Norton Mild, Best Bitter,
Old Hookey Ⓗ
Popular locals' pub near the
brewery ♠⅃♣⅊▩☗⑤ A

Juniper Hill
16B7

10–2.30; 6–10.30 (11 F, S)

Fox
(Off A43)
Hook Norton Best Bitter Ⓗ
Country pub mentioned in
'Lark Rise to Candleford'
♠⅃♣⅊▩

Kelmscott
15J7

10.30–2.30; 5.30–10.30 (11 F, S)

Plough
(Off B4449)
Arkell BBB Ⓗ
Hook Norton Best Bitter Ⓖ
Morland Bitter Ⓗ
Lively local off the beaten
track ♠⅃♣▣⅊▩Ⓖ☗⅂⑤ A

Kirtlington
16B8

10–2.30; 6–10.30 (11 F, S)

Oxford Arms
(A4095)
Halls Harvest Bitter Ⓗ
Friendly village pub
♠⅃♣▣⅊▩Ⓖ☗⅂⑤&

Langford
15J7

10.30–2.30; 6–10.30 (11 F, S)

Bell
(off A361) ⅁ Filkins 281
Cirencester Bitter Ⓖ
Morland Bitter
Wadworth 6X Ⓗ
Pleasant 17th-century
two-bar pub ♠⅃♣⅊▩▣Ⓖ☗⅂⑤

Lewknor
16C9

10.30–2.30; 6–10.30 (11 F, S)

Olde Leatherne
Bottel
(Off B4009/M40)

Morning opening: 11
Brakspear Pale Ale, Special
Bitter, Old Ⓗ
Friendly pub noted for its
curries
♠⅃♣⅊▩Ⓖ☗ (not Mon) ☗⑤

Little Coxwell
6C1

10–2.30; 6–10.30 (11 F, S)

Eagle Tavern
(Off A420) ⅁ Faringdon 20120
Opens at 11 am & 6.30 pm
Ind Coope Burton Ale
Morland Bitter
Ruddle Bitter Ⓗ
Rare Ruddles and interesting
food ♠⅃♣☷⅊▩◨Ⓡ Ⓖ☗⑤

Little Milton
16C9

10–2.30; 6–10.30 (11 F, S)

Plough
Thame Road (A329)
Morrell Light Ale, Bitter Ⓗ
Friendly local in attractive
village ♠⅃♣☷⅊▩Ⓡ⑤

Longcot
15J7

10–2.30; 6–10.30 (11 F, S)

Bricklayers Arms
The Green (off B4508)
Opens at 11 am & 7 pm
Wadworth 6X Ⓖ
Cheerful village free house
⅃♣⅊▩⑤

Long Hanborough
16A8

10–2.30; 6–10.30 (11 F, S)

Bell
Main Road (A4095)
⅁ Freeland 881324
Morrell Varsity Ⓖ
Busy pub, noted for food
♠⅊▩Ⓖ☗⑤

Swan
Combe Road (off A4095)
Morrell Light Ale, Bitter Ⓗ
Small, cosy locals' pub ⅂♣⅊▩

Lower Assendon
7F1

10.30–2.30; 6–10.30 (11 F, S)

Golden Ball
(B480) ⅁ Henley 4157
Morning opening: 11
Brakspear Mild, Pale Ale Ⓗ
Old Ⓖ
Splendid country pub with
good value food ♠⅃☗▩Ⓖ☗⑤

Maidensgrove
7F1

10–2.30; 6–10.30 (11 F, S)

Five Horseshoes
⅁ Nettlebed 641282
Brakspear Pale Ale, Special
Bitter Ⓔ Old Ⓖ
Attractive brick and flint
Chilterns pub
♠⅊▩Ⓖ☗ (not Mon) ⑤

Mapledurham
7F2

10.30–2.30; 6–10.30 (11 F, S)

Pack Horse
(A4074)

Gale BBB, HSB Ⓗ
Popular and attractive
country inn ▲♣🅗🅿🚗🄶🎵

Marsh Baldon 16B9

10–2.30; 6–10.30 (11 F, S)
Seven Stars
(Off A423)
Opens at 11 am & 6.30 pm
Usher Best Bitter, Founders Ale
Bulmer Cider Ⓗ
Popular one-bar pub
overlooking splendid village
green ▲🎵♣🅗🅿🚗🄶Ⓢ

Middleton Stoney 16B7

10–2.30; 6–10.30 (11 F, S)
Jersey Arms Hotel
(A43) ✆ 234
Marston Burton Bitter,
Pedigree Ⓗ
A delightful country hotel
▲🚗🅗🄶🎵Ⓢ

Noke 16B8

10–2.30; 6–10.30 (11 F, S)
Plough
(Off B4027) ✆ Kidlington 3251
Evening opening: 7
Courage Best Bitter,
Directors Ⓗ
Popular country pub
🎵♣🅿🄶🎵Ⓢ

Northmoor 16A9

10–2.30; 6–10.30 (11 F, S)
Dun Cow
(Off A415)
Morland Mild, Bitter Ⓖ
Charming and unspoilt, with
no serving counter ▲♣🅿🚗🎵

Oxford 16B8

10–2.30; 6–10.30 (11 F, S)
Bear
Blue Boar Street/Alfred Street
Morning opening: 10.30
Halls Harvest Bitter
Ind Coope Burton Ale
Coates Cider Ⓗ
Small, historic 15th-century
inn, famous for collection of
ties 🎵🅿🄶Ⓢ♦

Chequers
131 High Street ✆ 726904
Halls Harvest Bitter
Ind Coope Burton Ale Ⓗ
Well-restored 15th-century
inn with variety of bars
🎵♣🅿🄶🎵Ⓢ♦

Coach & Horses
62 St Clements Street
Morrell Light Ale, Varsity Ⓗ
Uncomplicated small town
local 🎵♣🅿🅁🎵

Cricketers Arms
43 Iffley Road
Opens at 11 am & 6.30 pm
Morland Mild, Bitter, Best
Bitter Ⓗ
Deservedly popular local ♣🎵

Gardeners Arms
39 Plantation Road (off
Woodstock Road) ✆ 259814
Morning opening: 11
Morrell Dark Mild,
Bitter Ⓗ College Ale
Weston Cider Ⓖ
Friendly, traditional
local; three rooms but only
one bar 🎵🅗🅿🄶🎵Ⓢ

Kings Arms
40 Holywell Street ✆ 242369
Draught Bass
Brakspear Pale Ale
Fuller London Pride
Glenny Eagle Bitter
Morland Bitter
Morrell College Ale Ⓖ
Wadworth 6X Ⓗ Old Timer Ⓖ
Younger No. 3
Weston Cider Ⓗ
Large popular pub 🅗🅁Ⓢ🎵🎵

Old Tom
101 St. Aldates ✆ 243034
Morning opening: 10.30
Morrell Bitter, Varsity Ⓗ
Comfortable city centre pub
🎵♣🅿🅗🄶🎵🎵

Prince of Wales
73 Church Way, Iffley
Archer Best Bitter
Wadworth 6X
Younger No. 3 Ⓗ
Popular free house in riverside
village; guest beers 🎵♣🅿🎵

Radcliffe Arms
Cranham Street, Jericho
Morning opening: 11
Usher Best Bitter, Founders
Ale
Bulmer Cider Ⓗ
Excellent North Oxford local
with musical flavour 🎵🎵♣🅿Ⓢ

Roebuck
8 Market Street ✆ 248388
Closed Sunday lunchtimes
Courage Best Bitter,
Directors Ⓗ
Busy city-centre pub next to
covered market 🎵🎵🅁🄶Ⓢ

Temple Bar
21 Temple Street, East Oxford
Wadworth IPA, 6X, Old
Timer Ⓗ
Shrine for lovers of
Wadworth's 🎵♣🄶🎵Ⓢ

Turf Tavern
10 Bath Place (off Holywell
Street) ✆ 243235
Hook Norton Best Bitter, Old
Hookey
Ruddle County
Wethered SPA
Weston Cider Ⓗ
Famous 13th-century tavern
in attractive setting; guest
beers ▲🎵🅿🄶🎵Ⓢ

Westgate
12 New Road ✆ 250099
Morrell Light Ale, Dark Mild,
Bitter, Varsity, College Ale Ⓗ

Modern one-bar pub, with
Morrells brewery mementoes
🎵♣🅿🄶🎵Ⓢ♦🎵

Rokemarsh 7E

10–2.30; 6–10.30 (11 F, S)
Horse & Harrow
(Off B4009)
Brakspear Pale Ale, Special
Bitter Ⓗ
Small traditional local
▲🎵♣🅿🎵

Sandford-on-Thames 16B

10–2.30; 6–10.30 (11 F, S)
Fox
25 Henley Road (off A423)
Morning opening: 11
Morrell Dark Mild, Light Ale,
Bitter Ⓖ
Simple, unaffected roadside
pub ▲🎵♣🅿🎵

Satwell 7F

10–2.30; 6–10.30 (11 F, S)
Lamb
(Off B481)
Brakspear Pale Ale, Special
Bitter, Old Ⓖ
Old cottage-style pub with
inglenook fire ▲🎵♣🅿🎵Ⓢ

Shepherds Green 7F

10–2.30; 6–10.30 (11 F, S)
Green Tree
(Off B481) OS 713833
Brakspear Mild, Pale Ale Ⓗ
No-nonsense local 🅗🎵

Shiplake 7F

10–2.30; 6–10.30 (11 F, S)
Baskerville Arms
Station Road (off A4155)
✆ Wargrave 3332
Morning opening: 11
Wethered Bitter, SPA,
Winter Royal Ⓗ
Smart pub, good food
🎵♣🅿🅗🄶🎵 (Tue–Sat)Ⓢ🎵

Shrivenham 6C

10.30–2.30; 6–10.30 (11 F, S)
Prince of Wales
High Street (A420)
Wadworth IPA, 6X, Old
Timer Ⓖ
Large and comfortable; note
interesting stillage
▲🎵♣🅿🅁🄶🎵🎵

Sonning Eye 7F

10–2.30; 6–10.30 (11 F, S)
Flowing Spring
(A4155) ✆ Reading 693207
Fuller Chiswick Bitter,
London Pride, ESB Ⓗ
Popular, tastefully refurbished
roadside pub ▲🎵♣🅿🄶🎵Ⓢ

South Leigh 16A

10.30–2.30; 6–10.30 (11 F, S)

Mason Arms
(Off A40) ℓ Witney 2485
Opens at 12 noon & 7 pm;
closed Mondays
Mason Arms Sowlye Ale Ⓗ
Delightful thatched country
pub with restaurant and own
brewery 🅰♪♣🅿🅰Ⓡ🄶↺🍴🅈

Steeple Aston 16B7

10–2.30; 6–11
Red Lion
South Street (off A423)
**Hook Norton Best Bitter, Old
Hookey**
Wadworth 6X, Old Timer Ⓗ
Friendly, attractive village pub
🅰♣🅰↺🅈Ⓢ

Steventon 6D1

10–2.30; 6–10.30 (11 F, S)
Cherry Tree Inn
High Street (off A34)
Brakspear Pale Ale
Hook Norton Best Bitter
Morland Bitter
Wadworth 6X Ⓗ
Comfortable and busy free
house, popular with young;
guest beers 🅰♪🎵🅿🅰Ⓡ↺🍴🅈Ⓢ

North Star
The Causeway (off A34)
Opens 10.30 am & 6.45 pm
**Morland Mild, Bitter, Best
Bitter** Ⓖ
Delightful old village pub
🅰🅿🅰Ⓡ↺ (weekdays)🍴

Stoke Lyne 16B7

10–2.30; 6–10.30 (11 F, S)
Peyton Arms
**Hook Norton Best Bitter,
Old Hookey** Ⓖ
Quiet, unchanged village local
🅰♣🅰🍴

Stoke Row 7F2

10–2.30; 6–10.30 (11 F, S)
Cherry Tree
(Off B481)
**Brakspear Mild, Pale Ale,
Special Bitter, Old** Ⓖ
Lively local with large garden
🅰♪♣🎵🅿🅰Ⓡ

Crooked Billet
Newlands Lane (off B481)
**Brakspear Mild, Pale Ale,
Special Bitter, Old** Ⓖ
Unique country pub with no
serving counter
🅰♣🅿🅰

Swerford 16A7

10–2.30; 6–10.30 (11 F, S and summer)
Masons Arms
(A361) ℓ Great Tew 212
Morning opening: 11
Mitchells & Butlers Brew XI Ⓗ
150-year-old stone roadside
pub 🅰♣🅿🅰↺🍴🍴Ⓢ♿

Swinbrook 15J6

10–2.30; 6–10.30 (11 F, S)

Swan
(Off A40) ℓ Burford 2165
Morland Mild, Bitter
Wadworth 6X Ⓗ
17th-century riverside inn
🅰♣🅿🅰🅰Ⓢ

Sydenham 16C9

10–2.30; 6–10.30 (11 F, S)
Crown
(Off A40/B4445)
Morning opening: 11
**Hall & Woodhouse Badger
Best Bitter**
Morland Mild
Ruddle County
Young Bitter Ⓗ
Charming 18th-century oak-
beamed free house 🅰♪♣🅿🅰Ⓢ

Thame 16C8

10–2.30; 6–10.30 (11 F, S)
Bird Cage
Cornmarket ℓ 2046
**Courage Best Bitter,
Directors** Ⓗ
13th-century former town
bridewell, steeped in history
♪♣↺ (not Sun)🍴Ⓢ

Towersey 16C8

10–2.30; 6–10.30 (11 F, S)
Three Horseshoes
Chinnor Road ℓ Thame 2322
Morning opening: 11
Aylesbury ABC Bitter
Everard Tiger Ⓗ
Substantial village pub with
licensed 13th-century barn
🅰♪♣🅿🅰Ⓡ↺🍴Ⓢ

Wallingford 7E1

10.30–2.30; 6–10.30 (11 F, S)
Coachmakers Arms
St. Marys Street (A329)
**Brakspear Mild, Pale Ale,
Old** Ⓗ
Good old-fashioned pub
🅰♪♣🅿Ⓡ🅈Ⓢ♿

Cross Keys
50 High Street (A4130)
**Brakspear Pale Ale, Special
Bitter, Old** Ⓗ
Three-bar pub with elevated
games room 🅰♣🅿🍴🅈Ⓢ

Wantage 6D1

10.30–2.30; 5.30–10.30 (11 F, S)
Shoulder of Mutton
Wallingford Street (A417)
Morning opening: 10.30
Morland Mild, Bitter Ⓗ
Delightfully basic; no frills
🅰🍴♣🅈🍴

Watlington 7F1

10.30–2.30; 6–10.30 (11 F, S)
Hare & Hounds
Market Place (B4009) ℓ 2329
Morning opening: 11
**Hall & Woodhouse Badger
Best Bitter**
Morrell Bitter
North Country Riding Bitter Ⓗ

17th-century coaching inn
near town hall; range of beers
may vary 🅰♪♣🅰🍴🍴Ⓢ

West Hanney 6D1

10–2.30; 6–10.30 (11 F, S)
Lamb Inn
School Lane (off A338) ℓ 540
Morning opening: 11
Hook Norton Best Bitter
Morland Bitter
Wadworth 6X
Weston Cider Ⓗ
Popular one-bar pub and
restaurant; guest beers
🍴♣🅿🅰↺🍴Ⓢ

Weston-on-the-Green 16B8

10–2.30; 6–10.30 (11 F, S)
Chequers
(A43) ℓ Bletchingdon 50319
Halls Harvest Bitter
Ind Coope Burton Ale Ⓗ
Large thatched roadside pub
🅰♣🎵🅿🅰Ⓡ↺🍴Ⓢ

Witheridge Hill 7F1

10–2.30; 6–10.30 (11 F, S)
Rising Sun
(Off B481)
Morning opening: 10.30
Brakspear Pale Ale, Old Ⓗ
Attractive, old cottage-style
pub 🅰♣🅿🅰↺🍴 (not Sun)Ⓢ

Witney 16A8

10–2.30; 6–10.30 (11 F, S)
Eagle Tavern
22 Corn Street
Glenny Eagle Bitter
Hook Norton Best Bitter
Morland Bitter Ⓗ
Undistinguished exterior hides
a delightful pub 🅰♣🍴Ⓢ

House of Windsor
31 West End (B4022)
Glenny Eagle Bitter
Hook Norton Best Bitter
Wadworth 6X
Younger No. 3 Ⓗ
Neat and comfortable two-bar
pub; range of beers may vary
🅰♣🅿↺🅈Ⓢ

Woodstock 16B8

10–2; 6–10.30 (11 F, S)
Queens Own
59 Oxford Street (A34)
**Hook Norton Mild, Best Bitter,
Old Hookey** Ⓗ
Small, friendly local ♪♣Ⓡ🍴Ⓢ

Wytham 16B8

10–2.30; 6–10.30 (11 F, S)
White Hart
(Off A34) ℓ Oxford 244372
Morning opening: 11
Halls Harvest Bitter
Ind Coope Burton Ale Ⓗ
Gaymer Cider Ⓖ
300-year-old pub of
character 🅰🅿🅰↺🍴Ⓢ

Shropshire

Albrighton 22E8

11–2.30; 6–10.30 (11 F, S)

Crown
High Street ✆ 2204
Banks Mild, Bitter Ⓔ
Attractive urban pub
🏠♣🅿🍴🆑Ⓡ🅖🕐Ⓢ♿

Alveley 15F2

11.45–2.30; 6.45–10.30 (11 F, S)

Royal Oak
(A442)
Banks Mild, Bitter Ⓔ
Small roadside inn between
Bridgnorth and Kidderminster
🏠♪♣🅰🅖Ⓢ⛺

Bishop's Castle 14C1

11.30–2.30; 6.30–10.30 (11 F, S)

Three Tuns
Salop Street ✆ 797
Three Tuns Mild, XXX, Castle
Steamer Ⓗ
One of the original home-brew
pubs, first mentioned 1642
🏠🍴♣🅿🅰🅖🆑Ⓢ

Bratton 22D8

11–2.30; 6.30–11

Gate
(B5063) ✆ Telford 44207
Wem Mild, Best Bitter Ⓗ
Friendly country pub
♪♣🅿🅰Ⓡ🅖Ⓢ

Bridgnorth 22D9

10.30–2.30; 6–10.30 (11 F, S)

Railwayman's Arms
Severn Valley railway station
Banks Mild
Batham Bitter
Davenports Bitter
Everard Old Original
Taylor Landlord Ⓗ
Smart freehouse on steam
railway platform; regular
guest beers 🏠♣🅰🅖Ⓢ

Shakespeare
West Castle Street ✆ 2403
Open until 4 pm Mon & Sat
Banks Mild, Bitter Ⓔ
Town pub with skittle alley
♪♣Ⓡ🆑🕐🍴Ⓢ

Vine
Mill Street, Low Town
Wem Mild, Best Bitter Ⓗ
Popular pub alongside River
Severn ♪♣🍴Ⓢ

Broseley 22D9

10.30–2.30; 6–10.30 (11 F, S)

Cumberland
Queen Street ✆ Telford
882301
Wem Mild Ⓔ Best Bitter Ⓗ & Ⓔ
Comfortable hotel near the
ironbridge ♪♣🅰🍴Ⓡ🆑🕐🍴Ⓢ

Cardington 22C9

12–2.30; 7–10.30 (11 F, S)

Royal Oak
(Off B4371) ✆ Longville 266
Closed Wed lunchtimes in
winter
Draught Bass
Mitchells & Butlers Springfield
Bitter Ⓗ
Superb example of an English
country pub 🏠♪♣🅿🅖Ⓢ

Church Stretton 22C9

10.30–2.30; 6–11

Kings Arms
High Street ✆ 722807
Wem Mild, Best Bitter Ⓗ
Well-appointed town-centre
pub ♪♣🍴🆑🕐🍴Ⓢ⛺

Claverley 22E9

12–3; 7–10.30 (11 F, S)

Crown
High Street ✆ 228
Hansons Mild, Bitter Ⓔ
Attractive Tudor-style inn
🏠♣🅿🅰Ⓡ🅖Ⓢ♿

Cleobury Mortimer 15E2

10.30–2.30; 6–10.30 (11 F, S)

Bell
Lower Street ✆ 305
Banks Mild, Bitter
Mitchells & Butlers Springfield
Bitter Ⓔ
Bulmer Cider Ⓗ
Small inn with character
🏠♣Ⓡ🍴

Clun 14C2

1.30–2.30; 6–10.30 (11 F, S)

Sun
(B4368) ✆ 277/559
Ansells Mild
Mitchells & Butlers Springfield
Bitter
Woods Special Bitter Ⓗ
15th-century cruck
construction, wealth of
exposed beams
🏠♣🅿🅿🅰🅖Ⓡ🕐🍴Ⓢ

Coalport 22D8

10.30–2.30; 7–10.30 (11 F, S)

Brewery Inn
53 High Street ✆ Telford
581225
Wem Mild, Best Bitter Ⓔ
Excellent pub with own
fishing rights
♪♣🅿🅰🕐🍴Ⓢ♿⛺

Woodbridge Inn
✆ Telford 882054
Opens 6 pm in summer
Banks Mild, Bitter
Courage Directors
Marston Pedigree
Simpkiss Bitter Ⓗ
Rambling pub in riverside
setting 🏠♪♣🅿🅖🕐🍴Ⓢ

Craven Arms 14D2

11–2.30; 6–11

Stokesay Castle Hotel
School Road (off A49) ✆ 2304
Davenports Mild, Bitter Ⓗ
Close to Stokesay Castle;
unusual beer engines in
lounge
🏠♪♣🅿🍴🅰🅖Ⓡ🆑🕐🍴Ⓢ⛺

Crosshouses 22C8

11.30–3; 6–11

Fox
(A458) ✆ 289
Wem Mild, Best Bitter Ⓗ
Busy roadside pub on tourist
route ♪🅿🅖🆑🕐🍴Ⓢ

Dawley 22D8

11–2.30; 6–11

Lord Hill
High Street ✆ Telford 503090
Closes 10.30 pm Mon–Thu
Banks Mild, Bitter Ⓔ
Lively pub decorated with
pictures of local hero Captain
Webb ♪♣🅿🅖🆑🕐Ⓢ♿

Ring O'Bells
King Street
Marston Mercian Mild,
Burton Bitter, Pedigree Ⓗ
Small busy local ♣🅿🅰🕐Ⓢ

Dorrington 22C8

10.30–3; 6–11

Bridge Inn
(A49) ✆ 209
Wem Mild, Best Bitter Ⓗ
Set in pleasant grounds off
main road ♪♣🅿🅰🕐Ⓢ⛺

Ellerdine Heath 22D7

10.30–2.30; 6.30–10.30 (11 F, S)

Royal Oak
(Off A442)
Wem Mild, Best Bitter Ⓔ
Classic country pub ♪♣🅿🅰🕐

Ellesmere 22B6

10.30–2.30 (3.30 F); 6–11

Market Hotel
Scotland Street ✆ 2217
Wem Pale Ale, Mild,
Best Bitter Ⓔ
Unspoilt pub; extends a
welcome to canal users
♪♣🍴🅿🅰Ⓢ

White Hart
Birch Road
Border Mild, Bitter Ⓗ
In side street, worth seeking
out ♪♣🅿🅰🕐🍴Ⓢ

Farley 22D9

12–2.30; 7–10.30 (11 F, S)

Rock House
1½ miles north of Much
Wenlock (B4378)
Closed weekday lunchtimes in
winter
Wem Best Bitter
Woods Special Bitter Ⓗ
Weston Cider Ⓖ

Enterprising free house with guest beers 🔥🔇♪♣🌼🚗

Ford 22B8

11.30–3; 6.30–11
Cross Gates
(A458) ☎ Shrewsbury 850332
Wem Pale Ale, Mild (winter), **Best Bitter** [H]
Unspoilt bar, splendid lounge facilities 🔥♪♣⊞🌼🚗[R]🕐🌙🍺Ⓢ

Grinshill 22C7

11–3; 6.30–11
Elephant & Castle
(Off A49) ☎ Clive 410
Tetley Bitter [H]
Large, well-appointed country pub, always a guest beer 🔥♪♣🌼🚗[R]🕐🌙🍺Ⓢ

Halfway House 22B8

10.30–3; 6–10.30 (11 F, S)
Halfway House & Seven Stars
(A458)
Burtonwood Light Mild [H] (Halfway House) [G] (Seven Stars)
Unusual combination – try them both 🔥♪♣🌼🚗🕐🌙🍺Ⓢ (Halfway House)

Harley 22C9

11–3; 6–11
Plume of Feathers
(A458)
Whitbread Flowers Original Bitter [H]
Attractive pub below Wenlock Edge 🔥♪♣🌼🚗🍺Ⓢ♿

Hengoed 22A7

11–2.30; 7–11
Last Inn
(Off A483/B4579) ☎ Oswestry 659747
Oak XL Bitter
Marston Burton Bitter
Woods Special Bitter
Weston Cider [H]
Large country pub near Offa's Dyke 🔥🔇♪♣🚗[R]🕐🌙🍺Ⓢ

Hookagate 22C8

11.30–2.30; 7–11
Royal Oak
Near Shrewsbury
Wem Mild, Best Bitter [H]
Old world village pub ♣🚗🕐🌙🍺Ⓢ⛺

Horsehay 22D8

11–2.30; 6.30–11
Foresters Arms
Wellington Road
Mitchells & Butlers Highgate Mild, Springfield Bitter [H]
Traditional multi-roomed local 🔥♣🌼🚗[R]🍺

Ironbridge 22D8

10.30–2.30; 6.30–10.30 (11 F, S)
Bird in Hand
Waterloo Street
Banks Mild, Bitter [E]
Friendly pub on the River Severn ♪♣🌼🚗🍺Ⓢ

Jackfield 22D9

11–2.30; 6–10.30 (11 F, S)
Half Moon
Salthouse Road
Ansells Mild, Bitter [H]
Hard-to-find pub with riverside garden 🔥🔇♪♣🌼🚗🍺Ⓢ

Little Stretton 22B9

10.45–2.30; 6–11
Ragleth
(B4370, off A49) ☎ Church Stretton 722711
Draught Bass
Manns Bitter [H]
Old country inn, set in delightful surroundings; occasional guest beer 🔥♣🌼🚗🕐🌙🍺Ⓢ

Loppington 22C7

12–3; 6.30–11
Blacksmiths Arms
(B4379) ☎ Wem 33762
Wem Pale Ale, Best Bitter [H]
A traditional pub in every respect 🔥♣🌼🚗🕐🌙🍺Ⓢ

Ludlow 14D2

10–2.30; 6–11
Church Inn
Butter Cross ☎ 2174
Marston Burton Bitter, Pedigree [H]
Comfortable lounge bar and restaurant with two Victorian beer engines; guest beer 🔥♪▣🕐🌙Ⓢ🚆

George
Castle Square
Ansells Mild, Bitter [H]
Unspoilt pub adjacent to castle ♪♣🌼🍺Ⓢ

Wheatsheaf
Broad Street ☎ 2980
Malvern Chase Ale
Robinson Best Bitter
Whitbread Flowers Original Bitter [H]
Built into town walls. Comfortable lounge bar ♪▣🕐🌙Ⓢ

Try also: Bull Hotel, Corve Street (Marston)

Madeley 22D8

10.30–2.30; 6–10.30 (11 F, S)
All Nations
Coalport Road
Opens at 12 noon & 7 pm
All Nations Pale Ale [H]
Long-established home-brew pub with strong local following ♣🌼🚗🍺

Market Drayton 22D7

11–3 (5 Wed); 7–11
Kings Arms
Shropshire Street (A53)
☎ 2417
Marston Mercian Mild, Burton Bitter, Pedigree, Owd Rodger [G]
Former coaching inn in town centre ♪♣🌼🚗[R]🕐🍺Ⓢ

Stags Head
Great Hales Street (A529)
Marston Mercian Mild, Burton Bitter, Pedigree, Owd Rodger [H]
Lively town-centre local with friendly atmosphere 🔥♪♣⊞🌼🚗[R]🕐🍺

Morville 22D9

11–2.30; 6–10.30 (11 F, S)
Acton Arms
(A458) ☎ 209
Banks Mild, Bitter [E]
Large, modernised country inn 🔥♪♣🌼🚗🕐🌙🍺Ⓢ♿⛺

Neen Sollars 14E2

12–2.30; 7–10.30 (11 F, S)
Railway Tavern
☎ Cleobury Mortimer 270254
Courage Directors [H]
Rural pub with skittle alley and duck suppers 🔥♪♣🌼🚗[R]🕐🌙Ⓢ

Newport 22D7

11–2.30; 6–10.30 (11 F, S)
Kings Head
Chetwynd End (A41)
Opens 11.30 am & 6.30 pm
Marston Mercian Mild, Burton Bitter, Pedigree [H]
Owd Rodger [G]
Friendly pub at the north end of town 🔥♪♣🌼🚗🕐🍺Ⓢ

Oakengates 22D8

10.30–2.30; 6–11
Alexandra
Slaney Street
Opens at 11 am & 7 pm
Banks Mild, Bitter [E]
Pleasant terraced pub ♪♣🌼🚗🍺Ⓢ

Caledonia
Lion Street ☎ Telford 613946
Opens at 11 am & 7 pm
Draught Bass [E]
Smart residential hotel 🚗▣[R]🕐🌙Ⓢ🚆

Oswestry 22B7

10.30–2.30; (4 Wed, Sat); 6–10.30 (11 F, S)
Five Bells
Willow Street
Border Bitter [H]
Homely town-centre pub ♪♣🚗🍺

Plough
Beatrice Street

Wem Pale Ale, Mild, Best Bitter [E]
Bustling town-centre pub opposite Indian restaurant
♪♣🚗▣[R][S]

Try also: Welsh Harp, Upper Brock Street (Border)

St Georges 22D8

11–2.30; 7–11

Turf Inn

School Street ☎ Telford 612497
Ansells Mild, Bitter [H]
Unspoilt backstreet inn with large beer garden
🔥♪♣✿🚗▣[R]🍴[S]♿

Selattyn 22A7

10.30–2.30; 6–11

Cross Keys

(B4579)
Banks Bitter [H]
Unspoilt rural alehouse, ½ mile from Offa's Dyke footpath
🔥♣✿🚗🍴

Shifnal 22D8

11.30–2.30; 6–10.30 (11 F, S)

Anvil

Aston Road
Opens at 12 noon & 7 pm
Banks Mild, Bitter [E]
Small and friendly backstreet local 🔥♣🚗🍴[S]⇌

Shrewsbury 22D8

10.30–3; 6–11

Acorn

St. Julian Friars
Draught Bass
Mitchells & Butlers Mild [H]
Unspoilt pub close to river
🔥♪♣🍴[S]

Admiral Benbow

Swan Hill
Ansells Bitter
Ind Coope Burton Ale
Tetley Mild [H]
Well-appointed lounge bar and restaurant; just off town centre ♪✿[R]☾◗[S]

Albert

Smithfield Road
Banks Mild, Bitter [E]
Marston Pedigree
Woods Special Bitter [H]
Shrewsbury's only real free free house; guest beer always available ♪♣[R]🍴[S]⇌

Boat House

Port Hill
Whitbread Bitter [H]
Riverside pub overlooking public park ♪♣✿🚗🍴[S]

Britannia

Castle Foregate
Wem Pale Ale, Mild, Best Bitter [E]
Excellent local, successfully refurbished ♣🚗[S]⇌

Loggerheads

Church Street ☎ 55457
Draught Bass
Mitchells & Butlers Mild [E]
Cosy town-centre pub; reputed smallest bar in county
♣☾◗🍴[S]⇌

Prince of Wales

Bynner Street
Border Mild, Bitter [H]
Complete with bowling green, overlooked by maltings
♪♣✿🚗🍴[S]

Try also: Cornhouse, Wyle Cop (Wilsons)

Stottesdon 15E2

12–2.30; 7–10.30 (11 F, S)

Fox & Hounds

Closed Monday lunchtimes except bank holidays
Fox & Hounds DDD Bitter, Dashers Extra (winter) [H]
Home-brew pub with guest beers 🔥♣🚗[R]☾🍴[S]

Trench 22D8

11–2.30; 6–10.30 (11 F, S)

Dun Cow

Trench Road (A518)
Banks Mild, Bitter [E]
Busy pub with comfortable lounge ♪♣✿🚗🍴[S]

Tweedale 22D8

12–2.30; 7–10.30 (11 F, S)

Three Furnaces

Bridgnorth Road (off A442)
Wem Mild, Best Bitter [E]
Spacious one-bar pub in industrial setting ♪♣✿🚗☾[S]

Wellington 22D8

10.30–2.30; 6–11

Red Lion

Park Street (A442)
Wem Mild, Best Bitter [E]
Drinkers' pub, formerly a local brewery ♪♣🚗🍴[S]♿

Three Crowns

High Street ☎ Telford 3209
Opens at 11 am & 7 pm
Ansells Mild, Bitter [H]
The only real Ansells in town
🔥♪♣☾◗[S]

Wem 22C7

10.30–3; 6–11

Dickin Arms

Noble Street
Open until 5 pm Thursdays
Marston Mercian Mild, Burton Bitter, Owd Rodger (winter) [H]
The only non-Wem pub in Wem ♪♣🍴[S]⇌

Wentnor 22B9

11–2.30; 6–10.30 (11 F, S)

Crown

(Off A489/A488)
Mitchells & Butlers Springfield Bitter [H]
Attractive pub in delightful surroundings; guest beers
🔥♪♣⊞✿🚗▣[R]☾◗[S]⛺

West Felton 22B7

10.30–2.30; 6–10.30 (11 F, S)

Fox & Hounds

(A5)
Banks Mild, Bitter [E]
Comfortable main road pub
♪♣🚗🍴[S]

Wheathill 14E2

10.30–2.30; 6–10.30 (11 F, S)

Three Horseshoes

(B4364) near Burwarton
Wem Mild, Best Bitter [E]
Rural pub overlooking Brown Clee 🔥♪♣⊞✿🚗🍴[S]♿⛺

Whitchurch 22C6

10.30–3; 6–11

Old Eagles

Watergate Street
Marston Mercian Mild, Burton Bitter, Pedigree [H]
Busy pub just off town centre
♪♣☾[S]

Old Town Hall Vaults

St. Mary's Street
Border Mild, Bitter [H]
Spacious pub in side street
⌐♪♣🚗🍴[S]

Try also: Highgate (Wilsons)

Wistanstow 14C2

11–2.30; 7–11

Plough

(Off A49)
Woods Special Bitter, Parish Bitter [H]
Well-appointed house, home of Wood's beers; occasional guest beers 🔥♪♣✿🚗☾◗🍴[S]

Woore 22D6

10.30–3; 6–11

Swan

(A51) ☎ Pipe Gate 220
Lunchtime opening: 12 noon
Wem Mild, Best Bitter [H]
Large, comfortable coaching inn with friendly landlord
🔥⌐♪♣✿🚗[R]☾◗🍴[S]

The 🔥 symbol denotes a pub with a real solid fuel fire

Appley 4C3

10.30–2.30; 6–11
Globe
OS 072216
Usher PA Ⓖ
Unspoilt village pub ♣♨🅿🛏Ⓢ

Ash 5F3

10.30–2.30; 5.30–11
Bell
Main Street (off A303)
Opens at 11 am & 7 pm
Whitbread Bitter Ⓖ
Old pub with collection of
clocks 🅰♪♣🅿🅑Ⓡ🅖➔Ⓢ

Axbridge 5F1

10.30–2.30; 5.30–11
Lamb Hotel
Market Square (off A371)
✆ 732253
Evening opening: 6.30
Nailsea Jacobs Best Bitter
Whitbread Flowers Original
Bitter Ⓗ
Interesting bar frontage of
labelled bottles ♣🔲Ⓡ🅖➔Ⓢ🅓♿Ⓐ

Barrington 5E3

11–2.30; 7–11
Royal Oak
(Off B3168) ✆ Ilminster 3455
Golden Hill Exmoor Ale
Hall & Woodhouse
Hector's Bitter
Ind Coope Burton Ale Ⓗ
Excellent village inn, next to a
thatcher's ♪♣♨🅑🅑Ⓡ🅖➔🅟Ⓢ

Binegar 5G2

11–2.30; 7–11
Horse & Jockey
(Off A37) ✆ Oakhill 840537
Draught Bass Ⓖ
Butcombe Bitter
Miners Arms Own Ale Ⓗ
Wadworth 6X Ⓖ
Pleasant country free house
♪♨🅑Ⓖ➔Ⓢ

Bridgwater 4E2

10.30–2.30; 5.30–11
Fountain Inn
1 West Quay (off A38)
Opens at 11 am & 7 pm
Berrow BBBB
Butcombe Bitter
Golden Hill Exmoor Ale Ⓗ
Excellent riverside pub; keen
landlord ♪♣🅟≷

North Pole
North Street (A39)
Courage Best Bitter, Directors
(summer)
Taunton Cider Ⓗ
Friendly town pub; folk club
Sundays ⎰♪♣♨🅑Ⓡ🅟Ⓢ

Quantock Gateway
Wembdon Road (A39)
Evening opening: 6
Draught Bass Ⓖ
Whitbread Bitter, Flowers
Original Bitter Ⓗ

Spacious and comfortable pub
on town outskirts
♪♣🔲♨🅑Ⓡ🅖➔Ⓢ

Bruton 5G2

11–2.30; 5.30–11
Castle Inn
High Street (A359) ✆ 2211
Draught Bass
Welsh Fussells Best Bitter Ⓗ
Thriving one-bar local, good
food ♪♣♨🅖➔Ⓢ

Buckland Dinham 5H1

10.30–2.30; 6–11
Fountain
(A362)
Closed Mon, Wed, Fri lunch
Eldridge Pope Dorchester
Bitter, Royal Oak
Wilkins Cider Ⓖ
Tiny pub with no bar – order
beer from kitchen ♣♨🅟Ⓢ

Burnham-on-Sea 4E2

10.30–2.30; 5.30–11
Lighthouse Inn
Highbridge Road (B3139)
Whitbread WCPA, Flowers
Original Bitter Ⓗ
Modern, comfortable pub
♪♣🔲♨🅑Ⓡ🅖➔🅟Ⓢ🅓

Cannington 4E2

10.30–2.30; 5.30–11
Blue Anchor
Brook Street (A39)
✆ Combwich 652215
Opens at 12 noon & 7 pm
Whitbread WCPA, Flowers
Original Bitter Ⓖ
Village inn with attractive
garden ♪♣♨🅑🅑Ⓡ🅖➔🅟Ⓢ🅓Ⓐ

Castle Cary 5G3

10.30–2.30; 5.30–11
Countryman
South Street (B3152)
Opens 11.30 am & 6.30 pm
Tisbury Local Bitter
Wadworth 6X Ⓗ
Small free house with railway
theme 🅰♪♣🔲♨🅑Ⓡ🅖➔🅟Ⓢ🅓Ⓐ

Catcott 5E2

10.30–2.30; 5.30–11
King William
(Off A39)
Opens at 11 am & 6 pm
Draught Bass
Eldridge Pope Dorchester
Bitter, Royal Oak
Halls Harvest Bitter
Wadworth 6X Ⓗ
Cosy pub with open fireplaces
🅰♣🔲♨🅑Ⓡ🅖➔🅟Ⓢ🅓

Chard 5E4

10.30–2.30; 5.30–11
Olde Ship Inn
94 Furnham Road ✆ 3135
Opens at 11 am & 6.30 pm

Golden Hill Exmoor Ale
Ind Coope Burton Ale
Wadworth 6X Ⓗ
Friendly old pub on Taunton
side of town 🅰♪♣♨🅑Ⓡ🅖➔Ⓢ

Charlton Musgrove 5H

11–2.30; 7–11
Smithy
(B3081) ✆ Wincanton 32242
Eldridge Pope Dorchester
Bitter, IPA, Royal Oak Ⓗ
Pleasant village local, good
value food 🅰♪♣🅑Ⓡ🅖➔🅟Ⓢ

Chiltorne Domer 5F

10.30–2.30; 5.30–11
Halfway House
Ilchester Road (A37)
Evening opening: 6.30
Devenish Wessex Best Bitter Ⓗ
Popular roadside pub
♪♣🔲♨🅑Ⓡ🅖➔🅟

Coleford 5G

11–2.30; 6–11
Rose & Crown
High Street ✆ Mells 812712
Butcombe Bitter Ⓗ
Large, rambling building,
guest beers ♪♨🅟➔🅟

Combe Florey 4D

10.30–2.30; 5.30–11
Farmers Arms
(Off A358)
Evening opening: 6
Draught Bass Ⓗ
Lovely old thatched inn
♪♨🅟➔Ⓢ

Combwich 4E

10.30–2.30; 5.30–11
Old Ship
Ship Lane (2 miles off A39)
OS 259425 ✆ 652264
Opens at 12 noon & 7 pm
Whitbread WCPA, Bitter,
Flowers Original Bitter Ⓖ
Well-kept village pub with
extensive menu
♪♣♨🅑🅑Ⓡ🅖➔🅟Ⓢ

Croscombe 5G

11.30–2.30; 6.30–11
Bull Terrier
(A371) ✆ Shepton Mallet 365
Butcombe Bitter
Eldridge Pope Royal Oak
Hook Norton Best Bitter
Wadworth 6X Ⓗ
Popular country free house
🅰♪♣🔲🅑🅑Ⓡ🅖➔Ⓢ🅓

East Lambrook 5F

10.30–2.30; 5.30–11
Rose & Crown
(Off A303)
✆ South Petherton 40433
Opens at 11.30 am & 7 pm
Eldridge Pope Dorchester
Bitter

Halls Harvest Bitter
and Coope Burton Ale Ⓗ
Large country pub, often
crowded ♨♣⊞⚲🏠®☾🍴🍽Ⓢ

Emborough 5G1

11–2.30; 7–11

Old Down
(A37) ℰ Stratton-on-the-Fosse
232398
Devenish Bitter, Wessex Best
Bitter
Miners Arms Own Ale Ⓗ
Pub of character built in
1640; guest beers
♨♪♣🏠®Ⓛ☾🍴🍽Ⓢ♿Å

Exford 4B2

10.30–2.30; 5.30–11

White Horse
(B3224) ℰ 229
Evening opening: 6
Courage Best Bitter
Hancock Cider Ⓖ
Rambling hotel in picturesque
village ♣⚲🏠Ⓛ☾🍴🍽Å

Faulkland 5H1

10.30–2.30; 6–11

Tuckers Grave
(A366)
Draught Bass
Whitbread WCPA
Cheddar Valley Cider Ⓖ
Old, unspoilt country pub
♨♣⚲🏠Å

Frome 5H2

10–2.30; 6–11

Angel
King Street (off A361)
ℰ 62469
Open until 4 pm Wednesday
Courage Best Bitter, Directors
Taunton Cider Ⓗ
300-year-old vine tree in
courtyard of former posting
inn ♨♪♣⚲🏠Ⓛ☾🍴🍽Ⓢ

Crown
Market Place ℰ 62156
Open until 4 pm Wednesday
Draught Bass
Welsh Fussells Best Bitter Ⓗ
Friendly market town local
♣🏠Ⓢ

Glastonbury 5F2

10.30–2.30; 5.30–11

Becketts
High Street (A39) ℰ 32928
Opens at 11 am & 6 pm
Draught Bass
Wadworth Devizes Bitter, IPA,
6X, Old Timer Ⓗ
Pleasant pub at top of high
street ♪⊞⚲®Ⓛ☾Ⓢ♿

Rifleman's Arms
Chilkwell Street (A361)
Opens at 11 am & 6 pm
Butcombe Bitter
Eldridge Pope Dorchester
Bitter, Royal Oak Ⓗ
Taunton & Wilkins Cider Ⓖ
Interesting 14th century inn
near Tor ♪♣⚲🏠☾🍴

Hardington Mandeville 5F4

10.30–2.30; 5.30–11

Mandeville Arms
High Street (off A30)
Opens at 11 am & 7 pm
Hardington Best Bitter,
Somerset Special Ⓗ
Popular home-brew pub in
pretty village ♨♪♣⚲🏠Ⓛ☾Ⓢ♿

Haselbury Plucknett 5F4

10.30–2.30; 5.30–11

Haselbury Inn
(Off A30) ℰ Crewkerne 72488
Evening opening: 6.30
Draught Bass
Welsh Hancocks Bitter Ⓗ
Modernised village local with
good food ♨♪♣⊞⚲🏠®Ⓛ☾🍴🍽Ⓢ

Henstridge 5H3

10.30–2.30; 5.30–11

Bird in Hand
(Off A30) ℰ Stalbridge 62255
Opens at 11 am & 6.30 pm
Draught Bass
Welsh Hancocks Bitter Ⓗ
Renovated village local; guest
beers ♨♪♣®Ⓛ☾🍴🍽Ⓢ

Hillfarrance 4D3

10.30–2.30; 5.30–11

Anchor Inn
(Off A361)
ℰ Bradford-on-Tone 334
Evening opening: 6 (summer),
7 (winter)
Courage Directors
Eldridge Pope Royal Oak
Golden Hill Exmoor Ale Ⓗ
Country pub specialising in
good and unusual food; jazz
Sundays ♪🍴♣⚲🏠®Ⓛ☾🍴🍽Å

Holcombe 5G1

12–2.30; 7–11

Duke of Cumberland
Edford OS 670487 ℰ Stratton-
on-the-Fosse 232412
Tisbury Local Bitter
Wadworth IPA, 6X Ⓗ
Well-kept country local
♪🏠Ⓛ☾🍴🍽Ⓢ

Keinton Mandeville 5F3

10.30–2.30; 6–11

Quarry Inn
(B3153, off A37)
Opens at 11.30 am & 7 pm
Usher Best Bitter
Founders Ale Ⓗ
Friendly welcome in popular
locals' pub ♪🍴♣⚲🏠®Ⓛ☾🍴🍽Ⓢ

Langford Budville 4D3

11–2.30; 6.30–11

Martlett Inn
(Off B3187) OS 110227

ℰ Milverton 400262
Eldridge Pope IPA, Royal Oak
Golden Hill Exmoor Ale Ⓗ
Old building sympathetically
modernised; good hot snacks
♨♣⚲Ⓛ☾ (not Sun) 🍴Ⓢ

Langley Marsh 4C3

10.30–2.30; 5.30–11

Three Horseshoes
(Off A361)
Opens at 12 noon & 6.30 pm
Cotleigh Tawny Bitter Ⓖ
Golden Hill Exmoor Ale
Hall & Woodhouse Badger
Best Bitter
Palmer IPA, Tally Ho
Perry Cider Ⓖ
Friendly, traditional local with
enthusiastic landlord, range of
beers may vary ♣⚲🏠Ⓛ☾🍴🍽Å

Litton 5G1

10.30–2.30; 5.30–11

Olde Kings Arms
(B3114)
Opens at 11.30 am & 6.30 pm
Draught Bass
Butcombe Bitter
Whitbread Flowers Original
Bitter Ⓗ
Picturesque pub on the
Mendips ♨♪⊞⚲🏠Ⓛ☾🍴🍽Ⓢ♿Å

Lovington 5G3

11–2.30; 7–11

Pilgrims Rest
(Off B3153) ℰ Wheathill 310
Wadworth Devizes Bitter, 6X,
Old Timer Ⓖ
Good local with cosy lounge
♨♪🍴♣⚲🏠Ⓛ®Ⓛ☾🍴🍽Ⓢ

Luxborough 4C2

10.30–2.30; 6–11

Royal Oak
OS 984377
ℰ Washford 40319
Morning opening: 11
Eldridge Pope IPA
Golden Hill Exmoor Ale
Whitbread Bitter, Flowers
Original Bitter Ⓖ
Old village pub, folk night
Friday ♨♪🍴♣⊞⚲🏠Ⓛ®Ⓛ☾🍴🍽

Lydford-on-Fosse 5G3

10.30–2.30; 5.30–11

Cross Keys
(A37/B3153)
Evening opening: 6
Usher Best Bitter Ⓖ
Fine renovated old pub with
restaurant 🍴♣⚲🏠®Ⓛ☾🍴🍽Ⓢ♿

Mells 5H2

11–2.30; 7–11

Talbot
(Off A362) ℰ 812254
Draught Bass
Butcombe Bitter
Eldridge Pope Royal Oak
Wadworth 6X Ⓖ
Delightful coaching inn with
guest beers ♨♪♣⚲®Ⓛ☾🍴🍽Ⓢ♿

Middlezoy 5E3

10.30–2.30; 5.30–11
George
Opens at 12 noon & 7 pm; closed Monday lunchtime in winter
Butcombe Bitter
Usher Best Bitter
Wadworth 6X [H]
Taunton Cider [G]
Busy, well-appointed village pub with stone floors
🔥♪♣🚗🛏🕐🌙 (Wed–Sun) 🍺Ⓢ⛺

Milborne Port 5G3

10.30–2.30; 5.30–11
Queens Head
(A30) ☎ 250314
Opens at 11 am & 6.30 pm
Hook Norton Mild, Best Bitter, Old Hookey
Smiles Best Bitter, Exhibition
Wadworth 6X [H]
Superb freehouse with regular guest beers 🔥♪♣✿🚗[R]🕐🌙🍺Ⓢ

Minehead 4C2

10.30–2.30; 5.30–11
Queens Head
Holloway Street ☎ 2940
Evening opening: 6
Whitbread Bitter
Bulmer Cider [H]
Well-kept, busy town pub
♪♣🚗🕐🌙🍺

Norton Fitzwarren 4D3

11–2.30; 6–11
Ring o' Bells
(A361) ☎ Taunton 75995
Whitbread Bitter, Flowers Original Bitter [H]
Pleasant roadside inn near church ♪♣✿[R]🕐🌙🍺Ⓢ

Odcombe 5F4

10.30–2.30; 5.30–11
Masons Arms
Lower Odcombe (off A3088)
Opens at 11 am & 7 pm
Draught Bass [H]
Friendly local near Brymptom House ♪♣🚗Ⓢ

Over Stratton 5F4

11–2.30; 7–11
Royal Oak
(Off A303)
Whitbread Bitter [G]
Delightful country pub in pretty village 🔥⚐♪♣✿🚗🍺Ⓢ

Pitminster 4D3

10.30–2.30; 5.30–11
Queens Arms
(Off B3170) OS 219192
☎ Blagdon Hill 529
Devenish Wessex Best Bitter [H]
Eldridge Pope Royal Oak [G]
Golden Hill Exmoor Ale
Hall & Woodhouse Badger Best Bitter [H]
Farmhouse Cider [G]
Friendly, enterprising village pub, weekly live jazz
🔥⚐♣🏠✿🚗🛏[R]🕐🌙Ⓢ⛺

Porlock 4B2

10.30–2.30; 5.30–11
Ship
High Street (A39) ☎ 862507
Evening opening: 6
Courage Best Bitter [H]
Ind Coope Burton Ale [G]
Welsh Hancocks Bitter
Perry Cider [H]
Old pub at bottom of Porlock Hill ♣🏠✿🚗🛏[R]🌙🍺Ⓢ

Priddy 5F1

10.30–2.30; 5.30–11
Hunters Lodge
OS 550502
Evening opening: 6
Draught Bass
Butcombe Bitter
Cotleigh Nutcracker
Hall & Woodhouse Badger Best Bitter [G]
Fine old pub, popular with cavers; frequent guest beers
🔥♪♣✿🚗[R]🍺♿

Queen Victoria
(Off B3135) ☎ 76385
Opens at 11 am & 6 pm (summer); 12 noon & 7 pm (winter); closed all day Monday in winter
Berrow BBBB
Butcombe Bitter
Devenish Wessex Best Bitter
Mendip Special Bitter
Nailsea Jacobs Best Bitter
Wadworth 6X
Thatcher Cider [G]
Fine old pub with church pews, folk club Thursdays
🔥⚐♪♣✿🚗🕐🌙🍺Ⓢ♿

Rimpton 5G3

11.30–2.30; 5.30–11
White Post Inn
(B3148)
☎ Marston Magna 850717
Opens at 11.30 am & 6.30 pm
Butcombe Bitter
Wadworth Devizes Bitter, 6X, Old Timer [H]
Isolated but superb free house with regular guest beers and good food 🔥✿🚗🕐🌙Ⓢ

Rode 5H1

11–2.30; 6.30–11
Red Lion
Main Street (off A361)
Usher PA, Best Bitter, Founders Ale
Bulmer Cider [H]
Cosy pub with fine collection of old enamel adverts
🔥♪♣🏠✿🍺Ⓢ

Shepton Beauchamp 5F4

10.30–2.30; 5.30–11
Duke of York
(Off A303)
Opens at 11 am & 7 pm
Courage Best Bitter [H]
Good village local 🔥♪♣🍺Ⓢ

Shepton Mallet 5G2

10–2.30; 6–11
Bell Hotel
3 High Street ☎ 2166
Courage Bitter, Best Bitter, Directors [H]
Taunton Cider [G]
Friendly atmosphere, warm welcome 🔥♪♣🏠🛏[R]🕐🌙🍺Ⓢ♿

Kings Arms
Leg Square ☎ 3781
Halls Harvest Bitter
Ind Coope Burton Ale
Wadworth 6X [H]
17th-century pub of character
🔥♪♣🛏[R]🕐🌙Ⓢ

Shepton Montague 5G3

10.30–2.30; 5.30–11
Montague Inn
(Off A359) OS 675316
Butcombe Bitter
Wadworth 6X [G]
Cosy country free house 🔥♣✿🚗🍺♿⛺

Shipham 5F1

10.30–2.30; 5.30–11
Miners Arms
The Square (off A38) OS 444576 ☎ Winscombe 2146
Opens at 11 am & 6 pm
Hall & Woodhouse Badger Best Bitter
Nailsea Jacobs Best Bitter
Thatcher Cider [H]
Pleasant village pub, recently renovated ✿🚗🕐🌙Ⓢ

Shurton 4D2

10.30–2.30; 5.30–11
Shurton Inn
OS 204444
Hall & Woodhouse Hector's Bitter, Badger Best Bitter, Tanglefoot [H]
Riches Cider [G]
Friendly rural pub, beer range may vary ♣✿🚗🕐🌙Ⓢ⛺

Staple Fitzpaine 4E3

10.30–2.30; 5.30–11
Greyhound
(Off B3170) OS 264184
☎ Hatch Beauchamp 480227
Devenish Wessex Best Bitter
Eldridge Pope Dorchester Bitter, Royal Oak
Golden Hill Exmoor Ale [H]
Taunton Cider [G]
Friendly pub, good food
🔥⚐♪♣🏠✿🚗🛏[R]🕐🌙🍺Ⓢ♿⛺

Stoford 5G4

10.30–2.30; 5.30–11
Royal Oak
The Green (off A37)
Opens at 11 am & 6 pm

raught Bass
/elsh Worthington Pale Ale [H]
nall village local opposite the
reen 🏠♪♣🚗🍷[S]🚉

togumber 4D2

30–2.30; 5.30–11
Vhite Horse Inn
)ff A358) OS 098373 ☎ 277
pens at 11 am & 6 pm
otleigh Tawny Bitter
olden Hill Exmoor Ale
eppey Cider [H]
pacious pub with restaurant
♪♣⊞🌳🚗[R]☾🍴[S]⛺

'aunton 4D3

30–2.30; 5.30–11
Harp
horeditch Road (B3170)
pens 11–2; 6–10.30
ourage Bitter, Best Bitter,
irectors [H]
easant pub on the outskirts
town ♪♣🌳🚗🍷[S]

Masons Arms
agdalene Street ☎ 88916
aturday evening opening: 6
raught Bass
olden Hill Exmoor Ale
iners Arms Own Ale
'adworth 6X [H]
nly freehouse in a town
ominated by big breweries
⊞🌳🛏☾🍴[S]🚉

Vood Street Inn
'ood Street ☎ 73011
sher Best Bitter, Founders
le [H]
usy, friendly local serving
ood food ⚑♪♣🌳🛏☾🍴[S]🚉

heale 5F2

30–2.30; 5.30–11
nooty Fox
3139) ☎ Wedmore 712220
pens at 11 am & 6 pm
raught Bass
utcombe Bitter
dridge Pope Royal Oak [H]
ush, comfortable Georgian
n, live jazz
⚑♪♣⊞🌳🚗🛏☾🍴[S]♿

Jpton Noble 5H2

30–2.30; 6.30–11
amb
)ff A359) OS 714395 ☎ 308
utcombe Bitter [H]
bbs Mew Bishops Tipple [G]
elsh Fussells Best Bitter [H]
xcellent country free house
ith restaurant
♪♣⊞🌳🚗[R]☾🍴🍷[S]♿

Vashford 4C2

30–2.30; 5.30–11
Vashford Hotel
39) ☎ 256
vening opening: 6.30
sher Best Bitter [H]
usy pub next to West
omerset railway station
♣⊞🌳🚗🛏[R]☾🍴🍷[S]⛺

Wellington 4D3

10–2.30; 5.30–11
Three Cups
Mantle Street ☎ 2066
Opens at 11 am & 6.30 pm
Usher Best Bitter
Whitbread Flowers Original Bitter [H]
Busy public bar, comfortable saloon, pool room
♪♣🚗🛏🍷[S]

Wells 5F2

11–2.30; 6.30–11
Crown Hotel
Market Place ☎ 73457
Draught Bass
Wadworth 6X [H]
Historic public house adjacent to cathedral
♪⊞🚗🛏☾🍴[S]

West Buckland 4D3

10.30–2.30; 5.30–11
Crown
(Off M5 exit 26) OS 174203
Opens at 11.30 am & 6.30 pm
Usher Best Bitter [H]
Basic two-bar local; hot snacks at all times
♪♣🌳🚗🍷[S]

West Chinnock 5F4

10.30–2.30; 5.30–11
Muddled Man
(Off A30) ☎ Chiselborough 235
Opens at 11 am & 7 pm
Usher PA [H]
Cosy local in attractive village
🏠♪♣[R]☾🍴[S]

West Coker 5F4

10.30–2.30; 5.30–11
Royal George
(A30) ☎ 2334
Opens at 11 am & 6.30 pm
Hall & Woodhouse Badger Best Bitter, Tanglefoot [H]
Attractive old pub on main road 🏠♪♣🌳🚗[R]☾🍴[S]

West Horrington 5G2

10.30–2.30; 6–11
Slabhouse Inn
(B3139) ☎ Oakhill 840310
Draught Bass
Butcombe Bitter [H]
Historic old farmhouse inn
🏠♪♣⊞🌳🚗🛏[R]☾🍴🍷[S]⛺

Winsford 4B2

10.30–2.30; 5.30–11
Royal Oak
(Off A391) OS 905347 ☎ 232
Opens at 11 am & 6 pm
Golden Hill Exmoor Ale
Whitbread Bitter, Flowers Original Bitter [H]
Comfortable thatched inn with good home-cooking; beer rather pricey
🏠♣🌳🚗🛏☾🍴🍷[S]⛺

Wiveliscombe 4D3

10.30–2.30; 6–11
Royal Oak
Church Street (A361)
☎ 23578
Usher Best Bitter, Founders Ale
Taunton Cider [H]
Excellent town local
♪♣🛏[R]☾🍴⛺

Wookey 5F2

10.30–2.30; 5.30–11
Burcott Inn
(B3139) ☎ Wells 73874
Opens at 11 am & 6 pm
Butcombe Bitter [H]
Superbly converted old farmhouse with cider press; guest beers
🏠♪⊞🌳🚗[R]☾🍴[S]⛺

Wrantage 4E3

10.30–2.30; 5.30–11
Wheelwrights Arms
(A378)
Opens at 11 am & 6 pm
Eldridge Pope IPA [H]
Golden Hill Exmoor Ale [G]
Whitbread Bitter [H]
Vickery Cider [G]
Congenial pub on Taunton side of village 🏠♪♣⊞🌳🚗[S]⛺

Yarlington 5G3

10.30–2.30; 5.30–11
Stags Head
(Off A359)
Opens at 11 am & 7 pm
Usher Best Bitter [G]
Traditional pub, remote but well worth finding 🏠♣🚗🍷[S]

Yeovil 5G4

10.30–2.30; 5.30–11
Bell Inn
Preston Road (A3088)
Evening opening: 6.30
Draught Bass
Welsh Hancocks Bitter [H]
Busy pub on western outskirts of town ♪♣🌳🚗[R]☾🍴🍷[S]

Black Horse
Reckleford (A30) ☎ 23878
Evening opening: 6
Draught Bass [H]
Good local near hospital, enthusiastic landlord
♪♣☾🍷[S]

Great Western
Cambourne Grove (off A30)
Evening opening: 6
Courage Bitter, Best Bitter [G]
Good local next to Penmill railway station
♪♣🚗[R]🍷[S]🚉

Hole in the Wall
Wine Street ☎ 75560
Courage Bitter, Best Bitter, Directors [H]
Small locals' pub in town centre ♪♣☾🍴🍷[S]

Abbots Bromley

23G7

11.30–2.30; 6–10.30 (11 F, S)
Coach & Horses
High Street (B5014) ☎ Burton 840256
Ind Coope Burton Ale Ⓗ
Lively 16th-century village pub ▲♩♣🌿🚅Ⓡ🕒🅘Ⓢ

Alrewas

23G8

11–2.30; 6.30–10.30 (11 F, S)
George & Dragon
High Street (off A38) ☎ Burton 790202
Marston Pedigree Ⓗ
Pleasing village pub with superb restaurant
♣🌿Ⓖ🕒🅘Ⓢ

Alstonfield

23G5

10.30–2.30; 6–10.30 (11 F, S)
George
(Off A515) OS 132556 ☎ 205
Ind Coope Burton Ale Ⓗ
17th-century inn facing the green ▲♣🌿🅰Ⓖ🕒🅘Ⓢ👗

Alton

23G6

11–3; 5.30–10.30 (11 F, S)
Talbot
☎ Oakamoor 702767
Opens at 11.30 am & 6 pm
Ind Coope Bitter, Burton Ale Ⓖ
Grade II listed building in Churnet Valley, near Alton Towers ▲♩♣🆔🌿🅰Ⓖ🕒🅘Ⓢ👗

Anslow

23G7

10.30–2.30; 5.30–10.30 (11 F, S)
Bell
Main Street (off B5017)
Marston Pedigree, Merrie Monk, Owd Rodger Ⓗ
Friendly village pub with gardens ▲♣🌿🅰🅘

Ashley

22E6

11–3; 6–10.30 (11 F, S)
Robin Hood
Lower Road (off A53) ☎ 2237
Closed weekday lunchtimes
Five Towns Bursley Bitter
Ind Coope Burton Ale
Winkle Saxon Cross Bitter Ⓗ
Comfortable free house with home-cooked food
♩♣🅰Ⓖ🕒Ⓢ

Barton-under-Needwood

23G7

10.30–2.30; 5.30–10.30 (11 F, S)
Royal Oak
74 The Green (off A38)
Marston Pedigree Ⓗ **Owd Rodger** Ⓖ
Unspoilt village local with unusual sunken bar
▲♩♣🌿🅰ⒾⓈ👗

Bishops Offley

22E7

11–3; 6–11

Brown Jug
(Off B5026)
Draught Bass
Mitchells & Butlers
Springfield Bitter Ⓗ
Ask about pub sign
▲♩♣🌿🅘Ⓢ

Brewood

23F8

11–2.30; 6–10.30 (11 F, S)
Admiral Rodney
Dean Street
Ansells Mild, Bitter Ⓗ
Cosy local with friendly welcome ▲♩♣🌿🅰Ⓢ

Bridge
High Green
Ansells Mild, Bitter Ⓗ
Village local next to Shropshire Union canal
▲♣🌿🅰Ⓢ

Brocton

23F7

11–3; 6–11
Seven Stars
Cannock Road (A34)
Ansells Mild, Bitter
Tetley Walker Bitter Ⓗ
Popular pub on edge of Cannock Chase ♩♣🅰🅘Ⓢ

Brownhills

23F8

10.30–2.30; 6.30–10.30 (11 F, S)
Anchor
Chester Road (A452)
Banks Mild, Bitter Ⓔ
Old local canalside pub
▲♣🅰Ⓢ

Chase
Watling Street (A5)
Banks Mild, Bitter Ⓔ
Lively one-room pub ♩♣🅰🅘Ⓢ

White Horse
White Horse Road (off A5)
Banks Mild, Bitter Ⓔ
Comfortable, friendly pub near Chasewater pleasure park ♩♣🅰🅘Ⓢ

Burton upon Trent

23H7

10.30–2.30; 5.30–10.30 (11 F, S)
Bridge Brewery
Bridge Street
Morning opening: 11
Burton Bridge IPA, Bitter, Porter, Festival Ale Ⓗ
Sampling room for brewery
🌿Ⓢ

Red Lion
Horninglow Road North
Marston Pedigree Ⓗ **Owd Rodger** Ⓖ
Lively suburban local
♩♩♣🅰🌿Ⓡ🅘Ⓢ👗

Royal Oak
Market Place ☎ 66932
Ind Coope Bitter, Burton Ale Ⓗ
Historic refurbished market pub ♩♣Ⓡ🕒🅘Ⓢ👗

Royal Oak
Newton Road (B5008)
Marston Pedigree Ⓗ **Owd Rodger** Ⓖ
Pleasant riverside pub with gardens ▲♩♣🆔🌿🅰Ⓖ🅘Ⓢ👗

Calf Heath

23F

11–2.30; 6–10.30 (11 F, S)
Dog & Partridge
(Off M6 exit 12) OS 942088
Mitchells & Butlers Highgate Mild, Springfield Bitter Ⓗ
Village pub with two bars and two snugs ▲♣🌿🅰🅘Ⓢ

Cannock

23F

11.30–2.30; 5.30–10.30 (11 F, S)
Royal Oak Hotel
Stafford Road (A34)
Mitchells & Butlers Highgate Mild, Springfield Bitter Ⓔ
No-nonsense pub
♩♩♣🅰Ⓡ🕒🅘Ⓢ

Unicorn
Church Street (A462)
Ansells Mild, Bitter Ⓗ
Friendly town bar with sporting theme ♩♩♣🅰Ⓖ🕒🅘

White Hart
Wolverhampton Road (off A34)
Banks Mild, Bitter Ⓔ
Popular side-street local
♩♣🌿🅰Ⓖ🕒🅘Ⓢ

Cauldon

23G

10.30–2.30; 6–10.30 (11 F, S)
Yew Tree
(Off A524/A523)
Draught Bass Ⓖ
Ind Coope Bitter
Mitchells & Butlers Mild
Winkle Saxon Cross Bitter Ⓗ
Country pub, full of working antiques including pianolas and polyphons ♩♣🌿🅰Ⓢ👗

Chase Terrace

23F

10.30–2.30; 6–10.30 (11 F, S)
Wych Elm
Cannock Road
Banks Mild, Bitter Ⓔ
Friendly modern pub
♩♣🌿🅰Ⓢ

Chasetown

23F

10.30–2.30; 6–10.30 (11 F, S)
Crown
High Street
Banks Mild, Bitter Ⓔ
Friendly town local ♩♣🅘

Cheadle

23F

11–3; 6–11
Miners Rest
Froghall Road (A521)
Lunchtime opening: 12 noon
Burtonwood Bitter Ⓗ
Small, friendly local on edge of town ▲♣🌿🅰🅘Ⓢ

heslyn Hay 23F8

.30–2.30; 5.30–10.30 (11 F, S)

Iary Rose
Ioon Lane
nsells Mild, Bitter
nd Coope Burton Ale
etley Bitter [H]
onverted old farmhouse with Iary Rose paraphernalia
🌳🚗🍷Ⓢ♿

Draycott-in-the-Clay 23G7

.30–2.30; 6.30–10.30 (11 F, S)

White Swan
A515)
nsells Mild
nd Coope Bitter [G]
nspoilt main road local
🌳🚗[R]🍷♿⛺

ccleshall 22E7

–3; 6–11

Bell
igh Street (B5026)
raught Bass
itchells & Butlers
pringfield Bitter [H]
usy pub with splendid ounge fireplace 🔥♣🌳🚗🍷Ⓢ

Railway Inn
reen Lane (off A519)
vening opening: 6.30
Vem Mild, Best Bitter [H]
Velcoming local; the railway was never built 🔥♣🌳🚗🍷

Four Ashes 23F8

.30–2.30; 6–10.30 (11 F, S)

Four Ashes
A449)
anks Mild, Bitter [E]
usy roadside pub
🌳🚗◔🍷Ⓢ

Gnosall 22E7

1–3; 6–11

Boat Inn
Wharf Road (off A518)
Marston Mercian Mild, Burton Bitter, Pedigree [H]
Comfortable canalside pub with bar billiards
🔥♪♣🌳🚗◔❥Ⓢ♿

Great Chatwell 22E8

1–3; 6–11

Red Lion
Off A41) ☎ 366
vening opening: 7
Vem Mild, Best Bitter [H]
plendid village local
🔥♪♣⊞🌳🚗[R]◔❥🍷Ⓢ⛺

Great Wyrley 23F8

0.30–2.30; 6–10.30 (11 F, S)

Royal Oak
Norton Lane (off A34)
Banks Mild, Bitter [E]
Pleasant, friendly local
♪♣🚗🍷Ⓢ

Halfpenny Green 22E9

11–2.30; 6–10.30 (11 F, S)

Royal Oak
Six Ashes Road ☎ Bobbington 318
Banks Mild, Bitter [E]
Popular old country local on crossroads, near Bobbington airport 🔥♪♣⊞🌳🚗◔❥🍷Ⓢ♿⛺

Handsacre 23G8

11–3; 6.30–10.30 (11 F, S)

Crown
24 The Green (off A513)
Draught Bass
Mitchells & Butlers
Mild [H]
Canalside pub with comfortable lounge and award-winning cellar
ſ♪♣⊞🚗[R]🍷Ⓢ

Hatherton 23F8

10.30–2.30; 6–10.30 (11 F, S)

Four Crosses
Watling Street (A5)
Banks Mild, Bitter [E]
Comfortable 17th-century coaching inn ♪♣🌳🚗◔🍷Ⓢ

High Offley 22E7

11–3; 6–11

Anchor
Old Lea OS 774256
Closed Sun Eve–Wed Eve, Nov–Mar
Ansells Bitter [G]
Marston Pedigree [H]
Owd Rodger
Wadworth 6X
Weston Cider [G]
Famous, unspoilt canalside pub with impromptu folk singing 🔥ſ♣🌳🚗🍷Ⓢ⛺

Hyde Lea 23E7

11–3; 6–11

Crown
Draught Bass
Mitchells & Butlers Highgate Mild, Springfield Bitter [H]
Popular village pub ♪♣🌳🚗◔🍷Ⓢ

Kidsgrove 23E5

11–3; 5.30–10.30 (11 F, S)

Blue Bell
Hardingswood (off A50)
Opens at 11.30 am & 7 pm
Boddingtons Bitter
McEwan 70/-
Younger No. 3 [H]
Friendly canalside pub on edge of town ſ♪♣⊞🌳🚗◔Ⓢ🚂

Kingsley 23F6

11–3; 6–11

Bulls Head
High Street (A52)
Closed weekday lunchtimes
Burton Bridge Bitter
Ind Coope Bitter [H]
Friendly village local, rare brew for the area ♪♣🚗

Kinver 15F2

11–2.30; 6–10.30 (11 F, S)

Cross
Dark Lane, off High Street
Hansons Mild, Bitter [E]
Weston Cider [G]
A real local, next to restored Tudor house 🔥♪♣🌳🚗🍷Ⓢ⛺

Elm Tree
Enville Road (off A458)
☎ 872480
Davenports Mild, Bitter [E]
Village pub with ex-bowling green garden 🔥♪🌳🚗❥Ⓢ⛺

Plough & Harrow
High Street ☎ 872659
Batham Bitter, Delph Strong Ale [H]
Weston Cider [G]
Split-level local, known locally as 'the Steps' ♪♣🚗◔❥🍷Ⓢ⛺

Vine
Dunsley Road (off A449)
Draught Bass
Mitchells & Butlers
Highgate Mild, Springfield Bitter [E]
Pleasantly decorated canalside pub ♪♣🌳🚗◔❥Ⓢ⛺

Knighton 22D7

11–3; 6–11

Haberdashers Arms
(Off A529/B5026)
5 miles west of Eccleshall
Banks Mild, Bitter
Five Towns Bursley Bitter [H]
Weston Cider [G]
Unspoilt country local selling home-grown produce
🔥♣🌳🚗🍷Ⓢ⛺

Knighton 22D6

11–3; 5.30–10.30 (11 F, S)

White Lion
(B4026) near Woore
Marston Burton Bitter, Pedigree [H] **Owd Rodger** [G]
Popular village pub in remote setting 🔥ſ♪♣🌳🚗[R]🍷Ⓢ⛺

Leek 23F5

10.30–2.30; 6–10.30 (11 F, S)

Angel (Yates)
Market Place
Open until 4 pm Wednesdays
Burtonwood Dark Mild, Bitter
Marston Pedigree, Owd Rodger [H]
Popular market pub with wine bar at rear ♪♣Ⓢ

Flying Horse
Ashbourne Road (A523)
Evening opening: 7
Marston Mercian Mild, Burton Bitter, Pedigree [H]
Smart pub with friendly local atmosphere ♪♣🌳🚗🍷Ⓢ

Park
Ball Haye Road
Open until 4 pm Wednesdays

Draught Bass
**Mitchells & Butlers Mild,
Springfield Bitter** Ⓗ
Cosy, traditional market town
pub ♪♠Ⓡ🅘Ⓢ

Wilkes Head

16 St Edward Street ☎ 383616
Opens at 12 noon & 7 pm;
open until 4 pm Wednesdays
**Ansells Mild, Bitter
Ind Coope Burton Ale
Tetley Walker Bitter
Coates Cider** Ⓗ
Thriving traditional inn with
shire horse bus service
🅰♪♠🅿🚲🅰Ⓡ🄶Ⓢ

Lichfield 23G8

11.30–3; 5.30–10.30 (11 F, S)

Carpenters Arms

Christchurch Lane (off A641)
Banks Mild, Bitter Ⓔ
Friendly, out-of-the-way
one-room local ♠🅰Ⓡ🅘

Duke of York

Church Street
Davenports Mild, Bitter Ⓗ
Weston Cider Ⓖ & Ⓗ
Friendly 16th-century beamed
pub with plenty of character
🅰♪♠🅿🅰🄶🅘Ⓢ≷

Earl of Lichfield

Conduit Street
Evening opening: 6.30
Marston Pedigree Ⓗ
Excellent arched frontage;
small, friendly pub ♪♠🅘Ⓢ

Kings Head

Bird Street ☎ 22314
**Marston Pedigree, Merrie
Monk, Owd Rodger** Ⓗ
Lively local, birthplace of
South Staffs regiment;
military paraphernalia
♪♠🅿Ⓡ🅘Ⓢ

Queens Head

Sanford Street
**Marston Pedigree, Merrie
Monk** Ⓗ
Large bar, comfortable
lounge, lively atmosphere
♪♠🅰🅘

Little Haywood 23F7

10.30–3; 6–11

Red Lion

(Off A51)
Ansells Bitter Ⓗ
Village local with lively public
bar ♪♠🅰🅘Ⓢ

Longdon 23G8

12–2.30; 7–11

Swan with Two Necks

Main Road (off A51)
**Ansells Mild, Bitter
Ind Coope Burton Ale** Ⓗ
Friendly village local just off
main road
🅰♪♠🅿🅰🅘Ⓢ

Longsdon 23F5

10–2.30; 6–10.30 (11 F, S)

Holly Bush

Denford (off A53) ☎ Leek
Ind Coope Burton Ale Ⓗ
Popular canalside pub in
pleasant valley 🅰♠🏕🅿🅰🅘Ⓢ🅰

Marston 23E8

11–3; 6–11

Fox

(Off A5) ☎ Wheaton Aston
840729
Opens at 12 noon & 7 pm
**Banks Mild, Bitter
Lloyds Derby Bitter, Country
Bitter
Marston Pedigree, Owd
Rodger
Wadworth 6X
Woods Special Bitter** Ⓗ
Weston Cider Ⓗ & Ⓖ
Excellent find; adjacent cider
barn has 11 ciders
🅰♠🅿🅰🄶🅘Ⓢ🅰

Milwich 23F7

10.30–3; 6–11

Green Man

(B5027)
Closes 10.30 pm Mon, Tues
**Draught Bass
Mitchells & Butlers Springfield
Bitter** Ⓗ
Small, friendly village pub
🅰♠🅿🅰🅘

Moreton 22E8

11–3; 6–11

Rising Sun

(Off A518)
Marston Burton Bitter Ⓔ
Pedigree, Merrie Monk Ⓗ
Well worth finding 🅰♪♠🅰🅘

Newcastle-under-Lyme 23E6

11–3; 5.30–10.30 (11 F, S)

Bear Hotel

West Brampton (off A34)
☎ 616334
Opens at 12 noon & 6.30 pm
**Ansells Bitter
Ind Coope Burton Ale** Ⓗ
Imposing multi-roomed pub
on outskirts of town
🅰♪♠🏕🅰Ⓡ🄶🅘Ⓢ

Boat & Horses

2 Stubbs Gate ☎ 610650
Lunchtime opening: 12 noon
**Ansells Bitter
Ind Coope Burton Ale** Ⓗ
Bulmer Cider Ⓖ
Popular pub with good choice
of rooms; folk music
Saturdays ♪♠🅿Ⓡ🄶🅘Ⓢ

Castle Mona

Victoria Street (off A34)
Opens at 12 noon & 7 pm
Wem Mild, Best Bitter Ⓔ
Cosy, quiet pub near town
centre ♪♠🅘

Jolly Potters

9 Barracks Road ☎ 631736
Evening opening: 6.30
(Mon–Fri)
Wem Mild, Best Bitter Ⓔ
Modern town pub opposite bus
station ♪♠Ⓡ🅘Ⓢ♿

Onecote 23F?

10.30–2.30; 6–10.30 (11 F, S)

Jervis Arms

(B5053, off A523) ☎ 206
Opens 12–2 (Thu–Sat);
evening opening: 7
**McEwan 70/-
Marston Pedigree
Ruddle County
Winkle Saxon Cross Bitter
Younger No 3** Ⓗ
Excellent home-made food
and riverside beer garden
🅰🏕🅿🅰Ⓡ🄶🅘Ⓢ

Oulton 23F?

11–3; 6–11

Brushmakers Arms

(Off A520)
**Draught Bass
Mitchells & Butlers
Springfield Bitter** Ⓗ
Village pub with Toby jugs
♠🅿🅰🅘Ⓢ

Penkridge 23F?

11–3; 6–10.30 (11 F, S)

Railway Inn

Clay Street (A449)
Ansells Mild, Bitter Ⓗ
Small, ambitious main-road
pub 🅰♪♠🅿🅰🅘Ⓢ≷

Star

Market Place (off A449)
☎ 2513
Banks Mild, Bitter Ⓔ
Old pub, modernised in
traditional style ♪🅿🅰🄶🅘Ⓢ≷

White Hart

Stone Cross (A449)
**Mitchells & Butlers
Highgate Mild, Brew XI,
Highgate Old Ale** Ⓔ
Popular, friendly pub in large
village 🅰♪♠🅿🅰🄶🅘Ⓢ≷

Rawnsley 23F?

10.30–2.30; 6–10.30 (11 F, S)

New Inn (The Rag)

Ironstone Road (off B5012)
Ansells Bitter Ⓗ
Small, popular country local
near Castle Ring iron-age fort
♪♠🅿🅘

Rough Hay 23G?

10.30–2.30; 5.30–10.30 (11 F, S)

Acorn

Henhurst Hill (B5017)
Draught Bass Ⓗ
Friendly pub on outskirts of
town ♪♠🅿🅰🅘

Rugeley 23F?

10.30–3; 6–10.30 (11 F, S)

lbion
bion Street
nks Mild, Bitter [E]
isy town pub ♪♣🍺

ed Lion
arket Street
nks Mild, Bitter [E]
0-year-old town pub of
eat character ♣🚗🍺

averley Green 23F6

3; 6–11

reyhound
ff A50)
aught Bass [H]
raightforward country pub
⌐♣🚗🍺Ⓢ

unter
ff A50) ☎ Blythe Bridge 2067
d Coope Bitter, Burton Ale
tley Walker Bitter [H]
terprising village pub which
kes care of its customers
♪♣⊞✿🚗[R]◔☛Ⓢ⛺

hebdon 22E7

3; 6–11

'harf
ff A519)
rtonwood Dark Mild,
ter [H]
aditional canal pub next to
ueduct ♪♣✿🚗🍺Ⓢ

afford 23F7

3; 6–11

oach & Horses
ll Bank (off A34)
aught Bass
tchells & Butlers
ringfield Bitter [H]
raightforward town-centre
b ♪♣🍺Ⓢ

arth Hotel
olverhampton Road (A449,
M6 exit 13) ☎ 56124
nks Mild, Bitter [E]
rge hotel with good food
✿🚗▣[R]◔☛🍺Ⓢ♿

olmcroft
olmcroft Road (off B5013)
nks Mild, Bitter [E]
easant estate pub
♣⊞✿🚗◔🍺

ings Arms
el Terrace (off B5066)
nsells Bitter [H]
nall backstreet pub north of
wn centre ♣✿[R]🍺

heasant Inn
iars Terrace (off A449)
ens at 12 noon & 7 pm
nsells Mild, Bitter
d Coope Burton Ale [H]
vely, progressive local
♣✿◔🍺Ⓢ⇌

un Inn
ichfield Road (A34)
aught Bass
tchells & Butlers
ringfield Bitter [E]

Cosmopolitan local
⌐♪♣⊞✿🚗[R]◔

Standeford 23E8

11–3; 6–10.30 (11 F, S)

Harrows
(A449) ☎ 790216
Ansells Mild, Bitter
Tetley Bitter [H]
Comfortable, friendly roadside
pub 🏛♪♣✿🚗◔🍺

Stoke-on-Trent 23E6

11–3; 5.30–10.30 (11 F, S)

Burslem:

Huntsman
13 Westport Road ☎ 84657
Banks Mild, Bitter
Five Towns Bursley Bitter
Marston Pedigree
Winkle Saxon Cross Bitter [H]
Drinkers' paradise; widest
choice in Burslem, including
two small breweries ♪♣[R]◔🍺Ⓢ

Travellers Rest
239 Newcastle Street
☎ 810418
Lunchtime opening: 12 noon
Ansells Mild
Ind Coope Bitter, Burton Ale
Gaymer Cider [H]
Popular local noted for
excellent beer and superb food
⌐♪♣⊞[R]◔☛🍺Ⓢ⇌

Fenton:

Terrace
192 City Road (A5007)
Draught Bass
Mitchells & Butlers Mild,
Springfield Bitter [H]
Deservedly popular local with
keen landlord ⌐♪♣🍺

Hanley:

Albion Hotel
2 Old Hall Street (A50)
☎ 24301
Banks Mild, Bitter [E]
Busy city-centre pub with
revolving doors ♪♣🚗◔🍺Ⓢ

Coachmakers Arms
64 Lichfield Street (A50)
Evening opening: 7
Draught Bass
Mitchells & Butlers Mild [H]
Good, old-fashioned, basic pub
🏛♣[R]🍺Ⓢ♿

Golden Cup
Town Road
Evening opening: 7
Draught Bass
Mitchells & Butlers Mild [H]
Fine building, fine atmosphere
♪✿🚗

Rose & Crown
Etruria Road (A53) ☎ 20503
Evening opening: 7

Ansells Mild, Bitter
Ind Coope Burton Ale
Tetley Walker Bitter [H]
Showpiece pub with
occasional guest beers
🏛⌐♪♣⊞✿🚗[R]◔☛🍺Ⓢ⇌

Longton:

Halfway House
132 Anchor Road ☎ 319576
Opens at 12 noon & 7 pm
Marston Burton Bitter,
Pedigree [H]
Large, popular pub with
comfortable lounge
⌐♪♣[R]🍺Ⓢ⇌

Stoke:

Glebe
Glebe Street
Banks Mild, Bitter [E]
Friendly, comfortable pub
next to Stoke Town Hall
♪♣🍺Ⓢ⇌

Greyhound
Manor Court Street, Penkhull
☎ 48978
Evening opening: 6.30
Ansells Mild, Bitter
Ind Coope Burton Ale [H]
Historic pub of character,
opposite church 🏛♪♣✿🚗☛🍺Ⓢ

Jolly Potters
296 Hartshill Road, Hartshill
Evening opening: 6 (7 Sat)
Draught Bass
Mitchells & Butlers Mild [H]
Multi-roomed pub of
character in conservation area
♣🍺Ⓢ

Uncle Tom's Cabin
91 Corporation Street
Evening opening: 6.30
Marston Mercian Mild,
Pedigree [H] **Owd Rodger** [G]
Popular multi-roomed local
outside town centre
🏛⌐♪♣🚗[R]🍺Ⓢ

Wellington
369 London Road
Morning opening: 11.30
Marston Mercian Mild,
Burton Bitter, Pedigree,
Merrie Monk, Owd Rodger [H]
Busy street-corner local ♪♣🍺

Tunstall:

Albion
77 High Street ☎ 85116
Evening opening: 7
Ind Coope Burton Ale
Tetley Walker Bitter [H]
Excellent local with keen
landlord ⌐♪♣⊞✿🚗[R]◔☛Ⓢ♿

White Horse
141 Brownhills Road (A527)
Opens at 12 noon & 7 pm
Mitchells & Butlers Mild
Springfield Bitter [H]
Spartan friendly alehouse ♣🍺

Stone 23E6

11–3; 6–11
George & Dragon
Meaford (A34)
Closes at 10.30 pm
Draught Bass
Burtonwood Dark Mild,
Bitter Ⓗ
Large roadside pub ♠🏠👤

Red Lion
23 High Street (A520 south)
Draught Bass
Mitchells & Butlers Mild,
Springfield Bitter Ⓗ
Basic town-centre pub ♪♠👤Ⓢ

Star
Stafford Street (off A34)
Draught Bass
Mitchells & Butlers
Springfield Bitter Ⓗ
Splendid small, two-roomed
canalside pub ♠🅿🏠Ⓢ

Stowe by Chartley
23F7

10.30–3; 6–11
Cock
(Off A518)
☎ Weston-on-Trent 270237
Ansells Bitter Ⓗ
Unspoilt country pub of
character ♠♣🅿🏠Ⓡ⑧

Stretton 23H7

10.30–2.30; 5.30–10.30 (11 F, S)
Beech
Derby Road ☎ Burton 61811
Marston Pedigree Ⓗ
Owd Rodger Ⓖ
Large, busy main-road pub
with beer garden
👤♪♠🅱🅿🏠Ⓡ👤⑧ Å

Sutton 22E7

11–3; 6–11
Red Lion
(A518) ☎ Newport 811048
Opens at 12 noon & 7 pm
Banks Mild, Bitter Ⓔ
Lively country pub
♠♪♣🅿🏠Ⓡ👤♿ Å

Swindon 15F1

11–2.30; 6–10.30 (11 F, S)
Greyhound
Wombourne Road (off
B4176) OS 863907
☎ Kingswinford 287243
Banks Mild, Bitter Ⓔ
Popular historic village local
♠♪♣🅿🏠Ⓖ⑧

Talke 22E5

11–3; 5.30–10.30 (11 F, S)
Swan
Swan Bank (off A34)
☎ Kidsgrove 2722
Burtonwood Dark Mild,
Bitter Ⓗ
Traditional village inn with
plush lounge and large public
bar ♪♠🏠Ⓖ👤⑧

Tamworth 23G8

10.30–2.30; 6.30–10.30 (11 F, S)
Bulls Head
Watling Street, Two Gates
(A5/A51) ☎ 287820
Marston Mercian Mild,
Pedigree Ⓗ
Exceptionally friendly local
♪👤🅿🏠Ⓖ👤⑧♿

Gate
Tamworth Road, Amington
Marston Pedigree, Merrie
Monk Ⓗ
Popular local with canalside
garden ♠♪♣🅿🏠Ⓖ👤

Globe
Watling Street (A5)
Opens at 11 am & 7 pm
Marston Mercian Mild,
Pedigree Ⓗ
Friendly local of character
♪♠👤⑧♿

Hamlets Wine Bar
Lower Gungate ☎ 52277
Burton Bridge Bitter
Samuel Smith Old
Brewery Bitter Ⓗ
Popular wine bar for the
young ♪♠Ⓖ👤⑧

Lamb
Kettlebrook Road (A51)
Draught Bass
Mitchells & Butlers Mild Ⓗ
Basic, friendly local
♪👤🅿🏠Ⓡ👤⑧

Tam O'Shanter
Cedar Drive, Gillway (off
A513)
Home Mild, Bitter Ⓔ
Friendly post-war pub; only
Home ales in the area
♪♠🅿🏠⑧

Tweedale Arms
Victoria Road ☎ 62748
Draught Bass
Mitchells & Butlers Mild Ⓗ
Popular local, basic but
friendly ♪♠⑧♿

Wiggington
Wiggington Road ☎ 62756
Banks Mild, Bitter Ⓔ
Large, modern friendly
suburban pub 👤♪♠🅿🏠Ⓖ👤⑧

Trysull 22E9

11–2.30; 6–10.30 (11 F, S)
Plough
School Road ☎ Wombourne
892254
Banks Mild, Bitter Ⓔ
Rambling country pub with
large garden ♠♣🅿🏠Ⓖ👤⑧

Tutbury 23G7

10.30–2.30; 6.30–10.30 (11 F, S)
Leopard
1 Monk Street (of A50)
Ind Coope Bitter, Burton Ale Ⓗ
Spacious village local near
Tutbury Castle ♪🅿Ⓡ

Uttoxeter 23⑥

10.30–2.30; 6–10.30 (11 F, S)
Plough
Stafford Road (A518) ☎ 238
Ind Coope Bitter, Burton Ale
Comfortable roadside inn
♠♪♣🅱🅿🏠Ⓖ👤👤⑧♣ Å

Roebuck
37 Dove Bank (A518) ☎ 556
Evening opening: 7
Burton Bridge IPA, Bitter,
Porter Ⓗ **Festival Ale**
Weston Cider Ⓖ
Free house of character
♠👤♪♣🅱🅿🏠🅳🏠Ⓡ👤⑧♣

Vaults
Market Square (A518) ☎ 29⑨
Draught Bass Ⓗ
Unspoilt town-centre pub wi
bottle collection ♠♪👤Ⓡ👤⑧♿

Waterfall 23⑥

10.30–2.30; 5.30–10.30 (11 F, S)
Red Lion
(A523) ☎ Waterhouses 279
Closed Mon–Fri lunchtimes
Draught Bass
Mitchells & Butlers Mild Ⓗ
Popular country pub in
attractive surroundings ♠♪♣
🅿🏠Ⓖ (weekends) 👤⑧ Å

Weston 23⑥

11–3; 6–11
Saracens Head
Stafford Road (A518)
Closes 10.45 pm Mon–Thu
Draught Bass Ⓗ
Multi-roomed country pub
near canal ♠♣🅿🏠Ⓡ👤⑧ Å

Wombourne 23⑥

11–2.30; 6–10.30 (11 F, S)
Vine
High Street (off A449)
☎ 892405 OS 878933
Draught Bass
Mitchells & Butlers Highgate
Mild, Springfield Bitter Ⓔ
Weston Cider Ⓖ
Smart, busy village local
♪♠🏠Ⓖ👤⑧

Woodseaves 22⑥

11–3; 6–11
Cock
(A519) ☎ 270
Banks Mild, Bitter Ⓔ
Bulmer Cider Ⓖ
Friendly village local
♠♪♣🅿🏠Ⓡ👤⑧

Wrinehill 22⑥

11–3; 5.30–10.30 (11 F, S)
Blue Bell
(A531) ☎ Crewe 820425
Greenall Whitley Dark Mild
Bitter Ⓔ
Roadside pub with interestir
collection of local photos
♠♣🅿🏠👤⑧ Å

Aldeburgh 19H6

30–2.30; 6–11
Mill
Market Cross Place
(off A1049) ✆ 2563
Adnams Mild, Bitter Ⓗ
d Ⓖ
As old as the Moot Hall
opposite ♪♣🅗Ⓖ➊①Ⓢ🅰

Sadingham 19G6

30–2 (2.30 summer); 6–11
White Horse
(1120) ✆ 280
Adnams Bitter, Old Ⓗ
Excellent country pub catering
for all tastes
♪♣🅿🅐Ⓖ➊①Ⓢ

Bardwell 19E5

30–2; 5–11
Dun Cow
Saturday evening opening: 7
Greene King XX, IPA, Abbot Ⓗ
All-purpose country inn
♣🅿🅐①Ⓢ🅰

Beccles 19H4

30–2.30; 6–11
Waveney Hotel
Pudding Moor
Adnams Bitter Ⓗ
Two-star riverside hotel,
excellent food 🅱🅿🅐🅗Ⓡ Ⓖ➊①Ⓢ

Blyford 19H5

–2.30; 6–11
Queens Head
(1123) ✆ Blythburgh 404
Winter evening opening: 7
Adnams Mild, Bitter, Old Ⓗ
Picturesque 15th-century
one-bar thatched smugglers
inn 🅰♪♣🅗🅿🅐Ⓖ➊①Ⓢ🅰

Blythburgh 19H5

30–2.30; 6–11
White Hart
(A12) ✆ 217
Adnams Mild, Bitter Ⓗ **Old** Ⓖ
Bulmer Cider Ⓗ
Lovely roadside pub, once the
village courthouse
♪🅿🅐Ⓖ➊①Ⓢ &

Boxford 19E7

30–2; 5–11
Compasses
Stone Street (off A1071)
210468
Morning opening: 11
Greene King IPA, Abbot Ⓖ
Old country village pub
♪♣🅿🅐🅗①Ⓢ

Bradfield Combust 18E6

–2; 5.30–11
Manger
Sudbury Road (A134)
✆ Sicklesmere 516
Morning opening: 11
Greene King XX, IPA, Abbot Ⓖ

14th-century timber-framed
building with inglenook
fireplace 🅰♪♣🅗🅿🅐Ⓡ Ⓖ➊①Ⓢ🅰

Bramfield 19H5

10.30–2.30; 6–11
Bell
The Street (A144)
Adnams Mild, Bitter, Old Ⓖ
Landlord knows what a good
pub is; 'ringing the bull'
played 🅰♣🅿🅐①Ⓢ🅰

Brandeston 19G6

10.30–2.30; 5.30–11
Queens Head
✆ Earl Soham 307
Opens 11–2 Mon–Fri;
Saturday evening opening: 6
Adnams Mild, Bitter, Old Ⓖ
Thoroughly deserving its
popularity
🅰♪♣🅱🅿🅐🅗Ⓡ Ⓖ➊①Ⓢ🅰

Brent Eleigh 19E7

10.30–2; 6–11
Cock
Lavenham Road (A1141)
Greene King XX, IPA, Abbot Ⓖ
Excellent unspoilt country pub
🅰♣🅿🅐🅰

Bungay 19H4

10.30–2.30; 6–11
Fleece
St Mary Street ✆ 2192
Adnams Bitter, Old Ⓗ
Old coaching inn ♪♣🅱🅿🅐Ⓡ Ⓢ

Bury St Edmunds 18E6

10.30–2; 5–11
Elephant & Castle
Hospital Road (off
A143/A134) ✆ 5570
Opens at 11 am & 7 pm
Greene King XX, IPA, Abbot Ⓗ
Cosy, popular pub – mild in
lounge only ♪♣🅿🅐Ⓖ➊①Ⓢ &

Glad Abbot
Glastonbury Road, Horringer
Court (off A143) ✆ 63377
Opens at 10 am & 6 pm
Adnams Bitter Ⓗ **Old** Ⓖ
Greene King IPA, Abbot Ⓗ
Modern free house
♪♣🅿🅐Ⓖ①Ⓢ

Butley 19H7

10.30–2.30; 6–11
Oyster
(B1084)
Morning opening: 11
Adnams Mild Ⓗ **Bitter, Old** Ⓖ
Quaint old inn with folk
singing Sundays ♪♣🅿🅐♥

Cavendish 18D7

10.30–2; 5.30–11
George
The Green (A1092)
✆ Glemsford 280248
Truman Bitter, Best Bitter Ⓗ

Popular summer trade;
enormous cigar decorates
bar 🅰♪🅱🅿🅐🅗Ⓡ Ⓖ➊①Ⓢ

Chelsworth 19E7

11–2; 6–11
Peacock
✆ Bildeston 740758
Evening opening: 5.30
(summer)
Adnams Bitter, Old
Greene King IPA, Abbot
Mauldons Bitter Ⓗ
14th-century timbered inn
with own art and crafts centre
🅰♪♣🅿🅐🅗Ⓡ Ⓖ➊①Ⓢ

Clare 18D7

11–2; 5–11
Bell Hotel
Market Hill (A1092)
✆ Sudbury 277741
Adnams Bitter, Old
Mauldons Bitter Ⓗ
Comfortable, beamed old
coaching inn
🅰♪🅱🅿🅐🅗Ⓡ Ⓖ①Ⓢ &

Claydon 19F7

10.30–2.30; 6.30–11
Crown Inn
Norwich Road ✆ Ipswich
830289
Greene King XX, IPA, Abbot Ⓗ
Busy village pub
♪♣🅿🅐Ⓖ➊①Ⓢ &

Coddenham 19F6

11–2.30; 6–11
Dukes Head
(B1078) ✆ 300
**Tolly Cobbold Mild, Bitter,
Original, Old Strong** Ⓖ
Attractive village local with
medieval features
🅰♣🅿🅐Ⓖ➊①Ⓢ

Combs 19F6

11–2.30; 6.30–11
Live & Let Live
Park Road OS 038564
✆ Stowmarket 615224
Greene King XX, IPA, Abbot Ⓖ
Unspoilt quiet country pub
♣🅿🅐🅗①Ⓢ

Debenham 19G6

10.30–2.30; 5.30–11
Red Lion
High Street ✆ 860113
**Tolly Cobbold Bitter,
Original** Ⓗ **Old Strong** Ⓖ
15th-century traditional inn
in unspoilt Suffolk village
🅰♪♣🅿🅐🅗Ⓖ➊①Ⓢ

East Bergholt 19F8

10.30–2.30; 6–11
Royal Oak
(The Dicky)
East End ✆ Colchester 298221
Morning opening: 11
Greene King IPA, Abbot Ⓗ
Friendly, pleasant village pub,
dominoes played ♪♣🅿🅐①Ⓢ🅰

Elveden 18D5

11–2; 5–11

Elveden Inn
Bury Road (B1106, off A11)
✆ 288
Greene King IPA, Abbot Ⓗ
Friendly, popular free house;
range of beers may vary
🏠♪♣🅿🏡🕒🍴Ⓢ♿

Ewarton 19G8

11–2.30; 6–11

Queens Head
✆ Shotley 550
Tolly Cobbold Mild, Bitter,
Old Strong Ⓗ
16th-century country inn
with views across the Stour
estuary 🏠♣🅿🏠Ⓡ①Ⓢ

Felixstowe 19G8

11–2.30; 6–11

Ferry Boat Inn
Felixstowe Ferry ✆ 284203
Tolly Cobbold Bitter, Original,
Old Strong Ⓖ
Old-world pub with a nautical
flavour 🏠♣🅿🏠Ⓡ🕒🍴

Felsham 19E6

11–2; 7–11

Six Bells
Church Road (off A45)
✆ Rattlesden 268
Greene King XX, IPA
Abbot Ⓖ
Traditional Suffolk pub, no
gas or fruit machines
🏠♪🅱🅿🏠Ⓡ①Ⓢ♿

Flempton 18D5

10.30–2; 5–11

Greyhound
The Green (off A1101)
✆ Culford 400
Opens at 11 am & 6.30 pm
Greene King XX, IPA, Abbot Ⓗ
Pleasant pub on the village
green ♪🅿🏠🅱🕒🍴Ⓢ

Forward Green 19F6

10.30–2.30; 5.30–11

Shepherd & Dog
(A1120) ✆ Stonham 361
Greene King XX, IPA, Abbot Ⓗ
Popular village pub, recently
extended 🏠♣🅿🏠🕒🍴Ⓢ♿

Framlingham 19G6

10.30–2.30; 6–11

Railway
Station Road (B1116)
Adnams Bitter, Old Ⓗ
Excellent traditional pub;
simple bar, smart lounge
🏠♪♣🅿🏠Ⓢ

Freston 19G7

11–2.30; 5–11

Boot
(B1456)
Evening opening: 6 (summer),
7 (winter)

Tolly Cobbold Mild, Bitter,
Original, Old Strong Ⓗ
Real country pub, just out of
town 🏠♪♣🅿🏡Ⓢ

Gislingham 19F5

11–2.30; 6–11

Six Bells
✆ Mellis 349
Adnams Bitter Ⓗ Old Ⓖ
Pleasant village inn; simple
bar, smart lounge
🏠♪♣🅿🏡🕒🍴Ⓢ♿

Glemsford 18D7

10.30–2; 5–11

Angel
Egremont Street (B1065)
Evening opening: 6
Greene King XX, IPA, Abbot Ⓖ
Friendly old country pub
🏠♣🅿🏠🍴

Great Glemham 19H6

11–2.30; 6–11

Crown
✆ Rendham 693
Adnams Bitter, Old
Greene King XX, IPA, Abbot Ⓗ
Christmas Ale Ⓖ
Tastefully restored pub in
rural conservation area
🏠♪♣🅿🏠🅱🕒🍴Ⓢ♿

Great Wratting 18C7

11–2; 5–11

Red Lion
School Road (B1061)
✆ Thurlow 237
Adnams Mild, Bitter, Old Ⓗ
Pleasant village pub,
westernmost Adnams' tied
house 🏠♪♣🅿🏠Ⓡ🕒🍴Ⓢ

Hadleigh 19F7

10.30–2; 5–11

Falcon
Benton Street ✆ 822312
Evening opening: 6.30
Ind Coope Bitter, Burton Ale Ⓗ
Cosy, friendly local
🏠♣🅿🏠🕒🍴Ⓢ

White Hart
Bridge Street ✆ 822206
Morning opening: 11;
Saturday evening opening: 7
Tolly Cobbold Mild, Bitter,
Original, Old Strong Ⓗ
Two pub signs, unique
fireplace and good atmosphere
🏠♪♣🅿🏠Ⓡ🕒Ⓢ♿

Hasketon 19G7

11–3; 6–11

Turks Head
Low Road (off A12)
✆ Woodbridge 2584
Closes 2 pm in winter
Tolly Cobbold Mild, Bitter, Old
Strong Ⓗ
Delightful country pub with
putting green in summer
🏠♪♣🅿🏠🕒🍴Ⓢ🅰

Haughley 19F

11–2.30; 5.30–11

Railway Tavern
Station Road (B1116) ✆ 577
Adnams Old
Greene King XX, IPA, Abbot Ⓗ
Christmas Ale Ⓖ
Mauldons Bitter Ⓗ
Friendly one-bar free house
with dog-breeding landlord
♪♣🅱🅿🏠🕒🍴Ⓢ

Haverhill 18C

11–2; 6–11

Queens Head
9 Queens Street ✆ 702026
Adnams Mild, Bitter
Draught Bass
Greene King IPA Ⓗ
Friendly town-centre free
house ♪♣🏠Ⓡ🕒Ⓢ

Hundon 18D

11.30–2; 7–11

Rose & Crown
North Street
Greene King XX, IPA, Abbot Ⓗ
Friendly 15th-century pub
♪♣🅿🏡Ⓢ

Ipswich 19G

11–2.30; 5–11

Greyhound
9 Henley Road
Adnams Bitter, Old Ⓗ
Popular local with no frills
♣🅿🏡🍴

Ipswich Arms
145 London Road ✆ 51187
Evening opening: 5.30
Ind Coope Bitter, Burton Ale Ⓗ
Friendly pub with gardens an
children's playground
♪♣🅿🏠🕒🍴Ⓢ

Queens Head
1 Civic Drive ✆ 54159
Closes 2 pm lunchtimes
Tolly Cobbold Mild, Bitter,
Original, Old Strong Ⓗ
Comfortable one-bar pub with
excellent food
♪♣🕒Ⓢ♿

Spread Eagle
1 Fore Street
Evening opening: 5.30 (7 Sa
Tolly Cobbold Mild, Bitter,
Original Ⓗ Old Strong Ⓖ
Splendid old pub with many
games; ask for handpumped
beer ♪♣🅿🍴Ⓢ

Station Hotel
Burrel Road ✆ 52664
Evening opening: 5.30
Tolly Cobbold Mild, Bitter,
Original, Old Strong Ⓗ
Hotel with excellent pub
atmosphere
♪♣🅱🅿🏠🅱Ⓡ🕒①Ⓢ♿🚆

Water Lily
100 St Helens Street ✆ 57035
Evening opening: 7

Tolly Cobbold Bitter, Old
Strong G
Country pub in town
♨♣♫♪⌂🕭🍴

Woolpack
Tuddenham Road (off A12)
Evening opening: 5.30
Tolly Cobbold Mild, Bitter,
Original, Old Strong H
Earliest brick-built pub in
town, with friendly village
atmosphere ♨♫♪♣♫♪🍴

Ixworth 19E5

11–2; 5.30–11
Crown
Thetford Road (A1088)
Evening opening: 7
Greene King XX, IPA, Abbot H
Fine small town locals' pub
♪♣♫🕭🍴🍴 (Mon–Fri)🍴🍴

Kirton 19G7

11–3; 7–11
White Horse
Bucklesham Road (off A45)
Tolly Cobbold Mild, Bitter,
Original, Old Strong H
Friendly country pub
♪♣♫🍴🍴

Lakenheath 18D5

11–2; 6–11
Plough
Mill Road (off B112)
Greene King XX, IPA, Abbot H
Large and lively pub
♪♣♫🕭🍴🍴

Try also: Half Moon
(Greene King)

Laxfield 19G5

10.30–2.30; 6–11
Kings Head
Low Street (off B1117)
Adnams Bitter, Old G
Fine old pub, unchanged for a
century ♨♣♫🍴🍴

Leiston 19H6

10.30–2.30; 6–11
Engineers Arms
Main Street (off B1069)
Adnams Mild (summer),
Bitter, Old H
Unpretentious town pub
♪♪♣🍴🍴

Levington 19G7

11.30–2.30; 7–11
Ship
Gun Hill (off A45) ☎ Nacton
573
Tolly Cobbold Bitter,
Original G
16th century pub with
nautical atmosphere
♨♣♫🕭♣🍴

Lidgate 18D6

12–2; 7–11
Star
(B1063) ☎ Ousden 275

Greene King IPA, Abbot H
Old-world village local with
unusual handpumps
♨♪♣♫♣🕭🍴🍴🍴

Lindsey 19E7

10–2; 5.30–11
White Rose
☎ Boxford 210387
Morning opening: 11
Adnams Bitter, Old
Mauldons Bitter G
700-year-old thatched village
pub ♨♫♪♣🍴🍴

Little Bradley 18C7

12–2; 7–11
Royal Oak
(A143) ☎ Thurlow 229
Mauldons Bitter
Paine Mild, EG
Taylor Landlord
Wadworth 6X H
Enthusiastic landlord,
excellent selection of guest
beers ♨♪♣♫🍴🍴

Long Melford 18E7

10.30–2; 5–11
Swan
Hall Street (A134)
Greene King XX, IPA, Abbot H
Lively village local, popular
darts venue ♪♣♫🍴🍴🍴

Lowestoft 19J4

10.30–2.30; 5.30–11
Hearts of Oak
Raglan Street (off A12)
☎ 61125
Wethered Bitter H
Busy town-centre local, good
value meals ♪♣♫🕭🍴🍴🍴

Royal Oak
London Road South (A12)
Opens at 11 am & 7 pm
Norwich Bullards Mild
Webster Yorkshire Bitter H
Pleasant pub near the seafront
♪♣🕭🍴🍴

Triangle
St Peters Street (A12)
Friendly, busy town centre
local; wide range of beers
include Adnams, Marston,
Woodforde, Greene King, plus
winter ales and ciders ♪♣🍴🍴🍴

Market Weston 19E5

11–2; 5–11
Mill Inn
(B1111) ☎ Coney Weston 464
Saturday evening opening: 7
Adnams Bitter
Greene King XX, IPA, Abbot H
Popular with drinkers and
diners; regular guest beers
♨♪♣♫♣🍴🍴

Mendlesham 19F6

10.30–2.30; 6–11
Fleece
☎ 511

Greene King XX, IPA G
Friendly, unspoilt country
local ♪♣♫♣🕭🍴🍴

Mildenhall 18D5

10.30–2; 5.30–11
Queens Arms
Queensway
Greene King IPA H
Tidy no-frills local ♣♫🍴

Naughton 19F7

11–2; 7–11
Wheelers Arms
Whatfield Road (off B1078)
☎ Bildeston 740496
Tolly Cobbold Mild, Bitter,
Original, Old Strong G
Bulmer Cider H
Picturesque 12th-century
thatched pub ♨♣♫♣🕭🍴🍴🍴

Newbourn 19G7

11–2; 6–11
Fox
OS 274431
Tolly Cobbold Mild, Bitter,
Original, Old Strong G
Popular country pub, well
worth finding ♣♫♣🕭🍴

Newmarket 18C6

10–2.30; 6–11
Black Horse
High Street
Tolly Cobbold Bitter, Old
Strong H
Old, basic local with racing
connections ♨♫♪♣🍴🍴

Occold 19F5

11–2.30; 6–11
Beaconsfield Arms
(Off B1077)
Norwich Bullards Mild, Castle
Bitter
Webster Yorkshire Bitter H
Traditional village local with
petanque pitch ♨♪♣♫🍴🍴

Orford 19H7

11–3; 6–11
Jolly Sailor
Quay Street (B1084) ☎ 243
Adnams Bitter H Old G
Popular haunt with snug
♨♪♪♣♫♣🕭🍴🍴🍴

Pin Mill 19G7

11–2.30; 6–11
Butt & Oyster
(Off B1456)
☎ Woolverstone 224
Tolly Cobbold Mild, Bitter,
Original, Old Strong G
Internationally-known
riverside inn ♨♨♣🕭🍴🍴

Ramsholt 19H7

11–2.30; 6.30–11
Ramsholt Arms
Dock Road
☎ Shottisham 411229

Adnams Bitter, Old Ⓗ
Free house in beautiful
riverside setting
🅰️🍴♪♣️📷🔌🅿️🚪🅶🍷❶Ⓢ

Rendham 19H6

10.30–2.30; 6–11
White Horse
(B1119) ℰ 497
Tolly Cobbold Mild, Bitter,
Original, Old Strong Ⓖ
Village pub with restaurant,
opposite church
🍴♪♣️🅿️🅰️🆁🅶🍷 (not Wed)❶Ⓢ🅰️

Shadingfield 19H5

10.30–2.30; 5.30–11
Fox
(A145)
Evening opening: 7
Adnams Mild, Bitter, Old Ⓗ
Friendly country local
🅰️🍴♪♣️🅿️🅰️Ⓢ

Shimpling 18E7

10.30–2; 5–11
Bush
(Off A134)
ℰ Cockfield Green 828257
Evening opening: 5.30
Greene King XX, IPA Ⓗ
Two pints in the Bush are
worth one in the hand
🅰️♪♣️📷🅿️🅰️🅶🍷❶Ⓢ🅰️

Shottisham 19G7

11–3; 6–11
Sorrel Horse
(Off B1083) ℰ 411617
Tolly Cobbold Mild, Bitter, Old
Strong Ⓖ
Picturesque 500-year-old
smugglers' inn with collection
of rural artefacts
🅰️♣️🅿️🅰️🆁❶Ⓢ🅰️

Snape 19H6

10.30–2.30; 6–11
Plough & Sail
The Maltings (B1069) ℰ 413
Adnams Mild, Bitter, Old Ⓗ
Next to Maltings and craft
shop ♪♣️🅿️🅰️🅶🍷❶Ⓢ

Southwold 19J5

10.30–2.30; 6–11
Lord Nelson
42 East Street ℰ 722079
Adnams Mild, Bitter, Old Ⓗ
Old-world pub near clifftop
♪🅸Ⓢ

Sole Bay Inn
East Green ℰ 723736
Adnams Mild, Bitter, Old Ⓗ
Friendly one-bar pub under
lighthouse; the brewery tap
♪♣️🅿️🅰️❶Ⓢ

All pubs in Southwold serve
real ale

Stansfield 18D7

10.30–2; 7–11

Compasses
High Street (off A143)
Lunchtime opening: 12 noon
Greene King XX, IPA, Abbot Ⓗ
Pleasant, friendly pub ♪♣️🅿️🅰️❶

Stanton 19E5

11–2; 7–11
Angel
(Off A143) ℰ 50119
Greene King XX, IPA, Abbot Ⓗ
Popular village centre pub;
good home-cooked meals
🅰️🍴♪♣️🅶🍷❶Ⓢ🅶

Stonham Aspal 19F6

10.30–2.30; 6–11
Ten Bells
(A1120) ℰ 601
Tolly Cobbold Mild, Bitter,
Original, Old Strong Ⓗ
Smart, extended pub, but
friendly atmosphere
unchanged 🅰️♪♣️🅿️🅰️🅶🍷❶Ⓢ🅰️

Stowmarket 19F6

10.30–2.30; 5.30–11
Royal William
53 Union Street
Greene King XX, IPA, Abbot Ⓖ
Backstreet pub, worth looking
for ♪♣️❶🚂

Stowupland 19F6

11–2.30; 6–11
Crown
Church Street (A1120)
Tolly Cobbold Mild, Bitter
Old Strong Ⓖ
450-year-old thatched
roadside country pub
♣️🅿️🅰️Ⓢ🅰️

Stutton 19F8

11–2.30; 6–11
Gardeners Arms
(B1080)
Adnams Bitter
Greene King IPA, Abbot Ⓗ
Friendly free house with guest
beers 🅰️♪🅿️🅰️❶Ⓢ🅰️

Kings Head
High Street (B1080)
ℰ Ipswich 328344
Tolly Cobbold Bitter,
Original Ⓗ Old Strong Ⓖ
Cosy old coaching inn
🍴♪♣️🅿️🅰️🅶 (Sun only)❶Ⓢ

Sudbury 18E7

10.30–2; 5–11
Horn
North Street ℰ 73802
Greene King KK, XX, IPA,
Abbot Ⓗ
Long tradition of popularity
and friendliness ♣️🅿️🅰️🆁❶Ⓢ🅶

Ship & Star
Friars Street ℰ 79269
Evening opening: 6
Adnams Bitter, Old
Greene King IPA Ⓗ

Deservedly popular town pub,
no gimmicks
🅰️♪🍴♣️🅿️🅰️🅶🍷❶Ⓢ🅶

Trimley St Martin 19G8

11–3; 5.30–11
Hand in Hand
High Road ℰ Felixstowe
275249
Tolly Cobbold Bitter, Original,
Old Strong Ⓗ
Friendly local with good food
♪🅿️🅰️🅶🍷❶Ⓢ

Walsham-le-
Willows 19E5

11.30–2.30; 7–11
Six Bells
ℰ 726
Greene King XX, IPA, Abbot Ⓗ
Fine old beamed pub in
pleasant village
🅰️♪♣️🅿️🅰️🅶🍷❶Ⓢ

Wangford 19H5

10.30–2.30; 6–11
Plough
ℰ 239
Adnams Bitter, Old Ⓖ
Pleasant pub, shirts must be
worn
♪🅿️🅰️🅶🍷Ⓢ🅰️

Suffolk Poacher
High Street (off A12) ℰ 636
Evening opening: 7
Greene King IPA, Abbot
Tolly Cobbold Mild, Bitter,
Original Ⓗ
Attractive coaching inn with
poaching curios
🅰️🍴♪♣️🅿️🅰️🆁🅶🍷Ⓢ🅰️

Washbrook 19F7

11–2.30; 6–11
Brook Inn
The Street (off A12)
ℰ Copdock 455
Tolly Cobbold Mild, Bitter,
Original Ⓗ Old Strong Ⓖ
Village pub with excellent
lunchtime food
♪♣️🅿️🅰️🅶❶

Wrentham 19J5

10.30–2.30; 6–11
Horse & Groom
London Road (A12) ℰ 279
Evening opening: 7 in winter
Adnams Mild, Bitter Ⓗ Old Ⓖ
Main road pub with good local
trade
♪♣️🅿️🅰️❶Ⓢ🅶🅰️

Yoxford 19H6

10.30–2.30; 6–11
Blois Arms
High Street (A1120)
Adnams Mild, Bitter, Old Ⓗ
Friendly country pub with
collection of old beer bottles
♪♣️🅿️🅰️🆁❶Ⓢ

Abinger 7H4

10.30–2.30; 5.30–10.30 (11 F, S and summer)

Abinger Hatch

(Off A25) OS 116460
Gale HSB
Hall & Woodhouse Badger Best Bitter
King & Barnes Sussex Bitter, Festive
Whitbread Pompey Royal [H]
Delightful setting in extensive grounds
🏨🔥♣🌼🚗◔🍽Ⓢ

Addlestone 7H3

11–2.30; 5.30–10.30 (11 F, S and summer)

Crouch Oak

138 Station Road (A319)
Watney London Bitter
Webster Yorkshire Bitter [H]
♪♣🌼🚗◔🍽♿🚆

Albury Heath 7H4

10.30–2.30; 5.30–10.30 (11 F, S and summer)

William IV

Little London (off A25)
OS 067468 ☎ Shere 2685
No summer extension
Courage Best Bitter, Directors [H]
Bulmer Cider [G]
Unspoilt, secluded village pub
🏨♣🌼🚗◔ (not Sun)

Alfold 7H5

10.30–2.30; 6–10.30 (11 F, S and summer)

Crown

(B2133) ☎ Loxwood 742216
Courage Best Bitter, Directors [H]
First-rate village local near village green
🏨♣👪🌼🚗◔🍽🎯Ⓢ⛺

Ash 7G4

10.30–2.30; 6–10.30 (11 F, S and summer)

Greyhound

1 Ash Street (A323)
Opens at 11 am & 7 pm
Friary Meux Bitter
Ind Coope Burton Ale [H]
Ornate lounge contrasts with basic public bar ♣🌼🚗🎯Ⓢ

Ashford 7H2

10.30–2.30; 5.30–10.30 (11 F, S and summer)

Ash Tree

Convent Road (B378)
Fuller Chiswick Bitter, London Pride, ESB [H]
Well-run, lively pub
♪♣👪🌼🚗[R]◔🍽🎯Ⓢ

Ashtead 7J3

10.30–2.30; 5.30–10.30 (11 F, S and summer)

Leg of Mutton & Cauliflower

48 The Street (A24) ☎ 77124
Charrington IPA
Draught Bass [H]
Large, comfortable old inn, popular with the young
♪🌼🚗[R]◔🍽Ⓢ

Banstead 7J3

10.30–2.30; 5.30–10.30 (11 F, S)

Victoria

High Street (off A217)
Courage Best Bitter, Directors [H]
Part of the original village, now a commuter town
♪♣🌼🚗◔🍽Ⓢ

Betchworth 7J4

10.30–2.30; 5.30–10.30 (11 F, S and summer)

Dolphin

(Off A25) ☎ 2288
Charrington IPA
Fuller ESB
Morland Best Bitter
Ruddle Bitter, County [H]
Historic pub; friendly and busy, but expensive 🌼🚗◔🎯

Bisley 7G3

10.30–2.30; 6–10.30 (11 F, S)

Hen & Chickens

Guildford Road (A322)
Courage Best Bitter, Directors [H]
600-year-old pub, tastefully modernised 🏨🔥♪♣🌼🚗◔🎯Ⓢ

Blackbrook 7J4

10–2.30; 6–10.30 (11 F, S and summer)

Plough

(Off A24) OS 181467
King & Barnes Sussex Mild, Sussex Bitter, Festive, Old Ale [H]
Splendid, cosy little pub
♣🌼🚗◔🍽🎯Ⓢ

Bletchingley 10B5

10.30–2.30; 6–10.30 (11 F, S)

William IV

Little Common Lane (off A25)
Charrington IPA
Draught Bass [H]
Excellent country pub with fine darts team ♪♣🌼🚗[R]◔🎯Ⓢ

Brook 7G4

10.30–2.30; 5.30–10.30 (11 F, S and summer)

Dog & Pheasant

(A286) ☎ Wormley 3364
Friary Meux Bitter
Ind Coope Burton Ale [H]
Pleasant country pub with restaurant 🏨♣🌼🚗◔🍽Ⓢ♿

Byfleet 7H3

10.30–2.30; 5.30–10.30 (11 F, S and summer)

Queens Head

2 High Road (A245) ☎ 45433
Friary Meux Bitter
Ind Coope Burton Ale [H]
Large, comfortable pub with weekend flower stall
♪♣🚗◔🍽🎯Ⓢ♿🚆

Camberley 7G3

10.30–2.30; 5.30–10.30 (11 F, S and summer)

Staff

London Road (A30) ☎ 28505
Friary Meux Bitter
Ind Coope Burton Ale [H]
Tastefully furnished saloon with Victorian and military theme 🔥♪♣🌼🚗◔🍽🎯🚆

Caterham 10B5

10–2.30; 6–10.30 (11 F, S)

Old Surrey Hounds

Croydon Road (B2208)
Courage Best Bitter, Directors [H]
Lively pub with mixed clientele 🔥♪🌼◔🍽Ⓢ🚆

Valley

7 Station Avenue (off A22)
Fremlins Tusker [H]
Expensive steakhouse
♪🚗◔🍽Ⓢ🚆

Chertsey 7H3

11–2.30; 5.30–10.30 (11 F, S and summer)

George

45 Guildford Street (off A320)
Courage Best Bitter, Directors [H]
Low-ceilinged, 14th-century former Windsor Forest hunting lodge
🏨♪♣🌼🚗◔🍽🎯Ⓢ🚆

Prince Regent

126 Guildford Street (off A320) ☎ 62015
Watney London Bitter, Fined Stag Bitter [H]
Modernised pub with a motor-racing theme
♪♣◔🍽Ⓢ🚆

Swan

Windsor Street (B375)
Evening opening: 6
Wethered Bitter, SPA [H]
Smart 17th century coaching house with polished copper bar 🏨 🚗◔🍽🚆

Chiddingfold 7G5

10.30–2.30; 5.30–10.30 (11 F, S and summer)

Winterton Arms

Petworth Road (A283)
Friary Meux Bitter
Ind Coope Burton Ale [H]
Many facilities, including a ghost 🔥♪♣👪🌼🚗[R]◔🍽🎯Ⓢ♿⛺

Chobham 7G3

10.30–2.30; 6–10.30 (11 F, S)

Sun

High Street (off A319) ☎ 7112
Courage Best Bitter, Directors [H]
Excellent village pub with restaurant 🏨♪🚗◔🍽🎯Ⓢ

White Hart

High Street (off A319) ☎ 8525
Courage Best Bitter, Directors [H]
Popular old pub near church and cricket green
♪♣👪🌼🚗[R]◔Ⓢ

Churt 7G4

10.30–2.30; 5.30–10.30 (11 F, S and summer)

Crossways

(A287) ☎ Headley Down 714323
Opens t 11 am & 6 pm
Courage Best Bitter, Directors [H]
Fine village local ♪♣℘🚗◔☽(must book)🍺Ⓢ⛺

Pride of the Valley
Jumps Road (A287)
☎ Hindhead 5799
Evening opening: 6
Courage Best Bitter
King & Barnes Sussex Bitter [H]
Ideal oasis for hikers and motorists ♣🎯℘🚗🛏[R]◔☽(not Sun)🍺Ⓢ♿

Claygate 7J3

10.30–2.30; 5.30–10.30 (11 F, S and summer)
Foley Arms
Foley Road ☎ Esher 63431
Young Bitter, Special Bitter [H]
Busy pub with large garden ♪♣℘🚗[R]◔(not Sat)🍺⇌

Compton 7G4

10.30–2.30; 6–10.30 (11 F, S and summer)
Harrow
The Street (B3000)
Friary Meux Bitter
Ind Coope Burton Ale [H]
Congenial old pub with good food 🔥♪℘🚗◔☽Ⓢ♿

Cranleigh 7H4

10.30–2.30; 6–10.30 (11 F, S and summer)
Leathern Bottle
Smithbrook (A281) ☎ 274117
King & Barnes Sussex Mild, Sussex Bitter, Festive, Old Ale [H]
Busy old roadside pub 🔥♣℘🚗◔☽🍺Ⓢ⛺

Critchmere 7G5

10.30–2.30; 5.30–10.30 (11 F, S and summer)
Royal Oak
Critchmere Hill (off A287)
Morning opening: 11
Courage Best Bitter, Directors [H]
Rambling one-bar local 🔥♪♣℘🚗◔☽Ⓢ

Crowhurst 10B5

10.30–2.30; 6.30–10.30 (11 F, S)
Brickmakers Arms
Tandridge Lane, near Lingfield
☎ South Godstone 3042
Devenish Wessex Best Bitter
Everard Old Original
Friary Meux Bitter [H]
Ruddle County [E]
Cosy free house noted for good food 🔥ſ♪℘🚗◔☽Ⓢ

Dorking 7J4

10.30–2.30; 5.30–10.30 (11 F, S and summer)
Prince of Wales
Hampstead Road (off A2003)
Courage Best Bitter, Directors [H]
Pub with good atmosphere, behind bus garage ſ♪♣℘◔☽Ⓢ

Earlswood 7J4

10.30–2.30; 5.30–10.30 (11 F, S)
Nags Head
Horley Road (A23)
Charrington IPA [H]
Main road pub with putting green ſ♪♣℘🚗[R]◔🍺Ⓢ⛺

Eashing 7G4

10.30–2.30; 6–10.30 (11 F, S and summer)
Stag
(Off A3)
Ind Coope Burton Ale [H]
Quiet pub with riverside garden 🔥♪♣℘🚗🍺Ⓢ

East Molesey 7J3

10.30–2.30; 5.30–10.30 (11 F, S and summer)
Streets of London
Bridge Road (off A309)
Gaffers Bitter
Wethered Bitter, SPA [H]
Large, interestingly decorated pub with home brew ſ♪🎯℘[R]◔⇌

Egham 7H2

11–2.30; 5.30–10.30 (11 F, S and summer)
Railway Hotel
40 Station Road ☎ 32401
Friary Meux Bitter
Ind Coope Burton Ale [H]
Modern, newly-improved house 🔥ſ♪♣℘🚗[R]◔☽🍺Ⓢ⇌

Elstead 7G4

10.30–2.30; 5.30–10.30 (11 F, S and summer)
Star
Milford Road (B3001)
Courage Best Bitter, Directors [H]
Cosy village local ſ♪♣℘🚗◔☽🍺Ⓢ

Englefield Green 7H2

11–2.30; 5.30–10.30 (11 F, S and summer)
Barley Mow
Barley Mow Road (off 328)
Evening opening: 6
Courage Best Bitter, Directors [H]
Popular pub facing village green 🔥♪♣℘🚗◔Ⓢ

Beehive
Middle Hill (off A30)
Brakspear Special Bitter
Gibbs Mew Wiltshire Bitter
Samuel Smith Old Brewery Bitter
Wadworth 6X
Young Special Bitter [H]
Small free house; range of beers varies, but usually six available 🔥♪℘🚗◔Ⓢ

Epsom 7J3

10.30–2.30; 5.30–10.30 (11 F, S)
Barley Mow
12 Pikes Hill, off Upper High Street ☎ 21044
Fuller London Pride, ESB [H]
Busy backstreet pub with pleasant garden ♪℘◔

Railway Guard
48 Church Road (off A2022)
Charrington IPA
Young Special Bitter [H]
Small, friendly free house with paintings by landlord ♪♣℘🍺Ⓢ

Ewell 7J3

10.30–2.30; 5.30–10.30 (11 F, S)
Green Man
71 High Street (off A24/A240) ☎ 01-393 1349
Courage Best Bitter, Directors [H]
Comfortable pub in village centre 🔥♪♣℘🚗[R]◔☽Ⓢ⇌

Farncombe 7G4

10.30–2.30; 5.30–10.30 (11 F, S and summer)
Three Lions
Meadrow (A3100)
Friary Meux Bitter
Ind Coope Burton Ale [H]
Old pub, venue for rock bands 🔥ſ♪♣℘🚗◔🍺⇌

Farnham 7G4

10.30–2.30; 5.30–10.30 (11 F, S and summer)
Nelson Arms
Castle Street (A287)
Courage Best Bitter, Directors [H]
Attractive 18th-century pub near castle ♪◔

Queens Head
The Borough (A287)
Gale Light Mild (summer), **BBB, HSB, XXXXX** [H]
Comfortable, inexpensive town-centre pub ♣🍺Ⓢ

Waverley Arms
Waverley Lane (off A31/A287) ☎ 715221
Courage Best Bitter, Directors [H]
Mouthwatering menu of house-cooked food 🔥♪♣℘◔☽🍺Ⓢ♿⇌

William Cobbett
Bridge Square (A287)
Courage Best Bitter, Directors [H]
Vibrant, gimmicky birthplace of Cobbett 🔥♪♣℘🚗[R]◔♿⇌

Fetcham 7H3

10.30–2.30; 5.30–10.30 (11 F, S and summer)
Bell
Bell Lane
Courage Best Bitter, Directors [H]
Large, friendly local ♪♣℘🚗◔🍺Ⓢ♿

Frimley 7G3

10.30–2.30; 6–10.30 (11 F, S)
Railway Arms
78 High Street (off M3)
Ind Coope Bitter, Burton Ale [H]
Neat, well-kept and welcoming ♪♣🚗◔🍺Ⓢ⇌

Surrey

Frimley Green 7G3

11–2.30; 6–10.30 (11 F, S)

Old Wheatsheaf
Frimley Green Road (A321)
Morland Mild, Bitter, Best
Bitter H
Comfortable pub with shove
ha'penny alcove ♪♣🛏
🍴(Mon-Fri)🍷 (must book)🍴&

Godalming 7G4

10.30–2.30; 5.30–10.30 (11 F, S and summer)

Railway
Meadrow (A3100) ✆ 6680
Courage Best Bitter,
Directors H
Large pub near River Wey
🛏♣🛏🍷⏰≷

Gomshall 7H4

10.30–2.30; 5.30–10.30 (11 F, S and summer)

Black Horse
Station Road (A25)
✆ Shere 2242
Evening opening: 6
Young Bitter, Special Bitter,
Winter Warmer H
Fine roadside house
🛏♣🎛🍷🛏🅿R⏰🍷🍴≷

Guildford 7H4

10.30–2.30; 5.30–10.30 (11 F, S and summer)

Robin Hood
Sydenham Road ✆ 576388
Friary Meux Bitter
Ind Coope Burton Ale H
Compact and handy for town
centre 🛏♪♣🍷🍴≷

Royal Oak
Trinity Churchyard (off
Sydenham Road) ✆ 66637
Courage Best Bitter,
Directors H
Popular, one-bar pub for all
generations ♪🍷⏰🍴≷

Sanford Arms
Epsom Road (A246)
Courage Best Bitter,
Directors H
Local catering for all tastes
🛏♣🍷⏰🍴≷

Star
Quarry Street
Friary Meux Bitter
Ind Coope Burton Ale H
Oldest pub in Guildford –
reputedly haunted ♪♣⏰🍴≷

Holmbury St. Mary 7H4

10.30–2.30; 6–10.30 (11 F, S and summer)

Kings Head
Pitland Street
Archer Best Bitter
Hall & Woodhouse
Badger Best Bitter
Ringwood Old Thumper
Usher Best Bitter
Young Special Bitter H
Local cider G
Characterful pub in
picturesque area
🛏♪♣🍷🛏⏰🍷(Wed–Sat)🍴&

Horley 7J4

10.30–2.30; 6–10.30 (11 F, S)

Foresters Arms
Victoria Road (A23)
Draught Bass
Charrington IPA H
Oldest building in town centre
♪🛏🍷⏰🍷≷

Gatwick
High Street (off A23) ✆ 3801
King & Barnes Sussex Mild,
PA, Festive, Old Ale H
Excellent town-centre pub
♪🛏🍷⏰🍷≷

Kings Head
63 Balcombe Road (B2036)
Charrington IPA
King & Barnes Sussex Bitter H
Lively 'local' atmosphere
🍴♪♣🍷🛏⏰🍷🍴&≷

Kingswood 10A5

10.30–2.30; 6–10.30 (11 F, S)

Pigeon Pair
Waterhouse Lane (B2032, off
A217) ✆ Burgh Heath 52696
Ruddle County
Watney London Bitter, Fined
Stag Bitter H
Popular stockbroker belt pub,
prices to match ♣🍷🛏⏰🍷🍴≷

Knaphill 7G3

10.30–2.30; 5.30–10.30 (11 F, S and summer)

Royal Oak
Anchor Hill (off A322)
Morning opening: 11
Courage Best Bitter,
Directors H
Distinctive local with
atmosphere ♪♣🍷🛏⏰

Laleham 7H3

10–2.30; 6–10.30 (11 F, S and summer)

Three Horseshoes
25 Shepperton Road (B376)
Ruddle County
Watney London Bitter, Fined
Stag Bitter
Webster Yorkshire Bitter H
Popular pub of character,
close to Thameside
recreational facilities 🛏🍷🛏⏰🍷

Leatherhead 7J3

10.30–2.30; 5.30–10.30 (11 F, S and summer)

Running Horse
38 Bridge Street (off A246)
Friary Meux Bitter H
Historic pub with friendly
atmosphere ♪♣🍷🛏⏰🍷≷

All pubs in Leatherhead sell
real ale

Leigh 7J4

10–2.30; 6–10.30 (11 F, S and summer)

Plough
King & Barnes Sussex Mild,
Sussex Bitter, PA, Festive, Old
Ale H
Lively, old-world rural local
♣🍷🛏⏰🍷🍴

Long Ditton 7J3

10.30–2.30; 5.30–10.30 (11 F, S and summer)

New Inn
Rushett Road, Thames Ditton
(Off A307) ✆ 1893
Wethered Bitter
Whitbread Flowers Original
Bitter H
Friendly local with resident
ghost ♪♣🍷⏰🍷

Lower Bourne 7G4

10.30–2.30; 5.30–10.30 (11 F, S and summer)

Spotted Cow
Bourne Grove
Morning opening: 11.30
Courage Best Bitter,
Directors H
Pleasant pub in rural setting
♪🎛🍷🛏⏰🍷🍴&

Merstham 10B5

10.30–2.30; 5.30–10.30 (11, F, S)

Railway Arms
London Road (A23)
Charrington IPA H
Family house in old village
♪♣🍷⏰🍷≷

Mogador 10A5

10.30–2.30; 6–10.30 (11 F, S)

Sportsman
Mogador Lane (off A217)
OS 241532 ✆ Reigate 46655
Courage Best Bitter,
Directors H
Small, cosy pub on the edge of
the heath 🛏♣🍷🛏⏰

Normandy 7G4

10.30–2.30; 5.30–10.30 (11 F, S and summer)

Duke of Normandy
(A323) ✆ Worplesdon 235157
Opens at 11 am & 6 pm
Friary Meux Bitter
Ind Coope Burton Ale H
Warm and welcoming
🍴♪♣🍷🛏⏰(not Sun)🍷

Oakwood Hill 7H4

10.30–2.30; 5.30–10.30 (11 F, S and summer)

Punchbowl
(Off A29) ✆ 249
Draught Bass
Hall & Woodhouse
Badger Best Bitter
King & Barnes Sussex Bitter
Young Special Bitter H
Upper-crust old country pub;
guest beer
🛏♪♣🎛🍷🛏R🛏⏰🍷🍴🍴&⛏

Ockham 7H3

11–2.30; 6–10.30 (11 F, S and summer)

Hautboy
Alms Heath (off A3) OS
076567 ✆ Guildford 224628
Eldridge Pope Royal Oak
Everard Old Original
Gibbs Mew Bishops Tipple
Hall & Woodhouse
Badger Best Bitter
Paradise Bitter H
Victorian folly with talkative

macaw; expensive, but 8 beers
usually available
♪♫♣⊞♪🚗®🅖♿🍴(not Mon)Ⓢ

Ottershaw 7H3

11–2.30; 5.30–10.30 (11 F, S and summer)
Castle
Brox Road ☎ 2373
Ind Coope Bitter, Burton Ale Ⓗ
Cosy, out-of-the-way pub
🏠♣♪🅖🚗🅖🍴🍴

Outwood 10B5

10.30–2.30; 5.30–10.30 (11 F, S)
Bell
Everard Old Original
Felinfoel Double Dragon
Fremlins Bitter
Taylor Landlord Ⓗ
Modernised, historic village
local ♪♫🅖Ⓢ

Oxshott 7H3

10.30–2.30; 5.30–10.30 (11 F, S and summer)
Victoria
High Street (A224) ☎ 3186
Courage Best Bitter,
Directors Ⓗ
Busy village pub with pleasant
garden 🏠♣♪🅖🚗🅡🍴🍴

Pirbright 7G3

10.30–2.30; 5.30–10.30 (11 F, S and summer)
White Hart
The Green (A324)
Opens at 11.30 am & 6 pm
Friary Meux Bitter
Ind Coope Burton Ale Ⓗ
Photogenic pub next to village
green
♪♫🅖🚗🍴 (Tue–Sat)🍴Ⓢ

Pyrford 7H3

10.30–2.30; 5.30–10.30 (11 F, S)
Anchor
Pyrford Lock (off A3) near
Ripley OS 053592
Opens at 11 am & 6 pm
Courage Best Bitter,
Directors Ⓗ
Large, popular pub near Wey
Navigation and Wisley
gardens ♪🅖🚗🍴🍴Ⓢ

Ramsnest
Common 7G5

10.30–2.30; 5.30–10.30 (11 F, S and summer)
Ramsnest Inn
Petworth Road, Chiddingfold
(A283) ☎ Haslemere 44610
Friary Meux Bitter
Ind Coope Burton Ale Ⓗ
Roadside pub with skittle alley
🏠♣♪🅖🚗🅡🅖🍴Ⓢ♿

Redhill 10A5

10.30–2.30; 5.30–10.30 (11 F, S)
Home Cottage
3 Redstone Hill (A25)
Young Bitter, Special Bitter,
Winter Warmer Ⓗ
Modernised pub with
character 🏠♣🅖🚗🅖🍴🍴Ⓢ♫

Jolly Brickmakers

60 Frenches Road (off A23)
Charrington IPA
**Mitchells & Butlers Springfield
Bitter** Ⓗ
Enthusiastic games pub near
industrial estate ♪♣🅖🍴Ⓢ

Lakers Hotel

Redstone Hill (A25) ☎ 61043
Charrington IPA
King & Barnes Sussex Bitter
**Mitchells & Butlers Springfield
Bitter** Ⓗ
Lively hotel
♪♫♣🅖🚗🅡🅖🍴🍴Ⓢ♫

Red Lion

Linkfield Corner (A35)
Draught Bass
Charrington IPA Ⓗ
Good pub, handy for town
centre 🏠♪🅖🅖🍴Ⓢ

Reigate 10A5

10.30–2.30; 5.30–10.30 (11 F, S)
Barley Mow
Eastnor Road, South Park (off
A217) ☎ 41891
Charrington IPA Ⓗ
Friendly pub on outskirts of
town ♪♣⊞🅖🚗🅖🍴🍴Ⓢ

Blue Anchor

27 West Street (A25) ☎ 47837
Draught Bass
Charrington IPA Ⓗ
Plush town pub ♪♣🅖🅖Ⓢ

Cobbles Wine Bar

Old Brewery Yard ☎ 44833
Opens 12–3; 7–10.30; closed
Sundays
Felinfoel Double Dragon
Hook Norton Best Bitter Ⓗ
Expensive haunt of young
people 🏠♪♣♪🅖🚗🅡🅖🍴Ⓢ

Nutley Hall

Nutley Lane (off A25)
☎ 41741
King & Barnes Sussex Mild
(summer), **Sussex Bitter,**
Festive, Old Ale Ⓗ
Pub of character, full of
characters
♪♫♣🅖🚗🅡🅖🍴 (must book)Ⓢ

Panther

Croydon Road (A242)
Courage Best Bitter,
Directors Ⓗ
Small, friendly local ♪♫♣🅖🍴

Yew Tree

Reigate Hill (A217)
Courage Best Bitter,
Directors Ⓗ
Cosy pub to north of town
♪♣🅖🚗🍴Ⓢ

Ripley 7H3

10.30–2.30; 5.30–10.30 (11 F, S and summer)
Half Moon
High Street (B2215)
Adnams Bitter
Brakspear Special Bitter
Fuller London Pride, ESB

King & Barnes Festive
Samuel Smith Old
Brewery Bitter
Wethered SPA
Young Special Bitter Ⓗ
Good alehouse at a price;
range of beers varies 🏠♪♣🅖

Ship

High Street (B2215)
Courage Best Bitter,
Directors Ⓗ
Friendly 16th century local in
village centre 🏠♪♣🅖🚗Ⓢ🍴♿

Send 7H3

10.30–2.30; 5.30–10.30 (11 F, S and summer)
New Inn
Send Road (A247)
Friary Meux Bitter
Ind Coope Burton Ale Ⓗ
One-bar pub with garden, by
Wey navigation ♪🅖🚗🅖🍴Ⓢ

Shackleford 7G4

10.30–2.30; 5.30–10.30 (11 F, S and summer)
Cyder House
Peper Harrow Road (off A3)
Courage Best Bitter
Fuller London Pride
**Ringwood Best Bitter, Old
Thumper** Ⓗ
Bulmer Cider Ⓖ
Friendly village local
🏠♪♣🅖🚗🍴🍴Ⓢ

Shepperton 7H3

10.30–2.30; 5.30–10.30 (11 F, S and summer)
Olde Kings Head
Church Square (off B375)
Courage Bitter, Directors Ⓗ
Old pub, parts dating from
14th century 🏠♪🅖🚗Ⓢ

Shere 7H4

10.30–2.30; 5.30–10.30 (11 F, S and summer)
Prince of Wales
(Off A25) ☎ 2313
Young Bitter, Special Bitter,
Winter Warmer Ⓗ
Imposing house in picturesque
village 🏠♪♣⊞🅖🚗🅡🅖🍴🍴Ⓢ♿

Staines 7H3

10.30–2.30; 5.30–10.30 (11 F, S and summer)
Bells
Church Street (off B376)
Courage Best Bitter,
Directors Ⓗ
Compact, friendly pub
opposite church ♣🅖🚗🅡🅖Ⓢ

Jolly Farmer

The Hythe (off A308)
Courage Best Bitter,
Directors Ⓗ
Small, friendly local near
Staines Bridge ♪♣🅖Ⓢ♿

Wheatsheaf &
Pigeon

Penton Road
Courage Best Bitter,
Directors Ⓗ
Well-run and comfortable
back-street local 🅖Ⓢ♿

Stanwell 7H2

10.30–2.30; 5.30–10.30 (11 F, S and summer)

Rising Sun
Riverside Road
Friary Meux Bitter
Ind Coope Burton Ale H
Opposite cargo terminal,
popular with airport staff
♪♣🏠🕒🍽(Mon–Fri)Ⓢ♿

Stoke d'Abernon 7H3

10.30–2.30; 5.30–10.30 (11 F, S and summer)

Plough
2 Station Road (off A245)
Manns IPA
**Watney London Bitter, Fined
Stag Bitter
Webster Yorkshire Bitter
Bulmer Cider** H
Pleasant pub near station
🏠♪♣🏠🕒🍽Ⓢ♨

Sunbury 7H2

10.30–2.30; 5.30–10.30 (11 F, S and summer)

Grey Horse
63 Staines Road East (A308)
**Courage Best Bitter,
Directors** H
Compact and lively
♪♣🏠🕒Ⓢ♨

Thames Ditton 8C7

10.30–2.30; 5.30–10.30 (11 F, S and summer)

Angel
Portsmouth Road (A307)
**Courage Best Bitter,
Directors** H
Happy, easy-going pub with
small beer garden
🏠🏠🍽

The Sands 7G4

10.30–2.30; 5.30–10.30 (11 F, S and summer)

Barley Mow
Littleworth Road (off A31)
Evening opening: 6
**Courage Best Bitter,
Directors** H
Country local with
prize-winning garden
♪♣🏠🍽

Tilford 7G4

10.30–2.30; 5.30–10.30 (11 F, S and summer)

Barley Mow
The Green
Evening opening: 6
**Courage Best Bitter,
Directors** H
Classic village pub with table
skittles
♣🏠Ⓢ♿

Virginia Water 7G2

11–2.30; 5.30–10.30 (11 F, S and summer)

Crown
Trumps Green Road (off
B389) ☎ Wentworth 3282
Friary Meux Bitter
Ind Coope Burton Ale H
Quiet pub with good garden
🏠♪🏠🕒Ⓢ♿

Walliswood 7H4

11–2.30; 6–10.30 (11 F, S and summer)

Scarlett Arms
(Off A29) OS 119382
**King & Barnes Sussex Bitter,
Old Ale, Draught Festive** G
Unspoilt country pub with
impressive flower displays in
summer
🏠♣🏠Ⓢ

Walton-on-Thames 7H3

10.30–2.30; 5.30–10.30 (11 F, S and summer)

Swan Hotel
50 Manor Road (off A3050)
**Young Bitter, Special Bitter,
Winter Warmer** H
Large, popular riverside pub
♪♣🏠Ⓡ🕒🍽Ⓢ

Walton on the Hill 10A5

10.30–2.30; 5.30–10.30 (11 F, S)

Bell (Rat)
Withybed Corner (off B2220)
OS 228557
Charrington IPA H
Fine old local
♣🏠Ⓢ

Chequers
Chequers Lane ☎ Tadworth
2364
Young Bitter, Special Bitter H
Large brewers' Tudor pub
with notable restaurant
🏠🏠🕒🍽(must book)🍽Ⓢ

Weston Green 7H3

10.30–2.30; 5.30–10.30 (11 F, S and summer)

Alma Arms
Alma Road, Esher (off A309)
**Courage Best Bitter,
Directors** H
Superb, unpretentious local,
off the beaten track
♣🏠🕒🍽Ⓢ♿♨

Greyhound
Hampton Court Way (A309)
Adnams Bitter
Arkell BBB
Brakspear Special Bitter
Greene King Abbot
Hall & Woodhouse Hector's
Bitter
King & Barnes Sussex Bitter
Wethered Bitter
Whitbread Castle Eden Ale H
Friendly Whitbread exhibition
pub
🍽🕒🍽

Weybourne 7G4

10.30–2.30; 5.30–10.30 (11 F, S and summer)

Elm Tree
14 Weybourne Road
☎ Aldershot 23537
**Courage Best Bitter,
Directors** H
Landlord is as good as the beer
♪♣🏠🏠🍽Ⓢ

Weybridge 7H3

10.30–2.30; 5.30–10.30 (11 F, S and summer)

Old Crown
83 Thames Street
**Courage Best Bitter,
Directors** H
Pleasant, friendly pub in
riverside setting
♣🏠🏠Ⓢ

Windlesham 7G3

10.30–2.30; 6–10.30 (11 F, S)

Surrey Cricketers
Chertsey Road (B386)
Friary Meux Bitter
Ind Coope Burton Ale H
Tastefully modernised village
pub
🏠♪♣🏠Ⓡ🕒🍽Ⓢ

Woking 7H3

10.30–2.30; 5.30–10.30 (11 F, S and summer)

College
College Road, Maybury (off
B382)
☎ 61730
Charrington IPA
Draught Bass H
Extensively altered pub
♪🏠🏠🕒🍽Ⓢ♿

Wotton 7H4

10.30–2.30; 6–10.30 (11 F, S and summer)

Wotton Hatch
(A25)
☎ Dorking 885665
Fuller London Pride, ESB H
Fine roadside pub with
restaurant
🏠♪♣🏠Ⓡ🕒🍽Ⓢ

Wrecclesham 7G4

10.30–2.30; 5.30–10.30 (11 F, S and summer)

Bat & Ball
Bat & Ball Lane, Boundstone
(off B3384) OS 834445
Opens at 12 noon (11 am Sat)
& 6 pm
Brakspear Pale Ale
Fuller ESB
Marston Pedigree, Owd
Rodger
Old Chidham Bitter
Shepherd Neame Bitter H
Former tally man's office
where hop pickers were paid in
cash and beer; hop fields have
gone but a fine pub remains
🏠♪♣🍴🏠🕒Ⓢ

Sandrock
Sandrock Hill Road (off
B3384)
Opens at 12 noon (11.30 am
Sat) & 6 pm
Batham Mild, Bitter
Gale BBB
Holden Special Bitter
King & Barnes Sussex Bitter
Simpkiss Bitter H
Woods Special Bitter
Selborne Cider G
Excellent beer drinkers' pub
🏠♣🏠🕒♿

Keg Buster by Bill Tidy

Alfriston 10C8

10–2.30; 6–10.30 (11 F, S and summer)

Star
High Street (B2108)
℡ 870495
Draught Bass
Hall & Woodhouse
Badger Best Bitter Ⓗ
Old hotel bar in tourist show
village ♪♣🎵♨🚪🅿🚾Ⓖ🌳Ⓢ

Arlington 10C8

10–2.30; 6–10.30 (11 F, S and summer)

Old Oak Inn
Cane Heath (off A22)
℡ Polegate 2072
Hall & Woodhouse Badger
Best Bitter
Martlet Brighton Special
Bitter, Regency Bitter Ⓖ
Pleasant country
pub/restaurant ♨🅿🌳Ⓢ

Battle 10D7

10–2.30; 6–10.30 (11 F, S and summer)

Chequers
Lower Lake (A2100) ℡ 2088
Fremlins Bitter, Tusker Ⓗ
Low-ceilinged pub
♠♪♣🚪Ⓡ🌳Ⓖ🌳Ⓢ🍴≹

Bells Yew Green 10D6

10.30–2.30; 6–10.30 (11 F, S and summer)

Brecknock Arms
(B2169) ℡ Frant 237
Harvey XX, BB, XXXX Ⓗ
Excellent pub opposite village
green ♪♣♨🚪Ⓖ🌳Ⓢ≹

Bexhill 10B8

10–2.30; 6–10.30 (11 F, S and summer)

New Inn
Sidley Green (A269)
Charrington IPA
Draught Bass Ⓗ
Little-changed pub in much
altered surroundings
♪♨🚪Ⓡ🌳Ⓢ

Traffers
19 Egerton Road ℡ 210240
Harvey BB
Young Special Bitter Ⓗ
Friendly bar opposite park and
near seafront ♪♨🌳Ⓖ🌳Ⓢ≹

Blackboys 10C7

10–2.30; 6–10.30 (11 F, S and summer)

Blackboys Inn
Lewes Road (B2192)
℡ Framfield 283
Harvey X, BB, XXXX Ⓗ
500-year-old smart country
inn ♪♣♨🌳Ⓖ🌳Ⓢ

Brede 10E7

10–2.30; 6–10.30 (11 F, S and summer)

Red Lion
(A28)
Courage Best Bitter
Fremlins Bitter
Harvey BB
Young Special Bitter Ⓗ

Pleasant village pub opposite
church 🏠🚪Ⓢ

Brighton 10B8

10.30–2.30; 5.30–11

Albion Inn
28 Albion Hill
Whitbread Flowers Original
Bitter, Strong Country Bitter,
Pompey Royal
Bulmer Cider Ⓗ
Traditional local, note the
trophy cabinet ♪♣Ⓢ

Basketmakers Arms
12 Gloucester Road
Gale BBB, HSB, Dark Mild,
XXXXX Ⓗ
Busy town pub, excellent hot
snacks 🍴Ⓢ≹

Eagle
125 Gloucester Road
℡ 607765
Opening hours vary
Eldridge Pope IPA, Royal Oak
King & Barnes Sussex Bitter,
Old Ale
Raven Bitter
Young Bitter, Special Bitter Ⓗ
Friendly, popular pub opposite
Basketmakers Arms 🏠♪Ⓡ🅪≹

Hand in Hand
33 Upper St. James Street
Fuller ESB
Hall & Woodhouse
Badger Best Bitter
King & Barnes Festive
Wadworth 6X
Young Special Bitter Ⓗ
Small, friendly, popular pub;
range varies ♪♣Ⓢ

Lord Nelson
36 Trafalgar Street (off A23)
℡ 682150
Harvey XX, PA, BB, XXXX
Bulmer Cider Ⓗ
Enthusiastic landlord, proud
of his mild ♪♣Ⓖ🅪Ⓢ≹

Oriental
5 Montpelier Road
Gale BBB, HSB
Tamplins Bitter
Usher Best Bitter
Webster Yorkshire Bitter Ⓗ
Friendly pub with unusual
decor; good snacks 🅪♣Ⓢ

Princess Victoria
Upper North Street
Whitbread Flowers Original
Bitter, Strong Country Bitter,
Pompey Royal Ⓗ
Friendly town pub close to
clock tower and shops ♪Ⓖ🅪≹

Rockingham Arms
24 Sillwood Street
Eldridge Pope IPA
Hall & Woodhouse
Badger Best Bitter
Harvey BB
King & Barnes Sussex Bitter,
Festive
Young Special Bitter Ⓗ

Comfortable pub with varied
clientele ♪♨

Sir Charles Napier
50 Southover Street
Gale BBB, HSB, Dark Mild,
XXXXX Ⓗ
Friendly street-corner local
with no smoking area
♪♣🅪Ⓢ

Stag
Upper Bedford Street
℡ 609673
Ballard Wassail
Boddingtons Best Bitter
Fuller ESB
Harvey BB
Marston Pedigree Ⓗ
Extremely popular pub with
extensive, variable range
♪♣Ⓖ🅪Ⓢ

Windsor Tavern
46 Windsor Street
Fuller London Pride, ESB
Gale HSB
Harvey BB
Whitbread Flowers Original
Bitter, Strong Country Bitter,
Pompey Royal
Young Special Bitter Ⓗ
Popular pub near clock tower;
intriguing collection of jugs
♪♣Ⓢ

Try also: **Bulldog Tavern**, St
James Street (free);
Prestonville Arms, Hamilton
Road (Gale)

Burwash 10D6

10–2.30; 6–10.30 (11 F, S and summer)

Bell
High Street (A265)
Beard XX, PA, BB, XXXX Ⓗ
Fine old award-winning pub
🅪♪♣♨🚪Ⓡ🌳Ⓖ🅪🌳Ⓢ

Chailey 10B7

10–2.30; 6–10.30 (11 F, S and summer)

Horns Lodge
South Chailey (A275)
℡ Barcombe 400422
Morning opening: 11
Hall & Woodhouse
Badger Best Bitter
Harvey BB
Usher Best Bitter Ⓗ
Popular with locals and
travellers ♪♣🎵♨🚪Ⓖ🌳Ⓢ

All pubs in Chailey sell real ale

Cowbeech 10D7

10–2.30; 6–10.30 (11 F, S and summer)

Merry Harriers
(Off A271) OS 619145
Charrington IPA Ⓗ
Out-of-the-way village local
🅪♣♨🚪Ⓢ♿

Crowborough 10C6

10.30–2.30; 6–10.30 (11 F, S and summer)

Boars Head
Eridge Road (A26) ℡ 2412
Fremlins Bitter, Tusker Ⓖ

Picturesque old country pub
♣🅿️🍺♿

Ditchling 10B7

10.30–2.30; 6–11
Bull
2 High Street (B2112)
Morning opening: 10.30
**Whitbread Strong Country
Bitter, Pompey Royal** Ⓗ
Quiet 16th century pub, smart
dress preferred 🅿️🍺Ⓢ

Try also: North Star, North
End Lane (free); White Horse,
West Street (Whitbread)

Eastbourne 10D8

10–2.30; 6–10.30 (11 F, S and summer)
Eagle
57 South Street (off A22)
☎ 23017
Fremlins Bitter, Tusker Ⓗ
Town-centre pub, tastefully
decorated ♪♣♿Ⓢ⇌

Hurst Arms
76 Hillingdon Road (A22)
Harvey XX, BB, XXXX Ⓗ
Lively turn-of-the-century
local ♪♣🍷Ⓢ

Star
Star Road
**Courage Best Bitter,
Directors** Ⓗ
Pleasant pub adjoining site of
old Star Brewery ♪♣🅿️Ⓢ

Eridge 10C6

10.30–2.30; 6–10.30 (11 F, S and summer)
Huntsman
(A26) ☎ Tunbridge Wells
25811
**King & Barnes Sussex Bitter,
Old Ale, Festive** Ⓗ
Small, friendly pub
♪♣🅿️🍺🍷⇌

Etchingham 10D6

10–2.30; 6–10.30 (11 F, S and summer)
De Etchingham
Arms
(A265) ☎ 292
**Draught Bass
Harvey XX, BB
King & Barnes Sussex Bitter
Young Bitter, Special Bitter** Ⓗ
Friendly pub, good location
♪♣🅿️🍺🅲🍺🍷Ⓢ⇌

Falmer 10B7

10–2.30; 6–10.30 (11 F, S and summer)
Swan
Middle Street (A27/B2123)
**Fuller London Pride
Harvey BB
King & Barnes Festive
Morland Best Bitter
Young Special Bitter** Ⓗ
Variable range, including mild
and old ♣🅿️🍷⇌

Fletching 10B7

10–2.30; 6–10.30 (11 F, S and summer)

Griffin Inn
(off A272) ☎ Newick 2890
Morning opening: 11
**Beard BB
Charrington IPA
Hall & Woodhouse
Badger Best Bitter
King & Barnes Sussex Bitter** Ⓗ
Oak-panelled village pub
with popular restaurant
🏠♪🎵♣🍺🅿️🅰️🍺🅲🍷🍺Ⓢ🅰️

Forest Row 10B6

11–2.30; 6–10.30 (11 F, S)
Foresters Arms
Hartfield Road (B2110, off
A22) ☎ 2792
Fremlins Bitter, Tusker Ⓗ
Lively and friendly village pub
🏠♪♣🅿️🅲Ⓢ

Golden Cross 10C7

10–2.30; 6–10.30 (11 F, S and summer)
Golden Cross Inn
(A22) OS 536125 ☎ 216
Harvey XX, BB, XXXX Ⓗ
Roadside pub ♪♣🅿️🍺🅲🍷🍺Ⓢ

Hadlow Down 10C7

10–2.30; 6–10.30 (11 F, S and summer)
New Inn
(A272)
**Fremlins Tusker
Harvey XX, XXXX** Ⓖ
Unusual if not unique ♣🍷

Hailsham 10C7

10–2.30; 6–10.30 (11 F, S and summer)
Kings Head
South Road (A295) ☎ 842487
Harvey XX, BB, XXXX Ⓗ
Old inn on town outskirts,
toad-in-the-hole played
♪♣🅿️🍺🅲🍷🍺Ⓢ

Hastings & St.
Leonards 10E7

10–2.30; 6–10.30 (11 F, S and summer)
Churchill Hotel
3 St. Helen's Crescent,
Hastings ☎ 439359
**Harvey BB
Martlet Brighton Special
Bitter** Ⓗ
Pleasant hotel bar in
Blacklands conservation area,
near Alexandra Park ♪🏠🅿️🍺⇌

Duke
Duke Road, Hastings (off A21)
Ind Coope Bitter, Burton Ale Ⓗ
Backstreet local in Silverhill
area ♪♣🔄

French's
Robertson Street, Hastings
(Off A259)
**Fremlins Bitter
Harvey BB, XXXX** Ⓗ
Oak-panelled Victorian wine
house 🏠Ⓕ🅱️🍺🅲🍷Ⓢ⇌

Lord Nelson
The Bourne, Old Town,
Hastings (A259)

**Courage Best Bitter,
Directors** Ⓗ
Lively and different – not a
tourist pub ♪♣🅿️Ⓡ🍷Ⓢ

Mr Cherry's
42/43 Marina Street, St.
Leonards (A259) ☎ 422705
**Courage Directors
Martlet Brighton Special Bitter
Ruddle County** Ⓗ
Lively free house with
enthusiastic landlord; jazz
Tuesdays, folk Sundays
♪♣🅱️🅿️Ⓡ🍺🍷Ⓢ🍷

Prince Albert
28 Cornwallis Street, Hastings
(off A259)
**Shepherd Neame Mild,
Bitter** Ⓗ **Stock Ale** Ⓖ
Street-corner pub near town
centre ♪♣🍷⇌

Queen Adelaide
20 West Street, Old Town,
Hastings (off A259)
Fremlins Bitter Ⓗ
Cosy little locals' pub ♣🍷

Hooe 10D7

10–2.30; 6–10.30 (11 F, S and summer)
Red Lion
☎ Ninfield 892371
**Charrington IPA
Draught Bass** Ⓗ
Comfortable village pub
♣🅿️🍺🅲🍷🍺Ⓢ

Hove 10A8

10–2.30; 6–11
Star of Brunswick
32 Brunswick Street West
☎ 771355
**Whitbread Strong Country
Bitter, Pompey Royal** Ⓗ
Friendly corner local with
quiet saloon and separate
poolroom ♪♣Ⓡ🅲🍷Ⓢ

Isfield 10C7

10–2.30; 6–10.30 (11 F, S and summer)
Halfway House
Rose Hill (A26) ☎ 382
Harvey XX, PA, BB, XXXX Ⓗ
Bulmer Cider Ⓖ
17th-century roadside inn
🏠♪🎵♣🅱️🅿️🅰️🍺🅲🍺Ⓢ🅰️🅰️

John's Cross 10D7

10–2.30; 6–10.30 (11 F, S and summer)
John's Cross Inn
(A21)
Fremlins Bitter, Tusker Ⓗ
Interesting roadside inn
♪♣🅿️🍺Ⓡ🍺Ⓢ

Lewes 10B7

10–2.30; 6–10.30 (11 F, S and summer)
Lansdown Arms
36 Lansdown Place ☎ 2807
**Whitbread Strong Country
Bitter, Pompey Royal** Ⓗ
Welcoming old single-bar pub
♪♣🅲Ⓢ⇌

Lewes Arms
Mount Place
Beard PA, XX, BB, XXXX [H]
Small, friendly 17th-century local 🔥♣℘🍷⇌

All Harvey/Beard pubs in Lewes sell real ale

Mayfield 10C6

10–2.30; 6–10.30 11 F, S and summer)
Carpenters Arms
Fletching Street (off A267)
King & Barnes Sussex Mild, Sussex Bitter, Old Ale, Festive [H]
Friendly, comfortable pub
🔥♣℘[R]◗(Thu–Sat) [S]⛺

Milton Street 10C8

10–2.30; 6–10.30 (11 F, S summer)
Sussex Ox
(Off A27) ☎ Alfriston 870840
Harvey BB, XXXX [H]
Splendid country pub with brick-tiled bar floor
🔥♪♣⊞℘🚗◷◗[S]⛺

Newhaven 10B8

10–2.30; 6–10.30 (11 F, S and summer)
Jolly Boatman
Lewes Road (off A259)
☎ 514457
Harvey XX, BB, XXXX [H]
Excellent, convivial street-corner local
🏠♪♣⊞[R]◷◗[S]⇌

Newick 10B7

10–2.30; 6–10.30 (11 F, S and summer)
Royal Oak
Church Road (off A272)
☎ 2506
Whitbread Flowers Original Bitter, Strong Country Bitter, Pompey Royal [H]
Traditional village pub
🏠♣℘🚗[R]◷🍷[S]

Ninfield 10D7

10–2.30; 6–10.30 (11 F, S and summer)
United Friends
(A271)
Courage Directors
Ind Coope Bitter, Burton Ale [H]
Sing-songs and play-arounds on Sunday nights 🔥♣℘🚗[S]

Pett 11E7

10–2.30; 6–10.30 (11 F, S and summer)
Royal Oak
(Off A259)
Fremlins Bitter
Young Special Bitter [H]
Classic village local ℘🚗🍷

Pevensey 10D8

10–2.30; 6–10.30 (11 F, S and summer)
Royal Oak & Castle
High Street (A27) ☎ 762374
Courage Best Bitter, Directors [H]
Next to Pevensey Castle and car park ♪♣℘◷[S]⇌

Smugglers
High Street ☎ 762112
Tamplins Bitter [H]
Old, low-ceilinged pub
♪♣⊞℘🚗[R]◷◗(not Thu) [S]⇌

Plumpton Green 10B7

10–2.30; 6–10.30 (11 in summer)
Fountain
Station Road ☎ 890294
Young Bitter, Special Bitter [H]
Cosmopolitan pub of character, only Young's tied house in Sussex
🏠♪♣℘🚗◷[S]⇌

Rottingdean 10B8

10.30–2.30; 5.30–11
Queen Victoria
54/56 High Street (B2123)
☎ 32121
Whitbread Flowers Original Bitter, Strong Country Bitter, Pompey Royal [H]
Where the locals drink
🔥♪♣◷◗🍷[S]

All pubs in Rottingdean serve real ale

Rye 11F7

10–2.30; 6–10.30 (11 F, S and summer)
Standard
The Mint (off A259) ☎ 3393
Fremlins Bitter
Young Special Bitter [H]
Old pub in historic town; guest beers 🔥♪♣[R]◷◗[S]⇌

Ypres Castle
Gun Garden (off A259)
Fremlins Bitter [H]
Excellent pub tucked away behind castle ♪♣⊞℘🍷[S]⇌

Seaford 10C8

10–2.30; 6–10.30 (11 F, S and summer)
Cinque Ports
49 High Street (off A259)
Charrington IPA
Draught Bass [H]
Traditional pub with comfortable saloon and unspoilt public bar 🏠♪♣℘🍷[S]⇌

Staplecross 10E7

10–2.30; 6–10.30 (11 F, S and summer)
Cross Inn
(B2165)
Charrington IPA
Young Special Bitter [H]
Low-beamed village pub
♣℘🚗🍷[S]

Telham 10E7

10–2.30; 6–10.30 (11 F, S and summer)
Black Horse
Hastings Road (A2100)
☎ Battle 3109
Fremlins Bitter, Tusker [G] & [H]
Friendly, good value pub in pleasant situation
♣℘🚗◷◗[S]⛺

Three Cups 10D7

10–2.30; 6–10.30 (11 F, S and summer)
Three Cups Inn
(B2096) ☎ Rushlake Green 252
Courage Directors [G]
Fine, unspoilt pub ♪℘🚗◷◗[S]

Ticehurst 10D6

10–2.30; 6–10.30 (11 F, S and summer)
Duke of York
The Square (B2099)
☎ 200229
Martlet Brighton Special Bitter
Ridley Bitter
Shepherd Neame Bitter [H]
Biddenden Cider [G]
Lively village local
🔥♪♣℘🚗◷◗🍷[S]

Uckfield 10C7

10–2.30; 6–10.30 (11 F, S and summer)
Alma Arms
Framfield Road (B2102)
☎ 2232
Harvey XX, PA, BB, XXXX [H]
Excellent, traditional local
♣℘🚗[R]◷(not Tue, Sat, Sun) 🍷[S]♿

Udimore 11E7

10–2.30; 6–10.30 (11 F, S and summer)
Kings Head
(B2089)
Ridley Bitter
Young Special Bitter [H]
Fine old country pub with excellent views
♣⊞℘🚗▣◷◗[S]

Wadhurst 10D6

10–2.30; 6–10.30 (11 F, S and summer)
Four Keys
Station Road (B2099) ☎ 2252
Four Keys 4K Bitter, Stallion
Ind Coope Bitter [H]
Friendly local with restaurant, home brew excellent value
♪♣🚗▣◷◗[S]⇌

Greyhound
High Street (B2099) ☎ 3224
Charrington IPA
Draught Bass [H]
One-bar village pub
🏠🔥♪♣⊞℘🚗[R]◷◗[S]

Wartling 10D7

10–2.30; 6–10.30 (11 F, S and summer)
Lamb
☎ Herstmonceux 2116
Courage Directors
King & Barnes Sussex Bitter
Ruddle County
Young Special Bitter [H]
Popular country inn
♣℘◷◗🍷[S]

Withyham 10C6

10.30–2.30; 6.30–10.30 (11 F, S and summer)
Dorset Arms
(B2110) ☎ Hartfield 278
Harvey BB, XXXX [H]
Fine old house in attractive setting ♣℘🚗[R]◷◗🍷[S]♿

Arundel 7H6

10.30–2.30; 6–10.30 (11 F, S and summer)
Swan Hotel
High Street (off A27)
✆ 882143
Hall & Woodhouse Badger
Best Bitter
King & Barnes Sussex Bitter
Young Special Bitter Ⓗ
Popular hotel near river; good
food ♫🗂️Ⓡ🕒🌳&♿

Ashurst 7J6

10–2.30; 6–11
Fountain
(B2135)
Whitbread Strong Country
Bitter, Pompey Royal Ⓗ
Unspoilt 15th-century inn
🏨♣🅿🚗Ⓢ

Bepton 7G6

10.30–2.30; 6–10.30 (11 F, S and summer)
Shamrock
(off A286)
Gale Light Mild, BBB, HSB Ⓗ
XXXXX Ⓖ
Easily missed, but should not
be 🏨♣🅿🚗Ⓢ

Binsted 7G6

10.30–2.30; 6–10.30 (11 F, S and summer)
Black Horse
Binsted Lane (off A27)
Gale Light Mild, BBB, HSB Ⓖ
Popular village pub with fine
views ♫♣🅿🚗Ⓒ🕒Ⓢ&

Bognor Regis 7G7

10.30–2.30; 6–10.30 (11 F, S and summer)
Royal Oak
336 Chichester Road (A259)
Friary Meux Bitter
Ind Coope Burton Ale Ⓗ
Busy roadside pub on outskirts
of Bognor ♫♣🏨🕒🌳Ⓢ

Terminus
26 Station Road ✆ 86574
Ind Coope Bitter, Burton Ale Ⓗ
Town centre pub with
oak-panelled saloon
♫♣🗂️Ⓡ🌳Ⓢ♿

Bucks Green 7H5

10.30–2.30; 6–11
Queens Head
(A281) ✆ Rudgwick 2202
Courage Directors
Hall & Woodhouse Hector's
Bitter, Badger Best Bitter
King & Barnes Sussex Bitter
Young Special Bitter Ⓗ
Comfortable pub with good
bar food; guest beers
🏨🗂️🚗Ⓡ🕒🌳Ⓢ

Burgess Hill 10B7

10.30–2.30; 6–11
Kings Head
London Road (A273)
Watney Fined Stag Bitter
Webster Yorkshire Bitter Ⓗ

Friendly roadside hostelry
♫♣🏨🕒Ⓢ

Burpham 7H6

10.30–2.30; 6–10.30 (11 F, S and summer)
George & Dragon
(Off A27) OS 038088
Charrington IPA
Draught Bass Ⓗ
In small village, good base for
walks 🏨♫♣🗂️🚗🏨🕒🌳Ⓢ&▲

Chichester 7G7

10.30–2.30; 6–10.30 (11 F, S and summer)
Bell Inn
3 Broyle Road (A286)
Morning opening: 11
Whitbread Flowers Original
Bitter, Strong Country Bitter Ⓗ
Lounge-bar local opposite
Festival theatre ♫🚗Ⓢ

New Inn
35 Whyke Road (B2145)
Gale BBB, HSB Ⓔ
Comfortable one-bar pub, folk
music Fridays ♫♫🚗🏨Ⓢ&▲

Wickham Arms
Bognor Road (A286)
Gale BBB, HSB Ⓗ
Good basic town local
🏨♫♣🚗🏨🌳Ⓢ▲

Cocking 7G6

10.30–2.30; 6–10.30 (11 F, S)
Greyhound
Cocking Causeway (A286)
Gale BB, HSB Ⓗ XXXXX Ⓖ
Air-conditioned cellar
🏨♫♣🗂️🚗🏨Ⓡ🕒🌳Ⓢ

Copthorne 10B6

11–2.30; 7–10.30 (11 F, S)
Hunters Moon
Copthorne Bank (off A264)
OS 322399 ✆ 713309
Everard Old Original
Hall & Woodhouse Hector's
Bitter, Tanglefoot
Wadworth IPA, 6X
Young Special Bitter Ⓗ
Trendy free house with disco
♫🏨🕒Ⓢ

Crawley 10A6

10.30–2.30; 6–10.30 (11 F, S)
Inn in the Park
Tilgate Park OS 276345
Gale BBB, HSB
Webster Yorkshire Bitter Ⓗ
Large, comfortably furnished
lakeside pub ♫🚗Ⓒ🕒Ⓢ

Maid of Sussex
Gales Drive, Three Bridges
Courage Best Bitter,
Directors Ⓗ
Large new town pub, good
food Ⓡ🕒🌳

Royal Oak
Ifield Green, Ifield OS 251379
Charrington IPA
Draught Bass Ⓗ

Friendly, popular local of
great charm ♣🚗🏨Ⓡ🕒🌳🕒Ⓢ

Dragons Green 7H5

10.30–2.30; 6–10.30 (11 F, S)
George & Dragon
Near Shipley ✆ Coulham 320
King & Barnes Sussex Mild,
Sussex Bitter, Old Ale, Festive Ⓗ
Old-world, friendly pub with
good food 🏨♫♣🗂️🚗🏨🕒🌳Ⓢ&

Eastergate 7G7

10.30–2.30; 6–10.30 (11 F, S and summer)
Wilkes Head
Church Lane (off A29) ✆ 3380
Friary Meux Bitter
Ind Coope Burton Ale Ⓗ
Historic village pub, excellent
food 🏨♣🚗🏨🕒🌳Ⓢ

East Grinstead 10B6

10.30–2.30; 6–11
Dunnings Mill
Dunnings Road (A264)
Harvey BB
Shepherd Neame Bitter
Young Special Bitter Ⓗ
Former 15th-century mill
with underground bar ♣🚗🏨Ⓢ

Elsted 7F6

10.30–2.30; 6–10.30 (11 F, S)
Three Horseshoes
OS 818196 ✆ Harting 746
Ballard Best Bitter
Devenish Wessex Best Bitter
Fuller London Pride
Bulmer Cider Ⓖ
Couldn't be more rural
🏨♣🚗🏨🕒🌳Ⓢ

Findon 7H6

11–2.30; 6–11
Village House Hotel
The Square (off A24) ✆ 3350
Fuller London Pride
Hall & Woodhouse Badger
Best Bitter, Tanglefoot
King & Barnes Sussex Mild
(summer), Sussex Bitter, Old
Ale, Festive
Bulmer Cider Ⓗ
Busy local in village with
horseracing connections
🏨♫♣🚗🏨Ⓡ🕒🌳Ⓢ▲

Ford 7H7

10.30–2.30; 6–10.30 (11 F, S and summer)
Ship & Anchor
Ford Marina (off A27)
Gale HSB
King & Barnes Sussex Bitter
Young Special Bitter Ⓗ
Old pub by River Arun with
campsite and marina
♫♣🗂️🕒🌳Ⓢ&▲♿

Graffham 7G6

10.30–2.30; 6–10.30 (11 F, S and summer)
Foresters Arms
(Off A285) ✆ 202
Courage Directors
Hall & Woodhouse

adger Best Bitter
Whitbread Strong Country
tter, Pompey Royal Ⓗ
5th-century oak-beamed inn
♪⚑☷♫🏠Ⓡ🅖🕘①⑤♿Å

Haywards Heath
10B7

30–2.30; 6–11

Liverpool Arms Hotel
air Road ✆ 413710
riary Meux Bitter
d Coope Burton Ale Ⓗ
mall, friendly local ♪♣Ⓡ①≷

tar Hotel
he Broadway (A272)
Whitbread Strong Country
tter, Pompey Royal Ⓗ
easant town pub ♨♣🏠①⑤

Hermitage
7F6

–2.30; 6–10.30 (11 F, S and summer)

ussex Brewery
6 Main Road (A27)
all & Woodhouse Badger
est Bitter
ermitage Bitter, 3X, Best
tter, Lumley Old Ale
arston Pedigree
orland Mild Ⓗ
ulmer Cider Ⓖ
mall, unspoilt and popular
cal with own brewery
♪♣☷♫🏠Ⓡ⑤

orsham
7J5

30–2.30; 6–10.30 (11 F, S)

oars Head Tavern
orthing Road (A224)
raught Bass
ing & Barnes Sussex Bitter Ⓗ
d Ale Ⓖ
itchells & Butlers Springfield
tter
adworth 6X Ⓗ Old Timer Ⓖ
Whitbread Pompey Royal Ⓗ
aunton Cider Ⓐ
easant pub on outskirts of
wn ♪♣🅖🏠①⑤

oot
erryfield Drive (off A281)
harrington IPA Ⓗ
riendly, busy pub on
utskirts of town, good food
♣🅖🏠①⑤

og & Bacon
orth Parade (off A24)
ing & Barnes Sussex Bitter,
d Ale, Festive Ⓗ
usy, comfortable pub; good
od ♨♣🅖♫🏠Ⓡ🕘①⑤≷

reen Dragon
2 The Bishopric (A281)
ing & Barnes Sussex Bitter,
d Ale, Festive Ⓗ
vely town pub near the
ewery ♨♣🅖🏠①⑤

orsted Keynes
10B6

–2.30; 6–11

reen Man
ff B2028) OS 384282

Harvey BB, XXXX Ⓗ
Bluebell railway connections
♣🅖🏠①⑤

Hurstpierpoint
10A7

10.30–2.30; 6–11

Poacher
High Street (B2116)
Gale BBB, HSB
Usher Best Bitter
Webster Yorkshire Bitter
Bulmer Cider Ⓗ
Small high street local, food
every lunchtime ♪♣🅖①⑤

Lagness
7G7

10.30–2.30; 6–10.30 (11 F, S and summer)

Royal Oak
Pagham Road (B2166)
Gale BBB, HSB, Dark Mild,
XXXXX Ⓗ
Large country pub
♨Ⓡ♪♣☷♫🏠🕘①⑤Å

Lindfield
10B6

10.30–2.30; 6–11

Linden Tree
High Street ✆ 2995
Everard Tiger
Fuller London Pride
Gale HSB
Ruddle County
Samuel Smith Old Brewery
Bitter
Young Special Bitter Ⓗ
Smart free house ♨🅖🕘①⑤

Littlehampton
7H7

10.30–2.30; 6–10.30 (11 F, S and summer)

Arun View Inn
Wharf Road ✆ 22335
Whitbread Strong Country
Bitter, Pompey Royal Ⓗ
Popular pub on River Arun
♪♪🅖🏠Ⓡ🕘①⑤≷♿

Lower Beeding
7J5

11–2.30; 6–10.30 (11 F, S)

Crabtree
Brighton Road (A281)
King & Barnes Sussex Mild,
Sussex Bitter, Festive,
Old Ale Ⓗ
Pleasant pub with attractive
garden, good food
♨♣🅖🏠Ⓡ🕘 (Mon–Sat) 🕘
(Wed–Sun) ①⑤

Loxwood
7H5

10.30–2.30; 6–10.30 (11 F, S)

Sir Roger
Tichbourne
Billingshurst Road, Alfold
Bars (B2133)
King & Barnes Sussex Mild,
Sussex Bitter, Old Ale,
Festive Ⓗ
Fine, friendly old-world village
local ♨♣🅖🏠🕘①⑤Å

Midhurst
7G5

10.30–2.30; 6–10.30 (11 F, S and summer)

Half Moon
Petersfield Road (A272)

Friary Meux Bitter
Ind Coope Burton Ale Ⓗ
Popular pub, good food
♨Ⓡ♪♣🅖🏠🕘①⑤

Nuthurst
7J5

10.30–2.30; 6–10.30 (11 F, S)

Black Horse
(Off A281)
Fuller London Pride
Hall & Woodhouse
Badger Best Bitter
King & Barnes Sussex Bitter
Marston Pedigree
Whitbread Pompey Royal
Bulmer Cider Ⓗ
Picturesque country free
house; guest beers
♣☷🅖Ⓡ🕘①⑤≷

Oving
7G7

10.30–2.30; 6–10.30 (11 F, S and summer)

Gribble Inn
(Off A259)
Morning opening: 11
Beard XX
Hall & Woodhouse
Badger Best Bitter
Hermitage Gribble Ale
King & Barnes Sussex Bitter
Ringwood Old Thumper Ⓗ
Picturesque 16th-century
thatched village local; guest
beers ♨♣☷🅖🏠Ⓡ🕘①⑤♿Å

Pagham
7G7

10.30–2.30; 6–10.30 (11 F, S and summer)

Lamb
144 Pagham Road
✆ Nyetimber 2168
Friary Meux Bitter
Ind Coope Burton Ale Ⓗ
Large, traditional pub
♨♪♣☷🅖🏠🕘①⑤♿

Pease Pottage
10A6

10.30–2.30; 6–10.30 (11 F, S)

Grapes
(Off A23/M23) OS 259329
King & Barnes Sussex Bitter,
Old Ale, Festive Ⓗ
Good village pub with
excellent food
♪♣🅖🕘①⑤

Petworth
7G5

10.30–2.30; 6–10.30 (11 F, S)

Angel Hotel
Angel Street (A283)
✆ 42153
Morning opening: 11
Courage Best Bitter
Whitbread Pompey Royal Ⓗ
13th-century beamed inn
♨Ⓡ♪♣☷🅖🏠Ⓡ🕘⑤

Plaistow
7H5

10.30–2.30; 6–10.30 (11 F, S and summer)

Bush
Rickmans Lane ✆ 246
King & Barnes Sussex Mild,
Sussex Bitter, Festive Ⓗ
Comfortable, friendly pub,
good food ♨Ⓡ♪♣☷🅖🏠Ⓡ🕘⑤

Pulborough   7H6

10.30–2.30; 6–10.30 (11 F, S)
Five Bells
London Road (A29) ☎ 2288
Courage Directors
Eldridge Pope Royal Oak
Gale HSB
Hall & Woodhouse
Badger Best Bitter
King & Barnes Sussex Mild,
Sussex Bitter, Festive
Old Chidham Bitter Ⓗ
Excellent 600-year-old free
house
🏚🍴♣🍽♿🅿Ⓡ🕒🎵

Pyecombe   10A7

10.30–2.30; 6–11
Plough
London Road (A23)
Fuller London Pride, ESB
Hall & Woodhouse Badger
Best Bitter
Sussex County Ale
Young Bitter, Special Bitter Ⓗ
Former coaching inn; guest
beers 🏚🍴♣🍽♿🅿Ⓡ🕒🎵Ⓢ

Rake   7F5

10–2.30; 6–10.30 (11 F, S)
Sun Inn
(A3) ☎ Liss 2115
Gale BBB, HSB, XXXXX Ⓗ
Old pub, well worth a visit
🍴♣🍽♿🅿Ⓡ🕒🎵🍖Ⓢ♿

Rogate   7F5

10.30–2.30; 6–10.30 (11 F, S)
Wyndham Arms
North Street (A272) ☎ 315
Friary Meux Bitter
Ind Coope Burton Ale Ⓗ
Small local with a sense of
humour
🏚🍴♣🍽🅿🕒🎵🍖Ⓢ

Rowhook   7H5

10.30–2.30; 6–11
Chequers Inn
(Off A29) ☎ Slinfold 790480
Whitbread Strong Country
Bitter, Pompey Royal Ⓗ
Bulmer Cider Ⓗ
Attractive 15th-century inn,
good bar food
🍴♣🍽🅿Ⓡ🕒🎵🍖

Rusper   7J4

10.30–2.30; 6.30–10.30 (11 F, S)
Star
Whitbread Strong Country
Bitter, Pompey Royal Ⓗ
Busy village pub with many
bars 🍴♣🍽🅿Ⓡ🕒Ⓢ

Selsey   7G7

10–2.30; 6–10.30 (11 F, S and summer)
Neptune
High Street (B2145)
☎ 602084
Ind Coope Bitter, Burton Ale Ⓗ
Popular pub in holiday village
🍴♣🍽🅿Ⓡ🕒🎵🍖Ⓢ♿🅰

Sharpthorne   10B6

10.30–2.30; 6–11
Bluebell
Station Road ☎ 810264
Courage Directors
Everard Old Original
Fuller ESB
Shepherd Neame Bitter
Young Special Bitter Ⓗ
Popular local, worth finding
🏚🍴♣🍽♿🅿Ⓡ🕒🎵Ⓢ♿🅰

Shoreham-by-Sea   10A8

10–2.30; 6–11
Bridge Hotel
87 High Street (A259)
Gale Dark Mild, BBB, HSB Ⓗ
XXXXX Ⓖ
Pleasant, well-run riverside
pub 🍴🍴♣🍽♿🕒🎵🍖♿🅰≈

Crab Tree
6 Buckingham Road ☎ 63508
Gale BBB, HSB, XXXXX Ⓗ
Comfortable family pub in
residential area
🍴♣🍽🅿♿🕒🎵🍖♿≈

Steyning   7J6

10–2.30; 6–11
White Horse
23 High Street
Whitbread Strong Country
Bitter, Pompey Royal Ⓗ
16th-century village inn
🍴♣🅿Ⓢ🅰

Stoughton   7F6

10.30–2.30; 6–10.30 (11 F, S and summer)
Hare & Hounds
(Off B2146) ☎ Compton 433
Gale Light Mild, BBB, HSB,
XXXXX Ⓗ
Remote Downland pub
🍴🍽🅿Ⓡ🕒🎵🍖Ⓢ

Sutton   7G6

10.30–2.30; 6–10.30 (11 F, S)
White Horse
(Off A29) OS 152978
Gale HSB
King & Barnes Sussex Bitter,
Festive, Old Ale Ⓗ
Delightful pub near Bignor
Roman villa 🍴♣🍽🅿Ⓢ♿

The Haven   7H5

10.30–2.30; 6–10.30 (11 F, S)
Blue Ship
(Off A281/A29)
King & Barnes Sussex Bitter,
Festive, Old Ale Ⓖ
Timeless retreat in remote
country setting 🏚♣🍽🅿🍴

Turners Hill   10B6

10.30–2.30; 6–11
Red Lion
Lion Lane (off B2028)
Morning opening: 11
Harvey BB, XXXX
Bulmer Cider Ⓗ

Good, friendly, popular local
🏚♣🍽♿Ⓢ

Walderton   7F

10.30–2.30; 6–10.30 (11 F, S and summer)
Barley Mow
(Off B2146) near Chichester
Friary Meux Bitter
Ind Coope Burton Ale Ⓗ
Fine village pub with skittle
alley 🏚🍴♣🍽♿🅿Ⓡ🕒🎵Ⓢ♿

Warnham   7J

10.30–2.30; 6–10.30 (11 F, S)
Sussex Oak
Church Road (B2199)
Whitbread Strong Country
Bitter Ⓗ
Busy, friendly pub in village
high street 🏚♣🍽🅿Ⓡ🕒♿≈

West Ashling   7F

10.30–2.30; 6–10.30 (11 F, S and summer)
Richmond Arms
Mill Lane (off B2146)
Alexandra Ashling Pale
Ballard Best Bitter, Wassail
Beard XX, PA
King & Barnes Sussex Mild,
Sussex Bitter
Taylor Landlord Ⓗ
Justly popular pub; guest
beers and cider 🍴♣🍽🅿Ⓡ🅿♿

Westergate   7G

10.30–2.30; 6–10.30 (11 F, S and summer)
Labour in Vain
Westergate Street (A29)
Ballard Best Bitter Ⓗ Wassail
Beard BB
Young Bitter, Special Bitter Ⓗ
Village local with good-value
food 🏚♣🍽🅿Ⓡ🕒🎵Ⓢ♿🅰

Wineham   10A

10.30–2.30; 6–10.30 (11 F, S)
Royal Oak
OS 236306
Whitbread Pompey Royal Ⓖ
Old country pub 🏚♣🍽🅿Ⓢ🅰

Worthing   7

10–2.30; 6–10.30 (11 F, S and summer)
Cobden Arms
2 Cobden Road
Whitbread Strong Country
Bitter, Pompey Royal Ⓗ
Excellent town local 🍴🍽Ⓢ≈

Warwick Arms
25 Warwick Street (off A259
Whitbread Strong Country
Bitter, Pompey Royal Ⓗ
Popular town-centre,
single-bar pub 🍴🍴♣🕒Ⓢ

Yapton   7G

10.30–2.30; 6–10.30 (11 F, S and summer)
Maypole Inn
Maypole Lane (off B2132)
Whitbread Strong Country
Bitter, Pompey Royal Ⓗ
Comfortable village pub,
worth finding 🏚🍴♣🍽🅿🕒Ⓢ♿

General opening hours: 11–3; 6–10.30

Birtley 33H9

Three Tuns
Durham Road (A6127)
Samuel Smith Old Brewery Bitter Ⓗ
Popular pub

Blackhall Mill 33G8

Mill Pub
(A694) OS 120569
Drybrough Pentland, Eighty Ⓗ
Tasteful three-roomed pub with restaurant

Cleadon Village 33H8

Cottage Tavern
Shield Road (A1018)
Vaux Samson Ⓗ
Small, smart pub

Cullercoats 33H8

Piper
Marrington Road, Marden Estate (off A193)
Whitley Bay 522513
Open until 11 pm F, S in summer
Bass Extra Light
Draught Bass
Stones Best Bitter Ⓗ
Modern, comfortable, suburban local with good lunches

Dudley 33H8

Clayton Arms
Dudley Lane 500416
Lorimer Best Scotch
Vaux Samson Ⓗ
Recently extended, much improved pub

Easington Lane 33H9

Free Gardeners Arms
High Street (A182)
Cameron Strongarm Ⓗ
Popular local with wood-panelled bar and pool table

Fawdon 33G8

Fawdon
Fawdon Park Road
Evening opening: 5.30
Tetley Bitter Ⓗ
Post-war estate pub with lively bar and small lounge

Fence Houses 33H9

Station
Morton Crescent (A1052)
Bass Extra Light
Stones Best Bitter Ⓗ
Friendly pub with beer garden

Gateshead 33H8

Five Wand Mill
102 Bensham Road (A692)
Tetley Bitter Ⓗ
Friendly local with keen landlord

Olde Fleece
High Street
Tetley Bitter Ⓗ
Basic bar with pool table and video, smart lounge

Gosforth 33H8

Gosforth Hotel
Salters Road/High Street (A6125)
Newcastle 856617
Evening opening: 5.30
Alloa Arrols 80/-
Tetley Bitter Ⓗ
Popular town pub

Millstone
Haddrick's Mill Road (A189)
Draught Bass
Stones Best Bitter Ⓗ
Popular pub with comfortable lounges

Houghton-le-Spring 33H9

Golden Lion
Broadway 842460
Lorimer Best Scotch
Vaux Samson Ⓗ
Welcoming small local near ancient parish church

Jarrow 33H8

Royal Oak
Grange Road/Staple Street
Samuel Smith Old Brewery Bitter Ⓗ
Town pub near Tyne Tunnel

Western
Western Road
Cameron Strongarm Ⓗ
Town pub with interesting murals

Kibblesworth 33G9

Plough
(Off A1) Birtley 402291
Bass Extra Light Ⓔ
Comfortable pub in former hill-top mining village (not Sun)

Monkseaton 33H8

Beacon
Earsdon Road (A192)
Draught Bass Ⓗ
Large, comfortable and friendly estate pub

Black Horse
Front Street
Whitley Bay 521867
Draught Bass Ⓗ
Cosy suburban pub with restaurant

Newbottle 33H9

Jolly Potter
(A182) Houghton 842587
Whitbread Castle Eden Ale Ⓗ
Pleasant village local

Newcastle upon Tyne: Byker 33H8

Cumberland Arms
Byker Buildings (off A193)
Big Lamp Bitter
Cameron Strongarm Ⓗ
Draught Bass
Marston Pedigree Ⓖ
Whitbread Castle Eden Ale
Bulmer Cider Ⓗ
Popular drinkers' pub; regular guest beers

Glendale
Potts Street (off A193)
Bass Extra Light
Draught Bass
Stones Best Bitter Ⓗ
Friendly and popular pub of character

Ship Inn
Stepney Bank (off A193)
Whitbread Castle Eden Ale Ⓗ
Tiny welcoming local tucked away under Byker Bridge

Newcastle upon Tyne: City Centre 33G8

42nd Street
Hood Street
Evening opening: 5.30
McEwan 70/-, 80/-
Younger No. 3 Ⓗ
Comfortable, flashy bar with good meals; beers available on rota

Bacchus
High Bridge
Evening opening: 5.30; closed Sunday lunchtimes
Samuel Smith Old Brewery Bitter
Younger No. 3 Ⓗ
Spacious, central pub, recently refurbished; guest beers

Bridge Hotel
Castle Square
Samuel Smith Old Brewery Bitter
Younger No. 3 Ⓗ

Superb building next to castle; guest beers in bar
🏛⌐♪♣✿[R]◷🍷Ⓢ🚆

Broken Doll
Blenheim Street
Matthew Brown Bitter, John Peel Bitter
McEwan 80/-
Younger No. 3 [H]
Refurbished pub near College of Art & Technology ⌐♪♣🍷Ⓢ🚆

Cooperage
The Close, Quayside
Big Lamp Bitter
Drybrough Pentland
Jennings Bitter [H]
Former cooperage in ancient part of city; guest beers
♪♣◷☛🍷Ⓢ🚆

Darn Crook
Stowell Street
Belhaven 60/-, 80/-
Drybrough Pentland, Eighty
Bulmer Cider [H]
Architecturally superb one-room bar, near coach station ⌐♪♣🍷Ⓢ🚆

Forth Hotel
Pink Lane
Tetley Bitter [H]
Cosy central pub near Central station ♪♣🍷Ⓢ🚆

Groat Bar
Groat Market
Evening opening: 5.30
Younger Scotch Bitter, No. 3, IPA [A]
Renovated town-centre bar with Scottish-style tall fonts, very popular 🏛♪[R]◷Ⓢ

Three Bulls Heads
Percy Street
Draught Bass [H]
Busy, city-centre pub, popular with students ♪♣🍷Ⓢ🚆

Newcastle upon Tyne: Shieldfield 33G8

Globe
Barker Street
Draught Bass [H]
Busy local, popular with students ♪♣🚗🍷Ⓢ

North Hylton 33H9

Shipwrights Arms
Ferry Boat Lane OS 350570
☎ Sunderland 495139
Vaux Samson [H]
Extensively refurbished pub on banks of the Wear
🏛♪♣⊞✿🚗[R]◷☛Ⓢ♿

North Shields 33H8

Wooden Doll
Hudson Street
Evening opening: 5.30; closes 11 pm in summer
McEwan 80/-
Younger No 3 [H]
Superb local above fish quay, excellent views out to sea
♪♣[R]🍷

Penshaw 33H9

Bird in Hand
Station Road
Bass Extra Light [E]
Popular local
♪♣🚗[R]🍷Ⓢ

Grey Horse
☎ Houghton-le-Spring 844882
Tetley Bitter [H]
Friendly, popular local near Penshaw monument
♪♣✿🚗[R]◷☛🍷Ⓢ

Ryhope 33J9

Mainspring
Ryhope Street South (B1286)
Matthew Brown Bitter, John Peel Bitter [H]
Old mainstreet local with busy, smokey atmosphere and pianola
🏛⌐♪♣[R]🍷Ⓢ

South Shields 33H8

Adam & Eve
Laygate
Samuel Smith Old Brewery Bitter [H]
Plain, friendly Victorian local
♪♣🍷

Smugglers
East Street ☎ 552876
Younger No. 3 [H]
Popular town pub with enthusiastic landlord
⌐♪♣⊞[R]◷🍷Ⓢ

Stags Head
Fowler Street (A1018)
Draught Bass [H]
Small, busy town-centre pub
♪♣🍷

Sunderland: Central 33J9

Rosedene
Queen Alexandra Road
Vaux Samson [H]
Large, luxurious pub in posh end of town
🏛♪♣✿🚗[R]◷🍷Ⓢ

Sunderland: Deptford 33H9

Saltgrass
36 Ayres Quay ☎ 657229
Closed Saturday lunchtimes
Lorimer Best Scotch
Vaux Samson [H]
Lively pub with friendly atmosphere, dwarfed by shipyards
🏛♪♣⊞✿[R]◷☛🍷Ⓢ

Sunderland: Hendon 33J

Salem Hotel
Nelson Street
Cameron Lion Bitter, Strongarm [H]
Modernised local in development area
♪♣[R]🍷Ⓢ

Sunderland: Seaburn 33J

Seaburn Hotel
Queens Parade
☎ Whitburn 292041
Vaux Sunderland Draught Bitter [H]
Large seafront hotel
♪♣⊞✿🚗▣[R]◷☛🍷Ⓢ

Tynemouth 33H

Dolphin
King Edward Road
Tetley Bitter [H]
Comfortable, friendly local
♪♣🚗🍷Ⓢ

Walbottle 33G

Percy Arms
Queens Road ☎ Newcastle 676451
Evening opening: 5.30
McEwan 80/- [H]
Modern pub decorated in traditional style
♪♣⊞✿🚗◷☛🍷Ⓢ♿

Wallsend 33H

Bush
Hadrian Park (off A1058)
OS 318687
Tetley Bitter [H]
New estate pub, tastefully decorated
♪♣🚗🍷Ⓢ

Rosehill Tavern
Churchill Street, Howden (A695)
Alloa Arrols 70/-
Tetley Bitter [H]
Large, friendly pub in tree-lined grounds
♪♣✿🚗◷🍷Ⓢ

Whitburn 33J

Jolly Sailor
East Street (A183)
Bass Extra Light [H]
Friendly local in attractive village ♪♣🍷Ⓢ

Whitley Bay 33H

Victoria
Whitley Road (A193)
Evening opening: 5.30
Tetley Bitter [H]
Magnificent, imposing pub in town centre, very friendly
⌐♪♣🚗[R]◷🍷Ⓢ♿

Alcester 15H3

10.30–2.30; 6–10.30 (11 F, S)
Dog & Partridge
Bleachfield Street (off A422)
Opens at 11 am & 7 pm
**Whitbread Bitter, Flowers
Original Bitter** Ⓗ
Bulmer Cider Ⓖ
Pleasant, backstreet local in
row of listed cottages
♪♣🅰Ⓡ🕓

Alderminster 15J4

10.30–2.30; 6–11
Bell
(A34) ✆ 414
**Davenports Bitter
Mitchells & Butlers Brew XI** Ⓗ
Free house with friendly
atmosphere
🅰♪♣🅿🅰Ⓡ🅒🕓🅢🅰

Ansty 16A4

11–2.30; 6–10.30 (11 F, S)
Sparrow Hall Hotel
Coombefields (off B4029)
✆ Coventry 611817
**Draught Bass
Everard Old Original
Ruddle County** Ⓗ
Modern motel with a fine
restaurant ♪🕓🎲🅰🅱🅒🕓🅢

Aston Cantlow 15H3

10–2.30; 6–10.30 (11 F, S)
Olde Kings Head
(Off B4089) ✆ Great Alne 242
Whitbread Bitter Ⓗ
Charming historic village inn
🅰🅿🅰🅒🕓🅢🅰

Atherstone 23H9

10.30–2.30; 6–10.30 (11 F, S)
Maid of the Mill
83 Coleshill Road
(B4116, off A5)
Davenports Mild, Bitter Ⓗ
Recently improved pub with
friendly bar ♪🕓🎲🅿🅡🕓

Old Swan
175 Long Street (off A5)
Banks Mild, Bitter Ⓔ
Fine old half-timbered pub
♪🕓🎲🅰🅡🕓

Austrey 23H8

11–2.30; 6–10.30 (11 F, S)
Bird in Hand
Main Road
**Marston Pedigree, Owd
Rodger** Ⓗ
500-year-old thatched inn in
unspoilt village
🅰🕓♣🅿🅰🅡🕓🅢🅰

Bedworth 16A3

2–2; 7–10.30 (11 F, S)
Boat
Black Horse Road, Exhall (off
A444)
**Ansells Mild, Bitter
Tetley Walker Bitter** Ⓗ

Unspoilt pub with character
🅰♪🕓🅿🅰Ⓡ🕓

Engine
90 King Street ✆ 314316
**Whitbread Flowers Original
Bitter** Ⓗ
Comfortable, friendly pub,
good food ♪🕓🎲🅰🅒🕓🅢

Railway Tavern
69 King Street
Manns Bitter Ⓗ
Bulmer Cider Ⓖ
Modernised town pub, known
locally as the 'Corner Pin'
♪🕓🅿🅰🕓

Bilton 16B4

11–2.30; 6–10.30 (11 F, S)
Black Horse
Main Street (A4071)
**Ansells Mild, Bitter
Ind Coope Burton Ale** Ⓗ
Large, comfortable lounge,
small basic bar
♪🕓🅰🅒🕓🅢

Bodymoor Heath 15H1

11–2.30; 6–10.30 (11 F, S)
Dog & Doublet
Dog Lane (off A4091)
**Mitchells & Butlers Mild, Brew
XI** Ⓗ
Popular canalside pub with
character ♪🕓🅿🅰🅒🕓🅢

Brinklow 16A4

11–2.30; 6–10.30 (11 F, S)
Raven
(A427) ✆ Rugby 832655
Ansells Mild, Bitter Ⓗ
Pleasant old pub at top of
village 🅰♪🕓🅿🅰🅒🕓

Bubbenhall 16A4

11–2.30; 6–10.30 (11 F, S)
Malt Shovel
✆ Coventry 301141
Ansells Mild, Bitter Ⓗ
Old pub with Italian food
🅰♪🕓🅿🅰🅒🕓 (Mon–Sat)🕓

Bulkington 16A3

10.30–2.30; 7–10.30 (11 F, S)
Old Chequers
12 Chequer Street (off B4029)
**Davenports Bitter
Mitchells & Butlers Mild, Brew
XI
Weston Cider** Ⓗ
Popular 18th century free
house ♪🕓🅿🅰Ⓡ🅢

Curdworth 15H1

10.30–2.30; 6–10.30 (11 F, S)
Beehive
Coleshill Road (off A4097)
✆ 70223
Ansells Mild, Bitter Ⓗ
Popular village pub; bar
extension for diners
♪🕓🕓🅿🅰Ⓡ🕓🅢

Eathorpe 16A4

11–2.30; 7–10.30 (11 F, S)
Plough
(Off A423) ✆ Marton 632557
**Ansells Mild, Bitter
Gibbs Mew Wiltshire Bitter** Ⓗ
Tastefully modernised old
village pub with excellent food
♪🕓🅿🅰🅒🕓🅢

Farnborough 16A6

12–2.30; 6–10.30 (11 F, S)
Butchers Arms
(Off A423) ✆ 615
**Draught Bass
Hook Norton Best Bitter
Litchborough Tudor Ale** Ⓗ
Stone-built village pub
🅰♪🕓🅿🅰🅒🕓🅢

Fillongley 15J1

10.30–2.30; 6–10.30 (11 F, S)
Weavers Arms
Nuneaton Road (B4102)
**Draught Bass
Mitchells & Butlers Mild,
Brew XI** Ⓗ
Basic village local off the
beaten track ♪🕓🅿🅰🕓

Fiveways 15J2

11–2.30; 6.30–10.30 (11 F, S)
Case is Altered
Rowington Road (off A41)
**Ansells Mild, Bitter
Whitbread Flowers Original
Bitter** Ⓗ
Rural pub with unique cask
pumps 🕓🅿🅰🕓

Grandborough 16B5

11–2.30; 6–10.30 (11 F, S)
Shoulder of Mutton
Sawbridge Road
Evening opening: 7
Whitbread Bitter Ⓗ
Unspoilt farmers' pub, families
welcome ♪🕓🎲🅿🅰🅒

Harbury 16A5

11–2.30; 6–10.30 (11 F, S)
Gamecock
Chapel Street ✆ 612374
Manns IPA, Bitter Ⓗ
Fine village pub 🅰🕓🅒🕓🅢

Henley-in-Arden 15H3

10–2.30; 6–11
Black Swan
(A34) ✆ 2350
**Davenports Mild, Bitter
Weston Cider** Ⓗ
Comfortable, attractive, 17th
century pub 🕓🅿🅰🅒🕓🅢

Golden Cross
High Street (A34)
Open all day Wednesdays
**Ansells Mild, Bitter
Ind Coope Burton Ale** Ⓗ
Friendly locals' pub with
interesting pictures of old
Henley 🕓🅿🅰🅱🅒🕓🅢

Hunningham 16A5

11–2.30; 6–10.30 (11 F, S)

Red Lion

Draught Bass
Mitchells & Butlers Brew XI [E]
Friendly country pub next to the river and medieval bridge
♪♣❀🚗🕐🌙 (not Tue)🍷[S]

Hurley 23H9

11–2.30; 6–10.30 (11 F, S)

Anchor Inn

Brick Kiln Lane
Draught Bass
Mitchells & Butlers Mild [H]
Friendly, comfortable old pub
🔥🛏♪♣❀🚗[R]🍷[S]

Kenilworth 15J2

11–2.30; 6–10.30 (11 F, S)

Coventry Cross

New Street (A429)
Ansells Mild, Bitter [H]
Traditional pub with large games room ♪♣❀🚗[R]🍷

Royal Oak

New Street (A429)
Marston Burton Bitter, Pedigree [H]
Bulmer Cider [G]
Comfortable local with folk club and free-and-easy
🛏♪♣❀🍷[S]

Wyandotte

Park Road
Marston Mercian Mild, Burton Bitter, Pedigree [H]
Bulmer Cider [G]
Friendly, backstreet local with bar billiards ♪♣❀🚗🍷

Keresley End 15J2

10–2.30; 6–10.30 (11 F, S)

Golden Eagle

Howats Road ☎ 3066
Banks Mild, Bitter [E]
Estate pub catering for all tastes ♪♣▣🚗🕐🍷[S]

Kingsbury 23G9

10.30–2.30; 6–10.30 (11 F, S)

Royal Oak

Coventry Road (A51)
Opens at 11.30 am & 7 pm
Marston Mercian Mild, Pedigree [H]
Friendly village local
♪♣▣❀🚗[R]🍷[S]⛺

White Swan

Coventry Road (A51)
Opens at 11 am & 7 pm
Draught Bass
Mitchells & Butlers Mild, Springfield Bitter [H]
Cosy, much-improved pub
🔥♪♣🚗[R]🍷[S]

Lapworth 15H2

10.30–2.30; 5.30–10.30 (11 F, S)

Navigation

Old Warwick Road (B4439)
Draught Bass [H]
Mitchells & Butlers Mild, Brew XI [H] & [E]
Delightful canalside pub catering for all tastes
♣❀🚗🍷[S]

Leamington Spa 16A5

10–2.30; 6–10.30 (11 F, S)

Black Horse

Princes Street
Hook Norton Best Bitter [H]
Bulmer Cider [G]
Busy bar with games and quiet lounge ♪♣🍷

Holly Bush

Holly Street
Marston Burton Bitter, Pedigree, Merrie Monk [H]
Modern pub with friendly landlord
♪♣❀🚗🕐🍷

Red House

Radford Road (A425)
Draught Bass
Mitchells & Butlers Mild, Springfield Bitter [H]
Basic pub with many alcoves but one bar ♪♣❀

Somerville Arms

Campion Terrace
Ansells Mild, Bitter
Ind Coope Burton Ale
Tetley Walker Bitter [H]
Friendly, old-fashioned local with the motto 'Per Ardua Disastra' ♪♣❀🍷[S]

Leek Wooton 15J3

11–2.30; 6–10.30 (11 F, S)

Anchor Inn

Draught Bass
Mitchells & Butlers Mild, Brew XI [H]
Modernised village pub with great character
♪♣❀🚗🕐🍷[S]

Little Warton 23H8

10.30–2.30; 6–10.30 (11 F, S)

Fox & Dogs

Orton Road
Marston Mercian Mild, Pedigree [H]
Recently extended village local
🔥♪♣❀🚗🕐🌙🍷[S]⛺

Long Itchington 16A5

11–2.30; 6.30–10.30 (11 F, S)

Green Man

(Off A423) ☎ Southam 2208
Davenports Mild, Bitter [H]
Fine, unspoilt village local
🛏♪♣▣❀🚗[R]🕐🍷

Harvesters

(Off A423) ☎ Southam 2698
Courage Directors
Everard Old Original [H]
Superb food in pleasant free house ♪♣🕐🌙🍷[S]

Marston Jabbett 15J1

11–2.30; 6.30–10.30 (11 F, S)

Corner House

454 Nuneaton Road (B4112)
Marston Burton Bitter, Pedigree, Merrie Monk, Owd Rodger [H]
Large friendly hotel with games room 🛏♪♣▣❀🚗[R]🍷[S]

Napton on the Hill 16B5

11–2.30; 6.30–10.30 (11 F, S)

Napton Bridge Inn

(A425) ☎ Southam 2466
Davenports Bitter [H]
Superb canalside pub and restaurant ♪♣❀🚗🕐🌙🍷[S]

Nether Whitacre 15J1

10.30–2.30; 6–10.30 (11 F, S)

Gate

(B4098 near Coleshill)
Opens at 12 noon & 7 pm
Mitchells & Butlers Mild, Brew XI [H]
Friendly country pub with collection of old clocks
🔥♪♣❀🚗[R]🍷♿⛺

Newbold-on-Avon 16B4

11–2.30; 6–10.30 (11 F, S)

Boat

(B4112) ☎ Rugby 76995
Davenports Mild, Bitter
Weston Cider [H]
Pleasant canalside pub
🔥♣❀🚗🕐🌙[S]

Newbold-on-Stour 15J4

10–2.30; 6–10.30 (11 F, S)

Bird in Hand

(A34) ☎ Alderminster 253
Whitbread Bitter, Flowers Original Bitter
Bulmer Cider [H]
Friendly pub with good food
🔥♣🚗🕐🌙🍷[S]

Newton Regis 23H8

11–2.30; 6.30–10.30 (11 F, S)

Queens Head

Main Road
Draught Bass [E]
Popular village pub ♪♣▣🚗🍷[S]

Nuneaton 16A3

11–2.30; 6.30–10.30 (11 F, S)

Brown's Wine Bar

Bridge Street ☎ 328444
Closed Sunday lunchtimes; evening opening: 6
Marston Pedigree
Whitbread Bitter, Flowers Original Bitter [H]
Good food and guest beers
🛏♪[R]🕐🌙[S]≷

Chetwynd Arms

Chetwynd Drive (off B4112)

Ansells Bitter
Ind Coope Burton Ale [H]
Big estate pub ♪🚗▮Ⓢ

Coniston Tavern
Pallet Drive, St Nicholas Estate
Marston Burton Bitter, Pedigee, Merrie Monk, Owd Rodger [H]
Large, pleasant estate pub
♪♣🚗◔▮Ⓢ

Pen & Wig
Church Street ☎ 381311
Evening opening: 7
Draught Bass
Mitchells & Butlers Mild, Brew XI [H]
Friendly town pub with skittle alley ♪♣🌿[R]▮Ⓢ≹

Rose Inn
Coton Road (A444) ☎ 383983
Marston Burton Bitter, Pedigree [H]
Friendly local; first CAMRA AGM met here in 1972
♪♣🌿🚗◔ (not Sun)▮Ⓢ

Priors Marston 16B5
11–2.30; 6–10.30 (11 F, S)

Holly Bush
Opens at 12 noon & 7 pm
Marston Mercian Mild, Burton Bitter, Pedigree [H]
Beautiful 15th-century pub
🏠♪🌿🚗◔❥Ⓢ

Radford Semele 16A5
11–2.30; 6.30–10.30 (11 F, S)

White Lion
Southam Road (A425)
☎ Leamington Spa 20230
Davenports Bitter [H]
Modernised Tudor village local with restaurant ♪♣🌿🚗◔❥▮Ⓢ

Ratley 16A6
10–2.30; 6–10.30 (11 F, S)

Rose & Crown
(Off A422)
Opens at 11 am & 7 pm
Draught Bass [H]
Litchborough Tudor Ale [G]
Wadworth 6X [H]
Single-roomed Cotswold village pub 🏠♪♣🌿Ⓢ

Rugby 16B4
11–2.30; 6–10.30 (11 F, S)

Half Moon
Lawford Road (A428)
Opens at 12 noon & 7 pm
Ansells Mild, Bitter
Ind Coope Burton Ale [H]
Small terraced town pub ♪♣Ⓢ

Raglan Arms
50 Dunchurch Road (A426)
Evening opening: 6
Marston Capital, Pedigree [H]
Tastefully modernised terraced pub ♪♣🚗◔

Shakespeare
7 Queen Street (off Chapel Street) (off A428) ☎ 4453
Evening opening: 7
Ansells Bitter [H]
Pleasant lounge pub, beware dartboard ♪♣🌿◔

Squirrel
Church Street (B5414)
Marston Pedigree [H]
Basic town local ♪♣

Shipston-on-Stour 15J4
10–2.30; 6–10.30 (11 F, S)

White Bear
The Square (A34) ☎ 61558
Draught Bass
Mitchells & Butlers Mild, Brew XI [H]
Lively atmosphere in converted coaching inn
🏠♣🌿▣[R]❥▮Ⓢ

Southam 16A5
11–2.30; 6–10.30 (11 F, S)

Old Mint
Coventry Street (A423)
Adnams Bitter
Everard Beacon
Whitbread Bitter, Flowers Original Bitter [H]
Stone-built 13th century free house, guest beers
🏠♪🌿🚗◔❥Ⓢ

Stockton 16A5
11–2.30; 6.30–10.30 (11 F, S)

Crown
High Street
Ansells Mild, Bitter [H]
Pleasant, untouched village local ♪♣⊞🚗▮

Stratford-upon-Avon 15H3
11–2.30; 6–11

Falcon Hotel
Chapel Street ☎ 205777
Morning opening: 11.30
Ansells Bitter
Manns Bitter
Tetley Bitter [H]
Old 16th century inn with modern additions
🏠♪⊞🌿🚗▣[R]◔❥▮Ⓢ≹

Old Tramway
Shipston Road (A34)
☎ 297593
Davenports Bitter
Weston Cider [H]
Friendly one-roomed pub
♣🌿🚗◔Ⓢ▲

Squirrel
Drayton Avenue ☎ 297893
Ansells Mild, Bitter
Tetley Bitter [H]
New estate pub with smart lounge ♪♣🌿🚗◔▮Ⓢ♿≹

White Swan
Rother Street ☎ 297022
Opens at 10 am & 5.30 pm
Draught Bass
Ruddle County
Wadworth 6X [H]
Fine town-centre hotel
🏠⊞▣[R]◔❥▮Ⓢ≹

Studley 15H3
10.30–2.30; 6–10.30 (11 F, S)

Bell
Alcester Road (A435) ☎ 2216
Mitchells & Butlers Highgate Mild, Brew XI [H]
Lively central village pub
♣🚗◔❥▮

Ufton 16A5
11–2.30; 6.30–10.30 (11 F, S)

White Hart
(A425) ☎ 612428
Davenports Bitter [H]
Modernised pub and restaurant with fine view
♪♣🌿🚗◔❥Ⓢ

Upper Brailes 15J4
10–2.30; 6–10.30 (11 F, S)

Gate
(B4035) ☎ Brailes 212
Opens at 11.30 am & 6.30 pm
Hook Norton Mild, Best Bitter, Old Hookey [H]
Tastefully rejuvenated, friendly village pub
🏠♪♣🌿🚗◔▮

Warwick 15J3
11–2.30; 6.30–10.30 (11 F, S)

Racehorse
Stratford Road (A429)
Banks Mild, Bitter [E]
Huge pub on outskirts of town
♪♣🌿🚗◔▮Ⓢ

Seven Stars
Friar Street (B4095)
Hook Norton Best Bitter
Marston Pedigree
Samuel Smith Old Brewery Bitter
Whitbread Flowers Original Bitter [H]
16th century free house next to racecourse, weekly guest beer ♪♣🌿🚗◔Ⓢ

Vine
West Street (A429) ☎ 491509
Whitbread WCPA, Flowers Original Bitter [H]
Fine Tudor pub 🏠♪♣🌿◔▮Ⓢ

Zetland
Church Street ☎ 491974
Davenports Bitter [H]
Pleasant town-centre pub
♪🌿▣◔▮Ⓢ

Withybrook 16A4
11–2.30; 6.30–10.30 (11 F, S)

Pheasant
(B4112) ☎ Hinckley 220480
Courage Directors
Everard Burton Mild, Old Original
Ind Coope Burton Ale [H]
Free house with excellent restaurant and guest beers
♪🌿🚗◔❥

Aldridge 24D6

11–2.30; 6–10.30 (11 F, S)

Hop'n'Grape
Unit 6, Anchor Road ✆ 58051
Banks Mild, Bitter
Marston Pedigree
Mitchells & Butlers Highgate Mild, Springfield Bitter Ⓖ
Modern pub/wine bar with real ale bar downstairs; guest beers ♪🍴Ⓢ

Bilston 24C7

11–2.30; 6–10.30 (11 F, S)

Swanbank Tavern
Lichfield Street (A41)
Banks Mild, Bitter Ⓔ
Bright and basic – a haven from recorded music ♠🍴

Birmingham: Aston 24E7

10.30–2.30; 5.30–10.30 (11 F, S)

Bartons Arms
High Street, 6 (A34)
✆ 021-359 0853
Mitchells & Butlers Mild, Brew XI Ⓗ
Spectacular tiled Victorian masterpiece ♠🍴♪♠RⒼ➘

Bulls Head
Pritchett Street, 6 (off A34)
Ansells Mild, Bitter Ⓗ
Renovated factory local with old theatre tip-up seats ♪♠🍴Ⓢ

Birmingham: Bordesley 25E8

Hen & Chickens
Lower Dartmouth Street, 9
Davenports Mild, Bitter Ⓗ
Quiet backstreet local ♪♠RⓈ

Horse & Jockey
Bordesley Park Road, 10 (Off A45)
Opens at 11 am & 6 pm
Davenports Bitter Ⓗ
Real Brummagem local, near St Andrews ☎♪♠🍴≷

Birmingham: Camp Hill 24E8

Brewer & Baker
Ravenhurst Street, 12 (Off A41) ✆ 021-772 7839
Draught Bass
Mitchells & Butlers Highgate Mild, Springfield Bitter, Brew XI Ⓗ
Lively pub with keen landlord ♪♠ⒼⓈ≷

Birmingham: City Centre 24E8

Australian Bar
Hurst Street, 5
Opens at 11 am & 6 pm
Davenports Mild, Bitter Ⓔ

Traditional bar, busy lounge
♪♠RⒾⓈ≷

Fountain
Wrentham Street, 5 (Off A38) ✆ 021-622 1452
Opens at 11 am & 6 pm
Ansells Mild
Ind Coope Burton Ale Ⓗ
Old-fashioned local near 'naughty' cinema ♪♠ⒼⓈ

Gough Arms
Gough Street, 1
Morning opening: 11
Courage Directors Ⓗ
Refurbished, quiet local
♪♠RⓈ

Holloway
Holloway Head, Lee Bank, 1
✆ 021-643 0432
Davenports Mild, Bitter Ⓗ
Modern pub near the brewery
♪♠RⒼⒾⓈ

Prince of Wales
Cambridge Street, 1
Ansells Mild, Bitter
Tetley Bitter Ⓗ
Refurbished local near the repertory theatre
♪♠🍴Ⓢ

Queens Tavern
Essex Street, 5 (off A38)
Morning opening: 11
Courage Directors Ⓗ
Small, comfortable corner lounge ☎♪ⒼⓈ≷

Roebuck
Hurst Street, 5
Opens at 11 am & 6 pm
Mitchells & Butlers Mild, Brew XI Ⓗ
Quiet, basic old pub, modern lounge ♪♠RⒼⒾⓈ≷

White Lion
Horsefair, 5 (A38)
Morning opening: 11
Davenports Bitter Ⓗ
Smart, friendly pub with theatrical connections
♪♠RⒾⓈ

Woodman
Albert Street, 5
Morning opening: 11; Saturday evening: 7
Ansells Mild
Tetley Bitter Ⓗ
Coates Cider Ⓖ
Old corner pub with fine etched windows ☎♪♠🍴Ⓢ

Birmingham: Five Ways 24E8

Bulls Head
Bishopsgate Street, 15
✆ 021-643 0038
Ansells Mild, Bitter
Tetley Bitter Ⓗ
Traditional pub, simple but becoming rare
♠☎♪♠RⒾⒼⒾⓈ≷

Birmingham: Handworth 24D7

Old Gate
Booth Street, 21
✆ 021-554 8139
Opens at 12 noon & 6.30 pm
Davenports Bitter Ⓗ
Modernised pub in a revitalised area ♪♠🍴🅿RⒼ➘Ⓢ

Red Lion
Soho Road, 21 (A41)
Ansells Mild Ⓗ
Unspoilt Edwardian brewers' baroque ♪♠R🍴

Birmingham: Jewellery Quarter 25G8

Brown Lion
Hall Street, 18 (off A41)
Courage Directors Ⓗ
Two-room pub with bar billiards ♪♠🍴Ⓢ

St Pauls Tavern
Ludgate Hill, 3
Saturday opening: 11.30 am & 7 pm
Draught Bass
Mitchells & Butlers Mild, Springfield Bitter, Brew XI Ⓗ
A gem in the jewellery quarter
♪♠RⒼ➘Ⓢ

Birmingham: Kings Norton 24D8

Navigation
Wharf Road, 30 (Off A441)
✆ 021-458 1652
Davenports Mild, Bitter Ⓔ
Lively, comfortable suburban pub ♪♠🅿R🍴Ⓢ

Birmingham: Moseley 24E8

Prince of Wales
Alcester Road, 13 (A435)
Ansells Mild
Ind Coope Burton Ale Ⓗ
Busy bohemian local ♪♠🍴Ⓢ

Birmingham: Northfield 24D8

Black Horse
Bristol Road South, 31 (A38) ✆ 021-475 1005
Davenports Mild, Bitter Ⓔ
Magnificent brewers' Tudor roadhouse ♪♠🅿RⒼ➘🍴🚻

Birmingham: Perry Barr 24D7

Wellhead Tavern
Franchise Street, 42
Sat morning opening: 11
Ansells Mild
Ind Coope Burton Ale
Tetley Bitter Ⓗ

raditional local, encroached
n by polytechnic
♣⚘🍷Ⓢ⇌

irmingham: hard End 25E7

rookmeadow
ld Forrest Way
Morning opening: 11
anks Mild, Bitter [E]
Modern estate pub in
raditional style ♪♣🚗🍷Ⓢ

Pack Horse
ackington Avenue
nsells Mild, Bitter
etley Bitter [H]
asic estate local ♪♣🚗🍷Ⓢ

irmingham: mall Heath 24E8

righton
oventry Road, 10 (A45)
Morning opening: 11
ourage Directors [H]
usy lunchtimes ♪♣⚘◔🍷Ⓢ

irmingham: tirchley 24D8

Three Horseshoes
ershore Road, 30 (A441)
021-458 1378
Morning opening: 11
avenports Bitter [H]
usy roadhouse catering for
ll tastes ♪♣⚘🚗[R]◔🍷Ⓢ⇌

irmingham: Winson Green 24D7

ellefield
Winson Street, 18 (off A457)
pens at 11.30 am (Mon–Fri);
1 am & 6 pm (Sat)
avenports Mild, Bitter [H]
ormer home-brew house
ith tiled interior ♪♣🚗[R]🍷Ⓢ

ricklayers Arms
knield Port Road, 16
Off A457)
avenports Mild, Bitter [H]
ively old three-bar local
♣[R]🍷Ⓢ

irmingham: Yardley Wood 25E8

herwood
ighfield Road, 14
pens at 11 am & 6 pm
ourage Directors [H]
ypical 1930s roadhouse with
nusual lounge ♪♣⚘🚗🍷Ⓢ⇌

lackheath 24C8

-2.30; 6–10.30 (11 F, S)
Old Bush Revived
owke Lane
ansons Mild, Bitter [E]
opular, friendly local
♣⊞🚗🍷⇌

Bloxwich 24D6

11–2.30; 6–10.30 (11 F, S)
Hatherton Arms
63 Reeves Street (off A34)
Opens at 11.30 am & 7 pm
Mitchells & Butlers Highgate Mild, Springfield Bitter [H]
Basic backstreet local
🏠♣🍷

Romping Cat
Elmore Green Road (off A34)
Banks Mild, Bitter [E]
Pleasant, round-corner pub
with interesting windows
♪♣🍷Ⓢ

Sneyd
Vernon Way, Mossley Estate
(Off A34)
Banks Mild, Bitter [E]
Basic one-bar pub ♪♣⊞⚘🚗🍷Ⓢ

Station
Station Street (off A34)
Ansells Mild, Bitter [H]
Cheerful one-roomed
backstreet local ♪♣⚘🍷Ⓢ

Brierley Hill 24C8

11–2.30; 6–10.30 (11 F, S)
New Inn
Dudley Road (A461)
Simpkiss Bitter, Supreme, Old
Wadworth 6X [H]
Small local near Civic Hall
🏠♪♣🚗🍷Ⓢ

Talbot
Brettell Lane (A461)
Simpkiss Bitter [E]
Comfortable pub, near the
brewery ♪♣🍷

Vine (Bull & Bladder)
Delph Road (off A461)
Batham Mild, Bitter, Delph Strong Ale [H]
Famous basic, popular Black
Country brewery tap; jazz
Mondays ⌐♪♣⊞⚘🚗🍷Ⓢ

Burton Green 25G9

10.30–2.30; 6–10.30 (11 F, S)
Peeping Tom
Cromwell Lane ☎ Coventry
466710
Manns Mild, Bitter [H]
Modern pub, lavishly
decorated; good food
♪♣⚘🚗◔

Chelmsley Wood 25F8

10.30–2.30; 5.30–10.30 (11 F, S)
Greenwood
Helmswood Drive,
Birmingham 37
Morning opening: 11
Ansells Mild, Bitter
Gibbs Mew Wiltshire Bitter
Tetley Bitter [H]
Keen darts pub with
downstairs lounge ♪♣🚗Ⓢ

Coseley 24C7

11–2.30; 6–10.30 (11 F, S)
Coseley Tavern
Upper Ettingshall Road
Evening opening: 6.30
Hansons Mild, Bitter [E]
Bright, vibrant Black Country
local 🏠♪♣🚗🍷

New Inn
35 Ward Street, (off
Birmingham New Road)
(A4123) ☎ Sedgeley 4511
Opens at 12 noon & 7 pm
Holden Mild, Bitter [E]
Special Bitter [H]
Small Black Country local,
partly hidden by a chapel
♪♣🚗🍷Ⓢ

Coventry 25G8

10–2.30; 6–10.30 (11 F, S)
Coombe Abbey
Craven Street, Chapelfields
Draught Bass
Mitchells & Butlers Mild, Brew XI [H]
Popular local with games
room ♪♣⊞⚘🍷

Craven Arms
Craven Street, Chapelfields
Whitbread Bitter, Flowers Original Bitter [H]
Streetcorner local ⌐♪♣⚘🍷

Earlsdon Cottage
Warwick Street, Earldsdon
Draught Bass
Mitchells & Butlers Mild, Springfield Bitter, Brew XI [E]
Large pub with old pub
photos; live music most nights
⌐♪♣⚘[R]🍷

Elastic Inn
Lower Ford Street, City Centre
☎ 27039
Ansells Mild, Bitter
Tetley Walker Bitter [H]
Popular pub near bus station
♪♣[R]Ⓢ

Greyhound
Sutton Stop
Draught Bass
Mitchells & Butlers Mild, Brew XI [E]
Weston Cider [G]
Popular pub in industrial
conservation area, of interest
to canal enthusiasts ♪♣⚘🚗🍷Ⓢ

Herald
Sir Henry Parkes Road, Canley
Draught Bass
Mitchells & Butlers Mild, Brew XI [E]
Popular pub with circular
lounge; opposite factory
where Triumph Herald was
made ♪♣⚘🚗🍷Ⓢ

Malt Shovel
Spon End ☎ 20204
Ansells Mild, Bitter
Tetley Walker Bitter [H]

Small, friendly local with weekend folk club 🔥♪♣✿🚗[R][S]

Maudsley
Allesley Old Road ☎ 75279
Draught Bass
Mitchells & Butlers Mild, Brew XI [E]
Basic pub, plush lounge ♪♣✿🚗[R]◔🍷[S]

Old Windmill (Ma Brown's)
Spon Street, City Centre
☎ 26237
Manns Bitter
Watney Fined Stag Bitter [H]
Reputedly the oldest licensed premises in Coventry
🏛♪⊞✿◔🍷

Open Arms
Daventry Road, Cheylesmore
Draught Bass
Mitchells & Butlers Mild, Brew XI [E]
Large, typical modern suburban pub ♪♣✿🚗🍷[S]

Pitts Head
Far Gosford Street (A46)
Draught Bass
Mitchells & Butlers Mild, Brew XI [H]
Large, basic bar, plush lounge, games room ♪♣✿🚗🍷

Sir Colin Campbell
Gosford Street
Draught Bass
Mitchells & Butlers Mild, Springfield Bitter [H] **Brew XI** [E]
Large, modernised late Victorian pub, good food
🔥♪♣[R]◔ (Mon–Sat) 🍷[S]

Three Tuns
Bull Yard, City Centre ☎ 20790
Draught Bass
Mitchells & Butlers Mild, Brew XI [H]
Modern pub with spit-and-sawdust bar and upstairs disco lounge
🔥♪♣[R]◔🍷[S]

Cradley Heath 24C8
11–2.30; 6–10.30 (11 F, S)

Swan
Providence Street (off A4100)
☎ 66685
Holden Mild, Bitter, Special Bitter [E]
♪♣◔🍷🚆

Darlaston 24C7
11–2.30; 6–10.30 (11 F, S)

Green Dragon
Church Street
Evening opening: 7
Mitchells & Butlers Highgate Mild, Springfield Bitter [H]
Traditional small town-centre pub ♪♣🍷

Prince of Wales
74 Walsall Road
Evening opening: 7
Holden Mild, Bitter, Special Bitter [H]
Lively bar, cosy lounge, occasional entertainment
🔥♪♣🍷[S]

Railway Tavern
Cemetery Road, James Bridge (off A4038)
Evening opening: 5.30 Mon–Fri
Mitchells & Butlers Highgate Mild, Springfield Bitter, Highgate Old Ale [E]
Good, honest Black Country pub near M5/M6 interchange
🏛♣✿🚗

Dudley 24C7
11–2.30; 6–10.30 (11 F, S)

Griffin
Stone Street (off A461)
Hansons Mild, Bitter [E]
Busy town-centre pub ♪♣🍷

Lamp Tavern
116 High Street (A459)
☎ 54129
Opens at 11.30 am & 7 pm
Batham Mild, Bitter [H]
Busy town pub with old brewery still standing
🏛♪♣🚗◔🍷[S]

Malt Shovel
Tower Street ☎ 52735
Banks Mild, Bitter [E]
Extended, popular old town local known as the 'Mad House' 🚗◔[S]

White Swan
Holland Street (off A461)
☎ 57049
Hansons Mild, Bitter
Old Swan Bitter [E]
Doris Pardoe's other outlet – small modern estate pub ♪♣🚗[R]🍷[S]

Earlswood 25E9
11–2.30; 6–10.30 (11 F, S)

Bulls Head
7 Limekiln Lane (off B4102)
OS 123744 ☎ 2335
Ansells Mild, Bitter
Ind Coope Burton Ale [H] & [E]
Country pub with modernised lounge and small, friendly bar
🏛♪♣✿🚗◔☽🍷[S]

Gornal Wood 24C7
11–2.30; 6–10.30 (11 F, S)

Pear Tree
New Street (off B4176)
☎ Dudley 231701
Evening opening: 6.30
Banks Mild, Bitter [E]
Popular Black Country pub, also known as the 'Stuffed Whippet' 🚗[R]🍷

Goscote 24D6
11–2.30; 6–10.30 (11 F, S)

Barley Mow
Goscote Lane, Walsall (Off B4155)
Mitchells & Butlers Highgate Mild, Springfield Bitter [E]
Old canalside local 🔥♪♣✿🚗🍷[S]

Halesowen 24C
11–2.30; 6–10.30 (11 F, S)

Beehive
Hagley Road (B4183)
☎ 021-550 1782
Hansons Mild, Bitter [E]
Comfortable modern pub
♪♣🚗◔🍷[S]

Hare & Hounds
Hagley Road (A458)
☎ 021-550 21550
Davenports Mild, Bitter [H]
Attractively designed pub wit comfortable lounge
♪♣✿🚗◔🍷[S]

Waggon & Horses
Stourbridge Road (A458)
Mitchells & Butlers Mild, Springfield Bitter [H]
Unspoilt, friendly corner local near Halesowen FC ♪♣[R]🍷[S]

Kingswinford 24B
11–2.30; 6–10.30 (11 F, S)

Park Tavern
Barnett Lane (off A4101)
Opens at 12 noon & 5.30 pm (Mon, Tue, Thu) 6.30 pm (Sa
Ansells Mild, Bitter
Gibbs Mew Wiltshire Bitter [H]
Busy local with collections of beer mats and bottles
♪♣✿🚗🍷[S]

Lower Gornal 24C
11–2.30; 6–10.30 (11 F, S)

Old Bulls Head
Red Hall Road ☎ Dudley 236092
Evening opening: 7
Ansells Mild, Bitter [H]
Excellent Victorian local, site of defunct Bradleys brewery
🏛🔥♪♣🚗◔🍷[S]

Red Cow
Grosvenor Road (off B4176)
Hansons Mild, Bitter [E]
Small, atmospheric Black Country local ♣🚗🍷

Lye 24
11–2.30; 6–10.30 (11 F, S)

Castle
Balds Lane (off A458)
Simpkiss Bitter, Supreme, Ol Ale [H]
Pleasant sidestreet local
♪♣🚗[R]🍷[S]

Hare & Hounds
Wynall Lane, Wollascote
Banks Mild, Bitter [E]
Large, comfortable pub in residential area ♪♣✿🚗◔🍷[S]

Swan with Two Necks
Dudley Road (A4036)
Banks Mild, Bitter [E]

ınpretentious local near ailway station ♪♣🚗[R]🍷Ⓢ🚆

Meer End 25F9

).30–2; 6–10.30 (11 F, S)

Tipperary
A4117) ☎ Berkswell 33224
Davenports Mild, Bitter [H]
solated pub, dedicated to Harry Williams of 'It's a Long Way to Tipperary' fame
♪♣✿🚗🕒🍷Ⓢ

Netherton 24C7

1–2.30; 6–10.30 (11 F, S)

Old Swan
Off A459) ☎ Dudley 53075
Old Swan Bitter [H]
Doris Pardoe's home-brew Victorian pub with enamelled eiling 🚗♣[R]🍷Ⓢ

Rose & Crown
Withymoor Road (off A459)
Ansells Mild, Bitter [H]
Well-preserved former ome-brew pub ♪♣🚗🍷

Oldbury 24D7

0.30–2.30; 6–10.30 (11 F, S)

New Navigation
Titford Road (off A4123)
Ansells Mild, Bitter [H]
Canalside pub ♪♣🚗🍷Ⓢ

White Swan
Church Street (off A4034)
Banks Mild, Bitter [E]
Friendly local in edevelopment area ♪♣🍷🚆

Olton 25E8

0.30–2.30; 5.30–10.30 (11 F, S)

Lyndon
Barn Lane
Opens at 12 noon & 6 pm
Ansells Mild, Bitter
Gibbs Mew Wiltshire Bitter [H]
Large pub with excellent children's playground
♪♣⊞✿🚗[R]🕒♞🍷Ⓢ

Pelsall 24D6

1–2.30; 6–10.30 (11 F, S)

Free Trade
Wood Lane
Ansells Mild, Bitter [H]
Bright and friendly ♪♣✿🚗🍷Ⓢ

Old Bush
Walsall Road (B4154)
☎ 682806
Ansells Mild, Bitter
Holden Special Bitter [H]
Popular pub overlooking Pelsall Common ♪♣✿🚗[R]🕒🍷

Old House at Home
Norton Road (B4154)
Banks Mild, Bitter [E]
Popular modern pub near the Common ♪♣✿🚗🍷Ⓢ

Rushall 24D6

1–2.30; 6–10.30 (11 F, S)

Manor Arms
Park Road (off A461)
Opens at 12 noon & 7 pm
Mitchells & Butlers Highgate Mild, Springfield Bitter, Brew XI [H]
Canalside pub with collection of saucy seaside postcards 🚗🍷

Shirley 25E9

11–2.30; 6–10.30

Bernies (off-licence)
266 Cranmore Boulevard (off A34)
Opens 12–2; 5.30–10
Adnams Bitter
Burton Bridge Bitter
Fuller London Pride, ESB
Marston Pedigree, Owd Rodger
Moorhouse Pendle Witches Brew [H] & [E]
100 beers and ciders rotated throughout the year; about 7 available at a time ♪

Solihull 25E8

10.30–2.30; 5.30–10.30 (11 F, S)

Golden Lion
Warwick Road (A41)
Morning opening: 11
Courage Directors [H]
Pub to suit all tastes
♪♣✿🚗[R]🕒♞🍷

Stourbridge 24C8

11–2.30; 6–10.30 (11 F, S)

Bulls Head
High Street, Wollaston (A461)
Davenports Mild, Bitter [H]
Comfortable three-roomed pub ♪♣✿🚗🍷Ⓢ

Foresters
Bridgnorth Road (A458)
Ind Coope Burton Ale
Tetley Bitter [H]
Cosy pub with good atmosphere ♪♣🚗🍷Ⓢ

Longlands Tavern
Western Road ☎ 2073
Banks Mild, Bitter [E]
Backstreet pub with comfortable lounge ♪♣✿🚗🍷Ⓢ

Plough & Harrow
Worcester Street (A458)
Ansells Mild, Bitter
Ind Coope Burton Ale [H]
Excellent small pub just out of town centre ♪♣✿[R]🍷Ⓢ

Royal Exchange
Enville Street (A458)
Batham Bitter [H]
Popular small pub ♪♣✿🚗🍷Ⓢ

Swan
Hagley Road, Oldswinford
Davenports Bitter [H]
Small bar, lounge popular with young ♪♣🚗[R]🍷Ⓢ🚆

Unicorn
Bridgnorth Road (A458)
Marston Pedigree
Mitchells & Butlers Springfield Bitter [H]
Former home-brew house; small and cosy ♣✿🚗[R]🍷Ⓢ

Sutton Coldfield 25E7

11–2.30; 5.30–10.30

Cork & Bottle
Boldmere Road, Boldmere (off A452)
☎ 021-382 4430
Evening opening: 6
Banks Mild, Bitter [E]
Popular wine bar, parking difficult ♪✿🚗🕒Ⓢ🚆

Duke
Duke Street
Ansells Mild, Bitter
Ind Coope Burton Ale
Tetley Bitter [H]
Friendly sidestreet local, popular and unspoilt ♪♣✿🍷Ⓢ

Plough & Harrow
Slade Road, Roughley (B4151) ☎ 021-308 1132
Banks Mild, Bitter [E]
Well-balanced local with something for all; excellent food ♪♣✿🚗🕒🍷

Station Hotel
Station Street
Saturday opening: 10.30 am & 6 pm
Mitchells & Butlers Mild, Brew XI [E]
Basic, popular pub with pool room ♪♣⊞✿🍷Ⓢ🚆

Three Tuns
High Street (A5127)
Ansells Bitter
Gibbs Mew Wiltshire Bitter
Ind Coope Burton Ale
Tetley Bitter [H]
Modernised, smart and expensive pub ♪🚗🍷🚆

White Horse
116 Whitehouse Common Road (off A453)
Davenports Mild, Bitter [E]
Comfortable multi roomed suburban pub ♪♣✿🚗🍷

Tipton 24C7

11–2.30; 6–10.30 (11 F, S)

Dew Drop
Toll End Road, Ocker Hill
☎ 021-520 1765
Draught Bass
Mitchells & Butlers Highgate Mild, Springfield Bitter [E]
Comfortable local with Darbys brewery windows, opposite Ocker Hill power station
🚗Γ♪♣✿[R]🍷Ⓢ

Horseley Tavern
Horseley Heath (A461)
Hansons Mild, Bitter [E]
Traditional Black Country pub with four rooms and cobbled archway, near Birmingham canal ♣✿🍷🚆

White Swan
Burnt Tree (A461, off A4123)
Hansons Mild, Bitter [E]
Small, compact former coaching inn ♪♣🍷Ⓢ≹

Upper Gornal 24C7
11–2.30; 6–10.30 (11 F, S)

Old Mill
Windmill Street (off A459)
☎ Sedgley 3000
Holden Mild, Bitter, Special Bitter [E] **Old Ale** [H]
Extensively modernised local ♪⚘🚗[R]◔◗Ⓢ

Walsall 24D6
11–2.30; 6–10.30 (11 F, S)

Butts Tavern
Butts Road (off A461)
Ansells Mild, Bitter [H]
30s pub with large bar and comfortable lounge ↱♪♣⚘🍷Ⓢ

Fountain
49 Lower Forster Street (off A461)
Mitchells & Butlers Highgate Mild, Springfield Bitter [H]
Small backstreet pub with cosy smoke room ♪♣🍷≹

Hamemakers Arms
Blue Lane West (A454)
Banks Mild, Bitter [E]
Comfortably modernised lounge, pleasant bar ♪♣🚗[R]🍷Ⓢ

Lamb
16 South Street, Palfrey (Off A461) ☎ 29867
Evening opening: 7
Mitchells & Butlers Highgate Mild, Springfield Bitter [H]
Small, homely local in redevelopment area ♪♣🚗[R]🍷Ⓢ

New Inns
John Street (off A34) ☎ 27660
Opens at 12 noon & 5.30 pm
Ansells Mild, Bitter
Ind Coope Burton Ale [H]
Pleasant back-street surprise – sometimes an instant party ↱♪♣[R]◔🍷

White Lion
Sandwell Street
Ansells Mild, Bitter
Ind Coope Burton Ale [H]
Large, popular backstreet local ♪♣⚘🍷Ⓢ

Wednesbury 24D7
11–2.30; 6–10.30 (11 F, S)

Cottage Spring
Franchise Street (off A4038)
Evening opening: 7
Holden Mild, Bitter [E]
Special Bitter [H]
Welcoming local in backstreet redevelopment area ♪♣⚘🚗[R]🍷Ⓢ♿

White Horse Hotel
48 Bridge Street (A41)
☎ 021-556 0092
Evening opening: 7
Draught Bass
Mitchells & Butlers Highgate Mild, Springfield Bitter [E]
Interesting, comfortable Victorian pub of character
🏨♪♣⚘🚗[R]◔🍷Ⓢ

Wednesfield 24C6
11–2.30; 6–10.30 (11 F, S)

Pyle Cock
Rookery Street (A4124)
Banks Mild, Bitter [H]
Rare outlet for handpumped Banks ↱♣⚘🚗[R]🍷

West Bromwich 24D7
11–2.30; 6–10.30 (11 F, S)

Flower Pot
Spon Lane (off A4031)
☎ 5261
Hansons Mild, Bitter [E]
Large, modern local just outside town
♪♣🚗◔🍷Ⓢ

Railway
Bromford Road
Mitchells & Butlers Mild, Springfield Bitter, Brew XI [H]
Old house, full of character
♪♣🚗🍷Ⓢ≹

Royal Oak
Newton Street (off A4041)
Morning opening: 11.30
Mitchells & Butlers Mild, Brew XI [H]
Small, homely and sociable house ↱♣🍷Ⓢ

Willenhall 24C6
11–2.30; 6–10.30 (11 F, S)

Falcon Inn
Gomer Street West (off A454)
Banks Mild
Marston Burton Bitter, Pedigree (summer), **Merrie Monk**
Mitchells & Butlers Highgate Mild [E]
Comfortable lounge, lively bar, friendly welcome guaranteed ♪♣⚘🚗🍷Ⓢ

Robin Hood
54 The Crescent, Shepwell Green (off A454)
Opens at 11.30 am & 6 pm
Ansells Mild, Bitter
Tetley Walker Bitter [H]
Comfortable, welcoming pub with enthusiastic landlord
🏨♪♣⚘🚗◔◗ (Mon–Fri) 🍷Ⓢ

Tiger
68 Stafford Street (off A454)
Opens 10.30 am & 5.30 pm (Mon–Fri)
Simpkiss Bitter, Old
Wadworth 6X
Bulmer Cider [H]
Town-centre local with real ale off-licence
♪♣⚘🚗[R]🍷Ⓢ

Wolverhampton 24C6
11–2.30; 6–10.30 (11 F, S)

Clarendon
Chapel Ash (A41) ☎ 20587
Banks Mild, Bitter [E]
Popular pub adjacent to Banks's Brewery, varied choice of rooms
♣⊞🚗[R]◔🍷Ⓢ

Feathers
Molineux Street
Banks Mild, Bitter [E]
Small, friendly local next to Wolves football ground
♪♣◔🍷Ⓢ

Forge Hammer
Spring Road, Ettingshall
Opens 12–3
Hansons Mild, Bitter [E]
Pleasant and friendly Black Country pub ♪♣🚗🍷Ⓢ

Goal Post
107 Waterloo Road (A449)
☎ 21833
Wem Mild, Best Bitter [E]
Splendidly renovated hotel next to Wolves football ground ♪♣⚘🚗◔Ⓢ♿

Homestead
Lodge Road, Oxley (Off A449)
Ansells Mild, Bitter
Holden Bitter [H]
Large, pleasant suburban pub
♪♣⚘🚗🍷Ⓢ

Jug & Bottle (off-licence)
Court Road, off Newhampton Road, Whitmore Reans
☎ 741897
Opens 6–10 pm Mon–Thu; 12–2, 6–10.30 Fri; 12–10.30 Sat, 12–2, 6–10 Sun
Batham Bitter
Hook Norton Old Hookey
Marston Pedigree
Woods Special Bitter [H]
Other guest beers always available ♪

Mitre
Lower Green, Tettenhall (off A41)
Draught Bass
Mitchells & Butlers Highgate Mild, Springfield Bitter [E]
Pleasant pub by the old village green ♪♣⚘🍷

Newhampton (O'Malleys)
Riches Street ☎ 755565
Courage Directors [H]
Bustling suburban pub with Irish music Sunday evenings
↱♪♣⚘[R]🍷

Parkfield
Parkfield Road (A4039)
Opens at 12 noon & 7 pm
Hansons Mild, Bitter [E]
Friendly and basic ♣🍷

osada
chfield Street ☎ 20926
nsells Mild, Bitter [H]
d-fashioned town-centre
ub with ornate tiling
♣[R]🍺Ⓢ🚆

ueens Arms
raiseley Row, off Penn Road
ff A449)
nsells Mild, Bitter
d Coope Burton Ale [H]
nall, friendly local ♪♣🚗🍺Ⓢ

illiers Arms
pper Villiers Street ☎ 23053
itchells & Butlers Highgate
ild, Springfield Bitter,
Highgate Old Ale [E]
Friendly suburban local
♪♣[R]◔🍺Ⓢ

Winning Post
Gorsebrook Road, Dunstall
☎ 710649
Wem Mild, Best Bitter [E]
Modern one-room pub
opposite racecourse ♪♣🚗◔Ⓢ♿

Woodsetton 24C7

11–2.30; 6–10.30 (11 F, S)

Brook
Bourne Street (off A463)
Lunchtime opening: 12 noon
Banks Mild, Bitter [E]
Unspoilt two-level pub, service
in bar through knee-level
hatch ♪♣⊞🚗🍺

Park Inn
George Street (off A4123)
Opens at 11.30 am and 7 pm
Holden Mild [E], **Bitter**
Special Bitter, Old Ale [H]
Brewery tap, highly decorated
with breweriana ♪♣✿🚗[R]🍺Ⓢ

Wordsley 24B8

11–2.30; 6–10.30 (11 F, S)

Rose & Crown
High Street (off A491)
Davenports Mild, Bitter [E]
Old pub on Charles II's escape
routefrom Worcester ♪♣⊞🚗🍺♿

GBBF

Where can you sample the widest range of well-kept traditional beers in Britain? At CAMRA's own Great British Beer Festival at Bingley Hall, Birmingham.

Every September, five hundred members of the Campaign for Real Ale give up part of their annual holidays to work a 90-hour week, unpaid and largely unthanked, to assemble, manage and run Europe's largest independent beer Festival. In five days, around 40,000 customers consume nearly 1,000 barrels of real ale at the show that has fast become the high spot of CAMRA's campaigning year.

Nine months planning and eight years experience make the Great British Beer Festival the biggest and the best. Deliveries from over 100 breweries converge on one hall – an administrative nightmare to produce a beer drinkers dream. Over 200 different beers appear on the bars – most of them served straight from the barrel. Where else could you follow a well-kept pint of a Scottish 70/– brew with a pint of best from a small Cornish brewhouse?

There is more to 'the national' than just beer, for each year we also feature some of the best traditional ciders. The increasingly rare drink, perry, is still made by a few companies and we go out of our way to acquire supplies of it in traditional form.

Our food stalls are increasingly popular – we sold over 300 'gallons' of mushy peas last year to accompany traditional 'local' pub foods. Less adventurous palates may prefer our prize Stilton, proper Cheddar and real bread. Hot pork rolls make a sharp contrast with the vegetarian specialities.

On the entertainment side there are good quality brass bands, Dixieland jazz groups and riotous assemblies of assorted players. For those who prefer to make their own entertainment we lay on an array of ancient and modern pub games, including five types of darts, long alley skittles, bat'n'trap, quoits and many others.

If you ask anyone who has been to a Great British Beer Festival what they remember the best, like as not they will say the atmosphere – huge but friendly – like some of our staff. If there is one lasting memory of this event, it must have been the sight of two nineteen-year-old football supporters leading a circle of fifteen or so octogenarian gentlemen from the British Legion Home in a last chorus of "Roll out the Barrel".

So if you want to make a date with the drinking experience of a lifetime, look out for the Great British Beer Festival, Bingley Hall, Birmingham in September 1984 and see what the real ale revolution is really about.

Amesbury 6B4

10.30–2.30; 6.30–10.30 (11 F, S)
Antrobus Arms Hotel
(Off A345/A303) ☎ 3163
Wadworth IPA, 6X [H]
Excellent cuisine and homely bar 🏠■🍴🚗▣[R]☾◗Ⓢ

Avoncliff 5H1

10.30–2.30; 6–11
Cross Guns
OS 805600
Opens 11 am & 6.30 pm (summer); 12 noon & 7 pm (winter)
Butcombe Bitter
Hall & Woodhouse
Badger Best Bitter, Tanglefoot
Tisbury Local Bitter
Wadworth 6X [H]
Fine old free house in Avon Valley 🏠♪♣🍴☾◗Ⓢ♿🚆

Badbury 6B2

11–2.30; 6–10.30 (11 F, S)
Bakers Arms
(Off A345/M4)
Arkell BB, BBB, Kingsdown Ale [H]
Small, neat pub 🏠♪♣🍴🚗☾◗Ⓢ

Barford St. Martin 6B5

10.30–2.30; 6–10.30 (11 F, S)
Green Dragon
(A30, off B3089)
☎ Salisbury 742242
Hall & Woodhouse Hector's Bitter, Badger Best Bitter, Tanglefoot [H]
Oak-beamed and panelled bar ♪♣🍴🚗▣[R]☾◗Ⓢ

Beckhampton 6B3

11.30–2.30; 6.30–10.30 (11 F, S)
Waggon & Horses
(A4) ☎ Avebury 262
Wadworth IPA, 6X, Old Timer [H]
Thatched coaching inn, good food 🏠♪🍴🚗☾◗🎯Ⓢ♿

Biddestone 15F9

11–2.30; 6–10.30 (11 F, S)
Biddestone Arms
(Off A420)
Usher PA, Best Bitter
Wadworth 6X
Whitbread WCPA [H]
Friendly pub in picturesque village ♪🍴🚗☾◗🎯Ⓢ♿

Bishops Cannings 6A3

11–2.30; 6–10.30 (11 F, S and summer)
Crown
(Off A361) ☎ Cannings 218
Wadworth IPA, 6X [H] **Old Timer**
Bulmer Cider [G]
Cheerful pub in pretty village 🏠♪♣🍴🚗☾◗🎯Ⓢ♿⛺

Bowdenhill 15G9

11.30–2.30; 7–10.30 (11 F, S)
Bell
(Off A350) OS 926680
☎ Lacock 308
Mole Cask Bitter
Wadworth IPA, 6X [H]
Friendly country local with guest beers 🏠🔥♪♣🍴🚗▣☾🎯Ⓢ⛺

Bradford-on-Avon 15G9

10.30–2.30; 6–11
Barge
17 Frome Road (B3109) ☎ 3403
Morning opening: 11.45
Usher PA, Best Bitter, Founders Ale [H]
Popular, comfortable pub with large garden; good food 🔥♪♣🍴🚗▣[R]☾◗Ⓢ♿🚆

Swan Hotel
Church Street (A363) ☎ 2224
Usher PA, Best Bitter, Founders Ale [H]
Elegant bar in old town-centre hotel 🏠🍴🚗▣[R]☾◗Ⓢ♿🚆

Bratton 5J1

10.30–2.30; 6.30–10.30 (11 F, S)
Duke
Melbourne Road (B3098)
Usher Best Bitter, Founders Ale [H]
Country pub with two very different bars ♪♣🚗☾◗🎯Ⓢ

Bremhill 6A2

10.30–2.30; 6–10.30 (11 F, S)
Dumb Post
(Off A4) OS 976727
Opens at 11.30 am & 6 pm
Archer Best Bitter
Arkell BBB
Wadworth 6X [H]
Hilltop pub with downland view ♪♣🍴🚗▣☾🎯Ⓢ

Broughton Gifford 15F9

11–2.30; 6–11
Bell
The Common (off B3107)
Wadworth IPA, 6X, Old Timer [H]
Taunton Cider [G]
Fine old village pub 🏠♪♣■🍴[R]☾◗🎯Ⓢ

Burbage 15J9

10–2.30; 6–10.30 (11 F, S)
Three Horseshoes
Stibb Green (A346)
Wadworth IPA, 6X, Old Timer [H]
Bulmer Cider [G]
Thatched inn near Savernake Forest 🏠♣🍴🚗☾◗🎯Ⓢ

Burcombe 6B5

10–2.30; 6.30–11
Ship
(Off A30) ☎ Salisbury 743182
Gibbs Mew Wiltshire Bitter, Premium Bitter [H]
Pub with riverside garden ♪♣🍴🚗[R]☾◗🎯Ⓢ⛺

Castle Combe 15F8

10.30–2.30; 6–10.30 (11 F, S)
White Hart
(Off B4039) ☎ 782295
Archer Village Bitter
Eldridge Pope Royal Oak
Hall & Woodhouse
Badger Best Bitter
Theakston Best Bitter
Wadworth 6X [H]
Well-equipped pub with good food ♪♣■🍴[R]☾◗Ⓢ♿

Chicksgrove 6A5

10.30–2.30; 6–10.30 (11 F, S)
Compasses
(Off A30) ☎ Fovant 318
Closed Tuesday lunchtimes
Halls Harvest Bitter
Ind Coope Burton Ale
Tisbury Local Bitter [H]
Wadworth 6X [H] & [G]
Old Timer
Bulmer Cider [G]
Picturesque country inn 🏠♪♣🍴🚗▣☾◗Ⓢ

Chippenham 15G8

10–2.30; 6–10.30 (11 F, S)
Rose & Crown
22 Market Place ☎ 653139
Usher PA, Best Bitter, Founders Ale [G]
Oak-beamed public bar ♪♣🍴🚗☾◗🎯Ⓢ

Collingbourne Ducis 6C3

11–2.30; 6–10.30 (11 F, S)
Shears
(Off A338/A346) ☎ 304
Bourne Valley Andover Ale
Wadworth IPA, 6X [G]
Attractive thatched flint-built pub 🏠♪🍴🚗☾◗Ⓢ

Collingbourne Kingston 6C3

10.30–2.30; 6–10.30 (11 F, S)
Cleaver
(A338)
☎ Collingbourne Ducis 368
Wadworth IPA, 6X [H]
Cheerful wayside inn 🔥♪♣🍴🚗▣☾◗Ⓢ

Crudwell 15G7

10–2.30; 6–10.30 (11 F, S and summer)
Plough
(A429) ☎ 229
Whitbread WCPA, Flowers Original Bitter
Weston Cider [H]
Friendly, comfortable pub, good food 🏠♪♣■🍴🚗☾◗Ⓢ♿

Devizes 6A3

10–2.30; 6–10.30 (11 F, S and summer)

Black Swan
Market Place ✆ 3259
Morning opening: 11
Wadworth IPA, 6X ⊞
Cosy bar in old coaching inn
🅿🍴🛏🅁🅖🌓⑤⚲

Three Crowns
Maryport Street ✆ 2688
Open until 4 pm Thursdays
Wadworth IPA, 6X, Old
Timer ⊞
Old-fashioned, cosy bars
🎵🍴🛏🅿🅁🅖🌓⑤♿⚲

White Bear
Monday Market Street ✆ 2583
Evening opening: 6.30
Wadworth IPA, 6X Old
Timer ⊞
Quaint Tudor inn – can get
crowded 🎵🍴🅖🌓⑤♿⚲

Downton   6B5

0–2.30; 6–11
White Horse
The Borough (off B3080)
Eldridge Pope Dorchester
Bitter, IPA, Royal Oak ⊞
Spacious pub near River
Avon 🚲🎵🍴🅿🅁🅖🌓⑤⚲

East Chisenbury   6B4

0–2.30; 6–10.30 (11 F, S)
Red Lion
Of A345) OS 141529
Whitbread Strong Country
Bitter ⓖ
Unspoilt village local ♣🍴🛏🅁❗

Fonthill Gifford   5J3

11–2.30; 6–11
Beckford Arms
(Off B3089) ✆ Tisbury 870385
Wadworth IPA, 6X, Old
Timer ⓖ
17th-century inn with blazing
log fires 🛏🎵🍴🅿🛏❗⑤

Ford   15F8

11–2.30; 6–10.30 (11 F, S)
White Hart
(Off A420)
✆ Castle Combe 782213
Archer Village Bitter
Fuller London Pride, ESB
Hall & Woodhouse Badger
Best Bitter
Wadworth 6X
Whitbread Flowers Original
Bitter ⊞
Inn of character by trout
stream 🎵♣🍴🛏🅁🅖🌓⑤

Heddington   6A3

10.30–2.30; 6–10.30 (11 F, S)
Ivy
(Off A3102) ✆ Bromham 276
Wadworth IPA, 6X, Old
Timer ⓖ
Thatched, half-timbered rustic
village pub 🛏♣🍴🛏❗⑤♿

Highworth   6B1

10.30–2.30; 6–10.30 (11 F, S)

Globe
Sheep Street (off A361)
**Courage Best Bitter,
Directors** ⊞
Contrasting bars, wild west
and naval themes 🚲🎵♣🍴🅖❗♿

Hodson   6B2

10–2.30; 6–10.30 (11 F, S)
Calley Arms
(Off B4005)
**Wadworth IPA, 6X, Old
Timer** ⊞
Modern village local with fine
views 🎵🍴♣🛏🌓❗⑤

Holt   5J1

11–2.30; 6–11
Old Ham Tree
(B3107)
✆ North Trowbridge 782630
**Eldridge Pope Royal Oak
Tisbury Local Bitter
Usher PA
Wadworth 6X** ⊞
Modernised 18th-century pub
🛏♣🍴🅿🛏🅖🌓⑤

Honey Street   6B3

11–2.30; 6–10.30 (11 F, S)
Barge Inn
OS 101616
✆ Woodborough 238
Courage Best Bitter, Directors ⊞
Canalside pub with landing
stage 🚲♣🍴🅿🛏🅁🅖🌓❗⑤⚲

Kilmington   5H2

11–2.30; 6–11
Red Lion
(B3092)
**Eldridge Pope IPA, Royal Oak
Fussells Best Bitter** ⊞
15th century inn with fine
meals 🛏♣🍴🅿🛏🅁🅖🌓⑤♿

Lacock   15G9

10–2.30; 6–10.30 (11 F, S)
George
(Off A350) ✆ 263
**Wadworth IPA, 6X, Old
Timer** ⊞
14th-century pub
🛏♣🍴🅿🛏🅖🌓❗⑤⚲

Limpley Stoke   15F9

11–2.30; 6–11
Hop Pole
Woods Hill (off A36) ✆ 3134
**Courage Bitter, Best Bitter,
Directors** ⊞
Small oak-panelled pub
🚲🎵🅿🛏🅖🌓❗⑤♿

Little Bedwyn   15J9

11–2.30; 6–10.30 (11 F, S)
Harrow
(Off A4)
**Arkell BBB
Fuller ESB
Hook Norton Best Bitter
Marston Pedigree** ⊞
Modernised Victorian free
house 🎵♣🅖🌓⑤

Malmesbury   15G8

10.30–2.30; 6.30–10.30 (11 F, S and summer)
Red Bull
Sherston Road (B4040)
**Archer Village Bitter
Draught Bass** ⊞
Popular, friendly pub, two
miles from town 🛏🎵🍴🛏🅖⑤♿

Market Lavington
                                  6A3

10.30–2.30; 6–10.30 (11 F, S)
Volunteer Arms
Church Street (B3098)
Wadworth IPA, 6X ⊞ **Old
Timer** ⓖ
Fine little pub ♣🍴🅿🛏🅁🌓❗⑤♿

Marlborough   6B3

10–2.30; 6–10.30 (11 F, S)
Roebuck
London Road (A4) ✆ 52610
**Usher Best Bitter, Founders
Ale** ⊞
Well-renovated roadside pub
🛏♣🎵🍴🛏🅖🌓❗⑤

Wellington Arms
High Street (A4) ✆ 52954
**Whitbread Flowers Original
Bitter, Strong Country Bitter,
Pompey Royal** ⊞
Bulmer Cider ⓖ
Friendly beamed bar, fine mug
collection 🎵🍴🅖🌓⑤

Melksham   15G9

10–2.30; 6–10.30 (11 F, S and summer)
Red Lion
3 The City (off A350)
Morning opening: 10.30
**Hall & Woodhouse
Hector's Bitter
Wadworth 6X, Old Timer** ⓖ
**Langton & Taunton
Cider** ⓖ & Ⓔ
Vibrant, stone-built town pub
🛏♣🍴❗⑤

Oare   6B3

11–2.30; 6–10.30 (11 F, S)
White Hart
(A345) ✆ Pewsey 2443
Wadworth IPA, 6X ⊞
A fine roadside inn
🎵♣🍴🛏❗⑤⚲

Pewsey   6B3

10–2.30; 6–10.30 (11 F, S)
Coopers Arms
Ball Lane (off B3087)
Morning opening: 10.30
Usher PA ⓖ
Superb rustic local in a back
lane 🛏🎵♣🍴🛏❗⑤♿

Poulshot   5J1

10.30–2.30; 6–10.30 (11 F, S)
Raven
(Off A361) OS 970601
**Wadworth IPA, 6X, Old
Timer** ⓖ
Attractive half-timbered inn
🎵♣🍴🛏🅁🅖🌓⑤⚲

Wiltshire

Salisbury 6B5

10–2.30; 6–10.30 (11 F, S and summer)
Bull Hotel
Fisherton Street ☎ 27518
Hall & Woodhouse
Hector's Bitter, Tanglefoot ℍ
17th-century hotel with
petanque 🏧♣🎵🅿🚗🍴🅑℞🕓♠🍽⛽

Haunch of Venison
Minster Street ☎ 22024
Courage Best Bitter ℍ & ⒼG
Directors ℍ
Ancient English chop house
🏧🅑℞🕓♠🍽

Railway Tavern
South Western Road ☎ 28120
Gibbs Mew Wiltshire Bitter,
Premium Bitter, Bishops
Tipple ℍ
Comfortable pub – country
and western Fridays and
Saturdays 🍴♣🏧🍽🕓🍽⛽

Sells Green 6A3

11–2.30; 6–10.30 (11 F, S)
Three Magpies
(A365) ☎ Seend 389
Wadworth IPA, 6X ℍ **Old**
Timer Ⓖ
Country pub near Kennet &
Avon canal 🍴♣🎵🅿🚗🕓♠🍽

Sherston 15F8

11–2.30; 6–11
Carpenters Arms
(B4040)
Whitbread WCPA
West Country Cider Ⓖ
Charming old-world local
🏧🍴♣🎵🅿🍽⛽

South Marston 6B1

10.30–2.30; 6–10.30 (11 F, S)
Carpenters Arms
(Off A420)
Arkell BB, BBB, Kingsdown
Ale ℍ
Pleasant, modernised family
pub 🏧♣🎵🅿🕓🍽⛽♠

Staverton 15F9

11–2.30; 6.30–11
Old Bear
(B3105)
Draught Bass
Usher PA, Founders Ale
Wadworth 6X ℍ
17th-century stone-built pub
🏧🍴♣🎵🅿🕓🍽⛽

Swindon 6B1

10–2.30; 6–10.30 (11 F, S)
Beehive
Prospect Hill ☎ 23187
Morrell Dark Mild, Varsity ℍ
Lively triangular pub behind
college 🍴♣🕓♠🍽

Glue Pot
Emlyn Square ☎ 23935
John Devenish Bitter, Wessex
Best Bitter ℍ

Busy pub in railway village
🍴♣🎵🅑🕓♠⛽♿🚆

Great Western
Station Road ☎ 22047
Arkell BB, BBB, Kingsdown
Ale ℍ
Plush bar and steakhouse
🍴🎵🏧🕓♠🍽🚆

Wheatsheaf
Newport Street ☎ 23188
Wadworth IPA, 6X, Old
Timer ℍ
Crowded one-bar pub 🎵🕓♠🍽⛽

The Green 5J3

10.30–2.30; 6–10.30 (11 F, S and summer)
Fox & Hounds
(Of A350) OS 871314
Usher Best Bitter, Founders Ale
Taunton Cider ℍ
Quaint local with good views;
guest beers 🏧🍴🎬🅿🚗🍽

Tisbury 5J3

10–2.30; 6–11
Crown
Church Lane (off B3089/A30)
Gibbs Mew Wiltshire Bitter ℍ
& Ⓖ **Premium Bitter, Bishop's**
Tipple Ⓖ
Tisbury Local Bitter
Bulmer Cider ℍ
Jovial pub with skittle alley
🏧🍴♣🎵🅿🅑℞🍽♿🚆

South Western
Station Road (B3089/A30)
☎ 870160
Everard Tiger
Tisbury Local Bitter ℍ
West Country Cider Ⓖ
Tisbury brewery's first tied
house; guest beers
🍴🎵♣🎬🅿🏧🅑🕓🍽♿🚆

Trowbridge 5H1

10.30–2.30; 6–10.30 (11 F, S)
Peewee's
Castle Street
Eldridge Pope Royal Oak
Mole Cask Bitter
Sussex County Ale
Tisbury Local Bitter
Whitbread Flowers Original
Bitter ℍ
Lively and noisy – guest beers
always available 🍴♣🎵🅿℞🍽

Wiltshire Yeoman
Chilmark Road (off A363)
Usher PA, Best Bitter,
Founders Ale ℍ
Converted farmhouse on
housing estate 🏧🎵🅿🕓♠🍽

Upavon 6B3

11–2.30; 6–10.30 (11 F, S)
Antelope
(A342/A345) ☎ 206
Evening opening: 6.30
Wadworth IPA, 6X, Old
Timer ℍ
Large converted malthouse
🏧🍴♣🎵🅿🅑℞🕓♠🍽

Urchfont 6A

11–2.30; 6–10.30 (11 F, S and summer)
Lamb
(Off B3098) ☎ Chirton 631
Wadworth IPA, 6X ℍ **Old**
Timer
Bulmer & Taunton Cider Ⓖ
Thatched village local
🏧🍴♣🎵🅿🅑℞🍽♿

Wanborough 6C

10–2.30; 6–10.30 (11 F, S)
Black Horse
(B4507) ☎ 305
Arkell BB, BBB ℍ
Kingsdown Ale Ⓖ
Cheerful little pub with fine
view
🍴♣🎵🏧🕓 (Mon–Sat)🍽♿♠

Warminster 5J

10–2.30; 6–10.30 (11 F, S)
Weymouth Arms
Emwell Street (off A362)
Usher PA, Best Bitter,
Founders Ale ℍ
Large town pub 🍴♣🎵🅑🕓♠🍽🕓

Westbury 5J

11–2.30; 6–10.30 (11 F, S)
Crown
Market Place
Wadworth 6X ℍ
Bulmer Cider Ⓖ
Busy town-centre pub
🍴♣🏧℞🍽

Whiteparish 6C

10–2.30; 6–11
Kings Head
(A27) ☎ 287
Whitbread Flowers Original
Bitter ℍ **Strong Country**
Bitter ℍ & Ⓖ
Welcoming small village local
🍴♣🎵🏧🅑℞🍽♿

Wilton 6B

10.30–2.30; 6–11
Bear
West Street (A30)
Hall & Woodhouse Hector's
Bitter, Badger Best Bitter ℍ
Welcoming local 🏧🍴♣🎵🍽♿

Wootton Bassett 6B

10.30–2.30; 6–10.30 (11 F, S)
Borough Arms
(A420) ☎ Swindon 852252
Arkell BB, BBB, Kingsdown
Ale ℍ
Noted chamberpot collection
♣🎵🅑🍽

Wroughton 6B

10–2.30; 6–10.30 (11 F, S)
Carters Rest
High Street (A361)
Archer Best Bitter, Golden
Eldridge Pope IPA, Royal
Oak ℍ
Two guest beers always
available ♣🎵🏧🕓♠🍽♿

Ainderby Quernhow 30C6

10.30–2.30; 6–10.30 (11 F, S and summer)

Black Horse
(B6267, off A1)
Thirsk 567313
Tetley Bitter
Webster Yorkshire Bitter Ⓗ
Black and white country inn
♣♠Ⓖ♥Ⓢ

Allerston 31F6

11–2.30; 6–10.30 (11 F, S)

Cayley Arms
(A170) OS 877830
Scarborough 85338
Cameron Lion Bitter Ⓗ
Popular residential local and
roadhouse ♠♪♣✠♠Ⓡ Ⓢ Å

Appleton-le-Street 31E6

10.30–2.30; 5.30–10.30 (11 F, S)

Cresswell Arms
(B1257) Malton 3647
Cameron Lion Bitter Ⓗ
Pub with a good local
reputation for meals
♣✠♠Ⓖ♥Ⓢ

Askrigg 29H5

11–3; 5.30–10.30 (11 F, S and summer)

Crown
Main Street (off A684)
Evening opening: 7
McEwan 80/-
Younger Scotch Bitter Ⓗ
Traditional Dales pub ♪♣♥

Austwick 29G6

11–3; 5.30–10.30 (11 F, S and summer)

Game Cock
(Off A65) Clapham 226
Yates & Jackson Bitter Ⓔ
Small, pleasant country pub
♣✠♠Ⓖ♥Ⓢ

Bedale 30B5

10.30–3; 6–10.30 (11 F, S and summer)

Old Black Swan
Market Place (A684)
Open all day Tuesday
Theakston Dark Mild, Best
Bitter, XB, Old Peculier Ⓗ
Rare outlet for Theakston's
Mild ♠♪♣Ⓡ Ⓖ♥Ⓢ

Bellerby 30A5

11–3; 5.30–10.30 (11 F, S and summer)

Cross Keys
(A6108)
Wensleydale 22256
Marston Burton Bitter,
Pedigree Ⓗ
Welcoming village inn of
character
♠♪♣✠♠Ⓡ♥Ⓢ Å

Bentham 29F6

11–3; 5.30–10.30 (11 F, S and summer)

Horse & Farrier
(B6480) 610381

Boddingtons Bitter
McEwan 70/-
Moorhouse Pendle Witches
Brew
Theakston Best Bitter
Younger No 3 Ⓗ
Comfortable rusticated pub
♪♣✠♠Ⓖ♥Ⓢ

Boroughbridge 30C7

11–3; 5.30–10.30 (11 F, S and summer)

Yorkshire Rose
St James Square 2734
May open 7 pm evenings
Cameron Lion Bitter,
Strongarm Ⓗ
Uniquely restored town pub
with original well
♠♪♣✠♠Ⓡ Ⓖ♥Ⓢ Å

Brearton 30C7

11–3; 5.30–10.30 (11 F, S and summer)

Malt Shovel
OS 322608 862929
Evening opening: 7
Vaux Sunderland Draught
Bitter, Samson Ⓗ
Unspoilt country inn in
isolated village
♠♪♣✠♠Ⓖ♥Ⓢ

Buckden 29H7

11–3; 5.30–10.30 (11 F, S and summer)

Buck
(B6160) Kettlewell 227
Theakston Best Bitter, XB, Old
Peculier
Younger Scotch Bitter, No 3 Ⓗ
Comfortable, beautifully
situated Dales inn
♠♪♣✠♠Ⓖ♥Ⓢ

Carleton 29H8

11–3; 5.30–10.30 (11 F, S and summer)

Swan
Webster Yorkshire Light,
Bitter Ⓔ
Attractive and pleasant village
pub ♠♪♣✠♠Ⓡ♥

Carthorpe 30C6

10.30–2.30; 5.30–10.30 (11 F, S and summer)

Fox & Hounds
(Off A1) Thirsk 567433
Sometimes closes weekday
lunchtimes
Cameron Lion Bitter
Tetley Bitter Ⓗ
Recently tastefully
modernised ♠♣✠♠Ⓡ♥Ⓢ

Castleton 30E4

10.30–3; 6–10.30 (11 F, S and summer)

Downe Arms
3 High Street Whitby 223
Opens at 11 am & 6.30 pm;
closes 2.30 pm in winter
Cameron Strongarm Ⓗ
Early 19th-century residential
country pub
♠♪♣✠♠Ⓡ Ⓡ Ⓖ♥Ⓢ

Cawood 30D8

10.30–2.30; 6–10.30 (11 F, S)

Bay Horse

Bishop Dike Road (B1222)
Tetley Mild, Bitter Ⓗ
Friendly, thriving village pub
♪♣✠♠♥Ⓢ

Cloughton 31G5

11–3; 5.30–10.30 (11 F, S and summer)

Falcon Inn
Whitby Road (A171)
OS 972982
Scarborough 870717
Cameron Lion Bitter,
Strongarm Ⓗ
Friendly moorland inn 3 miles
north of village
♠♪♣✠♠Ⓖ♥Ⓢ Å

Cononley 29H8

11–3; 5.30–10.30 (11 F, S and summer)

New Inn
(Off A629)
Opening hours vary
Taylor Golden Mild, Best
Bitter Ⓔ
Genuine low-beamed old
village pub ♠♪♣♥Ⓢ

Cray 29H6

11.3; 5.30–10.30 (11 F, S and summer)

White Lion
(B6160) Kettlewell 262
Theakston Best Bitter, Old
Peculier
Younger Scotch Bitter Ⓗ
Stone-floored Dales pub in
spectacular hill setting
♠♣✠♠Ⓢ

Dalton 30C6

10.30–2.30; 6–10.30 (11 F, S and summer)

**Jolly Farmers of
Olden Times**
(Off A168) Topcliffe 577359
Tetley Bitter
Webster Yorkshire Bitter Ⓗ
Village inn catering for all
tastes ♠♣✠♠Ⓡ Ⓖ♥Ⓢ Å

Darley 30B7

11–3; 6–10.30 (11 F, S and summer)

Wellington
(B6451)
Evening opening: 7
Tetley Bitter Ⓗ
A small country pub,
delightfully situated ♪♣✠♠Ⓢ

Easingwold 30D6

10.30–2.30; 5.30–10.30 (11 F, S)

George
Market Place (off A19)
21698
Cameron Lion Bitter,
Strongarm Ⓗ
Georgian market hotel
♠♪♣✠♠Ⓖ♥Ⓢ

East Marton 29H8

11–3; 5.30–10.30 (11 F, S and summer)

Cross Keys
(A59) Earby 3485
Theakston Best Bitter, XB, Old
Peculier

Thwaites Bitter Ⓗ
Popular free house near canal
🅿🍴⚲🏠Ⓡ©🚼⊙Ⓢ

Fearby 30B6

11–3; 6–10.30 (11 F, S and summer)
Kings Head
(Off A6108)
May open at 11.30 am & 7 pm
Theakston Best Bitter, Old
Peculier Ⓗ
Small, friendly free house two
miles west of Masham
🅿🍴🎲⚲🏠Ⓡ©🅰

Ferrensby 30C7

11–3; 5.30–10.30 (11 F, S and summer)
General Tarleton
(A6055) ☎ Copgrove 284
Cameron Lion Bitter
Taylor Best Bitter, Landlord
Tetley Mild, Bitter
Theakston Best Bitter, XB, Old
Peculier
Webster Yorkshire Bitter Ⓗ
Enthusiastic country
beerhouse 🅿🍴⚲©🚼Ⓢ

Filey 31H6

11–3; 5.30–10.30 (11 F, S and summer)
Foords Hotel
76 Queen Street
☎ Scarborough 512192
Evening opening: 7
Cameron Lion Bitter,
Strongarm Ⓗ
Friendly 18th-century hotel
with keen commitment to real
ale 🅿🍴🎲⚲🏠Ⓡ©🚼⊙Ⓢ🅰🚻

Fylingthorpe 31G4

10–3; 6.30–11
Fylingdales Inn
Main Street (B1447) ☎ Whitby
880433
Opens at 11 am & 6.30 pm
Draught Bass Ⓗ
Comfortable village inn,
children welcome
🅿🍴🎲⚲🏠Ⓡ©🚼⊙Ⓢ🅰

Glusburn 29H8

11–3; 5.30–10.30 (11 F, S and summer)
Dog & Gun
(A6068) ☎ Cross Hills 33855
Taylor Dark Mild, Golden
Mild, Best Bitter Ⓔ
Comfortable roadside inn
🍴⚲©🚼Ⓢ

Great Broughton 31D4

11–3; 5.30–10.30 (11 F, S)
Jet Miners
61 High Street
☎ Wainstones 427
McEwan 80/- Ⓗ
Unspoilt stone pub of 1750
🅿🍴🎲⚲🏠Ⓡ©🚼⊙Ⓢ🅰

Harmby 30A5

11–3; 6–10.30 (11 F, S and summer)
Pheasant
(A684) ☎ Wensleydale 22223

Tetley Bitter Ⓗ
Popular rural inn at gateway
to Wensleydale
🅿🍴🎲⚲🏠Ⓡ©🅰

Harome 30E6

10.30–2.30; 5.30–10.30 (11 F, S)
Star
(Off A170) ☎ Helmsley 70397
Cameron Lion Bitter
Lorimer Best Scotch
Theakston Best Bitter, Old
Peculier Ⓗ
Remarkable old thatched inn
🍴⚲🏠©🚼

Harrogate 30C7

11–3; 5.30–10.30 (11 F, S and summer)
Little Wonder
Ripon Road (A61/A59)
Cameron Lion Bitter Ⓗ
Large roadside pub named
after a racehorse
🍴🅿🏠Ⓡ©Ⓢ

Muckles Vaults
11 West Park (A61)
☎ 504463
Saturday evening opening:
7.30; closes 10.30 pm
Mon–Thu in summer
Tetley Mild, Bitter Ⓗ
Comfortable town house,
decorated with military
paraphernalia ⚲🏠©🚼

Nelson
Saltergate Hill (A59, 2 m west
of town) ☎ 500340
Tetley Mild, Bitter
Oliver John's Bitter Ⓗ
Welcoming pub; try the home
brew 🍴🎲⚲🏠©🚼🚻

New Inn
Otley Road (B6162) ☎ 503501
Tetley Mild, Bitter Ⓗ
Large Tetley house to west of
town 🍴🎲⚲🏠©Ⓢ

Old Tradition
Old Bath Road
Taylor Best Bitter, Landlord
Tetley Mild, Bitter
Theakston Best Bitter, XB Ⓗ
Two bars, popular with
younger set 🍴🎲⚲🚻

Squinting Cat
Whinney Lane, Pannal Ash
☎ 65650
Tetley Mild, Bitter Ⓗ
Old inn of great character
🍴⚲🏠© (not Mon)

Try also: Hales Bars (Bass)

Hawes 29H5

11–3; 5.30–10.30 (11 F, S and summer)
Board Hotel
Market Place (A684) ☎ 223
Open all day Tuesdays
Marston Burton Bitter,
Pedigree Ⓗ
Unpretentious, friendly
market town hotel
🍴🎲⚲🏠©🚼⊙Ⓢ🅰

Haxby 30D

11–3; 5.30–11
Tiger
Main Street (off B1363)
☎ York 768355
Samuel Smith Old Brewery
Bitter Ⓗ
Extensively renovated inn
🍴⚲©🚼⊙Ⓢ

Helmsley 30E

10.30–2.30; 5.30–10.30 (11 F, S)
Crown
Market Place (A170) ☎ 7029?
Cameron Lion Bitter Ⓔ
Attractive, lively old
residential hotel
🍴🎲🎲⚲🏠©🚼🚻Ⓢ

Helwith Bridge 26G

11–3; 5.30–10.30 (11 F, S and summer)
Helwith Bridge
(B6479) OS 811695
☎ Horton in Ribblesdale 220
Webster Yorkshire Mild, Bitte
Younger Scotch Bitter, No 3 Ⓗ
Homely country pub near
River Ribble
🅿🍴🎲🎲⚲🏠©Ⓢ🅰

Hornby 30C

11–3; 6–10.30 (11 F, S and summer)
Grange Arms
(Off A167) ☎ Great Smeaton
249
Webster Yorkshire Bitter
Younger Scotch Bitter Ⓗ
Cosy country pub
🅿🍴©🚼Ⓢ

Huby 30D

10.30–2.30; 5.30–10.30 (11 F, S)
Queen of Trumps
Tetley Mild, Bitter Ⓗ
Thriving village local
🍴🅰Ⓢ

Hutton Rudby 30D

11–3; 5.30–10.30 (11 F, S)
Kings Head
36 Northside ☎ 700342
Cameron Strongarm Ⓗ
Small, friendly local at top of
village 🍴🅰🅰Ⓢ

Ingleton 29F

11–3; 5.30–10.30 (11 F, S and summer)
Craven Heifer
1 Main Street ☎ 41427
Yates & Jackson Mild, Bitter Ⓔ
Popular, lively pub
🅿🍴🎲🏠Ⓡ©🚼⊙Ⓢ🅰

Kettlesing 30B

11–3; 5.30–10.30 (11 F, S and summer)
Queen's Head
(Off A59)
☎ Harrogate 770263
Theakston Best Bitter
Younger Scotch Bitter Ⓗ
Pleasant country inn, good
food 🍴🎲⚲🏠©🚼Ⓢ

ildwick 29H8

3; 5.30–10.30 (11 F, S and summer)
White Lion Hotel
.629)
tley Mild, Bitter Ⓗ
ell-maintained, spacious
ab near canal
♨🅰🅢

illinghall 30B7

30–2.30; 5.30–10.30 (11 F, S and summer)
Three Horseshoes
pon Road (A61)
Harrogate 56302
ameron Lion Bitter Ⓗ
omfortable and friendly
oadside pub ♪♣🅰🅖♥🅢

irkbymoorside 31E5

30–2.30; 5.30–10.30 (11 F, S)
lack Swan
arket Place (off A170)
31305
ameron Lion Bitter Ⓔ
ncient market inn with a
riking Elizabethan porch
♣🅓🅘🅢

naresborough 30C7

–3 (4 pm Wed); 5.30–10.30
F, S and summer)
ross Keys
heapside
etley Mild, Bitter Ⓗ
raditional local off market
quare ♪♣♥🅘

roves

arket Place ℰ 863022
ameron Lion Bitter,
rongarm Ⓔ
opular 18th century pub
♣🅖🅘

astingham 31E5

30–2.30; 5.30–10.30 (11 F, S)
lacksmiths Arms
247
etley Mild, Bitter
heakston Best Bitter, Old
eculier Ⓗ
lovely 200-year-old country
n ♨🅰🅓🅖♥

evisham 31F5

30–2.30; 5.30–10.30 (11 F, S and summer)
orsehoe Inn
ff A169) OS 833906
Pickering 60240
heakston Best Bitter, XB Ⓗ
omfortable inn between
llage green and moors
♪♣🅱♥🅰🅓🅡🅖♥🅢

inton-in-Craven 29H7

–3; 5.30–10.30 (11 F, S and summer)
ountaine Inn
ff B6160)
aylor Dark Mild, Best Bitter
heakston Best Bitter, XB,
ld Peculier
ounger Scotch Bitter Ⓗ

Popular old pub on village
green ♨🅰♣♥🅰🅢

Malton 31F6

10.30–2.30; 5.30–10.30 (11 F, S and summer)
Spotted Cow
Spitalgate, Cattle Market
ℰ 2100
Afternoon extension Tue, Fri,
Sat
Tetley Bitter Ⓗ
Superb old pub retaining
much character ♨🅰♣🅖🅘🅢

Masham 30B6

11–3; 6–10.30 (11 F, S and summer)
White Bear
Old Brewery Yard
**Theakston Light Mild, Best
Bitter, XB, Old Peculier** Ⓗ
Theakston's brewery tap;
full of fascinating
bric-a-brac ♨🅰♣♥🅰🅖🅘

Muker 29H5

11–3; 6–10.30 (11 F, S and summer)
Farmers Arms
(B6270) ℰ Richmond 86297
McEwan 80/- Ⓗ
Unspoilt pub in beautiful
countryside ♨🅰♣🅖♥🅘🅢🅰

Newton-on-Ouse 30D7

10.30–2.30; 5.30–10.30 (11 F, S)
Blacksmiths Arms
(Off A19)
**Cameron Lion Bitter,
Strongarm** Ⓗ
A well-patronised village local
in lovely setting ♨🅰♣♥🅰🅢

Normanby 31E6

10.30–2.30; 5.30–10.30 (11 F, S)
Sun
(Off A170)
ℰ Kirkbymoorside 31051
**Cameron Lion Bitter
Tetley Bitter
Theakston XB** Ⓗ
Welcoming old inn
♪♣🅱♥🅰🅖♥🅢🅰

Northallerton 30C5

11–3; 6–10.30 (11 F, S and summer)
Golden Lion
112/114 High Street (A167)
ℰ 2404
Open until 5 pm Wed
Tetley Bitter Ⓗ
Historic post house, now a
hotel ♨🅰♪🅱🅰🅓🅡🅖♥🅢≋

Norton 31F6

10.30–2.30; 5.30–10.30 (11 F, S and summer)
Buckrose Hotel
Church Street ℰ Malton 3706
Tetley Bitter Ⓗ
Town-style pub with good
reputations for meals
♪🅘♣🅰🅓🅡🅖♥🅢≋

Norwood 30B7

11–3; 5.30–10.30 (11 F, S and summer)

Sun
(B6451) OS 207538
ℰ Blubberhouses 220
**Tetley Mild, Bitter
Theakston Best Bitter, XB
Younger Scotch Bitter, No 3** Ⓗ
Modernised country inn in
pleasant setting
🅘♣🅱♥🅰🅖♥🅢

Osmotherley 30D5

11–3; 6–10.30 (11 F, S and summer)
Three Tuns
9 South End (off A19) ℰ 301
**McEwan 80/-
Younger No 3** Ⓗ
Bright and cosy local in 17th
century building
♨🅰♪♣♥🅡🅖♥🅘🅢

Oswaldkirk 30E6

10.30–2.30; 5.30–10.30 (11 F, S)
Malt Shovel
(B1363) ℰ Ampleforth 461
**Samuel Smith Old Brewery
Bitter** Ⓗ
Historic building dating from
1610, with colourful history
and genuine character
♨🅰♣♥🅰🅱🅡🅖♥🅘🅢

Pickering 31F6

10.30–2.30; 5.30–10.30 (11 F, S and summer)
Sun
Westgate (A170)
Afternoon extension Mondays
Tetley Mild, Bitter Ⓗ
Splendid roadside local; full of
life ♪♣🅖🅢

Raskelf 30D6

10.30–2.30; 5.30–10.30 (11 F, S)
Three Tuns
(Off A19) ℰ Easingwold
21335
**Tetley Mild, Bitter
Younger Scotch Bitter** Ⓗ
Enterprising, revitalised
village inn ♪♣♥🅰🅖♥🅘🅢

Reeth 29J5

11–3; 6–10.30 (11 F, S and summer)
Buck
(B6270) ℰ Richmond 84210
Webster Yorkshire Bitter Ⓗ
Prominent hotel on road
junction ♨🅰♪♣♥🅰🅖♥🅘🅢🅰

Richmond 30B4

11–3; 6–10.30 (11 F, S and summer)
Holly Hill
Sleagill OS 172003 ℰ 2192
**Theakston Dark Mild, Best
Bitter, XB, Old Peculier** Ⓗ
Modernised stone pub of
character, to south of town
♣🅰🅘🅢

Turf Tavern
Victoria Road (off A6108)
ℰ 3262
Draught Bass Ⓔ
Typical two-roomed market
town hotel ♪♣🅰🅱🅖♥🅘🅢

Ripon 30C6

11–3; 6–10.30 (11 F, S and summer)

Black Bull
Old Market Place ℰ 2755
Theakston Best Bitter, XB, Old Peculier Ⓗ
Modernised historic coaching inn ♨♪♣♒▣Ⓡ🅖♿

Studley Royal
Market Place ℰ 2044
Open until 4 pm Thursdays
Tetley Mild, Bitter Ⓗ
Traditional market-square hotel ♪♣▣Ⓡ🅖♋♉Ⓢ

Robin Hood's Bay 31G4

10.30–2.30 (3 summer); 6.30–10.30 (11 F, S and summer)

Bay Hotel
B1447, off A171) ℰ 880278
Morning opening: 11
Bass Brew Ten
Theakston Old Peculier Ⓗ
Perched at bottom of village overlooking the bay
♨♪♣▣♒▣Ⓡ🅖♋♉Ⓢ

Victoria
Cliff Top (B1447)
ℰ Whitby 880205
Opens at 11 am & 6 pm
Cameron Lion Bitter, Strongarm Ⓗ
Imposing seaside Victorian hotel ♨♣▣♒▣Ⓡ♋♉♉Ⓢ⚤

Rosedale Abbey 31E5

10.30–2.30; 5.30–10.30 (11 F, S)

White Horse Farm Hotel
ℰ Lastingham 239
Tetley Bitter
Vaux Samson Ⓗ
Enterprising converted farmhouse with fine views
▣♒▣Ⓡ🅖♋♉♉Ⓢ⚤

Ruswarp 31F4

10–3; 6.30–10.30 (11 F, S)

Unicorn
High Street (B1416, off A171)
Open 11 am–11 pm Wednesdays
Cameron Strongarm Ⓗ
Terrace inn in pretty village
♪♣▣♒♉

Ryther 30D8

10.30–3; 6–10.30 (11 F, S)

Rythre Arms
(B1223) ℰ Cawood 372
Tetley Mild, Bitter Ⓗ
Theakston Best Bitter Ⓔ
Old Peculier Ⓖ
Renovated free house with good restaurant ♪♒🅖♋♉Ⓢ

Sandsend 31F4

10.30–2.30; 6.30–10.30 (11 F, S)

Hart
East Row (A174)

ℰ Whitby 80304
Morning opening: 11
Cameron Lion Bitter Ⓗ
Strongarm Ⓔ
Picturesque pub overlooking beach ♨♪♣♒♋🅖♉♉Ⓢ

Scarborough 31G5

11–3; 5.30–10.30 (11 F, S and summer)

Cask
Cambridge Terrace, South Cliff ℰ 60198
Evening opening: 6
Tetley Mild, Bitter
Younger Scotch Bitter, No. 3, IPA Ⓗ
Modern old-world style pub with family holiday flats
♪▣♒Ⓡ♉⚤

Hole in the Wall
Vernon Road ℰ 73746
Theakston Best Bitter, XB, Old Peculier
Vaux Sunderland Draught Bitter Ⓗ
Small, popular gem away from main street ♪Ⓢ

Leeds Arms
St Mary's Street
Evening opening: 7
Draught Bass Ⓗ
Cosy old town pub with nautical theme ♨♪♣♉

New Tavern
Falsgrave Road ℰ 66965
Cameron Lion Bitter, Strongarm Ⓗ
Old pub away from the town centre ♨♪♣♒▣Ⓡ♉Ⓢ♿

Plough
St Thomas Street ℰ 73621
Cameron Lion Bitter Ⓗ
Town-centre pub, recently enlarged ♪♣Ⓡ♋Ⓢ

Prince of Wales
Castle Road
Cameron Lion Bitter, Strongarm Ⓗ
Two-roomed gem, small and friendly ♪♣♉Ⓢ

Scorton 30B4

11–3; 6–10.30 (11 F, S and summer)

Royal
(B1263)
Cameron Lion Bitter, Strongarm Ⓗ
Overlooking the village green
♨♪♣♒▣Ⓡ♉Ⓢ

Seamer 31G6

11–3; 5.30–10.30 (11 F, S and summer)

Londesborough Arms
Main Street (A64)
Evening opening: 7
Cameron Lion Bitter Ⓗ
Rambling old inn ♨♪♣▣♉♉

Selby 30E9

10.30–3; 6–10.30 (11 F, S)

New Inn
Gowthorpe (A19)
Tetley Mild, Bitter Ⓗ
Bustling town-centre house
♣♉Ⓢ⚤

Sherburn 31G6

10.30–2.30; 5.30–10.30 (11 F, S and summer)

Pigeon Pie
(A64) ℰ 383
Cameron Lion Bitter Ⓗ
Friendly local pub convenient for Woldsway and Ganton Golf ♪♣▣♒▣Ⓡ♉Ⓢ

Sicklinghall 30C8

11–3; 6–10.30 (11 F, S and summer)

Scotts Arms
Main Street (off A661)
ℰ Wetherby 62100
Taylor Best Bitter
Tetley Mild, Bitter
Theakston Best Bitter, Old Peculier
Whitbread Castle Eden Ale Ⓗ
Comfortable, up-market village inn with restaurant
♪♣▣♒▣Ⓡ♋♉Ⓢ

Skipton 29H8

11–3; 5.30–10.30 (11 F, S and summer)

Devonshire Hotel
Newmarket Street ℰ 3078
Tetley Mild, Bitter
Younger Scotch Bitter Ⓗ
Solid town-centre drinkers' pub ♪♣▣♒▣Ⓡ Ⓢ

Rose & Crown
10 Coach Street ℰ 2654
Evening opening: 7 (approx)
Tetley Mild, Bitter Ⓗ
A popular town pub opposite canal basin
♪♣Ⓡ♉

Royal Shepherd
Canal Street ℰ 3178
Chesters Bitter
Whitbread Castle Eden Ale Ⓗ
Friendly, traditional pub on canal-side ♪♣♒Ⓡ♉

Try also: Horse Close (Webster)

Stainforth 29G7

11–3; 5.30–10.30 (11 F, S and summer)

Craven Heifer
(Off B6479) ℰ Settle 2599
Evening opening: 6.15
Thwaites Best Mild, Bitter Ⓗ
Old pack horse inn in pleasant village
♨♪♣▣♒▣Ⓡ♉Ⓢ

Stapleton 30B4

11–3; 6–10.30 (11 F, S)

Bridge
(Off A66(M))
ℰ Darlington 50106
Lorimer Best Scotch
Vaux Samson Ⓗ
Village green inn on old A1
♨♪♣♒▣♋♉♉Ⓢ♿

Stockton-on-the-Forest 30E7

30–2.30; 6–10.30 (11 F, S)

Fox
York 768659
Tetley Bitter ℍ
Renovated village inn; smart
and popular ♪✦🅿🛏🕭♿⑤

Stokesley 30D4

–3; 5.30–10.30

Station
Station Road ☎ 710436
Evening opening: 7
Cameron Strongarm ℍ
Small and cosy bar
✦🅿🛏🕭⑤

Summerbridge 30B7

.30–2.30; 6–10.30 (11 F, S and summer)

Flying Dutchman
36165) ☎ Harrogate 780321
Morning opening: 11.45
Samuel Smith Old Brewery
Bitter ℍ
Friendly, comfortable country
pub ♪✦🅿🛏🍴♿🕭♿⑤Ⓐ

Tadcaster 30D8

.30–3; 6–10.30 (11 F, S)

Howden Arms
High Street (off A64)
Samuel Smith Old Brewery
Bitter ℍ
Bustling one-room pub,
luckily situated opposite John
Smith's brewery ♪✦🛏⑤

Thirsk 30C6

.30–2.30; 6–10.30 (11 F, S and summer)

Lord Nelson
0 St James Green ☎ 22845
Draught Bass
Cameron Lion Bitter
Stones Best Bitter
Theakston Best Bitter
Younger IPA ℍ
Popular pub in old Thirsk
✦🅿🛏♿🕭⑤

Thruscross 29J7

–3; 6–10.30 (11 F, S and summer)

Stonehouse Inn
Off A59) OS 159587
Blubberhouses 226
Theakston Best Bitter, XB, Old
Peculier
Younger Scotch Bitter, No 3 ℍ
Splendid old free house in
panoramic setting
✦♪✦🛏🅿🍴♿🕭⑤Ⓐ

Tunstall 30B5

–3; 6–10.30 (11 F, S and summer)

Bay Horse
Off A1) ☎ Richmond 818564
Opens at 12 noon & 7 pm;
closed Monday lunchtimes
Samuel Smith Old Brewery
Bitter ℍ
Cosy 18th-century village pub
✦🅿🛏🍴🅡⑤Ⓐ

Ugthorpe 31F4

10–3; 6.30–11

Black Bull
Main Street (off A171)
Cameron Strongarm
Tetley Mild, Bitter
Theakston Best Bitter, XB ℍ
Fine village pub in row of
cottages 🛏♪✦🅿🛏🕭⑤

Welburn 31E6

10.30–2.30; 5.30–10.30 (11 F, S)

Crown & Cushion
(Off A64)
☎ Whitwell-on-the-Hill 304
Cameron Lion Bitter,
Strongarm ℍ
Well-kept inn close to Castle
Howard ♪✦🛏♿🕭⑤

Well 30B6

11–2.30; 6–10.30 (11 F, S and summer)

Well Ox
☎ Bedale 70352
Theakston Best Bitter, Old
Peculier (summer) ℍ
Excellent traditional pub
🕭♪✦🅿🅡🛏⑤

Wheldrake 30E8

10.30–2.30; 6–10.30 (11 F, S)

Alice Hawthorne
(Off A19) ☎ 203
Cameron Lion Bitter ℍ
Popular village pub in pretty
setting ♪✦🅿🛏♿🕭⑤

Whitby 31F4

10–2.30 (3 summer); 6.30–10.30
(11 F, S and summer)

Black Horse
91 Church Street
Morning opening: 10.30
Tetley Mild, Bitter ℍ
Small fisherman's pub near
market 🕭♪✦🅡⑤

Board
Church Street
Morning opening: 10.30
Theakston Best Bitter, Old
Peculier ℍ
At the foot of the famous 199
steps 🕭♪✦♿🛏

Try also: **Jolly Sailor**; **Plough**
(Sam Smith)

Wighill 30D8

11–3; 6–10.30 (11 F, S)

White Swan
(Off A64)
Draught Bass
Stones Best Bitter
Theakston Best Bitter, Old
Peculier ℍ
Good country inn with many
small rooms
🛏✦🅿🛏🅿⑤

York 30D8

11–3; 5.30–11

Acorn
9 St Martins Lane, Micklegate

**Cameron Lion Bitter,
Strongarm** ℍ
Hardworking little
two-roomed local ♪✦🛏🕭♿≈

Bar Hotel
1 Micklegate
Tetley Bitter ℍ
Busy pub tucked inside city
walls ♪✦🛏≈

Bootham Tavern
29 Bootham ☎ 31093
Tetley Bitter ℍ
Compact, bustling
two-roomed pub ♪✦🕭🛏

Crystal Palace
66 Holgate Road ☎ 25305
Samuel Smith Old Brewery
Bitter ℍ
Comfortable, pleasant lounge
and large bar ♪✦🅿🛏🅡♿🛏⑤

Hole in the Wall
High Petergate ☎ 34468
North Country Riding Bitter ℍ
Riding bitter is the only
unfiltered beer 🛏♪♿⑤

John Bull
Layerthorpe (off A1036)
Darley Thorne Best Bitter
Franklins Bitter
Taylor Best Bitter, Landlord
Ward Sheffield Best Bitter ℍ
Recently re-opened, with
much memorabilia and guest
real ales 🕭🅿🛏

Punch Bowl
Lowther Street
Cameron Lion Bitter,
Strongarm ℍ
Busy two-roomed local
♪✦🅿🛏

Spread Eagle
98 Walmgate ☎ 37467
Taylor Best Bitter, Landlord ℍ
Thriving free house with a
wide choice of other real ales
♪✦🎲♿🕭⑤

Swan
Bishopsgate Street,
Clementhorpe
Tetley Bitter ℍ
Traditional street-corner local
♪✦🛏

Walkers Bar
55 Micklegate ☎ 28501
Theakston Mild, Best Bitter,
XB, Old Peculier ℍ
Busy pub with interesting
design ♪✦🅿🛏♿≈

Wellington
47 Alma Terrace, Fulford
Road
Samuel Smith Old Brewery
Bitter ℍ
Splendid, traditional
side-street inn ✦🅡🛏

Try also: **Richard III**
(Webster); **York Arms** (Sam
Smith)

In the Club?

From the Truss Testers Tabernacle in Truro to the Idle Working Mens Club, there are over 30,000 registered clubs in Britain. They range in size from tiny sports and social clubs to institutions as big as the Albert Hall. Some will admit only members and their guests, others operate a form of affiliate entry where belonging to one club gives automatic entry to all other linked ones. The largest chain – the Clubs and Institutes Union – has over 4000 affiliated clubs.

In some areas of the country, particularly the North East, clubs have a far greater volume of trade than the region's pubs, yet for many years the conventional wisdom was that clubs could not and would not sell cask conditioned beer. The result, actively encouraged by Newcastle's two major breweries – Scottish and Newcastle, and Federation was an unrelieved sea of bright beer throughout the North East clubs. The tide at last began to turn in 1981, when a CIU affiliated club became the first in Newcastle to re-install cask beer. Since then many others have begun to offer their members a choice between keg and real beer.

Away from Newcastle – the fizz capital of Great Britain – the club scene is far more encouraging. In the other bastions of the club, the Midlands, South Wales, the North West and Yorkshire, real beer is increasingly widely available. In Bradford, for example, two thirds of the clubs offer the real stuff, and in Blackpool a real beer unique to clubland – Blackpool Best Mild – is available in four clubs.

Club stewards and committees can no longer hide behind the claim that they can't obtain or keep real beer. Every brewery company in the country except Federation and John Smiths produces it and the chances are that the brewery that already supplies your club will provide real beer if they are asked for it. They are also usually happy to advise on cask sizes and keeping and serving methods, so there is no reason why all but the most slovenly club stewards should not serve real beer in just as good condition as the pub down the road. Give your taste-buds a treat – get your committee to join the real ale club!

CART it

You don't have to ask for McFizzie's lager. There are hundreds of real ale off-licences around the country with a range of regular and guest beers that you can drink at home, take to parties, or drink anytime and anywhere you want a decent pint.

Most real ale off licences will supply you with every thing from a barrel to a bottle and you can now even obtain draught beer by mail-order. The "beer-at-home" service long operated by Davenport's Brewery has been emulated by many milkmen. Even the supermarket chains have responded to the demand, by providing an ordering service for "polypins" (boxed, polythene containers).

The growth in outlets has been matched by the variety of containers now available. They range from casks which you can set up, tap and tend yourself, through stoneware, glass and plastic containers, "bags-in-a-box" and resealable, waxed-cardboard cartons.

Pubs have frequently neglected off-sales, but CART (CAMRA's "Campaign for Real Take-home") is urging them to get in on the act. Many now stock take-home containers, and some will also accept orders for casks. After all, Britain's biggest real ale off licence chain is the more than 30,000 real ale pubs special across the country.

Armthorpe 26B4

10.30–3; 6–10.30 (11 F, S)
Plough
Church Street
Darley Thorne Best Bitter Ⓗ
Colliery village pub with
traditional tap room
⌐♪♣▣Ⓡ❶⑧

Balby 26B4

10.30–3; 6–10.30 (11 F, S)
Spinney
Grenville Estate (off A630)
Home Bitter Ⓔ
Darts orientated estate pub
♪♣▣❶

Barnsley 23H2

11–3; 6–11
Drop Out (off-licence)
152 Sheffield Road (A61)
Open evenings only 7–10 pm,
closed Wed, Sun
Clark Bitter
**Marston Pedigree, Owd
Rodger**
West Riding Tyke Ⓗ
Barnsley's only real ale
off-licence; wide range of
guest beers

Silkstone
Park Road (off A61)
Tetley Bitter Ⓗ
Friendly estate pub ⌐♪♣⚘▣❶⚤

Wheatsheaf
Dodworth Road (A628)
Tetley Bitter Ⓗ
Friendly locals' pub with
enthusiastic landlady
⌐♪♣▣❶⑧

Blacker Hill 23H2

11–3; 6–11
Royal Albert
(Off A6096)
Ward Mild Ⓗ **Sheffield Best
Bitter** Ⓔ
Friendly local with cosy
wood-panelled lounge
♪♣▣❶

Bradway 23H4

11–3; 5.30–10.30 (11 F, S)
Old Mother Redcap
Prospect Road (off A621)
✆ Sheffield 360179
**Samuel Smith Old Brewery
Bitter** Ⓗ
Modern estate pub in stone
farmhouse style
♪♣⚘▣◖⑧

Chapeltown 23H3

11–3; 5.30–10.30 (11 F, S)
Thorncliffe Arms
135 Warren Lane, Sheffield
34 (off A6135)
Morning opening: 11.30
Ward Sheffield Best Bitter Ⓔ
Internally refurbished pub,
but retaining billiard room
▣♪♣⚘▣⑧

Conisbrough 23J3

10.30–3; 6–10.30 (11 F, S)
Red Lion
Sheffield Road (A630)
✆ Rotherham 864005
Opens at 12 noon & 7 pm
**Samuel Smith Old Brewery
Bitter** Ⓔ
Old coaching inn, popular
with all ages
♪♣⚘▣◖❶⑧

Crowedge 23G2

11–3; 6–11
Victoria
Huddersfield Road (A616)
Tetley Bitter Ⓗ
Pennine pub near West
Yorkshire border ▣♣▣❶⑧

Try also: Prince of Wales
(Tetley)

Darfield 23J2

11–3; 6–11
Victoria
Snape Hill Road (B6096)
Tetley Bitter Ⓔ
Popular mining village local
▣♪♣▣❶

Darton 23H2

11–3; 6–11
California
New Road (off A61)
Tetley Mild, Bitter Ⓗ
Large, basic bar, plush lounge
⌐♪♣▣❶

Denaby Main 26A4

10.30–3; 6–10.30 (11 F, S)
Denaby Main
Doncaster Road (A6023)
Tetley Bitter Ⓗ
Mining village pub with large,
basic bar ⌐♪♣▣Ⓡ❶

Doncaster 26B4

10.30–3; 6–10.30 (11 F, S)
Coach & Horses
5 Scot Lane ✆ 23456
Shipstone Mild Ⓗ **Bitter** Ⓔ
Lively town-centre tavern
with unusual collection of
customers ⌐♪♣▣Ⓡ⑧⚤

**Corporation
Brewery Taps**
135 Cleveland Street (A630)
**Samuel Smith Old Brewery
Bitter** Ⓗ & Ⓔ
Small cosy lounge, clubland
atmosphere in bar
▣⌐♪♣⚘▣⚤⚤

St. Leger Tavern
Silver Street ✆ 64556
Shipstone Mild, Bitter Ⓔ
Town-centre tavern with
racing decor ♪♣▣Ⓡ❶⑧

Vine
Balby Bridge (A630)
Darley Thorne Best Bitter Ⓗ
Proper pub surrounded by
concrete calamities ♪♣⚘▣❶

**Wellington Vaults
(Biscuit Billies)**
Bowers Fold
Draught Bass
Stones Best Bitter"
Cellar pub enjoying a new
lease of life ♪♣⑧

White Swan
Frenchgate
Ward Sheffield Best Bitter Ⓔ
Long thin pub, tallest bar in
Britain ⌐♪♣❶⑧⚡

Try also: Hallcross (home-
brew); **Yorkist** (Webster)

Ecclesfield 23H

11–3; 5.30–10.30 (11 F, S)
White Bear
46 Stockshill (off B6087)
Tetley Bitter Ⓗ
Fine stone-built pub on the
village square ♪♣⚘▣❶

Edenthorpe 26B

10.30–3; 6–10.30 (11 F, S)
Ridgewood
Thorne Road (A18)
**Samuel Smith Old Brewery
Bitter** Ⓗ
Post-war roadhouse with good
food ♪♣⚘▣◖❶⑧

Edlington 26E

10.30–3; 6–10.30 (11 F, S)
Tumbler
Broomhouse Lane (off B6376
Stones Best Bitter Ⓔ
Much-improved colliery
village local ♪♣▣❶

Elsecar 23H

11–3; 6–11
Market
Wentworth Road (B6097)
Stones Best Bitter Ⓗ & Ⓔ
Multi-roomed, friendly minin
village local ♪♣▣Ⓡ❶⑧

Finningley 26B

10.30–3; 6–10.30 (11 F, S)
Horse & Stag
Old Bawtry Road (off A614)
Bass Brew Ten Ⓔ
Right good pub in a pleasant
village ▣⌐♪♣▣Ⓡ❶⑧

Firbeck 26E

11–3; 6–10.30 (11 F, S)
Black Lion
(Off A634)
Opens 11.30 am & 7 pm
Tetley Bitter Ⓔ
Busy country pub near Roche
Abbey ▣♣⚘▣Ⓡ❶⑧

Grenoside 23H

11–3; 5.30–10.30 (11 F, S)
Cow & Calf
Skew Hill Lane (off A61)

☎ Sheffield 468191
Samuel Smith Old Brewery Bitter Ⓔ
17th-century farm buildings, unspoilt by conversion – fine views outside ♪♣▣♯🅰Ⓖ🍴⑧

Grimethorpe 23J2

11–3; 6–11
Red Rum
Cemetery Road (off A628)
Samuel Smith Old Brewery Bitter Ⓔ
Colliery village pub, formerly a doctor's house
♪♣♯🅰🍴

Harthill 26A5

10.30–3; 6–10.30 (11 F, S)
Beehive
Union Street (off A618)
Tetley Bitter Ⓔ
Old village pub with a snooker table ♪♣♯🅰🍴

Hatfield 26B3

10.30–3; 6–10.30 (11 F, S)
Green Tree
Bearswood Green (A18/A614)
☎ Doncaster 840305
Supper licence until 11.30 in restaurant
Darley Dark, Thorne Best Bitter Ⓗ
Former 17th-century posting house, emphasis on food
🅰♪▣♯🅰🅡Ⓖ🍴⑧♣🚹

Hatfield Woodhouse 26C4

10.30–3; 6–10.30 (11 F, S)
Robin Hood & Little John
Main Street (A614)
☎ Doncaster 840367
Stones Best Bitter Ⓔ
Friendly village pub, landlord a real character
♪♣♯🅰Ⓖ🍴⑧🚹

Higham 23H2

11–3; 6–11
Engineers
Higham Common Road (off A628) ☎ Barnsley 384204
Samuel Smith Old Brewery Bitter Ⓗ
Village pub with garden and good food ♪♣♯🅰Ⓖ🍴

Try also: Hermit (Tetley)

High Green 23H3

11–3; 5.30–10.30 (11 F, S)
Cart & Horses
2 Wortley Road, Mortomley
☎ Sheffield 848337
Opens at 11.30 am & 7 pm
Tetley Bitter Ⓗ & Ⓔ
Low beams and brasses, genuine atmosphere
🅰♪♣♯🅰Ⓖ🍴

Hoyland Nether 23H2

11–3; 6–11
Furnace
Milton Road (off B6047)
Ward Sheffield Best Bitter Ⓔ
Historic pub overlooking forge pond ♪♣♯🅰

Ingbirchworth 23H2

11–3; 6–11
Fountain
Wellthorne Lane (off A629)
☎ Barnsley 763125
Tetley Bitter Ⓗ
Attractive pub near reservoir
🅰♪♣🄴♯🅰🅡Ⓖ🍴⑧🚹

Jump 23J2

11–3; 6–11
Wellington
54 Church Street (off B6096)
Ward Sheffield Best Bitter Ⓗ
Characteristic mining village local, fine fire 🅰♪♣🅰🍴

Kilnhurst 23J3

11–3; 6–10.30 (11 F, S)
Terrace
Hooton Road (B6090)
Stones Best Bitter Ⓔ
Basic miners' local near river
🅰♪♣🅰🍴

Kiveton Park 26A5

10.30–3; 6–10.30 (11 F, S)
Forge
Wales Road (B6059)
Home Bitter Ⓔ
Friendly, modern local with large lounge ♪♣🅰🅡🍴

Maltby 26B5

10.30–3; 6–10.30 (11 F, S)
Toll Bar
Rotherham Road (A631)
Morning opening: 11.30
Stones Best Bitter Ⓔ
Post-war, street-corner local
♪♣🅰🅡🍴

Mexborough 26A4

10.30–3; 6–10.30 (11 F, S)
Ferryboat
Church Street (off A6023)
Stones Best Bitter Ⓔ
Comfortable old pub near the river ♪♣♯🅰🍴⑧

Moorends 26C3

10.30–3; 6–10.30 (11 F, S)
Winning Post
Marshland Road
Darley Dark Ⓗ
Thorne Best Bitter Ⓔ
Lively miners' pub with real landlord 🅰♪♣🅰🅡🍴⑧

Mosbrough 23J4

11–3; 5.30–10.30 (11 F, S)
British Oak
Mosbrough Moor (A616)

Shipstone Bitter Ⓔ
Comfortable, two-roomed local on busy road ♪♣♯🅰🍴

Munsbrough 23J3

10.30–3; 6–10.30 (11 F, S)
Buck & Griffin
Wagon Lane (B6089)
Home Bitter Ⓔ
Large modern pub on new estate ♪♣♯🅰🍴⑧🚹

Newington 26B4

11–3; 6–11
Ship
Mission Road (off A614)
Home Bitter Ⓔ
Excellent country pub near the River Idle ♪♣♯🅰🍴

Oughtibridge 23H3

11–3; 5.30–10.30 (11 F, S)
Hare & Hounds
6 Church Street (off A616)
Stones Best Bitter Ⓔ
Deservedly popular village local ♪♣🍴

Oxspring 23H2

11–3; 6–11
Travellers
Four Lane Ends (A629)
☎ Barnsley 762518
Ward Sheffield Best Bitter
Ⓔ & Ⓗ
Attractive pub at rural crossroads 🅰♪♯🅰Ⓖ⑧

Penistone 23H2

11–3; 6–11
Old Crown
Market Street (B6462)
☎ Barnsley 762422
Evening opening: 7
Tetley Bitter Ⓗ
Busy town pub, disco Tuesdays ♪♣Ⓖ

Rossington 26B4

10.30–3; 6–10.30 (11 F, S)
White Rose
Grange Lane
Samuel Smith Old Brewery Bitter Ⓔ
Totally in keeping with surrounding mining community ♪♣♯🅰🅡🍴

Rotherham 23J3

10.30–3; 6–10.30 (11 F, S)

Butchers Arms
Midland Road (A629)
☎ 560037
Tetley Bitter Ⓗ
Popular lounge, local tap room ♪♣🅰Ⓖ🍴🚻

Cross Keys
Moorgate (A618) ☎ 2296
Stones Best Bitter Ⓔ
Central pub renowned for home cooking
♪♣▣🅡Ⓖ🍴⑧

Junction
Milton Street ✆ 63078
Stones Best Bitter Ⓔ
Recently modernised, with an outside drinking area and aviary ♪♣♪🅿🅖Ⓢ

Moulders Rest
Masbrough Street (A6109)
✆ 560095
Stones Best Bitter Ⓔ
Tastefully modernised, with good local atmosphere
♪♣🅱🅖Ⓢ

Royal Standard
Masbrough Street (off A6109)
Stones Best Bitter Ⓔ
Town pub with interesting collection of trophies ♪♣🍴

Turners Arms
Psalters Lane (off A6109)
Ward Sheffield Best Bitter Ⓔ
Pleasant street corner local – 'The Green Bricks'
♪♣♪🅖Ⓘ Ⓢ

White Lion
92 College Road (A629)
Ward Sheffield Best Bitter Ⓔ
Comfortable atmosphere, landlord firmly committed to cask beer ♪♣♪🍴

Sheffield: Central
23H3

11–3; 5.30–10.30 (11 F, S)
Fat Cat
23 Alma Street, 3 (off A61)
Hardys & Hansons Bitter
Marston Pedigree, Owd Rodger
Ruddle County
Taylor Landlord
Theakston Old Peculier Ⓗ
Popular pub with no-smoking lounge, frequent guest beers and cider ʃ♣🎬🅿🅡🅖Ⓢ

Globe
Howard Street, 1
Stones Best Bitter Ⓔ
Cosy three-roomed pub close to polytechnic ♪♣🍴≋

Lord Nelson
Arundel Street, 1 ✆ 22650
Stones Best Bitter Ⓔ
Unspoilt local off town centre
♪♣🅡≋

Manchester
108 Nursery Street, 3
Ward Sheffield Best Bitter Ⓔ
Friendly, comfortable inn with active games teams ♪♣🅡🍴

Moseley's Arms
81 West Bar, 3 (A61)
Stones Best Bitter Ⓔ
Traditional local; snooker room upstairs ♪♣🅡🍴Ⓢ

Museum
25 Orchard Street, 1
Marston Pedigree
Whitbread Castle Eden Ale,

Durham Ale
Bulmer Cider Ⓗ
Popular city-centre meeting and drinking haunt ʃ♪🅖Ⓢ

Old Toad
40 Hoyle Street, 3 (off A61)
✆ 28217
Clark Bitter Ⓗ
Robinson Old Tom Ⓖ
Taylor Best Bitter
Theakston XB
Younger No. 3 Ⓗ
Bustling free house; other beers regularly available
♪♣🅖Ⓢ

Red Deer
Pitt Street, 1 (off A57)
Tetley Mild, Falstaff Best, Bitter Ⓗ
Small pub, traditional and friendly ʃ♪♣🅡Ⓢ

Red House
Solly Street, 3
Ward Sheffield Best Bitter Ⓗ
Traditional pub with Irish atmosphere ʃ♣🅡🍴

Red Lion
109 Charles Street, 1 ✆ 24997
Ward Sheffield Best Bitter
Ⓗ & Ⓔ
Comfortable lounge pub with small tap room ♪♣♪🅡🅖🍴≋

Shakespeare Hotel
Gibraltar Street, 3 (A61)
✆ 29048
Ward Sheffield Best Bitter Ⓗ & Ⓔ
Warm, friendly house with cosy atmosphere ʃ♪♣♪🅡🅖Ⓢ

Washington
Fitwilliam Street, 1
Tetley Mild, Falstaff Best, Bitter Ⓗ
Friendly local with an interesting collection of teapots ♪♣🍴Ⓢ

Sheffield: East

Cross Keys
400 Handsworth Road, 13 (A57)
Stones Best Bitter Ⓔ
Fascinating 12th-century local built in the corner of a churchyard ♠♪♣🍴

Excelsior
1 Carbrook Street, 9 (off A6178) ✆ 444152
Ward Sheffield Best Bitter Ⓔ
Welcoming haven in industrial area ♪♣🅖🍴Ⓢ

Fiery Fred
1 Clipstone Gardens, Darnall, 9 (off A6102) ✆ 446602
Evening opening: 6.30
Home Bitter Ⓔ
Plush estate pub featuring Yorkshire's famous bowler
♪♪🅖🍴Ⓢ⛵

New Inn
183 Duke Street, 2 (A616)
Tetley Bitter Ⓗ
Busy local with two rooms on different levels ♪♣🍴≋

Sportsman Inn
504 Attercliffe Road, 9 (A6178) ✆ 449177
Evening opening: 6.30
Ward Sheffield Best Bitter Ⓔ
Pleasant post-war local in declining area ♪♣🅡🅖🍴Ⓢ

Sheffield: North

Carlisle Hotel
Carlisle Street East, 4
Stones Best Bitter Ⓔ
Former hotel which has seen better days, but retains faithful locals ʃ♪♣🍴Ⓢ

Farfield
376 Neepsend Lane, 6
✆ 28779
Tetley Bitter Ⓗ
Tastefully renovated two-roomed local ʃ♪♣♪🅱🍴Ⓢ

Midland
2 Alfred Road (off A6109)
✆ 442800
Ward Sheffield Best Bitter Ⓔ
Comfortable, welcoming pub, isolated in industrial area
♠ʃ♪♣🅖🍴Ⓢ

Pitsmoor Hotel
448 Pitsmoor Road, 3 (Off A6135)
Tetley Bitter Ⓗ
Small, traditional two-roomed local ♪♣🎬♪🅱🍴Ⓢ

Sheffield: South

Byron House
16 Nether Edge Road, 7 (Off A621)
Draught Bass
Stones Best Bitter Ⓔ
Comfortable suburban local
♪♣♪🍴

Sheaf House
329 Bramall Lane, 2
Stones Best Bitter Ⓔ
Traditional local with snooker table and active games teams
♪♣🅱🍴Ⓢ

White Lion
615 London Road, 2 (A61)
Tetley Mild, Bitter Ⓗ
Variety of rooms to suit all tastes ʃ♪♣🍴

Sheffield: West

Banner Cross
971 Eccleshall Road
Tetley Falstaff Best, Bitter Ⓗ
Cheerful pub with two contrasting rooms ♪♣♪🍴Ⓢ

Firwood Cottage
279 Whitehouse Lane, 6
Tetley Bitter Ⓗ

Welcoming, comfortable local
♣♥📵♿

Hanover House
32 Upper Hanover Street, 3
Evening opening: 7
Stones Best Bitter Ⓗ
Busy street-corner local
♣Ⓖ📵♿

Noah's Ark
24 Crookes, 10
**Whitbread Trophy, Castle
Eden Ale
Bulmer Cider** Ⓗ
Popular with students; retains
atmosphere of small local
♣♪📵

Nottingham House
164 Whitham Road,
Broomhill, 10 (off A57)
℡ 663305
Tetley Mild Ⓔ **Falstaff Best,
Bitter** Ⓗ
Busy pub, close to University
♣♪Ⓖ🐕📵♿

Pomona
Ecclesall Road, 11 (A625)
Home Mild, Bitter Ⓔ
Popular, modern pub with
large conservatory
♣♠♪🅿Ⓖ📵

South Anston 26B5

10.30–3; 6–10.30 (11 F, S)
Loyal Trooper
Sheffield Road (off A57)
℡ Dinnington 562203
Tetley Bitter Ⓗ
17th-century coaching inn of
character ♪🅿Ⓖ🐕📵

Stainforth 26B3

10.30–3; 6–10.30 (11 F, S)
Peacock Hotel
East Lane
Morning opening: 11
**Samuel Smith Old Brewery
Bitter** Ⓗ
Typical modern estate pub
🛏♣♪🅿📵

Stannington 23H3

11–3; 5.30–10.30 (11 F, S)
Hollybush
Hollins Lane (off A6101)
Tetley Bitter Ⓗ
Comfortable local in Rivelin
Valley
♪♣🅿📵A

Try also: Robin Hood (Stones)

Swinton 23J3

10.30–3; 6–10.30 (11 F, S)
Sportsman
149 Fitzwilliam Street
Morning opening: 11.30
Stones Best Bitter Ⓔ
Lively oasis in a beer desert
♪♣♪🅿📵

Thorne 26C3

10.30–3; 6–10.30 (11 F, S)

Green Dragon
Silver Street (A614)
Darley Thorne Best Bitter Ⓔ
Pleasant pub near market
square, snooker table
♪♣🅿📵

Rising Sun
Hatfield Road (A614)
Darley Thorne Best Bitter Ⓔ
Pleasant pub by canal bridge
♪♣🅿Ⓡ📵

**Thornensians
(RUFC) Club**
Church Balk (off A614)
Darley Thorne Best Bitter Ⓔ
Non-affiliated rugby club, bar
under main stand; short-stay
membership on request
♪♣📵

Thorne High Levels 26C3

10.30–3; 6–10.30 (11 F, S)
Black Bull
(A18) ℡ Thorne 812744
Stones Best Bitter Ⓔ
Established roadside inn due
for extensive development
♪🅿ⒶⓇⒼ🐕📵A

Thorpe Hesley 23J3

10.30–3; 6–10.30 (11 F, S)
Horse & Tiger
Brook Hill (B6086)
Opens at 11 am & 7 pm
Tetley Bitter Ⓗ
Uniquely-named pub with
new games room
♪♣🅿📵

Thrybergh 26A4

10.30–3; 6–10.30 (11 F, S)
Reresby
Vale Road (off A630)
℡ Rotherham 850335
Home Bitter Ⓔ
Estate pub with strong local
trade ♪♣🅿Ⓖ🐕📵

Thurlstone 23H2

11–3; 6–11
Huntsman
Manchester Road (A628)
**Draught Bass
Marston Pedigree
Ruddle County
Stones Best Bitter** Ⓗ
Pennine roadhouse;
occasional guest beers ♪

Tickhill 26B5

10.30–3; 6–10.30 (11 F, S)
Buttercross
Northgate (A60)
**Whitbread Trophy, Castle
Eden Ale** Ⓗ
Pleasant tavern with
enthusiastic landlord
♪♣♪📵

Totley 23H4

11–3; 5.30–10.30 (11 F, S)

Fleur de Lys
Baslow Road, Sheffield 17
(A621)
**Draught Bass
Stones Best Bitter** Ⓗ
Large, popular pub on
outskirts of city ♪♣🅿📵

Wentworth 23J3

10.30–3; 6–10.30 (11 F, S)
George & Dragon
Main Street (B6090)
℡ Barnsley 742440
**Taylor Best Bitter, Landlord,
Ram Tam
Tetley Mild, Bitter** Ⓗ
Country inn with a wide
reputation for catering
♣🅿Ⓖ

Rockingham
Main Street (B6090)
℡ Barnsley 742075
**Theakston Best Bitter, Old
Peculier** Ⓗ
Rambling old village inn, with
bowling green and garden
♪♪♣🅿ⒶⓇⒼ📵

Whiston 23J3

10.30–3; 6–10.30 (11 F, S)
Sitwell
Pleasley Road (A618)
℡ Rotherham 77003
Tetley Bitter Ⓗ
Former coaching inn, now a
village pub
♪🅿ⒶⒼ🐕📵

Wombwell 23J2

11–3; 6–11
Railway
37 Station Road (off A663)
Evening opening: 7
Tetley Bitter Ⓗ
Friendly mining village pub
♪♣ⒶⓇ🐕

Woodhouse 23J3

11–3; 5.30–10.30 (11 F, S)
Junction
Station Road (off A57)
Tetley Bitter Ⓗ
Popular two-roomed local
♪♣🅿Ⓐ🐕

Woodlands 26B4

10.30–3; 6–10.30 (11 F, S)
Woodlands Hotel
Great North Road (A638)
℡ Doncaster 723207
Tetley Bitter Ⓗ
Caters for all local tastes, tap
room an eye-opener
🛏♣♪🅷ⒶⒹ🐕📵♿

Worsborough 23H2

11–3; 6–11
Edmunds Arms
(Off A61) ℡ Barnsley 6865
**Samuel Smith Old Brewery
Bitter** Ⓔ
Popular village inn with
restaurant ♪♪♣🅿Ⓖ🐕

Aberford 30C8

11–3; 5.30–10.30 (11 F, S)
Arabian Horse
Main Street (off A1)
Tetley Mild, Bitter
Younger Scotch Bitter, No 3 Ⓗ
Free house on old A1, next to
village green ▲⌂✦✿✿Ⓘ◉♿

Addingham 30A8

11–3; 5.30–10.30 (11 F, S)
Fleece
Main Street (A65) ✆ 830491
Tetley Mild, Bitter Ⓗ
Popular village pub with lively
atmosphere ▲⌂♪✦✿✿✿Ⓖ✿

Barkisland 23G1

11.30–3; 5–10.30 (11 F, S)
Griffin
Stainland Road (off A6025)
Open 12–2; evening opening
6.30; supper licence 11.30
Burtonwood Bitter Ⓔ
17th-century village pub
▲⌂✦✿✿Ⓘ◉

Batley 23H1

11–3; 5.30–10.30 (11 F, S)
Church Steps
Stocks Lane (off A638)
Opens at 11.30 am & 6.30 pm
Tetley Mild, Bitter Ⓗ
Refurbished pub near parish
church ♪✦✿✿Ⓖ◉

Birstall 23H1

11–3; 5.30–10.30 (11 F, S)
New Inn
High Street (off A643)
Tetley Mild, Bitter Ⓗ
Friendly local with fine urban
views ♪✦✿✿✿◉

Bradford 30B9

11–3; 5.30–10.30 (11 F, S)
Blue Pig
Fagley Road, Lower Fagley
Morning opening: 11.30;
winter evening opening: 6
Clark Bitter
Tetley Bitter
Theakston Best Bitter, XB, Old
Peculier Ⓗ
Bustling suburban free house
♪✦✿✿✿Ⓖ◉

Brown Cow
886 Little Horton Lane, 5
Opens at 12 noon & 7 pm
(Mon–Thu); 6 pm (F, S)
Samuel Smith Old Brewery
Bitter Ⓗ
Refurbished local with
popular games room ♪✦Ⓖ◉

Cock & Bottle
93 Barkerend Road, 3 (A658)
Saturday evening opening:
6.30
Tetley Mild, Bitter Ⓗ
Many-roomed pub with
ornate woodwork and glass
▲⌂♪✦Ⓡ Ⓖ◉

Fiddlers Three
Pasture Lane, Clayton
Bass Extra Light
Boddingtons Best Mild, Bitter
Stones Best Bitter Ⓗ
Stylish, original design
♪✦✿✿Ⓡ Ⓖ◉◉♿

Freshers
77 Listerhills Road, 7
Clark Bitter
Whitbread Trophy, Durham
Ale, Castle Eden Ale
Bulmer Cider Ⓗ
Revitalised, refurbished
hostelry near University,
formerly the Queen
⌂♪✦Ⓖ◉

Gladstone
City Road, 8 (off B6144)
Opens 11.30 am & 7 pm (Sat)
Bass Extra Light, Brew Ten
Stones Best Bitter Ⓗ
Basic working man's pub
▲⌂♪✦✿Ⓡ◉

Oakleigh
4 Oak Avenue, 8
(Off A650) ✆ 44307
Opens 12 noon & 6 pm (7 Sat)
Draught Bass
Franklins Bitter
Taylor Best Bitter, Landlord
Theakston Best Bitter
Thwaites Bitter Ⓗ
Lively, cosmopolitan free
house ✿✿Ⓖ

Royal
301 New Works Road, Low
Moor (off A641)
Opens 11.30 am & 7 pm (Sat)
Tetley Mild, Bitter Ⓗ
Pleasant pub with unusual
architecture ♪✦✿✿✿Ⓡ◉

Royal Oak
32 Sticker Lane, 4 (A6177)
Bass Extra Light
Taylor Golden Best
Tetley Bitter
Younger No 3 Ⓗ
Free house with varying range
♪✦✿✿Ⓖ◉

Shoulder of Mutton
Kirkgate, 1 ✆ 726038
Samuel Smith Old Brewery
Bitter Ⓗ
Splendid 19th century inn
♪✦✿✿✿Ⓡ Ⓖ◉

Wheatsheaf
Wardley House, Little Horton
Lane, 5 (A647) ✆ 721835
Darley Dark, Thorne Best
Bitter
Vaux Samson Ⓗ
Close to photographic
museum ⌂✦✿Ⓡ Ⓖ✿◉◉

Wild Boar
Bolton Road, 3 (A6176)
Trough Bitter, Wild Boar
Bitter Ⓗ
Refurbished and revitalised by
small brewery ♪✦✿✿Ⓡ◉◉

Bramham 30C8

11–3; 5.30–10.30 (11 Th, F, S)
Red Lion
The Square (off A1) ✆ Boston
Spa 843524
Samuel Smith Old Brewery
Bitter Ⓗ
Coaching house in a quiet
village ▲⌂✦✿✿Ⓔ Ⓖ✿◉◉

Brighouse 23G1

11.30–3; 5–10.30 (11 F, S)
Black Horse
6 Westgate, Clifton (off A643)
✆ 713862
Evening opening: 5.30 (7 Sat)
Whitbread Castle Eden Ale Ⓗ
Busy pub/hotel with noted
restaurant ▲⌂✿Ⓔ Ⓡ Ⓖ✿◉

Stotts Arms
Wakefield Road (A644)
Tetley Mild, Bitter Ⓗ
Many-roomed pub with plate
collection ♪✦✿✿Ⓖ◉

Burley-in-Wharfedale 30B8

11–3; 5.30–10.30 (11 F, S)
White Horse
Main Street (A65)
Saturday evening opening: 6
Tetley Mild, Bitter Ⓗ
Excellent small local in
pleasant village ▲⌂♪✦

Calder Grove 23H1

11–3; 5.30–11
Navigation
Broad Cut Road (off A636)
Opens at 12 noon & 7 pm
Tetley Mild, Bitter Ⓗ
Family pub in pleasant
canalside setting ✦✿✿✿

Castleford 30C9

11–3.30; 6–11
Crimea Tavern
Church Street (A655)
Boddingtons Bitter Ⓗ
Victorian town pub ♪✦Ⓖ◉

Rock Hotel
Rock Hill, Glasshoughton
(Off A639)
Darley Dark, Thorne Best
Bitter Ⓗ
Popular, traditional local; folk
music Weds ▲⌂♪✦✿Ⓡ◉◉

Churwell 30B9

11.30–3; 5.30–10.30 (11 F, S)
Commercial
78 Elland Road (A643)
Tetley Mild, Bitter Ⓗ
Classic village local ♪✦✿✿✿

Cleckheaton 30B9

11–3; 5.30–10.30 (11 F, S)
Commercial
Bradford Road (A638)
Tetley Mild, Bitter Ⓗ
Modernised town-centre pub
♪✦✿Ⓡ Ⓖ✿♿

Collingham 30C8

~3; 5.30–10.30 (11 F, S)
Old Star
Leeds Road (A58)
Theakston Light Mild, Best
Bitter
Younger Scotch Bitter, No 3 Ⓗ
Restaurant with firm
commitment to real ale
♪♨🅿Ⓖ🍴®

Denholme Gate 29J9

~3; 5.30–10.30 (11 F, S)
Brown Cow
370 Thornton Road (B6145)
Bradford 833077
Tetley Mild, Bitter Ⓗ
Wayfarer pub with good food
♪♨🅱🍴🅿🅰Ⓖ🍴🍺®Ⓐ

Dewsbury 23H1

~3; 5.30–10.30 (11 F, S)
George Hotel
Moorend Lane, Dewsbury
Moor (B6117)
Evening opening: 7
Bass Extra Light, Brew Ten
Draught Bass
Stones Best Bitter Ⓗ
Recently, but sympathetically,
refurbished local ♪♨🅰🍺♿

Market House
Church Street (A644)
Tetley Mild, Bitter Ⓗ
Town centre pub with five
handpumps ♪♨🅰🍺≷

Scarborough
Savile Road, Savile Town
(36409)
Tetley Mild, Bitter Ⓗ
Friendly pub near cricket
ground ♪♨🅰🍺

Station Hotel
Crackenedge Lane ℰ 450727
Evening opening: 7
Bass Brew Ten
Stones Best Bitter Ⓗ
Refurbished pub behind
market, nowhere near the
station ♪♨🅱Ⓖ🍺

Durkar 23H1

~3; 5.30–11
New Inn
Denby Dale Road East (off
A6361/M1 exit 39)
Tetley Mild, Bitter Ⓗ
Plain exterior belies pleasantly
refurbished lounge
♨🅰🍺

East Bierley 30B9

~3; 5.30–10.30 (11 F, S)
New Inn
South View Road
Saturday evening opening: 7
Tetley Mild, Bitter Ⓗ
Bustling, up-market village
local ♪♨🅿🅰Ⓖ

Elland 23G1

11.30–3; 5–10.30 (11 F, S)

Colliers Arms
70 Park Road (A6025)
Evening opening: 7 (6
summer)
Samuel Smith Old Brewery
Bitter Ⓗ
Popular canalside pub
♨♪♨🅿🅰Ⓖ🍴🍺®

Rawson Arms
Park Road (A6025) ℰ 78648
Webster Yorkshire Light,
Bitter Ⓗ
Friendly roadside pub; clock
and watch collection
🍴♨🅿🅰Ⓖ®

Wellington
Southgate
Evening opening: 7
Bass Extra Light Ⓔ
Draught Bass Ⓗ
Friendly, town-centre pub
♪♨🅿🅰Ⓖ🍺®

Esholt 30B8

11–3; 5.30–10.30 (11 F, S)
Commercial
(Off A6038) ℰ Bradford 582425
Whitbread Trophy, Durham
Ale, Castle Eden Ale Ⓗ
Smart pub/restaurant in
attractive village ♨♨Ⓖ (not
Sun) 🍴 (not Sun, Mon)

Featherstone 26A3

11–3; 6–11
White House
Pontefract Road, Purston
(A645)
Samuel Smith Old Brewery
Bitter Ⓗ
Whitewashed pub with
comfortable lounge ♪♨🅰Ⓖ®

Garforth 30C9

11–3; 5.30–10.30 (11 F, S)
Gaping Goose
Selby Road (off A63)
Tetley Mild, Bitter Ⓗ
Very popular ex-Melbourne
house ♨🅰🍺®≷

Gomersal 30B9

11–3; 5.30–10.30 (11 F, S)
Shoulder of Mutton
Oxford Road (A651)
Tetley Mild, Bitter Ⓗ
Village local, fine taproom
♪♨🅰🍺

Halifax 29J9

11.30–3; 5–10.30 (11 F, S)
Calder & Hebble
Huddersfield Road,
Salterhebble (A629) ℰ 72835
Saturday evening opening: 7
Tetley Mild, Bitter Ⓗ
Busy, single-room pub
♪♨🅿Ⓖ🍴 (Sat & Sun)

Crown & Anchor
Mill Lane, Mixenden
Evening opening: 6
Whitbread Durham Ale,
Castle Eden Ale Ⓗ

Cosy village pub in moorland
valley ♪♨🅿🅰Ⓖ🍺®

Shears Inn
Paris Gates, Boy Lane (A629)
Evening opening: 7
Taylor Best Bitter
Younger Scotch Bitter, IPA,
No. 3 Ⓗ
Popular pub by Hebble Brook;
dwarfed by mills ♪♨🅰Ⓖ®

Shoulder of Mutton
Towngate, Northowram
(A6036) ℰ 206229
Webster Yorkshire Dark,
Light, Bitter Ⓗ
Roomy village pub, good food
♨♪♨🅿🅰Ⓔ🍺®

Sportsman Inn
Lee Lane, Shibden (off A647)
ℰ 67000
Opens 12–2.30; evening
opening: 6 (7 Sat)
Goose Eye Dark Mild, Bitter
Ruddle County
Taylor Landlord
Theakston Old Peculier
Webster Yorkshire Light Ⓗ
Popular hilltop pub, squash
and sauna, guest beers 🍴♨🅰Ⓔ
♨🅰Ⓖ🍴 (weekends) ®

Three Pigeons
1 Sun Fold, South Parade
Evening opening: 6 (Mon–Thu)
Webster Yorkshire Light,
Bitter Ⓗ
Small, multi-roomed 30s-style
pub ♨♪♨🅿🅰Ⓔ🅖Ⓖ®≷

William IV
247 King Cross Road, King
Cross (A58)
Saturday evening opening: 7
Tetley Falstaff Best, Bitter Ⓗ
Popular pub in local shopping
street, split-level bar ♪♨🅰®

Haworth 29J9

11–3; 5.30–10.30 (11 F, S)
Fleece
Main Street (off A6033)
Taylor Best Bitter, Ram Tam Ⓗ
Thriving locals' beerhouse in
Brontë country
♪♨🅱Ⓖ (summer) 🍺

Royal Oak
2 Mill Hey ℰ Keighley 43257
Opens at 11.30 am & 7 pm
Webster Yorkshire Light,
Bitter Ⓗ
Modernised house by Worth
Valley Railway 🍴♪♨🅱♨🅰
Ⓖ🍴 (must book) 🍺≷

Hebden Bridge 29H9

11.30–3; 5–10.30 (11 F, S)
Cross Inn
Towngate, Heptonstall
ℰ 843833
Evening opening: 7
Taylor Golden Best, Best
Bitter Ⓗ
Smart pub in historic village
♪♨♨🅱Ⓔ🅖Ⓖ🍴🍺Ⓐ

West Yorkshire

Pack Horse
Widdop Road ✆ 842803
Closed winter lunchtimes;
opens 12 noon & 8 pm
Thwaites Bitter
Younger Scotch Bitter, IPA Ⓗ
Solitary pub, handy for
Pennine Way ♪✿🅰Ⓡ🅖Ⓖ➐Ⓢⓐ Ⓐ

Hemsworth 23J2
11–3.30; 6–11
Kinsley Hotel
Wakefield Road (B6273)
Boddingtons Bitter Ⓔ
Vast Edwardian pub ♪♪✿🅰🅘

Holmfirth 23G2
11.30–3; 5–10.30 (11 F, S)
Bareknuckle Boys
Woodhead Road, Hinchcliffe
Mill (A6024)
Evening opening: 5.30
Thwaites Best Mild, Bitter Ⓗ
Hospitable house
♪✿🅰Ⓡ🅘

Farmers Arms
Liphill Bank Road, Burnlee
(Off A635) ✆ 683713
Closed Monday lunchtime;
evening opening: 6 (7 Sat)
Draught Bass
Marston Pedigree, Merrie
Monk
Stones Best Bitter
Taylor Best Bitter
Tetley Mild, Bitter Ⓗ
Deservedly popular pub; guest
beers ♠♪✿🅰Ⓡ🅖➐Ⓢ

Rose & Crown (Nook)
Victoria Square (off A635)
Stones Best Bitter
Taylor Best Bitter, Landlord,
Ram Tam
Tetley Mild, Bitter
West Riding Tyke Bitter Ⓗ
Renovated basic boozer, guest
beers ♠♪✿♪

Honley 23G2
11.30–3; 5–10.30 (11 F, S)
Jacob's Well
16 Woodhead Road (B6024)
Bass Mild, Draught Bass Ⓗ
Small pub with interesting
bric-a-brac ♠♪✿♪ⓇⒼ

Horsforth 30B8
11.30–3; 5.30–10.30 (11 F, S)
Black Bull
The Green, Town Street (off
A6120) ✆ Leeds 586925
Tetley Mild, Bitter Ⓗ
Many-roomed pub with
children's play area
✿♪Ⓡ🅘Ⓢ

Huddersfield 23G1
11–3; 5–10.30 (11 F, S)
Black Bull
50 West Street, Lindley
Evening opening: 7
Tetley Mild, Bitter Ⓗ
Out-of-town local ♪✿🅘Ⓢ

Highgate Oakes
New Hey Road, Oakes (A640)
Bass Mild, Extra Light
Draught Bass Ⓗ
Modernised, comfortable local
♪Ⓖ

Plumbers Arms
Macauley Street ✆ 22968
Tetley Mild, Bitter Ⓗ
Comfortable town-centre pub
near bus station ♪✿Ⓖ🅘Ⓢ

Red Lion
260 Lockwood Road,
Lockwood Bar (A616)
Tetley Mild, Bitter Ⓗ
Modernised lounge, lively
taproom ♪✿🅰🅘

Star
Albert Street (off A616)
Bass Mild, Extra Light
Stones Best Bitter Ⓗ
Convivial pub with old photos
of Huddersfield ♪✿🅰Ⓡ

Walkers Arms
(Ben Idle's)
Parkwood Road, Golcar
Bass Mild Ⓗ **Extra Light** Ⓔ
Draught Bass
Stones Best Bitter Ⓗ
One-room village local ♠♪✿♪🅰

Ilkley 30A8
11–3; 5.30–10.30 (11 F, S)
Wharfe Cottage
Leeds Road (A65) ✆ 607323
Evening opening: 6
Taylor Best Bitter, Landlord
Thwaites Bitter Ⓗ
Comfortable, unusual pub
near the moor ♠♪✿♪🅰Ⓖ Ⓢ

Keighley 29J8
11–3; 5.30–10.30 (11 F, S)
Bridge Inn
Bradford Road, Stockbridge
(A650) ✆ 602300
Tetley Mild, Falstaff Best,
Bitter Ⓗ
Comfortable main road pub
with many rooms
♪✿🅓♪🅰Ⓡ🅘Ⓢⓐ Ⓖ

Eastwood Tavern
37 Bradford Road (A650)
Opens at 11.30 am & 6 pm
(Mon–Thu)
Taylor Golden Best, Best
Bitter, Landlord Ⓗ
Genuine basic locals' pub
♠♪✿🅓🅰Ⓡ🅘Ⓢ➐

Goose Eye Mint Bar
Goose Eye, Laycock ✆ 605807
Opens at 11.30 am & 7 pm
Goose Eye Mild, Bitter
Webster Yorkshire Bitter Ⓗ
Smart new bar attached to
restaurant and brewery
♠♪✿🅰🅓Ⓡ🅖➐🅘Ⓢ

Shoulder of Mutton
Parkwood Street, Thwaites
(Off A650) ✆ 602259

Thwaites Best Mild, Best
Bitter Ⓗ
Excellent homely pub
♪✿♠🅰Ⓖ🅘Ⓢ

Kirkheaton 23G1
11.30–3; 5.30–10.30 (11 F, S)
Beaumont Arms
Church Lane (off A642)
✆ Huddersfield 43502
Tetley Mild, Bitter Ⓗ
18th-century courthouse near
parish church ♪✿♪ⓇⒼ♠

Leeds 30B9
11–3; 5.30–10.30 (11 F, S)
Adelphi
Leeds Bridge, 10 ✆ 456377
Tetley Mild, Bitter Ⓗ
Superb Victorian 'Heritage'
inn ♪✿🅰Ⓡ🅘Ⓢ

Albion
Armley Road, 12 (off A647)
Tetley Mild, Bitter Ⓗ
Busy pub with beautifully
restored facade ♪✿🅘Ⓢ

Beech
Tong Road, 12
Tetley Mild, Bitter Ⓗ
Down-to-earth, cosmopolitan
and friendly ♪✿🅘Ⓢ

Brassmoulders
Arms
Church Street, 10
Tetley Mild, Bitter Ⓗ
Fine local with rugby league
connections ♪✿Ⓡ🅘Ⓢ

Brown Hare
Harehills Lane, 7
Samuel Smith Old Brewery
Bitter Ⓗ
Smart, new and busy ♪🅰🅘Ⓢ♠

Cardigan Arms
364 Kirkstall Road, 4 (A65)
Tetley Mild, Bitter Ⓗ
Large, busy local; a rugby
league haunt ♪✿Ⓡ🅘Ⓢ

Eagle Tavern
North Street, 7 (A61)
✆ 457142
Saturday evening opening: 7
Boddingtons Bitter
Clark Bitter
Samuel Smith Old Brewery
Bitter
Taylor Dark Mild, Best Bitter,
Landlord
Whitbread Castle Eden Ale Ⓗ
Zum Cider Ⓖ
Excellent lively local, guest
beers ♪✿♪🔲🅘Ⓢ

Fox & Newt
Burley Street, 3 ✆ 432612
Burley Bitter, Old Willow
Clark Bitter
Whitbread Durham Ale,
Castle Eden Ale Ⓗ
Well-renovated home-brew
pub with pianola
♪ⒼⓈ

Garden Gate
7 Waterloo Road, Hunslet,
0 (off A61)
Tetley Mild, Bitter ⒣
Magnificent Victorian
architecture, a 'Heritage' inn
♪♣⚑⒤⑧

Highland
Cavendish Street, 2
Tetley Mild, Bitter ⒣
Convivial backstreet
shift-workers' pub ♪♣⒤⑧

Nags Head
Town Street, Chapel Allerton,
7 ℓ 624938
Samuel Smith Old Brewery
Bitter ⒣
Very busy one-time coaching
inn ♪♣⚑⒢⑧

New Inn
68 Otley Road, Headingley, 6
(A660) ℓ 755035
Whitbread Trophy, Castle
Eden Ale ⒣
Re-vamped coaching inn with
unusual clock ♪♣⒢

New Inn
336 Tong Road, 12 ℓ 637084
Tetley Mild, Bitter ⒣
Full of tramcar photos and
street signs ♪♣⚑⒢⒤

Park
50 Hyde Park Road, 6
Bass Mild
Stones Best Bitter ⒣
Bustling ex-Melbourne house
♪♣⚑⒜

Pig & Whistle
Merrion Centre, 2 ℓ 445354
Cameron Lion Bitter,
Strongarm ⒣
Modern pub in office and shop
complex ♪⒢♿

Skinners Arms
Sheepscar Street North, 7
(A61)
Tetley Mild, Bitter ⒣
Popular pub with
prize-winning cellar
♪♣⚑⒤⑧

Spring Close Tavern
Ellerby Lane, Richmond Hill, 9
Tetley Mild, Bitter ⒣
Good down-to-earth pub,
popular and welcoming
♪♣⚑⒤⑧

Whitelocks
Turks Head Yard, off
Briggate, 1 ℓ 453950
Younger Scotch Bitter, No. 3,
IPA ⒣
Superb Edwardian luncheon
bar ⚑⒢⒤⑧

Wrens Hotel
Briggate, 1 ℓ 458888
Tetley Mild, Bitter ⒣
Pleasant pub, near Grand
Theatre ♪⒢⒤⑧

Liversedge   30B9
11–3; 5–10.30 (11 F, S)
Rising Sun
Norristhorpe Lane,
Norristhorpe (off A62)
Evening opening: 7
Tetley Mild, Bitter ⒣
Village local with warm
welcome ♪♣⚑⒜⒭

Luddendenfoot   30A9
11.30–3; 5–10.30 (11 F, S)
Coach & Horses
Burnley Road (A646)
Matthew Brown Mild, Bitter,
John Peel Bitter ⒣
Plush roadhouse, remarkable
brass collection ♪⚑⒭⒢⑧

Menston   30B8
11–3; 5.30–10.30 (11 F, S)
Menston Arms
26 Main Street (off A6038)
Samuel Smith Old Brewery
Bitter ⒣
Smart, well-appointed pub
with thatched bar
♣⚑⒢(not Sun)⑧

Mickletown   30C9
11–3; 5.30–10.30 (11 Thu, F, S)
Old Bay Horse
Main Street (off A639)
Tetley Mild, Bitter ⒣
Friendly pit-village pub with
own library ♣♪♣⚑⒜⑧

Middlestown   23H1
12–3; 7–11
Little Bull
New Road (off A642)
Tetley Bitter ⒣
An old village local, small
rooms and low ceilings
♪♣⚑

Mirfield   23G1
11–3; 5.30–10.30 (11 F, S)
Flowerpot
Calder Road, Lower Hopton
Tetley Mild, Falstaff Best,
Bitter ⒣
Popular riverside pub with
beer garden ♪♣⚑⒭⒜♿

Morley   30B9
11–3; 5.30–10.30 (11 F, S)
Fountain
Queen Street ℓ 533879
Samuel Smith Old Brewery
Bitter ⒣
Attractively modernised town
centre pub ♪⚑⒜⒢

Normanton   23J1
11–3; 5.30–11
Hark to Mopsey
Wakefield Road (A655)
ℓ Wakefield 892963
Bass Brew Ten
Stones Best Bitter ⒣
Roomy suburban local with
unusual facade ♪♣⚑⒧⒢⒤

Lee Brigg
Altofts
Darley Thorne Best Bitter ⒠
Cheerful local, popular with
older generation ♪♣⚑⒜⑧

Talbot
Talbot Street (off A655)
Tetley Mild, Bitter ⒣
Large, renovated local with
Victorian bar ♪♣⚑⒜⚷

Norwood Green   30A9
11.30–3; 5–10.30 (11 F, S)
Pear Tree
Station Road (off A641)
Evening opening: 7
Tetley Mild, Bitter ⒣
Modernised village local
♣♣⚑⒢ (Mon–Fri)

Ossett   23H1
11–3; 5.30–11
Fleece
Spa Street, Ossett Spa
(Off A648/M1 exit 40)
Tetley Mild, Bitter ⒣
Attractively modernised
pub in rural area ♪♣⚑⒜

Prince of Wales
South Parade
Wilsons Original Bitter ⒣
Thriving suburban local with
large lounge
♪♣⚑⒢⚷⑧

Otley   30B8
11–3; 5.30–10.30 (11 F, S)
Bay Horse
Market Place (off A659)
Closes 4 pm Mondays and
Fridays except bank holidays
Tetley Mild, Bitter ⒣
Small, friendly pub ♣⒜

Junction
Bondgate (A660)
Franklins Bitter
Taylor Best Bitter, Landlord
Tetley Mild, Bitter
Theakston Old Peculier ⒣
Thriving free house ♣♪♣⑧

Try also: Bowling Green
(Stones); Red Lion (Vaux);
Rose & Crown (Whitbread)

Oxenhope   29J9
11–3; 5.30–10.30 (11 F, S)
Dog & Gun
Denholme Road, Leeming
(B6141) ℓ Haworth 43159
Taylor Golden Best, Best
Bitter, Landlord ⒣
Welcoming pub on edge of
Brontë country
♣♪♣⚑⒢⒢⚷⑧⛺

Pontefract   26A3
11–3.30 (4 S); 6–11
Flying Horse
Salter Row ℓ 702142
Wilsons Original Bitter ⒣

Comfortable, attractive old pub ♪♠🅖(Mon–Fri)

Pool-in-Wharfedale 30B8

11–3; 5.30–10.30 (11 F, S)

Dyneley Arms
Pool Bank (A660)
Samuel Smith Old Brewery Bitter 🅗
Well-established roadhouse between village and airport
🏠♪✦🅐🅡🅖🍴◉

Pudsey 30B9

11–3; 5.30–10.30 (11 F, S)

Victoria
Hough Side Road/Swinnow Road, Lowtown (B6154)
Bass Mild
Stones Best Bitter 🅗
Lively pub with brass bric-a-brac, weekend discos
♪✦🅡◉

Queensbury 30A9

11–3; 5.30–10.30 (11 F, S)

Mountain Eagle
Brighouse and Denholme Road (A644)
Opens at 12 noon & 7 pm
Webster Yorkshire Light, Bitter 🅗
Friendly local with splendid views 🏠♪✦🅟🅖◉

Omnibus
Halifax Road, Amblerthorn (A647)
Tetley Bitter 🅗
Busy, unpretentious pub with collection of kettles ♪✦🅐🍴◉

Ripponden 23F1

11.30–3; 5–10.30 (11 F, S)

Blue Ball
Blue Ball Lane, Soyland (off A58) ☎ Halifax 823603
Opens at 12 noon & 7 pm; closed Tue lunchtimes
Boddingtons Bitter
Taylor Dark Mild, Golden Best, Landlord
Theakston Best Bitter, Old Peculier 🅗
Homely, 17th-century moorland inn
🏠♪✦🅗🅟🅐🅡🅖🍴◉⬦

Shadwell 30C8

11–3; 5.30–10.30 (11 F, S)

Red Lion
Main Street, Leeds, 17
Tetley Mild, Bitter 🅗
Archetypal village inn, always busy ♪✦🅟🅖◉

Sowerby Bridge 23F1

11.30–3; 5–10.30 (11 F, S)

Ash Tree
Wharf Street (A58) ☎ Halifax 831654
Moorhouse Premier Bitter
Stones Best Bitter

Taylor Dark Mild, Best Bitter, Landlord 🅗
Renovated pub, Indonesian restaurant 🏠♪✦🅐🅡🅖🍴◉🍴

Moorings
No 1 Warehouse, Canal Basin (off A58) ☎ 833940
Evening opening: 6.30
Clark Bitter
Younger Scotch Bitter, No 3, IPA 🅗
Converted canalside warehouse ♪🅗✦🅟🅐🅡🅖🍴◉🍴

Puzzle Hall
Hollins Mill Lane (off A58)
Evening opening: 7
Darley Thorne Best Bitter
Ward Best Mild, Sheffield Best Bitter 🅗
Quaint 'country' pub in industrial town ♪✦🅟🅐🅡◉

Stanley 23H1

11–3; 7–11

Thatched House
434 Aberford Road (A642)
Bass Brew Ten 🅗
Tidy, unspoilt former home-brew house ♪✦🅐🍴

Stanningley 30B9

11–3; 5.30–10.30 (11 F, S)

Sun
Town Street (B6157/B6155)
Tetley Mild, Bitter 🅗
Traditional three-roomed pub, agreeable atmosphere ♪✦🅐🍴

Thornton 30A9

11–3; 5.30–10.30 (11 F, S)

Great Northern
Thornton Road (B6145)
Evening opening: 6.30
Thwaites Best Mild, Bitter 🅗
Comfortable, modernised pub, snooker table ♪✦🅐🅡🅖🍴◉

School Green
1549 Thornton Road (B6145)
Opens at 12 noon & 7 pm (Sat)
Webster Yorkshire Light, Bitter 🅗
Suburban pub with pleasant lounge ♪✦🅐🅖🍴◉

Springfield
Bronte Old Road, (off B6145)
Evening opening: 7
Bass Extra Light
Stones Best Bitter 🅗
Lively, popular suburban village pub ♪✦🅡

Todmorden 29H9

11.30–3; 5–10.30 (11 F, S)

Bird i' th' Hand
Rochdale Road, Walsden (A6033)
Evening opening: 7
Whitbread Castle Eden Ale 🅗
Smart, popular roadside pub ♪🅗✦🅐🅖🍴◉⬦

York Hotel
Halifax Road (A646)

Evening opening: 7
Taylor Best Bitter
Tetley Bitter
Thwaites Best Mild, Bitter 🅗
Open-plan town centre free house ♪✦🅖(Mon–Fri)◉

Wakefield 23H1

11–3; 5.30–11

Albion
Stanley Road (off A642)
Samuel Smith Old Brewery Bitter 🅗
1930s estate pub
♪✦🅟🅐🅡🅖(Mon–Fri)🍴◉

Cock
Batley Road, Alverthorpe
Stones Best Bitter 🅗
Cheerful, thriving 1930s local ♪✦🅐🍴◉

Graziers
Market Street (A636)
Tetley Mild, Bitter 🅗
Popular, tastefully modernised town pub ♪✦🅐

Kings Arms
Heath Village (off A655)
Tetley Mild, Bitter 🅗
Historic gas-lit inn in picturesque village 🏠♪✦🅐🍴

Redoubt
Horbury Road (A642)
Tetley Mild, Bitter 🅗
Unspoilt Victorian local with four small rooms ♪✦🅐🍴

Swan with Two Necks
Westgate (A642)
Tetley Mild, Bitter 🅗
Busy two-roomed pub with stained-glass windows
♪✦🅐🍴◉🍴

Wilsden 29J

11–3; 5.30–10.30 (11 F, S)

New Inn
Main Street (off B6144)
☎ Cullingworth 272551
Lunchtime opening: 12 noon
Bass Extra Light, Draught Bass
Stones Best Bitter 🅗
Tastefully modernised village pub, good food ♪✦🅟🅐🅖🍴◉

Wragby 26A

11–3; 6–11

Spread Eagle
Doncaster Road (A638)
Samuel Smith Old Brewery Bitter 🅗
Homely 400-year-old stone pub 🏠♪✦🅐🍴

Yeadon 30B

11–3; 5.30–10.30 (11 F, S)

Nunroyd
New Road (A65)
Webster Yorkshire Bitter 🅗
Refurbished former mansion in attractive grounds
✦🅟🅐🅖🍴

Abergele 21H4

11–3; 5.30–10.30 (11 F, S)
Harp
Market Street ✆ 824080
✝Higsons Mild, Bitter ⊞
200-year-old pub, converted
from 700-year-old jailhouse
🏠♪♣🎯🐾🅟🅖♿️Å≷

Acrefair 22A6

11–3; 5.30–10.30
Hampden Arms
Llangollen Road (A539)
Opens 11.30 am and 7 pm
Banks Mild, Bitter ⊞
Modernised, friendly locals'
pub 🏠♪♣🅟

Bersham 22B5

11–3; 5.30–10.30 (11 F, S)
Black Lion
Hydes Best Mild, Bitter Ⓔ
Good village local with small
rooms 🏠♪♣🐾🅰🅡🅖♿ (not Sun)
🐾🅘🅢

Brymbo 22B5

11.30–3; 5.30–10.30 (11 F, S)
Black Lion
Railway Road (B5101)
Opens at 12 noon and 7 pm
**Burtonwood Dark Mild,
Bitter** ⊞
Friendly pub in shadow of
steelworks ♪♣🅰🅟

Buckley 22A5

11.30–3; 5.30–10.30 (11 F, S)
White Lion
Mold Road (A549)
**Greenall Whitley Mild,
Bitter** ⊞
Well-kept pub, rooms for all
tastes ♪♣🎯🐾🅰🅡🅖🐾🅘🅢♿

Burton 22B5

11.30–3; 5.30–10.30 (11 F, S)
Golden Groves
(Off A483) OS 354487
Evening opening: 7
**Bass Cask Bitter, Draught
Bass** ⊞
Remote inn with restaurant
🏠♣🐾🅰🅖🐾🅘🅢

Bylchau 21H5

11.30–3.30; 6.30–11
Sportsmans Arms
Bryntrillyn (A543)
Closed Mon–Fri lunchtimes in
winter
Lees GB Mild, Bitter ⊞
An oasis on high moorland
🏠🅟🎯🐾🅰🅡🅖🐾🅘🅢Å

Cilcain 22A4

11–3; 5.30–10.30 (11 F, S)
White Horse
(Off A541) ✆ Mold 740142
Opens at 12 noon & 7 pm
Greenall Whitley Bitter ⊞
Village inn in beautiful
surroundings 🏠♣🐾🅖🐾🅘🅢

Cymau 22B5

11–3; 7–10.30 (11 F, S)
Olde Talbot Inn
(Off A541) OS 297562
Hydes Mild, Bitter ⊞
Comfortable village local
♪♣🅰🐾🅰🅡🅖🐾🅘🅢Å≷

Cynwyd 21J7

11–3; 6–10.30 (11 F, S and summer)
Blue Lion
(B4401, off A5)
**Marston Capital, Mercian
Mild, Pedigree** ⊞
Ancient, comfortable and
friendly
🏠♪♣🅰🐾🅟🅘🅢♿Å

Denbigh 21J5

Summer: 11.30–3.30; 5.30–11
Winter: 11–3; 5.30–10.30 (11 F, S)
Masons Arms
Rhyl Road ✆ 2463
Ind Coope Bitter, Burton Ale ⊞
Small pub with loud jukebox
🏠♪♣🎯🅰🅟🅡🅖♿🐾🅘🅢

Old Vaults
High Street ✆ 2048
Open till 1 am Thu–Sat in
disco room
Lees Bitter ⊞
Lively, friendly atmosphere
♪♣🅡🅖🐾🅘🅢

Dyserth 21J4

11.30–3; 5.30–10.30 (11 F, S and summer)
Bodunig
High Street ✆ 570333
Ansells Mild
Ind Coope Bitter ⊞
Very popular, friendly local
🏠♪♣🅰🅡🅟🅘🅢♿

Cross Keys
High Street
Evening opening: 7 (Mon–Fri)
**Burtonwood Dark Mild,
Bitter** ⊞
Small, friendly local
🏠♪♣🅰🅟🐾🅰🅡🅟🅘🅢

Flint 22A4

11.30–3.30; 6–10.30 (11 F, S)
George & Dragon
Church Street (A5119)
**Burtonwood Dark Mild,
Bitter** Ⓔ
Comfortable lounge, 'men
only' bar ♪♣🅟≷

Froncysyllte 22A6

11–3; 6–10.30 (11 F, S and summer)
Britannia
(A5) ✆ Chirk 772246
**Border Mild, Bitter, Old
Master** ⊞
Near Pontcysyllte aqueduct
🏠♪♣🐾🅰🅟🅰🅡🅖🐾🅘🅢Å

Glan-Yr-Afon 21J4

11–3; 6–10.30 (11 F, S and summer)
White Lion
(Off A548) OS 119816

Evening opening: 7.15
Closed lunchtimes Mon–Sat
Marston Pedigree
Mitchells & Butlers Mild ⊞
250-year-old pub with ancient
beer engines
🏠♪♣🐾🅟🅰🅟

Graigfechan 21J6

11–3; 5.30–10.30 (11 F, S and summer)
Three Pigeons
(B5429) ✆ Ruthin 3178
Morning opening: 11.30
Border Bitter
Ind Coope Bitter Ⓖ
Excellent free house; beers
alternate
♪♣🅰🐾🅟🅰🅡🅟🅘🅢Å

Gresford 22B5

11.30–3; 5.30–10.30 (11 F, S)
Griffin
The Green (off A483)
**Greenall Whitley Mild,
Bitter** ⊞
Friendly, busy village local
♣🐾🅰

Gronant 21J4

12–3; 5.30–10.30 (11 F, S)
Bells of St. Mary's
Mostyn Road (A548)
Evening opening: 7
McEwan 80/-
Younger No. 3 ⊞
Comfortable 600-year-old pub
🏠♪🅰🐾🅰🅡🅖🐾🅘🅢

Gwernymynydd 22A5

11.30–3; 5.30–10.30 (11 F, S)
Owain Glyndwr
Glyndwr Road (off A494)
Opens at 12 noon and 6 pm
**Burtonwood Dark Mild,
Bitter** ⊞
Country pub of character with
fine views ♪♣🅰🅢

Halkyn 22A4

11.30–3; 6–10.30 (11 F, S)
Britannia
(Off A55) ✆ 780272
Evening opening: 7
Lees GB Mild, Bitter ⊞
500-year-old interesting rural
inn
🏠♪♣🅰🐾🅰🅡🅟🅡🅖♿🅘Å

Higher Kinnerton 22B5

11.30–3; 6–10.30 (11 F, S)
Swan
41 Main Road OS 327610
**Greenall Whitley Mild,
Bitter** ⊞
Small-roomed village local
♪♣🅰🐾🅰🅖🐾🅘🅢♿

Holywell 22A4

11.30–3.30; 5.30–10.30 (11 F, S)
Beaufort Arms Hotel
Well Street ✆ 710364
Evening opening: 7

Wilsons Original Bitter [H]
Modernised pub, popular with the young 🏛♪♣✿▣[R]☾◗Ⓢ

Volunteer Arms
Brynford Street ☎ 711735
Burtonwood Dark Mild, Bitter [H]
A must for lovers of traditional pubs 🏛♪♣⊞✿☾◗🍷Ⓢ

Llanarmon-yn-Lal 22A5

11–3; 5.30–10.30 (11 F, S)
Raven
(B5431) ☎ 235787
Burtonwood Dark Mild, Bitter [H]
Excellent 18th-century local
⌐♪♣⊞✿🚗[R]☾◗🍷Ⓢ⛺

Llanddulas 21H4

12–3; 5.30–10.30 (11 F, S)
Dulas Arms
Abergele Road (A55)
☎ Colwyn Bay 515747
Lees GB Mild, Bitter [H]
Well modernised, cheerful pub
⌐♪♣⊞✿🚗▣[R]☾◗🍷Ⓢ⛺

Llandyrnog 21J5

11.30–3; 6–10.30 (11 F, S)
Golden Lion
(B5429)
Marston Burton Bitter [H]
Friendly village local
♪♣🍷Ⓢ

Llanfair Talhaiarn 21H5

11.30–3; 5.30–10.30 (11 F, S and summer)
Swan
(Off A548) OS 927702
☎ 233
Marston Mercian Mild, Burton Bitter, Pedigree [H]
Unspoilt, traditional village local
🏛⌐♪♣⊞✿🚗[R]☾◗🍷Ⓢ⛺

Llansannan 21H5

12–3.30; 6–10.30 (11 in summer)
Red Lion
(A544) ☎ 365
Lees GB Mild, Bitter [H]
14th-century local
🏛♪♣✿▣☾◗🍷Ⓢ

Lloc 21J4

11.30–3.30; 6–10.30 (11 F, S)
Rock
(A55) OS 145766
Burtonwood Dark Mild, Bitter [H]
Good all-round pub
🏛♪♣⊞✿🚗[R]☾◗🍷Ⓢ

Meliden 21J4

11–3; 5.30–10.30 (11 in summer)
Melyd Arms
23 Ffordd Talargoch
Marston Burton Bitter [H]
Small, friendly local
♪♣⊞🚗[R]🍷Ⓢ

Mold 22A5

11.30–3; 5.30–10.30 (11 F, S)
Queens Head
Chester Road (A541)
Burtonwood Dark Mild, Bitter [H]
Welcoming old pub ⌐♣✿🚗🍷♿

Moss 22B5

11.30–3; 5.30–10.30 (11 F, S)
Bird in Hand
(Off B5101) OS 303538
☎ Wrexham 755809
Evening opening: 7
Hydes Mild, Bitter [E]
Refined pub with restaurant
♪✿🚗[R]☾◗(must book)Ⓢ

Nannerch 22A4

12–2.30; 6–10.30 (11 F, S)
Cross Foxes
(Off A541)
Younger Scotch Bitter [H]
Excellent free house 🏛♪♣🚗🍷

Rising Sun
Denbigh Road (A541)
Draught Bass [H]
Wayside inn specialising in meals 🏛♪♣⊞🚗[R]☾◗🍷Ⓢ♿

Old Colwyn 21G4

11–3; 5.30–10.30 (11 in summer)
Ship
Abergele Road (A55)
Mitchells & Butlers Mild, Brew XI [H]
Good public bar, comfortable lounge ♪♣✿🚗☾🍷♿

Sun
Abergele Road (A55)
Opens at 11.30 am & 6 pm
Marston Mercian Mild, Burton Bitter, Pedigree [H]
Good basic pub 🏛♪♣🍷

Pen-y-mynydd 22B5

11.30–3; 6–10.30 (11 F, S)
White Lion
(A5118)
Border Bitter [H]
Excellent traditional local
🏛⌐♪♣🚗🍷

Rhosesmor 22A4

11.30–3; 5.30–10.30 (11 F, S)
Red Lion
(Off A541) OS 213681
Burtonwood Dark Mild, Bitter [H]
Popular, friendly local, worth finding 🏛♣⊞✿🚗☾◗🍷Ⓢ⛺

Rhosllanerchrugog 22B6

11–3; 5.30–10.30 (11 F, S)
Black Lion
Church Street (B5097)
Border Mild, Bitter [E]
Pub with good atmosphere
♪🚗🍷Ⓢ

Rhos-on-Sea 21C

11–3; 5.30–10.30 (11 in summer)
Rhos Abbey Hotel
111 Rhos Promenade
☎ Colwyn Bay 46601
Moorhouse Premier Bitter, Pendle Witches Brew (summer) [H]
Smart three star hotel
⌐♪✿🚗▣[R]☾◗🍷Ⓢ♿

Rhyl 21H

11–3; 5.30–10.30 (11 F, S and summer)
Abbey Vaults
Abbey Street
Marston Pedigree [H]
Small, friendly local ♣🍷

Galley
Yale Road (A525)
Marston Mercian Mild, Burton Bitter [H]
Friendly, lively local ♪♣✿🚗🍷

Load of Mischief
High Street
Burtonwood Dark Mild, Bitter [H]
Large, friendly town pub
🏛⌐♪♣⊞🚗[R]☾◗Ⓢ⇌

Rossett 22B

11.30–3; 5.30–10.30 (11 F, S)
Butchers Arms
(A483)
Burtonwood Dark Mild, Bitter [H]
Small, friendly local ♪♣✿🚗🍷

Ruthin 21J

11.30–3.30; 5.30–11 (11.30 F, S)
Boars Head
Clwyd Street
Open all day 2nd Tue of the month, and Weds in summer
Burtonwood Dark Mild, Bitter [H]
Basic local ♪♣☾🍷Ⓢ

St. Asaph 21J

11–3; 5.30–10.30 (11 in summer)
Bull
Lower Street ☎ 583514
Marston Mercian Mild [G]
Burton Bitter, Pedigree [H]
Quaint, small, old and friendly
♪♣✿🚗☾🍷Ⓢ⛺

Treuddyn 22A

11.30–3; 7–10.30 (11 F, S)
Farmers Arms
Ffordd-y-Llan (off A5104)
Burtonwood Dark Mild, Bitter [H]
Friendly local 🏛⌐♣🚗[R]🍷Ⓢ

Wrexham 22B

11.30–3; 5.30–10.30 (11 F,S)
Oak Tree
Ruabon Road
Border Exhibition Mild [H] **4X** [E] **Old Master** [H]
Oasis in a beer desert ♪♣🚗🍷Ⓢ

Dyfed

Pubs that do not open on Sundays are marked *

Aberaeron 13F3

-3; 5.30–10.30 (11 F, S and summer)
Cadwgan Inn*
0 Market Street ☎ 570149
Felinfoel Double Dragon
Red Kite Original
Welsh Dark Mild Ⓗ
cosy lounge with restaurant
attached ♪�־♪❼⑤

Royal Oak*
orth Road (A487)
Felinfoel Double Dragon
Marston Pedigree Ⓗ
mall and friendly local ♪�־♪❶⑤

Aberporth 12E4

-3; 5.30–10.30 (11 F, S and summer)
Headland Hotel*
Off B4333) ☎ 810501
Welsh HB Ⓗ
mposing view of bay
�־♪❼⑤

Aberystwyth 13G2

.30–2.30; 5.30–11
Coopers Arms*
orthgate Street ☎ 4050
Draught Bass
Welsh Dark Mild, BB Ⓗ
enovated old local, centre for
azz and folk music ❢�־❽♪❶⑤

Crystal Palace*
ueens Road ☎ 615241
Draught Bass
Welsh HB Ⓗ
lain local ♪�־▣❼⑤

Nags Head*
ridge Street
anks Mild, Bitter Ⓔ
lain bar and cosy lounge
☖☰❶⑤

Weston Vaults*
orthgate Street ☎ 617641
anks Mild, Bitter Ⓔ
idy pub with a small lounge
☖▣❼⑤

Ammanford 13G6

.30–4; 6–10.30 (11 F, S and summer)
Telegraph
uay Street
losed Sunday evenings
uckley Mild, Best Bitter Ⓔ
omfortable, friendly pub
♪☖❶⑤

Amroth 12D7

-3; 5.30–11
New Inn
Saundersfoot 812368
Draught Bass
Welsh BB Ⓗ
6th-century seafront pub of
haracter
❢♪☖❽�־❶❼⑤

ry also: Temple Bar
Felinfoel, Welsh))

Borth 13G1

10.30–2.30; 5.30–11
Friendship*
(B4353)
Burtonwood Bitter
Red Kite Original
Worthy of its name
❢☖�־❶⑤☖

Burry Port 13F7

11–3; 5.30–10.30 (11 F, S and summer)
Pemberton Arms
Colbey Road (A484) ☎ 2129
Buckley Best Bitter Ⓗ
Tastefully renovated village
local ❢☖❽�־❶❼⑤☖

Burton Ferry 12C7

11–3; 5.30–11
Jolly Sailor
(Off A477) ☎ Neyland 600378
Ansells Bitter
Ind Coope Burton Ale Ⓗ
Pleasant, comfortable and
popular riverside pub
☖❢♪☖❽☰❼⑤

Bynea 13F7

11–3; 5.30–10.30 (11 F, S and summer)
Lewis Arms
90 Yspitty Road (A484)
☎ Llanelli 2878
Felinfoel Mild, Bitter, Double
Dragon Ⓗ
Smart, popular local with
enthusiastic landlord
♪☖❽❶⑤

Cardigan 12D4

11–3; 5.30–11 (Open all day Mon, Sat)
Bell Hotel*
High Street ☎ 612629
Closes 3–5.30 Mondays
Buckley Best Bitter Ⓗ
Friendly town centre hotel
♪☖❽☰▣☖❼⑤

Carew 12C7

11–3; 5.30–11
Carew Inn
(A4075)
Welsh BB Ⓗ
Small village pub with
character ❢♪☖❶⑤

Carmarthen 13F6

11 am–10.30 pm (11 F, S and summer)
Closes 3–5.30 pm Tue and Fri
Boars Head Hotel
Lammas Street ☎ 233147
Felingfoel Mild, Bitter, Double
Dragon Ⓗ
Two large, comfortable hotel
bars ♪▣☖≹

Coopers Arms*
Lammas Street
Buckley Mild, Best Bitter Ⓖ
Quiet, friendly and traditional
market pub ♪❶≹

Queens*

Queen Street ☎ 31800
Draught Bass
Welsh Dark Mild Ⓗ
Smart, friendly pub at rear of
castle remains ♪☖❶▣⑤≹

Cilgerran 12D4

11–3; 5.30–10.30 (11 F, S and summer)
Pendre
High Street ☎ Cardigan
614223
Opens at 12 noon and 7 pm
Welsh Dark Mild, BB Ⓗ
Friendly 14th-century inn
❢☖❽☰❼⑤

Cresswell Quay 12C7

11–3; 5.30–11
Cresselly Arms
(Off A4075) OS 051068
Welsh Dark Mild Ⓖ
Well-situated pub with lots of
character ☖❶❶

Crwbin 13F6

11–3; 5.30–10.30 (11 F, S and summer)
Three Compasses
(B4306)
☎ Pontyberem 870443
Felinfoel Mild, Bitter,
Double Dragon Ⓗ
Cosy friendly pub with superb
views ☖☖❽☖☰❼⑤

Cwmann 13G4

11–3; 5.30–10.30 (11 F, S and summer)
Ram Inn
(A482) ☎ Lampeter 422556
Whitbread Flowers Original
Bitter Ⓗ
Cosy, welcoming main-road
pub; restaurant open till
midnight ☖☖❽☰▣☖❼⑤☖

Tafarn Jem
(A482) OS 615437
☎ Pumpsaint 440
Buckley Mild, Best Bitter
Red Kite Original Ⓗ
A 'gem' of a pub
☖☖♪☖☰❼⑤

Cwmbach 13F7

12–3; 6–10.30 (11 F, S and summer)
Farriers Arms
(B4308) ☎ Llanelli 4256
Closed Mondays
Buckley Best Bitter
Felinfoel Bitter
Marston Pedigree Ⓗ
Idyllic country pub ♪☖❽☖❶

Dreenhill 12B6

11–3; 5.30–11
Masons Arms
(B4327) OS 922143
Welsh BB Ⓖ
Homely, nostalgic little
cottage pub ☖❽❶⑤

Fishguard 12C5

11–3; 5.30–11
Fishguard Arms
Main Street
Felinfoel Double Dragon
Marston Pedigree
Welsh BB [G]
Take a step back in time
🔥⌐♣[R]🍷Ⓢ

Ship
Cardigan Road
Lower Fishguard
Evening opening 6.30
Welsh Dark Mild, BB [G]
Low-ceilinged nautical gem
🔥♣🍷Ⓢ

Garnant 13G6

11.30–4; 6–10.30 (11 F, S and summer)
Lamb & Flag
Cwmamman Road (A474)
Buckley Bitter [G]
Old-fashioned pub, more like a private house ♣🍷

Goginan 13G2

10.30–2.30; 5.30–11
Druid*
(A44)
Draught Bass
Welsh Dark Mild [H]
Friendly, rural local ⌐♣▦🍷Ⓢ

Haverfordwest 12C6

11–3; 5.30–11
Bristol Trader
Old Quay, Quay Street (off Castle Square) ☎ 2122
Open until 4 pm Saturdays
Ind Coope Burton Ale [H]
14th century riverside inn
♪⚘🚗🕐◗🍷🚆

County Hotel
Salutation Square (A40)
☎ 3542
Open all day Tue & Sat
Felinfoel Double Dragon
Welsh BB [H]
Good old town hotel bar
🔥♣▦🚗■[R]🕐◗🍷🚆

Try also: Old Three Crowns; Bull; Belle View (Ind Coope)

Jameston 12C7

11–3; 5.30–11
Swan Lake
(A4139) ☎ Manorbier 262
Draught Bass
Felinfoel Double Dragon
Marston Pedigree
Welsh BB [H]
Outstandingly well-kept pub
♪♣▦⚘🚗[R]🕐◗🍷

Lampeter 13G4

11–3; 5.30–11
Old Quarry*
(Off North Road) OS579488
Ansells Bitter
Marston Pedigree
Red Kite Original [H]
Unusual pub/restaurant, hidden behind rugby club
♪♣⚘🚗🕐◗🍷Ⓢ

Lamphey 12C7

11–3; 5.30–11
Dial Inn
The Ridgeway ☎ 672426
Crown SBB [H]
Intriguing, unusual interior including squash court
♪▦🚗[R]🕐◗🍷

Laugharne 12E6

11–3; 5.30–11
Carpenters Arms
(A4066)
Buckley Best Bitter
Felinfoel Double Dragon
Whitbread Bitter [H]
Pleasant, popular pub
♪♣⚘🚗🍷Ⓢ⛺

Little Haven 12B6

11–3; 5.30–10.30 (11 F, S and summer)
Swan
☎ Broad Haven 256
Evening opening: 6.30
Draught Bass
Welsh BB [H]
Delightfully situated quayside pub ♪🕐◗ (Wed–Sat)

Try also: St Brides (Welsh)

Llanartheny 13F6

11–3; 5.30–10.30 (11 F, S and summer)
Paxton Inn
(B4300) ☎ Dryslwyn 591
Buckley Best Bitter
Whitbread Bitter [H]
Comfortable village pub
♪♣🕐◗🍷Ⓢ

Llanboidy 12D6

11–3; 5.30–11
Lamb
OS 216233 ☎ 243
Buckley Best Bitter [G]
Superb village pub
♪♣⚘🚗■[R]🕐◗🍷

Llanddewi Brefi 13G4

11–3; 5.30–11
Foelallt Arms*
(B4343)
Ansells Bitter
Ind Coope Burton Ale
Red Kite Original [H]
Friendly local on the main square ♪♣🚗🍷Ⓢ

Llanddowror 12D6

11–3; 5.30–11
Coopers Arms
(A477) ☎ St. Clears 230793
Buckley Best Bitter [G]
Quiet village pub on busy road
🔥♪♣🕐◗🍷Ⓢ

Llandeilo 13G6

11–3; 5.30–10.30 (11 F, S and summer)
Three Tuns
Market Street ☎ 2667
Open all day Mon. Sat
Felinfoel Bitter, Double Dragon
Marston Pedigree [H]
Tucked away in narrow street. Occasional guest beers
♪♣■🍷Ⓢ

Llandovery 13H5

11–3; 5.30–10.30 (11 F, S and summer)
White Swan
47 High Street (A40) ☎ 20816
Open all day Fridays, fairdays and alternate Tues
Everard Old Original
Hook Norton Best Bitter
Ind Coope Burton Ale
Marston Pedigree
Wadworth 6X [H]
Interesting free house; range may vary 🔥♪♣▦⚘🚗[R]🕐◗🍷Ⓢ

Llandyssul 13F5

11–3; 5.30–10.30 (11 F, S and summer)
Porth Hotel
(A486) ☎ 2202
Buckley Best Bitter
Felinfoel Double Dragon
Red Kite Original [H]
Plush hotel bar in town centre
♪▦⚘🚗■[R]🕐◗🍷Ⓢ

Llanelli 13F7

11–3; 5–10.30 (11 F, S and summer)
Clarence
42 Murray Street
Open all day Thu & Sat
Draught Bass
Welsh Dark Mild, BB [H]
Delightful town pub 🕐🍷Ⓢ

Railway Hotel
127 Station Road
Felinfoel Mild, Bitter, Double Dragon [H]
Friendly pub near level crossing ♣[R]🍷Ⓢ🚆

Rolling Mill
Station Road ☎ 51717
Usher PA, Best Bitter [H]
Friendly town pub
♪♣[R]🕐◗🍷Ⓢ

Llangadog 13G5

11–3; 5.30–10.30 (11 F, S and summer)
Castle Hotel
Queens Square (A4069)
☎ 377
Marston Pedigree
Whitbread Bitter [H]
Friendly old free house
🔥♪♣■[R]🕐◗🍷

Llangeitho 13G3

11–3; 5.30–11
Three Horseshoes*
(B4342) ☎ 244
Ansells Bitter [H]
Pleasant village local
♪♣▦⚘🕐◗ (summer) 🍷Ⓢ

Llanrhystyd 13F3

10.30–2.30; 5.30–11
Black Lion*
(A487) ☎ Llanon 338
Welsh BB [H]

omfortable hotel; supper
ence till midnight
♣✚❤♫🅟🏠🆓🆁🅖⬤🍴🅼⬤♿▲

lanwnen 13F4

-3; 5.30–11
ish & Anchor*
4337) ℰ Cwrt Newydd 233
pens 12–2; 6–11
uckley Best Bitter
ed Kite Original 🅷
.easant rural inn in good
shing locality
♣✚❤♫🅖🆓🍴⬤🅼▲

Maenclochog 12C5

-3; 5.30–11
Globe
4313)
Velsh BB 🅖
ocals are friendly and barrels
sible ♫♣🍴

Meinciau 13F6

-3; 5.30–10.30 (11 F, S and summer)
Black Horse*
4309)
uckley Mild
elinfoel Bitter 🅖
eat, homely country pub
♫🅟🍴🅼

Nevern 12C5

-3; 5.30–11
Trewern Arms
Newport 820395
elinfoel Double Dragon
Vhitbread Bitter 🅷
ttractive pub in idyllic
etting
♣✚❤♫🅟🅖🆓🆁🅖⬤🍴🅼⬤

Newcastle Emlyn 12E5

-3; 5.30–10.30 (11 F, S and summer)
Pelican Inn*
ycamore Street ℰ 710606
pen all day Friday
uckley Best Bitter
elinfoel Double Dragon
Veston Cider 🅷
ttractive, friendly old pub
♫♣✚❤🅟🆓🆁🅖⬤🍴⬤

Newport 12C5

-3; 5.30–11
Golden Lion
A487) ℰ 820321/820423
elinfoel Double Dragon
Vhitbread Bitter 🅷
ively, attractive, popular little
ub ♫♣✚❤🅟🆓🆁🅖⬤🍴⬤

New Quay 13E3

–3; 5.30–10.30 (11 in summer)
Black Lion*
Off B4342) ℰ 560209
Draught Bass
Marston Pedigree
Red Kite Original
Velsh BB 🅷
Vell-kept old free
ouse ♣✚❤♫🅟🅖🆓🆁🅖⬤🍴🅼⬤

Nolton Haven 12B6

11–3; 5.30–11
Mariners Inn
OS 859186 ℰ Camrose 469
Felinfoel Double Dragon
Usher Best Bitter 🅷
Attractive seaside pub
🍴♫♣✚❤🅟🅖🆓⬤♫▲

Pembroke Dock 12C7

11–2.30; 5.30–11
Charlton Inn
Bush Street
Welsh Dark Mild, BB 🅷
Popular man's pub ♣✚🍴🍴

Pisgah 13G2

10.30–2.30; 5.30–11
Halfway Inn
(A4120) ℰ Capel Bangor 631
Felinfoel Double Dragon
Gwynedd Anglesey Bitter
Marston Pedigree
Red Kite Original 🅷 & 🅖
Isolated but lively
🍴♣✚❤♫🅟🅖🆓🍴⬤🅼▲

Pontargothi 13F6

11–3; 5.30–10.30 (11 F, S and summer)
Cresselly Arms
Hotel
(A40) ℰ Nantgaredig 221
Draught Bass
Buckley Best Bitter 🅷
Coracle on ceiling for winter
floods ♫♣✚❤♫🅟🅖🆓🆁⬤

Pontfaen 12C5

11–3; 5.30–11
Duffryn Arms
(B4313) OS 026342
Draught Bass or
Ind Coope Burton Ale 🅖
As pubs were in grandfather's
day ♣

Rhydlewis 13E4

11–3; 5.30–11
New Inn*
Pentregat (A487)
ℰ Llangranog 285
Red Kite Original
Usher Best Bitter 🅷
Pleasant pub on main holiday
route ♫♣🅟🅖🆓🍴⬤

Rhydowen 13F4

11–3; 5.30–11
Alltyrodyn Arms*
(A415) ℰ Pontshaen 363
Buckley Mild, Best Bitter
Marston Pedigree
Red Kite Original 🅷
Comfortable, traditional
roadside inn
♫♣✚❤🅟🅖🆓🆁🅖⬤🍴⬤

St. Dogmaels 12D4

11–3; 5.30–11
White Hart
(B4546)

Nolton Haven (top right)

Buckley Mild (summer),
Best Bitter 🅷
Neat, well-kept free house
♫♣🅟🅖🍴⬤

Saundersfoot 12D7

11–3; 5.30–11
Royal Oak
Wogan Terrace (B4316)
Draught Bass
Welsh BB 🅷
Popular quayside pub
🍴♫♣✚❤🅟🆓🅖🍴≠

Solva 12B6

11–3; 5.30–11
Harbour House
Hotel
ℰ St Davids 721267
Ind Coope Burton Ale 🅷
Ex-servicemen should enjoy
this one 🅼🍴♣✚❤🅟🆓🆁🅖⬤🍴

Stepaside 12D7

11–3; 5.30–11
Stepaside Inn
(A477) OS 136077
ℰ Saundersfoot 813823
Welsh BB 🅖 & 🅷
Popular local with large
outdoor area
🅼🍴♫♣✚❤🅟🍴⬤≠

Tenby 12D7

11–3; 5.30–11
Coach & Horses
Upper Frog Street (off A478)
Draught Bass
Whitbread Bitter 🅷
Popular town-centre pub
♫♣⬤🍴≠

White Hart
(Off A478) ℰ 2698
Felinfoel Double Dragon 🅷
Friendly pub with good service
🍴♣✚❤🅟🆓🆁🅖⬤🍴⬤♿≠

Templeton 12D6

11–3; 5.30–11
Boars Head
(A478) ℰ Narberth 860286
Usher Best Bitter 🅷
Old world pub with pleasant
atmosphere
♫♣✚❤🅟🆓🆁🅖⬤🍴⬤♿

Tresaith 12E4

11–3; 5.30–11
Ship Inn*
(Off A487) OS 278515
ℰ Aberporth 810380
Buckley Best Bitter 🅷
Small seaside pub
🅼🍴♫♣✚❤🆁🅖⬤🍴⬤

Whitland 12D6

11–3; 5.30–11
Yelverton Arms
(Off A40) ℰ 240186
Buckley Best Bitter 🅷
Friendly pub next to station
♫♣✚❤🅟🅖🆓🆁🅖⬤🍴⬤≠

General opening hours: 11.30–4; 6–11

Aberaman 14A7

Temple Bar
Cardiff Road (A4224)
Courage Best Bitter
Samuel Smith Old Brewery Bitter
Usher Best Bitter [H]
Old-world homely pub
♣🚗♀Ⓢ

Aberdare 13J7

Bush
Commercial Street (off A4059)
Welsh BB [H]
Busy town-centre pub ♣♀Ⓢ

Bridgend 13J8

Two Brewers
Brackla Estate (off B4181)
☎ 61788
Brain Dark, Bitter, SA [H]
Smart, comfortable pub
🔥♪♣✿🚗◔◗♀Ⓢ♿

Victoria Hotel
Adare Street ☎ 59802
Courage Best Bitter, Directors [H]
Recently modernised one-room local 🔥◔Ⓢ⇌

Bryncethin 13J8

Masons Arms
(A4061)
Draught Bass
Welsh Dark Mild, PA, BB [H]
Bustling free house, full of atmosphere ♣[R]♀Ⓢ

Caerphilly 14B8

Goodrich
Van Road (off A469)
Whitbread Bitter [H]
Comfortable lounge and dining room, close to town centre ♪♣🚗◔♀Ⓢ⇌

Cefn Cribbwr 13H8

Farmers Arms
24 Cefn Road (B4281)
Draught Bass [H]
Friendly, unspoilt village local
♪♣⊞✿🚗♀Ⓢ

Cefn Rhigos 13J7

New Inn
(Off A4061) OS 916068
☎ Hirwaun 811007
Whitbread Flowers Original Bitter [H]
Friendly village pub renowned for its cow pie
♪♣🚗◔◗♀Ⓢ

Coychurch 13J8

White Horse
(Off A473) ☎ Bridgend 2583
Brain Dark, Bitter, SA [H]
Busy modern village local
♪♣✿🚗◔♀

Coytrahen 13H8

Nicholls Arms
Maesteg Road (A4063)
☎ Aberkenfig 720378
Courage Best Bitter, Directors [H]
Smart roadside pub, comfortable and friendly
♪♣✿🚗▣[R]◔◗♀Ⓢ♿

Cwmbach 14A7

Duffryn Arms
(A4059) ☎ Aberdare 861610
Welsh HB [H]
Comfortable roadside pub with a warm welcome
♪♣✿🚗◔◗ (Tue–Sat) ♀Ⓢ

Gelli 13J7

Gordon Hotel
Gelli Road ☎ Tonypandy 421155
Usher PA, Best Bitter [H]
Extensively renovated old valleys hotel
🔥♪♣▣[R]◔◗Ⓢ⇌

Gwaelod y Garth 14A8

Gwaelod y Garth
(Off (A470)
Welsh PA [H]
Friendly unspoilt village pub
♣✿🚗♀Ⓢ

Hirwaun 13J7

Glancynon
Swansea Road (off A4059)
OS 960055
Felinfoel Double Dragon
Fuller London Pride, ESB [H]
Enterprising free house with no sign ♪♣🚗♀Ⓢ

Llangeinor 13J8

Llangeinor Arms
(Off A4093) OS 925879
Courage Best Bitter, Directors
Welsh BB [H]
Remote but popular, with attractive views
✿🚗◔Ⓢ

Llangynwyd 13H8

Corner House Inn
(Off A4063) ☎ Maesteg 732067
Brain Dark
Courage Best Bitter
Felinfoel Double Dragon
Marston Pedigree [H]
Comfortable free house with interesting artefacts
🔥♪✿🚗◔◗Ⓢ

Llantrisant 14A8

Cross Keys
High Street (B4595)
Whitbread Bitter [H]
Popular, musical pub in centre of 'old' town
🔥♪♣◔♀Ⓢ

Pennyfarthing
Southgate, Pengawsi (Off A473) ☎ 228838
Usher PA, Best Bitter [H]
Comfortable modern pub in Victorian style
🔥♪✿🚗◔◗Ⓢ

Llantwit Fardre 14A8

Bush Inn
(A473)
Crown SBB [H]
Small, comfortable and friendly ♣🚗◔♀Ⓢ

Machen 14B8

Fwrrwm Ishta Hotel
Commercial Road (A468)
Courage Best Bitter, Directors [H]
Large, comfortable and friendly 🔥♪♣🚗[R]◔♀Ⓢ

Maesteg 13H8

Sawyers Arms
Commercial Street (off A4063)
Brain Bitter [H]
Unspoilt town-centre Victoriana ♣♀

Maesycwmmer 14B7

Angel
Main Road (off A4049)
Courage Best Bitter, Directors [H]
Friendly village local
♪♣✿🚗♀Ⓢ

Mawdlam 13H8

Prince of Wales
Main Street (off B4281)
Afan Bitter
Draught Bass [G]
Welsh PA, BB [H]
Interesting old pub opposite sand dunes
♣🚗♀Ⓢ

Methyr Tydfil 14A6

Anchor Hotel
High Street (off (A470)
Draught Bass [H]
Busy, basic town-centre local
♣♀⇌

Park View
Brecon Road (A4102)
Welsh PA [H]
Small, friendly local ♣♀

Mountain Ash 14A7

Jeffreys Arms
Jeffrey Street (off A4059)
Evening opening: 6.30
Welsh BB [E]
A warren of a pub, catering for all tastes ⚑♪♣◔🍺Ⓢ

Mwyndy 14A8

Castell Mynach
Cardiff Road (A4119, off M4 Jct.34) ☎ 222298
Draught Bass
Welsh PA, BB, HB [H]
Popular pub with a wide appeal ✿🚗◔Ⓢ

Nantyffyllon 13H8

Masons Arms
(Off A4063)
Whitbread Bitter [H]
Small and comfortable; ask for black handle
⚑♣✿🍺Ⓢ

Nant-y-Moel 13J8

Nant-y-Moel
(Off A4061)
Welsh PA [H]
Typical valleys local ♪♣🍺Ⓢ

Ogmore 13H9

Pelican
(B4524)
Courage Best Bitter, Directors [H]
Pleasant country pub
⚑♣✿🚗◔🍺Ⓢ

Penderyn 13J7

Red Lion
(Off A4059) OS 945085
Brain Dark, SA
Draught Bass
Everard Tiger, Old Original
Felinfoel Double Dragon
Marston Pedigree
Robinson Best Bitter
Wadworth 6X
Welsh HB [G]
Splendid hilltop pub; range of beers may vary
✿🚗🍺

Pentyrch 14A8

Kings Arms
Church Road
(Off A470/A4119)
Brain Dark, Bitter, SA [H]
Large country pub catering for all tastes
⚑♣✿🚗🍺Ⓢ

Pontypridd 14A7

Greyhound
The Broadway (A4058)
Draught Bass [H]
Small, popular pub with boxing memorabilia
⚑♣[R]🍺Ⓢ🚆

Llanover Arms
West Street (off A470)
Brain Dark, Bitter [E]
Classic old-fashioned inn, popular with all ages ♣🍺🚆

Pontycymmer 13J8

Ffaldau Arms
(A4064)
Whitbread Bitter [H]
Rambling town pub
⚑♪♣🍺Ⓢ

Porth 14A7

Britannia Hotel
(A4058) ☎ 5393
Brain Dark, Bitter [E]
Large, comfortable free house
♪♣🚗[R]◔🍺Ⓢ

Porthcawl 13H9

Jolly Sailor
Church Street, Newton
(Off A4106)
Brain Dark, Bitter, SA [H]
Nautical pub on village green
✿🍺Ⓢ

Rose & Crown
Nottage (off B4283)
☎ 4849/4850
Usher PA, Best Bitter [H]
Smart locals' local
♪✿🚗🛏◗

Royal Oak
South Road (B4283)
Draught Bass [G]
Welsh BB [H]
Delightful town pub with discriminating lounge
♪♣🍺

Rudry 14B8

Griffin Inn Motel
(Off A468) OS 187875
☎ Caerphilly 883396/869735
Marston Pedigree
Whitbread Bitter [H]
Friendly village inn with motel and restaurant attached
⚑♪♣⊞✿🚗🛏[R]◔◗🍺Ⓢ

Southerndown 13H9

Three Golden Cups
Llantwit Major Road
(B4524) ☎ 880432
Courage Best Bitter [H]
Popular pub in superb coastal scenery
♪♣✿🚗◔◗🍺Ⓢ

Taffs Well 14B8

Anchor Hotel
Cardiff Road (off A470/M4 exit 33) ☎ 860104
Restaurant licence until 12 pm
Whitbread Flowers Original Bitter [H]
Friendly family local with nautical bric-a-brac
♪♣🚗[R]◔◗🍺Ⓢ🚆

Tirphil 14B7

Dynevor Arms
(A469)
Welsh PA [E]
Small, popular local ♣🍺🚆

Treforest 14A8

Forest
Wood Road (off A473)
Brain Bitter [H]
Big, friendly pub with darters bar and plush lounge
♪♣[R]🍺Ⓢ🚆

Otley Arms
Forest Road (A473)
☎ Pontypridd 402033
Afan Bitter [H]
Brain Dark [E]
Crown SBB
Welsh HB [H]
Thatcher Cider [G]
Popular free house near polytechnic ♪♣[R]◔◗🍺Ⓢ🚆

Treorchy 13J7

Prince of Wales
High Street (A4058)
Whitbread Bitter, Flowers Original Bitter [H]
Splendid town pub, popular with all ages ♪♣🍺Ⓢ🚆

Troedyrhiw 14A7

Railway
Bridge Street (off A470)
Welsh PA [H]
Friendly valley local ♣🍺🚆

Wattstown 14A7

Wattstown Hotel
(B4277)
Welsh PA [E]
Impressive building with welcoming bar
♣🍺Ⓢ

Ynyswen 13J7

Crown Hotel
Ynyswen Road (A4061)
Draught Bass
Brain Dark [E] **SA**
Courage Directors [H]
Bulmer Cider [G]
Popular free house ♪♣🍺Ⓢ

Ystrad 13J7

Greenfield
Ystrad Fawr (A4058)
Welsh BB [H]
Popular valley local with comfortable lounge
♪♣🍺

Ystrad Mynach 14B7

Olde Royal Oak
(A469) ☎ Hengoed 814196
Draught Bass [H]
Modernised roadside pub, comfortable and popular
♪♣✿🚗◔🍺Ⓢ🚆

Aberthaw 14A9
Aberddawan

11.30–3.30; 5.30–10.30 (11 in summer)
Blue Anchor
East Aberthaw (off B4265)
Brain Dark, SA H
Gwent Druids Ale G
Marston Pedigree
Robinson Best Bitter
Wadworth 6X
Whitbread Bitter H
Bustling, popular old
smugglers' inn ▲▲🌢🏠🌜🌑🌑

Aberthin 14A8

11.30–3.30; 6–10.30 (11 in summer)
Hare & Hounds
(A4222, off A48)
Draught Bass
Welsh PA, BB G
Small, friendly country pub
🌜🌢🏠🌜🌑🌑

Barry 14B9
Barri

11.30–3.30; 5.30–10.30 (11 in summer)
Glenbrook Inn
Dobbins Road, Palmerston
(Off A4231) 🌜 746996
Evening opening: 6
Brain Dark, Bitter, SA
Welsh HB H
Attractive and comfortable
new housing estate local
🌜🌢🏠R🌜🌑🌑

Three Bells
Coldbrook Road, Cadoxton
Chesters Mild
Whitbread Bitter, Flowers
Original Bitter H
Modernised old village pub,
popular and cheerful
▲🌜🌢🏠🌜🌑🌑

Bonvilston 14A8
Tresimwn

11.30–3.30; 6–10.30 (11 in summer)
Red Lion
(A48) 🌜 208
Brain Dark, Bitter, SA H
Outstanding village pub
🌜🌢🌢🏠🌜🌑🌑

Boverton 14A9

11.30–3.30; 6–10.30 (11 in summer)
Boverton Castle Hotel
Eagleswell Road
🌜 Llantwit Major 2428
Ansells Bitter H
Spacious pub with bustling
bar 🌜🌜🌢🏠R🌜🌑🌑🌑▲

Cardiff 14B8
Caerdydd
City Centre

11.3; 5.30–10.30
Albert
St Mary Street 🌜 23032
Brain Dark, Bitter, SA H
The brewery tap, popular and
cheerful 🌜🌜🌜🌑🌑

Borough Arms
St Mary Street 🌜 21343
Closed Sundays
Usher Best Bitter H
Smart bistro-style bar
🌜🌜🌑🌑🌑

Bristol Hotel
9 Penarth Road (A4160)
🌜 373488
Brain Dark
Usher Best Bitter H
Impressive central hotel
lounge bar
🌜🌜🌢🏠R🌜🌑🌑

Brownhills Hotel
Saunders Road 🌜 33413
Brain Dark, Bitter H & E
Comfortable hotel bar
🌜🌑🌢R🌜🌑🌑

Duke of Wellington
The Hayes 🌜 27870
Brain Dark, Bitter, SA H
Recently modernised pub
adjoining brewery
🌜🌜🌑🌑🌑

St David's Hall
Working Street 🌜 42611
Usually closed Sundays
Brain Dark
Welsh HB E
Real ale in St David's Lounge
of new concert hall
🌜🌜🌑🌢R🌜🌑🌑🌑🌑

Westgate
Cowbridge Road East (A4161)
Brain Dark, Bitter, SA H
Prominent corner pub with a
variety of bars 🌜🌢🌜🌑

Cardiff: East

Crwys
34 Crwys Road, Cathays
(A469) 🌜 30893
Brain Dark, Bitter, SA H
Thriving local on the main
road 🌜🌢🌜🌑🌑

Gower
Gwennyth Street (off (A469)
Brain Dark, Bitter, SA H
Large backstreet pub with
snooker table 🌜🌢🌜🌑🌑

Heath
2 Whitchurch Road, Heath
(A469) 🌜 20902
Brain Dark, Bitter, SA H
Busy suburban pub with
modernised lounge 🌜🌢🌜🌑🌑

Rompney Castle
Wentloog Road, Rumney
(B4239)
Brain Dark, Bitter, SA H
Large, comfortable suburban
pub 🌜🌢🌢🏠🌜🌑

Royal Oak
Broadway, Roath (A4161)
Brain Dark, Bitter SA G
Bar a shrine to 'Peerless
Jim Driscoll' 🌜🌜🌢🌑

Cardiff: North East

Murrayfield
Pentwyn Drive, Pentwyn
Younger IPA, No 3 H
Tasteful new estate pub
▲🌜🌢🌢🏠🌜🌑

Ty Mawr Arms
Graig Road, Lisvane
(Off B4562)
OS 184845 🌜 756091
Robinson Best Bitter H
Hard-to-find pub in rural
setting 🌜🌢🏠🌜🌑

Unicorn Inn
Church Road, Llanedeyrn
(Off A48)
Ansells Bitter
Ind Coope Burton Ale H
Modernised and secluded
country pub ▲🌜🌢🏠🌑

Cardiff: North West

Black Lion
Cardiff Road, Llandaff (A411
Brain Dark, Bitter, SA H
Comfortable, well-modernise
hostelry 🌜🌢🌑

Butchers Arms
Heol-y-Felin, Rhiwbina (off
A469) 🌜 62526
Ansells Bitter
Ind Coope Burton Ale H
Busy pub in quiet residential
area 🌜🌢🌢🌜🌑🌑

Fox & Hounds
Old Church Road,
Whitchurch (off A4054)
Brain Dark, Bitter, SA H
Popular, comfortable local
🌜🌢🏠🌑

Pantmawr
Off Tyla Teg, Pantmawr Road
OS 148819 🌜 66542
Draught Bass, Welsh HB H
Excellent suburban pub,
worth finding ▲🌜🌢🏠🌜🌑

Pineapple
Station Road, Llandaff North
(A4054)
Draught Bass E
Welsh Dark Mild H **HB** E
Friendly suburban local
🌜🌢🌜🌑🌑🌑

Plough
Merthyr Road, Whitchurch
(A4054) 🌜 63017
Brain Dark, Bitter, SA H
Large popular pub with
village atmosphere ▲🌢🌜🌑

Royal Oak
Methyr Road, Whitchurch
(A4054)
Draught Bass
Welsh HB H & E
Genuine local pub 🌜🌜🏠🌑

Three Horseshoes
Merthyr Road, Gabalfa
(A470)
Brain Dark, Bitter, SA [H]
Friendly local on busy road
♣℘🚗🎯

ardiff:
outh West

Great Eastern
ietal Street, Adamsdown
Welsh HB [H]
Friendly backstreet local 🔥♪♣🎯

Inn on the River
Taff Embankment,
Grangetown (off A4119)
Brain Dark, Bitter, SA [H]
Large riverside pub with a variety of bars
♪♣℘[R]◷🎯[S]

Kings Castle
Cowbridge Road East
(A4161) ☎ 30291
Chesters Mild
Whitbread Bitter, Flowers Original Bitter [H]
Popular street-corner, art nouveau revival pub ♪◷

New Sea Lock
Harrowby Street, Butetown
(off A4119)
Brain Dark, Bitter [H]
Back-street local with strong nautical flavour ♣🎯🚉

Packet Hotel
93 Bute Street, Butetown
(A470) ☎ 23772
Brain Dark, Bitter, SA [H]
Superbly modernised dockland pub near museum
♣℘◷[S]🚉

Cowbridge 13J9
Y Bontfaen

11.30–3.30; 6–10.30 (11 in summer)
Horse & Groom
High Street (off A48) ☎ 2253
Evening opening: 5.30
Whitbread Bitter, Flowers Original Bitter [H]
Smart, lively pub ♪℘◷

Vale of Glamorgan
High Street (off A48) ☎ 2252
Welsh BB, HB [E]
Well-kept village pub, ask for cask BB ♪♣[R]🎯[S]

Dinas Powys 14B9

11.30–3.30; 5.30–10.30 (11 in summer)
Cross Keys
Elm Grove Road (off A4055)
Draught Bass
Welsh HB [H]
Busy local near the village green ♪♣🚗🎯[S]

Eglwys Brewis
Eglwys Brwys 14A9

11.30–3.30; 6–10.30 (11 in summer)
Fishersbridge Inn
(Off B4265)
☎ Llantwit Major 3921
Brain Bitter, SA
Whitbread Bitter [H]
Bulmer Cider [G]
Country pub near RAF camp
🔥♪♣℘🚗◷❥🎯[S]⛺

Llancarfan 14A9

11.30–3.30; 6–10.30 (11 in summer)
Fox & Hounds
(Off A48) OS 052704
☎ Bonvilston 297
Felinfoel Mild, Double Dragon [H]
Welsh HB [E]
Relaxed 16th century village pub with restaurant attached
🏠♪♣℘🚗◷❥ (must book)[S]

Llansannor 13J8

11.30–3; 6–10.30 (11 in summer)
City Inn
☎ Cowbridge 2437
Brain Dark, Bitter
Younger IPA [H]
Well-appointed motel in attractive countryside
🏠🔥♪♣℘🚗▣[R]◷❥[S]

Llysworney 13J9

11.30–3.30; 6–10.30 (11 in summer)
Carne Arms
(B4268) ☎ Cowbridge 2431
Whitbread Bitter [E]
Plush country pub
🏠♪℘🚗◷❥🎯[S]

Monknash 13J9
Yr As Fawr

11.30–3.30; 6–10.30
Plough & Harrow
(Off B4265)
Draught Bass
Welsh BB, HB [G]
Isolated rural pub in attractive setting ♪♣℘◷🎯[S]

Morganstown
Treforgan 14B8

11–3; 5.30–10.30
Tynant
Tynant Road (B4262)
☎ Cardiff 842313
Brain Dark, Bitter, SA [H]
Popular, comfortable out-of-town pub 🏠♣℘🚗[R]◷❥🎯[S]

Penarth 14B9

11.30–3.30; 5.30–10.30 (11 F, S in summer)
Plymouth
High Street ☎ Cardiff 702968
Draught Bass
Welsh HB [H]
Busy corner pub, undergoing gradual renovation ♪♣◷[S]

St Fagans
114 Glebe Street
Courage Best Bitter, Directors [H]
Comfortable town-centre pub
♪♣[S]

Penmark 14A9
Penmarc

12–3.30; 5.30–10.30 (11 in summer)
Six Bells
(Off A4226)
☎ Rhoose 710229
Welsh PA, BB [H]
Friendly, well-appointed country local 🏠🔥♪♣℘🚗▣◷🎯[S]

Peterston-super-Ely 14A8
Llanbedr-y-Fro

11.30–3.30; 6–10.30 (11 in summer)
Three Horseshoes
(Off A48) ☎ 760388
Brain Dark, Bitter, SA [H]
Unspoilt roomy village pub
🏠♪♣℘🚗◷❥🎯[S]

St Athan 14A9

11.30–3.30; 5.30–10.30 (11 in summer)
Three Horseshoes
The Square (Off B4265)
Welsh BB, HB [H]
Comfortable three-bar village pub ♪♣℘🚗◷🎯[S]

St Lythans 14A9

11.30–3.30; 5.30–10.30 (11 in summer)
Horse & Jockey
Twyn-yr-Odyn (off A4226)
OS 115738 ☎ Cardiff 593396
Welsh PA, HB [H]
Country pub with magnificent view of Cardiff ♪♣℘🚗◷🎯[S]⛺

St Mellons 14B8
Llaneurwg

11.3; 5.30–10.30
Star
Newport Road (B4487)
Welsh HB [H]
Cosy local in centre of village
♪♣🚗◷

Siginstone 13J9
Tresigin

11.30–3.30; 6–10.30 (11 in summer)
Victoria
(Off B4270)
Draught Bass
Welsh BB [H]
Comfortable village pub ♪🚗🎯[S]

Treoes 13J8
Tre-os

12–3.30; 5.30–10.30
Star
(Off A48)
Draught Bass
Welsh HB [H]
Thatched country pub ♣🚗🎯

Ystradowen 13J8

11.30–3.30; 5.30–10.30 (11 in summer)
White Lion
(A4222) ☎ Cowbridge 2540
Welsh BB, HB [H]
Comfortable main road pub
🔥♪♣▣℘🚗◷❥🎯

West Glamorgan

Aberavon 13H8
Aberafan

11.30–4; 6–10.30 (11 F, S)
Craddock
Green Park Estate (off B4290)
Whitbread Bitter [H]
Small, friendly old pub near shopping centre ♪♣🍷Ⓢ

Alltwen 13H7

11.30–4; 6–10.30 (11 F, S)
Butchers Arms
Near Pontardawe (off A474)
☎ Pontardawe 863100
Draught Bass
Everard Old Original [H]
One-bar village pub
🔥♪🚗[R]🕒🌙Ⓢ

Bishopston 13G8

11.30–3.30; 5.30–10.30 (11 F, S)
Bishopston Valley
Bishopston Road (off B4436)
Welsh Dark Mild, BB [H]
Attractive, busy pub
♣🌼🚗🕒Ⓢ⛺

Joiners
Bishopston Road (off B4436)
Buckley Best Bitter
Felinfoel Double Dragon
Marston Pedigree
Welsh Dark Mild [H]
Village inn with cast-iron spiral staircase ♣🌼🚗🕒🍷Ⓢ⛺

Plough & Harrow
Murton (off B4436) ☎ 4459
Brain SA
Usher Best Bitter
Welsh Dark Mild [H]
Sprawling village inn
♪♣🌼🚗[R]🕒🍷Ⓢ♿⛺

Briton Ferry 13H7
Morsawel

12–4; 6–10.30 (11 F, S)
Rose & Crown
Bethel Street (off A474)
Crown 4X, Pale Ale, SBB [H]
Only outlet for Crown 4X – PA darkened with caramel 🔥♪🌼🚗Ⓢ

Bryn 13H8

11.30–4; 6.30–10.30 (11 F, S)
Royal Oak
(B4282) ☎ Port Talbot 896712
Afan Bitter
Whitbread Bitter [H]
Large, solitary Victorian pub
♪♣🎲🚗[R]🍷Ⓢ

Cheriton 13F7

11.30–3.30; 5.30–10.30 (11 F, S)
Britannia
OS 450930 ☎ Llangenith 624
Draught Bass [G]
Friendly village local with good restaurant
♣🎲🌼🚗[R]🕒🌙🍷Ⓢ⛺

Clydach 13G7

11.30–4; 6–10.30 (11 F, S)
Bridge
High Street (A4067)
☎ 843372
Welsh Dark Mild [H]
Small, friendly Victorian pub
♣🛏Ⓢ

Carpenters
High Street (A4067)
Ansells Bitter [H]
Busy village local
♣🌼🚗🕒🍷Ⓢ

Old Glais Inn
Birchgrove Road (B4291, off A4067)
Usher Best Bitter [H]
Tastefully modernised pub
♪♣🌼🚗🕒🍷Ⓢ

Cwmgwrach 13H7
(Valley of the Witch)

11.30–4; 6–10.30 (11 F, S and summer)
Dunraven
High Street (off A465)
☎ Glynneath 720424
Whitbread Bitter [H]
Friendly village local
🔥♪♣[R]🕒🌙🍷Ⓢ

Star
(Off A465)
Buckley Standard Bitter [H]
Popular village local ♪♣🚗🍷Ⓢ

Dunvant 13G7

11.30–3.30; 5.30–10.30 (11 F, S)
Found Out
Killan Road (off B4296)
Whitbread Bitter [H]
Modern estate pub up the hill
♪♣🚗🍷Ⓢ

Glynneath
Glyn-Nedd 13H7

11.30–4; 6–10.30 (11 F, S and summer)
Dinas Rock
High Street (off A465)
☎ 720277
Whitbread Bitter [H]
Traditional village local
🔥♪♣[R]🕒🌙🍷Ⓢ

Gorseinon 13G7

11.30–4; 6–10.30 (11 F, S)
Tafarn-y-Trap
Swansea Road, Kingsbridge (A4070)
Buckley Mild, Best Bitter [E]
Modernised pub near local radio studios ♪♣🌼🚗🕒🍷Ⓢ

West End Hotel
High Street (A484/B4296)
Ansells Bitter [H]
Busy Victorian pub on crossroads ♪♣Ⓢ

Gowerton 13G7
Tre-Gwyr

11.30–4; 6–10.30 (11 F, S)
Commercial
Station Road (B4295)
Open all day Tue and second Friday of the month
Buckley Best Bitter [H]
Renovated Victorian inn
♪♣🎲🌼🚗[R]🍷Ⓢ🚆

Killay 13G
Cila

11.30–3.30; 5.30–10.30 (11 F, S)
Railway
Gower Road (A4118)
Opens 12 noon Mon–Fri
Draught Bass
Welsh Dark Mild, PA [H]
Former station house
♪♣🌼🚗🍷Ⓢ

Llanrhidian 13F

11.30–3.30; 5.30–10.30 (11 F, S)
North Gower
(B4295/B4271)
☎ Gower 390042
Buckley Best Bitter
Felinfoel Double Dragon (summer) [H]
Pleasant country house with magnificent views of the estuary 🔥♪🌼🚗[R]🕒🌙Ⓢ

Welcome to Town
(Off B4295)
Opens at 12 noon & 6 pm
Marston Pedigree [G]
Delightful unspoilt inn on village green ♣🌼🍷Ⓢ

Morriston 13G
Treforus

11.30–3.30; 5.30–10.30 (11 F, S)
Fountain
12 Woodfield Street
Buckley Mild, Best Bitter, Gold [H]
Busy town-centre pub
🔥♪♣🌼🕒🍷Ⓢ

Lamb & Flag
Morriston Cross ☎ 71663
Courage Best Bitter, Directors [H]
Large oak-panelled lounge
♪♣🛏[R]🕒🌙Ⓢ

Red Lion
Sway Road ☎ 73206
Welsh Dark Mild [E]
Friendly, renovated roadside inn ♪♣🎲🌼🚗[R]🕒🌙🍷Ⓢ

Smelters Arms
375 Trewyddfa Road (off B4489) ☎ 72728
Usher PA, Best Bitter [H]
Renovated large central bar
♪♣🛏[R]🕒🌙Ⓢ

Mumbles 13G

11.30–3.30; 5.30–10.30 (11 F, S)
Pilot
Southend
Usher Best Bitter [H]
Popular waterfront pub near yacht club ♪Ⓢ

White Rose
Newton Road
Draught Bass
Welsh Dark Mild [E]

ısy pub near waterfront and
stle ✿[R]Ⓢ

Neath 13H7
astell-Nedd

30–4; 6–10.30 (11 F, S and summer)

ull Moon
ıe Parade ☎ 2148
ıckley Mild, Best Bitter [H]
ıntral local with collection of
ıugs 🍺♣[R]🍴

hree Cranes
'ind Street
ourage Best Bitter,
irectors [H]
easantly refurbished pub
↺🍴Ⓢ

Velsh Bard
Commercial Street ☎ 2882
pen all day Wed and first and
ıird Friday in the month
uckley Mild, Best Bitter [H]
riendly, modernised pub
🍺🔥[R]↺◗🍴Ⓢ🚆

Vindsor Castle
'indsor Road
nsells Mild, Bitter [H]
raightforward street-corner
ıcal ♪♣↺🍴Ⓢ

Penclawdd 13F7
30–3.30; 5.30–10.30 (11 F, S)

erthlwydd
ı4295) OS 963562
uckley Best Bitter
ourage Directors
elinfoel Bitter [H]
easant roadside pub with
ews of estuary ♪↺Ⓢ

Royal Oak
4295 ☎ 782
raught Bass
Velsh Dark Mild [H]
easant estuary pub
♣✿🔥↺◗🍴Ⓢ⛺

Penllergaer 13G7
30–4; 6–10.30 (11 F, S)

Old Inn
ı48, off M4)
Gorseinon 894097
uckley Mild, Best Bitter [E]
arge, old, tastefully
odernised pub
🔥▣[R]↺◗🍴Ⓢ

Pontardawe 13G7
30–4; 6–10.30 (11 F, S)

Dynevor Arms
ımes Street
Vhitbread Bitter,
owers Original Bitter
ulmer Cider [H]
ld coaching house with
eekly live music 🍺♪♣✿[R]🍴Ⓢ

vy Bush Hotel
03 High Street
raught Bass
'elsh BB [E]
ood old-fashioned pub
♣[R]🍴Ⓢ

Victoria
James Street
Usher PA, Best Bitter [H]
Modernised public bar 🍺♪🍴Ⓢ

Pontardulais 13G7
Pontarddulais

11.30–4; 6–10.30 (11 F, S)

King
240 St Teilo Street (A483)
Buckley Mild, Standard Bitter, Best Bitter [H]
Friendly local with diverse display of water jugs 🍺♣🔥🍴Ⓢ

Wheatsheaf
St Teilo Street (A483)
Felinfoel Mild, Bitter [H]
Homely, traditional Welsh town pub ♪♣🍴Ⓢ

Pontneddfechan 13J7
11.30–4; 6–10.30 (11 F, S and summer)

Angel
(B4242) ☎ Glynneath 721142
Chesters Mild, Bitter [H]
Gateway to the waterfalls
🍺♪♣✿🔥▣[R]↺◗🍴Ⓢ

Port Talbot 13H8
11.30–4; 6–10.30 (11 F, S)

Bell Inn
Taibach (A48)
Afan Bitter [H]
Archer Best Bitter [G]
Bulmer Cider [H]
Real ale mecca; range of beers varies, but usually six available ♪♣🍴Ⓢ

Rhyd-y-Pandy 13G7
11.30–4; 6.30–10.30

Masons Arms
Near Morriston OS 668020
☎ Swansea 842535
Courage Best Bitter [H]
Popular, modernised, beautifully situated country pub ♪✿🔥↺◗Ⓢ

Skewen 13G7
Sgiwen

11.30–4; 6–10.30 (11 F, S and summer)

Crown
216 New Road
Brain Dark, MA [H]
Only outlet for MA, a brewery mix of SA and Dark ♣🍴Ⓢ

Swansea 13G7
Abertawe

11.30–3.30; 5.30–10.30

Adam & Eve
207 High Street
Brain Dark, SA [H]
Excellent, interesting pre-war city pub ♪♣🍴Ⓢ🚆

Bryn-y-Mor
Bryn-y-Mor Road
Ansells Bitter
Ind Coope Burton Ale [H]
Smart lounge pub, games in public bar 🍺♪♣↺◗🍴Ⓢ

Cockett
Waunarlwydd Road, Cockett (A4216)
Buckley Mild, Best Bitter [H]
Excellent, popular suburban inn ♣✿🔥↺🍴Ⓢ

Duke
Wind Street
Welsh Dark Mild, BB [H]
Victorian city pub, popular with dockers and businessmen ♣🍴Ⓢ

Robin Hood
Beach Street, Sandfields (Off B4290)
Buckley Gold [H]
Feared by the bad, loved by the good ♪♣↺◗Ⓢ

Singleton
1 Dillwyn Street ☎ 55987
Usher Best Bitter [H]
Comfortable pub close to the Grand Theatre 🍺♪[R]🍴Ⓢ

Star
Carmarthen Road, Fforestfach (A483)
Buckley Mild, Best Bitter [E]
Busy, friendly pub serving an industrial estate ♪♣🔥🍴Ⓢ

Upper Compass
Llangyfelach Road
Welsh Dark Mild [E]
Last honky-tonk local in town 🍺♣🍴

Vivian Arms
Sketty Cross, Sketty
Brain Dark, Bitter, SA [H]
Popular pub ♣↺🍴Ⓢ

Three Crosses 13G7
Y-Crwys

11.30–3.30; 5.30–10.30 (11 F, S)

Joiners
Joiners Road
Usher PA, Best Bitter [H]
Busy village pub
♪♣✿🔥↺◗🍴Ⓢ

West Cross 13G8
11.30–3.30; 5.30–10.30 (11 F, S)

Linden Tree
Fairwood Road
Draught Bass
Welsh Dark Mild [E]
Modern, spacious estate pub
♪♣✿🔥↺🍴Ⓢ

The 🔥 symbol denotes a pub with a real solid fuel fire

Gwent

Abergavenny 14C6

10.30–3 (10–4 Tue); 6–11
Britannia Inn
Frogmore Street
Whitbread Bitter Ⓗ
Well-run town-centre pub ♪♣Ⓢ

Hen & Chicken Hotel
Flannel Street ✆ 3613
Draught Bass Ⓗ
Small, friendly and
old-fashioned ♪♣ⓇⓈ

Station Hotel
Brecon Road (A40)
Davenports Bitter
Usher Best Bitter
Wem Bitter Ⓗ
Friendly local on road to
Sugarloaf Mountain ♪♣🏠🍴

Abertillery 14B7

11.30–4.30; 6.30–11
Commercial Hotel
Market Street ✆ 212310
Draught Bass
Welsh PA Ⓗ
Friendly locals' pub in town
centre ♪♣Ⓖ (Wed–Fri)🍴Ⓢ

Bassaleg 14B8

11–3; 6–11
Ruperra Arms
Caerphilly Road (A468)
✆ Newport 893374
Brain Bitter Ⓗ
Comfortable Whitbread house
🏠♣Ⓖ

Blaenavon 14B6

11.30–4; 6–11
Cambrian
Llanover Road
Brain Bitter, SA Ⓔ
Lively, friendly local in a
mining area ♪♣🍴Ⓢ

Caerleon 14C7

11–3; 5.30–11
Drovers
Goldcroft Common
Ansells Mild, Bitter Ⓗ
Popular pub on village
common ♯Ⓖ🍴Ⓢ♿

Caldicot 14D8

11–3; 6–11
Castle Inn
Church Road ✆ 420509
Whitbread Bitter Ⓗ
Pleasant pub at entrance to
Castle ♪♣♯🏠Ⓖ🍴🍴Ⓢ

Chepstow 14D7

11–3; 5.30–11
Coach & Horses
Welsh Street ✆ 2626
Brain SA
Nailsea Jacobs Best Bitter
Usher Best Bitter
Wadworth 6X Ⓗ
Lively free house ♪♣🔲Ⓖ🍴

White Lion
Bank Street
Draught Bass
Welsh PA Ⓗ
Oldest pub in town, dating
from 1630s ♪♣🍴

Crosskeys 14B7

11.30–4.30; 6.30–11
Eagle
High Street
Opens at 12 noon & 7 pm
Draught Bass
Welsh PA Ⓗ
Small, friendly local ♪♣🍴Ⓢ

Cwmbran 14C7

11–3; 6.30–11
Blinkin' Owl
Henlys Way, Coed Eva ✆ 4749
Brain Dark, Bitter, SA Ⓗ
Modern estate pub
♪♣♯🏠Ⓖ🍴🍴Ⓢ

Little Mill 14C7

11–3; 5.30–11
Halfway House
(A472) ✆ 252
Courage Best Bitter, Directors Ⓗ
Popular village local
♯♪♣♯Ⓖ🍴🍴Ⓢ

Llandegveth 14C7

11–3; 6.30–11
Farmers Arms
(Off A4042) OS 336957
✆ Tredunnock 244
Brain Dark, Bitter, SA Ⓗ
Comfortable country pub
♪♣♯Ⓖ🍴🍴Ⓢ

Llangybi 14C7

11–3; 6–11
White Hart
(B4596) ✆ Tredunnock 258
Marston Pedigree
Theakston Best Bitter Ⓗ
Historic pub with frequent
guest beers ♪♣♯🏠ⓇⒼ🍴🍴Ⓢ

Llantilio Crossenny 14C6

11.30–3; 6–11
Hostry Inn
(B4233) ✆ 278
Usher Best Bitter Ⓗ
Pleasant 15th-century pub
🏠♣♯Ⓖ🍴Ⓢ

Llanvapley 14C6

11–3; 6–11
Red Hart
(B4233) ✆ Llantilio 227
Morning opening: 11.30
(summer), 12 noon (winter)
Whitbread Bitter Ⓗ
Comfortable country pub
♪♣🏠Ⓖ🍴🍴Ⓢ

Llanvihangel Crucorney 14C6

11–3; 6–11

Skirrid Inn
(Off A465) ✆ 258
Felinfoel Double Dragon
Robinson Best Bitter
Wadworth 6X Ⓗ
Large roadside inn dating back
to 1110 🏠♣♯🏠Ⓖ🍴🍴Ⓢ

Llanwern 14C8

11–3; 6.30–11
Milton
(Off A455) ✆ 412432
Draught Bass Ⓔ
Popular local, real ale in bar
and snug only
🍴♪♣♯🏠ⓇⒼ🍴🍴Ⓢ

Lydart 14D6

11–3; 6–11
Gockett
(B4293) ✆ Trelleck 860486
Ansells Bitter
Theakston Best Bitter Ⓗ
Popular 17th-century inn
♪♣♯🏠Ⓖ🍴🍴Ⓢ♿

Magor 14C8

11–3; 5.30–11
Golden Lion
The Square ✆ Newport 880312
Courage Best Bitter,
Directors Ⓗ
Well-run pub facing village
square ♪♣ⓇⓈ🍴🍴Ⓢ

Marshfield 14B8

11–3; 5.30–11
Port o' Call
✆ Castleton 680204
Courage Best Bitter,
Directors Ⓗ
Large, comfortable pub with
several bars
♪♣♯🏠Ⓖ🍴🍴Ⓢ

Monmouth 14D6

10.30–3; 5.30–11
Beaufort Arms Hotel
Agincourt Square ✆ 2411
Draught Bass
Courage Best Bitter
Usher Best Bitter Ⓗ
Comfortable bar in large
central hotel
♪♣🔲♯🏠🔲ⓇⒼ🍴🍴Ⓢ

Punch House
Agincourt Square ✆ 3855
Evening opening: 6
Draught Bass
Wadworth 6X
Welsh BB Ⓗ
Large, comfortable pub
🏠ⓇⒼ🍴🍴Ⓢ

Queens Head Hotel
St. James Street ✆ 2767
Opens at 11 am & 6 pm
Marston Pedigree
Queens Head 1035, Piston
Bitter Ⓗ
Large, comfortable pub dating
from 1630, with own brewery
♪♣🔲🏠🔲ⓇⓈ🍴🍴Ⓢ

Newport 14C8

-3; 5.30–11

Conti's
40/41 Llanarth Street
℄ 55652/63684
Draught Bass
Welsh HB, BB Ⓗ
Busy town-centre pub in
pedestrian precinct Ⓖ Ⓢ

Crown Inn
Crown Street, Maindee
℄ 67002
Ansells Bitter Ⓗ
Busy local ♪♣Ⓖ🐕Ⓢ

Lamb
Bridge Street ℄ 66801
Courage Best Bitter,
Directors Ⓗ
Busy town pub ♪ⒼⒼⓈ≉

Lyceum Tavern
112 Malpas Road ℄ 858636
Courage Best Bitter,
Directors Ⓗ
Large, busy local
♣𝒫ⒺⒼ🐕Ⓢ

Murenger House
High Street ℄ 63977
Samuel Smith
Old Brewery Bitter Ⓗ
Large busy pub dating from
1530 ♪Ⓔ Ⓖ Ⓢ≉

Prince of Wales
2 Cardiff Road
Draught Bass
Welsh BB Ⓗ
Well-run town pub ♪♣🐕Ⓢ

Roundabout
Spytty Road ℄ 273613
Opens 11.30–2.30 Mon–Fri
Brain SA
Usher Best Bitter Ⓗ
Large and airy, but cosy
♣🍴ⒶⒼ🐕Ⓢ

Royal Albert Grill
164 Commercial Street
℄ 64261
Draught Bass
Welsh BB Ⓗ
Berni Inn; real ale in Victoria
bar only Ⓖ🐕Ⓢ

Pandy 14C5

1–3; 6–11

Pandy Hotel
A465) ℄ Crucorney 208
Brain Dark, Bitter, SA Ⓗ
Pleasant, simple country pub
♣𝒫ⒶⒺ Ⓖ🐕Ⓢ

Pant-yr-Esk 14B7

1.30–4.30; 6.30–11

Pant-yr-Esk Inn
℄S 202956
Evening opening: 7; closed
Mon–Sat lunchtimes
Crown SBB Ⓗ
Small, friendly local on top of
mountain ♪♣🐕Ⓢ

Penallt 14D6

11–3; 6–11

Boat
Lone Lane (off A466)
Butcombe Bitter Ⓗ
Hook Norton Best Bitter
Marston Pedigree
Robinson Best Bitter Ⓖ
Theakston Best Bitter Ⓗ
Small, friendly pub on River
Wye ♪♣𝒫ⒶⒾⓈ

Penhow 14C7

11–3; 5.30–11

Groes Wen
(A48, off M4)
Welsh PA Ⓗ
Pleasant main-road pub
♪♣ⒶⒾⓈ

Pontymister 14B7

11.30–4.30; 6.30–11

Masons Arms
Mill Terrace
Draught Bass
Welsh BB Ⓗ
Busy local, only real ale for
miles around ♪♣𝒫ⒶⒼ🐕Ⓢ

Porkskewett 14D8

11–3; 6–11

Portskewett Hotel
Main Road ℄ Caldicot 420300
Courage Directors Ⓗ
Large, pleasant pub ♪♣ⒶⒼ🐕

Rhiwderin 14B8

11–3; 6–11

Rhiwderin Inn
Caerphilly Road (A468)
℄ Newport 893234
Welsh BB Ⓗ
Comfortable pub with friendly
public bar ♪♣ⒶⒼ🐕

Rogerstone 14B8

11–3; 6–11

Tredegar Arms
(A467) ℄ Newport 893417
Morning opening: 11.30
Courage Best Bitter,
Directors Ⓗ
Comfortable pub on the main
road ♪𝒫Ⓖ (Mon–Fri) Ⓢ

St. Bride's Wentlooge 14C8

11–3; 6–11

Church House
(B4239) ℄ Castleton 680807
Brain Dark, Bitter, SA Ⓗ
Popular country pub
♪𝒫ⒶⒼ🐕 (Tue–Sat)🐕Ⓢ

Sebastopol 14C7

11.30–4; 6–11

Open Hearth
Wern Road (off A4051)
℄ Pontypool 3752
Closes 3 pm
Butcombe Bitter
Courage Best Bitter

Felinfoel Double Dragon
Hook Norton Best Bitter
Marston Pedigree Ⓗ
Friendly canalside pub, guest
beers ♪𝒫ⒶⒼ🐕Ⓢ

Shirenewton 14D7

11–3; 5.30–11

Tredegar Arms
The Square ℄ 274
Smiles Best Bitter
Usher PA
Wadworth 6X Ⓗ
Friendly village local
♪♣𝒫ⒶⒼ🐕Ⓢ

Tintern 14D7

11–3; 6–11

Cherry Tree
Devauden Road (off A466)
Evening opening: 7
Welsh PA Ⓗ
Bulmer Cider Ⓖ
Small pub in excellent walking
area ♣𝒫Ⓐ🐕

Moon & Sixpence
(A466) ℄ 288
Evening opening: 7
Marston Pedigree Ⓗ
14th-century pub with
tasteful furnishings
♪𝒫ⒶⒹⒼⓈ

Rose & Crown
(A466) ℄ 254
Courage Best Bitter Ⓗ
Picturesque pub by the River
Wye ♪♣ⒶⒹⒺⒼ🐕Ⓢ

Trelleck 14D7

11–3; 6–11

Lion
(B4293) ℄ 860322
Gwent Pub Brew
Whitbread Bitter Ⓗ
Pleasant village local; Gwent
is a house beer ♪♣𝒫ⒶⒹⒼ🐕Ⓢ

Usk 14C7

11–3; 7–11

Kings Head Hotel
18 Old Market Street
℄ 2963
Felinfoel Double Dragon
Marston Pedigree Ⓗ
Robinson Old Tom Ⓖ
Hotel with contrasting bars
♪♣𝒫ⒶⒹⒺⒼ🐕Ⓢ

Royal Hotel
New Market Street ℄ 2931
Evening opening: 7
Draught Bass
Felinfoel Double Dragon
Welsh PA, BB Ⓗ
Comfortable, well-run free
house Ⓐ♪♣Ⓖ🐕Ⓢ

Three Salmons
Bridge Street ℄ 2133
Gwent Best Bitter, Special
Bitter, Exhibition Ⓗ
Druids Ale Ⓖ
Large comfortable hotel
♪𝒫ⒶⒹⒺⒼ🐕Ⓢ

Aberffraw 20D5

11–3.30; 6–10.30 (11 F, S in summer)

Prince Llewellyn

(A4080)

Burtonwood Dark Mild, Bitter [H]

Quiet pub with several rooms

⌐♪♣🌿🚗🍺Ⓢ

Bangor 21F5

11–3; 5.30–10.30 (11 F, S in summer)

Bulkeley Arms

Caernarfon Road (A4087)

Marston Burton Bitter, Pedigree [H]

One-room working men's pub

♪♣🍺Ⓢ🚆

Union

Garth Road (off A5) ☎ 2462

Burtonwood Dark Mild, Bitter [H]

Small sitting rooms, interesting bric-a-brac

♣🌿🚗🛏🍺Ⓢ

Barmouth 21F8

10.30–3; 6–10.30 (11 F, S in summer)

Tal-y-Don

St. Anne's Square, High Street (A496) ☎ 280508

Burtonwood Bitter [H]

Pleasant hotel with covered outdoor drinking area

♪♣🌿🛏☾🍴🍺Ⓢ🚆

Beaumaris 21F4

11–3.30; 6–10.30 (11 F, S in summer)

Olde Bull's Head

Castle Street ☎ 810329

Draught Bass [H]

Historic inn dating from 1472

🏠🚗🛏🍴

Bethesda 21F5

11–3; 5.30–10.30 (11 F, S in summer)

Victoria Hotel

High Street (A5)

☎ 600481

Evening opening: 6

Greenall Whitley Mild, Bitter [E]

Friendly, welcoming village pub

♣▦🛏🍺Ⓢ

Betws-y-Coed 21G6

11–3; 5.30–10.30 (11 F, S and summer)

Pont-y-Pair

(A5) ☎ 407

Opens at 12 noon weekdays in winter

Younger Scotch Bitter, IPA, No. 3 [H]

Cheery hotel bars, good snacks

♪♣▦🌿🚗🛏☾🍴Ⓢ

Blaenau Ffestiniog 21G6

10.30–3; 6–10.30 (11 F, S in summer)

King's Head

Glan-y-Pwll (off B4414)

Ansells Mild

Ind Coope Bitter, Burton Ale [H]

Basic pub beside the Festiniog railway ♪♣▦🍺Ⓢ

Bodedern 20D4

11–3.30; 6–10.30 (11 F, S in summer)

Crown Hotel

(B5109)

☎ Valley 740734

Burtonwood Dark Mild, Bitter [H]

Well-run, friendly, popular pub 🏠⌐♪♣▦🌿🚗🛏[R]☾🍴🍺Ⓢ

Caernarfon 21E5

11–3; 5.30–10.30 (11 F, S in summer)

Black Boy

Northgate Street ☎ 3604

Draught Bass

Gwynedd Anglesey Bitter [H]

Well-appointed hotel with lively taproom 🏠♪▦🛏☾🍴🍺♿

Crown

17/19 High Street

Ind Coope Burton Ale

Tetley Walker Bitter [H]

Very busy at night

🏠♪♣▦Ⓢ

Try also: Palace Vaults (Marston)

Capel Curig 21G5

11–3; 6–10.30 (11 F, S and summer)

Tyn-y-Coed Hotel

(A5) ☎ 255

Gwynedd Mild, Anglesey Bitter [H]

Comfortable hotel with stagecoach outside

🏠♪♣▦🌿🚗🛏☾🍴🍺Ⓢ

Corris 21G9

11–3; 6–10.30 (11 F, S in summer)

Slaters Arms

Lower Corris (off A487)

Banks Mild, Bitter [E]

Friendly local in former slating village ♣🍺Ⓢ

Criccieth 21E7

11–3; 5.30–10.30 (11 F, S in summer)

Prince of Wales

High Street (A497)

Evening opening: 6; closed Sundays

Whitbread Castle Eden Ale [H]

Popular with tourists and locals 🏠♪♣🍺Ⓢ🚆

Deganwy 21G4

11–3; 6–10.30 (11 F, S and summer)

Maggie Murphy's

Tywyn Hill (off B5115)

Ind Coope Bitter

Tetley Walker Bitter [H]

Popular pub with atmosphere

♪♣🌿🚗Ⓢ

Dolgellau 21G8

10.30–3 (4F); 6–10.30 (11 F, S in summer)

Stag

Bridge Street

Burtonwood Dark Mild, Bitter [H]

A warm welcome 🏠♪♣▦🌿🍺Ⓢ

Dulas 20E4

11–3.30; 6–10.30 (11 F, S in summer)

Pilot Boat

(A5025)

Winter evening opening: 7

Robinson Best Mild, Best Bitter [E]

Busy old roadside pub with fine views 🏠♪♣🌿🚗🍺Ⓢ

Fairbourne 21F8

10.30–3; 6–10.30 (11 F, S in summer)

Fairbourne Hotel

(Off A493) ☎ 250203

Draught Bass

McEwan 70/-

Younger No. 3 [H]

Large and comfortable hotel

🏠♪♣▦🌿🚗🛏🍴🍺⛺🚆

Gaerwen 21E5

11–3.30; 6–10.30 (11 F, S in summer)

Dinam Arms

(½ mile off A5) OS 485709

Burtonwood Dark Mild, Bitter [H]

Small, comfortable local beside goods station

🏠♪♣🚗🍺

Harlech 21F7

10.30–3; 6–10.30 (11 F, S in summer)

Castle Hotel

Castle Square ☎ 780529

Gwynedd Anglesey Bitter [H]

Comfortable lounge, large public bar ♪♣▦🌿🚗

🛏 (summer) 🍺Ⓢ

Holyhead 20D4

11–3.30; 6–10.30 (11 F, S in summer)

Boston

London Road

Ansells Mild

Ind Coope Bitter [H]

Busy, open-plan local ♪♣🍺🚆

George

Market Street ☎ 2005

Burtonwood Dark Mild, Bitter [H]

Town pub with central bar serving several rooms

♪♣▦🛏🍺Ⓢ

Llanbedrog 20D7

11–3; 5.30–10.30 (11 F, S in summer)

Ship

Bryn-y-Gro (B4413) ☎ 270

Closed Sundays

Burtonwood Dark Mild, Bitter [H]

Pleasant old pub

🏠⌐♪♣🌿🚗☾🍴🍺Ⓢ♿

Llanbedr-y-Cennin 21G5

11.30–3; 6–10.30 (11 F, S and summer)

Olde Bull Inn

(Off B5106)

✆ Dolgarrog 508
Winter evening opening: 6.30
Lees GB Mild, Bitter Ⓗ
16th-century inn, excellent
food
🅰 ♪ ♣ 🎲 ✎ 🅰 Ⓛ Ⓡ Ⓖ ⤴ ⑨ ♿ ⚓

Llandudno 21G4

11–3; 5.30–10.30 (11 in summer)
King's Head
Old Road (off Church Walks)
✆ 77993
Evening opening: 7
Ansells Mild
Ind Coope Bitter, Burton Ale
Tetley Walker Bitter Ⓗ
Imaginatively refurbished pub
next to Great Orme tramway
station; oldest pub in town
🅰 ♪ 🎲 ✎ 🅰 Ⓖ ⤴ ⑨

Snowdon Hotel
Tudno Street ✆ 75515
Draught Bass Ⓗ
Superb town pub
♣ ✎ 🄴 Ⓖ ⑨ ♿ ⚓

Washington Hotel
Clarence Road
Ansells Mild
Ind Coope Bitter
Tetley Walker Bitter Ⓗ
Comfortable and interesting,
Lloyd & Trouncer style
🅰 ♪ ♣ ✎ 🅰 ⑨

Try also: Albert Hotel
(Greenall Whitley); Hydro
Hotel (Whitbread); Links
Hotel (Lees)

Llanfaethlu 20D4

11–3.30; 6–10.30 (11 F, S in summer)
Black Lion
(A5025)
Burtonwood Dark Mild,
Bitter Ⓗ
Interesting, friendly old pub
🅰 ♪ ♣ 🎲 ✎ 🅰 ⑨

Llanfrothen 21F7

11–3; 6–10.30 (11 F, S in summer)
Bron Danw Arms
(A4085)
Mitchells & Butlers Mild, Brew
XI Ⓗ
Modern lounge and
slate-floored bar, open-plan
🅰 ♣ 🎲 ✎ 🅰 ⑨

Llangefni 20E4

11–3.30; 6–10.30 (11 F, S in summer)
Railway Inn
High Street
Lees GB Mild, Bitter Ⓗ
Cosy, well-kept pub with
several small rooms
♪ ♣ 🎲 ✎

Llanrwst 21G5

11–3; 6–10.30 (11 F, S and summer)
Pen-y-Bryn
Ancaster Avenue (A470)
Open till 4.30 pm market and
fair days

Bass Cask Bitter
Mitchells & Butlers Mild Ⓗ
Lively pub, popular with
locals ♪ 🎲 ✎ ⑨ ⚓ ≹

Try also: Queens (Wilson)

Llanwnda 20E6

10.30–3; 6–10.30 (11 F, S in summer)
Mount Pleasant
(A487)
Morning opening: 11.30
Draught Bass
Mitchells & Butlers Mild Ⓗ
Renovated, comfortable
lounge with oak beams
🅰 ♪ ♣ 🎲 ✎ 🅰 Ⓡ Ⓖ ⤴ ⑨

Maentwrog 21F7

11–3; 6–10.30 (11 F, S in summer)
Grapes Hotel
✆ 208
Draught Bass
Mitchells & Butlers Mild
(summer) Ⓗ
Traditional bar,
cathedralesque lounge
🅰 ♪ ♣ 🎲 ✎ 🅰 🄴 Ⓖ ⤴ ⑨

Menai Bridge 21F5

11–3.30; 6–10.30 (11 F, S in summer)
Anglesey Arms
Hotel
(A5) ✆ 712305
Lees Bitter Ⓔ
Pleasant lounge bar
♪ ♣ 🎲 ✎ 🅰 🄴 Ⓖ (not Mon) ⤴ ⑨

Nefyn 20D7

11–3; 5.30–10.30 (11 F, S in summer)
Sportsman
Stryd Fawr (High Street)
(B4417)
Closed Sundays
Ind Coope Bitter
Tetley Walker Bitter Ⓗ
Friendly pub with small
lounge 🅰 ♪ ♣ ⑨

Newborough 20E5

11–3.30; 6–10.30 (11 F, S in summer)
White Lion
(A4080)
Lunchtime opening: 12 noon
(Mon–Fri)
Marston Mercian Mild,
Burton Bitter Ⓗ
Unpretentious village pub
🅰 ♪ ♣ ✎ ♿

Penmaenmawr 21G4

11–3; 5.30–10.30 (11 F, S and summer)
Alexandra
High Street (A55)
Draught Bass
Mitchells & Butlers Mild Ⓗ
Basic, unspoilt local
♪ ♣ ♿

Bron Eyri
Bangor Road (A55)
Marston Burton Bitter,
Pedigree, Merrie Monk Ⓗ
Pleasant, tiny pub ♪ ♣ ✎ ♿ ⑨

Penrhyndeudraeth 21F7

10.30–3; 6–10.30 (11 F, S in summer)
Royal Oak
High Street ✆ 770501
Burtonwood Dark Mild,
Bitter Ⓗ
Good welcome, good beer
🅰 ♪ ♣ 🎲 🄴 ⑨

Penrhynside 21G4

11–3; 5.30–10.30 (11 in summer)
Cross Keys
Pendre Road
Ansells Mild
Banks Bitter
Ind Coope Bitter
Tetley Walker Bitter Ⓗ
Fantastic local with great
barmaids
♪ ♣ 🎲 ✎ Ⓖ ⑨

Port Dinorwic 21E5

Y Felinheli

11–3; 5.30–10.30 (11 F, S in summer)
Gardd Fôn
Beach Road (off A487)
Burtonwood Bitter Ⓗ
Small pub by the Menai Straits
♪ ♣ ⑨

Pwllheli 20D7

11–3; 5.30–10.30 (11 F, S in summer)
Penlan Fawr
Penlan Street
Closed Sundays
Ansells Mild
Ind Coope Bitter Ⓗ
Popular old pub used by
young people
🅰 ♪ ♣ 🎲 ✎ Ⓡ Ⓖ ⑨ ≹

Talysarn 21E6

11–3; 5.30–10.30 (11 F, S in summer)
Nantlle Vale
(B4418)
✆ Penygroes 310
Closed Sundays
Marston Mercian Mild,
Pedigree Ⓗ
Hotel bar used by locals
♪ 🎲 ✎ 🅰 🄴 Ⓡ Ⓖ ⤴ ⑨

Tan-y-Bwlch 21F7

11–3; 6–10.30 (11 F, S in summer)
Oakeley Arms
(A487) ✆ Maentwrog 277
Bass Cask Bitter
Draught Bass
McEwan 70/- Ⓗ
Modernised 18th-century
coaching inn with lovely
views
♪ 🎲 ✎ 🅰 🄴 Ⓡ Ⓖ ⤴ ⑨ ⚓

Trawsfynydd 21G7

10.30–3; 6–10.30 (11 F, S in summer)
White Lion
(Off A487) ✆ 277
Burtonwood Dark Mild,
Bitter Ⓗ
Unspoilt village pub
🅰 ♪ ♣ 🎲 Ⓖ ⤴ ⑨ ⚓

Powys

Abercrave 13H6

11.30–4; 6–10.30 (11 F, S and summer)
Copper Beech
(Off A4067)
Courage Best Bitter,
Directors Ⓗ
Country pub close to
Dan-yr-Ogof caves ♪♣Ⓖ🐾⑨⑧

Abermule 14B1

10.45–2.45; 5.30–10.30 (11 F, S and summer)
Abermule Hotel
(B4386) ☎ 273
Banks Mild
Wem Best Bitter Ⓗ
Attractive locals' pub
♣♪♣🅿🅰Ⓡ🅳Ⓖ🐾⑨⑧🅰

Arddleen 22A8

11.30–3; 5.30–10.30 (11 F, S and summer)
Horseshoe
Guilsfield (A483) ☎ Guilsfield
318
Border Mild, Bitter, Old
Master Ⓗ
Cosy old pub with adventure
playground
♣♪♣🅴🅿🅰🅳Ⓡ🅲Ⓖ🐾⑨⑧

Brecon 14A5

11–3; 5.30–11
Open all day Tuesdays and Fridays
Gremlin
The Watton (A40) ☎ 3829
Evening opening: 6; open all
day Bank holiday Saturdays
and Mondays only
Draught Bass
Robinson Best Bitter Ⓗ
Old, comfortable family pub
♪♣🅰🅳Ⓡ🅲Ⓖ🐾⑨⑧

Sarah Siddons
47 High Street ☎ 2009
Whitbread Bitter, Flowers
Original Bitter Ⓗ
Busy pub with one
lounge-type bar ♪♪Ⓖ⑧

Builth Wells 14A4

11–3; 6–11
**Llanelwedd Arms
Hotel**
(A483) ☎ 553282
Gwent Special (occasional) Ⓖ
Whitbread Bitter Ⓗ
Pleasant riverside hotel
♪♪♣🅰🅳Ⓖ🐾⑨⑧

Castle Caereinion 22A8

12–3; 6–10.30 (11 F, S and summer)
Red Lion
(B4385) ☎ Welshpool 233
Draught Bass
Welsh PA, BB
Bulmer Cider Ⓗ
Cosy, traditional local
♣♪♣🅿🅰Ⓡ🅲🐾⑨⑧

Church Stoke 14B1

11–2.45; 6–10.30 (11 F, S and summer)
Horse & Jockey
(A490) ☎ 324

Draught Bass
Mitchells & Butlers Mild Ⓗ
Large, comfortable old pub
♣♪♣🅿🅰🅳Ⓖ🐾⑨⑧

Crickhowell 14B6

10.30–3 (4 Thu); 6–11
Beaufort Arms
Beaufort Street (A40)
☎ 810402
Open all day Bank holidays
Davenports Bitter Ⓗ
Hotel with a local pub
atmosphere ♪♣🅰🅳Ⓡ🅲⑧

Bridge End
(A4077) ☎ 810338
Morning opening: 11.45
Draught Bass Ⓗ
Brain Dark Ⓔ SA
Robinson Best Bitter
Bulmer Cider Ⓗ
16th-century pub overlooking
the river 🐾🅰🅳⑧🅰

Cwmtaff 13J6

11–3; 5.30–11
Nant Ddu Lodge
(A470) ☎ Merthyr Tydfil
79111
Draught Bass Ⓗ
Country house hotel with
restaurant
♣🅴🐾🅰🅳Ⓡ🅲🐾⑨

Defynnog 13J5

11–3; 6–11
Lion
(A4067)
Open all day Wednesdays
Whitbread Bitter
Bulmer Cider Ⓗ
Old, comfortable roadside inn
♪♣🐾🅰⑧

Guilsfield 22A8

11–3; 6–10.30 (11 F, S and summer)
Oak Inn
(Off B4392)
Wem Pale Ale, Mild, Best
Bitter Ⓔ
Large oak-beamed public
house ♪♣🅲Ⓖ🐾⑨

Hay-on-Wye 14B4

11–3; 6–11
Blue Boar Hotel
Castle Street ☎ 820884
Open until 5.30 pm Mon, Thu
Whitbread Bitter
Bulmer Cider Ⓗ
Friendly central pub
♣Ⓖ🐾

Llanbrynmair 21H9

11.30–2.30; 5.30–10.30 (11 F, S and summer)
**Wynnstay Arms
Hotel**
(A470) ☎ 431
Banks Mild
Draught Bass
Gwynedd Anglesey Bitter Ⓗ
Friendly village local
♣♪♣🅴🐾🅰🅳Ⓡ🅲🐾⑨⑧🅰🅰

Llandinam 14A1

11–2.30; 5.30–10.30 (11 F, S and summer)
Lion Hotel
(A470) ☎ Caersws 233
Draught Bass Ⓗ
Unspoilt old country local,
home cooking ♣♣🅴🐾🅰🅳
Ⓡ🅲Ⓖ🐾(must book) ⑧⑧🅰🅰

Llandrindod
Wells 14A3

11–3, 6–11
Llanerch
Waterloo Road ☎ 2086
Draught Bass
Brain Bitter
Robinson Best Bitter Ⓗ
Pleasant 16th-century
coaching inn
♣♪♣🅴🐾🅿🅰🅳Ⓡ🅲Ⓖ🐾⑨⑧≈

Llandyssil 14B1

11–3; 6–10.30 (11 F, S and summer)
Upper House
(Off B4386)
Weekday lunchtime
opening: 12–2
Woods Special Bitter Ⓗ
Busy village local
♣♪♣🐾🅰⑧

Llanfair Caereinion 21J9

11–3; 5.30–10.30 (11 F, S and summer)
Wynstay Arms
Watergate Street
Ansells Mild, Bitter Ⓗ
Imposing corner pub with
restaurant ♣♪♣🅴🐾🅰Ⓡ🅲🐾⑨⑧

Llanfyllin 21J8

11–3; 5.30–10.30 (11 F, S and summer)
Cain Valley Hotel
High Street (A490) ☎ 366
Draught Bass
Burtonwood Bitter
Ind Coope Bitter
Bulmer Cider Ⓗ
Superb 17th-century
coaching inn
♣♪♣🅴🐾🅿🅰🅳Ⓡ🅲🐾⑨⑧🅰

Llangenny 14B6

10.30–3; 6–11
Dragons Head
(Off A40)
☎ Crickhowell 810350
Draught Bass
Butcombe Bitter
Welsh BB Ⓗ
Weston Cider Ⓖ
Pleasant, comfortable
village pub ♣🐾🅰🅳⑧

Llangorse 14B5

11–3; 6–11
Red Lion
(B4560) ☎ 238
Felinfoel Double Dragon
Whitbread Bitter Ⓗ
Superb inn in a picturesque
village ♪♣🐾🅰🅳🅲Ⓖ🐾⑨⑧🅰

Llangurig 13J2

30–2.30; 5.30–10.30 (11 F, S and summer)
Blue Bell
(A44) ☎ 254
Banks Mild, Bitter Ⓔ
16th-century fishing inn
♪✦♨🅿🅐🅑Ⓖ➋❶Ⓢ⑧

Llanhamlach 14A5

1–3; 6–11
Old Ford
(A40) ☎ Llanfrynach 220
Felinfoel Double Dragon
Robinson Best Bitter
Wem Pale Ale, Mild,
Best Bitter Ⓗ
Bulmer Cider Ⓔ
Well-appointed free house
with occasional guest beers
♨🅿🅐🅑Ⓖ➋❶Ⓢ

Llanidloes 13J2

30–2.30; 5.30–10.30 (11 F, S and summer)
Angel Hotel
High Street ☎ 2381
Open all day Saturday
Burtonwood Best Bitter Ⓗ
Lounge has old pennies
mounted into top of bar
✦🅐🅑🅘Ⓖ➋❶Ⓢ⑧⑤

Mount
China Street ☎ 2247
Open all day Saturdays
Welsh PA, Dark Mild Ⓗ
Boasts a fascinating old cast
iron stove ♨✦♨🅿🅐🅑🅘⑧

Queens Head Hotel
40 Long Bridge Street ☎ 2383
Open all day Saturday
Ansells Mild
Burtonwood Light Mild
Tetley Bitter
Weston Cider Ⓗ
Friendly hotel ♪✦♨🅿🅑Ⓖ➋⑧⑤

Llanwrtyd Wells 13H4

1–3; 6–11
Neuadd Arms Hotel
(A483) ☎ 326
Welsh BB Ⓗ
Central hotel with two large
bars ♪♨🅐🅑🅘🅑Ⓖ➋❶Ⓢ

Machynlleth 21G9

10.30–2.30; 5.30–10.30 (11 F, S and summer)
Dyfi Forester
Doll Street ☎ 2004
Banks Mild, Bitter Ⓔ
Draught Bass
Border Bitter Ⓗ
Enterprising free house
♪✦♨🅿🅐🅑Ⓖ➋❶Ⓢ❄

Red Lion
Maengwyn Street
Open till 4 pm Wednesdays
Banks Mild, Bitter Ⓗ
Friendly local opposite Post
Office ✦♨🅿🅐♨❄

Manafon 21J9

1–3; 6–10.30 (11 F, S and summer)

Beehive
(B4390) ☎ Tregynon 244
Wem Mild
Woods Special Bitter Ⓗ
Delightful country pub with
occasional guest beers
♨✦♨🅿🅐🅑Ⓖ➋⑧

Meifod 21J8

11–3; 6.30–10.30 (11 F, S and summer)
Kings Head
(A495) ☎ 256
Wem Pale Ale, Best Bitter Ⓔ
Bustling village local
♪✦🅐🅑Ⓖ➋❶Ⓢ⑧⑤

Montgomery 22A9

11–3; 6.30–10.30 (11 F, S and summer)
Bricklayers Arms
Chirbury Road (B4386) ☎ 442
Burtonwood Bitter Ⓗ
Friendly local ♨♪✦❶

Crown
Bishops Castle Street
(B4385) ☎ 533
Wem Pale Ale, Best Bitter Ⓔ
Locals' pub: old and friendly
♪✦Ⓖ➋❶Ⓢ⑧

New Radnor 14B3

11–3; 6–11
Radnor Arms
High Street (A44) ☎ 232
Draught Bass
Tetley Bitter
Weston Cider Ⓗ
Well-appointed country pub
♨♪✦♨🅐🅑🅑Ⓖ➋❶Ⓢ⑧Å

Newtown 14A1

10.30–2.30; 5.30–10.30 (11 F, S and summer)
Open all day Tuesdays
Cambrian Vaults
Shortbridge Street
Wem Mild, Best Bitter Ⓗ
Small town-centre pub with
pool room ♪✦⑧❄

Pheasant
Market Street ☎ 25966
Burtonwood Bitter Ⓗ
Old pub backing onto new
shopping precinct
♨♪✦♨🅿🅑Ⓖ⑧⑤❄

Sportsman
Severn Street (off A483)
Tetley Bitter Ⓗ
An excellent small
town-centre pub
✦⑧❄

Pant Mawr 13H2

10.30–2.30; 5.30–10.30 (11 F, S and summer)
Glansevern Arms
(A44) ☎ Llangurig 240
Evening opening: 6.30
Draught Bass
Welsh Dark Mild Ⓗ
A comfortable, isolated hotel
♨♨🅐🅑Ⓖ➋(must book) ❶⑧

Pontdolgoch 14A1

10.45–2.45; 6–10.30 (11 F, S and summer)

Mytton Arms
(A470) ☎ Caersws 253
Banks Mild, Bitter
Draught Bass Ⓗ
A taste of the past
♨♪✦♨🅿🅐🅑Ⓖ➋❶Ⓢ⑤

Rhayader 13J3

11–3; 5.30–11
Cornhill
West Street ☎ 787
Open all day Weds and
alternate Fridays
Burtonwood Bitter
Whitbread Bitter Ⓗ
Comfortable 17th century inn
♨♪✦♨♨🅑Ⓖ➋❶⑧

Try also: Horsehoe (Bass, Red
Kite)

Talgarth 14B5

11–3; 6–11
Radnor Arms
(B4560)
Open all day Fridays and
alternate Fridays
Whitbread Bitter Ⓗ
Bulmer Cider Ⓖ
Basic village local ✦♨🅐❶

Talybont-on-Usk
14A5

11–3; 6–11
Star
(B4558) ☎ 635
Open all day Thu and Bank
Holiday Sat and Mon
Felinfoel Double Dragon
Gibbs Mew Bishops Tipple
Marston Pedigree
Smiles Best Bitter,
Exhibition
Welsh Fussells Best Bitter Ⓗ
Friendly village pub,
other beers always available
♨♪✦♨Ⓖ➋❶⑧

Trecastle 13J5

11–3; 6–11
Castle Hotel
(A40) ☎ Sennybridge 354
Lunchtime opening: 12 noon
Usher Best Bitter Ⓗ
Pleasant old hotel with high
class food ♨🅐🅑Ⓖ➋❶⑧

Try also: Three Horseshoes
(Everard)

Welshpool 22A8

11–3; 5.30–10.30 (11 F, S and summer)
Green Dragon
Mount Street ☎ 2531
Open all day Monday
Burtonwood Light Mild,
Bitter Ⓗ
Recently revamped family-run
pub ♪✦♨🅑Ⓖ⑧⑧❄

Talbot
High Street ☎ 3711
Banks Mild, Bitter Ⓗ
Friendly 15th century town
pub ♪✦♨♨Ⓖ➋❶⑧❄

Heavy Heaven

Scottish drinkers have a legendary faith in the superiority of their beers over the English ones. Despite this, the Scots made virtually no resistance to the takeovers and rationalisations of the 50s and 60s, which saw the disappearance of 24 breweries and countless beers.

The Campaign for Real Ale, though formed in 1971, had little impact in Scotland until a couple of years later. CAMRA took root north of the border during the early stages of the 1973/4 Scottish football season. Two people determined to do something about the apparently lost cause of real ale, John Whitecross and Alan Watson (now revered in CAMRA circles as a legend in his own lunchtime), feverishly signed up supporters of Glasgow's other lost cause, Partick Thistle F.C., as new CAMRA members.

An official Glasgow CAMRA branch was formed in August 1974 – Scotland's first. It was led by the footballing fans along with Iain Dobson, now CAMRA's company secretary, and Tony Dean, now a director of the Leith Brewing Company. Mr Dean's Edinburgh connections led to the formation of a branch there in 1975.

The early campaigners opened on a very poor wicket but active campaigning on the ground together with close liaison with the brewers soon put the efforts of the campaign in Scotland into the public eye. The publication of Scottish beer guides and several successful Scottish traditional beer festivals have involved the general public with the aims of CAMRA, and handsome dividends have been paid to the drinker as a result. Today, both Edinburgh and Glasgow boast around 180 real ale outlets and there is keen competition to be first to record 200.

Branches now exist in most areas of the country where there is a sizeable population.

The legacy for the drinker at large is that Scotland has moved a long way from 1974, when it was rightly regarded as one of the major 'beer deserts' of the U.K. into being one of the better areas for ale. The range of real ales and pubs now enjoyed in both Edinburgh and Glasgow is thought by many to be bettered only by London and Manchester. While there remains much still to be campaigned for in Scotland, the dark days of 1974 surely feel to be further than ten years away.

SCOTTISH

BREWING ARCHIVE

Scottish Brewers

SCOTLAND boasts a brewing history second to none, but the scale of 'public' brewing remained small in Scotland, until the 19th-century when, as the demand for beer grew with industrialisation, many more brewers for public sale were established. As local brews appeared, suited to local tastes and preferences and brewed in local traditions, differences between Scottish and English beers developed, especially in those rural areas that relied on very local barleys for their malt.

Scottish beer was traditionally both mashed at a higher temperature and fermented longer at a lower temperature than in England. This suited the dark, heavy-gravity 'Scotch Ales' that became popular in much of England and the Low Countries. A by-product of these 'Scotch' ales was table beer, or small beer – sometimes known as 'two penny' ale from its price per quart in the 18th-century. This beer, very popular on the domestic market, was basically a second-mash brew. Porter was another popular brew. A porter brewery was established in Glasgow in 1775 and the drink remained widely sold for most of the 19th-century.

Edinburgh, with its hard, mineral rich water was always the core of Scottish brewing and Edinburgh Ale – like Alloa Ale – became a well known and respected name both abroad and throughout the U.K. Edinburgh water was found to be particularly suitable for India Pale Ale brewing, and William Youngers led a group of Scottish brewers who were quick to seize the chances of the overseas markets.

By the turn of the twentieth century, the Scottish industry was concentrated in Edinburgh, Alloa and Glasgow, and many of the smaller rural companies had disappeared. The older Scots beers – strong ales, porter and table beers – had decreased in popularity and most brewers offered pale ales of a generally lighter colour and lower gravity, though mild remained dark.

The process of takeover and rationalisation quickened in the inter-war period, but the post second world war years saw the greatest concentration and loss of the small regional independents.

The largest company, Scottish Brewers Ltd., formed in 1931 by bringing Wm. Youngers together with Wm. McEwan, were heavily involved in take over and amalgamation toward the end of the 1950s. Amalgamation with Newcastle Breweries Ltd., made the powerful Scottish & Newcastle Breweries – the only Scots-based member of Britain's Big Six.

Northern Brewers, who eventually led into Bass Charrington and absorbed J. & R. Tennent of Glasgow were even more involved in take over. On one dark day in 1963, they acquired the brewing firms of Fowler of Prestonpans, George Younger of Alloa and Aitkens of Falkirk. All were closed.

One closure that irks many to this very day was that of the famous and much revered Edinburgh brewer Archd. Campbell, Hope & King. Campbells was a name synonymous with style and great beer and their cruel and unforgivable closure, by Whitbread in 1971, has left many

Scots with a more than passing resentment for the London based giant.

Since then, only one major closure has taken place – Thos. Usher of the Park Brewery in Edinburgh – sold by Vaux to Ind Coope Scotland in 1980 and immediately closed.

The re-awakening of interest in traditional beer in Scotland has helped to preserve the two surviving long standing independents, Maclay of Alloa and Belhaven from East Lothian, but these are all that remain to remind us of a once rich collection of local traditional beers suited to local tastes.

Small is beautiful

Belhaven has been established at Dunbar since 1719, and still produces 60/-, 70/- and 80/- ales and an occasional 90/-strong ale.

Maclays have brewed in Alloa since 1830. The company was built upon a reputation for Oatmalt Stout, now sadly discontinued, but a 60/-, 70/- and 80/- range of cask beers is made along with keg and bottled beers.

New independents have opened up in all corners of Scotland. The Broughton Brew-

ing Co. the Leith Brewing Co., Strathalbyn in Clydebank, Devanha from Aberdeenshire, and the Alice Brewery in Inverness have all sprung up since 1980 and new breweries are planned at Dundee, Cumbernauld and Melrose. Scotland's first pub brewery since the 1870s, the Rose Street Brewery in Edinburgh, opened in July 1983, while the Traquair House Brewery, mainly using 18th-century equipment continues to brew excellent strong ales from Scotland's oldest inhabited house. 'The Laird', Peter Maxwell-Stuart, re-commenced brewing in 1965 – and looks like going on strong for some time to come.

A Scottish Brewing Archive was set up at Heriot-Watt University in 1981, to record and preserve information on Scotland's brewing heritage. Enquiries and donations of archive material are welcomed.

Fount of All Knowledge

FOR well over a century in Scotland, air pressure and the tall pillar fount has been the principal means of dispensing cask conditioned beer. Air pressure involves an electric compressor or water engine forcing air into the cask to push out the beer.

The beer is served via a Tall Fount – pronounced Font but derivative of fountain. This application of pressure may provoke some feelings of doubt in southern drinkers minds, but Air Pressure does not 'gas' the beer at all. Indeed pubs using the system are noted for their softer tasting, very smooth beer with a tight creamy head.

A crude form of air pressure dispense was in use in the early decades of the 19th-century, involving the use of a well-type pump to apply compressed air to the casks. The benefits of the system, ease, cheapness and an improved preserving condition in the beer, were enough for the Scottish licensed trade to persevere with it, though air pressure only boomed in the 1870s, after several Water Engines, which converted ordinary mains water into air pressure, came onto the market.

As cask-conditioned beer continues to grow in popularity (each Scottish Brewery now brews at least one), a system combining tall founts with air pressure or electric pump is, in many Scottish eyes, the best way to serve cask-conditioned beers.

The 'return trays' which returned over-spills of beer into the next pint poured have become extremely rare, but the tall fount with its undoubted visual appeal and association with real ale, is certain of a long life.

Happy Days

BREWERS seem to have another term for everything. Water is known as liquor, hop sacks are pockets and so on. Scotland has her own range of beer terminology.

The 'Shilling' is the traditional method by which beers have been categorised in Scotland. The system started in the 1880s, when Beer Duty replaced sugar and malt taxes, and it referred to the *invoice* price of a barrel only, not the real price.

The net price to the publican depended on duty payable and discounts allowed. Thus a barrel invoiced from the brewery to the publican at 80 shillings, may have had 10/- duty added and 40/- discounts; giving him a net price of 50/-. The stronger ales, which carried far higher duty tended to be those quoted with the high 'shilling' price. The system was complicated by the fact that it referred to barrels (36 gallons) and to hogsheads (54 gallons). A 120/- ale could really have been a hogshead of 80/- type beer.

The use of 'shillings' was largely superceded by the terms light, heavy and export after the Second World War, but the coming of CAMRA and the 'real ale boom' brought about a resurrection of the system. Today a 'light' or 60/- ale is usually a dark low gravity beer around 1030–33° O.G. A 70/- 'heavy' (the term really only in use since the 1940s) is a light coloured beer, akin to ordinary bitter, with an O.G. around 1034–39°. An 'export' or IPA (India Pale Ale) is a stronger, usually light coloured beer with an O.G. from 1040–50° – today's 80/- ale. 'Special' is a keg version of heavy, as seen in Younger's Tartan.

It has also been traditional in Scotland to drink 'wee heavies'. These are usually bottled, very potent ales available in 'nips' of 1/3 pint imperial measure (6 fl. oz.).

Wee Heavies are an ingredient necessary for another institution, the "Happy Day". This drink is a pint, made up by around 2/3 of a pint of draught light beer with a bottle of wee heavy beer added. Scottish pubs teem with other local terms and phrases. These are best discovered by some ground work – in the bar.

Opening hours in Scotland are 11 a.m.–2.30 p.m. & 5 p.m.–11 p.m., but many pubs have extensions and are open all day during the week. Pubs with Sunday licenses usually open from 12.30 p.m.–2.30 p.m. & 6.30 p.m.–10.30 p.m.

Borders

Burnmouth 35J5

Flemington
(A1) ☎ Ayton 277
Ind Coope Burton Ale Ⓗ
Historic, modernised
first/last pub in
Scotland ♪♣🅱♙🅰🅁Ⓖ🍴Ⓢ⅄

Cockburnspath 35H5

Cockburnspath Hotel
(A1) ☎ 217
Drybrough Pentland Ⓐ
Plain three-roomed bar with
nets, starfish and crabs on
ceiling ♪♣🅱🅰🅔Ⓖ🍷🍴⅄

Coldstream 35H6

Besom Inn
High Street (A697) ☎ 2391
McEwan 70/-
Younger No. 3 Ⓐ
Hospitable pub; strangers
treated like locals ♣♙🅔🍷Ⓢ

Commercial
30–32 Main Street (A697)
Belhaven 70/-, 80/- Ⓐ
Noisy and friendly border
pub ♙♪♣🅱🅰🅁Ⓖ🍷🍴Ⓢ♣⅄

Greenlaw 35H6

Cross Keys
(A697) ☎ 247
Alloa Arrols 70/- Ⓗ
Plain village bar ♙♣🅔Ⓖ🍷🍴Ⓢ

Hawick 35G7

High Level
Green Terrace
McEwan 80/- Ⓗ
Bonny Borders backstreet
boozer 🍷

Mansfield Bar
Mansfield Road
McEwan 80/- Ⓗ
Well-worn wood-walled
waterhole 🍷Ⓢ

Queens Head
High Street
McEwan 80/- Ⓐ
Heady, hearty Hawick howff;
tall fonts 🍷Ⓢ

Oxton 35G5

Tower Hotel
(Off A68) ☎ 235
Open Sundays
Alloa Arrols 70/-
Ind Coope Burton Ale Ⓗ
Friendly country hotel with
interesting stained glass
windows ♙♣♣🅔🅁Ⓖ🍷🍴Ⓢ♣

Peebles 35G6

Park Hotel
Innerleithen Road ☎ 20451
Open Sundays
Lorimer & Clark 70/- Ⓗ
Well-appointed hotel with
putting green ♪♙🅱🅰🅔Ⓖ🍷♣⅄

St Boswells 35H6

Buccleuch Arms
(A68) ☎ 22243
Open Sundays
Broughton Greenmantle Ale Ⓗ
Large, wood-panelled cocktail
bar ♙♣🅱🅰🅁Ⓖ🍷Ⓢ

Selkirk 35G6

Town Arms
(Off A7)
Open all day Sundays
Belhaven 80/- Ⓗ
Mirrored, traditional
horseshoe bar 🍷

Stow 35G6

Manorhead Hotel
(A7) ☎ 201
Open Sundays
Darley Dark
Lorimer & Clark 70/-, 80/- Ⓗ
Well-run hotel on main
Edinburgh road 🅰🅔Ⓖ🍷Ⓢ

Town Yetholm 35H6

Plough Hotel
Main Street ☎ 215
Open Sundays
Alloa Arrols 70/- Ⓗ
Cosy inn full of character and
characters ♙♣🅔Ⓖ Ⓢ

West Linton 35F5

Linton Hotel
(Off A702) ☎ 60228
Broughton Greenmantle Ale
Tennent Heriot 80/- Ⓗ
Popular village hotel 🅔ⒼⓈ

Yarrow 35G6

Gordon Arms Hotel
(A708) ☎ 222
Open Sundays
Broughton Greenmantle Ale Ⓗ
Front-room bar with pictures
of sheep; good taste has
passed it by ♙🅱🅰🅔🍷⅄

Central

Aberfoyle 34D4

Altskeith Hotel
3 miles west of Aberfoyle on
Kinlochard Road
☎ Kinlochard 266
Open Sundays
Broughton Greenmantle Ale
McEwan 80/- Ⓗ
Attractive country hotel on
the banks of Loch Ard; fishing
♙♪♣🅱♙🅰🅔🅁Ⓖ🍷🍴Ⓢ⅄

Alloa 35E4

Thistle Bar
1 Junction Place

Maclay 80/- Ⓐ
Brewery tap, with busy lounge
and McGlashan fonts ♪♣🍷Ⓢ

Bridge of Allan 35E4

Queens Hotel
Henderson Street
Open Sundays
Broughton Greenmantle Ale
Ind Coope Burton Ale
Younger IPA Ⓐ
Spacious lounge bar with tall
fonts; guest beers ♙♪🅁Ⓖ🍷🍴

Westerton Arms
Henderson Street
Alloa Arrols 70/-
Ind Coope Burton Ale Ⓗ
Large, well-appointed lounge
bar ♙♪🅁Ⓖ🍷

Callander 34E4

Bridgend House Hotel
Bridgend ☎ 30130
Open Sundays
Broughton Greenmantle Ale
Strathalbyn Ale Ⓗ
Cosy pub on banks of River
Teith, beautiful scenery
♙♪♣🅱♙🅰🅔🅁Ⓖ🍷🍴Ⓢ♣⅄

Clackmannan 35F4

County Hotel
1 Main Street ☎ Alloa 722912
Open Sundays
Maclay 80/- Ⓔ
Excellent village local; historic
clack just outside ♪♣🅔🅁🍷

Falkirk 35E5

Burns Bar
Vicar Street
Open Sundays
Maclay 60/-, 70/-, 80/- Ⓐ
Strathalbyn Ale Ⓗ
Town-centre bar, popular
music spot 🍷Ⓖ🍴Ⓢ♣

Woodside Inn
High Station Road
Belhaven 60/-, 70/-, 80/- Ⓔ
Fine, wood-panelled bar with
old mirrors ♣🅁🍷Ⓢ≉

Grangemouth 35F5

Oxgang House Hotel
Oxgang Road ☎ 73131
Open Sundays
Belhaven 80/-
Broughton Greenmantle Ale
Ind Coope Burton Ale Ⓗ
Real ale in attractive
Ballantyne bar
🍴♣♙🅰🅔🅁Ⓖ🍷Ⓢ

Stirling 35E4

Barnton Bar & Bistro
Barnton Street ☎ 61698
Open Sundays
Maclay 80/- Ⓐ
Stylish cafe bar with keen
owners ♪🅱Ⓖ🍷Ⓢ≉

Birds & Bees
Easter Cornton Road,
Causewayhead ☎ 3663
Open Sundays
Younger IPA Ⓐ
Unique rustic pub with farm-
yard furnishings, fine French
restaurant ♪🍴🍺🕓🏧🛏🅿️

Rob Roy Bar
2 Wallace Street
Open Sundays
McEwan 80/-
Younger No. 3 Ⓐ
Hospitable town-centre pub in
historical setting ♪🍴

Settle Inn
91 St Mary's Wynd
Belhaven 70/-, 80/- Ⓗ
Stirling's oldest coaching inn,
tastefully renovated 🍴♪🏧🔔🍴

Dumfries & Galloway

Annan   35F8

Blue Bell
High Street (A75)
Open Sundays
Theakston Dark Mild, Best
Bitter, XB, Old Peculier Ⓗ
Lively ex-state brewery pub
🍴🏧🔔Ⓢ🅰️≈

Canonbie   35G8

Riverside Inn
(A7) ☎ 295
Theakston Best Bitter Ⓗ
Fine hotel specialising in food
🅿️🅰️Ⓑ🔔🕓🍴🅢

Dumfries   35F8

Douglas Arms
Friars Vennel
Open Sundays
McEwan 80/- Ⓐ
Small, friendly pub in a busy
shopping street 🏧🍴

Ship Inn
97 St Michael's Street
Open Sundays
McEwan 70/-, 80/-
Younger IPA, No. 3 Ⓐ
Friendly local opposite Robert
Burns' mausoleum 🏧🍴

Tam o' Shanter
117 Queensberry Street
Broughton Greenmantle Ale Ⓗ
McEwan 80/-
Younger No. 3 Ⓐ
Homely pub close to town
centre 🏧🔔🍴

Eastriggs   35G8

Graham Arms
(A75) West end of village
Open Sundays
McEwan 70/-
Younger IPA Ⓐ
Friendly, comfortable two-
roomed inn 🅰️♪🏧🏨🅿️🍺🕓🍴🅢🅰️

Gretna   35G8

Solway Lodge Hotel
Annan Road (off A74) ☎ 266
Theakston Best Bitter Ⓗ
Comfortable lounge bar with
restaurant facilities
🍴♪🏨🅿️🍺🏧🔔🕓🍴🅢🅰️

Lockerbie   35F8

Kings Arms Hotel
High Street ☎ 2410
Open Sundays
McEwan 80/- Ⓐ
Old coaching inn of great
character 🍴♪🏧🔔🔔🕓🍴🅰️≈

Moffat   35F7

Star Hotel
High Street ☎ 20156
Open Sundays
Marston Pedigree Ⓗ
Friendly hotel near war
memorial 🍴♪🏧🔔🔔🕓🍴🅰️

New Abbey   35F8

Criffel Inn
(B710) ☎ 244
Younger No. 3 Ⓗ
Owner is a traction engine
enthusiast; real ale in public
bar 🏧🏨🅿️🏧🔔🕓🍴🅢

Fife

Aberdour   35F4

Aberdour Hotel
High Street (A92) ☎ 860325
Open Sundays
Belhaven 80/- Ⓗ
Fine old coaching inn
🅰️♪🏧🅿️🏧🔔🔔🕓🍴🅢≈

Cupar   35G3

Findlay's
43 Bonnygate (A91) ☎ 52830
Belhaven 80/-
Broughton Greenmantle Ale
Maclay 70/- Ⓗ
Interesting, quality pub with
excellent bar food ♪🕓🔔≈

Dunfermline   35F4

Old Inn
Kirkgate, opposite Abbey
Open Sundays
Younger IPA, No. 3 Ⓔ
Excellent pub with fine gantry,
oldest pub in city ♪🏧🕓🍴🔔≈

Inverkeithing   35F4

Volunteer Arms
61 High Street ☎ 412834
Open Sundays
Maclay 70/- Ⓐ
Friendly locals' bar in village
square ♪🏧🔔🕓≈

Kettlebridge   35G4

Kettlebridge Hotel
☎ Ladybank 30232

Maclay 60/-, 70/-, 80/- Ⓗ
Friendly, well-run, traditional
village inn 🏧🏨🅿️🏧🔔🔔🕓🍴🅢

Kirkcaldy   35G4

Novar Bar
17 Nicol Street ☎ 260545
Open Sundays
McEwan 80/- Ⓔ
Friendly, modern and spacious
wood-panelled bar
♪🏧🔔🕓 (Thu–Sat)🍴🔔≈

Largo Ward   35G4

Staghead Hotel
(A915) OS 465073
☎ Peat Inn 205
Ind Coope Burton Ale Ⓗ
Picturesque Victorian hotel
🅰️🍴♪🏧🏨🅿️🏧🔔🔔🕓🍴🅢🅢

Limekilns   35F4

Bruce Arms
Main Street (off A985)
Open Sundays
McEwan 80/- Ⓔ
Small, curved bar with fine
view of River Forth
♪🏧🅿️🏧🔔🕓🍴

Lochgelly   35F4

Silver Tassie
(Central Bar)
49 Main Street (A910)
Open Sundays
Belhaven 60/- Ⓐ
Fine pub in the heart of Fife
mining area ♪🏧🏨🔔🅢🅢

Lower Largo   35G4

Railway Inn
Station Wynd (off A915)
Open Sundays
McEwan 80/- Ⓗ
Traditional one-room pub
beneath old viaduct 🏧♪🏧

St Andrews   35G3

Kates Bar
Market Street ☎ 72110
Open Sundays
McEwan 80/-
Younger No. 3 Ⓗ
Popular with students;
restaurant attached
♪🏧🏨🔔🕓🍴🔔

Russell Hotel
The Scores ☎ 73447
Open Sundays
Broughton Greenmantle Ale
Theakston Old Peculier Ⓗ
Comfortable hotel lounge
♪🏨🕓🔔

Grampian

City of Aberdeen   37J8

Bobbin Mill
500 King Street (A92)
Open Sundays

Drybrough Pentland [A]
Renovated mill with three busy bars ↱♪♣🚗[R]🥃Ⓢ

Carriages
101 Crown Street ☎ 55440
Open Sundays
Whitbread Castle Eden Ale [H]
Comfortable basement lounge, good value meals ♪▣🚗■◔❥Ⓢ

Ferryhill House Hotel
Bon Accord Street ☎ 50867
Open Sundays
Devanha XXX
Maclay 80/-
McEwan 80/- [A]
Theakston Best Bitter [H]
Younger No. 3, IPA [A]
Popular, pricey hotel near city centre ▣⚘🚗■[R]◔

Grill
213 Union Street
McEwan 80/- [A]
Well-kept Edwardian one-bar pub 🥃

Olde Frigate
57 Netherkirkgate
Lorimer & Clark 80/- [H]
Excellent beer; outnumbered by malt whiskies ♪♣[R]🥃Ⓢ

Pittodrie Bar
339 King Street ☎ 638836
Younger IPA [H]
Island bar with fine collection of mirrors ↱♪♣🥃Ⓢ

Prince of Wales
7 St. Nicholas Lane ☎ 640597
Open Sundays
Devanha XXX
Lorimer & Clark 80/-
Tennent Heriot 80/-
Theakston Best Bitter, Old Peculiar [H]
Younger No. 3 [A]
Best beer in town – excellent service ↱♪♣◔🥃Ⓢ

Yardarm
40 Regent Quay
Open Sundays
Alloa Arrols 70/-
Ind Coope Burton Ale
Maclay 80/- [H]
Popular dockside pub with friendly staff ♪Ⓢ

Aboyne 37H9

Boat Inn
Charleston Road ☎ 2137
Open Sundays
Drybrough Eighty [A]
Friendly inn by the Dee
🏛♪♣▣🚗■◔❥🥃Ⓢ⛺

Balmedie 37J8

Coach & Horses
(A92) ☎ 3249
Open Sundays
Younger IPA [H]
Former country cottage, north of village ↱♪♣⚘🚗◔❥🥃Ⓢ⛺

Banchory 37H9

Scott Skinner Bar
North Deeside Road (A93)
Open Sundays
Devanha XXX [H]
Small, cosy and intimate
🏛↱♪♣▣⚘🚗[R]◔❥Ⓢ♿⛺

Bucksburn 37J8

Craighaar Hotel
Waterton Road (off A947)
☎ Aberdeen 712275
Open Sundays
Maclay 80/-
Theakston Best Bitter [H]
Up-market lounge bar
♪▣⚘🚗■[R]◔❥♿

Elgin 37F7

Braelossie Hotel
2 Sheriffmill Road (off A96)
Younger IPA [H]
Fine hotel with sauna, west of town ♪▣⚘🚗[R]◔❥⛺

Crown Bar
Batchen Street (off A96)
Younger IPA [H]
City centre pub, handy for thirsty shoppers ♪♣[R]◔🥃Ⓢ⛺

Elrick 37H8

Broadstraik
(A944)
Open Sundays
McEwan 80/- [E]
Maclay 80/- [H]
Real ale in public bar
🏛♣▣🚗[R]◔🥃

Forres 37F7

Red Lion Hotel
2 Tolbooth Street (off A96)
Open Sundays
McEwan 70/- [H]
Younger No. 3 [E]
Two traditional, unspoilt bars
♪♣[R]🥃Ⓢ

Fraserburgh 37J7

Crown Bar
45 Broad St./125 Shore St.
Open Sundays
Younger IPA [H]
Traditional long Scottish bar with friendly service ♣🥃Ⓢ

Lossiemouth 37G7

Clifton Bar
Clifton Road
Alice Ale
Alloa Arrols 70/-
Ind Coope Burton Ale [H]
Younger IPA, No. 3 [A]
Bulmer Cider [H]
Busy seafront pub, keen landlord ♪♣🚗🥃Ⓢ⛺

Huntly House Hotel
Stotfield Road (B9040) ☎ 2085
Maclay 80/- [H]
Tudor-style family hotel, with magnificent view of Sutherland hills
↱♪▣⚘🚗■[R]◔❥Ⓢ⛺

Newburgh 37J8

Udny Arms
(A975) ☎ 444
Open Sundays
Alice Ale
Younger IPA [H]
Country hotel by the Ythan
↱♪♣▣⚘🚗■[R]◔❥🥃Ⓢ⛺

Peterhead 37J7

Grange Inn
West Road ☎ 3472
Open Sundays
McEwan 80/- [E]
Excellent modern pub
♪♣🚗[R]🥃Ⓢ♿⛺

Stonehaven 35J1

Marine Hotel
9/10 Shore Head (off A92)
☎ 62155
Open all day Sundays
Devanha XXX
McEwan 80/-
Tennent Heriot 80/- [H]
Small, friendly hotel overlooking picturesque harbour
🏛↱♣⚘🚗■[R]◔❥🥃Ⓢ♿⛺

Highlands

Aviemore 37E8

Winking Owl
Grampian Road ☎ 810646
Alloa Arrols 70/-
Ind Coope Burton Ale [H]
Modern, winter-sports orientated pub with fine restaurant
♪⚘🚗◔❥Ⓢ⛺🚉

Fort William 34C2

Nevis Bank Hotel
Belford Road (off A82) ☎ 2595
Younger IPA [A]
Convenient for thirsty Ben Nevis climbers 🚗■❥🥃Ⓢ

Glencoe 34C2

Clachaig Inn
(Off A82) OS 127567
☎ Ballachulish 252
McEwan 80/- [H]
Popular climbers' pub on site of the massacre
♣🚗■❥🥃Ⓢ⛺

Inverness 36E7

Gellions Hotel
Bridge Street
Alice Ale
Alloa Arrols 70/-
Ind Coope Burton Ale
Tennent Heriot 80/- [H]
Younger IPA, No 3 [E]
Busy pub with bottled beers from all over the world
♪♣◔🥃Ⓢ

Scotland

Kingsmills Hotel
amfield Road (off B9006)
37166
lice Ale Ⓗ
ounger IPA Ⓔ & Ⓗ No. 3 Ⓔ
mart hotel near golf club
🆓🍴🍺🏠🍴Ⓡ🕓🔵🅰🔥

Phoenix Bar
08 Academy Street
ounger XXPS Ⓐ
raditional public bar 🆓Ⓡ🍴🔁

Thurso
37F3

Station
rinces Street
ounger IPA, No. 3 Ⓐ
raditional farmers' bar; most
ortherly outlet in the UK
naybe the world!) 🍴🍴🔥🔁

Lothian

Balerno
35F5

Grey Horse
Main Street (off A70)
Belhaven 60/-, 80/- Ⓗ
Friendly, low-ceilinged village
nn; a wee gem 🎵🆓Ⓡ🔥

Marchbanks Hotel
Marchbanks Road (off A70)
☎ 031-449 3970
Open Sundays
Lorimer & Clark 70/-, 80/- Ⓗ
Superb hotel, a mile from
Balerno 🍴🎵🆓🍺🏠🕓🔵🔥🔵

Bathgate
35F5

Glenmavis Tavern
51 Gideon Street
Belhaven 60/-, 80/- Ⓔ
Refurbished 18th-century
building, comfortable lounge
🍴🎵🆓Ⓡ🔥🔵🔵

Dirleton
35G4

Castle Inn
(Off A198) ☎ 221
Open Sundays
McEwan 80/- Ⓐ
Inn with fine mirrors and tall
fonts 🍴🆓🏠🔵🔥🔵

East Linton
35H5

Railway Hotel
5 Bridge Street (off A1)
Open all day Sundays
Ind Coope Burton Ale Ⓗ
Popular pub in small
agricultural village 🍴🍴🔥

City of Edinburgh
35G5

Athletic Arms
(Gravediggers)
Angle Park Terrace
McEwan 80/- Ⓐ
Mecca 🆓🔥🔵

Bennet's Bar
1a Maxwell Street,
Morningside

Belhaven 60/-, 70/-, 80/- Ⓐ
Sonsie, smokey, stand-up shop
with tall fonts 🆓🔥🔵

Cafe Royal
(Circle Bar)
West Register Street
McEwan 70/-
Younger No. 3, IPA Ⓐ
Fine Victorian pub with island
bar and pictorial tiling 🔁

Clarks
Dundas Street
Younger IPA Ⓐ
Classic Edinburgh bar with tall
fonts 🔥🔵

Coppers
19 Cockburn Street
Alloa Arrols 70/-
Ind Coope Burton Ale
Lorimer & Clark 70/-, 80/- Ⓗ
Well-run one-room pub in city
centre 🎵🔵🔁

Cramond Inn
Cramond Glebe Road,
Cramond ☎ 031-336 2035
Lorimer & Clark 80/- Ⓐ
Lounge bar in beautiful village
overlooking Firth of Forth
🎵🔵🕓🔥🔵

Fiddlers Arms
9/11 Grassmarket
Open Sundays
McEwan 70/-, 80/- Ⓐ
Mellow enclave of conviviality
with mature ceiling and
magnificent fonts 🍴🆓🔥🔵

Green Mantle
133 Nicholson Street
Open Sundays
Alloa Arrols 70/-
Ind Coope Burton Ale
Lorimer & Clark 70/-, 80/- Ⓗ
Popular southside bar with
colourful management 🎵🕓

Guildford Arms
West Register Street
Open Sundays
Broughton Greenmantle Ale
Lorimer & Clark 70/-, 80/- Ⓐ
Younger IPA, No. 3 Ⓔ
City-centre bar with some fine
Victorian features 🔁

Jinglin' Geordie Bar
Fleshmarket Close, EH1
☎ 031-225 2803
Maclay 60/-, 70/-, 80/- Ⓐ
Smart, relaxed bar frequented
by journalists; tall fonts 🔵🔁

Kay & Company
Jamaica Street
Belhaven 70/-, 80/-
Lorimer & Clark 70/-, 80/- Ⓗ
Younger No. 3, IPA Ⓐ
Smart re-creation of a
Victorian pub 🍴Ⓡ🔵

Leslie's Bar
Ratcliffe Terrace
Lorimer & Clark 70/-, 80/-
Younger No 3 Ⓐ

Outstanding pub with fine
woodwork and ceiling 🍴🔥🔵

Liberton Inn
Kirkbrae, Liberton
McEwan 70/-, 80/- Ⓐ
Cask beers in two out of three
bars of fascinating wood-
panelled inn 🆓🕓🔥🔥🔵

H. P. Mather's Bar
Queensferry Street, West End
McEwan 80/- Ⓐ
Inspiring city-centre bar
with superb gantry 🔥

Mill
Slateford Road
Lorimer & Clark 80/- Ⓐ
Modern pub close to the
brewery, traditionally run 🔥🔵

Navaar House Hotel
12 Mayfield Gardens,
Newington ☎ 031-667 2828
Open Sundays
Broughton Greenmantle Ale Ⓗ
Lorimer & Clark 80/- Ⓐ
Caledonian Strong Ale Ⓗ
Maclay 80/- Ⓐ
Younger No. 3 Ⓗ
Smart suburban hotel with
friendly lounge 🎵🍴🏠Ⓡ🔵

Olde Inn
Main Street, Davidson's Mains
(off A90)
Drybrough Pentland, Eighty Ⓐ
Tasteful local in village suburb
🎵🆓🕓🔵🔥🔵

Piershill Tavern
(Porter's)
Portobello Road (off A1)
Open Sundays
McEwan 80/-
Younger No. 3 Ⓐ
Robust, timeless boozer; an
inspiration to its often lyrical
clientele 🍴🆓Ⓡ🔵

Raeburn Bar
Raeburn Place, Stockbridge
Open Sundays
Alloa Arrols 70/-
Ind Coope Burton Ale
Lorimer & Clark 80/- Ⓗ
Friendly corner local; oasis in
a trendy district 🆓🔥🔵

Rutherford's Bar
3 Drummond Street
Broughton Greenmantle Ale
Younger IPA Ⓐ
Friendly local with genial staff
and customers, tall fonts 🆓🔥🔵

Sheep's Heid Inn
Duddingston
Tennent Heriot 80/- Ⓗ
Bar with skittle alley, near
Arthur's Seat 🎵🆓🏠🔵

Sinclairs
1 Montrose Terrace
Open Sundays
Drybrough Pentland, Eighty Ⓗ
Worthwhile, cosy local in
small baronial building 🎵🆓🔵

Southsider
West Richmond Street
Maclay 60/-, 70/-, 80/- [A]
Busy, popular bar with tall fonts [R]🍷Ⓢ

Starbank Arms
Starbank Road, Newhaven
Open Sundays
Belhaven 70/-, 80/-
Leith Heavy
Taylor Best Bitter, Landlord, Ram Tam, Porter [H]
Well-run, up-market bar, fine view over Firth of Forth
[R]◷🍽Ⓢ

Station Bar
320 Gorgie Road
Drybrough Pentland, Eighty [A]
Canny local in downtown Gorgie [R]🍷Ⓢ

Walk Inn
Leith Walk
Open Sundays
Leith Heavy
Lorimer & Clark 80/-
McEwan 80/-
Tennent Heriot 80/- [A]
Superbly-run, with tall fonts and good mix of clientele 🔥🍷Ⓢ

Windsor Buffet
Leith Walk
Closes 10.30 pm
Younger IPA [A]
Nice windows and gantry, seating in alcoves 🍷

Kirkliston 35F5

Newliston Arms
Main Street ☎ 031-333 3214
Open Sundays
Lorimer & Clark 70/-, 80/- [A]
Flourishing semi-rural local with panelled ceiling 🛏♣▣🍷Ⓢ

Linlithgow 35F5

Champany Inn
Champany Corner (A803, off M9 exit 3) ☎ Philipstoun 4532
Belhaven 70/-, 80/-
Leith Heavy [H]
Converted farmhouse with Victorian antique furniture
🛏♪🎯🚗◷🍽Ⓢ🚉

Four Mary's
67 High Street ☎ 842171
Belhaven 80/- [H]
Tasteful wine bar/bistro
🔥♪[R]◷🍽Ⓢ🚉

Midcalder 35F5

Black Bull
Market Street (A71) ☎ 882170
McEwan 80/- [E]
Low-ceilinged, mellow bar
▣[R]◷🍽🍷♿

Musselburgh 35G5

Hole in the Wall
170 New Street
McEwan 80/- [A]
Friendly back street pub near the shore Ⓢ

Penicuik 35G5

Carnethy Inn
John Street (A703) ☎ 76838
Drybrough Pentland [A]
Interesting public bar ♪♣🚗[R]🍷

Wester Howgate 35G5

Old Howgate Inn
(Off A703) ☎ Penicuik 74244
Belhaven 60/-
McEwan 80/- [H]
Restored old coaching inn
🛏🚗◷🍽Ⓢ

Strathclyde

Alloway 34D7

Bellisle House Hotel (Tam 'o Shanter Bar)
(A719) OS 332195 ☎ 42331
Open Sundays
Tennent Heriot 80/- [H]
Golfer's bar attached to hotel in extensive park ♪🚗▣◷🍽🍷

Ayr 34D6

Matha Dickie's
High Street (A79)
McEwan 80/- [A]
Basic but friendly, lively town-centre pub 🍷🚉

Balloch 34D5

Balloch Hotel
Balloch Road (off A811)
☎ Alexandria 52579
Open Sundays
Alloa Arrols 70/- [H]
1820s building, on River Leven source
🔥♪♣🚗▣◷🍽🍷Ⓢ♿🚉

Bearsden 34D5

Burnbrae Hotel
Milngavie Road
☎ 041-942 5951
Open Sundays
McEwan 70/-, 80/-
Younger No. 3 [A]
Large, modern Reo Stakis Hotel ♪♣🚗▣◷🍽🍷⛺

Beith 34D5

Eglinton Inn
48 Eglinton Street (B7049) OS 348539 ☎ 2736
McEwan 80/- [H]
Busy pub catering for all ages, enthusiastic staff ♪🎯🚗[R]🍷Ⓢ

Biggar 35F6

Elphinstone Arms Hotel
145 Main Street (A702)
☎ 20044
Open Sunday evenings
McEwan 80/-
Younger No. 3 [A]
Popular old hotel in pleasant market town
🛏🔥♣⊞▣[R]◷🍽🍷Ⓢ

Bothwell 34E5

Cricklewood Hotel
27 Hamilton Road ☎ 853172
Broughton Greenmantle Ale
Lorimer & Clark 80/- [H]
Converted house with genteel atmosphere 🛏♪🚗▣◷🍽Ⓢ

Brodick, Isle of Arran 34C6

Ormidale Hotel
(Off A841) ☎ 2226
McEwan 70/- [A]
Victorian sandstone hotel with unusual conservatory
🔥♪♣🎯🚗▣[R]◷🍽🍷Ⓢ♿⛺

Caldercruix 35E5

Railway Tavern (Taylors)
67 Main Street (B825, off A89)
Open Sundays
Belhaven 60/-, 80/- [A]
The coalmines have gone but the 60/- remains
🔥 (occasional)♣🚗[R]🍷♿

Cambuslang 34E5

Sefton Bar
40 Main Street (off A724)
Belhaven 60/- [A]
Only pub in Glasgow area that never abandoned beer
♣🍷

Castlecary 35E5

Castlecary House
(Off A80) ☎ Banknock 840233
Open Sundays
Belhaven 80/-
Broughton Greenmantle Ale
Maclay 70/-
Tennent Heriot 80/-
Theakston Best Bitter [H]
Popular village hotel with new, public bar
♪♣🚗▣◷🍽🍷Ⓢ♿

Clachan-Seil 34B

Tigh-an-Truish Hotel
Isle of Seil
McEwan 80/- [H]
Just a short walk over the Atlantic ♪♣🚗Ⓢ

Coatbridge 34E

Carson's
4/6 Whifflet Street ☎ 22867
Broughton Greenmantle Ale
Tennent Heriot 80/- [A]
Well-designed modern interior 🛏♪🚗◷🍽🍷Ⓢ♿

Dumbarton 34D5

Stags Head
116 Glasgow Road
Open Sundays
Drybrough Pentland [H]
Open-plan pub, skilfully designed ♪♣🚗☾♟Ⓢ♿🚉

Gatehead 34D6

Cochrane Inn
43/47 Main Road (A759)
Open Sundays
Maclay 60/- [A]
Busy village local with a strong following for darts and dominoes ♪♣🚗♟Ⓢ

City of Glasgow 34E5

Allison Arms
720/722 Pollokshaws Road
Belhaven 80/-
Maclay 60/- [A]
Superb local, threatened with imminent closure for over a quarter of a century ♣♟Ⓢ

Arlington
130 Woodlands Road
Maclay 70/- [A]
Probably the oddest pub in Glasgow

Athena Tavern
780 Pollokshaws Road, 41
Open Sundays
Belhaven 80/-
Broughton Greenmantle Ale
Lorimer & Clark 80/- [H]
Dix Cider [G]
Small wickerwork bistro, family licence ♪♣Ⓢ🚉

Blythswood
Hope Street
Belhaven 70/-, 80/-
Lorimer & Clark 70/-, 80/-
Strathalbyn Ale
Taylor Best Bitter, Landlord, Ram Tam [H]
Quantity with quality, at quality prices Ⓢ🚉

Bon Accord
153 North Street (off M8)
Belhaven 80/-
Ind Coope Burton Ale [H]
Maclay 60/-, 70/-, 80/- [A]
Marston Pedigree, Merrie Monk
Whitbread Castle Eden Ale [H]
Up to 14 real ales; most Glaswegians cut their teeth here ♪[R]☾Ⓢ

Cameron's
129 St George's Road (off M8)
Belhaven 60/-, 80/- [A]
Friendly West End local, traditional island bar ♟Ⓢ

Horseshoe Bar
17/19 Drury Street
Tennent Heriot 80/- [H]
Magnificent example of Victorian 'gin palace' decor ☾♟Ⓢ🚉

Mitre
12 Brunswick Street
Belhaven 80/-
Ind Coope Burton Ale [H]
Small is beautiful, and the Mitre proves it ♪♣[R]☾◗♟Ⓢ♿

Outside Inn
1256 Argyle Street
Open Sundays
Belhaven 60/-, 70/-, 80/-,
Caledonian Strong Ale
Broughton Greenmantle Ale [H]
Well-weathered trendy bar ♪♣[R]☾◗♟

Victoria
157 Bridgegate, 1
Maclay 60/- [H] **70/-, 80/-** [A]
Strathalbyn Ale
Theakston Best Bitter [H]
Fine, friendly free house with folk music 🔥[R]♟Ⓢ

Wee Mann's
167 Stockwell Street
Open Sundays
Drybrough Pentland [H]
Friendly family-run pub on Clydeside 🔥♪♣[R]☾◗♟Ⓢ♿

Gourock 34D5

Spinnaker Hotel
131 Albert Road (A78)
☎ 33107
Open Sundays
Belhaven 80/- [A]
Seafront hotel with renowned food 🔥♣⊞⚘■[R]☾◗♿

Hamilton 34E5

Ranche
18 Strathaven Road (A723)
Belhaven 60/-
Younger No. 3 [A]
Floor gets steeper with every pint consumed 🏠♣♟

Helensburgh 34D5

Royal Bar
8 West Clyde Street
Open Sundays
Younger No. 3 [A]
Modern, friendly pub with naval connections ♪♟♿

Houston 34D5

Fox & Hounds
Main Street
Open Sundays
Drybrough Pentland, Eighty [A]
Tastefully decorated three-bar pub, beware of mynah bird 🔥♪♣⊞🚗[R]♟Ⓢ♿

Irvine 34D6

Turf Hotel
34 Eglinton Street (off A737)
Open Sundays
Broughton Greenmantle Ale [H]
Traditional Scottish pub with service to match 🏠♣☾♟Ⓢ

Johnstone 34D5

Coanes (Masonic Arms)
26 High Street
Open Sundays
Broughton Greenmantle Ale [H]
McEwan 80/-
Younger No. 3 [A]
Friendly pub with enthusiastic staff ♪♣♟Ⓢ♿🚉

Kilmarnock 34D6

Hillhead Tavern
Hill Street
Maclay 60/- [A]
Suburban local ♣🚗♟Ⓢ🚉

Kilmun 34C5

Coylet Hotel
Loch Eck (A815)
OS 144885 ☎ 322
McEwan 80/- [A]
Country hotel in idyllic setting ⚘■[R]☾◗♟♿⛺

Kilwinning 34D6

Alton Arms
Byres Road (A738) ☎ 53160
Open Sundays
McEwan 80/- [A]
Friendly local ♪☾♿🚉

Kirkoswald 34D7

Kirkton Jean's Hotel
(A77) OS 238075 ☎ 220
Open Sundays
Younger No. 3 [A]
Interesting country hotel with Burns connections ♣⊞🚗■[R]☾◗♟

Lanark 35E6

Wallace Cave
11/13 Bloomgate
Tennent 80/- [H]
Architecturally interesting, with golf and fishing clubs ♣♟

Largs 34C5

Clachan
Bath Street (B7025)
Open Sundays
Broughton Greenmantle Ale
McEwan 80/- [H]
Younger No. 3 [A]
Cheery sidestreet pub with vast whisky selection 🔥♪♣☾Ⓢ🚉

Loans 34D6

Dallam Tower Hotel
Old Loans Road (off A78)
OS 349321 ☎ Troon 312511
Open Sundays
Broughton Greenmantle Ale
Lorimer & Clark 70/-, 80/-
Traquair House Bear Ale [H]
Hillside hotel with extensive Clyde views; guest beers 🏠♪⊞⚘🚗■[R]☾◗Ⓢ♿

Oban 34B3

Lorn Hotel
Stevenson Street (off A85)
✆ 62094
Open Sundays
McEwan 80/- Ⓗ
Attractive old building with
lots of tradition
ⓘ♪♣☐Ⓖↄ≈

Paisley 34D5

Argyll Bar
16 Old Sneddon Street
Open Sundays
McEwan 80/-
Younger No. 3 Ⓗ
Fine collection of historic
photos of Paisley
Ⓨ◉♿≈

Stags Head
11 Renfrew Road
Open Sundays
Drybrough Pentland, Eighty Ⓐ
Comfortable lounge, quiet
atmosphere
♪♣Ⓡ◉≈

Wee Howff
53 High Street
Open Sundays
Alloa Arrols 70/-
Ind Coope Burton Ale Ⓗ
Handy for shoppers;
enthusiastic landlord
♪♣◉♿

Saltcoats 34D6

Windy Ha'
31 Bradshaw Street (off
A738)
Open Sundays
McEwan 80/- Ⓗ
Typically Scottish island bar in
pub with a tower ⓘ♣◉≈

Torrance 34E5

Wheatsheaf
(B822)
Open Sundays
McEwan 80/- Ⓗ
Maclay 70/- Ⓐ
Attractive village inn; original
stained glass windows now
set into a panel inside
♿♣♠◉

Troon 34D6

Harbour Bar
169 Templehill (B749)
Maclay 60/-, 80/-
Strathalbyn Ale Ⓐ
Excellent local near marina,
landlord a real ale enthusiast
for 25 years ♪♣♠◉

Twechar 34E5

Quarry Inn
Main Street
Open Sundays
Maclay 60/-, 70/-, 80/- Ⓐ
Fine wood-panelled public bar,
renovated lounge ♿ⓘ♣♠◉

Tayside

Almondbank 35F3

Almondbank Inn
Main Street (off A85)
OS 065262 ✆ 242
Broughton Greenmantle Ale Ⓗ
Well-kept village pub with
good bar lunches
♪♣♠♨ⓇⒼↄ (weekends)◉♿

Arbroath 35H3

St. Thomas Bar
17 James Street (off A92)
Open Sundays
Maclay 80/- Ⓗ
Cosy, friendly pub near
Arbroath Abbey ♣◉◉

Bridge of Earn 35F3

Cyprus Inn
Back Street (off M90 exit 9)
OS 133184
Open Sundays
Belhaven 80/-
Broughton Greenmantle Ale
Maclay 70/-
Younger IPA Ⓗ
200-year-old inn with cosy
lounge ♿♪♣♠◉

Broughty Ferry 35G3

Fisherman's Tavern
12 Fort Street (off A930)
Open Sundays
Broughton Greenmantle Ale
McEwan 80/-
Maclay 80/- Ⓗ
Younger No. 3 Ⓔ
Small, unique and popular
bar, new lounge ♣◉◉

Carnoustie 35H3

Station Hotel
Station Road ✆ 52447
Open Sundays
McEwan 80/- Ⓔ
Maclay 80/- Ⓐ
Friendly, busy public bar
♣☒♠Ⓗ Ⓡ Ⓖↄⓘ◉♿≈

City of Dundee 35G3

Ladywell Tavern
16 Victoria Road ✆ 23586
Open Sundays
McEwan 80/- Ⓐ
Younger No. 3 Ⓔ
Busy central bar, small lounge
♿♣Ⓖↄⓘ◉

Speedwell Bar
165–167 Perth Road
Open Sundays
Belhaven 80/-
Ind Coope Burton Ale Ⓗ
McEwan 80/- Ⓐ
Busy Edwardian bar, known
as Mennie's ♣Ⓡ◉

Dunkeld 35F3

Atholl Arms Hotel
Bridge Street (off A9) ✆ 219

Open Sundays
Alloa Arrols 70/- Ⓗ
Real ale in bar only
♪♣☒♠Ⓡ Ⓖ

Kinnesswood 35F4

Lomond Country Inn
✆ Scotlandwell 317/253
Open Sundays
Belhaven 70/- Ⓗ
Friendly inn at foot of Lomond
Hills ⓘ♪♣☒♠Ⓡ Ⓖↄⓘ◉♿

Kinross 35F4

Green Hotel
2 The Muirs (A90, off M90
exit 6) ✆ 63467
Open Sundays
Broughton Greenmantle Ale Ⓗ
Modernised coaching inn with
extensive sporting facilities
ⓘ♣☒♠Ⓡ Ⓖↄⓘ◉♿

Letham 35G2

Commercial Inn
The Square
Open Sundays
Maclay 70/- Ⓐ
Cosy, friendly country pub
♠♪♣♨

Monifieth 35G3

Crown Bar
49 High Street ✆ 534361
Open Sundays
Maclay 80/- Ⓐ
McEwan 80/- Ⓐ
Comfortable home from
home, busy weekends
♪♣Ⓖⓘ♿≈

Montrose 35H2

Three Craws
1–4 Wharf Street (A92)
Open Sundays
Devanha XXX
Tennent Heriot 80/- Ⓗ
Pleasant pub by Montrose
Bridge ♪♣☒Ⓡ Ⓖↄⓘ◉

Perth 35F3

Hal o' the Wynd
7 George Street ✆ 29914
Maclay 70/-, 80/- Ⓐ
Recently modernised lounge;
games room ♪♣☐Ⓖↄ◉

John Moir's (Central)
189 South Street (A9)
McEwan 80/- Ⓐ
Fine Victorian interior; five
minutes walk from rail and
bus stations ♪♣◉≈

Scone 35F3

Scone Arms
Cross Street (A85)
Open Sundays
McEwan 80/- Ⓔ
Scottish decor, traditional
music weekends
♿ⓘ♪♣☒♠Ⓡ Ⓖↄⓘ◉

Though it's too early to predict a collapse of the stout party, the Guinness stranglehold on Dublin drinkers has been broken. Dempseys have brought a whiff of competition and a taste of the real thing to beleaguered Dubliners who were previously dependent on imported Theakstons as their only relief from the black stuff or keg bitter.

If holidaying in the Republic, rejoice! The pubs are open all day except for the "holy hour" – an beers from the Hilden, Down Royal and Herald breweries awaiting them.

In the Isle of Man the pubs are open all day and the island's famed Pure Beer Act protects the drinker from artificial additives. Only hops, malt, and sugar may be used in brewing beer, and the two breweries – Okells and Castletown – serve their natural beer in the natural way in all but a couple of the island's pubs. And now the bad news...Sunday

hours hiatus in mid-afternoon. While the Irish are not noted for their reticence in pursuit of the milk of the barley, there is nothing to suggest that their relaxed licensing hours have led to an excessive consumption – English MPs please note.

North of the borders, licensing hours stretch from morning to night, with no interruption at all, though, by way of revenge, the pubs are shut all day on Sunday. Thirsty travellers to the province will find a choice of

opening hours are severely restricted.

In the Channel Islands, too, the pubs are open all day, though visitors to Guernsey and Herm should beware – Sunday is a dry day. While the Jersey brewers Randalls seem to be backpedalling on real ale, with Draught Bass the only cask ale on the island, the Guernsey Randalls (no relation) and the Guernsey brewery provide many welcome refuges after a hard day admiring the tomato crop.

Isle of Man

General opening hours: 10.30am–10.45 pm (summer);
12noon–10 pm (10.45 F,S) (winter). Sunday: 12–1.30; 8–10

Andreas 20C1

Grosvenor
Jurby Road (A17)
✆ Kirk Andreas 227
Okell Mild, Best Bitter Ⓗ
Modern pub with wooded
lounge and restaurant
♫♣✿🅿🚗Ⓡ☺🍴🍺Ⓢ♿

Ballasalla 20B3

Whitestone Inn
✆ Castletown 822334
Okell Best Bitter Ⓗ
Historic inn in village centre
🏠🅿♣♿Ⓢ♿

Douglas 20C2

Albert Hotel
Chapel Row
Okell Mild, Best Bitter Ⓗ
Local pub near the quay ♫♣🍴

Bridge Inn
North Quay
Castletown Bitter Ⓗ
Quayside pub with good food
and atmosphere
🏠♫♣🚗Ⓡ🍴🍺Ⓢ

British Hotel
North Quay
Okell Mild, Best Bitter Ⓗ
Trendy quayside pub,
interesting characters in
taproom ♫♿🍴

Clarendon
North Quay
Okell Mild, Best Bitter Ⓗ
Lively quayside local ♫♣🍴

Douglas Head Hotel
✆ 3405
Okell Best Bitter Ⓔ
Friendly atmosphere,
panoramic view of Douglas
bay ♫♣🚗🅰Ⓡ♿🍺Ⓢ

Help keep real ale alive by
joining CAMRA. Your voice
helps encourage brewers big
and small to brew cask beer
and offer all beer drinkers a
better choice. Send £7 for a
year's membership or use the
form on page 319.

Queens Hotel
Promenade
Castletown Bitter Ⓗ
♫♣🅿🍴♿Ⓢ

Woodbourne Hotel
Alexandra Drive ✆ 21766
Okell Mild, Best Bitter Ⓗ
Splendid Edwardian pub with
gentlemen-only bar
🅿♿🍴🍺

Kirk Michael 20B2

Mitre
Castletown Bitter Ⓗ
Oldest pub in IOM
♫♣🚗🅰Ⓡ🍴

Laxey 20C2

Mines Tavern
Mines Road
Okell Mild, Best Bitter Ⓗ
Tram theme in bar, mining
relics in lounge 🏠♣♿Ⓢ🅰

New Inn
New Road
Okell Best Bitter Ⓗ
Friendly pub with plush
mock-Tudor lounge
🏠🍴♣🚗Ⓖ♿Ⓢ🅰

Queens Hotel
New Road ✆ 781195
Castletown Bitter Ⓗ
Comfortable local sponsoring
TT riders ♫🚗🅰Ⓡ🅰

Maughold 20C1

Glen Mona Hotel
Ramsey Road ✆ 781283
Okell Mild, Best Bitter Ⓗ
Residential hotel, discount for
CAMRA members
🏠♫♣🚗🅰🅱Ⓖ♿🅰

Peel 20B2

Creek Inn
Station Place
Okell Mild, Best Bitter Ⓗ
Modernised pub
♫♣🚗Ⓖ🍴🍺Ⓢ🅰

Neptune's Tavern
Castle Street
Castletown Mild, Bitter Ⓗ
Small, unspoilt local 🍴♣Ⓡ🍴🅰

Whitehouse
Douglas Road
Okell Mild, Best Bitter Ⓗ
Comfortable pub in outskirts
🍴♣🅰🅰

Port Erin 20A3

Station Hotel
Station Road ✆ 832236
Okell Mild Ⓗ
Best Bitter Ⓔ

Comfortable residential pub
opposite steam railway
🏠♫♣🅿🅱Ⓡ♿🍴Ⓢ⇌

Port St. Mary 20A3

Bay View Hotel
Bayview Road ✆ 832234
Okell Mild, Best Bitter Ⓗ
Excellent hotel with sea views
🏠♫♣✿🚗🅱🅿Ⓖ🍴

Station Hotel
Station Road ✆ 832249
Castletown Bitter Ⓗ
Friendly hotel by steam
railway station 🏠♣🅿🅱Ⓖ♿⇌

Ramsey 20C1

Bridge Inn
Bowring Road
Okell Mild, Best Bitter Ⓗ
Attractive lounge with
nautical flavour ♫♣🚗🅿Ⓢ

Royal George
Market Square
Castletown Bitter Ⓗ
Town-centre pub with
old-world lounge 🏠♫♣Ⓖ♿Ⓢ

Saddle Inn
West Quay
Okell Mild, Best Bitter Ⓗ
Imaginatively renovated West
Quay local 🏠♫♣✿🅱🍴Ⓢ

St. Johns 20B2

Central (Farmers Arms)
Castletown Road ✆ 372
Castletown Mild, Bitter Ⓗ
Popular village local
🏠♫♣🅱🚗ⓇⒼ🍴🍺Ⓢ🅰

Sulby 20C1

Ginger Hall
✆ 231
Castletown Bitter Ⓗ
Large Victorian pub with fine
brass handpumps
🏠♫♣✿🅿🍴Ⓢ🅰

The 🏠 symbol denotes a pub
with a real solid fuel fire

Northern Ireland

General opening hours: 11.30 am–11pm Mon–Sat, closed Sundays

Ballymena 36C1

Montgomery's
Tower Centre
Hilden Ale Ⓗ
Comfortable new pub in
spacious shopping centre
ⓇⒼ♥Ⓢ

Belfast 36C2

Botanic Inn
23 Malone Road (off B23)
℘ 660460
Hilden Ale Ⓗ
Busy pub near Queens
University ♠Ⓡ♪Ⓖ♥Ⓢ

Linen Hall
9 Clarence Street ℘ 248458
Hilden Ale, Linenhall
Special Ⓗ
Friendly Edwardian-style bar
in town centre ⓇⒼ♥

Glengormley 36C2

Crown & Shamrock
584 Antrim Road (A6)
Hilden Ale Ⓖ
Traditional Irish country pub,
family-owned ♠♥♥Ⓢ

Hillsborough 36C2

Hillside Bar
Main Street ℘ 682765
Lunchtime opening: 12 noon
Hilden Ale Ⓗ
Comfortable country town bar
♠♣♥Ⓖ♥♥♦

Holywood 36C2

Seaside Tavern
Stewarts Place (off A2)
Hilden Ale Ⓗ
Popular bar near seafront
♪♠Ⓖ♥Ⓢ

Lisburn 36C2

Down Royal Inn
Ballinderry Road ℘ 82473
Down Royal Local, Export,
Special Brew Ⓗ
Pub-brewery; Ulster pub of
the year 1983 Ⓡ♪♥♠ⓇⒼ♥Ⓢ

Newtownards 36C2

Old Cross
Castle Place ℘ 8·11320
Hilden Ale Ⓗ
Quaint 18th-century village
pub ♠Ⓡ♪♠Ⓖ♥Ⓢ

Portrush 36C1

Harbour Bar
6 Harbour Road
Herald Ale
Hilden Ale Ⓗ
Unspoilt traditional Irish
fisherman's pub ♠Ⓡ♥♠♥Ⓢ

Portstewart 36C1

Cashlandoo Inn
Coleraine Road (A2) ℘ 3077
Open Sundays 12–12.30;
4.30–10 (with meals only)
Herald Ale
Hilden Ale Ⓗ
Pleasant ranch-style inn
Ⓡ♪♥♠ⓇⒼ♥Ⓢ♦

Saintfield 36C2

Whitehorse Inn
Main Street (A21) ℘ 510417
Hilden Ale Ⓗ
Splendid village inn with good
food ♠ⒼⒼ♥Ⓢ♦

Try also: Carrickfergus:
Dobbins Inn; Lisburn:
Maghaberry Arms; Newry:
McGinty's Speakeasy

Republic of Ireland

General opening hours: 10.30–2.30; 3.30–11 (11.30 in summer)

Cabinteely 36C3

Horse & Hound
Bray Road, Dublin 18
Dempseys Real Ale Ⓗ
Former wayside inn now in
suburbs but with retained
character ♪Ⓖ♥Ⓢ

Dalkey 36C3

Sorrento Lounge
Sorrento Road
Dempseys Real Ale, Porter Ⓗ
Well-run pub, popular with
businessmen and fishermen
♪♠Ⓢ♦

Dublin 36C3

George Chaney
1/2 Chancery Place, 7
℘ 775274
Dempseys Real Ale, Porter Ⓗ
Tastefully renovated pub by
historic Four Courts
♠ⒻⓇⒼ♥Ⓢ

Norseman
29 Essex Street, Dublin 2
Dempseys Real Ale, Porter Ⓗ
Homely Victorian pub near
site of ancient Norse
settlement Ⓡ♪Ⓖ♥Ⓢ

O'Dwyers
8 Lower Mount Street, Dublin
2 ℘ 762887
Dempseys Real Ale, Porter Ⓗ
Tastefully renovated, popular
pub in old Georgian area
♪ⓇⒼ♥Ⓢ

O'Dwyers
104 Lower Leeson Street,
Dublin 2 ℘ 766390
Dempseys Real Ale Ⓗ
Busy pub beside picturesque
St. Stephen's Green
♪ⓇⒼ♥Ⓢ♦

Rainbows
Exchequer Street, 1
Dempsey's Real Ale, Porter Ⓗ
Popular disco pub with billiard
tables ♪♣Ⓢ♦

Sally O'Briens
Thorncastle Street, Ringsend
Dempseys Real Ale, Porter Ⓗ
Huge pub with friendly bar
staff
ⓇⒼ♥Ⓢ♦

Dun Laoghaire 36C3

Paddy McCormack
Mounttown
Dempseys Real Ale Ⓗ
Pre-war pub 1 mile from ferry
terminal
♪♠Ⓢ♦

Howth 36C3

Lighthouse Bar
Opens 10 am–10.30 pm
Dempseys Real Ale Ⓗ
Fishermen's local with good
view of the harbour ♥

Stillorgan 36C3

**Byrne's of
Galloping Green**
Bray Road
Dempseys Real Ale, Porter Ⓗ
Suburban pub of character
♪♠Ⓢ

Pubs on Guernsey and Herm are closed on Sundays

Alderney

St Anne 5J8

11–2; 5–12
Coronation
High Street ☎ 2630
Randall Bitter [G]
Real locals' pub 🏠↱♣⊞🍷⛺

Guernsey

Castel 5F7

10.30 am–11 pm
Vazon Bay Hotel
Vazon Bay ☎ 57120
Guernsey LBA, Draught Bitter (summer) [H]
Friendly hotel with pool
♪♣🌿🚗▬[R]🍷Ⓢ

Forest 5G8

10.30 am–11 pm
Deerhound Inn
Le Bourg ☎ 38585
Closes 2.30–5 pm
Guernsey Draught Bitter [H]
Cosy country inn 🌿🚗▬[R]☾◗

St Andrews 5G8

10.30 am–11 pm
Hangman
Bailiffs Cross
Closes 2–5 pm Mon–Fri
Guernsey LBA, Draught Bitter [H]
A pleasant, friendly pub
♪♣🚗🍷Ⓢ

Last Post
Les Buttes ☎ 36353
Randall Mild, Bitter [E]
Comfortable, friendly pub
🏠↱♪♣⊞🌿🚗☾🍷Ⓢ⛺

St Martins 5G8

10.30 am–11 pm
L-Auberge Divette
Jerbourg Road ☎ 38485
Guernsey LBA, Draught Bitter [H]
Beautifully situated, keen real ale house 🏠♪♣⊞🌿🚗[R]☾◗🍷Ⓢ

Try also: Greenacres Hotel

St Peter Port 5G7

10.30 am–11 pm
Beehive
Rohais Road
Closes 2–4.45 pm Mon–Fri
Guernsey LBA [G]
Busy, friendly little local ♣🍷Ⓢ

Britannia Real Ale Bar
Trinity Square
Draught Bass
Guernsey LBA, Draught Bitter [H]
Renovated Victorian-style pub
♪🍷Ⓢ

Dorset Arms
Hauteville
Closes 2–5 pm Mon–Sat
Guernsey Draught Bitter [H]
Worth the long steep climb
🏠↱♪♣⊞🚗[R]🍷Ⓢ

Golden Lion
Market Street ☎ 26862
Guernsey LBA, Draught Bitter [H]
Attractive, one-bar, bow-windowed pub
🏠♪♣☾🍷Ⓢ

Harbour Lights/ Farmer's Bar
South Esplanade
Guernsey LBA [G]
Draught Bitter [H]
Handy for bus station; formerly two pubs
↱♪♣☾🍷Ⓢ

Kosy Korner
Church Square
☎ 23518
Guernsey Draught Bitter [G]
Plush harbourside pub with cellar upstairs
↱♣[R]☾◗🍷Ⓢ

La Couture Inn
Couture Road
Guernsey LBA [H]
Pleasant, lively local
↱♪♣🌿🚗🍷Ⓢ

Ship & Crown
Crown Pier ☎ 21368
Guernsey Draught Bitter [H]
Comfortable, lively pub
♪♣☾◗Ⓢ

Try also: Plough; Rohais

St Sampsons 5G7

10.30 am–11 pm
Mariners
The Bridge
Closes 2–5 pm
Randall Mild [H]
Pleasant, basic harbour pub
♣🍷⛺

Pony Inn
Les Capelles ☎ 44374
Guernsey LBA, Draught Bitter [H]
Large, agreeable modern pub
↱♪♣🌿🚗[R]☾◗🍷Ⓢ⛺

Vale 5G7

10.30 am–11 pm
Trafalgar Inn
North Side ☎ 48144
Closes 2–3 pm Mon–Fri
Guernsey LBA
Randall Mild [G]
Basic, sociable pub with cheapest ale on island
↱♣[R]☾Ⓢ⛺

Try also: Coq du Nord Hotel

Herm

Herm Harbour 5G7

10.30 am–11 pm
Mermaid Tavern
☎ 6
Guernsey Draught Bitter [H]
Handy for yachtsmen and day-trippers – the only pub on the island
🏠↱♪♣⊞🌿[R]☾◗🍷Ⓢ⛺

Jersey

St Brelade 5H9

9 am–11 pm
Old Portelet
Portelet Bay
☎ 41899
Draught Bass [G]
Old farmhouse overlooking spectacular bay
↱♪♣⊞🌿🚗[R]☾◗🍷Ⓢ

Smugglers Inn
Ouaisne Bay
☎ 41510
Draught Bass [H]
Old inn serving good food
♣⊞☾◗🍷Ⓢ

St Helier 5J9

9 am–11 pm
Cosy Corner
Royal Square ☎ 22184
Draught Bass [H]
Only Ann Street Brewery pub with real ale (public bar only)
↱⊞☾🍷Ⓢ

Esplanade
The Esplanade
Closes 3–5 pm
Draught Bass [H]
An old town pub with great character ♪♣🍷

St John 5H9

9 am–11 pm
Les Fontaines Tavern
Route du Nord ☎ 62707
Draught Bass [H]
Fine converted farmhouse with views of French coast
🏠♪♣⊞🌿🚗☾🍷Ⓢ

St Martin 5J9

9 am–11 pm
Rozel Bay Hotel
Rozel Bay ☎ 62205
Draught Bass [H]
Small, friendly pub near the sea 🏠♪♣🌿🚗☾🍷Ⓢ

Welcome Inn
Coast Road, Gorey
Draught Bass [H]
Busy pub by the beach
♪♣⊞🌿🚗🍷Ⓢ

Time for a Change?

If my father had known Lloyd George, he'd have punched him in the nose. The teetotal Welsh wizard introduced restrictions on licensing hours during the First World War, as a temporary measure to control the drinking of munitions workers. 70 years later, the 'temporary measure' is still in force, responsible for a rag-bag of differing opening and closing times that would drive half the population to drink if they could only find somewhere open.

Apart from the annoyance to landlord and customers, the present laws hardly help our tourist trade, for if there's one thing that foreign visitors find harder to understand than cricket, it's the fact that for large parts of the day and night, they can't even get into a British pub, let alone buy a drink in one. Our licensing laws might be a little more bearable if they were more consistent, but they are riddled with so many variations, inconsistencies and contradictions that the kindest thing would be to have them quietly put to sleep.

English and Welsh pubs may open for a total of around nine hours on weekdays and there must be a break of two hours in the afternoon. The actual hours in each district are decided by the local licensing bench. In Weymouth you can call in for a pint at 10 am, in Liverpool you'll have to wait another hour and a half. Head for Holyhead and you can carry on drinking until 3.30 pm, linger in Loughborough and you'll be out on your ear at 2. Even when you've discovered the hours for the area you're in, there's nothing to make the landlord open on time, or advertise what hours he does keep. On Sundays – a day of rest – the hours are a miserly 12–2 and 7–10.30, and in Northern Ireland and two districts of Wales the pubs stay firmly shut all day. Some police forces rigidly enforce the laws, others turn a blind eye to unofficial extensions at pubs in their area.

If you want a drink when the pubs are closed, there are many ways, of course, that you can legally buy one. Supermarkets and off licenses can sell you alcohol anytime between 8.30 am and 10.30 pm. Members clubs can open 24 hours a day if the steward can stand the pace, and, surprise, surprise, Members of Parliament can have all day and all night sittings in their very

own bar at the House of Commons. Despite or possibly because of this, twice in recent years they have failed to emerge from it in sufficient numbers to pass private members bills aiming to allow the rest of us the right to a drink when we'd like one.

Constant protests by members of the public, consumer organisations, tourist authorities, overseas visitors, brewers and the licensed trade have left our legislators curiously unmoved. Even the government-inspired Erroll report, which recommended that pubs should be permitted to sell alcohol any time between 10 am and midnight, made no impression on our legislators.

CAMRA believes that the interests of pub customers and landlords would be far better served by a licensing system which allowed flexibility in the choice of opening hours within reasonable limits. The pattern of trade varies so much from pub to pub that it is only sensible that the landlord should decide the most suitable opening hours for his house. Having selected his hours, he should stick to them and advertise them inside and outside the pub so that we all know where we stand.

If this was to happen, farmers could use the summer daylight to the full and still be able to get a pint after work, office and factory workers could have a drink on the way home, tourists could find pubs open in mid-afternoon and theatre and film-goers wouldn't find all the pubs closing just as the performance ends. Sunday supping could become a leisurely pleasure instead of an unholy race against the clock.

The advantages of flexibility are obvious from the Scottish experience. Until the late seventies, Scottish opening hours were even more restricted than those in England and Wales. Changes were introduced in the wake of the Clayson Report, relaxing the laws, and transforming Scottish drinking habits for the better.

By liberal use of permitted extensions of the basic opening hours, a few bars now open as early at 6 am, others remain open as late as 4 am, and many more also open the hours that best suit their landlords and customers. Not only has this resulted in a much improved service to the drinker, but some of the more unsavoury problems associated with Scottish pubs in the past have been dramatically reduced.

The notorious '10 o'clock swill' – the rush to cram as many drinks in as possible before closing time – has disappeared. Violence in pubs and on the streets has decreased. The atmosphere and pattern of alcohol consumption is generally more relaxed. Perhaps even more telling is the fact that the anti-alcohol lobby, vociferous in opposing any improvement in conditions for the vast majority of the adult population who enjoy a social drink, have been unable to pinpoint any adverse consequence of these changes.

Scottish experience suggests that our licensing laws are counter-productive. CAMRA's thousands of members will keep up the fight to change our out-dated licensing laws. With a little more help from our friends, that change will come sooner rather than later.

The Year of the Pub

What makes a good pub? Anyone who could pin down the answer to that would soon be richer than even a brewer's dreams, but the formula is an elusive one. While bad architecture and design can make a pub a joyless place, even the best cannot, on its own, make a joyful one. Some are carefully designed, smart and comfortable, but have as much atmosphere as a Batley versus Huyton match on a wet day in February. Others are as apparently unpromising as a British Rail pork pie, but turn out to be full of atmosphere and character, a delight to drink in.

The aim of all pub design should be to produce a relaxing, friendly and pleasant atmosphere for the customer. The use of the available space, the lighting, the colours, textures and materials, the quality of the licensee and the beer, even the bric-a-brac, all contribute to the feel of a pub. Some are welcoming even when empty, others can have a hundred customers and still not feel right.

The strength of the British pub is its ability to be all things at once. The snugs, saloons, lounges and taps allow it to cater for many different kinds of customers, and even an open plan area can be subdivided to create semi-private space. A good pub will enable its customers to have a quiet tête-a-tête, play a game of darts or doms, or join in with the conversation at the bar as the mood takes them.

Brewery architects have often seemed to think that atmosphere can be introduced by the wholesale use of ersatz oak beams and horse brasses, whereas what is really needed is a sympathetic eye for the character of each individual building.

The current dream of some designers – theme pubs and fun pubs – cater for a particular sector of the market, the young, but at the expense of all other possible customers. No-one would describe a fun pub as a local. They are briefly very popular, but, like all gimmicks, are prone to fall out of fashion as quickly as they came in, requiring a fresh infusion of capital and gimmickry to re-attract custom. They have as much relevance to good pub design as junk food does to good eating.

CAMRA's Pub Preservation Group make two annual awards for Best New and Best Refurbished Pub, with the aim of encouraging brewers and pub owners to take a critical look at their pub design. The Best New Pub has to be either a new building or a sensitive conversion of an existing one that has not previously been a pub. The Best Refurbishment category celebrates those houses of architectural merit which have survived modernisation and changes to the exterior or interior, and retained features of enduring delight and fascination.

Breweries and pub owners have responded enthusiastically to the scheme and the successful pubs highlight the ways in which interior design can be used to complement and develop the character of a building, rather than simply ripping out the interior walls and installing the company livery or imposing a 'brewers' Tudor' interior on every pub. Pubs don't have to be old to be good. There are many new ones that have all the virtues of the typical British pub but there are also many modern horrors that perfectly reflect the poverty of imagination of the housing built around them.

The PPG awards highlight the need for all pub design and refurbishment work to be carried out in a sensitive and sympathetic way. As long as designers put the essential ingredients of a pub in a setting that is appropriate to the character of the building and the locality, the future of the British pub is assured. Good beer and a good landlord can make up for a lot of design imperfections in a pub, but good beer, a good landlord and good design is an unbeatable combination.

Further information on CAMRA'S Pub Preservation Group can be obtained from Jenny Greenhalgh, 2 Roseberry Avenue, Lancaster LA1 RDJ.

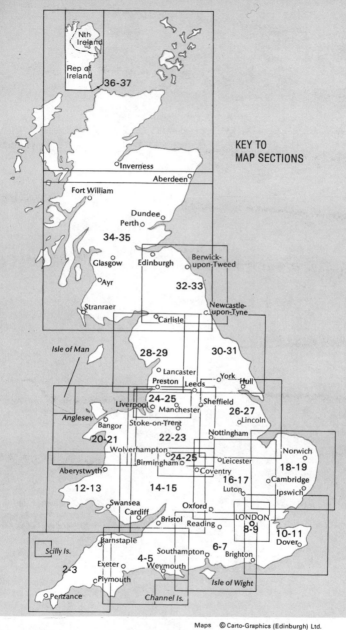

KEY TO
MAP SECTIONS

36-37

Inverness

Aberdeen

Fort William

Dundee
Perth

34-35

Glasgow Edinburgh Berwick-upon-Tweed

Ayr

Stranraer Newcastle-upon-Tyne

Carlisle

Isle of Man

28-29 **30-31**

Lancaster York
Preston Leeds Hull

Liverpool **24-25** Sheffield

Manchester **26-27**

Anglesey Lincoln

Bangor Stoke-on-Trent

20-21 **22-23**

Nottingham

Wolverhampton Norwich

Aberystwyth **24-25** Leicester **18-19**

Birmingham Cambridge

12-13 Coventry **16-17** Ipswich

Luton

Swansea Oxford

Cardiff **LONDON** **10-11**

Bristol Reading **8-9** Dover

Barnstaple **6-7**

Scilly Is. Southampton Brighton

Exeter **4-5** Weymouth

2-3 Plymouth Isle of Wight

Penzance Channel Is.

Maps © Carto-Graphics (Edinburgh) Ltd.

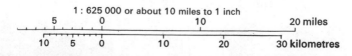

M6	Motorway with junction number and service area	
M6	Motorway junction with limited interchange	
A6	Primary routes	
A495	'A' class roads	
	'B' class roads	
⁄⁄⁄⁄⁄⁄⁄⁄⁄⁄⁄⁄⁄⁄⁄⁄	Regional and county boundaries	
◀	Good Beer Guide entry locations	

1 : 625 000 or about 10 miles to 1 inch

5   0   10   20 miles

10 5 0   10   20   30 **kilometres**

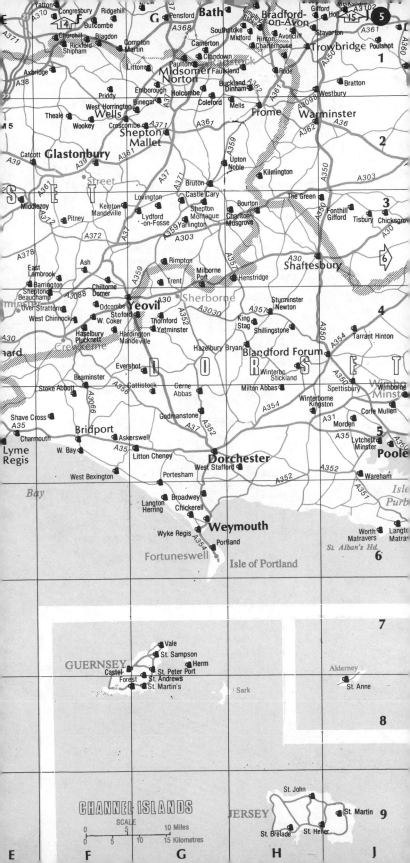

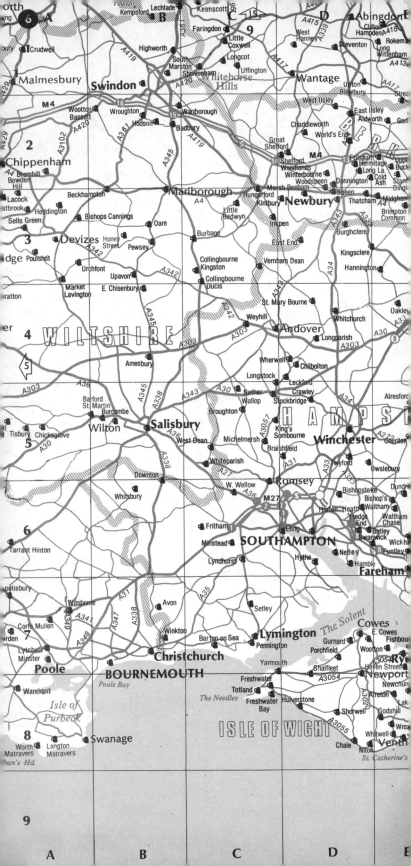

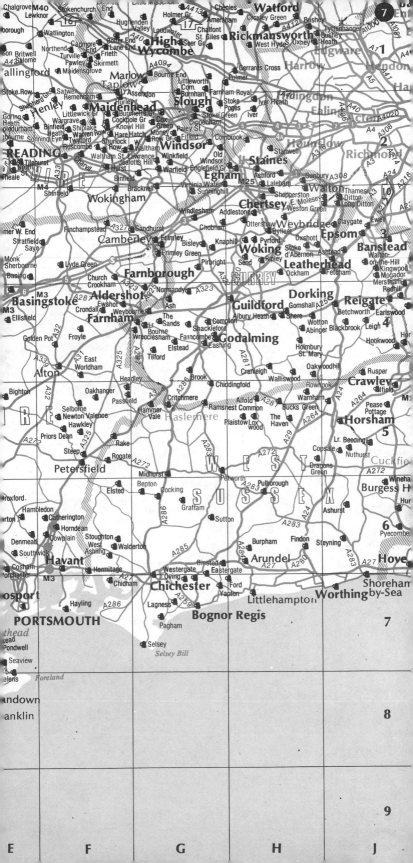

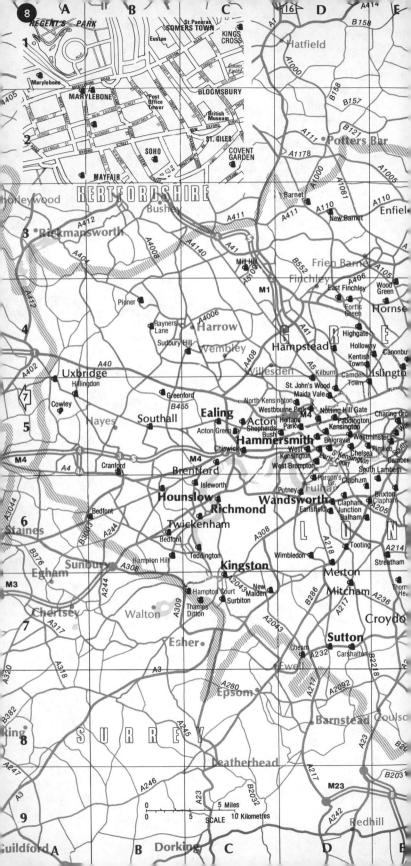

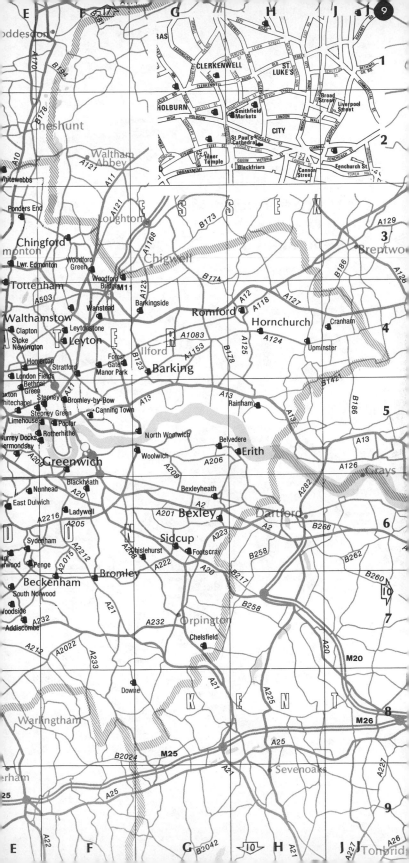

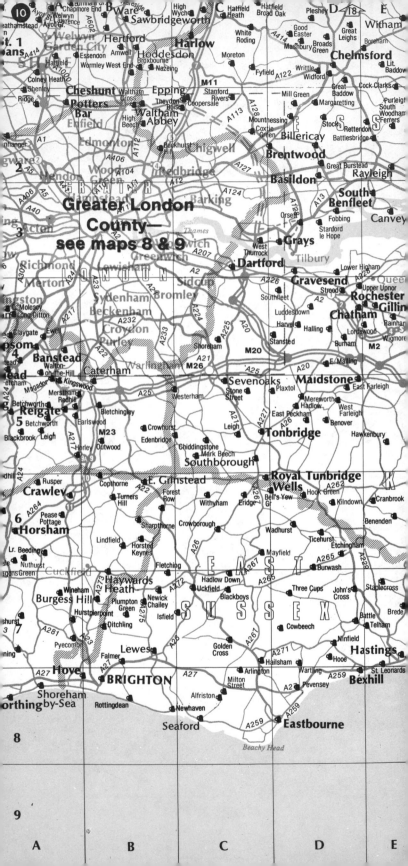

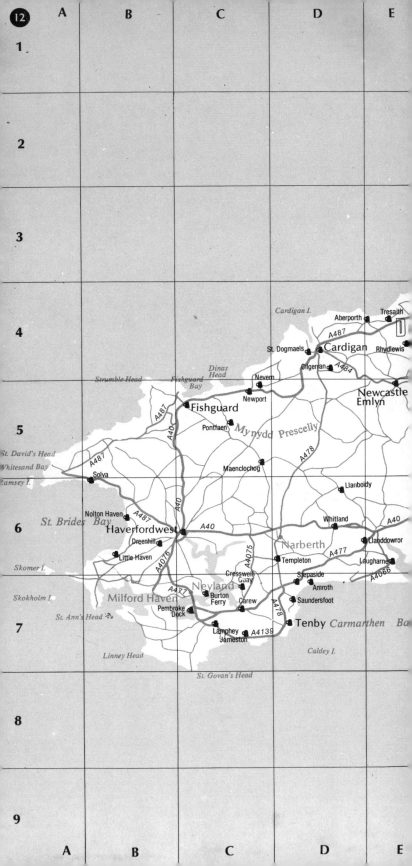

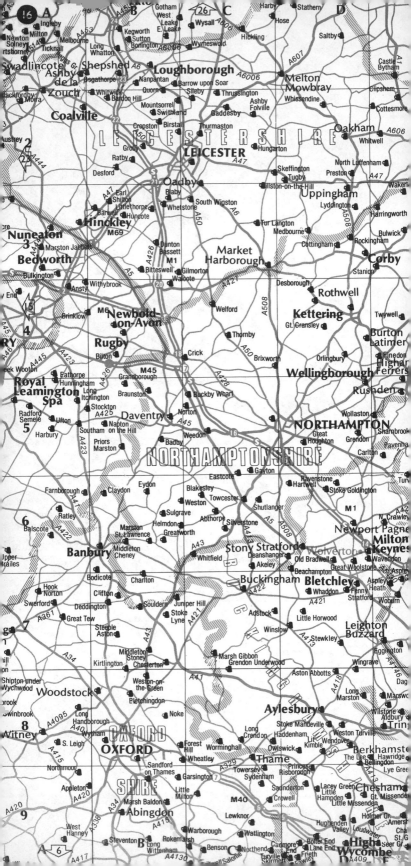

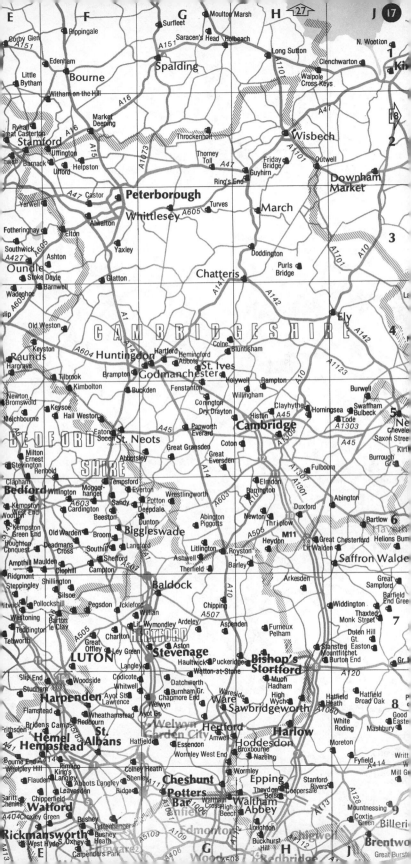

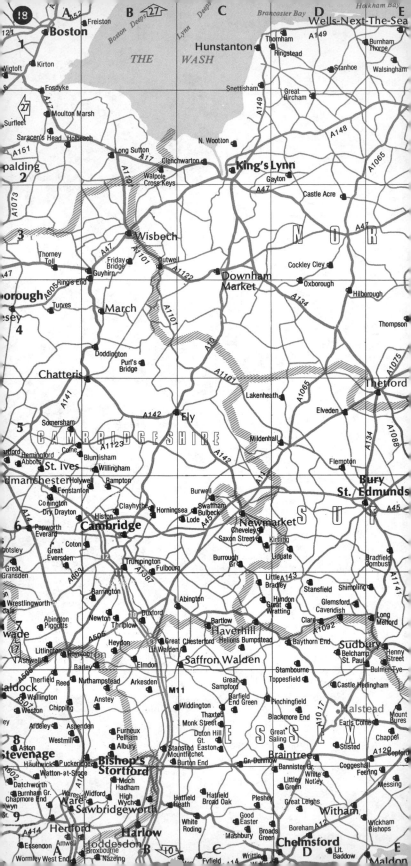

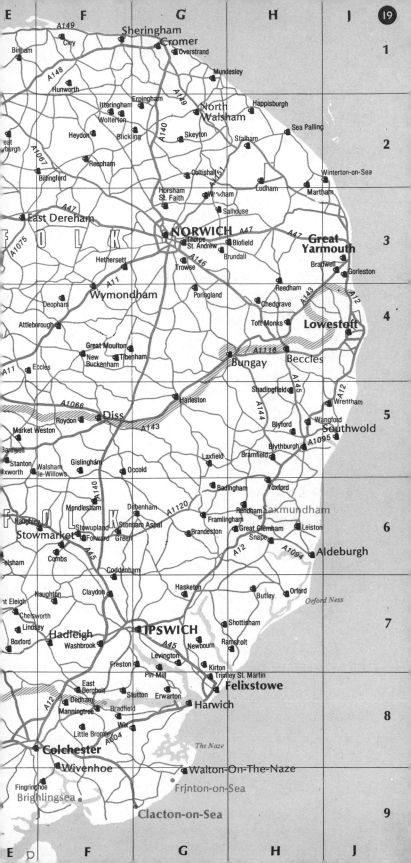

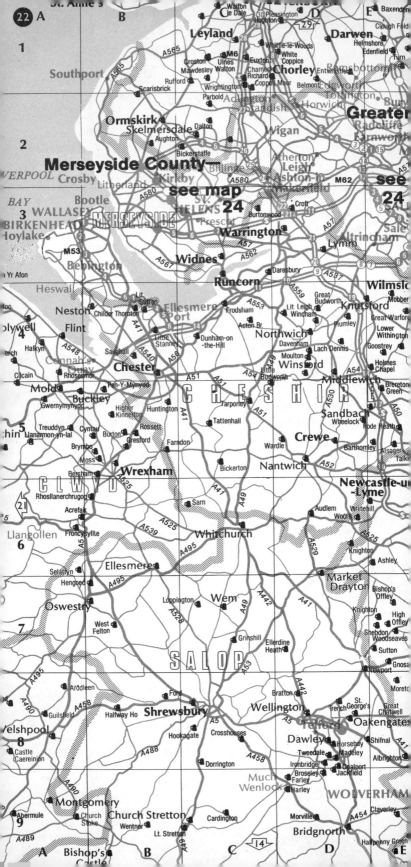

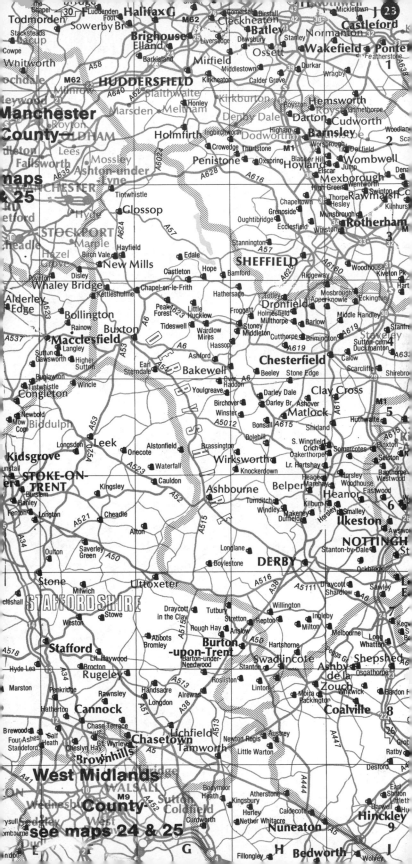

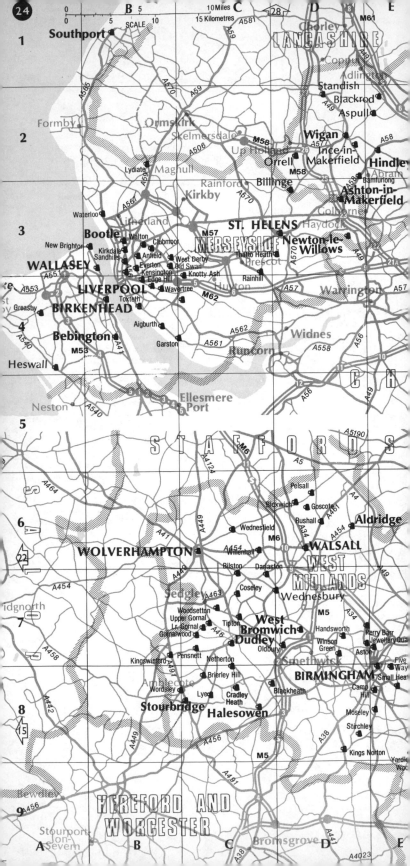

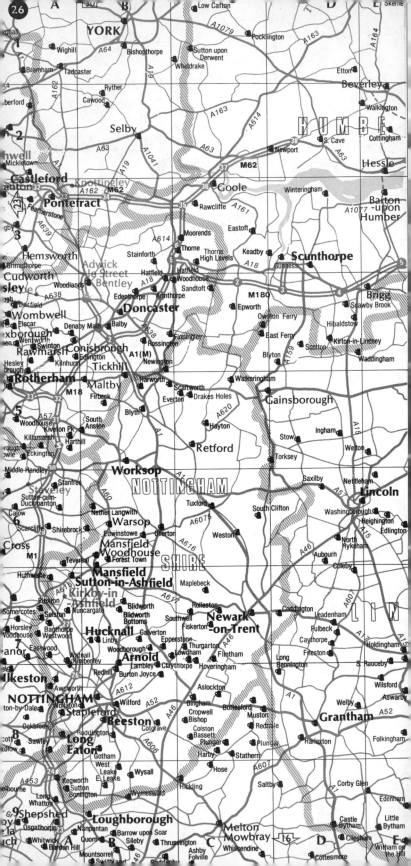

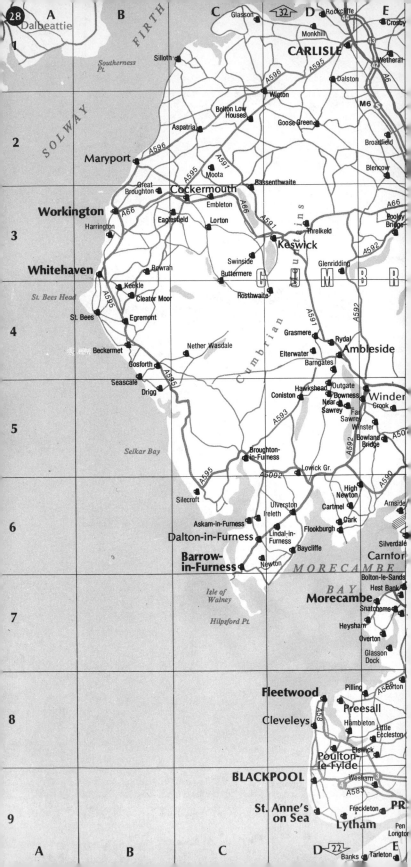

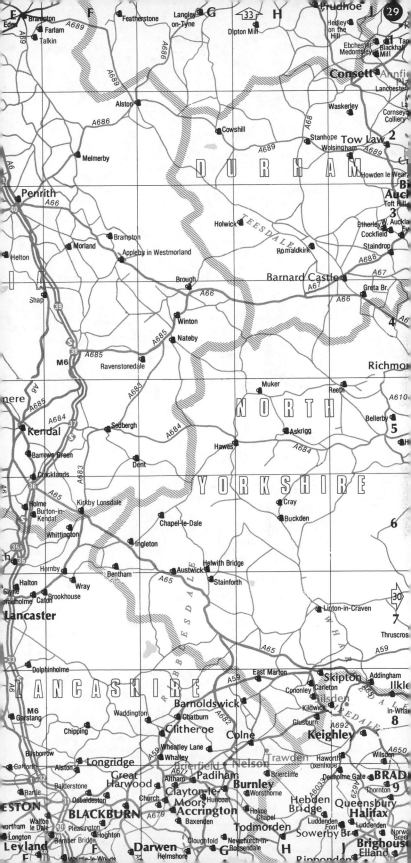

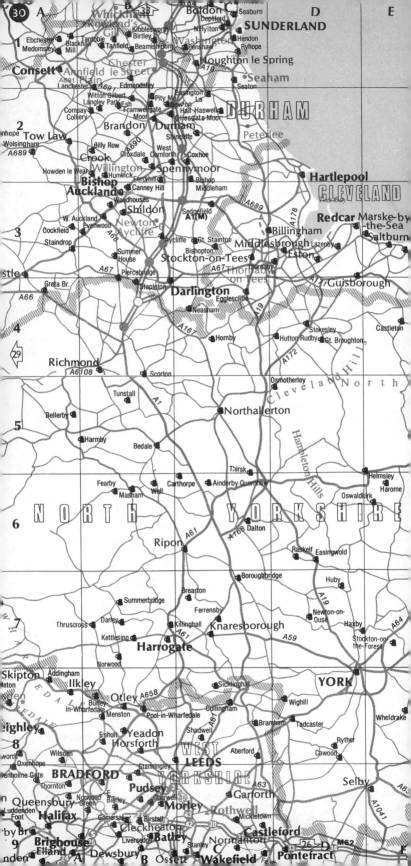

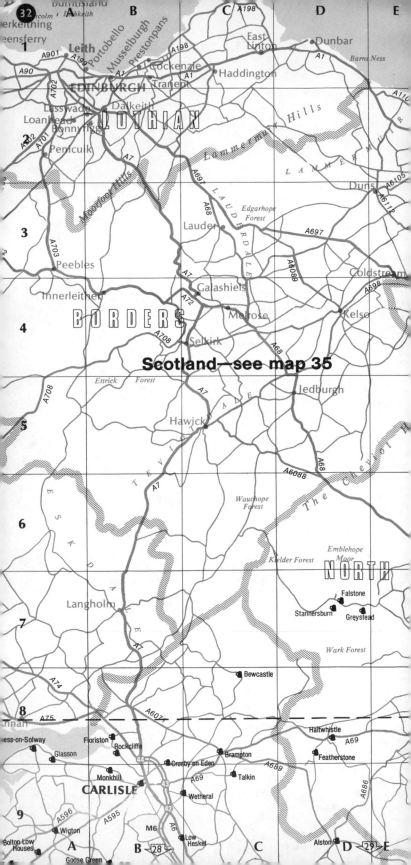

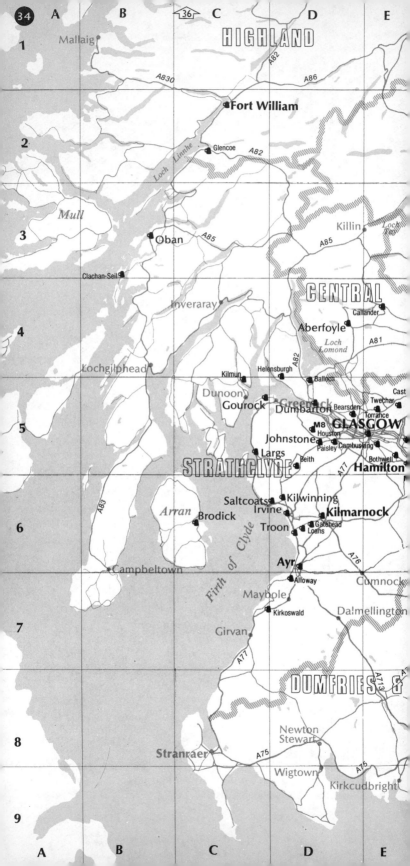

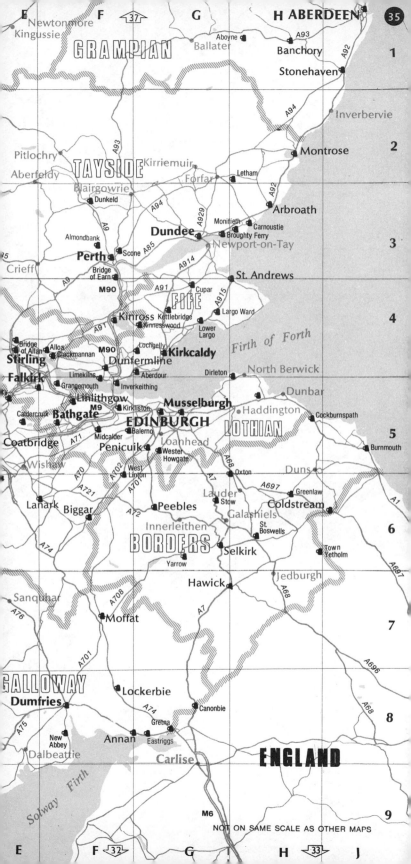

A   B   C   D   E

1

Portrush

Portstewart   A2   Ballycastle

Londonderry

A6

A5   Ballymena

A8   Holywood

Glengormley   BELFAST

NORTHERN   Lisburn   Newtownards

IRELAND   Saintfield

A4   M1   Hillsborough

A1

2

REPUBLIC

OF   N1

IRELAND

N6   Howth

DUBLIN   Stillorgan

Dundrum   Dun Laoghaire

Cabinteely

3

A838

A894

A836

4

A835

Lairg

5

Ullapool   Bonar

A832   Bridge

HIGHLAND

A832   A836

6

A9

Loch

Maree   Dingwall

A896

A890   Muir of Ord

Portree   INVERNESS

7

Skye

Kyle of

Lochalsh

A87   Loch Ness

8

A82

A87   A82

Mallaig   A8

9

NOT ON SAME SCALE AS OTHER MAPS   A82

A   B   34   C   D   E

ORKNEY
ISLANDS

Thurso   A836

A882

A897   A895   A9   Wick

A9

Tain

Moray   Firth   Lossiemouth   Fraserburgh

Cromarty   Elgin   A98   A98   A952   A97   A952   Peterhead

Forres   A96   Turriff   A952

A96   A941   Huntly

Grantown-   A95   A941   Newburgh

on-Spey   A96   Balmedie

GRAMPIAN

A9   Bucksburn

A95   Elrick

Aviemore   ABERDEEN

A93   Aboyne   A93

Ballater   Banchory

A94   Stonehaven

Inverbervie

Why Join CAMRA?

'What's the point in joining CAMRA? It's only a load of old bores droning on about beer, and most British pubs sell real ale anyway now. Why join an army when the battle's already been won?'

If that's what you think about CAMRA, you're wrong. The truth is that the battle has only just begun.

CAMRA aims to do much more than just campaign for pubs to serve real ale. No longer is it real ale at any price – but good quality real ale at value-for-money prices. CAMRA wants to preserve the local and regional identities of breweries, and the distinctive tastes of the beers they brew – not see them submerged in a tide of bland and boring beer.

CAMRA is campaining to get our antiquated licensing laws changed so that licensees can open the hours that suit themselves and their customers. Only in England could a law laid down by a teetotaller to regulate the drinking of munitions workers during the First World War, still be in force 70 years later, to the despair of landlords, locals and tourists alike.

CAMRA is fighting to protect the local pub from the ravages of brewery rationalisation and development schemes, which destroy the character of pubs and leave some town and village communities without a local pub at all.

CAMRA is battling to prevent beer being priced out of the market by the greed of the brewers and the efforts of the EEC to redistribute beer and wine duty. Beer is already taxed far more heavily in Britain than in most European countries, and CAMRA will not allow the British pint to be sacrificed to empty a European wine lake.

CAMRA is fighting in short, to ensure that you, the customer, have a genuine freedom to choose where you drink, what you drink and when you drink. Whether you are eighteen or eighty, and whether you drink a pint of Crudgingtons or a Pina Colada with a cherry on top, CAMRA helps to protect your heritage and your drinking pleasure.

The cost of joining CAMRA is only £7 for a single or joint membership, and this modest sum brings you:

- **A member's handbook.**
- **12 copies of *What's Brewing* – the Campaign's entertaining and highly regarded monthly newspaper.**
- **Generous discounts on a wide range of CAMRA products and publications (including the best selling *GOOD BEER GUIDE*).**
- **An invitation to join in all CAMRA activities such as brewery trips, branch meetings, socials, conferences and beer exhibitions.**
- **and the chance to add your voice to the continuing Campaign for Real Ale.**

CAMRA Products

If you're looking for a present for that special person in your life – the landlord of your local – how about a fullsize CAMRA mirror painted in gold, green, brown and black, in a wooden frame 28 × 22 inches? At £20 including post and GPO-proof packing it's a snip!

While you're admiring your reflection in the mirror, why not try a CAMRA tie round your neck at £2-50? In blue or brown with a gold CAMRA logo.

Now you can pull a pint in the privacy of your own home with the CAMRA mini beer-engine. It delivers $\frac{1}{4}$ pint each stroke and has the CAMRA logo on the white porcelain handle. It costs £27-50, and for another £1-15 you can have a cream and brown CAMRA bar towel to catch the drips as well.

Use the order form on page 320 to acquire the drinker's complete CAMRA tool kit – you know it makes sense!

Membership Form

Full membership £7.00.
Joint husband/wife membership £7.00.
I/We wish to become members of CAMRA Ltd.
I/We agree to abide by the memorandum and articles of association of the company.
I/We enclose a cheque/p.o. for £7.00.

Name(s)
Address
Signature

Questionnaire

We'd like your views on the Good Beer Guide. Please help us to make the guide even more useful to you by answering these questions.

1	Is this the first GBG you have bought?
2	Do you buy it every year?
3	When was the last time you bought the GBG?
4	Did you buy it to use in your home area?
	Did you buy it for work and travel?
	Did you buy it for holiday travel?
5	Do you buy any other national guides?
	If so, which ones)?
6	Are you a CAMRA member?
7	What other information would you find useful in the GBG?
8	What other improvements would you make to the GBG?

Order Form

Local Guides

	Quantity	Price ea.	Amount
Reference number			
Reference number			
Reference number			
Reference number			
Reference number			
Reference number			
Please add postage and packing See opposite page for details			

CAMRA Items

	Quantity	Price ea.	Amount
Good Beer Guide Covers		£1.50	
CAMRA Mirrors		£20.00	
CAMRA Ties: Blue ☐ Brown ☐		£2.95	
CAMRA Mini-Handpumps		£27.00	
CAMRA Bar Towels		£1.15	

Send to CAMRA Ltd. 34 Alma Road St. Alban's,
Herts. AL1 3BW.
Make cheques payable to CAMRA Ltd and allow
3 weeks for delivery.

£ ☐

Name	
Address	
Signature	

New Pub Submission

Pub Name
Address
Reason
Please supply your name and address above